PARADIGM LOST

PARADIGM LOST

A Cultural and Systems Theoretical Critique of Political Economy

Kenneth Michael Stokes

LONDON AND NEW YORK

First published 1995 by M.E. Sharpe

Published 2015 by Routledge
2 Park Square, Milton Park, Abingdon, Oxon OX14 4RN
711 Third Avenue, New York, NY 10017, USA

Routledge is an imprint of the Taylor & Francis Group, an informa business

Copyright © 1995 Taylor & Francis. All rights reserved.

No part of this book may be reprinted or reproduced or utilised in any form or by any electronic, mechanical, or other means, now known or hereafter invented, including photocopying and recording, or in any information storage or retrieval system, without permission in writing from the publishers.

Notices
No responsibility is assumed by the publisher for any injury and/or damage to persons or property as a matter of products liability, negligence or otherwise, or from any use of operation of any methods, products, instructions or ideas contained in the material herein.

Practitioners and researchers must always rely on their own experience and knowledge in evaluating and using any information, methods, compounds, or experiments described herein. In using such information or methods they should be mindful of their own safety and the safety of others, including parties for whom they have a professional responsibility.

Product or corporate names may be trademarks or registered trademarks, and are used only for identification and explanation without intent to infringe.

Library of Congress Cataloging-in-Publication Data

Stokes, Kenneth M.
  Paradigm lost : a cultural and systems theoretical
critique of political economy / Kenneth Michael Stokes.
        p.   cm.
  Includes bibliographical references (p.   ) and index.
  ISBN 1-56324-483-7 (hardcover). — ISBN 1-56324-484-5 (pbk.)
  1. Marxian economics. 2. Bogdanov, A. (Aleksandr), 1873–1928.
  3. Bukharin, Nikolaĭ Ivanovich, 1888–1938. I. Title.
      HB97.5.S743   1995
      335.4—dc20   94-23385
                      CIP

ISBN 13: 9781563244841 (pbk)
ISBN 13: 9781563244834 (hbk)

Dedicated to the organic intellectualism of Michael Bader

We must stress that the importance of a historical understanding stems not from an antiquarian interest, but from a deep commitment to understand the present.

Contents

ACKNOWLEDGMENTS   xiii

INTRODUCTION   3

1. SELECTED ISSUES IN THE PHILOSOPHY OF SCIENCE AND ECONOMIC METHODOLOGY

Introductory Remarks	17
The Paradigmatic Conceptual Framework	20
Revolution Versus Reform in a Scientific Community	41

2. SYNTHESES AND INVERSION IN POLITICAL ECONOMIC THOUGHT

Introductory Remarks	44
The Ascendancy of the Mechanical Paradigm	45
The Enlightenment's Mechanicalism	49
The Inversion of Economic Analysis	52

3. PHILOSOPHICAL COUNTERCURRENTS

Introductory Remarks	56
Archaeology of Knowledge	59

Kant's Critique of Reason ... 71
Holistic Philosophy ... 76
Hegelian Totality ... 78
Marx's Holism ... 83

4. HOLISM AND THE NATURAL UNITY OF SCIENCE   91

5. THE PHILOSOPHICAL HERITAGE OF CRITICAL MARXISM

An Introductory Overview ... 102
Critical Theory and Political Economy ... 104
Critical and Scientific Marxism ... 109

6. TOWARD THE NATURAL UNITY OF SCIENTIFIC KNOWLEDGE

Introductory Remarks ... 115
The Discovery of Thermodynamics ... 116
Evolution Versus Mechanics: Irreversibility of Life Processes ... 118
Search for the Unification of Natural Scientific Knowledge ... 120
The Collapse of the Laplacean Prototype ... 124
The Search for the Natural Unity of Scientific Knowledge ... 126
The Energeticist School ... 128
Ostwald's Social Energetics ... 133

7. NARODNIK AND NIHILIST DIMENSIONS: A CRITICAL KERNEL IN RUSSIAN MARXISM

Introductory Remarks ... 140
Narodnik Influences ... 141
Unity of Science and Nihilist Strains ... 146
A Critical Kernel in Russian Marxism ... 155
A Keystone to Russian Critical Marxism ... 162

8. SOCIAL ENERGETICS: A MARXIAN VARIANT   169

9. THE PHENOMENOLOGICAL MARXISM OF BOGDANOV

Machian Influences	178
A Response to the Crisis of Russian Marxism	193
Rival Concepts of Dialectical Materialism	204

10. FROM PHENOMENOLOGY TO TEKTOLOGY

The Systems Practice of Bogdanov	214
Forces of Production: Technology and Social Energetics	217
Social Consciousness, Ideology, and Culture	222

11. TEKTOLOGY: THE METASCIENCE OF PRAXIS

Introductory Remarks: A Philosophy of Praxis	267
Dimensions in Tektology	276
Tektology: Basic Concepts and Methods	282
Tektology and the Formulating Mechanism	283
Tektology and the Regulating Mechanism	286
Bogdanov's Counterpart: Nikolai Bukharin	287
Tektology and the Theory of the Economy as a Metabolic System	295
Bukharin's Contribution to Open Systems Analysis	296
Tektology and Open Systems	303

12. TEKTOLOGY AND SOVIET PLANNING   305

13. TECHNO-UTOPIA: AN ATHENS WITHOUT SLAVES   319

14. DYSTOPIAN WARNINGS   330

15. DYSTOPIA REALIZED   335

16. CONCLUDING REMARKS   339

NOTES   349

BIBLIOGRAPHY   395

INDEX   413

ABOUT THE AUTHOR   425

Acknowledgments

I wish to acknowledge an intellectual indebtedness to Russian academician N.N. Moiseev, former director of the Research/Computer Center of the USSR Academy of Science; Professor P.I. Medow of the Department of Economics at York University; and Dr. I. Yu. Egorov of the Dobrov STEPS Center of Kiev, whose recondite remarks and constructive critiques of the A.A. Bogdanov and N.I. Bukharin materials were instrumental in bringing this project to a close. I am also thankful for the useful comments of my students and for the editorial assistance of Ms. Christine Florie of M.E. Sharpe, Inc. Finally, I wish to thank my wife, Rhonda, for the constancy of her encouragement and her patience, not a minor form of despair, but a virtue to be witnessed in other than my conscience.

PARADIGM LOST

Introduction

The social sciences, in general, and political economy, in particular, are currently undergoing a period of self-analysis and self-doubt in which the traditionally prized shibboleths of academic discourse have become the subject of critical reflection.[1] Indeed, there exist serious rifts in the community of political economists and in their relationship to society at large. These rifts are threaded backward in time by philosophical, epistemological, and methodological controversies.

In his general introduction to *La Nature de la Nature*, Edgar Morin speaks of a *"paradigme perdu"* and the need for its reconstruction.[2] His reminiscence was of a lost sense of wholeness, of the lost integral unity of man, society, and nature. In *La Nature de la Nature*, Morin attempted, without reducing the anthropological to the biological, a reconstruction of a multidisciplinary synthesis that, unknown to him, constitutes a long-neglected, original, and foundational contribution to Critical Marxism.

A central point made in much of the discourse on Marxism is the flawed distinction drawn between "Western" and "Russian" Marxism. These two are also occasionally denoted as Critical and Scientific Marxism, respectively.[3] In the more usual histories of these Marxisms the Second International (1889–1914) is cited as a turning point; thereafter, a doctrinal, scientistic approach was evident in the "Russian" edition, and only in the Western Marxism, which emerged in the 1920s, did there develop a Critical and oppositional appreciation of what later became the institutionalized and thus orthodox edition, an edition that admitted no qualifications or eclectic revisions. It matured into a theoretical degeneration that presented a rigid, nondialectic abstract formalism. It is, however, important to note that this canvas has been painted with a broad brush. Absent from this history is an acknowledgment of the significant contributions of Nikolai I. Bukharin and the lesser known but august theorist, Alexandr A. Bogdanov.

This book constitutes a project in the archaeology of knowledge; for *Para-*

digm Lost is an account of the origins and development of a cultural, social energetic, and systems theoretical contribution to Critical Marxism. Contrary to the widely accepted yet faulted Eurocentric view that Critical Marxism was wholly a product of Western theorists, Critical Marxism matured first not in Western Europe in the 1920s, but in Russia during and following the period of the Second International.

The Russian philosophers A.A. Bogdanov and N.I. Bukharin were deeply engaged intellectuals whose works responded to the events of their day. Their search for a Marxian epistemology was influenced by and, in some cases, anticipated the later developments in Western Critical Marxism. They were attracted to more libertarian modes of political activism out of a sober realization that the Soviet Union's sorry history had compromised Leninism irreparably. The despotic insistence on a Marxism that would not surrender its theoretical purity meant a desperate search for historical "subjects" who would regain the momentum lost when the Soviets were defeated. And while it meant an abandoning of the blessed faith that a subject could be discovered, it also represented a retreat into hollow theorizing. It was from this retreat that a seminal contribution was made to a cultural and systems theoretical critique of political economy.

Critical Marxism in pre- and post-revolutionary Russia derived much of its strength from its nondoctrinaire openness to the rich Russian traditions of multidisciplinary intellectuality. Accordingly, it was not presumed that Marxism was itself an impermeable theoretical totality with nothing to gain from dialogue with its competitors.

While Western Marxism, finding in Freud's psychological analysis points of contact with Hegel,[4] added forms of psychological estrangement to the other expressions of alienation in the experience of everyday life, the central figure in this text, A.A. Bogdanov, centered his attention on what would in Piaget's hand become identified with genetic structuralism. Indeed, Bogdanov's structuralism was subsequently identified with general systems theory. Both psychoanalytical and structuralist categories were, in fact, manifestations of an essential readiness to draw on non-Marxist intellectual currents to make up for deficiencies (or develop incipient leads) in the inheritance from the nineteenth century. This process, to be sure, had already begun during the Second International with the revisionists' attempt to link Marx and Kant, with Plekhanov's interest in Spinoza, Kautsky's interest in Darwin, and Bogdanov's social energetics and structuralism. But it was only after 1918 in Western Europe that the practice became widespread. Those engaged in one or another of these cross-fertilizations defended their position as a synthetic enrichment that helped Marxism to adjust to the changed circumstances of the modern world. To their opponents, however, the results were a divisive eclecticism that defiled Marx's teaching. Some Western Marxists, notably Lukács, looked askance at the synthesizing efforts of their peers. Indeed, in general, Critical Marxists were uncharitable toward their fellows, if they deigned to notice them at all. Like their Russian cousins, Western

Critical Marxists frequently maligned and deprecated each other, often after misrepresenting the positions they attacked. Potential allies were thus lost in the eagerness for theoretical correctness, a failing that is still manifest in the assertion of absolute opposition between Critical and Scientific Marxism. The reverse side of this internecine quarreling has been the enormous creative fecundity of the tradition, which sharply sets it apart from messianic Marxism. Critical Marxism has been open and experimental in a way that is not comparable with anything in this century except perhaps aesthetic modernism, which also exploded in a whirl of movements and countermovements. But with the means to impose "intellectual conformity," the various subcurrents and critical dialogue of Russian Critical Marxists were repressed. It was this repressed dialogue that was institutionalized in the frozen ontology of Stalinism.

Ontology is situated at the beginning of any critical inquiry. For we cannot define a problem without presupposing a certain basic structure consisting of the significant kinds of entities involved and the form of significant relationships among them. We think, for example, about a system whose basic entities are states situated in an interstate system and of a hypothesized mechanism once called the balance of power through which their relationships may be understood to constitute a certain kind of world order. From such ontological beginnings, complex theories have been constructed and specific cases—particular interstate relationships—examined. There is always an ontological starting point. Any ontological standpoint is open to question. Indeed, all of the terms just used have ontological meanings.

Theory follows reality. It also precedes and shapes reality. That is to say, there is a concrete historical world in which things happen; and theory is informed through deliberation upon what has happened. The separation of theory from the historical record is, however, only a way of thinking, because theory feeds back into the making of history by virtue of the way those who make history think about what they are doing. Ontology is therefore important. Their understanding of the historical context allows, requires, even encourages them to act, prohibits their actions, and formulates the purposes of action. These are the products of theory whether it be scholarly and esoteric or merely common-sense.

The often unquestioned ontologies with which people work obtain from their historical experience and in turn become embedded in the world they construct. What is subjective in understanding becomes objective through action.

The embedded structures of thought and practice—the nonphysical realities of political and sociocultural life—may persist over long periods of time, only to become problematic when people confront new sets of problems, which the conventional ontologies do not seem able to account for or cope with. In such periods, the old certainties about ontology give place to skepticism. We are today confronting a new set of problems.

Our challenge is not to contribute to the construction of a universal and absolute knowledge, but to devise a daring vision practical for contextualizing the problems of the present. To deconstruct the ontological constructs of the ever-fleeting present is a first step toward a more substantive though, nevertheless, contingent knowledge. The task of clearing the ground should not become an obstacle to constructing a new perspective that can be useful even though it, in turn, will ultimately be open to critical reevaluation.

An ontological shift is inherent in the very process of historical structural change. The entities that are significant are the emerging institutions and the processes through which they emerge. Reflection upon change discredits received ontologies and provides a clue for a possible new ontology. Use of a new ontology becomes the heuristic for strategies of action in the emerging (dis)order.

In the historic development of economic thought from the feudal and modern epochs, it is possible to identify the waxing and waning of broad themes and a clash between two forms of rationality. After a review in chapter 1 of selected issues in the philosophy and sociology of science and the methodology of economics, it is argued, in chapter 2, that from the Enlightenment two paradigms presented themselves: mechanicalistic atomism and holism. And whereas conventional economic thought aligned itself with mechanicalistic atomism, holistic appreciations were also present. Fixing its attention upon mechanicalism and atomism was the first step toward creating a paradigm and an important victory for positivist methodology.

Thus, not only are there ontological issues, there are epistemological ones to be resolved in an era of structural change. Positivism may offer an epistemological approach of a certain practicality for periods of relative structural stability. The state of the social whole can be taken as given in order to center our attention on those particular variables that frame the specific and limited object of inquiry. Positivism facilitates a detailed empirical investigation of ostensibly discrete problems. The observing subject can be thought of as separated from, and not directly involved with, what is investigated. The purpose of positivist inquiry is conservative: to bring the aberrant activity back into a compatible relationship with the relatively stable whole. In positivism there is an implicit identity between the observer-analyst and the stable social whole. This identity, at the level of the whole, abides the fiction of a separation between subject and object at the level of the specific issue.

But positivism is less well adapted for uncritical inquiry into systemic (i.e., structural) change. For this we need an epistemology that does not disguise, but rather explicitly affirms, the dialectical relationship of subject and object in the historical process. Where positivism separates the observing subject from the observed object of inquiry, this other historically oriented, interpretative epistemology sees subject and object in the historical world as a coevoluntionary whole. Such an epistemology is more adequate as a guide to action toward structural change, even though it may not attain the degree of precision expected of positivism.

In chapter 2 we also recount the neglect of holism, which obtained from the Newtonian thrust, a thrust in which the universe was represented by man as a huge mechanism that had been wound up once and for all time. People saw, as the basis of all existence, mechanical motion, the displacement of bodies in space, taking place according to Newton's laws of motion. Life was discussed, from this point of view, as being merely a special kind of mechanical motion.

But with the advance of rational mechanics the philosophical criticism of science gradually became harsher. Positivism and mechanicalism were being criticized not for their limitations but for their ontological presuppositions, and a rival knowledge based on holism was sought. Two cultures coalesced, and knowledge was fragmented into two opposed modes of inquiry.

While more conventional appreciations of the Enlightenment have, with good reason, emphasized its positivist and mechanicalist thrust, an opposing counter-current (addressed in chapter 3) was also apparent in Enlightenment thought—a countercurrent that was to provide the philosophical grounding for the "knights of totality." While "totality" or "holism" has enjoyed a privileged and nostalgic place in the discourse of the Cultural West, it is a concept not without a methodological appreciation. The issue of totality has been at the center of the Marxist debate. It is to the concept of totality that we can look for a compass to help us traverse the vast and uncharted intellectual territory that is Russian Critical Marxism. Although totality has been of enormous importance for Critical Marxists, other key concepts such as social energetics, praxis, phenomenology, and dialectics will also be explored in the tradition of the history of ideas. But each of these taken in isolation would not be sufficient to give us a complete view of the topography. Though working our way through the complicated analyses of how all of these concepts were used by Critical Marxists, it is apparent that they come together in a grand synthesis. Our project is, at one level, a critique of Marxism that rests upon aesthetic and productionist assumptions of Marxism itself and is thus, in part, an autocritique of Marxism.

To accomplish this task, and after a review of holism, we shall review the transit of the concept through the Enlightenment referring to the instrumental contributions of Montesquieu, Rousseau, Kant, Hegel, and Vico. It was the tradition defined by these philosophers in which Marx grounded himself and that later invested Critical Marxism.

The further development of economic thought marked the beginning of a paradigmatic challenge to political economy. This challenge, on the one hand, gave rise to the marginalist revolution, which constituted a detour from the more substantive categories of economic analysis, but it also marked the beginning of a reemergent theme in political economy, that of holism.

Chapter 4 speaks to the reemergence of a Marxist-inspired holism and to the Comtean search for a unity of scientific knowledge associated most forcefully with the evolutionary dynamic of Engels's dialectic of nature.

In chapter 5 we turn from this account to an overview of the philosophical heritage of Critical Marxism and its grounding in the problematic relation between theory and practice. From this perspective we turn to the place of critical theory in political economic analysis and seek to distinguish between Critical and Scientific Marxism. The intent here is to establish a basis for the (re)construction that follows.

Even while the Darwinian perspective of the evolution of life was developing from the physical sciences, from industry there was a growing awareness that Newton's laws of motion did not provide for a complete understanding of all physical phenomena. In particular, the rigorous principles of thermodynamics were found to be alien to the Newtonian world. Consequently, both in biology and in evolution theory, the second principle of thermodynamics presented a major obstacle to the understanding of life itself. This in turn led to a monist effort to synthesize the unification of scientific knowledge. While it led to the flourishing of neopositivist concepts, it also led to attempts to elaborate a general theory of organization and to a formulation of the dialectics of energy and organization. Pointedly, it meant the reassertion of the Aristotelian systems problematique and the collapse of the Laplacean prototype for political economic thought. These are the issues addressed in chapter 6. Recounted therein are the complex events that variously informed Russian Critical Marxism.

Influenced by the cosmological monism expressed by members of the Vienna Circle and the concepts of *Kulturwissenschaften* and social energetics, a powerful influence was felt on the revision of Marxism, but also on Anglo-American appreciations of political economy. However, the early reconstruction of economic thought consistent with a thermodynamic paradigm came to be regarded as an unwarranted and malicious attack upon the established mechanical paradigm —an attack upon science, in general, and materialism, in particular. The most interesting of the substantive contributions to this emerging paradigm arose in prerevolutionary Russia and are identified with the philosopher, translator of *Capital*, and challenger to Lenin, Alexandr A. Bogdanov. Standing head and shoulders above all the other revisionists, Bogdanov attempted to systematically introduce his revisionist views in philosophy, political economy, and sociology. Although he expressed admiration for Marx's theories, he refused to accept Marxism as a prescribed thought. An active member of the Socialist Academy of Sciences, he was among the founding members of the Proletariat Culture movement, an organization dedicated to advancing the labor movement—the creative role of the workers' class in culture and ideology.

It is at this juncture that we turn, in chapter 7, to a detailed analysis of a singular contribution, which is identified with both Critical Marxism and a critical systems theoretical challenge to political economy. It is argued that Russian Critical Marxism and systems theory was a synthetic creation that absorbed elements of Narodnism and Nihilism; it was a response to the crisis of science but also constituted a response to the economist determinism of "Engelsism." Moreover, its cultural dimension anticipated and possibly informed Western Marxism.

Insofar as the crisis of science enjoined Marxism in that crisis the search for an alternate paradigm included recondite Marxian social energetics. In chapter 8 we take a brief look at nineteenth-century Russian contributions that sought not only to synthesize the ultramaterialistic Kulturwissenschaft philosophy of W. Ostwald with Marxian thought but also made original contributions to an understanding of the energy basis of the livelihood of man. These developments, together with others, provided a basis for the later emergence of A.A. Bogdanov's phenomenological Marxism.

In chapter 9 we shall consider at length the development of phenomenological Marxism as a response to the late-nineteenth-century crisis of Marxism. Bogdanov's embryonic phenomenological Marxism was a countercurrent to the fixity of doctrinal Marxism. For to the extent that social and historical content conditions theoretical form, the elevation of doctrinal Marxism to the plane of a metaphysics revealed an ideological remnant of somewhat dubious value—a frozen articulation of abstract categories of diminished meaning. Sustaining a holism grounded in traditional Russian thought, Bogdanov's phenomenology was a mélange of social energetics and empirio-criticism. It was a redirection of attention from abstractions to the world of lived experience. Arguing that Marx had failed to provide a rigorous theory of knowledge, Bogdanov synthesized Mach's and Avenarius's epistemology with its psychological dimensions with Marx's theory of social history. The "phenomenological" qualification appended to Marxism, far from being a mere afterthought, is an expression of the conceptual otherness of a determinate sociohistorical problem—the need to develop and sustain a critical approach to social reality.

Turning, in chapter 10, from phenomenological Marxism (though never departing from its insights), we reflect on the praxiological dimensions of other aspects of Bogdanov's social thought. After acquainting ourselves with a "Kantian" dimension in his thought, we turn to considerations of social consciousness, the concept and role of ideology, culture, and hegemony. At this juncture it is worth mentioning that Bogdanov's appreciation of ideology and culture in social revolution anticipated, and in some instances surpassed, the later contributions more usually associated with such names as Gramsci, Lukács, Korsch, Brecht, and Block.

In chapter 11 we shall consider at length an original systems theoretical challenge to political economy. A constant in the critical Marxism of Bogdanov was social praxis. From his understanding of social energetics, his formulation of phenomenological Marxism, and his appreciation of the broader meaning of a cultural revolution, Bogdanov conceived of a metascience—Tektology.

An idiosyncratic Marxist committed to the construction of socialism, Bogdanov's abiding theoretical interest was the formulation of a metascience of organization—Tektology—that would permit balanced regulative (i.e., planning) mechanisms to preserve stability and prevent cataclysmic change in any of life's major processes. Following Marx's dictum, Bogdanov contended that the intent of Tektology was not merely to describe the structure of the social world but to produce reliable information for changing it. In developing his concept of "Tektology," Bogdanov tried to find through structural analogies, metaphors, and models the organizational principles that would unite under one conceptual scheme "the most disparate phenomena" in the organic and inorganic worlds. This monist metascientific approach apparent in Bogdanov's, and later in Bukharin's, theory of equilibrium was years later identified in the cybernetics of Norbert Wiener. Alien in its universality to the scientific thinking even of today, the idea of a general theory of organization was fully understood by only a handful of people and did not therefore spread. It became a *paradigm lost*. In this chapter we shall review the various conceptual and methodological dimensions of Tektology and grow to understand that it constituted, in fact, a general theory of organization.

Embodying policy choices of a theoretically informed political will and social action, the formulation of Soviet planning in the early 1920s was of considerable ideological importance to the self-description of Bolshevism. It was in a search for a methodical approach to planning that Tektology first gained adherents. In chapter 12 we shall cast our eye to the early Soviet planning debates and the role that Bogdanov's Tektology played therein.

Both methodologically and philosophically Bogdanov contributed to the early Soviet planning under Bukharin, Bazarov, and Groman. He anticipated the possibility of a socialist state surrounded and beleaguered by capitalist states and thought that were socialism to prevail in such circumstances it would be a perverted edition shorn of its ebullience. Though committed to socialism, he appreciated the multiple problems facing a socialist state. He expressed concern about the rise of dangerous technologies, an exploding population whose rapid growth would trigger food shortages and decade-long famines, and the exhaustion of natural resources. He discerned, albeit somewhat ambiguously, Stalin's embrace of a technocratic trend, a potentially threatening fusion of technology with authoritarianism. A plaintive constant in much of Eurocentric philosophizing is a nostalgia for an antiquity lost. Philosophers and technocrats alike are haunted by dreams of an Athens without slaves. Indeed, this was certainly an abiding theme among late-nineteenth-century socialists. Bebel, Engels, and Kautsky enthused about the possibility. As we shall see in chapter 13, neither Lenin nor Bogdanov entirely escaped from the dream, nor from the exaltation of technologizing everyday life. However, with respect to Gastev's exaggerated man-the-machine Taylorism, Bogdanov expressed serious misgivings.

In constructing his socialist techno-utopia, Bogdanov was not indifferent to the dangers of collectivism and advanced technology projected by some dystopian fantasies. In chapter 14 we shall consider the dystopian warnings present in Bogdanov's science fiction works. These were consistent with the genre established by Chernishevsky's utopian novel *What Is to Be Done?* Unlike some utopian socialists, he believed that even after socialism had been successfully created, civilization would be plagued by a whole series of problems recognized as problems of "technified societies." Were a triumphant socialism to flow through the floodgates, which the bourgeoisie cast open, what dreadful impulses might flow in along with it, or in its wake? He imagined that a society committed to a radical socialist individualism might develop its own distinctive varieties of nihilism, a nihilism potentially far more explosive and culturally disintegrative than its bourgeois precursor. A daring and original socialism might launch the liberated self into immense unknown human spaces without legislated limits.

Insofar as there exist comprehensive histories that recount the lurid history of Stalinism, chapter 15 is intended merely to provide readers with a brief sketch of selected historical events, events speculatively addressed in Bogdanov's utopian novels.

Written from an explicitly Leninist point of view, the history of Russian Social Democracy was presented as a vindication of Leninism. Since Western historians also tended to focus their attention on Lenin, the histories of Social Democracy in Russia do not yet provide the historical context that the study of Bogdanov's ideas requires. In its own small way this volume seeks to redress this deficiency.

Insofar as Nikolai I. Bukharin is a well-recognized political figure, our treatment of him herein concerns itself more with his critical appreciations of Marxism and his contribution to systems theory.

A "seeking Marxist," N.I. Bukharin, "the darling of the Party" alongside Bogdanov, has also been regarded as one of the founders of systems thinking. *Historical Materialism*, among Bukharin's later works, showed Bogdanov's substantial influence on his intellectual development. Bukharin was not, however, Bogdanov's disciple, as his party enemies were later to argue. He did not accept the older theorist's philosophical arguments but rather admired and was influenced by his capacity for creative innovation within the framework of Marxist ideas. The mature Bukharin refused to regard scientific Marxism as a closed, immutable system and was alert both to its inadequacies and to the accomplishments of rival doctrines.

In his remarks on Bukharin's *Historical Materialism*, Lenin repeatedly reacted critically to Bukharin's borrowings of the Tektological vocabulary, calling it "organizational gibberish." Bukharin attempted to reconcile Marxism with scientific advances of the period. Whereas Bogdanov sought to revise Marxism initially on the basis of social energetics, and later on the basis of his general theory of organization, Bukharin sought to also modernize it in light of the achievements of Western sociology.

Bukharin formulated a metabolic and ecologically oriented theory of open system dynamics and located these propositions within the context of economic reproduction and his general theory of equilibrium. Incorporating into his work the Bogdanovian concept of equilibrium, Bukharin came under sustained attack. In their desire to slander Bogdanov, Lenin's successors seized on the theory of equilibrium as a symbol of anti-Soviet activity. That a growth model based on conditions of economic equilibrium could be derived from volume 2 of *Capital* was not a unique point of view.

Distinct from Walrasian general equilibrium, Bukharin's theory of equilibrium was a general "formulation of the laws of motion of material systems." Every system, he argued, is involved in two stages of equilibrium: internal and external. The first refers to the relationship between different components within a system, the second to the entire system in its relationship with its environment. In neither case is there ever an "absolute, unchanging equilibrium." It is always "in flux"—a dynamic or moving equilibrium. However, this appreciation of the dialectic was attacked on the basis that it was subject to forces of change external to the system in question. For Bukharin, it is the relation between a system, such as society, and its environment—an external contradiction—that is a decisive and basic historical factor.

In defining stable and unstable equilibrium, Bukharin specifically employs energy and ecological analogies together with the principle of conservation and feedback concepts. It becomes relatively clear that for Bukharin the role of feedback mechanisms is to regulate the tendency toward disorganization. In other words, to produce a temporary and local reversal of the normal direction of entropy.

In the conclusions to his *Imperialism and the World Economy*, Bukharin notes that "the process of subjugating nature to man's domination on an unprecedented scale begins to choke the capitalist grip." Effectively, he supplemented the dialectic of class conflict with the dialectic of man and the biosphere.

For Bukharin "society is unthinkable without its environment," which is nature. Society adapts itself to nature, strives toward equilibrium with it, by extracting energy from it. Presenting a highly contemporary argument, he asserted that a society grew when it extracted more energy from nature than it put back in. Following Marx's lead, he referred to this material process as metabolic, a life-sustaining relation between society and nature, between "external conditions" and human society. It was a relation mediated by an artificial system of organs—technology. If society extracts from nature precisely as much energy as it consumes, the contradiction between society and nature will be reproduced; the society will mark time, and a state of stable equilibrium results.

Though in a somewhat problematic form, the basic theoretical elements for an ecologically centered Critical Marxism were present in such formulations. The reference image of the economy is systemwide, that the economy is an open system with respect to the natural world. Occasionally it was even acknowledged obliquely by Bukharin's opponents. What was more easily denounced as "un-Marxist" was Bukharin's extrapolation of this limited concept into a macrosociological model.

The *idée fixe* of Bolshevism, the class struggle, was in both Bogdanov's and Bukharin's analysis attenuated. The nexus of class dominance with legal ownership of property would later hamper the critiques of neo-Marxists for decades.

Like Bogdanov before him, Bukharin cautioned against "a new ruling class" based not only on the juridical rights, which attach to property, but also on authority and privilege—what Bogdanov referred to as "organizational" forces. While Bukharin had in his earlier study of capitalism ignored the problem of "the managerial class" and of "power without property," he now saw that an exploiting organizational class could emerge on the basis of nationalized property. His discussion was prompted by the "different élite" theories of Bogdanov. This is not to suggest that Bukharin was merely an admiring student of the elder philosopher; for Bukharin suspected that Bogdanov had, like West European sociologists, "psychologized" the human side of the mode of production and that his phenomenological empirio-criticism was distinctly un-Marxian.

Bukharin grasped that there was something beyond the political hegemony that Lenin and Stalin secured. He worried about a possible degeneration of the body politic and the rise of a "new class" composed of NEPmen, specialists, and distressingly of the party itself. But the emergent crises were increasingly apparent to Bukharin, who regarded these as a kind of mirror image of those of capitalism; for in both Stalinism and capitalism there were disproportions between production and consumption. Anticipating elements of the "convergence" discourse, and with something of a Bogdanovian flourish, he conjectured that there was a formal resemblance between some of the organizational problems of capitalism and those of socialism. He railed against "economic arteriosclerosis" and "a thousand small and large stupidities" associated with "organized mismanagement" and Stalin's "theory of the permanent revolution." While defending the principle of economic planning, he opposed "hypertrophied planning" and argued that "centralization has its limits and it is necessary to give subordinate agencies a certain independence."

While the cogency of the anticipatory arguments of Bogdanov and Bukharin are, since the axial year of 1991, apparent for all, our knowledge of their broad socio-economic theorizing is somewhat less conspicuous.

The nineteenth-century Industrial Revolution augmented labor's natural energy with artificial ones, in the process of which it presented a critical problem for the institutionalization of the corresponding process technologies. In the contemporary situation artificial forms of knowledge are progressively amplifying those of labor. And whereas the nineteenth-century revolution was an energy-based one, the contemporary one is a knowledge- and information-based phenomenon. The full consequences of the cybernetic revolution, with its impact on process technologies, are not fully appreciated within economic thought. For conventional economic analysis is only now coming to grips with the particular theoretical implications of the Industrial Revolution and its meaning for a sustainable coevolution of man and the biosphere. It has yet to substantially address what may be termed the cybernetization of production processes. While conventional contemporary theorists struggle with the issues that undergird these phenomena, aspects of both a socio-energetic and a systems theoretical appreciation were already apparent in the works and the Critical Marxian thought of A.A. Bogdanov and N.I. Bukharin.

Though they themselves contributed to both mechanistic and organismic analogies that subsequently infused systems theory, Bogdanov and Bukharin sought to transcend these limitations and to formulate a purposeful systems paradigm that could be employed by planners to reflect upon the existing social system and to explore alternative socialist designs. It was with a (re)construction of Marx's totality theory that Bogdanov sought to build his critical systems theory.

Bogdanov's and Bukharin's contributions, while constituting an elaboration of a genuine Marxian critique, began a search for a unity of scientific knowledge and constituted a paradigmatic change from closed mechanical systems to an open systems paradigm. Their scholarly efforts offered an early formulation of a systems theoretical interpretation of the economy replete with an appreciation of social autopoiesis. Their considerable efforts are noteworthy, for in some respects they transcend the orthodox reductionism that has piqued attention.

In relatively recent years the Hungarian political economist Janos Kornai offered a critique of orthodox economic theory, urging the application of systems theory.[5] His appeal was neither new at that time nor unheard, and it has been repeated occasionally by others.

Contemporary systems thinking is without neither insights nor ambiguities, for there are a variety of approaches in the application of systems thinking and the usual family disputes among system theorists. Appearing mechanistic on the one hand and, on the other hand, conservative and functionalist where it is "much more like causal thinking than systems thinking,"[6] it would be reckless to suggest that system theorists have been altogether successful in surmounting these somewhat eccentric derivations. To some extent, the very contemporary effort is, once again, in the fashion of a (re)construction of the Critical Marxist systems thinking explored at some length herein.

For these reasons, it is necessary to avoid making exaggerated claims for the potency of system theory as a miracle cure for a complex but bedraggled economic "science." It is not an instant remedy, nor does it represent a single or unified philosophy or technique. It is not a panacea, nor does it offer an alternative formal framework that the theorist of mathematical or formalistic inclination can readily dissect and evaluate. Instead, it involves a paradigmatically incommensurable alternative, embracing a holistic style and habit of thought divorced from Cartesian mechanicalism.

In systems science, the "systems idea" is used in the context of "instrumental reason" to help us decide how to do things. It refers to a set of variables to be controlled. Though his formulation of systems science embodied this functionalist Parsonian aspect, Bogdanov's Tektology embodied the systems idea of "practical reason"—that which helps decide what we ought to do. Bogdanov's Tektological approach was critical in the sense that it demands reflection upon the ontological presuppositions that enter into social systems design. And though

Bogdanov and Bukharin, like Marx, were held in the orbit of Comtean positivism, concerned with the *logos* underpinning "theoretical reason," they also subscribed to a critical approach to the *empire of reason*. For the positivist the only "rational" application of theoretical reason is in its instrumentality. As far as social systems design is concerned, therefore, reason can only encompass technical questions of means and their efficient use. Praxiological discourse about ends, and even about the value content of means, is concealed. The central question of practical reason, "What ought we to do?" for positivists is situated beyond the scope of critical reflection. Rational social action is thus defined by what it is possible to do. The efficient choice of means is a matter of instrumental reason, whereas the issue of what we ought to do is a matter of practical reason. For the positivist, the domain of practical reason collapses into instrumental reason. It is this positivism that still pervades contemporary systems science. For the goals served by systems science too often go unexamined, as effort is put into finding the most efficient means for achieving predetermined but unquestioned ends. Bogdanov's Tektology sought to make the question of what we ought to do subject to critical reflection.

Bogdanov's critical theorizing contributes to the enterprise of practical systems thinking insofar as he recognized that instrumental reason is not the exclusive domain of the *empire of reason*. Practical reason and "emancipatory reason" (aiming at freedom from alienation) are no less important.

While some branches of contemporary critical systems theory are critical in terms of the idealism of Kant and Hegel, absent from their critique is a grounding in the historical materialism of Marx. Though such contributions allow us to reflect upon the ideas that enter into any social systems design, they do not help us to reflect upon the micro- and macropolitical conditions that give rise to those ideas and lead to ideological hegemony. While such an analysis will help give focus to such material conditions, it cannot provide an examination or explanation of the essential nature and development of those conditions. Thus, it assumes a static rather than an evolutionary perspective.

This neglect of the structural aspects and development of social systems means that explanations and recommendations grounded in a Kantian approach embody a utopian element absent from Bogdanov's formulation. The question of which class, group, or agency has the power, the will, and the interest to bring about the *empire of reason* has vexed philosophers of history throughout the modern era. It may be an entirely obfuscating question.

At this juncture let me depart from this sketch of *Paradigm Lost* and note that any work of scholarship begins somewhere and ends somewhere and thus presents a sense of closure and completion. This is, in fact, inevitable, for no text is detached from its intertextual context, a context that differs for the writer and for each of his readers. While this is true in the domain of the aesthetic, it is no less so for works of scholarship, especially those that enter into an ongoing theoretical dialogue. This study does not aspire to the status of a "definitive" work, foreclosing further discussion of the issues it treats; instead, its more modest aim is to contribute to and (re)construct elements of a historic intellectual juncture, a *paradigm lost*.

In seeking to describe the emergence of Russian Critical Marxism and systems thinking, it will be best to give a kind of historical account of its development. In doing so, however, we must be aware of the inevitable bias that enters into the construction of any historical record. It is important to acknowledge that the pattern "discerned" herein will, to a certain degree, be one the author has created. It is then one that in the terms of a hermeneutic distinction is a *Nachkonstruktion* rather than an ascetic *Rekonstruktion*. That is, rather than being a neutral rendering of history "as it actually happened," it bears all the frailties of a rhetorical reenactment inevitably shaped by the author's own concerns. The inevitability of such a (re)construction in the crafting of historical accounts has been emphasized by a variety of theorists whose common premise is that although the historian does not construct his or her narrative out of whole cloth, he or she nonetheless imagines a coherence that the participants in the account may well have failed to perceive. Any historical narrative tends to meld and temper the disparities in the rusting iron of the past, and it inevitably does so from the finite perspective of the historian's present. Although unraveling the history of a concept recalls the approach identified with the controversial History of Ideas School, it would do violence to the history of the systems theoretical critique of political economy were a restricted methodology adopted. A "fusion of horizons" between past and present makes historical thinking a never-completed, infinitely interpretative process.

This account is not an attempt to present an "unvarnished" truth. It is neither a vilification nor an attempt to lionize the characters that enter into the record presented herein. Rather the author seeks to merely convey to the reader the events and drama that have hitherto characterized a footnote in the history of ideas. Our appreciation of the Soviet controversies of the 1920s is one largely dependent upon post-Stalinist and largely Western perspectives. This is due, in part, to the proleptic nature of much of the Western literature on the ideas of the period. The most interesting and significant aspect of the debate was its anticipation of relatively recent developments in economic ideas. Ours is something of an anticipatory reading of the characters who strut across our stage. The appeal of the characters does not obtain merely from their oppositional stance but from the cogency and contemporary relevance of their ideas.

Whether or not this account is able to illuminate the darkened passages that may have led to the turmoil that today cleaves the remnants of the Soviet Union remains a matter of speculation that is history's tantalizing game of "What if?" Nonetheless, speculative thought leads us to consider that had the events of the Russian cultural revolution taken a different turn, had Critical rather than Scientific Marxism informed the nascent structures of the Soviet Union, its history of socio-economic development could have been remarkably different.

1

Selected Issues in the Philosophy of Science and Economic Methodology

Introductory Remarks

In 1898, in the *Quarterly Journal of Economics*, Thorstein Veblen's essay entitled "Why Is Economics Not an Evolutionary Science?" was first published. At the very least, Veblen must be credited with asking a poignant question, a question that has tried the patience of conventional economic theory. The field of inquiry we currently refer to as economics has had a much more turbulent evolution than other fields of intellectual inquiry. Indeed, the enduring powers of conventional economic theory are legendary. Its durable nature has not been without considerable criticism and though such heresy has accumulated, the heretics have not succeeded in bringing about the paradigmatic changes they sought. They have, nonetheless, established an impressive critical literature. Despite the formidable nature of the heresy the conventional wisdom continues rather undisturbed; the critics themselves have either been reabsorbed into economic orthodoxy or become marginalized fringe dwellers. The extreme durability and apparent immunity to criticism of conventional theory has led some observers to liken it to theology. "Man cannot live," noted Galbraith, "without an economic theology—without some rationalization of the abstract and seemingly inchoate arrangements which provide him with his livelihood."[1] This suggests that economic ideas and beliefs are cultural phenomena rather than elegant logical constructs.[2] There are further distinctions.

Modernity takes it for granted that the so-called hard sciences provide the epistemological foundations upon which to build our view of nature and humanity. In addition, modernity accepts scientific data and predictions as reliable grounds for the purpose of making decisions concerning the present and future. Last, modernity has elevated scientists to the status once secured for the high priests and saints who communicated to humanity the revealed word of God.

Science and scientists assume a culturally preferred position. If we view scientists as those having access to revealed truths of one sort or another, then economists will have the elevated political stature of those whose predictions and policy recommendations are epistemologically sound and beyond doubt. However, unsettling doubts are present in the minds of some of its most distinguished practitioners, and discursive epistemic communities are fracturing, for problems emerge when attempts are made to justify knowledge claims.

Once celebrated as the "Queen of the Social Sciences," economics is struggling to come to grips with a paradigmatic crisis that obtains, in part, from its trenchant recalcitrance.

> The trouble with modern economics is its ultra-narrow doctrinal basis. Proclaiming itself a science, it is grounded in a form of logical positivism which elsewhere was superseded 20 to 30 years ago. Neoclassical economics especially survives in almost total intellectual isolation from neighboring disciplines.... The effect of modern (neoclassical) economics has really been to uncouple the economy from both its socio-cultural and political life support systems, to confer on it a self-determining reality of its own.[3]

Its failure to examine its conceptual structure and frames of reference undermine even its most innocent "factual" inquiries. It is a failure that jeopardizes its practical usefulness. For in some circles its "usefulness" is of a parochial character, which cultivates a callow professionalization, one that seeks to root out alternative discourse. Characterized by its fragmentary approach, by its loss of totality, and by its unquestioned ontological substratum, the more formally intricate economics becomes, the more resolutely it turns its back on the problems of its own sphere of influence, the more it will become a formally closed system of partial "laws." It suffers from Sorokin's "quantiphrenia."

> Present-day economics is characterized by the fragmentary and reductionist approach, which typifies most social sciences. Economists generally fail to recognize that the economy is merely one aspect of a whole ecological and social fabric; a living system composed of human beings in continual interaction with one another and with their natural resources, most of which are, in turn, living organisms. The basic error of the social sciences is to divide this fabric in fragments, assumed to be independent and to be dealt with in separate academic departments.[4]

Were society led to an unquestioning acceptance of certain theories concerning the economic domain, as it was led to accept certain religious doctrines, then we may create and support an environment in which a "guardian" minority (no matter how esteemed) will be able to dominate and manipulate the majority. This potential situation, one might hasten to add, may be welcomed by the majority and may come about in a seemingly democratic way. That is, the majority routinely accepts the verdicts of experts, feeling incompetent to challenge them.

The majority thereby enhances the political power of experts, while simultaneously debilitating its power to control them. This potential political problem has, of course, many ethical corollaries, which have occupied the philosophers and social theorists of this century.

It is reasonable to insist that we reconsider economics as political economy and acknowledge the intimate relationship that both fields of inquiry, politics and economics, have maintained over the past two centuries. We ought to evaluate economic theories in much broader terms than that which relies on conventional methodological discourse, for there is no economic theory devoid of ideology or ontological presuppositions. Theory is always theory "for" someone or something.

Because economic theories may be enacted into policies, we ought to consider anew the scientific status of economics. In a society that worships science and technology, as it once worshiped stone idols, one's only chance to put doubt in the public's mind about the feasibility and validity of any proposal is to question the scientific foundations upon which that proposal is made. If one is merely left to argue about the particularities of a theory, one can be rebuffed by the excuse that this or that particular aspect is only an approximation. The broader context for examining economic theories should include at the very least the history, sociology, and philosophy of science. One might view current debates on the philosophy of science to be of both a micropolitical and a macropolitical character. Insofar as economic knowledge is a political activity, it is the expression of power and its disciplinary techniques. French philosopher Michel Foucault wrote that "there is no power-relation without the correlative constitution of a field of knowledge, nor at the same time any knowledge that does not presuppose and constitute at the same time power-relations."[5] The dominant economic paradigm cannot be divorced from power. It is an expression of Foucault's "disciplinary power." It fosters a convoluted exercise in "truth-seeking," for it is linked in a circular relation with veiled systems of power that produce and sustain the paradigm's "hard core."[6] Pointedly, the very disciplinary nature of economic science must be eschewed. It must become "undisciplined" and admit other than the received knowledge.

Formalist economics is recalcitrant; its professionalized nucleus impugns criticism and potential change. So deeply entrenched is the disciplinary mode of domination, so pervasive is it in its operation, and so ubiquitous is it in its location, that changing any part of the power field leaves the basic form untouched. Consequently, the plight of rehabilitating the discipline of political economy is not merely affected by demonstrating that orthodox methods attach to a special case, the formidable intellectual task is the construction (or reconstruction) of an alternative paradigm.

Political economy should not be constituted by fixed methods or axiomatic assumptions. It should be the study, as Karl Polanyi argued, of the nature, processes, and social relations governing the appropriational and locational movements of the requisites of human life.[7] It must again embrace the ethical imperative that it once articulated. Political economy should be a campaign to address aspects of the reality of society.[8] This is not a rigid definition, and it is not intended to be. The livelihood of man is, as Polanyi taught us, necessarily embedded within broader social relations, culture, and institutions, and the real boundaries between the "economy" and "society" and "polity" are ambiguous. But it is also grounded upon the biophysical processes of the biosphere. This shifting away from a method-centered to a subject-centered definition is critically necessary if we are to make sense of the present and invent a sustainable future. There is a pressing need for a more tolerant and permissive atmosphere, and for genuine competition among rival paradigms in the discipline.

Economic science is jeopardized by an intellectual hegemony. Economists, who are proselytizers of free competition, will not admit that very ethos into the province of ideas. A new spirit of pluralism in political economy is required, involving critical conversation and tolerant communication between different paradigms. Such pluralism should not undermine the standards of rigor; for a political economy that requires itself to face all the arguments will be a more, not a less, rigorous science.

To emancipate political economy from its scientistic hegemony requires us to critically examine elements of the philosophical and methodological underpinnings that constitute its paradigm and to reflect upon the continuing historical relevance of the Aristotelian tradition of praxis. In this chapter, after introducing the paradigmatic conceptual framework as it pertains to political economy and addressing the social psychological dimensions of scientific revolution and reform, we shall sketch the syntheses and inversion in political economic analysis. This exercise begins with an evaluation of paradigmatic change in economic thought and then reviews selected dimensions of the European history of economic thought as it matured from the period of the Enlightenment to embrace, on the one hand, the mainstream mechanicalist paradigm and, on the other hand, a countercurrent holistic paradigm. It was against this background that the progress of economic "science" made particular methodological advancements even while obscuring a certain category of problems. But the enigmatic qualities of mechanicalism evoked a Kantian and Hegelian critique that addressed the alleged universalism of the mechanical paradigm. The critique of the philosophy of nature diagnosed the misplaced concreteness, which obtained from an alleged universality and sought to reaffirm the long-obscured Aristotelian systems problematique. However, it was not until the last decades of the nineteenth century that from a confluence of insights there arose a humanist (re)construction of Aristotelian praxiology whose method of inquiry merged with the pursuit of a natural unity of scientific knowledge.

The Paradigmatic Conceptual Framework

A "science" is customarily identified as an inquiry into a specific realm of objective reality. Insofar as modern science inquires into the phenomena of life, whether inanimate, brute, or human, it is occupied with questions of genesis and cumulative change, and it converges upon a theoretical formulation in the shape of a life-history drawn in causal terms. Insofar as it is a science in the current sense of the term, political economy occupies itself with a partial analysis of human conduct. It is an inquiry into the human scheme of life, where the subject of inquiry is the conduct of man in his dealings with the material means of life. It is often an inquiry into the life-history of material civilization. But, as John Dewey wrote in *The Quest for Certainty*, it is "only recently that there has been sufficient understanding of physical relations (including the biological under this caption) to provide the necessary intellectual instrumentalities for effective intellectual attack upon social phenomena." Before the "necessary intellectual instrumentalities" were accessible, the "theoretical formulation" more often than not did violence to the facts. Ignorance was the wellspring of invention, for knowing scandalously little about his world, man was free to construct his own beliefs and myths about it. But as he assembled his data, as his awareness grew, the domain of belief has allegedly diminished. With the expanding compass of his knowledge, he "discovered" that new phenomena tallied with causal sequences. Related causal sequences were conjoined into the sciences, wherein each phenomenon obtained meaning in terms of its relation to the other phenomena in its sequence. Thereafter, no magical revelation was necessary to give significance to phenomena whose correlation with other existential items had been established.

Political economy is, allegedly, one of the latest disciplines to attain sufficient correlative data with "obvious" and "mandatory" causal relations to stand alone, that is, to stand without occult interpretation to give it meaning. However, political economy is, even now, still struggling with the goblins of its childhood. Failure to examine the conceptual structure and frames of reference that are unconsciously implicated in even the most innocent factual inquiries is the greatest single defect that can be found in any field of inquiry. This failure is a hindrance to the development of any science, but it occurs very easily in political economy. And it occurs there more easily because the domain of political economy is closely identified with frames of reference the validity of which is conjectured to be beyond dispute. Individual phenomena in the subject matter of political economy are, even yet, thought to have intrinsic meaning within themselves. For while physics alleges to be descriptive of the nature and properties of matter and energy and biology descriptive of living open systems, the conventional practice has been to regard political economy as being not a study of the livelihood of man but a method or formal type of analysis: equilibrium theorizing with fixed tastes and technology.

The basic difference between economic "science" and the physical sciences is perhaps revealed in a maxim of Wesley Clair Mitchell's: "The only reason, the only excuse, for the study of economic theory is to make this world a better place in which to live."[9] Whether or not it is "the only excuse," Mitchell clearly put his finger on the fundamental motive underlying the theoretical endeavors of the great figures in economics. We start with the premise that political economy is fundamentally an instrument for making this world a better place in which to live.

Keeping in mind this maxim, we would be wise to dwell on the fact that there appears to be an economic crisis in the real world that is not unrelated to the widely appreciated and long-acknowledged crisis in positivist economic theory.

Upheavals in scientific theory often occur in times of crisis for both the science and the social system that support it: Edmund Burke responded to the forces for democratization; Adam Smith provided a theoretical justification of a laissez-faire ideology; Marx attempted to explain the more disturbing consequences of capitalism; and so forth.

From the perspective of the philosophy of science, the issue is more, not less, clouded. "Logicians cannot make sense of science—but they make sense and so they stipulate that science must be presented in terms of their favorite logical system. This would be excellent comedy material were it not the case that by now almost everyone has started taking the logician seriously."[10]

Neither can orthodox neoclassical economists make sense of the livelihood of man, but they too can make sense of logic; so they stipulate that economics must be presented in terms of their favorite logical system—logical empiricism—and therein lies one of the fundamental stumbling blocks to progress within the discipline of economics. The neoclassical paradigm that now dominates the Anglo-American profession is purportedly based on a methodological foundation of logical empiricism, which the neoclassical economists themselves cannot conform to, but which nonetheless has proven politically instrumental in undercutting the legitimacy of those alternative research programs that do not support the ontological premises or ideological conclusions of neoclassicism. Indeed, logical empiricism retains its hegemony within the discipline of economics and continues to provide conventional economists with the rationale to dismiss alternative paradigms.

One cannot help but ask why neoclassical economics continues to invoke positivism as the only acceptable methodology when positivism has been in decline for more than twenty years within the philosophy of science. The answer, we believe, is that the positivist tradition has been instrumental in allowing orthodox economists to castigate those alternative research programs that do not support the conclusions of neoclassicism. Indeed, the systems theoretical approach to economics has been conveniently dismissed as illegitimate because it is not "scientific"; that is, it does not conform to the disciplinary demands of logical empiricism.

It may be argued, for instance, that the present crisis corresponds to the logic of the neoclassical synthesis, a logic essentially pre-Keynesian in its character. And insofar as the pre-Keynesian systems were inadequate for analyzing the real-world economic problems of the 1930s, it is not surprising that they are incapable of dealing with the more complex problems of the 1990s. This is not to suggest for a moment that the crisis lies purely in the domain of macroeconomic analysis, for it undoubtedly permeates the whole of conventional economic thought. The acknowledgment of the crisis, as such, no longer evokes the heated discussion that it did a scant few years ago. It has now grown so conspicuous that it may seem somewhat banal to make the argument. For as necessary as such pronouncements remain, they are often of merely parenthetical interest; an explicit treatment of the nature of the crisis seems more worthy of attention. Moreover, beyond groping with the crisis per se, it is constructive to explicate the nature of the malaise that frustrates current economic thought. Clear understanding of the cause of the problems is necessary to achieve the redirection that the word "crisis" evokes.

Crises are resolved by redirection. The grave character of contemporary socioeconomic problems and dilemmas of governance makes it imperative that theorists embark on this expedition. To begin, we shall employ the customary, serviceable, though not undisputed, lexicon of Thomas S. Kuhn to derive a conceptual outline with which to address the issue at hand. And one might add, we shall decline any invitation to rigorously contest the Popperian reflections on science. Such a debate is outside the context of this work. The important aspects of the philosophy of science framework will be highlighted in the first section. I invite those readers familiar with the philosophy of science debate to proceed to "Syntheses and Inversion in Political Economic Thought," chapter 2.

The conceptualization of scientific change in the philosophy and sociology of science may be analyzed in terms of three bipolar frames of reference: the scientific process seen as (1) cumulative versus noncumulative; (2) rational versus nonrational; and (3) internal versus external in substance.[11] Philosophers and scholars have traditionally expressed the opinion that scientific progress is due largely to the rationality with which scientific goals are pursued. The rationalist model of scientific change assumes that the methodology adopted in the pursuit of a desired goal is justified. Karl Popper, for example, in his *The Logic of Scientific Discovery* apparently thinks that science may be the only human activity in which mistakes are regularly challenged and corrected, and that regulation from within the discipline makes progress possible. Indeed, for many years logical empiricism, associated with this appreciation, dominated the philosophy of science.

The philosophy of science in the twentieth century has encompassed the rise of logical positivism, its maturation in logical empiricism, and a fundamental attack thereon through the "growth of knowledge tradition" of Thomas Kuhn, Paul Feyerabend, and others. Logical empiricism grew in the 1940s and 1950s out of the tradition of logical positivism, which argued that science progresses through the application of logical analysis to empirical phenomena. In constructing scientific theories, only those statements that can be verified—that is, empirically observed—are accepted as meaningful statements in a theory. Logical empiricism evolved within this tradition in an effort to explicate the derivation of meaningful (verifiable/falsifiable) sentences for theory construction. The evaluation of theories rested upon a determination of the correspondence between theory claims and reality. But much of the empirical work in economics is like "playing tennis with the net down" and produces what Mark Blaug has called "innocuous falsificationism."[12]

According to Bruce Caldwell, "logical empiricists concerned themselves with the elaboration of universal models and procedural rules which they believed aptly characterized legitimate scientific practice."[13] As Feyerabend describes the process, the aim of positivists such as Karl Popper is to "develop a special point of view, to bring that point into logically acceptable form . . . and then to discuss everything in its terms."[14] Both the natural and the social sciences have cherished a positivist epistemology according to which scientific knowledge addresses the presentism of the phenomenal world. Disciplined objectivity, as this criterion might be called, requires that a "proper" scientific description should not include man in any capacity whatsoever. The crux of the scientific method lies in the disputed idea of the complete neutrality between the observer and the observed. However, for a science of man to altogether exclude man from the picture is a patent incongruity. Nevertheless, those who subscribe to a positivist appreciation of the economy take special pride in operating in a man-less universe. As Vilfredo Pareto overtly claimed, once we have determined the means at the disposal of the individual and obtained "a photograph of his tastes . . . the individual may disappear."[15]

True, the ideal of a man-less science has been discredited by post-positivist philosophers of science, particularly since Heisenberg's formulation of the Indeterminacy Principle.[16] Feyerabend notes that "according to Kuhn, science is a historical tradition . . . it is not subjected to external rules, the rules that guide the scientist are not always known, and they change from one period to the next."[17] Post-positivists are less concerned with developing a universal "scientific method" and more concerned with "the growth of knowledge over time, the dynamics of change within individual disciplines and the actual practices of scientists."[18] By stressing the historical aspect of inquiry, post-positivists minimize the prescriptive role of philosophy of science and, by acknowledging the heterogeneous process of inquiry, advocate methodological pluralism. The growth-of-knowledge tradition exposes the weakness of the Cartesian system that underlies positivism/objectivism and its forced separation of fact and value, normative and positive.

In recent times the exalted view of narrowly interpreted scientific rationality has been criticized as a dangerous myth by T. Kuhn and P. Feyerabend, among others. Science, in their view, is seen not a system of statements but rather a "skillful knowing." The traditional conception of the relation between theories and practices is that practices are successful insofar as they are based on theories that give factual representations of the world. This conception has been criticized on various grounds, including political ones, and some authors, (e.g., Paul

Feyerabend) have described theories as fairy tales from which no issue of truth can meaningfully arise.[19] As Kuhn has shown, new approximations, new theories, will not bring us any closer to an absolute truth.

Whether economics can be considered a science remains controversial.[20] The question requires that we first define more precisely what we mean by science. It seems that economists historically have tried to imbue their studies with what they took to be standard scientific methods. It remains unclear whether the field as a whole has been able to follow any of these methods precisely or to fulfill any of its criteria for scientific practice. That is, the striving to fulfill its criteria may be viewed as insufficient in itself for the sake of conferring scientific status on this field.

But before we hasten to condemn economics as a pseudoscience or to claim that its practitioners have routinely failed to live up to their own scientific expectations and the expectations of other scientists, we should take note of a peculiar situation concerning the scientific status of any field of inquiry, not only economics. It can be argued that many other fields of inquiry, even astronomy and physics, according to some, also fail to fulfill the standard criteria that allow us to confer on them scientific status.[21] That is, it may be impossible to find any field fully qualified to be called a science in a narrow and fixed sense of the term. In this respect, then, all fields of intellectual inquiry, be they of empirical content or not, continuously struggle to position themselves within the established and "normal" scientific community while still (implicitly) admitting large portions that are not "scientific" at all.

Science is criticized by Feyerabend because of its: monopoly on determining the "natural"; monopoly of access to investigation of the natural; and lack of a critical reflexivity. Some see science as an internally consistent set of beliefs that has no more validity than any other. They argue that the nonrationalist criticism usually proceeds through either "stodgy" or "inspiring" attacks. Their main hypothesis, though with some variance, is a Darwinistic scheme of evolution. Drawing from historical studies, Feyerabend contends that science does not proceed according to a rational method, rather progress occurs only when scientists adopt an "anything goes" philosophy. It is competition between incompatible theories that facilitates scientific progress, though scientific progress sometimes occurs in the absence of any solution to a previously recognized problem. Feyerabend also believes that all theories should be given equal attention, not just those that are commonly accepted.[22]

However, realizing that the "value free" position of "everything is permitted" leads to the destruction of every system of thought, including his own, Feyerabend's position compares with that of K. Popper, who argued that any effort to prove a statement empirically eventually comes up against underlying theories and assumptions that cannot be empirically proven. Feyerabend bases his rejection of empirical experience on the proposition that all experience is deceptive. He did not go beyond the established criticism of predominant positions in the theory of knowledge (e.g., logical positivism and critical rationalism). Rather he set out to find a stable social core, which led him to his concept of tradition. While it is possible to agree with much that Feyerabend says, his dissatisfaction with modern science causes him to advocate a position that potentially admits irrationalism and mysticism. Feyerabend's claim is that some anomalous facts will remain hidden in the absence of alternatives to the theories to be tested. For Feyerabend, tradition is not just a framework for the functioning of norms and institutions passed from one generation to the next but an "elementary social relationship" of a normative character that allows its interpreters to judge concrete values and institutions.

Scientific development may be conjectured to be part of social evolution, in which the actual sociological arguments against a Darwinistic logic of social development have considerable impact on a philosophical theory of scientific evolution. The arguments of N. Luhmann, J. Habermas, and K. Marx make it quite clear that Darwinism cannot be a clue to the explanation of social (and scientific) evolution. Science and scientific standards cannot be separated from the institutional context and practice of science; their use presupposes immersion in this practice. In fact, and contrary to accepted opinion, the relativism of science is not the result of a newly developed sensitivity on the part of philosophers of science for the history of science but merely expresses the problems endemic to Popperian progeny.

However, before descending further into the debate it would be helpful to render as unambiguous as possible the meaning herein associated with the word *paradigm*. It first entered the vernacular of economics in the wake of the widespread discussion of Thomas Kuhn's *The Structure of Scientific Revolutions*. Kuhn himself used the term to connote the "disciplinary matrix," that is, the constellation of shared beliefs and practices, i.e., the culture, structuring the scientific activity of an "invisible college" of scientists.[23] Unfortunately, it has not been generally understood that an important modification, or at least a shift in emphasis, must be made to Kuhn's conception of a disciplinary matrix, or paradigm, before it can be applied to the "scientific activity" of political economy.

When the appreciation of a system's structural or behavioral performances or properties is incomplete, where the variables, their character, magnitudes, and interaction are unknown, a particular class of problems is involved: these problems are called *metaphysical*. While we are no doubt familiar with the cynical meaning of *metaphysical*, there is also a meaning that is less appreciated by science. Consider, for instance, the concepts of political economy that could not be properly treated inside the mechanistic framework, like social ethics, finalism, or essentialism. They were/are regarded as *metaphysical* because there were/are no means for submitting them to economic analysis narrowly defined. Many social science theories, including much of economic theory, are in a *metaphysical* stage of development in that their problems are essentially imaginative or purely conceptual in character. For instance, the formalist aspect of much of conventional economics, that is, its ahistorical dimension, binds it to the dominion of the metaphysical. The fact that they were once considered metaphysical did not in any case prevent them from subsequently becoming focal concepts in the discipline. They reflect a need to develop methods for creating as well as appraising methodological proposals. These considerations are meta-methodological; they are related to questions of theoretical change or paradigm shift. Correspondingly, controversies of a meta-methodological nature can be defined as disputes regarding the epistemological nature of methodology, in which the empirical sciences form the "object of attention" of meta-methodological subjects. These subjects are analytical in that they are concerned with developing guidelines or criteria for "doing science." They are concerned with developing "good ideas about ideas about reality." Thus, for instance, epistemology, logic, mathematics, and, important for this work, cybernetics and general systems theory qualify as relevant meta-methodological studies for social sciences. The central epistemological meaning of systems theory for economic analysis is that having been successful in the difficult task of "concretizing" such concepts as totality, finality, and autopoiesis, concepts that did not previously possess a status, it secures them a transition from the metaphysical to the scientific.

The related metasystem concept is an attempt to emphasize the ontological, epistemological, and methodological differentiation of sciences. Such a concept suggests that every science has a lower level of inquiry, where observations and descriptive models obtain; an object level of inquiry, where we seek to formulate explanatory hypotheses and models; and a metasystemic level of inquiry, where the prescriptive efforts take place. Moreover, it is possible to refer to a subsequent level associated with the conceptualization of the epistemological mode, where the paradigms of science and metamodeling are of the essence and elaborated.

Joseph A. Schumpeter, in his analyses of business cycles, argued that a doctrinal series maps the path of equilibrium points and neighborhoods, where each succeeding point is associated with a higher level than the preceding one, the path being therefore descriptive of an evolutionary process. With regard to the evolution of political economy, he believed that during the feudal ages, scholastic thought contained all the germs of capitalism; it developed slowly but steadily by small increments. Classical political economy evolved on the basis of earlier and more simple structures or theses (feudalism, mercantilism) that were no longer functionally viable or became otherwise untenable.

In his opus, *History of Economic Analysis*, Schumpeter ponders the issue of change in economic thought:

> The most obvious way in which science advances is by new departures, that is, by the discovery of new facts, or new aspects of old facts, or new relations between facts. . . . But there is another way.
>
> When we use the concepts and theorems that we have inherited from our

predecessors ... we add here and correct there and so this apparatus slowly develops into a different one.[24]

The two modes of change to which Schumpeter alludes bear a similarity to the view of scientific disciplinary change laid out by Thomas Kuhn in his modern classic, *The Structure of Scientific Revolutions*. While Popper's view is redolent with classical liberal ideas, Feyerabend uses notions of "uneven development" and "permanent revolution," and Kuhn draws on a "crisis" model of political revolution and describes the articulation of a discipline's developmental path up to the point at which an exemplar fails to furnish or adjudicate provocative problems. This, the crisis of normal science, provokes extraordinary science and the way is then cleared for scientific revolution—the institution of a new developmental exemplar. There seems to be in Kuhn a singular lack of appreciation of the broader institutional and sociological context. It is this, in the case of economic thought, which forms a further constraint on paradigm change. Kuhn's paradigmatic dynamic appears rather insulated from the macro- and micropolitics to which we have alluded.

The fundamentals of Kuhn's history of science paradigm are the following: pre-paradigm; normal science; crisis and, possibly, extraordinary science; and normal science again with the resolution of the crisis. For Kuhn, a paradigm, i.e., disciplinary matrix, is a worldview, a set of implicit and explicit guides or examples defining the world and the questions and methods for analyzing the world. It may be conjectured to be the corpus of theoretical knowledge and analytical and empirical techniques customary to the dominant scientific community. The paradigm provides a legitimating consensus, a system of shared values necessary for the group's endurance.

The pre-paradigmatic phase of the dynamics of science is guided by the growth of experience with the use of apparatus and instruments, through the systematic ordering of empirical data, and through the formation of heuristically meaningful analogies and modes of reasoning. Thus, for instance, the explorative phase associated with Schumpeter's remarks about feudalism already has certain structures, but it lacks a comprehensive theory. In it, tools are transformed into instruments, phenomena into effects, and ideas into concepts. The unity of pre-scientific experience, that is, the common sense rooted in everyday life is shattered, and a disciplinary field of scientific inquiry emerges.

In the subsequent phase of paradigm articulation, the search for the fundamental theory of an experimentally structured discipline becomes dominant. This theory must be capable of resolving all the fundamental problems of that discipline, thereby reconstituting the objectified fragments of experience into a theoretical unity. In this phase science follows an autonomous path of development, and it is postulated that such autonomy is necessary from the cognitive point of view. The various theoretical approaches, each with its own internal problems and confrontations, give rise to a clear-cut research path. The individual scientist has, by then, come to realize that the most important and most interesting problems of the discipline are those that will provide it with the theoretical foundations it has, up to then, lacked.

The pre-paradigm phase is identified with the fleeting existence of several competing schools of thought, each offering an alternative paradigm, none of which is persuasive enough to garner a consensual acceptance that attaches to normal science. There is a lack of direction as to what research should be done and as to the appropriate methods for doing it. Each competing group tends to seize upon a set of problems, facts, and methods. Published works take the form of calloused theses that define and justify the scope and method of the research and protect its vital core. This work itself may, in fact, be so characterized.

With little incentive to exhume recondite data, and no guide to assure its relevance once attained, there is a near-paranoid insecurity exemplified by the tendency to limit fact gathering to existent or easily accessible data. Within the physical sciences, in particular, it is with technological advances that the store of accessible data in the professions and crafts assumes critical importance to the conception of new sciences. Though it may be too critical a remark, it may nonetheless be the case that those in each school, though practicing science, when taken as a whole do not, in fact, form a science.

Kuhn's theory of scientific revolutions has been criticized as being irrational and a matter of psychological processes void of quantitative verification. Each Kuhnian paradigm has its own standards, making rational comparisons impossible. Kuhn's method of scientific change from one paradigm to another possesses an alleged spiritualness.

Might not this be the expression of a phenomenon that situates itself in the realm of social psychology, that is, the theory of cognitive dissonance? If we cautiously eliminate—not as nonexistent but as unsatisfactory—the conspiratorial motivation of a conscious fabrication to mislead others (and ourselves) to hide the concrete reality from them, we may inquire into the mechanism of cognitive dissonance. It may permit us to understand the phenomenon.

The theory of cognitive dissonance, formulated by Leo Festinger in the 1950s to address issues removed from paradigmatic change, may prove useful and may be reduced to the following thesis. If scientific community finds itself in a situation of conflict (which occurs often not only to individuals but also to specifically structured groups of people), when its ideas, beliefs, and attitudes (in the sense of readiness to act) do not correspond to the concrete reality and are falsified by this reality, then three possibilities present themselves:

1. To change "reality" in such a way that it corresponds with our ideas, beliefs, and attitudes; this normally proves to be impossible.

2. To change our ideas, beliefs, and attitudes to make them correspond with "reality"; this is easier, but often it would mean an ideological catastrophe for the person or group of people involved, and therefore they will resist the acceptance of such a solution to the utmost.

3. To ignore the evidence of facts, to close one's mind to them, to become immune to the voice of "reality" that falsifies our beliefs.[25]

The third possibility—which is not a theoretical speculation but an empirically verified theory—is the defense mechanism of cognitive dissonance that interests us. It encourages a sort of schizophrenia—a social schizophrenia—when a person understands intellectually what we are telling him but erases emotionally the content of the statement heard or read because its acceptance would demolish those beliefs that are central to his being—a typically schizophrenic situation in which a person knows something and at the same time does not "know" it.

Corresponding to the second category of Festinger's theory, when an association of practitioners of competing schools or a synthesis of schools reaches a critical mass, the transition to normal or mature science begins. The knowledge accumulated in the preceding phase of cognitive autonomy makes it possible to formulate the fundamental theory of a particular discipline. "Scientization" of the discipline having thus achieved a stage of theoretical maturity, its further theoretical development can be linked with specific social interests. Thus, the strategic direction of fundamental research is established in the post-paradigmatic phase. The cognitive resistance to external direction (which marks autonomous fundamental research) becomes obsolete when the fundamental theory has "in principle" resolved all the problems of that discipline.

Paradigms gain acceptance by being considered more capable of solving a set of problems that have come to be accepted as the most compelling. To place this in perspective, let us refer to neoclassic economics. Its formalism defines the set of problems as those characterized by choice under constraint. Other problems stand outside of the paradigm.

Elevating formalism and axiomatics to unwarranted heights, the formal definition of economics becomes a recipe for intolerance.[26] The issue is one not of analytical technique but of analytical focus or substance. Formalism in this sense emphasizes the economizing or maximizing connotation of the term *economic*, with the familiar presumption of scarcity and insatiable wants (not needs) in the face of limited resources. Coupled with the further proposition of rationality, economics becomes the "science of choice," where its typical concern is the deductive exploration of the logic of maximization under the constraint of scarcity. In this view, calculated choice, oriented toward maximization, is *the* economic problem, and the economy is said to consist of a series of choices imposed by scarcity situations. But this formalist perspective is conspicuously ahistoric and ethnocentric. For insofar as it universalizes the historically specific culture of market capitalism, it limits itself to the concerns and motivations characteristic of capitalist society. Consequently, the formalist perspective constitutes a subtle ideological expression of that society. Formalism constrains inquiry with respect to the objective meaning of the livelihood of man—past, present, and future. It obscures the institutional structure of the economy with its preoccupation with economizing or calculative behavior. It prefigures all economic systems as being essentially concerned with *the* economic problem of efficient resource allocation and equitable distribution of the products that result. This ethnocentrism leads to the presumption that market exchanges must have existed in the past and it leads to the search for functional equivalents to the market process therein. The actual institutions that provide the context for the economic process are excluded from analysis. Thus it abstracts precisely those concrete phenomena that should be the axial concern of analysis.

Even as formalism inhibits scholarly appreciation of past economies, it obscures our understanding of the present. In idealizing the self-regulating market economy, its blinkered approach denies the hegemonic dimensions of the market economy, for it treats the economy as an autonomous entity. There is no methodological mandate for examining the interaction of society and the economy or for appreciating the metabolic interaction of the economy and the biosphere. Formalism cannot possibly come to grips with the essential features of the livelihood of man today.

There is yet a further myopia of formalism—the future. If the market mode of economic integration is receding in the wake of a societal and environmental protective response, it is necessarily being replaced by alternative integrative modes. Consequently, the future is being born along fault lines invisible to the formalist. Moreover, the solutions to the problems of emergent and alternative modes of economic integration may well be in the socioeconomies of the past. But here formalism absents itself, for it neglects the essential past and misreads much of the essential present. Consequently, it is of no use in the *architectonik* effort of designing an alternative future.[27]

Let us return to our main theme. The transition to normal science is marked by a withering away of rival schools caused by conversion of old adherents or lack of recruits from a new generation. Normal science is consummated when the discipline more or less universally accepts the paradigm and then escorts the practitioner down the pathways relevant to address the allegedly key questions with the approved methodology of normal research. As a discipline it may assume an ever narrower definition. This more spartan definition changes the character of scientific publications as general books are replaced by shorter articles or research reports that assume prior knowledge of the paradigm on the part of the reader. The textbook tradition also arises. Novices learn from texts, not by perusing original treatises. The discipline assumes a myopic professionalized dimension, with its own symbolisms, standards, and communications system increasingly detached from the lay public.

Normal science encompasses a period of paradigm articulation involving the manipulation of fact and theory to expand its scope and precision and to resolve the ambiguities internal to the paradigm. Significantly, normal science typically seeks to uncover phenomenal or theoretical novelties. The accepted paradigm defines the appropriate problems to pursue and the procedures to be used for this pursuit. It guarantees that by using these procedures, solutions to the problems can be found, publication offers received, and tenure more or less assured. Normal science is a kind of riddle solving. When a practitioner fails to produce the anticipated result, the riddle solver, not the riddle paradigm, is contrived to be inadequate. This point, corresponding to category three of Festinger's theory, is not without importance, for paradigm changes are repudiations of previous paradigms, which infrequently redeem themselves.

A "cultural crisis" occurs with the interruption of normal science. The existence of one or several anomalies marks the first stage of a crisis. An anomaly is a repudiation of expectations or failure of a set of paradigm riddles to resolve themselves. As such, an anomaly may be associated with conflicting experimental or empirical discoveries or with a persistent theoretical ambiguity, an ambiguity that defies resolution by paradigm articulation and that raises hard questions about ontology.

An anomaly, of course, may not lead to crisis; it may exist and be recognized but be considered peripheral and as such possibly corresponds to the third category of the above rendition of Festinger's theory of cognitive dissonance. Or, the paradigm may be adjusted to resolve the anomaly. To evoke a crisis, an anomaly must: question explicit fundamental generalizations and ontology of the paradigm; be instrumental to the solution of a pressing practical problem; or be plagued with internal incoherences that defy resolution within the paradigm. When, for these or other reasons, an anomaly becomes recognized as more than merely an intransigent problem, the transition to crisis and Kuhnian extraordinary science occurs. More attention is afforded the anomaly, and it may come to be recognized as the critical subject matter of the discipline.

The period of extraordinary science is similar in many ways to the preparadigm state. Corresponding to category two of Festinger's theory, there occurs a relaxation of the rules of normal science that results in more speculative, expansive research. Increasingly divergent articulations occur that may involve the formation of dissonant schools of thought. This pattern often leads to an increase in discoveries and a shift to philosophical analyses or explicit methodological debates on the rules of the paradigm. In essence, then, a state of flux exists in which the (un)discipline searches for a new departure by reconsidering its ontology, questioning structural institutions, and evaluating received doctrine.

The period of extraordinary science ends in one of three ways. The anomaly may be resolved by normal science; it may resist all offered approaches, in which case the discipline accepts it as insoluble given the state of the art; or, tentative paradigms may be conjectured and a confrontation for their acceptance ensue. Parenthetically, it is an examination of such a provocative episode of this phase to which we shall devote considerable study in the subsequent chapters of this work. In the last case, the ascension to dominance of a new paradigm constitutes the synthesis of a scientific revolution.

Within the context of a scientific revolution a number of interesting properties deserve some remarks. First, according to Kuhn, the old paradigm is sustained until and unless a new paradigm arises to replace it. For to relinquish a paradigm without a redefinition forfeits the power and/or status of the disciplinary community. Second, the new paradigm does not reduce to merely an accretion of layers on an existing skeleton. Rather, the ideation of fundamental laws, generalizations, and behavioral functions; original methods and applications; and a redefinition of the character and standards of the science constitute the construction of a new episteme for the discipline. The new paradigm is a change in worldview to the extent that the appreciative world has changed.

Pedagogically speaking, scientific revolutions may be obscured insofar as the textbook tradition dominates our institutes of higher learning. Textbooks, in their glossy presentation of appropriated knowledge, generally include only that past scientific work relevant to the dominant paradigm. This conjures the illusion of a homogeneous discipline. For instance, within economics it has been acknowledged that the so-called Keynesian synthesis is a misrepresentation; for in focusing on consumption, marginal efficiency of capital, liquidity preference, and labor supply aspects of John M. Keynes's *General Theory*, interpreters assiduously neglected the enveloping commentary, observations, and asides. And it was precisely those latter elements that sharply distinguish Keynes from the neoclassical fraternity. What has been referred to as the synthesis of neoclassical economic and Keynesian ideas was not really the synthesis it was purported to be but, more correctly, the reassertion of the neoclassical framework garnished with Keynesian "macro" terminology. The elements selected for textbook treatment are more or less consistent with the neoclassical orthodoxy.

More generally, the weathered scientists of history are perceived as sharing a common worldview, studying, though in a less artful manner, the same riddles, data, and phenomena as contemporary scientists. Even Schumpeter's *History of Economic Analysis* creates this illusion, insofar as it takes a "development of theory approach" rather than a relativist approach.

There are three persuasive arguments for a new paradigm: that it is capable of addressing the crisis-producing anomaly, i.e., market failure; that it permits the admission of new phenomena inadmissible under the old paradigm; and that it is aesthetically more pleasing and elegant, more suitable, or simpler than the old paradigm. More generally, to gain acceptance the new paradigm must be seen as preserving most or all of the problem-solving capacity of the old paradigm while offering an additional capacity of its own. Of course, its chances for success increase with the amount of importance that can be attached to this additional capacity.

The new paradigm emerges in the minds of one or a few individuals, often newcomers, whose research is customarily preoccupied in the area of anomalous phenomena. The true testing in a science occurs within the paradigm battle. Normal science shuns deep questioning of the paradigm. It is a process of matching fact and theory with the burden of failure resting upon the tool user, not the tool. Introspection occurs in the paradigm battle when competing paradigms are tested for the allegiance of the disciplinary community. It is an assumption of Popperian falsability and the Kuhnian notion of paradigm that scientific theories are superseded by new conceptual structures that are more general or fundamental. But, while Popper holds science hostage to disciplined observation, Kuhn admits the possibility of methodological pluralism. Scientific theories are supposedly bypassed in the endlessly provisional, and sometimes revolutionary, development of science. But paradigm testing cannot be done by proof of either the Popperian falsifiability criterion or the probability of accurate prediction types, insofar as competing paradigms are incommensurate. For a scientific paradigm is defended according to accepted norms and thus is virtually impenetrable so long as those norms are maintained. Insofar as the autonomy of a theory is strengthened by the separation of observation and meaning, it is therefore necessary to develop a new theory before the old one can be refuted. The fact that each theory has its own set of "facts" to support it means that differing theories generally cannot be compared with each other—they are incommensurable.

Imre Lakatos's model of "hard core" scientific postulates, which may be conceived of as irrefutable metaphysical presuppositions and a "protective belt" of refutable and flexible sets of hypotheses, is by now commonplace, though not without problematic dimensions. This model is in many ways a refinement of the dominant view on scientific demarcation, as formulated by Karl Popper. Lakatos's model argues that there is a central hard core that is seldom challenged, while scientists may continuously challenge, test, revise, and replace any of the hypotheses or theories they encounter in the unprotective belt. The protective belt becomes the focus of scientific attention and serves in some ways to distract our attention and to shield the hard core from potential criticism. "Scientific research," according to this formulation, invites empirical testing and critical analysis of only part of science, thereby allowing another part to remain beyond reproach.[28] And when, for instance, social scientists challenge the ontological kernel of the hard core, they are attacked as ideologues. It is harder to do this with those critics situated outside of the discipline in question. Today in economics an alternate paradigm—nonequilibrium dissipative systems—is challenging not from within the discipline but from outside. This makes the attack on the hard core so much more important and threatening to the received paradigm.

In its attempt to emulate a defunct positivist methodology in the hope of appearing scientific, economics has become a sterile game played for the entertainment of economists. Presenting "core" assumptions as incontrovertible and given, positive economics reconstructs reality to fit theoretical perspectives. Problem solving for the orthodox economist becomes one of simply drawing internally consistent, that is, logical, conclusions from a concoction of preordained and more malleable secondary assumptions. For practitioners, attempts to address concrete reality, or to evaluate ontological presuppositions on the basis of a deep questioning of "reality" serves to depreciate one's professional standing. For an idiosyncratic appreciation of "science" provides a serviceable means for dealing with iconoclasts. Mavericks who do not accept the axiomatic assumptions, methods, and theories have diminished stature. They may be disparagingly regarded as *auslanders*, of not being members of the disciplinary community, of not being "economists."[29] Having acquired an imperial status in our midst, scientific formulations face less fundamental challenges than theoretical ones. Criticism may be leveled against this or that formulation, yet, however severe, it remains limited to the protective belt. The criticism remains internal to the endeavor and thereby avoids the potentially devastating results that await any intellectual endeavor exposed to unrestrained criticism. A relevant, yet external, view of economics can be forwarded through the philosophy of science.

According to Kuhn, one can perceive the history of science as having long periods of "normal science" in which scientists work within a given paradigm—of problems and accepted metaphysical framework (Lakatos's hard core)—and occasional "revolutions" in which there is a paradigm shift.

Kuhn's normal scientists uphold the principles and methods prescribed by their period's paradigm. They are reluctant to give up their normalcy, and they discourage dissent or revolution. Their normalcy is a powerful political position in addition to being a scientific position proper. Those who disagree are ostracized—transported to an intellectual ghetto. The sociological description, whether accurate or not, can be politically viewed and thereby shed some new light on any preconceived ideas concerning scientific objectivity and value neutrality. Lakatos's hard core is guarded by the normal establishment within the paradigm and is difficult to reproach. The protective belt is political in nature and hardly a methodological tool with which to test hypotheses. The protective belt of scientific theories and models is a political shield the normal scientific establishment employs to persuade society of the validity of its claims in order to retain its social power and political authority.

The incommensurability of scientific concepts was advocated by such philosophers as Kuhn and Feyerabend. That is, holding different worldviews, standards, delineations of the science, and connotations of terminology, practitioners cannot agree on evaluative procedures to test their paradigms. Frequently, members of the old generation remain unpersuaded and either seek sanctuary within the discipline's hard core or, conferred with tenure, manage to stave off conversion.

Choosing among competing paradigms may be something of an act of faith, based upon the paradigms' comparative explanatory power. However, there is more to the sociology of political economy than acts of faith. As we have already implied, relations of power also play an important role. In this connection one may speak of pluralist and hegemonic approaches to the subsumption of paradigms. Whereas hegemonists seek to maintain an original methodology in a dominant position, with other subsumed methodologies being reserved for "special case" applications, pluralists attempt to give equal weight to all subsumed methodologies. At the same time, the so-called pluralists claim theoretical commensurability is possible, though in practice this can only be attained at the expense of the worldviews of the subsumed theories. Thus, the practice of pluralism, as opposed to the meta-theoretical ideal, cannot help but turn out to be an advanced form of hegemony.

It is argued that modern scientific research suggests that the *empire of reason* is not the key to understanding natural phenomena. From Feyerabend's analysis it appears that the substitution of "market forces" for reason reigns supreme in the selection process. This form of epistemological anarchy is a recent concept in scientific knowledge supported by Feyerabend, Kuhn, and others and has been attributed to the Popperian tradition. Anarchy signifies the existence of irrationality in creating and deciding among scientific theories. This obtains from the "incommensurability thesis," which argues that there is no logical contact between theories nor standards outside theory to guide a choice among different theories.[30]

Feyerabend has brought together a number of arguments embodying his admittedly Dadaist approach to philosophy. The heart of these arguments is methodological pluralism carried to the point of outright rejection of all the standard concepts of rational procedure used in science. He claims that rejection of method is the best way to advance knowledge; this amounts to rational selection by a kind of natural selection. His basic position is rejection of modernity's intellectual standards, together with a postmodernist rejection of objectivism and methodological rules. Feyerabend contends that the arguments used against inductive methodology also apply to deductive approaches to science. This, however, leads to the view that a standard of explanatory validity is unattainable. Arguing from an ethical standpoint, he insists that Popperian methodism reduces freedom, but his is a narrowly individualistic concept of freedom, though, like that of political anarchism.[31] The form of epistemological anarchy that issues therefrom finds its roots buried deep in the vacant nihilist tradition.

Assuming an oppositional posture with respect to any philosophy of science that proposes universally valid rules for the pursuit of knowledge, and favoring an anarchist or Dadaist rule that anything goes, Feyerabend proposes a number of epistemological arguments. One of these is that scientific knowledge has in the past been advanced by means other than the methods favored by philosophers of science. This leads to an essentially imperial approach to science with a skeptical conclusion, a position that rests on a confounding of concrete reality with theoretical reality, an error allegedly avoided in so-called praxiological theories of knowledge. A second epistemological argument is that non-argumentative processes have been involved in the growth of science and that arguments depend on structures that attach to culture. In a praxiological approach, however, these two are not seen as incompatible. It is on occasion argued that an understanding of the relation of theory and praxis can be found in historical materialism. However, this proposition is not without technocratic elements, for the demand that political praxis be based on scientific standards may lead to elitism. A final epistemological argument that deflates this view is that successive theories are incommensurable in content; the investigation of modes of production of scientific discourse, however, may offer a resolution of this problem. Finally, this prevents Feyerabend from recognizing the deeper problematic nature of methodism, its occlusion of the social relations of theory production.[32]

Kuhn's analysis is also distanced from an intercontextual appreciation. His central thesis is that knowledge does not accrue in an additive or cumulative fashion. Faced with an anomaly, the disciplinary community searches for a new theory that explains both the anomalies and whatever the previously existing theory satisfactorily explained. The new theory does not necessarily offer the old view plus a little bit extra; it may propose a different view of the world. In other words, a new worldview can be created.

The conversion process is one of a cumulative, intergenerational drift in the distribution of affiliations. The relative volume of experiments, research, curricula, and publications based on the new paradigm swells until it acquires a purported universality. Universal acceptance of the new paradigm, of course, culminates the revolution and initiates a new period of normal science. In this process one cannot blithely delineate the social structure of a scientific community from its paradigm and break the definitional circularity of the two spheres.

As Karl Mannheim insisted, the social structure acquires import in any discourse of a scientific community. For example, an image of socialization or acculturation emerges from the discussion of the intergenerational process of recruitment and accreditation. The self-maintenance of a disciplinary community involves two processes. The one of higher profile refers to the structure and function of a penalty-reward and status system in the discipline's hierarchy of journals, departments, and sinecure. The second, less distinct process, encompasses the internalization of a group's tacit knowledge. Shared commitments, values, and research guides endure as tacit knowledge in a period of normality. In periods of crisis and extraordinary science their specificity and functionality can be consciously appreciated and their ontology scrutinized. In this context, however, Kuhn's paradigmatic approach may be criticized insofar as it is incapable of appreciating the production of knowledge from within a scientific problematic or from within a social perspective. Social theory per se is not a scientific phenomenon, as it claims to be, but a product of cultural and specifically institutional contexts. This appreciation raises an awareness of the crucial role of "tribal standards" in the formation, validation, and finalization of scientific knowledge. It thus intermingles science and ideology. The claim that scientific knowledge is valid only in certain institutional contexts, however, does not entail the argument that science is indistinct from ideology. Scientists cannot be expected to welcome such an appreciation, insofar as it denies their claims to privileged knowledge, which is the basis of their careers and their claims to social status and possible political influence.

A disciplinary community's paradigm influences, and is influenced by, the *Weltanschauung* of the cultural and institutional milieu. This, the so-called historicist tradition, is perhaps best represented by K. Mannheim's sociology of knowledge. For Mannheim, all thoughts—with the exception of mathematics and some branches of the natural sciences—reflect the ideological context in which they were formed. In particular, Mannheim criticized Marx for not raising the problem of the social determination of the socialist ideology. In brief, as historical periods succeed each other, so do ideas in an endless chain. Today's "truths" are tomorrow's "errors." The sociology of knowledge has, in fact, been described as a sociology of errors. In this connection, Ludwig Wittgenstein is a rich source:

> One must start out with error and convert it into truth. That is, one must reveal the source of error, otherwise hearing the truth won't do any good. The truth cannot force its way in when something else is occupying its place. To convince someone of the truth, it is not enough to state it, but rather one must find the path from error to truth.[33]

Consequently, development itself results in a further development. Understanding is therefore not merely reproductive but also productive.

The practitioners of economics, for instance, are also part of a broader culture, and they retain their cultural conditioning in their practice of economics. But they also carry over their socialization within the economics community in their various social roles. This interface between paradigm and Weltanschauung rivets our attention to the consistency or inconsistency of the two vantage points. Some degree of consistency is required in periods of normality, within both a scientific community and society at large. On the one hand, a disciplinary perspective inconsistent with the cultural *Gestalt* almost inevitably diminishes the dissonant's stature, leading to his or her ostracism. However, while ostracized disconsonant theorizing may lead to crisis and extraordinary science, it may just as well leave merely an obscure footnote in the discipline, a footnote that only years later may evoke a challenge. And it is just such a footnote that we shall content ourselves with in this work. On the other hand, a cultural perspective is likely to be unstable if it is inconsistent with the Gestalt of a major subsystem, such as a disciplinary community of practitioners.

At issue is a requisite degree of coherent discourse between a social system and its constituent subsystems. Dissonance along any systemic interface contains the potential for tension and change. The extent to which this potential is realized or suppressed, and the character of change or stability, depends upon the specific desiderata of particular cases. One such particular case, that of the economics profession in relation to the extant social anxiety about economic phenomena, is a subterranean theme present in this work and reminds us of Mitchell's dictum referred to above.

Ultimately, in cases of a rupture between disciplinary and cultural views, the Weltanschauung assumes an authoritative perspective. Though examples surely exist in which a disciplinary perspective has altered the vantage point of society, no science could long exist that did not enjoy the succor provided by society. Truth seeking, the role of critical assessment, and the freedom of inquiry, communication, and social responsibility are fundamental to the scientific enterprise. They possess a transcendent quality. In a pluralist society these principles have a particularly compelling force, and they are fundamental to the social ethos.

Social structure locates itself in the discussion in much the same way as perspectives. Any paradigm or Weltanschauung coevolves with social institutions, and in this connection the role of ideology cannot be dismissed out of hand.[34] The received paradigm of the economics community provides criteria by which its practitioners achieve "success" and by which they are recognized for their achievements. The resultant distribution of status and power is legitimated by the paradigm and in turn legitimates the paradigm and enforces the strictures of the hard core. The same is true of the Weltanschauung and the wider social structure. In either case, ideological and practical friction engenders adaptation and deviation, though most usually on the protective belt, rather than the hard core.

We may consider science and scientific activity as a social institution and as one of the forms of the existence and development of culture because we believe that, in discussing the ethical problems of science, the naive view of science as merely a sum of knowledge divorced from the context of the instrumental activity of people who create, impart, and use that knowledge is completely inadequate. It is such a view that underlies much of the insistence on the ethical neutrality of science. If knowledge is regarded as a thing-in-itself, independent of the richness of its intercontextual framework, and if this knowledge is further equated with science, any discussion of the ethical imperative of science becomes decontextualized.

A scientific community as a differentiated subsystem secures some degree of autonomy from society at large. While this autonomy is on occasion a hackneyed concern of the scientific community, this legitimate concern for scientific autonomy does not imply that science is impervious to its social responsibility and unaccountable to the social order that sustains it. It does emphasize, however, the need to provide sufficient degrees of freedom for the scientific community to execute its responsibility to assist society in resolving social problems and in shaping social evolution. A scientific community that is excessively finalized, politicized, or socialized may not be able to serve as a relatively disinterested information basis for political and social discussion. At the same time, a scientific community that is excessively detached from social and political issues may be socially irresponsible and not respond to the charge of providing assistance in this discussion. Science is not the quest of absolutes. It is a product as well as a creator of its social milieu. Science does not issue from a social vacuum in this view, rather it emerges from a socially conditioned atmosphere. It seems clear that the social function of science requires that it be neither reduced to partisan rhetoric nor sequestered to distill scholastic esoterica.

The fact that, as socioeconomists, we have not (yet) a knowledge of humankind, society, and history comparable to that celebrated in natural science may be that they just are not knowable in the sense that we can know nature. Human, social, and historical knowledge is of a different kind, it is less incremental and cumulative than that of the physical world. Factual knowledge, to be sure, may increase in the humanities too, but the "truth" about human beings that it conveys reflects more what they happen to be at the time of looking at themselves than what they are once and for all. The knowledge of things human, of the subject/agent of history, is a historical phenomenon itself, as it springs from the shifting self-interpretation of the changing historical subject. The Popperian image of progressively superior theories, each a better approximation than its predecessors to an always self-same given, does not apply here. Suffice the statement: What we have here, compared with the unequivocally "progressing" knowledge of reality in the natural sciences, is not a cognitive lag but a cognitive heterogeneity that no progress will bridge. While a generation has the sciences it inherits, each generation may well have the humanities it deserves. Though this is not to suggest that solipsism permeates the humanities.

A social science, like economics, incessantly faces the peril of failing to keep up with social evolution. That is, the structure and function and the values and meanings of society undergo persistent change and may simply move on, leaving behind an ossified and obsolete paradigm and disciplinary community. Insofar as this is descriptive of the received economic paradigm, and insofar as it condones an ahistorical vision, this problem is particularly acute for the community of practitioners and society at large.

The more intricate a modern science becomes and the better it appreciates itself methodologically, the more resolutely it neglects the ontological problems of its own sphere of influence, the more it becomes a formally closed system of partial "laws." And whereas in the physical sciences, where researchers supposedly seek laws that are part of a realm of truth that exists independent of society, it is not so with the social sciences such as economics. In these areas the objects of attention are social artifacts, as are the laws and theories that are invented to disclose phenomena. If we recognize that the economist investigates socially designed phenomena (inventing rather than discovering reality), then it becomes necessary to consider criteria to guide our inventing.

But the effect of Popperian arguments insisting on value-free science has discouraged scholars from inquiring into the social and political underpinnings of their theorizing, for knowledge and truth are decontextualized by the assumption that an objective reality exists independent of its social setting. This is particularly true of the mechanicist/disciplined observationalist approach, which combines the Cartesian analytic method with the positivist alleged separation of fact and value.

The Cartesian sciences are first characterized by their fragmentation of reality, by their loss of totality, and by an unquestioned "ontological substratum." This is not to argue that totality signifies all facts. But it does signify reality as a structured, i.e., concrete, whole from and within which particular facts can be appreciated. An appropriation of "facts" does not amount to an appreciation of concrete reality. Neither does the corresponding inventory sum to a totality. Facts provide an appreciation of reality only conditionally, that is, provided they are understood as structured parts of a concrete whole. This distinguishes them from allegedly immutable and further reducible atoms that, agglomerated, inform reality. The totality is not equal to all the facts, that is, to an appropriation of facts or to an accumulation of aspects and relations, for this bundle lacks the salient features, i.e., the concreteness, of totality.

Without comprehending the signification of facts, that is, without appreciating that reality is a concrete totality, which for the purpose of knowing individual facts or sets of facts threads into a structure of meanings, appreciation of the concrete totality itself amounts to no more than mysticism or to an unknowable thing-in-itself.[35] Consequently, it does not address directly the problem of meaning for the observer of any variation in the relations posited by theoretical models and validated by empirical observation. In other words, the mechanicist paradigm ignores the intercontextual and representational character of scientific theories, thereby confusing a constructed image of the world with concrete reality. To quote Whitehead, it rests on the "fallacy of misplaced concreteness." Thus, it offers no strategy for critically assessing the arbitrariness inherent in its determination of what constitutes factual evidence; for it reduces reason to merely method. In particular, the social sciences have been subject to what Sorokin called "quantiphrenia": the abstraction of reality into abstruse formulae, concepts, and jargon.[36]

In this connection it seems that periods of crisis in economic thought have been marked by a striking regard for historical change and institutional structure. This not only supports the importance accorded to ossification and obsolescence in social science but also suggests that the formalist mainstream of economic analysis must be reoriented by its more historically minded advocates.

Revolution Versus Reform in a Scientific Community

Focusing on instances involving sharp cleavages of tradition, Kuhn's discussion may seem to imply the prevalence of abrupt sea changes in scientific communities, much in the same way that some politicohistorical discussions seem to emphasize discontinuity in institutional changes.

At any given time, within the interrelationships, anomalies and controversies may exist. These may be likened to fault lines, and they may exist anywhere along the interfaces between paradigm and social structure within a discipline, and between paradigm and Weltanschauung. Along such fault lines there exist tension, controversy, and alignments or factions among practitioners of a discipline. Any social system moves upon the energy generated by myriad inconsistencies and frictions. Change creates tension and tension creates change. Differences make a difference.

Within a community of practitioners, there are many subsystems, the interaction of which may generate friction. A disciplinary tree has a trunk that is fundamental and many branches that bifurcate from this trunk. There can be anomaly and change within given branches that do not call into question any of the disciplinary foundations analogous to the trunk of a tree. If so, there is still considerable coherence for the practitioners of a given branch or specialty, and the problems of paradigm incommensurability and translation may be mitigated and managed. For any structure or synthesis contains its past, present, and future in elements that have been superseded, in elements that have been preserved, and in elements that are still unrealized potentialities. Popper refers to this as the principle of correspondence. For example, it is always possible to question a structure or a thesis and what it asserts about reality. As a result a higher-level structure or thesis will evolve that again will be subject to testing. To assume differently would be to admit the existence of an absolute limit to knowledge.

Even in the extreme case of polarization about some schism over fundamental matters, some coherence exists. If it did not, there would be a clear case for emphasizing two social systems rather than two polarized subsystems of one system. No doubt considerable problems of incommensurability and translation would exist, but they should not be intractable. The coherence may or may not be sufficient or sufficiently employed to bring about a smooth transition of disciplinary power and emphasis. If there is sufficient coherence, then this might be what Kuhn had in mind in his discussions of the resolution of an anomaly within a given paradigm. Certainly such resolution makes sense only in light of a structuring social environment.

Kuhn drew an explicit analogy between scientific and historicopolitical revolutions. That analogy per se indicates yet a further analogy between orderly transfer of power in the sociopolitical realm and in a scientific community. Obviously, to return to the disciplinary structure, change in one field may immediately generate friction and change in a related field. In a social science, friction and change may be generated by the articulation of the dominant paradigm or by social change, that is, change in the object of study itself. At any time there may be several areas in which related inconsistencies are at work. These areas will differ as to the pace and pattern required for resolving such anomalies. Some disciplines will lead and some will lag; some will be more responsive or more immediately affected than others. And, as we shall see later, the contemporary penetration of the systems theoretical challenge to political economy, a challenge that precipitated out of nineteenth-century science and Marxist analysis, has suffered a particularly long lag.

Within disciplines, there is frequently sufficient interpenetration to make it difficult to separate the representatives of the dissenting traditions from those with more orthodox proclivities. There are issues and periods that sharpen the distinction between orthodox and dissident opinion.

More formalized disciplines, possibly owing to their high level of abstraction, are more insulated from changing social circumstance. Practitioners in these more insular disciplines play a reasonably warranted conservative role within the disciplinary hard core. Within a discipline the function of hard-core conservatism, when confronted with vogue and external influences, is to assure that practitioners do not casually abandon the discipline's traditions and established practices. However, the objective reification that corresponds to such practitioners nonetheless promotes a professional mystique: it supplies respectability in the form of alleged scientific objectivity, an aura of aloof detachment from partisan interests and human frailties. But revolutions do occur. Having matured and festered with ad hoc tampering, they occur when the fissures running from a critical fault line have evidently ruptured the hard core of the discipline. In the case of intractable divisions, the previously ubiquitous value system atrophies, leaving incommensurability.

In the social system at large, such revolutionary transformations occur at the expense of grim hardship and misery. Within a scientific community, the scale of the trauma is incomparably less, but there is still potential for considerable mischief and dislocation. There surely must be, within all but the most vindictively radical or truculently reactionary souls, a reform conscience that seeks progress and preservation within a framework of cooperation, dialogue, and compromise.

The argument that unfolds in the following chapters is that there exist fundamental fissures within the community of political economists and in their relationships to society at large. These fissures are not altogether new; they are threaded backward in time by many controversies, especially for our purposes, those involving a number of Russian Marxian critical systems theorists. For it was they who challenged the notion that the methods of scientific knowledge and changes of concepts should be interpreted via formal logic and analytical philosophy. They inquired into the epistemological relevance of the positivist interpretation of Marxian dialectics for the philosophy of science and whether or not Hegelian dialectics was serviceable for the advance and autocritique of political economy. Since these fissures were first identified, there has been a great deal of change in the substance of the social economy. An alternative paradigm articulated in the first quarter of this century reasserts its relevance today. There has been substantial methodological and philosophical reflection within the community of political economists. These reflections are sufficient to warrant a reevaluation of the drama and personae that surrounded a *paradigm lost*.

2
Syntheses and Inversion in Political Economic Thought

Introductory Remarks

In the historic development of political economy it is possible to identify the waxing and waning of three broad themes, or Weltanschauung. The first theme corresponds to a holistic appreciation of a hierarchy of finalities, which attaches to Platonic and Aristotelian praxis theory. The second theme corresponds to an abandonment of praxiological holism, formerly the hard core of economic thought. This abandonment was complemented by the development, during the Age of Reason, of the mechanical materialist paradigm. Finally, the furtive reemergence from its peripheral existence of praxiological holism in its dialectical materialist guise and nascent critical systems theory is recounted.

Whereas the second theme progressed along lines contingent with what may be termed Galilean or scientific rationality, the third followed the heritage of Aristotelian praxis and ensued from criticisms of the second theme. The general contention is that, while Galilean rationality abandoned the praxiology of "becoming" in pursuit of "being," and moreover suppressed the Aristotelian problem of "wholes," reconstructed Aristotelian holism pursued "being." However, the ghost of the Aristotelian systems problem haunted science. From the resulting philosophical confusion over being and becoming, there emerged, in the nineteenth century, a rekindled and romantic interest in Platonic idealism, vitalism, and finalism. Moreover, it was from this state of confusion that a general interest in evolution theory developed and a particular interest in dialectical materialism emerged. Today, both a rekindled interest in the systems problem and praxiological dialectical materialism are progressively penetrating economic thought, revising and overthrowing its long-accepted mechanical paradigm.

The Ascendancy of the Mechanical Paradigm

While worldviews have long been an essential feature of human society, it is necessary to draw some distinctions between the pre-industrial and industrial reference of human beings and nature. In pre-industrial feudal society the relationship of human beings with nature was more participatory than exploitative. Constrained by its physical capacity to purposively manipulate and redirect nature, society's preoccupation was with coexisting with the forces of nature. In fact, its very survival depended, on the one hand, on its ability to conform to the norms of the biosphere and, on the other hand, on a deep sense of the society-integrating role of social and religious ethics.

The conception of the economy that follows from such an approach is that of an activity setting physical flows into motion, an activity that can perpetuate itself only through the reproduction of a natural environment.

The conception of "nature as ideal" found its grand expression in Aristotle's philosophy—and Aristotelian thought set the dominant pattern for intellectuality throughout the Middle Ages. However, the scientific synthesis of knowledge as it evolved from the late Renaissance and Baroque periods was grounded in a form of rationality (and reason) that represented a departure from that embodied in classical Greek thought.

Seventeenth-century science arose in opposition to idealism and was confronted with another fundamental alternative whose articulation turned on questions of order.[1] Are nature and history intrinsically random? Is ordered behavior merely the transient result of chance collisions of atoms and of their unstable associations? One of the main sources of fascination in modern science was the singular conviction that it had discovered eternal laws at the core of nature's transformations and, thus, had exorcised time and becoming. However, this confidence in the reason of nature created a deep rift within science and estranged it from philosophy. What had originally been a daring wager with the Aristotelian tradition gradually became a dogmatic assertion directed against all those chemists, biologists, and physicians for whom a qualitative diversity existed in nature. At the end of the nineteenth century, this conflict had shifted from within the midst of scientific inquiry to the relation between science and the broad expanse of the Cultural West.

The world of classical science was a world in which the only events that could occur were those deducible from the instantaneous state of the system. Curiously, this notion, which we can trace back to Galileo and Newton, was not new in their time. Indeed, it can be identified with Aristotle's conception of a divine and immutable heaven. In Aristotle's opinion, it was only the heavenly world to which we could hope to apply an exact mathematical description. Science disenchanted the world. But this disenchantment was paradoxically due to the glorification of the earthly world, one worthy of the kind of intellectual pursuit Aristotle had reserved for heaven.

As Koyre asserts, the clash between the Aristotelians and Galileo was a clash between two forms of rationality. Classical science denied becoming and natural diversity—both considered by Aristotle as attributes of the sublunar, inferior world. In this sense, classical science brought heaven to earth. However, this apparently was not the intention of the celebrated fathers of modern science. In challenging Aristotle's claim that mathematics ends where nature begins, they did not seek to discover the immutable concealed behind the changing, but rather to extend changing corruptible nature to the boundaries of the universe.[2]

In particular, the Aristotelian appreciation of a hierarchy of norms was arrested by scientific development in the Cultural West. However, the problems contained in it, such as order and "directedness" of living matter remain problematic, for these issues were bypassed rather than solved. Thus, the basic systems problem was obscured by hegemonic scientific rationality. Indeed, the spirit of Aristotelian thinking was very opposite of the one that animated the later development of science and technology.

Francis Bacon laid the groundwork for the machine paradigm with his attack on the worldview of the ancient Greeks. For the Greeks, science was one of answering the question of the why of things. Bacon's concept of science and learning was that it should answer the question of the how of things. From an ends-oriented pursuit it became a means-oriented one. For a reflective inquiry a disciplined observational one was substituted. Bacon sought to make clear that the new method for dealing with the world, the new worldview, was one that should "enlarge the bounds of human empire to the effecting of all things possible."[3] It was this that most notably contrasts with the praxis orientation in Greek thought. The scientific method proposed by Bacon would separate the observer from the observed and provide an ostensibly neutral forum for the development of objective knowledge. By about A.D. 1500, European minds became infused with the application of instrumental reason to the study of nature and the search for an alleged underlying mathematical precision in God's design.

Bacon's kindred spirit, René Descartes, succeeded in turning all of nature into a simple matter of motion. He reduced all quality to quantity and then confidently proclaimed that only space and location mattered. Bacon's objectification of nature was reinforced by Descartes, who elaborated on why the world must be accessible to mathematics. Mathematics represented total order, and so, in a fit of genius, Descartes had successfully eliminated everything in the world that might be thought of as messy, chaotic, and alive.

To fix attention upon a mechanical system was the first step toward creating a new paradigm and an important victory for modernity's scientific rationality. By centering its effort on the nonhistoric and the dead, the physical sciences clarified the entire procedure of analysis. The field to which they confined their attention was one in which the method could be pushed furthest without being too obviously inadequate or encountering too many special difficulties. However, the real physical world was still not simple enough for the scientific method in its first stages of development. It was necessary to reduce it to such elements as could be ordered in terms of space, time, mass, motion, and quantity. In other words, physical science confined itself to the Cartesian coordinates of extension in space and motion in space and time.

The objects chosen by the physicists to explore the validity of a quantitative description were simple machines, like the ideal pendulum with its conservation of motion. Simple machines and planetary orbits were allegedly found to correspond to unique mathematical descriptions that reproduced the divine order of Aristotle's heaven.

Like Aristotle's gods, the objects of classical dynamics are concerned with themselves; closed atoms, they can learn nothing from the outside. At any instant, each point in the system knows all it will ever know—that is, the distribution of masses in space and their velocities. Each state contains the whole truth concerning the possible states, and each can be used to predict the others, whatever their respective positions on the time axis. This description leads to a tautology, for time, both future and past, is contained in the present. History becomes nothing more than extension.

The Age of Renaissance marked the beginning of a long series of synthetic scientific constructions that today makes it possible to perceive a synthetically integrated unity of the world in which we live and the mutual interdependence of the various processes that occur within it. They have made possible the gradual construction not only of the foundations of an analysis of processes taking place in the world that surrounds us but also of the required technology that makes it possible for us to solve the concrete problems in a world grown complex.[4]

It was Newton who transformed the general ideas of motion that appeared in the ancient world into a point of departure for analyzing the processes of the external world. At first this related strictly to mechanics and astronomy. But, if it is possible to calculate and to establish precisely when and where in the solar system a planet would appear, or where a stone of known momentum would fall, then why should it not be possible to establish the fact of a more complex mechanical motion and the causes that produce it? Humankind acquired the possibility of creating theories on the basis of which scientific forecasting developed.

The pre-Socratic speculations were immersed in the problem of change: Is change, whereby things are born and die, imposed from the outside on some kind of inert matter? Or, is it the result of an intrinsic and independent activity of matter? Is an external driving force necessary, or is becoming inherent in matter?

The theology of naturalism, expressed by seventeenth-century philosophers, to a considerable extent addressed the arcane question, What are the forces active throughout the history of the biosphere? Are these the same forces that act throughout the material universe, different in their results only to the extent that the matter they are acting on is differently organized? Or, do they include forces peculiar to and inherent in life, essentially different from the mechanistic forces of cause and effect of the purely material realm?

The doctrine of cause and effect has been invoked throughout history to explain the behavior of nature. Thus we try to find causes, because this knowledge would enable us to bring about desired effects. Causality is a somewhat more vague doctrine than mechanism. It asserts cause and effect, although it does not insist on knowing the mechanism. For many centuries, until the emergence of the theory of relativity, causality was supported by the belief in mechanism. Originally, causality implied contact between cause and effect, or spatial contiguity. However, this was soon extended to action at a distance, as in the case of gravitation, and, in other hands, to a philosophy of history.

Like most doctrines causality had its origin in Greek thought. Aristotle distinguished four kinds of causes operating in the universe: formal causes, which are plans or designs; final causes or purposes; material causes, which reside in matter; and efficient causes, which effect changes or events.

While Cicero wrote, "Nothing happens without a cause, and nothing happens unless it can happen. When that which can happen does in fact happen, it cannot be considered a miracle,"[5] the search for causes in modern science begins with Galileo. He spoke of the earth's gravitational force as a cause of terrestrial motions, but he was compelled to ignore causality and had to be content with mathematical descriptions of the motions.

Newton and his contemporaries gave substance to Cicero's musing, destined to remain essentially unchanged over the following two centuries, that causality is inherent in the nature of the physical world itself. It was in his search for causes that Newton introduced the universal force of gravitation as the cause of the elliptical motions of the planets, which might otherwise move along straight lines. Leibniz, too, asserted that nothing happens without a cause; however, in his day, belief in cause and effect was just that, a belief.

A radically different understanding of cause and effect was advanced by Immanuel Kant. He advocated Newton's system of celestial mechanics and even supplemented it in his scientific treatise *A Theory of the Heavens*. In his major philosophical work, *A Critique of Pure Reason*, he asserted that causality was a logically necessary precondition for all rational thought. Therefore, it was in no need of support by factual evidence. In his second edition he wrote, "All changes happen according to a law of connection between cause and effect."

These appreciations of causality involve, in various ways, the idea of a nexus whereby a cause brings the effect into being. The Scottish philosopher David Hume sought to purge causality of any metaphysical basis in his epistemological treatise *Enquiry Concerning Human Understanding*. He wrote:

> The only immediate utility of all science is to teach how to control and regulate future events by their causes.... Similar events are always conjoined with similar, of this we have experience; therefore we may define a cause to be an object followed by another and where all the objects similar to the first are followed by objects similar to the second.[6]

In this wording, "object" might be better rendered as "event." The inclusion of the word "similar" in his definition was in order to render causality experimentally verifiable, for he realized that a given situation cannot be found to reoccur if it is too precisely defined.

It was Hume's conviction that just because we have become aware of a particular cause-and-effect sequence is no proof that the cause will be followed by the effect on future occasions. With this observation, Hume concluded that causality is no more than a habit; it is not an adequate basis for belief.

A more recent and devastating attack on causality was made by the English philosopher, mathematician, and Nobel laureate Bertrand Russell. In a paper *On the Notion of Cause*, he wrote:

> All philosophers, of every school, imagine that causation is one of the fundamental axioms of science, yet, oddly enough, in advanced science, such as gravitational astronomy, the word "cause" never occurs.... The Law of Causality, I believe, like much that passes among philosophers, is a relic of a bygone age, surviving like the monarchy, only because it is erroneously supposed to do no harm.[7]

With the advance of rational mechanics the philosophical criticism of science, like that of Diderot, gradually became harsher, resembling certain modern forms of antiscience. It was no longer a question of refuting rather naive and shortsighted generalizations that "only have to be repeated aloud to make even children laugh"—to use Diderot's quip. Rather it was one of refuting the paradigm that produced experimental and mathematical knowledge of nature. Scientific knowledge was being criticized not for its limitations but for its nature, and a rival knowledge based on another approach was sought. Two cultures coalesced, and knowledge was fragmented into two opposed modes of inquiry.[8]

Principally owing to its diagnostic and predictive achievement, Western science, on the one hand, fostered an immense technological payoff with profound socioeconomic effects. However, the penetration of scientific rationality into political economy shifted its focus from a concern with policy-oriented, substantive, qualitative studies to those that merely reflect a subset of formalistic problems bearing little relation to the substantive issues of the livelihood of man.

The Enlightenment's Mechanicalism

If Newton, Descartes, and Bacon formulated the physics of the mechanical paradigm, then one must search no further than Locke and Smith to seek the analogy in social relations. These men sought the discovery of the relationship between universal mechanics and the workings of society. Together Locke and Spinoza brought the workings of government and society in line with the mechanical paradigm, and Adam Smith, together with Robert Townsend and later luminaries, attempted the same for the economy.

Referring pointedly to the so-called economic motive, Townsend dismissed the institutional and societal dimensions of the economy and, invoking the laws of nature into human affairs, succeeded where others had failed. For while Hume, Hartley, and Smith had metaphorically sought Newtonian laws in society, Townsend had used a biological analogy to contend that social harmony, i.e., equilibrium, could be maintained without the intervention of government. Hunger and scarcity were the operative mechanisms.

With Smith the penetration of scientific rationality into the problem of the livelihood of man explicitly removed any notion of morality. Moreover, the narrower focus shifted attention away from the Aristotelian problem of wholes and societal norms to an atomistic appreciation of man. Man was seen as a utilitarian atom whose material self-interest was assumed to be constant in society. Individualism was vaunted for its innate propensities, which came to be regarded as normative, and society, where it survived as a concept, was conceived as a cluster of individuals.

The place of the economic system in society came to be defined strictly by economic motives of hunger and gain. They alone accounted for the economic laws of rent and the iron law of wages. Society was governed by the dynamics of the market and in turn dominated by natural laws. The motives of man, seen as an atom, were perceived to be solely of a material character, which thereby determined his participation in economic activity and hence in society. Society, being the agglomeration of these "economic" atoms, was perceived as fundamentally "economic." These ideas, which shaped the liberal doctrine, were augmented by the belief that society's institutions were determined by the economic system. The notion of economic determinism as a societal law shaped the minds of the classical economists and, through Ricardo, impressed themselves upon Marx.[9] It is from this perception of society that "real" man was seen as "economic" man, who behaved according to a definite, if not an ethnocentric, rationality.

"Economic" man was endowed with certain natural tendencies to "truck, barter, and trade." Inclined by some force akin to gravity, trade would flow, creating a pool of goods organized in markets. Money would appear, and all things would be drawn into the giddy whirl of wealth-generating, price-making exchanges, or so it was alleged. In such circumstances neither political, religious, nor ideological strivings to change the course of the economic system were deemed effectual. Culture, other than that materially defined, was eschewed. Nonetheless, beyond the domain of economistic motivations, valuations, and calculations, there exists a universe of inspiration, aesthetic, ethical, and moral coordinates within which man locates his reason for life. It was Plato's reference image, the *City of Pigs*, however, that ironically came to be theorized as the very epitome of the emergent capitalist edition of the modernity project.[10]

Smith was enamored by the mechanical worldview and was determined to formulate a theory of economy that would reflect the universals of the Newtonian paradigm. His initiative found its resolve in the adoption, in the hands of mathematical economists, of those unnatural abstractions that reduced man's livelihood to a crude clockwork mechanism, automatically allocating capital, resources, and production.

However, the images of Townsend and Smith were distinct from pre-industrial economies. For millennia man's productive activities, based on hunting, fishing, and gathering, and later agriculture and animal husbandry, have followed the narrow mechanisms of the natural ecosystem. Economic thinking, as such, was simultaneously thinking about nature. This was reflected in the Physiocratic model, one that was inspired by biology and, following Aristotle and Confucius, argued for the pre-eminence of the natural order, whose rules human societies must obey. For the Physiocratic mind, production could provide for the continuity of man's livelihood only by respecting nature, and the finality of production was self-evident: to meet the organic needs of man.

However, as humankind began to develop the mechanical arts, its relationship to nature changed, and so too did its view of nature. With increasing reliance on technology and the corresponding dependence on fossil fuels, humanity began the slow process of wresting away from its dependence on the biosphere's cycles and flows of solar energy. Though not without other institutional influences, the power of science and Promethean technology encouraged human beings to believe they could distance themselves from nature's rhythms. The intimate relationship of man and nature was undermined and finally ruptured by the mediating role of technology between society and the living planet. Humanity used science and technology to create an artificial environment, one cast in its own image. Its view of nature, in turn, came more and more to resemble the newly technified form of civilization.

As organic needs were progressively met, the Aristotelian-Physiocratic image was eclipsed. Production activities serving comfort or well-being came to replace those serving survival. The notion of need itself came to be transformed; rather than referring to substantive and physiological imperatives, it related to psychological aspirations, to which newly institutionalized monetized and productive structures sought to respond.

From the throes of the Industrial Revolution there emerged a way of life whose practical requirements bound it to market phenomena. It was no longer in organic needs, but rather in subjective considerations, that most production activities derived their justification. The context of reproduction, moreover, was abstracted from biophysical realities and limited to market factors. The ubiquitous supply-demand mechanism, which had previously been restricted to various ports of trade and fairs, showed a staggering capacity for organizing both man and nature, as if they too were commodities. This caused the problem of value to become the leading problem.

The logic of the economic apparatus thus fundamentally transformed itself in three respects: First, by confusing the means with the end, it ceased to relate to biophysical realities and responded to monetary values. Second, it draws away from the dimensions of the biosphere, whose laws of reproduction it previously sought to respect, to the dynamics of the market, whose equilibrium it sought to assure. The economic machine created an artificial autojustified ecosystem animated by its own logic and progressively subjected the natural ecosystem to its laws. Third, the community was no longer conceived of as an organism articulated and integrated in accord with a socioethical imperative. The idea grew that society was composed of various parts acting in concert, of a machine whose function could be manipulated. Cartesian atomism replaced praxiological holism.

In brief, there was a reversal in the situation: Through the evolution of technology man appeared to have liberated himself from the constraints of the biosphere. However, this was only a self-induced narcotic phantasm. Imposing himself as nature's finality, man now subjects nature to the play of his wishes. He projects himself as the ultimate link, whose appearance was creation's sole objective and within whom the finality of the cosmos resides. His mastery depends solely on the state of knowledge. The mystery (and ethics) of religions retreats before his thirst for scientific knowledge, and there emerges the age of scientific and economic rationality by which he imposes on nature his laws of efficiency and material productivity. Both in terms of its content and its finality, after assuming an abstract form, economic rationality radically dissociates itself from holistic appreciations. And, evidently that divorce is becoming increasingly acute. As the impact of economic activities is extended and the scope of economic analysis paradoxically narrows, a multiplicity of events present themselves no longer as insular but as the unavoidable consequence of the confrontation of the logic of the biosphere and the price-making market economy. The collision of the biospheric imperative with the economic imperative is forcing on us a reassessment of holism.

The Inversion of Economic Analysis

Progressively both the philosophical and the analytical underpinnings of political economy were transformed. Philosophically political economy retreated from Platonic-Aristotelian praxiological holism, while analytically its reference image adjoined mechanics. The inversion of economic thought may be intuited as the subversion of Kant's world of noumenal knowledge for the phenomenal.

Political economy was appreciated in metaphoric terms as more closely associated with mechanical systems, systems that seek their justification in their own equilibrium. The equilibrium of market economies, being a consequence of the price mechanism and the cybernetic mechanism of the reestablishment of the balance of trade, appears analogous to a mechanical system. The Platonic-Aristotelian and Physiocratic perception of a natural and coherent order was subverted. The autojustified economic system treated nature as mere data.

The system justifies itself through its own equilibrium, for it is within itself that the system finds its own coherence. Its variability is attributable not to divine intervention or to collective reason, but rather to the pursuit of private interests whose convergence was theorized to assure the realization of the interests of the great collective. The Law of Markets, formulated by J.B. Say, together with Ricardo's theory of trade, maintained that the price mechanism and the balance of trade drove the market to a narrow equilibrium. Removed from interest is the socioethical imperative; it is merely the system's equilibrium that constitutes its justification.

The economy was no longer seen to be embedded in society and polity and ultimately in nature. Rather, the economic system was the determinant of social relations, while holism was expunged from mainstream economic thought.[11] Indeed, the biosphere was made to be dependent on the laws of one of its subsystems—namely, the economic system. This constituted a complete inversion of the Platonic-Aristotelian praxiological reference image.

The inversion of economic thought, which was the labor of Townsend, Malthus, and Ricardo, among others, established the modern concept of the autonomous economic system governed by purely economic motives and subject to the economic principle of formal rationality—in short, economism. The descendent of seventeenth-century scientific rationality and eighteenth-century political rationality, economic rationalism was no less unrealistic than its predecessors. Scientific rationality chose as its referent mechanics and thereby failed to account, for instance, with open living systems. Political utopians ignored the economy, while the market utopians abstracted the livelihood of man from both nature and politics. The twin liberal postulates of rationalism and atomism, which had found their ultimate expression in the physical sciences, were conjectured to provide the foundation of "economic" society. Their transference to social science conveyed an image of society as a mere agglomeration of human atoms whose behavior conformed to an individualized kind of rationality relating ends to means—assumed to be scarce. The eclipse of political economy was the consequence of the economistic fallacy; the idea of the economic sphere was seen as the source of moral law and political obligation. The primacy of economic rationality is postulated as the ultimate criterion and the finality governing both the behavior of the individual and the great collective. The economistic doctrine, the synthesis of Bentham and Ricardo, among others, fostered this, the central myth. While intellectually the myth was hailed as a triumph of the Enlightenment, it meant the eclipse of ethics, moral valuations, and holistic appreciations of political economy.

A social philosophy erected on such foundations is nothing short of fantastic, for it meant the individualization of society—to interpret every member of society as an atom subject to Benthamite principles of economic rationalism. In effect, it made the marketplace the sole referent for the whole of social existence, whereas previously the "economy" had functioned as a by-product of kinship, political, and religious obligation. In primitive and archaic economies one's livelihood was in effect guaranteed as a moral right of membership in the community. An institutionally enforced utilitarian practice warped Western man's understanding of the reality of society.

By confining his operations to those aspects of reality subject to quantification, and by isolating and dismembering the corpus of experience, the physical scientist created a habit of mind favorable to practical inventions. By its consistent metaphysical principles and its alleged methodological factuality, the Enlightenment denuded the world of natural and organic subjects and turned its back on real experience: It substituted for the body and blood of reality a skeleton of malleable abstractions. What was left was the bare, depopulated world of matter and motion, a veritable wasteland.

The mechanical paradigm proved irresistible. It was simple, predictable, and above all it worked. There was an order to things, and that order could be ascertained by mathematical formulations and scientific observation. The penetration of the mechanical paradigm into economic science was not an isolated instance, for it was adopted more generally. Indeed, few nineteenth-century scientists escaped the compulsion to reduce, to quantify, and to formalize.

Economic science in the late nineteenth century sought to strengthen itself, to be viewed as a science of no less significance than celestial mechanics. Prestige was sought for a science that had lingered in the backwaters of a general scientific advance. The solution was to apply the philosophy and those methods of inquiry that had proved themselves so successful in the first field of scientific advance—mechanics.

In the age of clocks, the Newtonian universe was represented as a colossal mechanism that had been wound up once and for all time. Physical scientists saw mechanical motion as the basis of all existence, the displacement of bodies in space, taking place according to Newton's laws of motion. Life itself was discussed from this point of view. According to the idea of the time, the organism was nothing but a complicated machine whose structure was nevertheless completely comprehensible. Its movement depended entirely on its structure and on the pressure and the collision of particles of matter, like the wheels of a water clock.

The mechanistic paradigm found its ideal in the Laplacean spirit, the conception that all phenomena are ultimately aggregates of actions of elementary physical units. The philosophers thereupon proclaimed matter that behaved in accordance with fixed mathematical laws as the sole reality. Theoretically, this conception did not lead to exact sciences outside the field of physics. It failed to lead to laws of other levels of reality, to biology, psychology, sociology, and to economic science. Practically, its consequences have been catastrophic for civilization. For the attitude that considers physical phenomena as the sole standard of reality has led to the mechanization and alienation of humankind and to the devaluation of ethical and moral values.

Nonetheless, much of social science remains in the grip of the machine model of reality. Values, purpose, inner experience, and meaningful units of behavior are not accommodated by the machine model of reality. No wrong prediction, no inability to account for much of human life, creativity, love, courage, dignity, and so on, seems to discourage social scientists from adhering to this narrow view of how to organize reality, a Cartesian view inherited from the early stages of the physical sciences.

While it is possible to interpret the development of the scientific synthesis and systemic thinking in a number of ways, we shall turn to a particular theme in the advance of thought and the critique of political economy.

3
Philosophical Countercurrents

Introductory Remarks

While more conventional appreciations of the Enlightenment have with good reason emphasized its positivist and mechanicalist thrust, an opposing countercurrent was also apparent in Enlightenment thought. Indeed, in the works of Spinoza through to Kant, and boldly evident in Hegel and Marx, one may detect a holistic discourse. It was this theme, which was to inform Marxist theorizing, that provided the philosophical grounding for Critical Marxism and later infused a systems theoretical critique of political economy. The intent in this chapter is not to offer a comprehensive overview but rather to merely acquaint the reader with a brief history of a philosophical countercurrent to modernity's mechanicalist enterprise.

The term Critical Marxism is a signifier that connotes no particular body of doctrine. Its historical function has been linked to the anti-Leninist movements of the twentieth century as both the object of accusation and, less often, a self-description of a mélange of dissenters. Its theoretical status is not only ambiguous, it is also problematic. It has been identified solely with a subterranean tradition of humanist, subjectivist, and nondoctrinal Marxism, which was the negation of its official Soviet counterpart. The latter was twisted into a doctrinaire ideology legitimated through its institutionalization, whereas Critical Marxism, nowhere in power, retained emancipatory ambitions. Those ambitions were preserved in its challenge to the scientific self-understanding of its orthodox rivals. In this reading, therefore, Critical Marxism opposed not only the economism of the Second International but also the vanguardism of the Third. In contrast to both, it insisted that true praxis was a collective expression of self-emancipation involving all humankind. The reawakening of the potential for such a collective subject was thus a central preoccupation of Critical Marxists. Moreover, rather than trying to mimic the methods of mechanicalism, Critical Marxism recognized its certain origins in the tradition of philosophical critique initiated with Kant and German Idealism.

"There is no single tendency in the history of modern social thought," notes Robert Unger, "more remarkable in its persistence or more far-reaching in its influence than the struggle to formulate a plausible version of the idea of totality."[1] "Totality" or "holism" has indeed enjoyed a privileged place in the discourse of the Cultural West, motivated perhaps by a Hellenic nostalgia for a primal unity and a stubborn attraction to its implicit reliance on totalistic associations. Presenting totality as a normative goal, Lukács contended that "what is crucial is that there should be an aspiration towards totality."[2] Notably, Russian Critical Marxists provided a methodological appreciation that adequate understanding of complex phenomena can come only from an appreciation of their relative integrity.

That concept of "holism" or "totality" had a privileged place in the lexicon of Marxism. In privileging it as they did, they betrayed their unmistakable status as intellectuals; throughout modern history, only "men of ideas" have combined the time (and material support) to reflect on matters beyond their immediate material concerns with the hubris to believe they might know the whole of reality. Often only marginally related to their class of social origin, frequently tending to the cosmopolitan rather than the provincial in their loyalties, intellectuals have rarely been reluctant to impute to themselves a universal function in society. Along with this self-image has gone a willingness to assume a holistic perspective and speak for all members of the relevant whole, whether it be local, national, or global. It is not only that intellectuals can take the standpoint of the "whole" by reason of their special culture, they may occupy privileged positions that induce them to define themselves as representatives of the larger whole. They are in Nietzsche's phrase "knights of totality." Notable among the intellectual elite who labored for the Russian Revolution were those motivated by a totalistic imagining normally absent among the more self-interested and myopic. Marx and Engels justified themselves in these terms when they wrote in *The Communist Manifesto* that "a portion of the bourgeoisie goes over to the proletariat; and in particular a portion of the bourgeois ideologists, who have raised themselves to the level of comprehending theoretically the historical movement as a whole."[3]

A totalistic stance has not, of course, had only revolutionary political implications. In the twentieth century, holistic perspectives of a nonradical kind have been developed by a wide range of thinkers, including Karl Mannheim, Othmar Spann, Talcot Parsons, and the adherents of such movements as structuralism and conventional systems theory. The celebrated claim made by Lukács in *History and Class Consciousness*, that Marxism is differentiated from bourgeois thought by its adoption of the point of view of totality, is a modest exaggeration.[4]

However, by and large it is correct to say that the issue of totality has been at the center of the Marxist, or more correctly Critical Marxist, debate as it has not been with bourgeois thought, especially in its positivist or neo-Kantian guises. Possibly because of their marginal relation to both the class of their origin and the class to which they gravitated, the intellectuals in the Critical Marxist tradition were particularly prone to think holistically. But if collectively drawn to the concept of totality, they were by no means unified in their understanding of its meaning or in their evaluation of its merits. Indeed, it might be said that the family quarrel of this subterranean tradition has been waged over this concept's implications. It is to the concept of totality that we can look for a compass to help us traverse the vast and uncharted intellectual territory that is Russian Critical Marxism. It is, to be sure, not the only guide that we might use, for although totality has been of enormous importance for Russian Critical Marxists, other key concepts such as social energetics, praxis, subjectivity, or dialectics might also be explored profitably by historians of the tradition. But each of these taken in isolation would not be sufficient to give us an unblemished view of the topography. Working our way through complicated analyses of how all of these key terms were used by Russian Critical Marxists, however, it is apparent that they come together in an integral synthesis.

When Western Marxists talk of bourgeois society as totalizing, they obviously do not mean that this society has achieved the harmonious order of a true whole. Instead, they suggest that the various component parts of bourgeois society, as disparate and unconnected as they appear, are inextricable elements in a larger complex whole. How that whole is itself to be conceived is, to be sure, problematic. What is its internal structure? How is one to understand its boundaries, its relation to human agency? How may it be connected with other totalities? How is its concreteness captured in human thought? All of these questions were and still are very much in dispute. But that Marxism is a holistic rather than an atomistic theory has been and remains an article of common faith among Western Marxists.

Totality has, of course, figured in non-Marxist schools of thought in a similar way. In fact, the word *holism* was coined by the South African politician and scientist Jan Smuts in his 1926 study *Holism and Evolution*.[5] This reminds us that the Marxist subscription to totality must be placed in the larger tradition of holistic thought. Indeed, many of the issues fought over by Western Marxists were introduced by earlier theorists, if in significantly different contexts. It would be wrong, therefore, to isolate Marxist from non-Marxist holisms, although it would be equally dangerous to indiscriminately equate them. Changed historical circumstances, which, in part, account for the autocritique of Marxism itself, make such an equation clearly erroneous. And although there are significant parallels between other twentieth-century holisms and those of Critical Marxism, here too no simple equivalence can be posited. From the perspective of positive or atomistic thought, all holisms may seem alike, but from within the discourse the differences are extremely important. To enter into the Critical Marxist debate over totality, it is imperative to make some sense of its background without, however, reducing the dynamics of the debate to a mere repetition of that of its predecessors.

Insofar as political economy is once again experiencing a rediscovery of a systems theoretical critique (a proposition that pervades this work), we should tender some conceptual appreciation of "critique," for it is central to a deeper understanding of the modernity project. Whereas the interpretivist approach takes worldviews as given, the critical approach to knowledge asks to what extent those views may be distorted, and in whose interests the distortions may serve. In the vernacular, the word *critique* has a negative connotation. To criticize is usually to reveal negative features of something. However, in the authentic sense, a sense present in the interpretation of the philosophers Kant, Hegel, and Marx, it meant a lifting and separating of an object in order to examine its properties, so as to distinguish it from other things.[6] This is very near to the meaning of the term *aufgehoben* (lifted up). In the Gestalt ground-figures, what is being distinguished is possible only against the background of its distinction. Similarly, a system is perceived as such only insofar as it is distinct from its environment. But for Kant critique was the examination of the possibilities and limits of our way of experiencing something. Critique pushes us to the edge of the abyss that opens in front of us in the uncertain space of the concealed. Therefore, doubt is the starting point, the measure, and the limit of critical thought. It is the attempt to see not that which as an objective thing we are looking at, but rather how we are looking at it. Thus, critique is an impossible accomplishment, if by "accomplishment" we infer something that is totally performed and finished. A critique is an always ongoing project whose finality is achieved only in the process itself.

Archaeology of Knowledge

The background of this debate is crucial enough for us to linger with it for some time. Yet it would be unwise to attempt an exhaustive history of the concept of totality and holism in European thought; not only would such an account tax the reader's patience but it would also convey the misleading impression that a unified and coherent history of holism could be written with Critical Marxism as its telos. There were a number of versions of totality available for revisionists to claim as their own. For, as we will see, defending their interpretation of Marxism by reference to its debt to, or compatibility with, certain of the great traditions of European thought was a strategy common to all.

The usual place to start any project in the archaeology of European thought is with some ancient and illustrious Greek philosopher.[7] Wishing not to disappoint our audience, we will also begin such an investigation here. For it is here in the musings of the ancient Greeks that holism's philosophical roots lie. As early as Parmenides's attempt to dissociate the One as an indivisible unity from the concept of wholeness, which included the presence of parts, Greek philosophy was concerned with the nature of the *holos*. In addition to descriptive analyses of the whole or the One, Greek thought entertained normative ideas of totality as well, which culminated in the elaborate neo-Platonic attempts to overcome the contingency of man's finite existence through recovering his lost unity with the gods of the mythical Greece.

The first stage in the development of systems theory and the problem of wholes, parts, and complexity may be associated with the Greek philosophers. The Greeks were also holistically inclined in much of their thinking about more mundane matters, such as politics. Both Plato and Aristotle focused on the state, rather than on what a later age would call society, as the significant totality of human life. To Aristotle, in particular, the state (society) was likened to an organism that was differentiated into complementary parts subordinate to the whole. "The state," he contended in *Politics*, "is by nature clearly prior to the individual, since the whole is prior to the parts."[8] In an argument that would be repeated many times, he wrote: "The proof that the state is a creation of nature and prior to the individual is that the individual, when isolated, is not self-sufficing; and therefore he is like a part in relation to the whole."[9]

Both Plato and Aristotle employ the word *systema* in the sense of a whole compounded of several parts or members. And Aristotle, for instance, says that a "whole means that which so contains its contents that they form a unity; and this in two ways, either in the sense that each of them is a unity, or in the sense that the unity is composed of them."[10] In the latter sense the whole cannot be understood as a mere arithmetical sum of its parts. The parts are, as it were, held together in such a way that it would be properly impossible for them to exist otherwise. Aristotle expresses this state of affairs as the *priority* of the whole to its parts. The whole is prior because it possesses or is endowed with an *arche* (first principle), which alone forms the basis of its unity, just as the heart is the *arche* of the living organism (whole, system), according to Aristotle. A whole (system) then is a collection of parts that exist—both individually and as a whole—only insofar as they are related through the agency of the first principle. As can be seen, this interpretation focuses its attention solely upon the internal organization of the system. The system's environment is neglected.[11]

Holism, in contrast to classical atomism, seeks explanations at the level of the totality of things and not at the level of basic constitutive elements. In a parallel manner holism reduces everything to the whole in the same way that atomism reduces everything to its parts. Both are reductive principles, both are simplifiers, and both mutilate and manipulate the parts and the whole.

What must, above all, be appreciated is that the whole can be understood only in terms of its parts and the parts can be understood only in terms of the whole. This tacitly understood concept was never really put to use in positive science because of its inherent ambiguity with its "mission." In the logic of analytical-empirical science, the conjunction of whole to parts canceled each other out in vicious circularity. But it is within this very circularity of complementarity and antimony that one can begin to perceive the constructive forces necessary for achieving an understanding of the whole and the parts.

Consequently, what Greek thought lacked was a belief that history could be understood as a progressively meaningful whole with a beginning and a millennial end. Preferring to see time as repeating itself in infinite cycles without any progress or, in the case of Hesiod and others, stressing decline, the Greeks failed to develop an optimistic, "longitudinal" concept of totality. Here Hebrew and, more important, Christian thought provided a corrective, although St. Augustine limited the progress he posited to the spiritual realm of the City of God and denied it to the mundane City of Man.

Though lacking this historical longitudinal dimension, Aristotle's naturalism still had a profound impact on late medieval thought after the translation of his *Politics* c. 1260 and its assimilation into scholasticism. Medieval organicism perhaps reached its peak in the work of the Florentine Dominican Remigio di Girolemi, Aquinas's pupil and Dante's teacher, who wrote: "If you are not a citizen you are not a man, because a man is naturally an evil animal," and, "The whole is more fully united to the part than the part is to itself."[12]

It suffices to note that organic theory based on the analogy between the state and a living organism provided one vital source of later holistic thought. It informed the so-called social physics of Hobbes but also the socioeconomic thought of François Quesnay and the Physiocrats.[13] It reemerged during the Romantic era in the early nineteenth century, often for conservative purposes. The expediencies of reason were appropriated by social thinkers, such as Saint-Simon and Comte, whose concern was their application to the increasingly weighty problems of governance brought about by the complexification of society. No less indebted to organicism was the new science of sociology, which set out to restore a sense of order after the initial trauma of the French and Industrial revolutions. Although Saint-Simon and Comte were important figures in the rise of positivism, they nonetheless combined their allegiance to the scientific method, as they understood it, with an organic and holistic vision of the reality of society.

For our later purposes it is important to note that Comte, perhaps the first philosopher of organization, saw industrial organization—the scientific organization of labor and knowledge for the production of wealth—as the source of human unity and progress. More particularly, his was a theory of organization applied to the administration of society as a whole that laid down detailed specifications at the level of the microfunction: the precise roles of politicians, industrialists, bankers; the optimum number of people in each city, etc. The spirit of this functional reason was well captured at the time by Goethe in the character of Faust, who translated passive reason, mere thought, into active reason, the accomplished deed, through the technological transformation of the entire world.[14] The capitalist edition of the modernity project thus appeared early on as the organization of knowledge expressed in terms of the appropriative needs of large-scale technological systems.

It has sometimes been argued that Marxism, because of its links to Romantic conservatism through Hegel and to the early positivists through French socialism, shared an essentially organic vision of the social whole. And insofar as all these movements did have a common disdain for the fragmentation and atomization caused by the emergence of bourgeois society, there is some truth to this contention. But in crucial ways Marx's use of totality clashed with that of the organicists, even though at times he labeled his position naturalist and even evoked the organic metaphor. Indeed, in the first preface to *Capital* Marx writes: "The present society is no solid crystal, but an organism capable of change, and is constantly changing." In *Grundrisse*, he finishes a discussion of exchange and circulation with the remark: "Mutual interaction takes place between different moments. This is the case with every organic whole." While the sense of wholeness and community to be found in Aristotle, with its underlying naturalistic and normative sense of totality, was conservative, Marx's holism was clearly a critical one and less naturalistic than that of his organicist predecessors.

To be sure, Marx read Spinoza with apparent enthusiasm in 1841, was attracted to his liberal critiques of religion and censorship, and initially saw him as a corrective to Hegel's authoritarian statism,[15] but when it came to deriving the lineage of his materialism, he preferred French *philosophes* like Diderot, Holbach, and Helvetius.

For Spinoza, the intelligible order of reality was understood as eternal and without development. Spinoza's totality was in permanent existence, whereas for Marx, it was emergent and articulated by a historical subject. Along with his denial of a Divine Creator in the Judeo-Christian sense, Spinoza also dismissed the possibility of social action, of creative human agency, to change the world. Rather than a reciprocity between the whole and the parts, Spinoza's whole dominated the parts entirely. Despite his liberal stress on the value of free thought, there was no place in his system for human agency; indeed, free will itself was an illusion that an appreciation of logic and concrete reality would dispel.

Marx's materialism obtained less from Spinoza's than from the radical philosophers. Unencumbered by a depth of knowledge, the Enlightenment seems an unlikely source for an idea of totality, Marxist or otherwise. The traditional image of the Enlightenment, despite countless revisions and reevaluations, is of a movement whose major intellectual impulses included the critical, analytic, scientific, mechanistic, and antimetaphysical. Indeed, the modern epoch was born at that moment when man invented himself, when he no longer saw himself as a reflection of God or Nature. Its historical impulse lies in the eighteenth-century philosophy of the Enlightenment, which chose reason as the highest of human attributes. Reason, according to Kant, is when we think for ourselves and cease depending on an external authority to make up our minds for us; it thus implies a critical sense in which we have to develop both our powers of rational discrimination and our courage and the autonomy to express them. "Dare to know," said Kant.

Epistemologically, the Enlightenment is normally seen as sensationalist and associationist, with a straight line running from Locke to the skepticism of Hume.[16] The deductive reasoning characteristic of seventeenth-century metaphysicians like Spinoza and Leibniz was replaced by empiricist induction. The classical scientific method, as we have seen, is based on an analytic approach to problem solving: the focal feature is isolated; the whole decomposed into elements; linear causation supplies the logic; reductionism the path of explanation.[17] This model cannot explain system connectedness, which is concerned with interdependencies and the way parts are related to wholes.[18]

Positivist methodology, born of seventeenth-century scientific advance, insists on the primacy of the simple. That is, theory must begin with the particular and build (synthesize) up toward greater generality. Consequently, positivism "turns us away from any attempt to understand our social situation as a whole, a whole that could never be elucidated by the study of the parts alone."[19]

Politically, the Enlightenment is usually associated with social contract theory, civil society, individualism, natural right theory, and the pursuit of self-interest, rather than the search for community or wholeness. Although Aristotle was important for the Enlightenment in a number of ways, his view of man as a political animal subordinate to the whole was not.

Yet the concept of totality, which seems on the surface foreign to the Enlightenment, can be said to have emerged in its interstices. In fact, it is possible to isolate many different Enlightenment sources for later concepts of totality in Critical Marxism. Among these, perhaps the most obvious is the *philosophes'* essential confidence in the capacity of humankind to know the world as a whole. Despite its scorn for the hollow deductive systems of the seventeenth century, the Enlightenment did not hold a modest view of the *empire of reason*. In Ernst Cassirer's words, for the Enlightenment,

> reason cannot stop with the dispersed parts, it has to build from them a new structure, a true whole. But since Reason creates this whole and fits the parts together according to its own rule, it gains complete knowledge of the structure of its product. Reason understands this structure because it can reproduce it in its totality and in the ordered sequence of its individual elements.[20]

No better monument to the belief in the thrust of reason exists than the great encyclopedia of Diderot and D'Alembert, which paid tribute to what Cassirer calls the Enlightenment's *libido sciendii*, its lust for knowledge. Marxism was to emphasize praxis more than knowledge. This was by no means foreign to the Enlightenment itself, for there is more than a trace of the *philosophes'* hubris in the claims of Marxist intellectuals to know the whole.

The confidence behind this claim was grounded in part in the Enlightenment belief in the essential unity of humankind. The concept of progress held by Turgot, Condorcet, and others was predicated on the assumption that the course of human history was a unified whole with a common destiny. Jettisoning Augustinian divisions between cities of God and of man, they conceived of history as a unified process, the epic of a single subject, mankind or humanity. To speak of progress at all demanded a faith in a universal standard by which to measure advance or decline. Although Marxism would later challenge the ahistorical homogenization of humankind implicit in the Enlightenment view of progress, there would be enough of an evolutionary dimension left in its own assumptions to warrant comparison.

Another contribution of the *philosophes* to the holistic tradition can be noted in their expansion of the scope of historical inquiry. Although generally maligned by nineteenth-century critics, the Enlightenment clearly possessed a historical sense well in advance of its predecessors. Instead of merely chronicling the deeds of kings and popes, Voltaire and some of his peers investigated the cultural life of the entire society of the period he studied. The belief that cultures were, in fact, coherent unities whose common features were expressed in their art, religions, institutions, social mores, and political constitutions animated the work of Herder and others who fed directly into nineteenth-century historicism. Indeed, the very notion of a *Zeitgeist* or "spirit of the times," with its implication that each era was a coherent whole, can be traced beyond the Romantics to the eighteenth century. Although the Enlightenment thinkers tended to simplify the unity of the culture they isolated, a holistic appreciation is nonetheless present in their cultural appreciations. In this regard, Marxism can be said to have more closely approximated the Enlightenment's balance between a universalization of humankind and an interest in specific cultures than had the Romantics.

The Enlightenment produced several thinkers whose ideas would later resonate in Marxist totality theory. Prominent among them were Montesquieu, Rousseau, Kant, and Vico.[21] One might add Quesnay and the Physiocrats, who were the first to isolate the economy as a system capable of holistic analysis, although the very isolation of the economy from the rest of society was a target of Marx's holism, properly understood. Vico and Montesquieu were the earliest of their number and can be said to have inaugurated, or at least anticipated, traditions that produced divergent Marxist concepts of totality. It is thus necessary to pause with each of them before examining the other Enlightenment thinkers whose links to Critical Marxism have been more frequently traced.

Giambattista Vico's impact on Marx and Marxism has been difficult to gauge, but there can be little doubt that he anticipated Marx's stress on totality. Most obviously, Vico's recognition of the importance of history at a time when the dominant paradigm was Cartesian, and thus ahistorical, opened the possibility of totality as a historical category, thus incorporating an aspect omitted from the naturalistic and Spinozist traditions. Beyond merely defending the validity of historical thought, Vico's *New Science* attempted to plot the "ideal eternal history traversed in time by the history of every nation in its rise, development, maturity, decline and fall." In so doing, Vico assumed that history made sense as a whole—an anticipation of similar assumptions in Hegel and, to a certain extent, in Marx. Where Vico differed from both, however, was in his cyclical view of the course of that history, which went through a circuit from barbarism to culture and back again. Descending from the level of a universally traversed "ideal eternal history" to that of specific societies, Vico clearly anticipated Marx's idea that the components of those societies could be understood only in relation to each other, that is, as part of a coherent whole. Furthermore, he recognized that pure thought was not the dominant element in the totality. "The order of ideas," he contended, "must follow the order of institutions."[22]

Vico insisted that human creativity was at the root of social and cultural institutions. Institutions were not the product of conscious and deliberate contrivance, as social contract theorists from Locke to Rousseau argued. They arose instead in the course of a historical process ruled more by imagination and passion than by reason. Vico's stress on "making" history was, as other commentators have observed, his seminal contribution to the philosophy of history, and by extension to Marxism and, in particular, Critical Marxism (at least in its Hegelian guise).

In his quarrel with Descartes and Spinoza, Vico advanced a most revolutionary epistemological principle, *verum et factum convertuntur*—the true and the made are interchangeable. Vico argued that men can know history, which they have made, better than they can know nature, whose cause is God alone. Vico's belief in the human origins of history and the concomitant superiority of historical over natural knowledge might then seem compelling, as indeed, it was for Lukács and the Critical Marxists. Vico denied a technically rational interpretation of the word *made* in his thesis. The poet-creators of culture were not Cartesian thinking machines. His was a *making* found in the intellectual heritage of pre-Socratic Greece.[23]

If society is not a divine institution, it is made by man, and man is free to do with society as he likes. Consequently, for Vico, and later for Marx, there is no excuse for having an invidious society, and we must make a noninvidious one without delay. For this purpose you must take power, and you can take power over an invidious society only by a revolution. Moreover, to achieve a comprehensive improvement of society you need comprehensive powers; so you must regard all resistance as treason. This was the meaning of total revolution, which for zealots from Robespierre to Hitler was transmuted into messianic violence.

Vico, who included the "barbarism of reflection" in his *corsi* and *ricorsi* did not hold out any hope for a future determination of history by rational intentionality. Although Marx agreed about deliberate creation in the past—he too had no use for social contract theory or the Physiocrat's myth of the wise legisfactor—he clearly thought otherwise about the future. Indeed, he spoke of true history beginning only when men gained conscious control over the social process. Unreflective "making" would then give way to reflective creation. The implications for knowing the totality of history, especially before the onset of communism, were thus clouded, for, in the famous words from *The Eighteenth Brumaire*:

> Men make history, but they do not make it just as they please; they do not make it under circumstances chosen by themselves, but under circumstances directly encountered, given and transmitted from the past. The tradition of all the dead generations weighs like a nightmare on the brain of the living.[24]

Until they awaken from that nightmare, Marx implied, men will not fully make their own history.[25]

Vico's formula about knowing what we have made cannot be unequivocally applied to all previous history. And thus the perfect symmetry between cognition and production posited by Vico must await some future state when true history can be said to have begun. His positing of an "ideal eternal history" for all societies suggests prediction as well as retrospection; the linkage of making with knowing has other epistemological implications. It suggests that the object of historical knowledge is entirely in the past: what men have made, not what they are making or will make, is the truth. The well-known implication, which Hegel drew from this promise, is that the owl of Minerva flies only at dusk, when the story is already over. This motif could not be adopted by a future-oriented Marxism, which stressed a philosophy of praxis over interpretation or recognition. Vico's holism was thus better suited to a retrospective theory of knowledge than to one with a practical orientation.

Although Vico freed the idea of totality from its naturalist envelope and tied it to human artifice—certainly a critical step in the development of Marxist totality theory—he left unresolved a number of problems. For instance, the real identity of the agent or authentic maker of history and the proper relationship between that making and the domination of nature were also to trouble Critical Marxists.

No less obscure than Vico's, was Montesquieu's contribution to the concept of totality. A contemporary of the Neapolitan, Montesquieu shared with Vico an interest in history and believed that it possessed a discernible order. Like Vico, Montesquieu had no use for social contract theory and rejected the then fashionable notion of a natural man antecedent to society. Finally, Montesquieu joined with Vico in holding that societies could be understood as coherent wholes whose elements were meaningfully interrelated. In *The Spirit of the Laws*, of 1748, Montesquieu presented his celebrated typology of governmental forms, each ruled by a specific principle. The totalizing impulse behind his typology was his correlation of specific social organizations with those principles. In linking governmental form, social organization, and ruling principle, Montesquieu acknowledged, as had Vico, the necessity of viewing man's collective life in holistic terms.

But whereas for Vico the origin of totalities lay in man's poiesis, for Montesquieu they obtained from natural relations. Presaging the Physiocrats, one of the primary goals of *The Spirit of the Laws* was to establish the primacy of natural over human law. To Montesquieu, law was discovered, not created. Far closer to Descartes than Vico in his epistemology was Montesquieu's new variant on the naturalist and organic version of totality. According to Althusser:

> Montesquieu was probably the first person before Marx who undertook to think of history without attributing to it an end, i.e., without projecting the consciousness of men and their hopes onto the time of history. This criticism is entirely to his credit. He was the first to propose a positive principle of universal explanation for history; a principle which is not just static: the totality explaining the diversity of the laws and institutions of a given government; but also dynamic: the law of the unity of nature and principle, a law making it possible to think of the development of institutions and their transformations in real history, too.[26]

As we have already indicated, Vico's understanding of the making of history was approvingly received by Marx, whose theory of totality is congruent with holism and, moreover, with systems theory. While appropriating both the successes and failings of earlier analyses, Marx, in the context of a totality theory, and in his critique of the capitalist mode of production, referred to issues and categories of analysis that are finding their way into contemporary discussions of political economy.[27] However, Marx was not among the first of the German philosophers to propose a totality theory. Kant, opposing the methodology of Descartes in *Critique of Pure Reason*, refers to the "art of systems" in opposition to "technical unity."[28] While the mechanical system, says Kant, starts from single elements and particles, the whole, depending on indifferent unchanged elements, is a motionless, stationary system; the organic system starts from the concept of the whole and then sees in the elements, which interact according to their quality, an organic structure that determines the dynamics of the system. The Kantian principle of the organic system provided a definition of the theory of totality. It was, however, limited in scope; for it contained no clear distinction between material and theoretical systems. It was particularly theoretical; "the architectonic plan of all scientific concepts deriving from pure reason."[29]

Ernst Cassirer's studies of Jean-Jacques Rousseau's relation to Immanuel Kant were singularly successful in exploring the influence of the apostle of pre-Romanticism upon German Idealism.[30] Perhaps no one in the eighteenth century posed the question of individual or personal totality as acutely as did Rousseau. Perhaps no one did more than Rousseau to dramatize the anomie, the agony of personal fragmentation, or searched as frantically for an escape. His constant goal, pursued by various means, was to find a framework in which, as he put it in *Emile*, "I shall be me without contradiction, without division."[31] Although dimly echoing the ideal of the universal man in classical and Renaissance thought, Rousseau's appreciation of that ideal was not without a proto-existentialist dimension, an awareness of the virtual impossibility of attaining it. It was perhaps this that marked him as a clearly modern figure. Indeed, inasmuch as he perceived the integrity of the individual to be fragile, he was set apart from those *philosophes* who saw more confidently what a later age would call "ego integration," fostered by the growing power of reason. Their confidence is not surprising, for, after all, the individual had only recently emerged as a discrete entity during the Renaissance and Reformation, an individual whose unction was found in Kant's categorical imperative. In Rousseau's time the dissemination of the bourgeois notion of self-interest, "possessive individualism," was only beginning and thus was not yet prominent enough for critical scrutiny. Nonetheless, Rousseau was able to comprehend the brittle quality of emergent individualism. He denounced the shallowness implicit in the rationalist's definition of personality. Just as bitterly, he called into question the compromises demanded of personal integrity by the modern, urbane society of his day. To live in the civilized world of the Enlightenment, the world of fashionable salons and literary politics, meant to live unauthentically and estranged from one's deeper self. To break free from that estrangement meant ending one's dependence on external values, the desire for status in the eyes of others.

By so insistently vilifying the society of his day, Rousseau gave the impression that he placed no faith in social answers to personal fragmentation, whence his popular reputation as a primitivist extolling the noble savage. To those who interpreted him in this way, among them the poets of the *Sturm und Drang*, personal totality could be regained only through individual rebellion against society or escape from it into art. But the Rousseau who had a more immediate impact on Marxist notions of totality offered a very different remedy, which can best be understood as nonindividualist. In *The Social Contract* of 1762, Rousseau's solution to personal dissociation was clearly holistic and collectivist. Here he turned his back on "natural man" and embraced the artificial citizen as the answer to his dilemma. The road to personal wholeness, he argued, could only come through the transcendence of the empirical self with all its petty needs and desires and the achievement of a new moral personality through allegiance to a higher moral community. As he put it in *The Social Contract*:

> He who dares to undertake the making of a people's institutions, ought to feel himself capable so to speak, of changing human nature.... Transforming each individual, who is by himself a complete and solitary whole, into part of a greater whole from which he in a manner receives his life and being.[32]

In *Emile*, written the same year, he remarks:

> Civil man is only a fraction of a whole, his value lying in his relation to the whole, which is the social body. Good institutions are those which best strip man of his nature, taking away his absolute existence to give him a relative one, and transferring his *Self* into a common unity; so that each individual no

longer believes himself to be one, but a part of a unit, and is no longer aware except of the whole.³³

Turning from an earlier nostalgia for a lost bucolic age before the alleged civilizational decline to a political moral community, his reference image of wholeness has been ungenerously interpreted as a progenitor of totalitarian democracy.³⁴ Appreciating societies as unique wholes, Rousseau realized that the democratic principle could operate in a state the size of the Greek *polis*. It was only therein that a social contract allegedly made sense, where a public life among equals was possible. It was on the basis of this insight that he rejected the proposition that there could be no solution to personal fragmentation within the context of giant nation-states. Without faith in Turgot's and Condorcet's idea of progress, or Vico's concept of history, Rousseau was a moralist without hope that his utopia might be realized. Eleven years after his death the great French Revolution gave the lie to Rousseau's disdain for history. Indeed, meaningful transformation was now understood to be a possibility, and new totalities in the normative sense might be hoped for; a collective agent of history was no longer a utopian whimsy.

The line from Rousseau's *Social Contract* to Marx's "On the Jewish Question," with its impatient critique of political emancipation and the continued split between man and citizen, was a direct one. Indeed, Rousseau's expressive critique of liberal representative parliamentary institutions may well have been a source of Marx's critique of bourgeois democracy.

Rather than surrendering to the organicist's natural totality, Rousseau proposed a surrender to an artificial totality of man's collective creation, one that would allegedly realize the authentic self. Unlike Vico's poiesis contribution to the concept of cultural wholes, Rousseau emphasized the deliberate, conscious action involved in their realization. Consequently, the solution to alienation lay less in a return to rustic nature than in the creation of a "second nature" transcendent of the first. In this connection, it was German Idealism that was to seek the realization of that which Rousseau had posited as an unrealizable dream.

It was in the substantial figure of Immanuel Kant that Rousseau's meditations on totality most influenced German Idealism. Lukács, in *History and Class Consciousness*, identified in Kant's ambiguous and ambivalent work the bourgeoisie's inability to achieve a totalistic appreciation of reality. Kant's rejection, in *Critique of Pure Reason*, of dialectics as a meaningful mode of cognition, its separation of the noumenal from the phenomenal, plus its stress on scientific as opposed to historical thought, seemed to Lukács to be an ahistorical transformation of the specific contradiction of bourgeois society into eternal categories. It depicts Kant as hostile to holism. Moreover, in *Critique of Practical Reason* the impression is reinforced. For here Rousseau's concern for a moral community to be created by the general will was with Kant transformed into a private and personal moral sense instilled in man by God, i.e., the categorical imperative. With starry heaven above him and the moral law within, the first enveloping the empirical being, the second linking the intelligible self to a higher reality beyond the sensate, the duality of the human condition was bound by external reality and internal freedom. But this served only to reaffirm the alleged primacy of the individual. Not responding, but seeking to escape the anguished civil conscience, Kant defined personal self-responsibility empty of socioethical imperative. He created a notion of duty to principle that remained indifferent to the consequences of the actions taken.[35]

The morality expressed by Rousseau appeals to, and is finalized in, social ethics, by which he sought to evaluate the content of social practice. His theory sought to ground its standards in the reality of society. But what if that social reality embodies rationality in a one-sided—and to that extent, irrational—way? What happens when instrumental rationality, for instance, that which attaches to science and technology, ceases to be one legitimate type of reason and becomes the hegemonic mode of thought and practice? If by Kant's categorical imperative moral decision is relegated to the sphere of arbitrary (private) preference, then instrumental rationality, logical and calculating thought, may lay claim to the *empire of reason*. In a society in which the validity of basic goals and values is assumed to be beyond rational assessment, social practice itself—however scientifically enlightened it may be—hinges on the irrational. Insofar as instrumental rationality dominates social life, it too easily dismisses the validity of social ethics. This is the ethical dilemma of Kant's categorical imperative.

In 1790, *Critique of Judgment* optimistically argued that underlying the apparent chaos was a coherence determined by universal natural laws. But the nature to which Kant referred was not that described by Newtonian mechanics, a universe knowable to man through a priori synthetic judgments of pure theoretical reason. Rather Kant's nature was teleological; it implanted in man capacities that were to be self-cultivated over time. Man, Kant insisted, was distinguished by his reason, which would be completely developed through the collective work of the species, rather than through the efforts of the isolated individual. Self-cultivation of the species meant the progressive transcendence of man's animal existence and the increased perfection of his rational faculty, which implied practical or moral reason—the phenomenal self would be transcended by the noumenal self. This he argued was the product of the "unsocial sociability." This formulation provided a justification of struggle as a means to achieve the ultimate totalization of humankind, and it would later not only constitute the basis of Hegel's idea of dialectical contradiction but also inform Marx's notion of class struggle as the agency of history.

History, Kant contended, must be conceptualized as an endless process of totalization in which practical reason determined the movements of the whole.[36] History possessed coherence and structure as a whole. It was as well a normative totality whose end was an international community of civil societies. And whereas earlier thinkers had attributed providential intervention to the movement of history, for Kant the instrument of totalization was humankind, for "nature has intended that man develop everything which transcends the mechanical ordering of his animal existence, entirely by himself and that he does not partake of any happiness or perfection except that which he has secured himself by his own reason and free of instinct."[37] Kant placed his normative totality firmly in the future.

While the legacy of Kant's thought continued to inform Austrian Marxism, the Vienna Circle, and thereby the Russian Critical Marxists, Lukács and later Marcuse, sought to distance themselves from Kant. This rejection by the Western Marxists was not, however, uniform. Lucien Goldman sought in Kant's work evidence of an appreciation of the concept of totality and its relation to social community. Kant, according to Goldman, "was the first modern thinker to recognize anew the importance of the Totality as a fundamental category of existence, or at least to recognize its problematic character."[38] But allegedly Kant was dissuaded from fully developing a philosophy of totality by the impact of Humean empiricism, which convinced him that no theoretical or practical totality existed as a given fact. Insofar as empiricism did not carry the day,

> totality retained all its reality and all its importance. Kant had merely been seeking it in the wrong direction. It is not external to man, but in him; it is not given and existing, but an ultimate goal which gives man his human dignity. It is a transcendental ideal, a practical postulate.[39]

Rousseau's nostalgia for a once-accomplished totality was replaced by Kant's for an imminent totalization in the normative sense. Fusing this ideal with a concept of progress absent from Vico and Rousseau, Kant earned the label of philosopher of the French Revolution.

Kant's Critique of Reason

How to restore order in the intellectual landscape left in disarray with the expulsion of God, conceived as the rational principle that links science and nature, became a weighty question. How could scientists ever have access to global truth when it could no longer be asserted, except metaphorically, that science deciphers the word of creation? God was now silent or at least no longer spoke the same language as human reason. Moreover, in a nature from which time itself was eliminated, what remained of subjective experience? What was the meaning of freedom, destiny, or social ethical values?

Kant's *Critique of Pure Reason* was written in response to a "rationality crisis" captured in these questions. The crisis was rooted in a disagreement between rationalists and empiricists over the proper foundations of knowledge. Both schools of thought believed that in order for knowledge to be legitimated, it had to be founded on truths whose certainty could be directly intuited.

The rationalists held that such truths were intuited by pure reason unaided by sensory experience. In his *Meditations on First Philosophy*, Descartes had argued that nothing attested to by his senses—even the very existence of his corporeal being and the surrounding world—was certain, since it was logically possible that he could be dreaming. Worse yet, he could be deceived by an evil deity into falsely believing that a world existed outside his mind. He observed, however, that he could not doubt his own existence as a thinking thing. Using this foundational belief as a test case for all authentic knowledge, he then proceeded to show that he knew other things with certainty as well. These were the truths of mathematics, geometry, and, above all, the existence of a perfect God who would not deceive him into believing there was an external world if there was not one. Having thus established a metaphysical warrant for believing in the existence of the material world, Descartes felt that he had discovered the scientific foundation for which he was looking. More important, he felt that he had shown why mechanistic science posed no threat to freedom and immortality of the soul. For how could one possibly doubt that the very act of thinking—which confirmed one's being—was logically distinct from physical extension? If thoughts and ideas do not possess physical extension, how can they be subject to its causal mechanism? At this juncture the skeptical implications of empiricism made their appearance.

The empiricists contested the possibility of founding scientific knowledge on pure reason. Their most sophisticated and radical representative, David Hume, maintained that the truths of reason consisted of relations of ideas that, though certain, were not necessarily informative. Tautologies, statements such as "All bachelors are unmarried," though necessarily true by definition of the terms (ideas) contained in the statements, fail to advance our appreciation. Knowing that "unmarried" is contained in the idea of "bachelor" does not extend our knowledge about bachelors. It does not even tell us whether such things as bachelors exist or not. Beliefs regarding the existence of things and their properties —what Hume called "matters of fact"—are truly informative. Therefore, he concluded that they must have their source in sense experience, not reason.

From a philosophical point of view, the transition from Diderot to the Romantics and, more precisely, from one of these two types of critical attitudes toward science to the other, can be found in Kant's transcendental philosophy. The foundational proposition being that the Kantian critique identified science in general with its Newtonian realization. It, thereby, branded as impossible any opposition to classical science, which was not antithetical to science itself. Any criticism against Newtonian physics must then be seen as aimed at devaluing the rational understanding of nature in favor of metaphysics. Kant's approach had repercussions, which still reverberate in our day, captured in the awareness that science has become the ideology of the nonideology. Let us, therefore, summarize his point of view as presented in *Critique of Pure Reason*.

The focus on mechanics plagued philosophy and evoked the Kantian critique.

Kant's critical philosophy, while it ratifies all the claims of science, actually constrains scientific pursuit to problems that can be considered both easy and futile. It condemns science to the tedious task of deciphering the monotonous language of physical phenomena while retaining for itself the questions of human "destiny." The world studied by science, the world accessible to positive knowledge is "only" the world of phenomena. Kant's contention was that not only is the scientist unable to know things-in-themselves, but even the questions he asks are irrelevant to the real problems of humankind. Beauty, freedom, and ethics cannot be objects of positive knowledge. Positive knowledge itself is impossible, for it is crippled by systemic disjunction and simplification.

Kant's *Critique of Pure Reason* attempts to resolve the crisis of knowledge by combining rationalism and empiricism in a manner that avoids dogmatic metaphysics and radical skepticism. The empiricists, he notes, were correct in denying that reason could provide informative knowledge about the world without sensory experience. Metaphysical beliefs about God, soul, and the totality of things unobserved can be topics of moral speculation and articles of faith but cannot rightly claim to be true or false, argued Kant. Nevertheless, the rationalists were correct to point out that the possibility for judging a cluster of discrete sensory properties as belonging to one and the same temporally perduring object necessarily presupposes a rational intuition (or judgment) of unity.

Kant argued that there were two levels of reality: a phenomenal level that corresponds to science and a noumenal level corresponding to ethics. This constituted an uneasy truce between philosophy and science. The phenomenal order is created by the human mind. The noumenal level transcends man's intellect; it corresponds to a spiritual reality that supports his ethical and religious way of life. In a way, Kant's solution was the only one possible for those who asserted both the necessity of ethics and the reality of the objective world. Instead of God, it is now man himself who is the source of the order he perceives in nature. Kant justifies both scientific knowledge and man's alienation from the phenomenal world described by science. From this perspective we can see that Kantian philosophy explicitly situates the philosophical content of classical science.[40]

Kant defines the subject of critical philosophy as transcendental. It is not concerned with the objects of experience but is based on the a priori fact that a systematic knowledge of these objects is possible (this is, for Kant, proved by the existence of physics). Kant further argued for the a priori conditions of possibility for this mode of knowledge. To do that a distinction must be made between the direct sensations we receive from the outside world and the objective mode of knowledge. Objective knowledge is not passive; it informs its objects. When we take a phenomenon as the object of experience, we assume, a priori before we experience it, that it obeys a given set of principles. Insofar as it is perceived as a possible object of knowledge, it is the product of retrojection. The object is a "re-cognition" of a priori synthetic cognitive process, of an unreflective ontology. We find ourselves in the objects of our knowledge, and the socially informed scientist himself is thus the source of the universal laws he discovers. This appreciation of intersubjectivity, however, seems to have escaped positive economics in its pursuit of scienticity.

The a priori conditions of experience are also the conditions for the existence of objects of experience. This statement sums up the "Copernican Revolution" achieved by Kant's transcendental inquiry. The subject no longer "revolves" around its object, seeking to discover the laws by which it is governed or the language by which it may be deciphered. Now the subject itself is at the center, imposing its laws, and the world perceived speaks the language of that subject. No wonder, then, that Newtonian science is able to describe the world from an external, almost divine point of view! Or that political economy acquired an invidious "naturalness."

That all perceived phenomena are governed by the laws of our mind does not mean that a concrete knowledge of these objects is useless. And though, according to Kant, science does not engage in a dialogue with nature but imposes its own language upon it, still it must discover, in each case, the specific message expressed in this general language. A knowledge of the political economy of a priori concepts alone is vain and empty.

From the Kantian point of view, Laplace's demon, the symbol of the scienticity, is an illusion, but it is a rational illusion. Although it is the result of a limiting process, it is still the expression of a legitimate conviction, which is the driving force of science—the conviction that, in its entirety, nature is rightfully subjected to the laws that scientists have succeeded in deciphering. Wherever it goes, whatever it questions, science will always obtain, if not the same answer, at least the same kind of answer. There exists an exclusive syntax that includes all possible answers.

Transcendental philosophy thus ratified the physicist's claim to have found a definitive form of positive knowledge. At the same time, however, it secured for philosophy a dominant position in respect to science. It was no longer necessary to look for the philosophic significance of the results of scientific activity. From the transcendental standpoint, those results—that is, the subject of philosophy, science taken as a repetitive and closed enterprise—provide a stable foundation for transcendental reflection.

Science in general came to be identified with its Newtonian realization. It thereby confused any opposition to rational mechanics as antithetical to science itself. Any criticisms directed against mechanicalism were then seen as aimed at depreciating the rational understanding of nature and the repudiation of what constitutes a major mode of intellectuality in favor of an allegedly spurious metaphysical form of knowledge.

The seventeenth century produced a scientific paradigm formulated by mathematicians for mathematicians. The idiosyncratic characteristic of the mathematical mind lies in its capacity for manipulating abstractions and for distilling from them concise internally cohesive corollaries. The master physicist, physician, and mathematician Herman von Helmholtz declared, in an address reproduced in his *Popular Lectures on Science*, that the final aim of all natural science is to resolve itself into mathematics.[41]

Why did the eighteenth- and nineteenth-century scientists cling to mechanics in spite of its patent failings? For though Newton had made strenuous efforts to explain the action of gravity, his efforts failed to penetrate the problem of how the sun's attraction acted on planets millions and hundreds of millions of miles away. Newton's efforts failed, and he closed his endeavor with his famous "I frame no hypotheses." One answer is that "hope springs eternal." More relevant is that they were so flushed with success in following Newton's lead that they lost sight of the problem of explaining the physical nature. Instead, they resorted to the descriptive mathematics, and their successes (most notably those of Lagrange and Laplace) in deducing some known regularities in the heavenly motions and in encompassing new phenomena were so great, so remarkably accurate, that the problem of explaining the physical action was buried under a mountain of mathematical formulations.

In general, the reliance on mathematical description, even though concrete understanding was singularly lacking, made possible remarkable contributions in science.[42] Parenthetically, as René Passet has remarked, the penetration of positivist mathematical description into conventional economic thought brought esoteric developments similarly detached from the substantive (noumenal) problematique of the livelihood of man.[43] What these practitioners did was to sacrifice concrete intelligibility for mathematical description and prediction. With its putative scientific status shielding it, economic theory repulsed any criticism that threatened to expose its ontological hard core.

The Newtonian concept of a universe, consisting of hard, indestructible particles acting one upon another by well-determined, calculable forces, was made the basis of a rigorous determinism by the French astronomer and mathematician the Marquis Pierre-Simon de Laplace. In his classic statement on the nature of determinism he wrote:

> An intelligence knowing, at any given instant of time, all forces acting in nature, as well as the momentary positions of all things of which the universe consists, would be able to comprehend the motions of the largest bodies of the world and those of the smallest atoms in one single formula, provided it were sufficiently powerful to subject all data to analysis; to it nothing would be uncertain, both future and past would be present before its eyes.[44]

The enormous success of positivism and scientific abstraction has foisted onto philosophy the indulgent task of accepting mathematical description as the most concrete rendering of fact. This vanity evoked diverse responses both from outside science and from within it. Voltaire, in his *Ignorant Philosopher*, speculated: "It would be very singular that all nature, all the planets, should obey eternal laws, and that there should be a little animal, five feet high, who, in contempt of these laws, could act as he pleased, solely according to his caprice."

Denis Diderot, at the height of the Newtonian triumph, emphasized that the problem of living systems, that is, wholes, was repressed by the mechanical paradigm, and that its image would haunt the ardent practitioners of rational mechanics. The vitalist's—and for that matter, the dialectic materialist's—forceful contention was that unlike a living being, a Cartesian automaton's finality does not lie within itself, rather its finality is imposed from without.

The birth of rational mechanics was thus marked by the abandonment of the Aristotelian holism as well as its vitalist inspiration. However, the vitalist issue, reconstituted as the organization of living matter, remained problematic and became a challenge for classical science. According to the mechanistic paradigm, the understanding of life in general comprises simply a complete explanation in terms of principles of physics and chemistry; in short, a mechanistic account of all living phenomena as physical and chemical processes. The rift was considerable for rational mechanics, and the generalized laws of motion had become synonymous with artificiality and nonliving systems.[45] Indeed, the Cartesian description of nature had its logical counterpart in the conception of man as an "economizing" automaton, ultimately alienated both from the reality of society and from nature, rendering man a creature suitable only to inhabit Plato's *City of Pigs*.

Holistic Philosophy

The Kantian truce between science and philosophy was a fragile one. Post-Kantian philosophers broke the truce in favor of a new philosophy of science, presupposing a path to knowledge that was distinct from mechanicalism and occasionally hostile to it. Speculation, released from the constraints of any experimental dialogue, reigned supreme, but with tragic consequences for the dialogue between scientists and philosophers. For most scientists the philosophy of nature became synonymous with an arrogant, absurd speculation riding roughshod over facts, and, indeed, was regularly proven wrong by the facts. On the other side, for the philosophers, it has become a symbol of the dangers involved in dealing with nature and competing with science. The rift among science, philosophy, and humanistic studies was thus made greater by mutual disdain and anxiety.

As an example of this speculative approach to nature, let us consider further Hegel's contribution. His most important contribution to critical theory consists in conceiving reason as both an institutionalized social practice and a living dialectic. For Hegel, the cognitive, as well as moral, concepts by which we impose meaningful order on ourselves and our world are intertwined in the totality of our "way of life." In everyday life one cannot rigorously distinguish facts from values, what *is* from what *ought* to be. Our moral ideals are substantiated in the institutions and practices in which they are factually embedded. Social institutions and practices, in turn, circumscribe our traffic with the world and determine the way we perceive it. Hegel's philosophy distanced itself from that of Kant, for whom the "abstract" distinction between science and morality, necessity and freedom, and historical change and universal reason was ambiguously consistent with Cartesian foundationalism. It constituted a nuanced reproduction of the Enlightenment's own unresolved enigma and failed to do justice to the dialectical unity and dynamic tension informing the whole of our historical experience.

Akin to the Kantian critique, the Hegelian philosophy of nature in reasserting elements of Aristotle's theory of praxis systematically incorporated all that was denied by mechanicalism. In particular, it rests on the qualitative difference between the simple behavior described by mechanics and the behavior of more complex wholes. It rejects reductionism and the idea that differences are merely apparent and that nature is basically homogeneous, simple, and fully explicable through mechanical description. It affirms the existence of a hierarchical yet intercontextual simultaneity in which each level of complexity coevolves with others, constraining in the process some possible future structures while admitting others. It denies the possibility of collapsing those levels, where each level is characterized by qualitatively distinct finalities and comes to be regulated by what we now understand as specific cybernetic mechanisms. But Hegel's philosophy was not without idealistic and finalistic dimensions. In his system, increasing levels of complexity are specified, and nature's finality is the eventual self-realization of its spiritual dimension.

Unlike the mechanicalist world-embracing panoramas ranging from gravitational interactions to human passions, Hegel knew perfectly well that his distinctions ran counter to the day's mathematical science of nature. He therefore set out to limit the significance of mechanics, to show that mathematical description is restricted to the most trivial situations. Mechanics can be mathematized because it attributes only space-time properties to matter. It is precisely this interchangeable quality, which Hegel sets as a condition for mathematization, that is no longer satisfied when the mechanical level of description is abandoned for a metasystemic one involving a luxuriant spectrum of physical, social, and psychical properties.

In a sense, Hegel's system provides a measured philosophic response to the crucial problems of complexity and wholes. However, for generations of scientists Hegelian holism represented the epitome of abhorrence and contempt. And in the course of time, the intrinsic difficulties of Hegel's philosophy of nature were aggravated by the obsolescence of the metaphysical ontology on which his system was based. Hegel, of course, based his rejection of the Newtonian system on the scientific conceptions of his time. And it was precisely those conceptions that were to fall into oblivion with astonishing speed. It is difficult to imagine a less opportune time than the beginning of the nineteenth century for a reevaluation of Aristotelian holism as a paradigmatic alternative to atomistic mechanicalism.

Hegelian Totality

After the German Enlightenment, the objective idealist Georg Wilhelm Friedrich Hegel came to dominate German thought. Hegel taught that nothing was real but the "whole," the "Absolute"; that history was a series of advances toward the unobtainable but essential goal of both the historical development of mind and the continuous becoming of God, the Absolute Idea; that all things proceed from a less to a perfect "Oneness." Moreover, in the preface to *Phenomenology of the Spirit* Hegel inscribed that "the truth is the whole."[46] This truth appeared in all facets of the realized totality: epistemological, ontological, political, and ethical.

For Hegel, Kantianism was identified with abstract and ahistorical antinomies, which only dialectical thought, with its appreciation of totality, could best. Whereas Kant had condemned dialectical thinking as a source of illusion, Hegel asserted that only by employing the dialectic could the distinctions between knowledge of the world of appearances (phenomena) and of the world of essences or things-in-themselves (noumena), between the sensible and the intelligible, and between the moral *ought* and the empirical *is* be reconciled. An appreciation of the centrality of totality was necessary to transcend these and other dichotomies.

From his triadic dialectic construct of thesis, antithesis, and synthesis, "being" and "nothing" generate "becoming," wherein the necessary or essential dimension of concrete reality is revealed and achieves a synthesis. For beneath the "abstract" world of description, of proportions and causal events, there lies a deeper subjectivity—the essential in the concrete totality—possessing its own dynamic and logic inaccessible to mere observation. For disciplined observational, rationalist, and objectivist inquiry gives us access only to surface appearances. These may correspond to statistical "laws" describing events taken in isolation from the totality of relations constitutive of their essential meaning, unity, and purpose. The nondialectical method integrates the partial—and to that extent, false—perspectives of analytic reason into a synthetic whole. And whereas the empirical/positivist notion of concreteness is equated to the unmediated facticity-of-the-given, for Hegel the realization of the essence was complexly mediated and richly articulated. It was in concrete totality, the web of relations among seemingly discrete entities, that Hegel alleged was the proper focus of a philosophy isomorphic to reality. Therefore, he distanced himself from that mode of thought expressed in general, empty, and formal universals that conceal the potential for contradiction and the emergent essence buried within the whole.

Throughout social history, science and religion, i.e., social ethics, achieve a unity in the dialectic as a comprehensive and rational view of the essential in reality. The dialectical implies a unity of opposites whose essence is apparent from the very beginning but only in a very undeveloped and imperfect sense. Thus, for Hegel a genuinely critical knowledge of reality presupposes a comprehensive dialectical grasp of the totality of relationships, the logical and the historical, that sustain its unity even while threatening its disunity. His triadic view of reality presents a cosmic teleology, a reconciliatory spiraling toward ever greater degrees of freedom, unity, and reason in which the finalization of nature is found in the self-realization of its spiritual element. Thus, for Hegel, the "reconciliation" of man and nature comes only with the mastering of nature. In his *The Philosophy of History*, he wrote:

> Nature is to be regarded as a system of grades, of which the one necessarily arises out of the other, and is the proximate truth of the one from which it results; but not so that the one were naturally generated out of the other.... It has been an inept conception of earlier and later "Naturphilosophie" to regard the progression and transition of one natural form and sphere into a higher as an outwardly actual production.[47]

Nature's history is finalized with the consummate realization of man—that is, with the coming of Spirit apprehending itself. The reconciliation, if we may call it that, obtains from stamping man's identity on it and appropriating it to man's needs through science and technology. Reconciliation with other totalities occurs on a different plane. For instance, the reconciliation of man and state requires the establishment of legal, moral, economic, and political institutions guaranteeing universal equality and freedom.

Hegel's vision of the concrete in political and social terms involved the creative interplay of various levels of social reality—the family, civil society, and the state—rather than the reduction of some in the name of the alleged universality of one of the others. The state, as a political entity, was seen as assuming an instrumental role in reconciling or mediating the interests of the whole. Thus, unlike Rousseau, Hegel was content with a series of countervailing social and political institutions that resisted abstract homogenization. The separation of man into bourgeois and citizen, private and public, was not a source of embarrassment for him, as it was to be for Marx. Neither was the maintenance of a sphere of personal, private subjectivity seen as corrosive to the fundamental unity of the whole. Moreover, neither was class struggle nor the persistence of war between sovereign states seen as an impediment to the rationality of the whole, rather they were moments in the realization of the Absolute.

Central to Hegel's system was the assumption that the ontological process was ultimately knowable by the human subject, whose rationality participates in the rationality of the whole. Thus, the method of *Wissenschaft* was comparably holistic, circular, and dialectical. Each of the parts of philosophy is a philosophical whole, a circle rounded and complete in itself. In each of these parts, however, the philosophical idea is found in a particular medium. The single circle, because it is a real totality, bursts through the limits imposed by its special medium and gives rise to a wider circle. The whole of philosophy in this way resembles a spiral sweeping toward the realization of the Absolute.

A self-contained philosophic circuit conceives of substance subjectively; that is to say, it defines the principle of a dialectical identity. The subject moves in a world created by itself that assumes full objectivity. For Hegel the unity of human subjectivity and natural objectivity was constitutive of free rational agency and signifies a potential realizable in history. Because of the dynamic character of reality for Hegel, history was given axial importance. The historical totality, understood as the self-reflexive subjective totality at the beginning of the process, was transmuted into the objective totality at the end. In the process, different ontological levels emerge as totalities according to the measure of their development. Central to Hegel's totality was the assumption that the ontological process was ultimately knowable by the subject, whose rationality partakes of the general rationality permeating the whole (i.e., systems rationality). Thus, the method of science was holistic, circular, cumulative, and dialectical. A theory of totality, which was at once a doctrine of history, was grounded on an emergent reality animated by necessity rather than freedom.

Thus, for Hegel, grounded in an assumption that hearkened back to Vico's *verum-factum* principle, the subject and object of knowledge were intertwined insofar as the latter was produced out of, and constituted, the former. He insisted that the distinction between the spiritual and the material obliterated man's capacity to see the dichotomy itself as a topic that emerges from man's role as the producer of such conceptions. But distancing himself from Vico, Hegel did not posit an ultimate subordination of man-the-maker to God-the-maker in terms of their relative ability to know what they had made. Man was himself a moment in the Absolute Spirit—a combination of the Greek Logos and the Christian divinity who served as the unifying ground of *Being*. The self-recognition of the Absolute was also the recognition of man's own *Being*. All subsequent humanizations of Hegel's totality entered through the door opened by this identification.[48]

Hegel's objective idealism—a concept not then hostaged to positivism—undermined the Cartesian and philosophical duality between objectivity and subjectivity.[49] More specifically, it meant that the Cartesian dualisms, mind-and-body, man-and-nature, and man-and-society, ontologized by modern thought were, for Hegel, moments in the dialectic of self-recognition in which contradiction, fragmentation, estrangement, and alienation were real, lamentable, but nonetheless necessary, aspects of the reconciliation of the progress of the Absolute Spirit. Indeed, for Hegel, the "agent" of history was contradiction and determinate negation. When the dialectic, paradoxically, was at an end, the contradictions and dualisms that had manifested themselves along the way would be (re)conciled, a (re)conciliation by which they were simultaneously retained, canceled, and transcended. Thereby, for instance, the Cartesian dualities would be recognized as false dichotomies; for they are the products of historically contextualized appreciations of man and "other"; whereby nature-as-other, body-as-other, and society-as-other are merely accorded residual status. Thus, a final identity would be reached in the curious gap between identity and nonidentity.[50]

For Kant, nature was opposed to spirit and was spirit's emanation. Whereas for Hegel, the Absolute Spirit was the meta-spirit, both the creator and the created, which served as the synthesizing ground of *Being*; it was dynamic and subjective, the protagonist in a cosmic drama of its own invention. The Absolute Spirit's ultimate function was to differentiate its primal immediacy into a richly articulated universe of mediated particulars, then recognize itself therein. Indeed, only after differentiation and recognition was the Absolute Spirit truly itself, for "of the Absolute it must be said that it is essentially a result, that only at the end is it what it is in very truth."[51] Thus, truth makes its appearance at the conclusion of a history whose actual meaning, at least as far as the participants are concerned, is one of unreason and unfreedom. Or, to use Hegel's epigram: "The owl of Minerva only takes wing at dusk." That is, hidden truth knows itself as truth only when it has become manifest.

Because of the importance of the dynamic of reality for Hegel, history was given a privileged place while nature was awarded a lesser place in the emergence of truth. In *Philosophy of History*, he stated:

> The changes that take place in nature, how infinitely manifold however they may be, exhibit only a perpetually self-repeating cycle; in nature there happens nothing new under the sun and the multiform play of its phenomena so far induces a feeling of ennui; only in those changes which take place in the region of Spirit does anything new arise.[52]

In a connected manner, and with a chauvinism perhaps surpassed only by Herder, Hegel maintained that the development of the spirit of man, and thus truth and reason, was best represented by German achievements. For Hegel, the "great" men of history were all German: Theodoric, Charlemagne, Barbarossa, Luther, and Frederick the Great. These men, all "heroes," the best a nation could produce, were the finest examples of the "health" of a country. Indeed, in Hegel's interpretation of Platonic thought, the "whole" was represented by the state (Plato's *Republic*). Its purest form was the Prussian monarchy, which was absolute. Moreover, he indicated that: "The German spirit is the spirit of the new world. Its aim is the realization of absolute truth as the unlimited self-determination of freedom—that freedom which had its own absolute form itself as its purpose."[53]

Significantly, it was over Hegel's proposition on "the end of history" that Marx and later critical theorists broke rank with Hegel. He had argued that the basic contours of rational life were in the process of being finally established in Europe's liberal monarchies. Not surprisingly, the notion that the dialectic of reason (and history) was coming to an end struck the Left Hegelians as manifestly undialectical. Others found irony in Hegel's Smithian belief in the "cunning of reason" as determining the destiny of Western civilization. In Hegel's reading, free rational insight into the emancipatory potential inherent in the historical process is denied to the "makers" of history. Such insight is limited to the retrospective reflection of the philosopher. For them, the general course of a history, all but completed, is necessarily regarded as the inevitable outcome of necessity, of the logic of the essence buried in the totality. Thus, reason and freedom make their appearance at the conclusion of a history whose actual meaning, at least as far as the participants are concerned, is one of unreason and unfreedom.

For Hegel progress in morality and ethics obtains from the poetic force of cultural ideas, not in the production of material necessities. The struggle for recognition (*thymos*) attached to the "cunning of reason" is a social activity whereby individuals allegedly come to realize that their very identity as free subjects depends on social recognition. So long as domination exists, recognition will at most be limited and imperfect.[54] No one will be truly free, not even the masters, because their own freedom and sense of self will be continually challenged by the will of oppressed people. For Hegel, it is primarily at the level of culture that this Enlightenment dilemma—the problematic mediation of individual freedom and moral community—is resolved. For it is at this level, he argues, that a people (as a political entity) or state articulates its ideal self-image or self-concept. More specifically, this self-concept expresses the level of freedom that a nation feels it has ideally attained. The ideal, whether ethical or moral, is prior to the real insofar as it lends the real, the whole, unity, meaning, legitimacy, and purpose. In short, it lends "truth" to existing economic, social, and political relations. For they are necessary to the further moment in the dialectic. Here the "true" and the "necessary" collapse into one.

When applied to the more concrete historical development of humankind, Hegel's totality theory permeated his judgment about past, present, and future cultures and societies. While he took as his source of inspiration the image of the Greek *polis*, his Hellenophilic nostalgia was tempered by an appreciation that Greek society was insufficiently self-conscious, ensnared in the immediacy of its presence. From Herder and Schiller he came to appreciate its naive unity, grounded in an aesthetic that, though extremely beautiful in its manifestations, lacked an element of the sublime, a formlessness of infinity, of self-consciousness and self-reflection. Hegel contended that with the cunning of reason the development of inwardness, individuality, and self-consciousness could obtain a mediated totality.

Hegel's contribution to holistic tradition was profound in its multidimensionality. By referring to all coherent entities within the cosmic whole, he encouraged the vision that lesser or partial totalities existed on all levels of the meta-totality. This meant that any part in a larger whole might itself be considered an organized whole from a perspective internal to that totality. Concrete reality was thus populated by multitudes of hierarchically linked and juxtaposed totalities. Pointedly, it was this meta-totality that was annihilated by Cartesian reductionism. Therein concreteness was falsely understood as merely existence of internally related but differentiated lower-order atomic entities. Society was not a mass society. Its movement was generated through the intercontextual simultaneity of the various lower-ordered totalities, whose relations became richer and more complicated as the process pressed forward.

The articulations of the meta-totality were united in their common source as emanations of the Absolute Spirit. From the individual's perspective this meant that personal totalization (freedom) was impossible outside of the context of global totalization (freedom). It was for this reason that Hegel ridiculed the Romantic's search for personal wholeness in a flight from the world.[55] The expressive notion of totality meant the existence of a collective subject of history—whose objectifications were the source of the social whole—as well as the denial of personal totalization detached from institutional contexts and processes. This proposition implied that the intercontextuality between totalistic knowledge and the "real" totality of the objective world was one uncomplicated by the dualism inhabiting the center of Kant's design. Hegel's optimism obtained from Vico's principle that the "maker" of reality and the made reality found their unity in the One—the Absolute Spirit.

Hegel's "totality theory," though not without theoretical value, was doubly faulted. On the one hand, a contradiction lies in the fact that due to its idealist conception it was oblivious to the essential difference between material and theoretical systems; Hegel even insisted on their conceptual unity.[56] On the other hand, Hegel, following Aristotle, expressed the totalitarian view that priority attaches to the whole rather than to its parts. The whole (state) is prior because it allegedly possesses or is endowed with an arch that alone forms the basis of its unity, just as the heart is the arch of the living organism (whole system), according to Aristotle.[57]

Marx's Holism

Marx and Engels aimed at a comprehensive and critical appraisal of political economy. It was Marx who referred to Hegel's "totality theory," of which Ricardo's views on political economy were merely a "special system."[58] Marxism from its inception was attracted less to the content of Hegel's system than to the procedure—the critical dialectics—by which he claimed to have derived its content. Marx, radicalizing the critique of reason undertaken by Kant and Hegel, sought to show how ideas themselves were ideological manifestations of real intercontextual socioeconomic forces. Although profoundly influenced by the Hegelian dialectic, Marx objected to the way in which Hegel had elevated ideal philosophical activity (cultural poiesis) above material labor (scientific and economic production) as the primary vehicle of historical progress. In particular, he showed that these aspects reflected a politically charged and class-based content. In effect, this amounted to transforming philosophy into social science and the idealistic critique of knowledge into a materialistic critique of political economy.

Though at the center of Hegel's method was an emphasis on holism, in stressing the ideal over the material Hegel could delude himself into thinking that, at least from the vantage point of pure philosophical reason, the contradiction between the individual and civil society, freedom and natural necessity had been subdued. For Hegel, though workers and capitalists might be mortal enemies in the workplace, they were otherwise reconciled by fraternal membership in the ideal communities of church and state.

Marx's own holism emerged in critical confrontation with his partial assimilation of Hegelianism. Whereas for Hegel bourgeois civil society was the manifest totality, for Marx civil society itself is an unfinished whole whose deep structure is its concrete totality. For Marx, Hegel's ideal communities lack a basis in real everyday life, the life of work and consumption. They are mere ideologies, or illusory or invidious legitimations of the status quo. They mask real inequality and domination behind a veneer of purportedly necessary and universal laws ostensibly designed to advance the interests of all persons equally and impartially. The critique that underlay this proposition was the keystone of his own intellectual edifice.

Hegel's claim that "the truth is the whole" inspired the reflective practice of the concrete totality that formed the basis of the distinction in Marx's thought between the abstract concepts of perception and observation and the concrete concepts of materialist dialectical reflection. Marx apparently felt it necessary to distinguish between thought and thinking, on the one hand, and the concept, on the other, and does so in a manner that generates many more questions for us than it does answers. In *Grundrisse*, Marx distinguished between concrete totality as a totality of thoughts, concrete in thought, that are, in fact, a product of thinking and comprehending and the concept that thinks and generates itself outside or above observation and conception. Whereas the concrete totality is a product of the working up of observation and conception into concepts, which for Marx is synonymous with thinking and comprehending, the concept exists independently of concrete totality while at the same time being of the essence of the process of concrete totalization. But the concreteness of the whole is something that positivists frenetically reject. Its denial leads to the false dichotomies of mind and body, man and nature, and man and society, where the whole is either impossible to know, given the infinitude of facts to be appropriated, or some prior and/or superior entity that constitutes a different reality from the facts.

In his review of Marx's *Critique of Political Economy* for the newspaper *Das Volk*, Engels insisted that Marx's intention was not to discuss merely some noteworthy economic problems of capitalist society. "His aim," wrote Engels, "has ever been to give a systemic survey of the whole complex of economic science."[59] The theoretical critique of capitalism had to be a critique of the whole or it would be nothing but a facile repetition of the whole. The method of reasoning that Marx addresses critically leads him to equate political economy with a systematic unwillingness to reflect on its alleged point of departure. Marx says that political economy's point of departure is false, even though it appears to be true and correct. It is to the idea of beginning that Marx addresses his initial concerns in *Grundrisse*. He acknowledges that were he to begin in the manner of political economists, he too would end where they end. Marx's methodological point of departure is a method of reasoning made up of sequential steps, all constitutive of a process with unavoidable points along the way and an inescapable terminus. Marx shows that he believes this to be the case when he states the following:

> Thus, if I were to begin with the population this would be a chaotic conception (*Vorstellung*) of the whole, and I would then, by means of further determinations, move analytically towards ever more simple concepts (*Begriff*) from the imagined, concrete towards even thinner abstractions, until I had arrived at the simplest determinations. From there the journey would have to be retraced until I had finally arrived at the population again, but this time not as a chaotic conception of the whole, but as a rich totality of many determinations and relations.[60]

When Marx notes that this path is the one "historically" followed by economics at the time of its origins, he implies that it is both mistaken and untrue because of the way it is determined in its process from beginning to end. It "appears" to be the correct method, to be sure, but only given the social and historical circumstances, Marx implies. Begin with the whole as chaotically conceived and discover through the application of a specified sequence of reasonings a given, generally preordained outcome in the person of a whole that is characterized by abstract general relations rather than a chaotic conception. When Marx argues that this alleged terminus is really the point of departure, he implies that the so-called chaotic whole that is the ostensible beginning for political economy is in reality already a determination of abstract general relations. All of this means that a new theoretical structure was under construction whose author recognized the problematic methodological issues arising from the classical political economist's method, and the paradox of bourgeois philosophy ensued therefrom.[61]

In effect, Marx was saying that, given its object, political economy really could not be a science as long as it simply recapitulated the alleged life history of its now abstracted object, instead of concretely reflecting on it as an already appropriated object.

It is a generally uncontended proposition that Marx was a holistic thinker.[62] The term *totality* and synonyms such as *the whole* appear frequently and affirmatively throughout his writings. "We are concerned," he wrote, "with bourgeois society as it emerged and is moving along its pedestal" and in a systematic exposition we must follow its "definitions" up to their "totality."[63] He explains the emergence of totality as the homogeneous development of society on a new and higher level. From the individual's perspective this meant that personal totalization (freedom) obtained only in the context of global totalization (freedom).

Marx's theory meets the basic requirement of "system" on the concrete level. He stated, "Society is not merely an aggregate of individuals; it is the sum of the relations in which these individuals stand to one another."[64] As a student of law he wrote:

> In the concrete expression of a living world of ideas, as exemplified by law, the state, nature and philosophy as a whole, the object itself must be studied in its development; arbitrary divisions must not be introduced, the rational character of the object itself must develop as something imbued with contradictions in itself and find unity in itself.[65]

and:

> A social revolution involves the standpoint of the whole because it is a protest of man against dehumanized life even if it occurs in only one factory district, because it proceeds from the standpoint of the single actual individual because the community against whose separation from himself the individual reacts is the true community of man, human existence.[66]

For Marx the world of an abstract one-sided man gave expression to partial-rationalism and eventually irrationalism.[67] Similarly, the world of concrete universal man, with his production hinging on the correlation of all the functions, placed in the center of Marx's inquiry the intercontextuality of human and social functions. Consequently, Marxist totality theory, as an anticipatory system theory, is juxtaposed to the Marxist theory of socialism, denoting simultaneously a new type of logic of scientific systems and the positivist resolution of segregated sciences into a unified science.[68]

Turning his attention to the theorizing of the political economists, Marx notes that they fail to appreciate that behind their seemingly immutable laws lies a historical flux that is the totality of actual life.

> Society as it appears to the political economist is civil society, in which every individual is a totality of needs and only exists for the other person, as the other exists for him, in so far as each becomes a means for the other. The political economist reduced everything . . . to man, i.e., to the individual whom he strips of all determinateness so as to class him as capitalist or worker.[69]

Ridiculing his opponents for their inability to grasp the intercontextuality of the whole of meaningful relations, which meant understanding it historically, in *German Ideology* he remarked:

> Our conception of history depends on our ability to expound the real process of production, starting out from the simple material production of life, and to comprehend the form of intercourse connected with this and created by this (i.e., civil society in its various stages), as the basis of all history; further, to show it in its action as State; and so, from this starting-point, to explain the

whole mass of different theoretical products and forms of consciousness, religion, philosophy, ethics, etc., etc., and trace their origins and growth, by which means, of course, the whole thing can be shown in its totality (and therefore, too, the reciprocal action of these various sides on one another).... The result we arrive at, is not that production, distribution, exchange and consumption are identical, but that they are all elements of a totality, distinctions within a unity. Production predominates ... from it, the process continually recommences ... but there is interaction between the various elements. This is the case in every organic whole.[70]

Moreover, for Marx,

The liberation of man is not advanced a single step by reducing philosophy, theology, substance and all the trash to "self-consciousness" and by liberating man from the domination of these phrases, which have never held him in thrall ... in reality and for the practical materialist, i.e., the communist, it is a question of revolutionizing the existing world, of practically attacking and changing existing things.[71]

Recognizing, with Hegel, that alienation and estrangement were necessary way stations on the road to a higher level of fulfillment, and having no use for simpering Romantics who fantasize a restoration of a lost wholeness, for Marx, history was to be appreciated as a totality and normatively as the promise of a new and future emancipatory totalization. Marx's holism was not a counterfeit of his philosophical mentor, for he rejected Hegel's idealistic premises. This he made in clear in *The German Ideology*:

[Our conception of history] has not, like the idealistic view of history, in every period to look for a category, but remains constantly on the real ground of history; it does not explain practice from the idea but explains the formation of ideas from material practice.[72]

Further emphasizing the materiality of his holistic understanding, elsewhere in *The German Ideology*, he writes:

If in a fully developed bourgeois system each economic relation takes the other for granted in a bourgeois-economic form, so that each requisite is at the same time a precondition, the same is true as far as organic systems are concerned. An organic system as totality has its own prerequisites and its emergence as totality is due to the fact that it can place under its influence all the elements of society, i.e., it can produce from them the previously missing organs. In this way it becomes a historical totality.[73]

Marx's system, as he himself states, points beyond the existing capitalist society to earlier social structures, on the one hand, and to future social structures, on the other hand. Capitalist society, for Marx, was a self-evolving system, a historically given totality, achieving processlike existence, in the dual negation of its emergence and dissolution.

In "On the Jewish Question," Marx challenged the social implications of Hegel's valorization of bourgeois totality, i.e., civil society, and stressed that the split between man as bourgeois and man as citizen, the distinction between civil society and the state, meant that a truly human totality had not yet been achieved. He rejected the contemplative attitude toward totality registered in Hegel's famous remark about Minerva's owl. Challenging the contemplative epistemology of Hegel, which was grounded in the belief that the whole could be understood retrospectively and only in its transcendence, he asserted that:

> By investigating the "whole as such" to find the conditions for its existence, Critical Criticism is searching in the genuine theological manner, outside the whole, for the conditions for its existence. ... Critical Criticism dispenses with the study of this real movement which forms the whole in order to be able to declare that it, Critical Criticism as the calm of knowledge, is above both extremes of the contradiction, and that its activity, which has made the "whole as such," is now alone in a position to abolish the abstraction of which it is the maker.[74]

For Hegel, those who acted in history were not the same as those who "made" it; those who made history and those who understood it were disparate. Marx, to the contrary, saw knowledge as active and alive rather than passive and dead; instead of waiting for dusk to fall, the owl of Minerva accompanied the creators of history as they made it. It is for this reason that Marxism was identified as a philosophy of praxis.

Marx described his own materialist approach to history as standing Hegel's dialectic "right side up." It is not ideas and philosophical reflections that determine the course of history but the forces and relations of material production. Productive forces include labor and its instruments and their organization. Productive relations designate forms of ownership that regulate access to the means of production and the distribution of wealth. Together the forces and relations constitute a definite mode of production. Modes of production can be ranked on an evolutionary scale, depending on how much they advance the emancipation and realization of the totality of human freedom. They ostensibly begin with the communal mode of production, characteristic of primitive societies, and advance through primitive, archaic, feudal, capitalist, socialist, and communist modes of production. The mode of production thus comprises the real foundation on which rises a legal and political superstructure and to which correspond definite forms of social consciousness (and conditions the social political and intellectual life processes in general).

For the political economist committed to disciplined observation, technology and the economy appear to develop in a decontextualized manner, that is, independent of any societally integrative coordinates. Consequently, technology takes on an almost autonomous existence, towing the rest of the social system in its wake. In the preface to *Critique of Political Economy*, the relationship between the economic factor and the whole of the social system even takes on the appearance of unilinear causality, with the economic function allegedly determining the entire social structure. And, indeed, Marx wrote that "the economic structure of society, is the real basis on which the juridical and political superstructure is raised, and to which definite social forms of thought correspond."[75] Writing to Engels, Marx noted: "Current society, seen economically, becomes pregnant with the new higher form [and] thereby shows socially the same gradual process of transformation that Darwin provided in natural sciences."[76] However, he nonetheless unequivocally stated:

> Man himself is the basis of his material production, as of all production which he accomplishes. All circumstances, therefore, which affect man, the subject of production, have a greater or lesser influence upon all his functions and activities as the creator of material wealth, of commodities. In this sense it can truly be asserted that all human relations and functions, however, and whenever they manifest themselves, influence material production and have a more or less determining effect upon it.[77]

The economic factor allegedly plays a leading role, but superstructural elements, maturing from and contingent with changing economic conditions and the various material factors determining these conditions, in their turn both react on and exert a decisive influence on the structure of economic life. Nor is there doubt that a simultaneous and reverse process is at work: a process of mutual cause and effect among various categories of social phenomena. Marx referred to such in both *Capital* and *Grundrisse*.[78]

Moreover, the effect of the economic factor on the other elements in the system seems to be more of a "boundary effect" than a determination or simple causality. That is, it is the determination within limits within which the system may function. Marx, in *Critique of the Gotha Programme*, wrote:

> It is always the direct relationship of the owners of the conditions of production to the direct producers—a relation always corresponding to a definite stage in the development of the methods of labour and thereby its social productivity—which reveals the innermost secret, the hidden basis of the entire social structure, and with it the political form of that relation of sovereignty and dependence, in short, the corresponding specific form of the state. This does not prevent the same economic basis, from the standpoint of its main conditions ... from showing infinite variations and gradations in appearance which can be ascertained only by analysis of the empirically given circumstances.[79]

The particular causality that Marx attributed to the economic factor in the richly interactive whole that formed his working model of society can be seen to be more complex than has been previously assumed. The complexity of this relationship is attributable to Marx's use of what we now understand to be a systems model. This was a breakthrough in nineteenth-century social thought and a sharp contrast to the causal monism of Comtean positivism and Social Darwinism. The elements of Marx's model are neither cause nor effect; rather, they engage in a complex intercontextual simultaneous interaction in which the economic factor is a dominant, though not exclusively, determining factor.[80]

The various coexisting elements of Marx's theoretical model are ultimately irreducible structures. The noneconomic elements cannot simply grow out of the economic structures as epiphenomenal relations. Nor can the effect on the economic factor be interpreted as simply causal.[81] There is an interaction of independent, though unequal, forces. In his correspondence with Bloch, Engels noted that:

> According to the materialist conception of history, the ultimately determining element in history is the production and reproduction of real life. More than this neither Marx nor I have ever asserted. Hence, if somebody twists this into saying that the economic element is the only determining one, he transforms that proposition into a meaningless, abstract, senseless phrase.[82]

Marx's critique of Hegel's philosophical idealism does not signal an indiscriminate abandonment of philosophically critical theory. Philosophical ideas are still accorded an important role in guiding practice. Thus, it would be wrong to assume that for Marx the economic base causally determines the social, legal, political, and cultural-ideological superstructure. As Marx repeatedly points out, the state's monopoly over education, i.e., its disciplinary approach, sanctioned through coercion, violence, law and order, is vital to the preservation of the economic system. He also notes that the predominance of economy over polity fully obtains only under capitalism. Therein the engine of progress ultimately resides within the economy. To this point, Marx's theory of historical materialism maintains that progressive advances in the ideological sphere—above all, in religion, morality, and law—reflect deeper advances in the economic and political spheres. The entrance of new social and economic classes gave rise to new modes of governance that, in turn, reflected advances in the mode of production.

For Marx himself the substructure does not strictly "determine" the superstructure; it constrains and is the key to an appreciation of the social structure that generalizes its norms. Far from Marx being a rigid "abstract" determinist on the matter of laws, it is the political economists who believe in "general laws" that hold for all periods of human development. The essence of man's natural history can thus be grasped only through a materialist dialectics that is after the thing-in-itself in its wholeness. This procedure requires, among other things, that concepts be reflected into their own history, which is part of the natural history of man. The laws that hold in an organic sense only within discrete historical periods of collective life are revealed through concrete totalization. Laws are neither valid nor appropriate beyond given wholes, given formations.

4

Holism and the Natural Unity of Science

It took some twenty-five centuries for the idea of evolution to gradually erode the crystalline splendor of the mathematical cosmos. What is left of it, preserved in strongholds of determinism, will clash more and more threateningly with the dynamics of reality. The idea that every process generates its own norms and measures as it unfolds—that process creates structure, not vice versa—has, since Darwin, sunk its roots into part of modern science. While, it is only in recent years that a confluence of insights points to a grand synthesis, elements of this synthesis were already apparent in the latter half of the nineteenth century.[1] Today this flow of insights is stimulating the physical and the life sciences—including political economy—to elaborate a unity of science, a paradigm of far-reaching consequences.

The question of the desirability or possibility of a unity of science is not the issue here. The question is rather of how the unity is characterized and how to do justice to similarities and differences among natural and social phenomena captured by such a unity. But we would be betraying our later interests were the reader not made aware that the concept of the unity of science was foundational to a Critical Marxist and systems theoretical critique of political economy.

In logical positivism and empiricism, the thesis of the unity of science is intimately related to the program of reductionism and mechanicalism. From such a perspective, rival claims to knowledge must satisfy the stringent logical requirements for translation or reduction to an ideal universal physics. However, the thesis of the unity of science has also assumed a non-, even anti-, reductionist dimension in its embrace of holism. Here rival claims to critical knowledge must not satisfy appropriative interests, but rather adopt a praxiological dimension. From both perspectives there is, in principle, only one science.

In addition to the many criticisms internal to science, for instance, of what is meant by "reduction" and whether it is possible, the entire project loses its credibility as a universalizer when we fully appreciate the image of science as endorsed by positivists. Theirs is a discredited reference image. One way of characterizing the post-objectivist post-positivist philosophy and history of science is to realize that the natural sciences exhibit many of the characteristic features of what were originally taken to be pseudo-sciences, i.e., the human sciences. In this respect the recovery of the hermeneutical dimension of the science transforms the question of how the unity of the sciences is to be characterized. And at this juncture one can begin to speak of a unity of science grounded not in mechanicalism, nor a reductionist biologism, but in general theory of organization.

The imagination of evolutionists among philosophers and social scientists was first captured by the upward sweep of time in the Darwinian theory. Impressed by Darwin's theory, Marx and Engels transmuted an evolutionary optimism latent in Hegelian thought into their encompassing theory of evolution in nature and society, understood in terms of dialectical and historical materialism. Welcoming the method of Darwin in biology, they sought to explicate an evolutionary political economy that penetrated beneath surface particularities to the essence of the whole.[2]

The logic of their method led Marx and Engels to investigate the economic relations of man and societies to their natural environments and to pose questions about the foremost of the nature-society relations. The nature-society nexus is intercontextual; not only does nature influence society but society influences nature in an unremitting process.

Nature and species-being for Marx was a totality. It included a conscious, active, sensate-modifying part—the human species—and an unconscious, inorganic, insensate, inactive part—that part of nature external to man. The two could not be divorced. They were both integral parts of an encompassing unity. To speak of man was, by definition, to speak of man's productive praxis, his modification of and influence on insensate nature. To speak of insensate nature was, by definition, to reflect on how and in what fashion this passive material was altered and "humanized" by the activity of man. The stress was always on the active, practical activity of men, the changes wrought by them in their environment or their attempts to extract from their surroundings objects that fulfilled their needs.

> In the process of production, human beings do not only enter into a relation with nature. They produce only by working together in a specific manner and by reciprocally exchanging their activities. In order to produce they enter into definite connections and relations with one another and only within these social connections and relations does their connection with nature, i.e., production take place.[3]

Insensate nature was both the condition of human labor and the source of human realization. As the condition of human labor, insensate nature supplied man with materiality. It was the substance in which human objectification assumed form. Labor could only be fulfilled, could only realize itself in an object. Insensate nature was the basis of mediation, the materiality that afforded labor the possibility of objectification.[4]

In relation to the history of insensate nature, Marx wrote: "Nature, as it develops in human history, in the act of genesis of human society, is the actual nature of man; thus nature, as it develops through industry, though in an alienated form, is truly anthropological."[5] Industrial production, the change of material forms, had altered the condition of insensate nature itself. In this sense, insensate nature had become anthropological; that is, it bore the stamp of human praxis. That part of insensate nature that became involved in human activity and production was historized, for it was continuously modified by human praxis in the course of time.[6]

Insensate nature had two sides, the historical and the nonhistorical. History for Marx, as we have seen, was synonymous with the autogenesis of the species through its own activity. Therefore, only that part of insensate nature that was humanized could also be historized. Laws of chemistry and physics could produce change and process, but history could not because it lacked a conscious agent or purposeful praxis. Marx's view of the man-nature metabolic nexus led him to an ontological view of human nature.

To quote again that phrase that resonates with his ontological stance: "Men make their own history, but they do not make it as they please; they do not make it under circumstances chosen by themselves, but under circumstances directly encountered, given and transmitted from the past."[7] Beginning with the assumption that man is a conscious change-inducing agent, Marx could easily move to a praxiological multilineal concept of history. He could understand in Promethean terms that *Homo faber* could give rise to different societies, could so act on similar material as to fashion alternative futures.

If ontologically man was *Homo faber*, then history could be nothing but the manifestation of that making, the continuous self-creation of man by man, a process of autopoiesis. "Since [the] relationship between man and nature is the precondition for the relationship between man and man, the dialectic of the labour-process as a natural process broadens out to become the dialectic of human history in general."[8] Man forms the connecting link between the instrument of labor and the object of labor. Nature is the Subject-Object of labor. The dialectic consists in this: that man changes his own nature as he progressively deprives external nature of its mystery and externality; as he mediates nature through himself, he makes nature itself work for his own purposes. When Marx wrote that "man has his own process of genesis, history,"[9] he meant that since the essence of man was productionist, history itself could only be the autogenesis of man.[10]

Marx indicated that society itself was a natural environment. This was meant not only in the immediately critical sense that man is still not in control of his own productive forces vis-á-vis nature, that these forces confront him as the organized, rigid form of an opaque society, as a "second nature" that sets its essence against its creators, but also in the "metaphysical" sense that Marx's theory is a theory of the world as a whole.[11] It is, in other words, a "totality theory" in the grand tradition.

Marx never fully formulated the logic of the totality of man's coevolution with the biosphere; for the demands for a rigorous science of political economy were so monumental as to call for concentration on the intrasocial relations, political concern and theory, and for a resignation from a more intensive study of the complexities of man-nature intercontextualities.[12] Engels, however, undertook the project. In this undertaking, he breathed life anew into the holism that marked Platonic-Aristotelian thought and hesitantly constructed a unity of science.

Joravsky comments that the preface to the second edition of Engels's *Anti-Dühring* was, in effect, the synthesis of Engels's philosophy of natural science.[13] Schmidt came to the same conclusion: "Engels, by introducing dialectics into the natural sciences, was inventing a philosophy of nature."[14] As such, it was an attempt to apply dialectics to physical processes.[15]

Engels claimed that Hegel's dialectic method could be extracted from its idealist framework and formulated in terms of three fundamental laws of dialectic processes: (1) the principle of contradiction; (2) the interpenetration of opposites; and (3) the negation of the negation. Thus, he took over several categories and principles from Hegel's *Logic*, purged their idealist content, and claimed they constituted a "method" that could be applied to concrete reality.[16] This apparently distinguishes his position from that of Marx, who never tried to codify dialectics as a formal methodological schema, but instead tried to reveal the dialectical character of history by unfolding its alleged conflict-ridden course of development.[17]

Engels's analysis contained the following three elements:

1. Dialectic systems required a motivation or propelling force. For Hegel the "energizing principle" in the dialectics of logic was desire.[18] The "energizing principle" in the dialectics of history for Marx was human activity. Motion, for Engels, was the "energizing principle" in materialistic dialectics.[19] Motion, then, corresponded to the first dialectical law: the transformation of quantity into quality.[20]

2. Even though the universe and everything in it could be reduced to the mono-substance "motion," contradiction was still a basic part of organic and inorganic existence. For Engels, the second law of dialectics, the law of interpenetration of opposites, demonstrated that reality was constituted of contending and contradictory forces.[21] Moreover, the law of interpenetration of opposites implied the mutual balancing of contradictory forces. In the law of the conservation of force, Engels assumed that physicists had discovered empirical proof of the dialectical thesis of the interpenetration of opposites: negative forces must be equal to positive forces.[22]

3. The dialectical law of the negation of the negation required that nature be in continual motion. Negation of the negation meant growth, that the contradiction would be moved to a higher level of opposition. Growth involved disjunction as well as reestablishment of equilibrium.

Insofar as such a philosophy expresses a metaphysical point of view, Schmidt notes that it consists of the following theses, as developed in *Anti-Dühring*:

a. the unity . . . of the world consists in its materiality;[23]

b. the basic forms of all beings are space and time, and a being outside time is just as nonsensical as a being outside space;[24] and

c. motion is the mode of existence of matter. Never and nowhere has there existed, or can there exist, matter without motion. The statement that all rest, all equilibrium is only relative, has meaning only in relation to this or that definite form of motion.[25]

Engels's formulation presented man as having entered into a dialectical relation with Nature, into a dynamic and evolutionary interaction with it. Such a relation, when critically analyzed, reveals Nature in continuous motion, interconnected and constantly transforming.[26]

> When we reflect on Nature, or the history of mankind, or our own intellectual activity, the first picture presented to us is of an endless maze of relations and interactions, in which nothing remains what, where and as it was, but everything moves, changes, comes into being and passes out of existence. This primitive, naive yet intrinsically correct conception of the world was that of ancient Greek philosophy, and was first clearly formulated by Heraclitus: everything is and also is not, for everything is in *flux*, is constantly changing, constantly coming into being and passing away.[27]

With Engels the historical dialectic of subject and object was transformed into a course of development operating deterministically within objects driven by necessary and universal laws of motion. He was prompted to write that "dialectics is nothing more than the science of universal laws of motion and evolution in nature, human society and thought."[28] We might contend that Engels's dialectic is a "meta-methodology" unifying the Kantian duality of the noumenal and phenomenal worlds. Only because he allegedly lost sight of the constitutive role of the active subject in the Marxian dialectic could Engels seek to develop a purely objective dialectics of nature. Moreover, he was led to argue that the same dialectical laws were transhistorical, thereby again obscuring the role of the subject in history.[29] Though he admitted that the laws that operate as blind unconscious forces in nature are, in history, mediated through the will and consciousness of men, he denied that this difference undermined the fundamental parallelism between the two realms.[30] In Engels's view, social laws do not differ from scientific law by dint of their historicity. Rather, "the eternal laws of nature also become transformed more and more into historical ones."[31] This "historicization of nature" is similar to that of the younger Marx, who argued:

"History itself is a real part of natural history—of nature's coming to man."[32]

In *Ludwig Feuerbach and the End of Classical German Philosophy*, Engels argued that the laws that operate in nature and history are "identical in substance."[33] Historical evolution is, therefore, simply an aspect of the more general processes of development, just as historical materialism is but one branch of a more general theory of evolution. In this conception, history becomes reified as a second nature governed deterministically by objective laws like first nature. This implies, according to Mendelson, that Marx's concept of historical laws had slipped from Engels's grasp.[34] On this issue, Engels argued that the unity of nature in motion could be achieved, in any meaningful sense, only by dialectics: "Dialectics divested of mysticism becomes an absolute necessity for natural science, which has forsaken the field where rigid categories sufficed."[35]

For dialectical materialism, as opposed to mechanical materialism, motion, that essential category, is "not merely a change of place, but also, in fields higher than mechanics, a change of quality."[36] One of the limits of mechanical materialism for Engels was "its inability to comprehend the universe as a process, as matter undergoing uninterrupted historical development [that is] eternal motion."[37] In other words, mechanical materialism was a nonevolutionary paradigm. Critical to Engels's view is that this motion can never be created, only transferred, while for Eugen Dühring, "the restoration of the uniformity of matter to mechanical force has the further advantage that a force can be conceived at rest, as tied up, and, therefore, inoperative."[38] But, asks Engels, how could matter pass from this motionless state to movement? "An initial impulse must, therefore, have come from outside, from outside the universe, an impulse that sets it in motion. But as everyone knows the 'initial impulse' is only another expression for God."[39] This critique was, as we shall see, to become central to both a philosophical and a planning debate on equilibrium in Russia in the 1920s.

Engels spoke of "the world" and "everything." The dialectic is the expression of the general laws of motion and development of nature, human society, and thought. In this conception the dialectic, given its materialist foundation, becomes a Weltanschauung. Marxism was ostensibly transformed from a critical theory into a materialist metaphysics comprised of a theory of nature, a theory of history, and an epistemological theory of the "laws" of the development of mind (logic represented in Reflection Theory). Engels, assuming an Aristotelian posture, admitted that each domain had laws peculiar to it, but he believed that the dialectic grasped the overarching laws of motion that asserted themselves in the movement of nature and history.[40] In accord with this conception, Engels attempted to complement Marx's dialectic of history with his own dialectics of nature.

Engels believed he was consistent with Marx's insight and wrote of dialectical materialism that: "[It] constitutes the most important form of thinking for present-day natural science, for it alone offers the analogue for, and thereby the method of explaining, the evolutionary processes occurring in nature, inter-connections in general and transitions from one field of investigation into another."[41]

The notion of the dialectic of Marxism as a Weltanschauung, which included an independent science of nature, was, as we have seen, factually at variance with Marx's own views. In his historical materialism and critique of political economy dialectics referred specifically to human history, and nature had a history only in relation to its intercontextual processes. Marx focused on the interaction of man and nature as mediated by processes of social labor facilitated by technology. Nature entered into human history both internally, in the form of organic needs, and externally, as that physical environment in which man is situated and upon which he labors in order to appropriate the means of subsistence. In both realms nature exhibited historical variation, but this was by virtue of its intercontextuality with human activity. For Marx, "nature, taken abstractly for itself, rigidly separated from man, is nothing for man."[42] He seemed not to have thought he was developing a Weltanschauung that contained a theory of nature alongside a theory of history. However, for Engels the dialectic of history is merely one discipline alongside nature and logic.[43]

After mentioning his projected treatise on the dialectics of nature, Engels remarked:

> [To] me there could be no question of building the laws of dialectics into nature, but of discovering them in it and evolving them from it.... To do this systematically and in each separate department is a gigantic task.... It may be, however, that the advance of theoretical natural science will make my work to a great extent or even altogether superfluous.[44]

In Engels's monist conception of the unification of science, the moments of the dialectic are divorced from the concrete historical situation and collapse into the three hypostatized "fundamental laws" laid down in *Dialectics of Nature*. These categories conform to laws that force their way through natural transformations. For Marx, however, "there is no general law formulated by abstraction from the principle of interaction itself," for nature itself is devoid of negativity and emerges only with man's transformation of it.[45] Hence, Engels's dialectic becomes a distinct and encompassing Weltanschauung. Carver, for instance, claims that "there is no evidence that Marx was working towards a unification of all scientific laws on some 'dialectical' basis."[46] Schmidt, arguing to the contrary, notes: "Marxist theory itself already contains the dialectic of nature with which Engels believed it had to be supplemented,"[47] and:

> Engels's historicization of nature led to a naturalization of human history. This did not occur in the manner of Social Darwinism, whose social function and origin were spotted by both Marx and Engels. Here the naturalization of history means that Engels reduced history to the special area of application of nature's general laws of motion and development.[48]

Indeed, Engels's search for the unification of scientific knowledge led him to the holism of the French encyclopedists. He wrote: "The idea of the Encyclopedia was characteristic of the eighteenth century; it rested on the awareness that all these sciences were interconnected, yet no one was capable of making the transitions, and hence, the sciences could only be placed side by side."[49]

On the empirical level, Engels believed that the actual data for such a unified or totality theory of the natural universe already existed.

> If we wish to speak of general laws of nature that are uniformly applicable to all bodies—from the nebula to man—we are left only with gravity and perhaps the most general form of the theory of transformation of energy into heat [*first law of thermodynamics*]. But on its general consistent application to all phenomena of nature this theory itself becomes converted into a historical presentation of the successive changes occurring in a system of the universe from its origin to its passing away, hence into a history in which at each stage different laws, i.e., different forms of the same universal motion, predominate and so nothing remains absolutely universally valid except motion.[50]

The older mechanical materialism and corresponding natural science had seen only cyclical or mechanical movement in nature while missing its processes of development. However, the total comprehension of the natural world was heralded by two fundamental scientific concepts:

1. The Darwinian theory of evolution.
2. The theory of transformation of energy, which meant that heat, radiation, electricity, magnetism, and chemical energy were different forms of the same basic energy supply, that is, all were reducible to motion. This law was equated to the first law of dialectics, that quantitative changes made for qualitative changes.

The theory of evolution and the discovery of the cell as the generative source of all plant and animal life gave man the opportunity to systematize the growth of all organisms into a single general law and allowed us to see that the entire range of organic life was the result of germ plasmas that had gone through a long process of evolution.[51] Natural science, through its own immanent development, seems to be becoming a science of processes and interconnections in which the classical notion of cause and effect are being replaced by relations, interaction, and development.[52]

Beginning with motion, we could derive every form of matter and, therefore, every form of inorganic life. Moreover, beginning with motion we could derive the cell and from the cell every form of organic existence. Indeed, Engels felt he had discovered a grand evolution theory, a metaphysical nature of the cosmos. In fact, what he had formed was a metaphysical monistic view of nature. He tried to explain the total function of the universe in 1888 in *Ludwig Feuerbach*.[53] He was a materialistic monist and said as much in his own words:

> Thanks to three great discoveries and other immense advances in natural science, we have now arrived at the point where we can demonstrate the intercon-

nection between the processes in nature not only in particular spheres but also the interconnection of these particular spheres on the whole, and so can present in an approximately systematic form a comprehensive view of the interconnection in nature by means of the facts provided by empirical natural science itself.[54]

Employing the concept of metabolism, notably present in much of Marx's work, Engels referred to life as the conversion of matter from one form into another. Matter was conceptualized as congealed motion or energy. Thus, life itself was reducible to the dialectic laws of motion. The same was true of the mind, which for Engels was simply another "mode of energy."[55]

A central idea that distinguished Marx's interpretation of nature from Engels's was the notion of praxis. Whereas Marx spoke of a pre-given natural and social environment in which man coexisted, Engels described a micromacrocosmic determinism in which thought was merely the epiphenomenon of physical forces. Marxism referred to humanistic and programmatic naturalism,[56] the belief that man modified the organic and inorganic world, while Engels referred to a metaphysical monism, the belief that organic and inorganic existence were all reducible to a universal monosubstance. The Marxian vision was always on man who acts, while Engels's vision tended to cosmological monism.[57]

Marx aimed to keep physical science and its laws within a human, social perspective, alerting us to the enormous importance of scientific discoveries in improving the productivity of human labor and, in certain cases, such as the physiology of labor, assisting us in our understanding of socially productive activity itself. Engels's synthetic argument asserted that human thought and behavior could not be other than emanations of matter and thus subject to the same dialectical laws.[58]

In postulating that the laws of nature themselves were dialectic, Engels was attempting something that Marx himself did not attempt.[59] For Marx the dialectic was not in nature itself, but in the ontological metabolic interaction between man and nature. The dialectic process for Marx was the motion of form and content; species-being was the content, while nature was the form. When Marx said that he stood Hegel on his head he did not mean that he had erased the subjectivity of history. What Marx did was to keep the subjective element: man who modifies— *Homo faber*. But instead of modifying in a strictly logical form, as Hegel believed, man modified because he had to labor to produce use-values to provide for his livelihood. Engels, therefore, lessened the subjectivist dimension. For Engels the essence of nature was dialectical, and all other existence proceeded from these laws.[60]

The claim may be made that Engels's metaphysical monism shaped his view of man's history and that his monism projected a deterministic philosophy of history. In the grand style, Engels can be compared with Plato, Aristotle, Comte, and Hegel. Indeed, in *The Origin of the Family, Private Property, and the State*, he adopted a modified Comtean thesis.[61] Borrowing the Comtean formula of a three-stage development sequence (theological, metaphysical, positive), Engels fit it into a nineteenth-century anthropological frame of reference. In this thesis, history was linear: all societies must pass through certain fixed stages. It was a universally deterministic scheme of historical development. Engels declared his faith in this proposition, saying it introduced "a definite order in the prehistory of man"[62] and, consequently, capitulated to macroscopic determinism that was at once a millennial optimism. Such a view corresponded to his monistic view expressed in the *Dialectics of Nature*. The physical and the historic processes were of the same order.[63]

The Marxism that emerged in the work of Marx's immediate successors in the period of the Second International did not dwell with any sustained interest on the issue of totality. While there was, to be sure, interest in the dialectics of nature, and such logical categories as the integration of opposites and the negation of the negation, and the Dialectical Materialism of Engels, the ambiguity of "Engelism" was a fertile ground for the ripening of Scientific and Critical Marxism. In the process Marx's own concept of totality was eclipsed. By transmuting Marx's historical materialism into a consummated metaphysics of matter and by reducing social consciousness and culture to an epiphenomenal status, dialectical materialism avoided dealing with the troublesome question of the role of subjectivity in the totality. By arbitrarily equating Marx's method to that of the natural sciences, vulgar Marxists failed to examine the ontological premises of their epistemology and to justify their knowledge of the social whole. Moreover, the effort of presenting Marxism as an absolute historicism unleashed a chain reaction that reduced and flattened out the Marxist totality into a variation of the Hegelian totality, and that, even allowing for more or less rhetorical distinctions, ultimately diluted, discounted, or erased the real differences between them.

Erwin Ban presents a philosophical-biographical analysis of Engels's role in the gestation of Marxian theory and concludes that to the extent that Engels was not, like Marx, an "heir to classical German idealism," his role was nil, indeed, negative.[64] Engels, Ban argues, had a positivist-naturalist conception of the dialectic—a dialectic of causation from lower to higher forms—and a mechanistic-instrumental conception of praxis. It may be argued that Engels set the course that German Social Democrats in the 1890s and so-called vulgar Marxists later followed. Lukács believed that human subjectivity and intersubjectivity had been liquidated, i.e., reduced to functions of the economy, in Kautskian Marxism. Indeed, some Marxists declared that "history" was determined independently of free will and that socialism is inevitable because of the march of economic forces. Such a view had, of course, particular propagandistic value for Stalinists.[65]

The over-reliance on economic determinism among vulgar Marxists, though discredited first by Marx's own and then by Lenin's very different perspective, did little to dissuade. Indeed, the determinism and economism of Engels, Kautsky, Plekhanov, etc., contributed to the bureaucratic, nonrevolutionary, and ultimately impotent politics of the Second International's mass parties, most notably the Social Democratic Party of Germany, and thence to a deep questioning of the dynamic and resilience of "late capitalism." The restoration of the totality concept to a central role in Critical Marxist theory must, therefore, be understood in relation not only to the repudiation of Marxist economism and determinism, and to the interplay of social forces, but also to the role played by individual theorists.

Deemphasizing the creative activity of man, subjectivity, and consciousness and referring to a metaphysical monism, Engels logically contrived an "automatic" or Scientific Marxism, that history was controlled by universal law. Thus, it was Engels who was the economic determinist. It is alleged that he intuited in economic laws the allegedly determinate causal laws of history in the same way that he found in motion the determinate causal laws of the physical universe. However, in fact, Engels's work is replete with statements qualifying such a determinism as asserting the historicity of social laws.[66]

5

The Philosophical Heritage of Critical Marxism

An Introductory Overview

Let us briefly recapitulate the ground we have covered so far. The driving force behind the philosophical genesis of critical theory can be traced to several key problems revolving around the relationship between theory and practice. During the Enlightenment this problem took the following form: How does one reconcile the idealistic and largely ethical heritage of philosophical/practical reason with the materialistic heritage of instrumental reason? Or how does one reconcile the democratic and communitarian thrust of a socioethically informed concept of reason emphasizing universal equality with the individualistic and acquisitive thrust of an instrumental reason emphasizing self-preservation? Or how does one reconcile the notion of freedom with necessity and historical causation?

Kant attempted to solve the contradiction inherent in Enlightenment rationality philosophically by means of a critique of reason itself. Reason, he argued, is not merely a passive faculty of analysis. It is also an active faculty of synthesis. Transcendental reason is not wholly transcendent; it is not independent of and cut off from reality. Rather, it is directly productive of reality, including the material world.

Kant's transcendental idealism enabled him to affirm the radical freedom of the rational subject against the objectivism of empirical science. However, the price he paid for endowing humanity with radical freedom was a new metaphysical dualism separating socioethical reason from instrumental reason and ideal from material reality. Once again, a gap was introduced between the intentions of social ethics and everyday practice.

Hegel sought to bridge the gap by integrating philosophy and history—a strategy that Kant himself had anticipated in his writings on history. Reason, Hegel argued, was not a transcendent subjective faculty, but consisted of real objective institutions whose development was propelled by contradictions inherent in the ideas they embodied. These contradictions between freedom and necessity, communality and individuality, philosophy and science, spirit and nature, were precisely those that achieved their expression during the Enlightenment. Imperiously regarding his own philosophy as the culmination of Enlightenment thought, Hegel believed that the contradictions inherent in instrumental reason had, in fact, been more or less resolved in the constitutional monarchy of early nineteenth-century Prussia. The reconciliation of individual freedom and ethical community, he believed, was now a fact for reflective contemplation, rather than a yet-to-be-accomplished task.

The conservative implications of Hegel's philosophy, however, still seemed to contradict social reality. For Marx, at any rate, the fulfillment of the emancipatory aims of the Enlightenment remained a task that could not be dismissed philosophically, for the contradictions besetting the Enlightenment reflected contradictions inherent in capitalism itself. In capitalism, the contradictions between individual and community, freedom and necessity, morality and science are enveloped in the principle of private property. Production is social, but consumption is private. Private entrepreneurs are instrumental in calculating the profitability of their enterprises, but the cumulative impact of their decisions results in irrationality, an anarchy of overproduction. Freedom to buy and sell is circumscribed by the law of supply and demand. One's individuality as proprietor demands alienation of those social powers that truly individuate.

Marx takes what appears to be the decisive step in resolving the theory-practice problem. The critique of reason must move beyond philosophy and become the scientific critique of political economy. The overcoming of Cartesian objectivism and the realization of Enlightenment's unaccomplished *empire of reason* could only be achieved politically, by abolishing capitalism.

Marx's and Engels's observations on society and the economy were comprehensive in many respects. Their totality theory joined a line of philosophy that connected them with the holism of Plato and Aristotle. Theirs foreshadowed and provided the impetus for the later appearance of a general theory of organization and a formative open system or metabolic appreciation of the livelihood of man. To some extent their efforts also enabled a systems theoretical challenge to political economy. However, in some cases they failed to go beyond mechanical conceptualizations. For unlike Engels, who had some understanding, albeit confused,[1] Marx was unaware of the economic-ecological-social significance of the second law of thermodynamics, which had been formulated in France and Germany; and no wonder: Marx lived in the age of unprecedented expansion of industrial production due to coal and iron.[2] Thus, economics and political economy have continued to posit that production and reproduction are carried out perpetually without constraint and that spiraling technological advances may eventually lift the burden of man.

Marx's envisaged political struggle for emancipation was an optimistic forecast. Workers would achieve rational insight into their world historical destiny and establish a humane socialist state. That this did not happen, critical systems theorists argued, was due to two dimensions missing from Marx's thought: the openness of capitalism, which would admit state intervention in the economy, and the possibility of its contradiction originating with humankind's interaction with the biosphere.

All this raises new philosophical questions: What role does philosophy continue to play in the aftermath of Marx's critique of Hegel? If Hegel blunted the revolutionary force of moral reason by assimilating it to existing social reality, must we then turn to a more transcendent notion of reason? Are there agencies within existing social reality that embody this rationality? Or does the heritage of the Enlightenment ultimately present us with an unsolvable set of contradictions pitting individual against society, science against morality, negative freedom against positive freedom?

Critical Theory and Political Economy

Theory work is not done just by "adding another brick to the wall of science" but often involves throwing bricks as well. It involves not only a paying of one's intellectual debts but also (and rather differently) a "settling of accounts."

Critical theory offers a distinctive approach to understanding the livelihood of man. Of course, not all social political theories are critical; in fact, most are not for the reasons apparent above. In contrast to critical theory, their primary aim is to provide the faithful description and explanation of social and political events. Empiricists working in these fields collect "factual" data by means of disciplined observation. These are then used to classify the memberships and corresponding attitudes of particular groups. They also yield statistical information about general behavioral patterns and probabilities that can be used to explain why a given event was or is to be expected. This knowledge is warranted by those who seek to control or influence the behavior of others, for it is alleged that by changing one variable in a social pattern (e.g., the amount of available money in a society), one can alter other variables—the rates of inflation, interest, investment, and consumption.

Unlike descriptive and explanatory theories, critical theories are chiefly concerned with evaluating the goodness of societies. In this respect they bear more of a resemblance to philosophy than to science. Philosophy, as it is traditionally conceived, involves reflecting upon the "essential" meaning of life and the subordinate activities and terms whereby it is sustained as an ongoing process. The essential means the most basic, the most necessary, and/or the most universal features of some activity or thing. This is what defines something in its innermost identity, relating it to things that are like it and distinguishing it from things that are not. Although this defining activity is similar to the social and political scientists' penchant for constructing classifications, it involves considerably more than mere disciplined observation. It prescribes an ethical norm or ideal to which the activity or thing being defined must conform in order for it to be truly what it is. Therefore, the definitions sought by philosophers have a critical edge.

Critical theory is like other forms of social and political philosophy in that it reflects on the basic meaning of social and political life in order to discover standards of evaluation. Its primary aim is not the discovery of surface phenomena, of statistical patterns enabling the prediction and technical control of social and political processes, but the proffering of critical enlightenment regarding the goodness of social and political institutions. Yet critical theory distinguishes itself from social and political philosophy in being "truth-realistic" and critical about its own philosophical assumptions.

This takes us to the key problem underlying critical theory—its problematic relationship to philosophy. By its very nature philosophy is idealistic. This means it abstracts from, or goes beyond, the limitations of observed reality in prescribing ideal goals which ought to be attained. Such idealism can be problematic. It tends to be utopian in its demand for perfection. But how can persons be expected to take seriously goals that are so ideal as to be impossible of any practical implementation? Suppose we say that an ideal democracy must satisfy conditions of perfect justice in which everyone has an equal say in all decision making affecting them. Such a goal might be implemented only by greatly reducing the vastness and complexity of modern societies. All hierarchies based on technical expertise would have to be eliminated, as well as those based on wealth, social status, and natural circumstance. For each person the network of social relations would have to be reduced to a minimum, so that he or she would be guaranteed a direct say in all decisions affecting him or her. Life would be simple—but difficult—under such radically egalitarian conditions. Indeed, one cannot help but wonder whether democracy would even be relevant in a world in which the individual's literacy and scope for political action is subordinated to the narrow task of providing for his livelihood.

Critical political economy cannot avoid addressing the philosophical problem of goodness. This is a philosophical problem because the mere fact that people in a given society think with contentment that their social relations are just and mutually fulfilling does not necessarily make them so. Slaves may be taught to accept slavery as the most just and fulfilling system for people "like themselves," who are "by nature inferior in intelligence, weak, and dependent." Likewise, business executives, no less than ordinary criminals, may deceive themselves into thinking that the acquisition of power and wealth is all that matters in achieving true happiness. In short, people can rationalize invidious relations, existing injustice, and unhappiness by convincing themselves that it is the "natural thing" that all human beings, or at least all human beings of a certain rank, ought to want.

Thus from a philosophical point of view, commonly shared assumptions about what constitutes goodness must be viewed with suspicion as potentially ideological. Those opinions, cultural values, practices, and institutions are ideological that appear to be generally true or valid for all persons but are not. Accepted out of ignorance or sheer force of habit, these opinions and values may reflect nothing more than the interests of an elite few who benefit—or think they benefit—from the social relations that constrain their acceptance.

Our project, our "brick throwing," is, at one level, a critique of Marxism that rests upon some assumptions of Marxism itself and is thus, in part, an autocritique of Marxism. Indeed, the very idea of a critique, as we have seen, was originally rooted in Kant's critique of pure and practical reason transmitted and reshaped by Marx. At another level, of course, our project is an archaeological one that seeks to reveal a lost paradigm.

Yet critique is not a pedantic effort to debunk or unmask a theoretical system; it is never undertaken as an occasion in which the critic outsmarts his subject and certainly never views the subject's work as the mere product of a historical mistake or ignorance. A critique searches for Marxism's rationality. At the same time, a critique, seeing a theory as a human product, can have no impulse to canonize it. Conceiving theory as a poetic enterprise by persons enveloped in some specific historical era, critique searches for the limits no less than the achievements of a theory. It strives to discern and strike off from any doctrine its flawed, erroneous, and irrational parts, so that it may rescue its productive and rational side, polishing and resituating this in a new intellectual setting. To view Marx or Marxism as having shadows, silences, and subtexts beneath the text is thus in no way to debase it but only to see it as sharing in the common human condition.

For Marxists reflexive efforts at historical self-appreciation are often taken as narcissistic, diverting enquiry from the praxiology of the philosophy. Marxism is, indeed, a historical and social product shaped by the social needs no less than it is molded by reason and research. It is part of the tissue of its time rather than an eruption without precedent. This perspective may not be congenial to those who celebrate Marx's discovery as the greatest event in the history of human knowledge, or who shroud Marxism's origin in the mystique of an unaccountable rupture in epistemology, setting it altogether apart from other achievements of its time. Like other social theories, Marxism emerged in an ambivalent relationship to different parts of its productionist tradition and to the culture of everyday life. Marxism established its own identity only by distinguishing itself from the traditions of Hegel's philosophical idealism and English political economy. More than most theories, Marxism emerged in the form of an ambitious polemic against other views. To understand Marxism, as any theory, then, requires an appreciation of the accomplices in its intellectuality and the forefathers from whom it draws its capital. In viewing Marxian holism, as a system of either propositions or actions, as potentially contradictory, the intent is not to render a verdict against Marxism's flaws but to demonstrate that the flaws are of themselves important.

Marx conceived of the emergence of socialism as depending on the prior maturation of certain objective conditions, especially the structures of an advanced industrialism, while also conceiving of capitalism as producing these conditions through the operation of its own blind, impersonal, and allegedly necessary laws. Thus viewed, capitalism is a stage in a social evolution destined to give rise to another, higher society—socialism. However, at the same time, Marx's was a praxis-oriented philosophy. He did not think of his theory simply as a social science, for theoretical enlightenment might cast the scales from the eyes of the masses and strike the shackles from their limbs, but theory might make man free. It was also a doctrine of violent revolution. Marxism is not attempting simply to understand society; it not only predicts the rise of a revolutionary proletariat that will overturn capitalism but also actively mobilizes persons to do this. It intervenes to change the world. It is, indeed, as Gramsci remarked, a philosophy of praxis.[3]

In his famous eleventh *Thesis on Feuerbach* Marx urged persons to undertake action, that is praxis, and held that, "The philosophers have only interpreted the world in various ways; the point is to change it." Implicit in Marx's philosophy of praxis are, in fact, two disparate meanings. $Praxis^\alpha$ is the unreflective laboring process on which capitalism rests, where wage labor is imposed by necessity and operates within a narrow institutional framework and division of labor. Reproducing a crippled freedom, it constitutes the foundational basis of that society. Here workers are shackled to the very system that alienates them. This conception of praxis is congenial to Scientific Marxism. In the second, more heroic concept, one more affable to Critical Marxism, $Praxis^\beta$, emphasis is on a practice more freely chosen, that is on political struggle. If $Praxis^\alpha$ is the constrained labor that reproduces the *status quo*, $Praxis^\beta$ is the free labor contributing toward emancipation from it.

On the one hand, Marxism is a philosophy of praxis; on the other hand, it is a "science," the political economy of the laws of capitalism. Marxism is thus a conjunction of science and politics, of theory and practice. Its topic is the objective socioeconomic conditions imputedly requisite for socialism. Its object in addressing this topic, however, is not only understanding but also revolutionary practice aimed at changing the world. Science and ideology, rational understanding and political practice, these are the orbits of Marxism. As science, it premises that some things will happen without men's rational foresight and whatever their efforts. As a dimension of politics, however, it also premises the centrality of people's efforts, struggle, capacity for sacrifice, and self-discipline. Indeed, while all politics premises that men "must seize the time," science premises that things have their own cadence and rhythm.

The Marxist community has been divided into roughly two orbits: one conceiving Marxism as "critique" and the other conceiving it to be some kind of social "science." The conjunction of the scientific and the critical in ordinary Marxism is recurrently productive of tensions and of a tension-reducing segregation of the inconsistent elements by insulating them from one another into two distinct and boundaried systems of "elaborated" Marxism, Critical and Scientific. While Scientific Marxism and Critical Marxism are bearers of the noble traditions of European thought and culture, it is the dichotomous juncture between the praxis-oriented and the scientific interpretations that is problematic. The problem between these is that if capitalism is indeed governed by lawful regularities that doom it to be supplanted by a socialist society (when the requisite infrastructures have matured), why then stress that the point is to change it? Why go to great pains to arrange capitalism's funeral if its demise is guaranteed by science? Why must persons be mobilized and exhorted to discipline themselves to behave in conformity with necessary laws by which, it would seem, they would in any event be bound?

Marx employed two concepts of change: one gradualistic, evolutionary, and continuous; the other more discontinuous, abrupt, and catastrophic. The first situates itself within Scientific Marxism's conception of historical change and is coincidental with Darwinism; the second approximates Critical Marxism's appreciation of historical change and is allegedly grounded in a Hegelian perspective.

Hegel's notion of contradiction is one in which later forms incorporate parts of earlier forms, which are synthesized in a new, more encompassing totality. This concept of progress is that all that is true or still of value in the past is carried forward and preserved in the new entity, so that the more recent form embodies and transcends the truth of the past. A rupture is introduced.

The two readings of Marxism, in part, ripened around the essential tension between voluntarism and determinism, between freedom and necessity. Both of these readings, let us hasten to add, are a bona fide part of Marxism. We are not faced with only a seeming contradiction, which can be glibly resolved by asserting that one side is false, revisionist, opportunist, misguided, and not-really-Marxist, while the other is the genuine revolutionary article.

For some vulgar Marxists, to speak of a dichotomous Marxism is slanderous. Perhaps Marxism shares something of the flawed existence of the very life it wishes to dismantle. But a consistent autocritique of Marxism can do no other; it must insist that Marxism is not without its problematic dimensions. Any effort to grapple with these must grope with Marxism's living contradictions, not simply the vestigial remnants of Marxism's birth, its bourgeois heritage, or prejudices. It must view Marxism's own contradictions as a living part of Marxism today and as an essential key to its present diminished condition and still-future prospect. Indeed, to critique it implies a concern with identifying the contradictions, strains, or dissonances embedded in Marxism with a view to seeing certain other parts of the theory as efforts to reduce, control, or remove these, as well as a concern with the resulting development of the theory.

However, in distinguishing Critical and Scientific Marxisms, there is no intention of suggesting that voluntarism, on the one hand, and determinism, on the other hand, are the deepest "essence" or legitimate meaning of that which distinguishes these two editions of Marxism. Neither is this the unique burden of

Marxism, for other sociological theories may be similarly identified. Some express a view of society as a network of human meanings and embodiment of human action. Others present us with society conceived as a thinglike fact, standing against its individual members and invidiously molding them in its socializing processes. The first view presents us with man as the social being and with society as being "made" by him. The second view sets society apart from man, as an entity over and against him and conjectures that man is made by society.

This dichotomy, the tension between voluntarism and determinism in Western socioeconomic thought, may be seen as part of the deep structure of the Cultural West evidenced in the tension between "necessity" and "freedom" that reaches back to ancient Greek philosophy. Therein, there was a sacred law by which men were bound, there was a division of the cosmos by fate into distinct spheres by which even the gods themselves were bound. There was, in short, "necessity." Yet to pursue a course of conduct simply out of "necessity" was a slave's way, and a free people insisted on going to their fate, even if it were death itself, out of their own free will. It was slavish for persons to be dragged to their fate; free people would face it unblinkingly. The Greek necessity, then, did not contain the idea of the absolutely impossible. The boundaries around people, their "destiny," could indeed be stretched or breached, at least momentarily; the law could only ensure retribution for the breach but could not prevent it from happening. The legislated against and the forbidden are not the same as the impossible; they are merely costly.

Critical and Scientific Marxism

Hegelian philosophy has continued to infuse Marxism. Indeed, both Russian and Western Critical Marxism emerged out of two different Hegelian currents, designated the "historicist" and the "scientific." Critical Marxism inherited the Hegel of subjectivity rather than the Hegel of science. For Lukács, science itself is saturated with bourgeois ideology, and any attempt to make Marxism scientific in this sense is misplaced.[4] With Lukács, Korsch, and Gramsci, but also Bogdanov and Bukharin, this shared appreciation posed a threat to Soviet Marxism, i.e., Stalinism. Indeed, defined in this way, Western Critical Marxism was created by a loose band of theorists who took their cue from Lukács and the other founding fathers of the immediate post–World War I era, Antonio Gramsci, Karl Korsch, and Ernst Bloch.[5] Included in their number were the members of the Frankfurt School, notably Max Horkheimer, Theodor W. Adorno, Herbert Marcuse, Leo Lowenthal, and Walter Benjamin.

Wittgenstein's notion of "family resemblances" tells us that no perfectly uniform set of characteristics need be found to identify members of a collective entity. Insofar as both neo-Hegelians and anti-Hegelians share certain traits that cut across their antagonism over Marx's debt to German Idealism, they can be understood as cousins, if not brothers, in an extended family. Thus, rather than contending that Critical and Scientific Marxists are two separate species, one calling for a revolution against *Capital* and the other defending its continued relevance, as we shall see, the Russian Critical Marxists, Bogdanov and Bukharin, sought a synthesis of the two themes. Moreover, their edition of Critical Marxism was, in fact, open to influences from non-Marxist schools of thought such as psychoanalysis, phenomenology, environmentalism, and structuralism, according to the coincidence of those competing systems with their own intellectual development. It was understood that Marxism was founded on an awareness of the historical limits of the Cultural West in relation to its social content: namely, the rationalization of the capitalist project. But Marxism was formed both out of and against the Enlightenment and, as a result, is marked by this origin and remains an unfinished construct.

As differently elaborated paradigms of Marxism, Critical and Scientific Marxism, a dualism, emerged under different sociohistorical conditions and among different persons and groups. And while it has become the convention to refer to Lukács, Korsch, Gramsci, Goldman, and the early and later Frankfurt School as the authors of Critical Marxism, we maintain that Russian contributors contributed to both normative and methodological Critical Marxism.

Some part of the theoretical dualism is appreciated as a conflict between those theorists supporting the central importance of Hegel for Marx and those opposing that view, but also between those using and those rejecting a Hegelian conception of ideology critique.

Scientific Marxism is often taken to view ideology as a distorted reflection of the world, as a world turned upside down and projected through the reflecting lens of self-interest. Western Critical Marxism maintains that even as men go about fashioning ideological masks for class domination, they do so under the scrutiny of their own and others' critical reason.

The difference between Critical and Scientific Marxism reflects, as well, a conflict between those viewing Marx as the culmination of German Idealism and those emphasizing Marx's superiority to that tradition. It is, therefore, also a difference between those accepting the "young" (and allegedly more Hegelian) Marx as the genuine article and those who regard the young Marx as "immature" and ideologically bound.

Critical Marxists (or Hegelianizers) conceive of Marxism as critique rather than science; they stress the continuity of Marx with Hegel, the importance of the young Marx, the significance of the young Marx's emphasis on alienation and the allegedly more historicist views. The Scientific Marxists (anti-Hegelians) have stressed Marx's epistemological break with Hegel. For them, Marxism is a science entailing a structuralist methodology whose full maturity is apparent in *Capital* rather than the still ideologized *Economic and Philosophic Manuscripts of 1844*. The controversy about the young versus the mature Marx is a metaphor for the more analytical distinction between Critical and Scientific Marxism.

However, it is important to note that for the Russian Critical Marxists the tension cannot be characterized by the metaphor of the young and the mature.

Unlike the Critical Marxist—the Hegelian Marxist—the resurrection of Marx's early writings in the late 1920s and the subsequent publication of the *Grundrisse* a generation later helped strengthen the above equation, as they sought to demonstrate that Marx had been what Lukács and the others had said he was: a radical Hegelian. Accordingly, such terms as alienation, mediation, objectification, and reification were understood to have a special place in the lexicon of Critical Marxism. Culture, defined both broadly as the realm of everyday life and narrowly as man's most noble aesthetic and intellectual achievement, was also a central concern of the tradition, which tended as a result to diminish the economic and political dimensions. Critical Marxism, therefore, meant a Marxism that was far more dialectical than materialist, far more holistic than Cartesian. It celebrates the dialectic and defines social situations in a manner maximizing the role of the "subjects." As a "theory of praxis," it focuses on the shifting dialectic of subject and object.

Critical Marxists stress a historicism that emphasizes social fluidity and change, a kind of organicism calling for intercontextual appreciation of phenomena, while Scientific Marxism searches for firm social structures that recur and are presumably intelligible in decontextualized ways.

Scientific Marxism tends to divide the sociocultural world of objects and events into two basic structures: the economic infrastructure, centering on the mode of production, and the superstructure, involving the ideological and the state, with the firm insistence that the former controls the latter. In contrast, Critical Marxism tends to:

1. reject such a dichotomous division of the social world as a vulgar oversimplification,
2. stress holism, and
3. argue that those engaged in the dichotomy have unduly narrow conceptions of the elements that enter into either side of it.

Accenting the density of social structure and the weight of history, Scientific Marxism sees the social world as imposing itself on persons, rather than being a plastic medium open to human intervention. This sets apart Critical Marxism and Scientific Marxism in terms of their politics, in their conception of revolution and how it is made, and no less in their imagining of the meaning and reality of socialism. For Scientific Marxism politics is treated as an epiphenomenon, insofar as the transformation of capitalist society into socialism is seen as taking place via an inevitable worldwide economic collapse. It failed historically to develop a political theory that explains how the working class would struggle for and appropriate state power. Politics as an epiphenomenon corresponds to the proposition that changes in the mode of production and the maturing of development need only be consummated by commandeering state power in order to establish socialism. Indeed, some Marxists actually made a virtue out of refusing to think about the future. Theirs was an ontologicalization of the present, an abstention from a more than furtive anticipation of historical time and the meaning of the future. "The Socialist Party," said Kautsky, "can make positive propositions only for the existing social order. Suggestions that go beyond that cannot deal with facts, but must proceed from suppositions; they are accordingly fantasies and dreams."[6]

Paradoxically, the theorists of the Bolshevik party, before it came to power, appear to have set out to establish what conditions were necessary for a socialist society and whether those conditions existed in Russia. These questions only began to be tackled during the 1920s, most notably in the works of Trotsky, Stalin, Bukharin, and Preobrazhensky. The omission of any clear indication of the rational preparation and political organization required to produce socialism presents Scientific Marxism as a kind of political utopianism. But the absence of a theory of socialism is not as absolute as it might seem. In the period of the First World War the perspectives for socialism and the conditions necessary for its attainment were discussed within the framework of theories of imperialism or finance capital (Hilferding) and culture (Bogdanov).[7] It was generally believed at that time that the contemporary evolution of the capitalist system was laying the foundations for the future socialist society. Behind this belief was the Second International's assumption that world history was moving inexorably from capitalism to socialism and that socialism would emerge from a matured capitalism in a way that would require comparatively little intervention by human agency. Attention was fixed on current developments within capitalism to discover the contours and character of the emergent socialist system. Socialism was to be delivered through the trapdoor of history by some *deus ex machina*.

In the vivid language of one of its most celebrated founders, Antonio Gramsci, Critical Marxism demanded a revolution against the false belief that objective economic laws would automatically bring about the collapse of capitalism and the victory of the proletariat. For if the automaticism of history will thrust upon the proletariat the accomplished fact without struggle, why exercise oneself, why sacrifice? Philosophical critique showed instead that radical change could come only when human actions overthrow the man-made structures oppressing humankind. Scientific Marxism has, then, ambiguous consequences: It leads adherents to wait for the inevitable unfolding of history, but its intentions are broader.

Marxism, as science, seeks to link science and technology more broadly to the institutions on which they depend. Scientific Marxism is disposed to assume that science and technology—forces of production—are central in defining the essential character of modernity. Oriented to modern science and technology, it seems to accept the great value placed upon the "civilizing instrumentalities" allegedly obtained therefrom. It sought to recontextualize the topics and issues it analyzed and was thus drawn to a systems analytical appreciation.

Rather than being obsessed with the certainty of its knowledge, Scientific

Marxism is less concerned with the dangers of uncertainty-induced Hamletian procrastination associated with Critical Marxism. Scientific Marxism risks disengaging the emancipatory ends addressed by socialism and revolution in order to secure the means, the organizational instrument—the "vanguard party." Indeed, Lenin was led to the conclusion that the working class could not itself generate a socialist consciousness (and that this had to derive from the bourgeois intelligentsia). Yet, insofar as members of the vanguard accept a radical popular sovereignty, in principle they cannot acknowledge that they are usurpers of the proletariat's sovereignty. They then conceal their usurping by proclaiming themselves the servants of that sovereignty and justify it with their self-imputed possession of superior knowledge or theory. Theirs is not an ordinary knowledge or theory but, allegedly, an extraordinary and superior knowledge immunized against corruption of the social conditions from which it was born. Their knowledge claims the status of a science that rises above its social origins. As a science it allegedly escapes the distortions of social circumstance. The pathology of this tendency is a political ritualism in which what was originally regarded as an instrument, the party, in time became an end in itself. It obviates the moral issue. Leninism, as such, itself grew out of a disillusionment with the results of the Second International's theory-practice nexus. But whereas Leninism tended to change its practice without seriously questioning the theory it had inherited, Russian Critical Marxists rarely, if ever, deluded themselves into believing that theirs was a time in which the unity of theory and practice was effortlessly achieved.[8] In fact, in the clouded years of the 1920s, Russian Critical Marxism was marked by a growing pessimism. Its authors, nonetheless, directed a great deal of their intellectuality toward investigating the means by which advanced capitalism prevented the unity of theory and practice from being achieved. The critical role of culture in this process was affirmed as it could not have been during the era of the Second International, when the primacy of the economy was an article of faith. Having originally come to Marxism in the hope that it would address the crisis in bourgeois culture, many Russian Critical Marxists continued to be preoccupied with cultural questions.

Scientific Marxism confidently relies on social evolution and on the unfolding of certain tendencies, allied with history and nature, to fulfill socialist millennial expectations. Regarding men as the products of structures, rather than as producers (makers) of social structures, Scientific Marxism is sedimented with a tacitly dour judgment on human nature as somehow falling short of history's requirement. Critical Marxism, to the contrary, relies not on objectified history, social structures, or nature but on human will to overcome the deficiencies of nature, history, and socioeconomic structures.

Scientific Marxism was a theory about certain historically specific entities: about advanced industrial capitalism, about the proletariat and its socialist revolution. But the revolution betrayed the Marxist expectation that it would occur in advanced capitalist society and be "made" by the proletariat. Modern revolution has largely been an affair of industrially backward societies enacted under tutelage of radicalized intellectuals. Critical Marxism was a response to this phenomenon. Moreover, it was Eduart Bernstein's "bad news" about capitalism—that its "crash" was not inevitable—that was conducive to Lukács's and Gramsci's reconceptualization of Marxism as a method focused on the totality of social relations rather than the narrower sphere of economic relations.

Critical Marxism, with its orientation to the more literary and more philosophic traditions of European thought, explores a different layer of modernity linked to a humanistic culture displaced by the parvenu of science and technology. It is concerned with the preservation of "culture" and aims at a moral reinvigoration that may be dissonant with technical modernization. For Critical Marxism, science is part of the modern condition and not exempt from a dissonance-generating critique, for it violates the value so widely awarded science in liberal society. Since science has ascended to the dominant form and the very epitome of rationality, i.e., constituting an ideology of the nonideology, any critique of it exposes the critic to condemnation as antiscientific, as harboring anti-intellectual sentiment, and certainly as irrational. Critical Marxism pursues an oblique critique by focusing on the more diffuse "positivism" rather than on science itself. Critical Marxism rejects the dominant decontextualized concept of science, that is, that science is autonomous and value free and the ultimate form of rationality.

The principal aim of critical theory is to expose such ideologies for what they are. In order to do this, however, it must be that the ideals of goodness—appealed to by the ideology in question—are in some sense false or irrational. In that case, critical theory will have to possess true knowledge of these ideals. But this, as we have seen, is problematic. Ideals that so totally transcend reality are practically impossible. Being neither true nor rational, they are themselves ideological. Therefore, the trick for critical theory is to show how true ideals of goodness are somehow implicit in ideological opinions and practices that constitute and are constitutive of the reality of society.

The paradox of critical theory is that, in some sense, it is a part of the very society it wishes to criticize. The crisis that it exposes in modern society—the contradiction between scientific and moral rationality—is its own. Critical theory has renounced its claim to being pure moral philosophy and has taken on the burden of scientific verification. At the same time, however, it cannot but contradict its own scientific identity in the name of a higher reason. This is especially so when science and technology have become ideological. For this reason, critical theorists are faced with the necessary task of engaging in philosophical reflections that are historically responsible. Just how this is to be accomplished is itself problematic. Where does one locate moral reason? From the physical sciences other issues also present themselves.

6
Toward the Natural Unity of Scientific Knowledge

Introductory Remarks

Let us return to an apprehended theme and note that even while the Darwinian perspective of the evolution of life was developing, from the physical sciences and industry there was a growing awareness that mechanicalism did not provide for a rigorous understanding of all physical phenomena. In particular, the principles of thermodynamics were found to be alien to the Newtonian world.

Consequently, in both biology and evolution theory, the second principle of thermodynamics presented a major obstacle to the understanding of life and led to an ad hoc revision of mechanics. While the discovery of the celebrated second law of thermodynamics presented a number of theoretical difficulties in the late nineteenth century, it also stimulated a search for the natural unity of scientific knowledge.

There later developed theories of "energeticism" and "cosmological monism," which asserted, contrary to Cartesian dualism, that the world is one great whole ruled by the principles of thermodynamics. The monist effort to synthesize the unification of scientific knowledge led to the flourishing of positivist concepts, to attempts to elaborate a general theory of organization, and to a formulation of the dialectics of energy and organization. Moreover, in the first quarter of this century, a nonvitalist branch of "energeticism" led to an evaluation of the economic process in terms of the general principles of thermodynamics. Furthermore, it stimulated an interest in trophism and an understanding of the economy as an autopoietic process.

In essence, the recognition of the thermodynamic dimension of the economy of man is a reassertion of the Aristotelian systems problem and of "becoming." While the discovery of the second law presented merely a paradox for biology, its fuller appreciation bankrupted the mechanical paradigm and depreciated it as the reference image for economic science. Finally, it has led to an emergence of an economic paradigm embracing a concept of holism that attaches to "open" and "living systems."

The Discovery of Thermodynamics

In the age of clocks the Newtonian universe was represented by man as a huge mechanism that had been wound up once and for all time. Some saw, as the basis of all existence, mechanical motion, the displacement of bodies in space, all taking place according to Newton's laws of motion. Life was discussed, from this point of view, as being merely a special kind of mechanical motion. According to the idea of the time, an organism was nothing but a "very complicated machine, the structure of which is, nevertheless, completely comprehensible. Its movement depends entirely on its structure and on the pressure and on the collision of particles of matter like the wheels of a water clock."[1]

While anatomy occupied the most important place in the study of life at that time, in the next period of the development of science, that is, in the age of steam engines, physiology began, to an ever-greater extent, to aspire to that place. Subsequently, the role of mechanics in the study of life was taken over in many sciences by what was known as "energetics."[2]

It is of interest to note that while Adam Smith was working on his *Wealth of Nations* and collecting data on the prospects and determinants of industrial growth, at the same university James Watt was putting the finishing touches on his steam engine. Yet, the only use for coal that Adam Smith could find was to provide heat for workers.[3] In the eighteenth century, wind, water, and animals, and the simple machines driven by them, were still the only conceivable sources of power.

With rapid dissemination of Watt's invention, there was brought about a new fascination with the mechanical effect of heat. Thermodynamics, born out of this interest, was not so much concerned with the nature of heat, as with heat's latent potential for producing mechanical energy.

Ilya Prigogine dates the birth of the first form of energetics—the "science of complexity"—to 1811, the year Baron Jean-Joseph Fourier won the prize of the French Academy of Sciences for his mathematical treatment on the propagation of heat in solids.[4] Fourier's result was simple and elegant: Heat flow is proportional to the gradient of temperature. This simple law applies to matter, irrespective of its state, whether it be solid, liquid, or gaseous. Moreover, it remains valid whatever the chemical composition of the body. It is only the coefficient of proportionality between the heat flow and the gradient of temperature that is specific to each substance.[5]

The universality of Fourier's law was unrelated to the dynamic interactions as expressed by Newtonian mechanics and Laplace's eternal Platonic universe. It is for this reason that Fourier's formulation may be considered the starting point of a new type of science. This law was formulated when Laplace's school dominated European science. Laplace, Lagrange, and their disciples vainly joined forces to criticize Fourier's theory, but they were forced to retreat.[6] At the peak of its glory, the Laplacean dream met with its first setback. A physical theory, every bit as mathematically rigorous as the mechanical laws of motion, had been discovered, but whose character was alien to mechanicalism.

The early nineteenth century was characterized by an unprecedented experimental ferment. Physicists realized that motion does more than bring about changes in the relative position of material bodies in space. New processes identified in laboratories gradually formed a synthesis that ultimately linked all the new fields of physics with the more traditional mechanics. Indeed, Galvani's, Volta's, and Faraday's diverse experimentation with electricity gradually lay bare a whole network of new effects.[7]

Because matter in motion was the key to the mathematical description of falling bodies and planetary motion, science attempted to fit a materialist explanation to phenomena whose nature they did not at all understand.[8] Heat, light, electricity, and magnetism were regarded as imponderable kinds of matter. "Imponderable" meaning merely that the densities of these kinds of matter were too small to be measured. The "matter" in heat, for example, was called *caloric*. A body, when it was heated, soaked up this matter, just as a sponge soaks up water. Similarly, electricity was matter in the state of a fluid or two fluids, and these fluids flowing through wires were electric current. Moreover, mechanicists, asserting the material unity of the world, sought to reduce the different levels of organization of nature to the progressive complexification of material substance directed by the laws of the motion of dead matter.[9] Matter was set in motion and generally kept in motion by the action of external forces. A billiard ball hitting another billiard ball imparts motion by the force of impact. To account for the continuing motion of planets, Newton introduced, in particular, the force of gravitation. To account for electric and magnetic phenomena, Faraday introduced lines of electric force and magnetic force that he believed were real.[10]

Of the three concepts, matter, force, and motion, force acted on matter, and motion was a behavior of matter; hence, matter was fundamental. The positivist philosophers, thereupon, proclaimed matter, which behaved in accordance with fixed mathematical laws, as the sole reality.

In 1847 a linkage among chemistry, the science of heat, electricity, magnetism, and biology was speculated on by Joule.[11] Joule recognized the "conversion" of a potential as a generalization of that which occurs during mechanical motion. Joule's contribution was to identify a general equivalent for physicochemical transformations, thereby making it possible to measure the quantity conserved. This quantity was later to become known as "energy." As we are all aware, total energy is conserved, while potential energy is converted into kinetic energy or vice versa. In the midst of a bewildering variety of new discoveries, a unifying element had been identified. The conservation of energy, throughout various transformations undergone by physical, chemical, and biological systems, was to provide a guiding principle in the study of new processes.[12]

It is no wonder that the principle of conservation of energy was so important to the nineteenth-century scientists. For many of them it meant the unification of the whole of nature. Moreover, it fostered a belief in a new golden age, which would lead to the ultimate generalization of mechanics. The cultural implications were far-reaching, and they included a conception of society and man as energy-transforming engines.[13]

The grand design was, however, incomplete, for energy conversion represents but the peaceful or controllable aspects of nature, which echoes with the creations and destructions that go beyond the mere conservation and conversion of energy. The focus on conservation principles concealed another aspect of nature: life and death. Here we reach the most original contribution of thermodynamics to the economic process—the concept of irreversibility.

Evolution Versus Mechanics: Irreversibility of Life Processes

The idea that the life process can be reversed seems so entirely preposterous to the human mind that it does not even appear as myth. The evidence that life proceeds in one direction suffices as proof of the irreversibility of the life process. However, this reality has been obfuscated by the advance of the mechanical paradigm. For, if science were to discard a proposition that follows logically from its theoretical postulates, merely because its concrete realization has never been observed, modern technology might not exist.

Impossibility is not a password in science. Consequently, if one cornerstone of science is the doctrine that all phenomena are governed by mechanical laws, science has little alternative but to admit that life itself is reversible. That such an admission would cause considerable intellectual discomfort is evidenced by the fact that not a single scholar of the classical school has ever overtly made such a claim.[14]

Shortly after Laplace extolled the power of mechanics, an officer in the French Engineer Corps, Sadi Carnot, became interested in affairs of less celestial interest—in quite pedestrian problems.[15] The problem was the efficiency of steam engines, of the power of fire, as Carnot described it. His memoirs of 1824 were ultimately to force the realization upon physicists that Laplacean mechanics cannot account for every phenomenon in the universe. It is unable to explain faithfully the constant phenomenon of heat always passing by itself from a hotter to a cooler body, never the reverse.

That the laws of mechanics allow any mechanical phenomenon to operate in reverse is best exemplified by a simple pendulum.[16] To wit, the earth could very well have moved spontaneously in the opposite direction on its ecliptic; no mechanical law would have been violated in its transit. However, if heat moved by itself from a colder to a warmer body, the second law of thermodynamics would be annulled.

Thermodynamics is that branch of natural science that deals with the flow and transformation of energy. This was the origin of the entropy law and, parenthetically, by the same token, the negation of the perpetual-engine hypothesis of the economy. It was Carnot who developed the basic principles of what came to be later known as the second law of thermodynamics.[17] And in the process he discovered irreversible Time, heterogeneous to Newtonian Time.

Carnot pointed out that thermal energy can do no work unless a temperature gradient exists. The basis of the second law of thermodynamics has led to several formulations of available energy, a quantity more related to the ability to do work than thermal energy. In a general sense, any kind of gradient represents available energy or potential work. Carnot's observation was that an *engine* can be inserted and some of this "falling apart" can be converted into a "putting together" of something else; in short, it can be made to do work. Broadly interpreted, the economy of man in its totality may be considered a Carnotian *engine*.

The reference image of the economy operating as a heat engine is particularly relevant when the lifelines of modern industrialized societies are the far-flung stocks of fossil fuels. It becomes apparent that from a purely physical viewpoint the economic process is entropic: it neither creates nor consumes matter or energy but only transforms low entropy into high entropy. Consequently, the wealth of nations, which has so animated economic analysis, is nothing more, but no less either, than temporary appropriations from nature. We must make a sharp distinction here, for whereas the entropic processes of the biosphere are spontaneous, the economic process is dependent upon the conscious activity of humankind. The entire industrial effort is no less than the shuffling and sorting of environmental low entropy.

In 1850, Rudolf Clausius described the Carnot cycle from the new perspective provided by the conservation of energy.[18] Then, in 1865, he introduced the concept of entropy. Clausius's formulation was actually the advent of a new set of ideas concerning irreversible phenomena, heterogeneous to mechanicalism. He recognized the need for two heat sources and that the formula for theoretical efficiency, as stated by Carnot, expressed but a specific problem with heat engines: the need for a process compensating for conversion (in the present case, cooling by contact with a cold source) to restore the engine to its initial mechanical and thermal conditions. Carnot's balance relations were now joined by the conservation principle. Thus, a new science, thermodynamics, which linked mechanical and thermal effects, was advanced.

Clausius implied that we cannot use, without real constraints, the seemingly inexhaustible energy reservoir that nature provides us. In the history of economic thought, Clausius's observation found its expression in W.S. Jevons's *The Coal Question*. It was an investigation into the economic dimensions of the increasing physical scarcity of Great Britain's nineteenth-century energy reservoir. Clausius recognized that not all energy-conserving processes are possible. An energy difference, for instance, cannot be created without the destruction of at least an equivalent energy difference. Thus, the price paid for the work produced is, in the ideal Carnot cycle, the heat that is transferred from one source to another.[19] Introducing the concept that the earth is a thermodynamical machine, Clausius noted that: *"Die Energie der Welt is konstant. Die Entropie der Welt strebt einen Maximum zu."* (The energy of the world is constant. The entropy of the world strives to a maximum.)

In a closed system—closed to the influx of energy or information—all organization eventually, irreversibly, and monotonously dissipates, and energy cannot be directed any more to act as power; it all ends up as high-entropy dissipated heat. And since the ultimate system, the universe, is closed (Boltzmann's *Warmtod*),[20] as the end point toward which the evolution of the universe incessantly moves, seemed inevitable.[21] So deeply ingrained became this belief that the word *entropy* was deliberately chosen as a synonym for *evolution*, and T.H. Huxley penned the epigram that "Evolution encourages no millennial expectations."[22]

Like all life processes, the economic process is firmly anchored in the material environment—the biosphere. There is also a balance equation of the life process expressed in physical units based on the law of conservation of matter-energy. However, more significant than the physical balance, from the viewpoint of the livelihood of man, is the one-way, noncircular, irreversible nature of the flow of matter-energy through all divisions of the life process. Since useful (low entropy) matter-energy is finite, the total life process could be brought to a halt by what the late American economist Kenneth Boulding has called "the entropy trap." Thus, one of the ultimate natural sources of scarcity and, hence, of economic activity is the second law of thermodynamics. The entropic nature of the economic process is due to the irrevocable degradation that matter and energy undergo from available into unavailable forms. Economic activity cannot be characterized as a wealth-producing circular flow, but rather one in which matter and environmental energy are irreversibly transformed. This is what is meant by the entropy trap.

The economic process, like any other life process, is irreversible; hence, it cannot be explained in accord with mechanical principles. It is classical thermodynamics that recognizes the qualitative distinction that political economists should have made from the outset between the inputs of provisionally valuable resources and the final outputs of valueless waste—though to make this assertion is somewhat absurd, for this is only the material side of the story. From an Aristotelian perspective, the true product of the process is not the material flow that results but the immaterial flux—the enjoyment of life itself.

Search for the Unification of Natural Scientific Knowledge

The attempt to reconcile thermodynamics with classical mechanics and, hence, resolve that paradox of life became science's quest. The determinism of classical mechanics was not fated to endure. There were unstable factors, which Hegel referred to as "nodal" points in his *Wissenschaft der Logik*. Clerk Maxwell referred to them as "singular points" in the dynamics of nature.[23] For instance, the match that starts a conflagration, the command that might unleash the terrors of a holocaust, and the obscure gene that makes us philosophers or idiots are quasi-stable phenomena. Such quasi-stabilities were viewed as flaws in the deterministic world of Laplace. Laws break down in these instances, and effects, which are negligible under other circumstances, can be dominating. Compensating for the inconvenience, and in an ad hoc reversion, strict causal determinism yielded to *statistical laws*. The use of statistical laws in physics started with mechanics, where one could at least believe that if we could embrace millions of collisions of molecules, each behaving deterministically, we could determine the "mass effect" of a gas.[24] In its fullest interpretation this problematic development constituted an attack on classical mechanic's hard core, an attack countered by Boltzmann's statistical reconstruction of mechanics.

The first significant use of statistical laws was made by Ludwig Boltzmann in his work on gases. In 1866, he offered an alternative formulation of the second law, in which it was linked with probability theory and statistical mechanics. This was a radical step in a world seemingly at ease with mechanism and determinism. Indeed, it caused fierce debates. So it was that Boltzmann's statistical mechanics was, in his time, derided as the speculation of a "mathematical terrorist."[25] H. Poincaré addressed Boltzmann's doctrine of mathematical probability of complex phenomena:[26]

> If by ill luck I happen to know the laws which govern them I should be helpless, I should be lost in endless calculations and could never supply you with an answer to your questions. Fortunately for both of us I am completely ignorant about the matter. I can therefore supply you with an answer at once. This may seem odd. However, there is something odder still, namely, that my answer will be right.[27]

Boltzmann's was an alternative formulation of classical thermodynamics. Based on considerations of space and velocity distributions of individual molecules, "statistical mechanics" combined some mechanical postulates with notions of probability to define entropy as thermodynamic probability.[28] Accordingly, free energy is associated with low entropy and low probabilities, while bound energy is attached to high entropy and high probabilities. Later, Werner Heisenberg's Indeterminacy Principle of 1927 played an important role in discrediting the doctrine of mechanical determinism. In an article published that year, Heisenberg attacked both causality and determinism:

> But in the strong formulation of the causal law, if we know the present exactly, then we can calculate the future; it is not the final cause which is wrong, but the assumption. It is impossible for us in principle to know the present in all its

determined pieces. Therefore, all perception is a selection from among a large number of possibilities and a restriction on future possibilities. As the statistical character of the quantum theory is so closely linked to the imprecision of all perception, one is tempted to suspect that another "real" world is hidden behind the perceived, statistical world in which the causal laws are valid. But such speculations appear to us . . . pointless and sterile. Physics must give only a formal description of the connection between perceptions. A much better description of the real facts is: because all experiments are subject to the laws of quantum mechanics, quantum mechanics definitely shows the invalidity of the causal law.[29]

Heisenberg's Indeterminacy Principle does not merely state that the causal links of quantum phenomena are beyond our powers of detection; it clearly implies that these links do not exist. This was Heisenberg's own inference. Classical causality and determinacy become meaningless. And if Kant were right in his *Critique of Pure Reason* (that causality was a necessary precondition for rational thought), rational thought itself is jeopardized by the Indeterminacy Principle. While quantum mechanics could be a statistical discipline, the meaning of rationality had to be radically reconceptualized.

In no uncertain terms, formalized economics has also become something of a statistical discipline, for it has generally adopted the same principles. Moreover, as Georgescu-Roegen asserts, the statistical inferences and tests are based on some special assumptions in addition to one general assumption, that of randomness.[30] Yet in many cases there seems to be a great gulf between what one knows and what one does. The technique presents neither an exact description nor an exact prediction of an individual particle or its behavior. However, it can make occasionally reliable short-term predictions regarding the behavior of large aggregates of particles. Economist Kenneth Boulding writes:

> And in the mass, human behavior is fairly regular—which explains, incidentally, why so much of economics assumes the mass—interactions of perfect competition and why indeterminacy appears in the theory of oligopoly—i.e., in the interaction of few exchangers. It may be incidentally noticed that the same difficulty crops up in physics, where the law of behavior of gases, being a statistical law involving enormous numbers of molecules ("perfect competition") is nicely determinate, but where much less is known about the behavior of individual molecules, and where the strangest indeterminacies crop up in the oligopolistic interactions of the few in the atom. This remoteness from human behavior is seen most clearly in the Keynesian economics, which consists of "models" whose component variables (national income, consumption, investment) are vast statistical aggregates which enjoy cozy relationships among themselves but which are only distantly related to the millions of flesh-and-blood people whose experiences these aggregate variables are in some sense a sum.[31]

Anatol Rapoport argues more acerbically, noting that from its methodological individualism the resulting model, which has become central to applied behavioral social science and almost obligatory in Anglo-American academic environments, resembles a kinetic gas theory of society.[32] It assumes that the behavior of statistically significant groups can be imputed with statistical accuracy no matter how far individuals may deviate from the average. This is the analog of the "mass effect." Statistical mechanics has become "the inductive technology of social science." All determinate laws became viewed as nothing more than approximate and purely passive reflections of the probabilistic relationships associated with the laws of chance. As Arthur Eddington predicted in *The Nature of the Physical World*, "Science has made determinism untenable."[33] For Jacques Monod:

> The probabilistic ideas of modern science are plainly even more offensive than were the mechanistic theories of the early nineteenth century. Laplace's world was less frightening than ours. In it man had his inevitable place, prepared for him since the beginning of time.... But that man might be the sum product of an incalculable number of previously preserved random events, how are we to believe this, how can we face it otherwise than by testing it against biological man, at least against his works?[34]

There has been some argument among scientists about the validity of the underlying assumptions and theoretical consequences of statistical mechanics. The most perplexing of such problems was identified by the Soviet scientist A.I. Oparin as the reversibility of evolutionary sequences.[35] While classical thermodynamics is identified with irreversible and indeed irrevocable spontaneous processes, reformulated in Boltzmann's model, time once again became reversible. Physicists could once more rest easy, satisfied that thermodynamics might after all be formally consistent with Laplace's certain cosmos.[36] Classical thermodynamics, by offering evidence that even in the physical domain there are irreversible processes, reconciled science's stand with generally shared common sense.[37] However, as statistical mechanics began teaching, with great aplomb, that all phenomena are virtually reversible, universal reversibility became the object of a prominent controversy. For there were a number of logical contradictions. Nor was statistical mechanics free of epistemological difficulties. From physics the controversy spread into biology, where the issue is clearly more crucial, particularly for evolutionary biology.[38] And from biology, in turn, there arose questions to which only recently has economic thought turned.

It is because science began to speak of evolution, first in connection with biological phenomena,[39] that by evolution we generally understand "the history of a system undergoing irreversible changes."[40] The existence of evolutionary laws in nature depend then upon whether there are irreversible phenomena. All the stronger, therefore, is the negation of evolutionary laws by the universal reversibility proclaimed by statistical mechanics. Many a scientist was thus induced to argue that evolution is "appearance."[41] A disruptive phenomenological perspective was intruding on the concrete reality.[42]

The Collapse of the Laplacean Prototype

In the age of clocks the world of Laplace was eternal, an ideal perpetual-motion machine. Laplace's image of nature had likened it to an ideal mechanical system. However, because of the celebrated second law of thermodynamics, some physicists of the nineteenth century were caught up with the dismal image of Boltzmann's *Warmtod* of the earth and the universe as a whole. Max Planck wrote:[43]

> Nature seems to favor certain states. The irreversible increase in entropy describes a system's approach to a state that attracts it, which the system prefers and from which it will not move of its own "free will." From this point of view, nature does not permit processes whose final states she finds less attractive than their initial states. Reversible processes are limiting cases. In them, nature has an equal propensity for initial and final states; this is why the passage between them can be made in both directions.[44]

The prototype of living nature was now thought of not as a mechanical automaton but as a heat engine.[45] The analogy put forward by Lavoisier between respiration and the burning of fuel was a great step forward.[46] Food is simply the fuel we throw into the furnace of our organism, and its organic importance can, therefore, be assessed in terms of calories. The guiding principles of that time, in connection with the understanding of life, were those of the conservation and degradation of energy. The first law of thermodynamics, that of the conservation of energy, was found to be applicable to both organisms and mechanical systems.[47]

The second law was a more complicated matter. This law expresses the tendency of nature toward disorder, the tendency to even out energy and, thus, to devalue it in isolated systems. If one were to put such a system in uniform conditions and leave it alone, then all phenomena occurring within it would come to an end. It would thus attain the unchanging state in which nothing would happen. This corresponds to a state of "thermodynamic equilibrium" or the condition of "maximum entropy."

As Planck noted, the irreversibility of the second law of thermodynamics upset the Laplacean ideal. It became apparent that natural open systems, characterized by irreversible thermodynamical processes, were the norm and that closed, mechanical, and reversible processes were the exception.[48] When applied to closed systems, the second law of thermodynamics is absolute, for all naturally occurring and artificial metabolic processes lead to a gradual destruction of organization, to chaos, and to complete disorder. This is the meaning of the law of increasing entropy. In concurrence, we shall interpret the second law as a tendency toward the destruction of organization, a process of decomplexification. Indeed, such an interpretation also constitutes its generalization. No other law occupies a position in science as singular as that of the second law of thermodynamics—the entropy law. It is the only natural law that recognizes that even the material universe is subject to an irreversible morphological change, to an evolutionary process.[49]

By the mid-nineteenth century the physical and the life sciences found themselves embroiled in a paradigmatic dispute regarding the nature of change.[50] Among the physical sciences, classical thermodynamics dealt with irrevocable processes in nature and admitted the irreversibility of time.[51] In the life sciences, Darwin's theories of speciation, based on irreversible processes of cumulative change in the world of the living, created a bona fide revolution distinct from Herbert Spencer's more general theory of evolution. Some idealist philosophers, including Henri Bergson and Herbert Spencer, defined life as "the struggle against entropy" and saw in this a contradiction between physics and biology and a reason for accepting a metaphysical philosophy of nature. The universe, according to Bergson, showed two tendencies: there is a "reality which is making itself in a reality which is unmaking itself." The general tendency to repetition and the dissipation of energy, discovered by thermodynamics, is the characteristic of "matter" to counter tendencies within it. As documented by Darwin and Wallace, among others, this is the tendency of life itself. The evolution of life is the result of the workings of a basic impulse Bergson termed the *élan vital*.[52]

The paradox of life remained. In organic systems not only does organization not decrease, it apparently increases.[53] Thus, one might say that the fundamental law of physics was a tendency toward disorder or an increase in entropy, while that of biology was a counterentropic tendency to increasing levels of organization. The evolutionary processes postulated in classical thermodynamics and Darwinian biology conflicted with mechanics, but they also conflicted with each other. The irrevocable processes discovered by classical thermodynamics and Darwinian biology were apparently irreconcilable. In classical thermodynamics, Eddington's "arrow of time" points downward, toward Boltzmann's state of *Warmtod*, to disorganization and randomness, while in Darwinian biology it apparently points upward, toward higher levels of complexity. Since Newtonian mechanics went largely unchallenged until the beginning of the present century, nineteenth-century natural science found itself confronted with the paradox of life and two arrows of time.

The discovery of the second law collapsed the physicist's ideal. But the conceptual significance of entropy extended far beyond mere heat engines, for it implied that Locke's, Condorcet's, and Montesquieu's cosmology of progress went completely counter to the real workings of the world.[54] While the entropy law states that all things in nature can be transformed only from a usable to an unusable state, Locke (and those who followed him) argued the opposite. Claiming that everything in nature was waste until man took hold of it and transformed it into usable forms, Locke, and later architects of sociomechanics, argued, in fact, that the world and history were progressing from chaos to order. All organic and inorganic activities on the earth—creative and destructive—are entropy-increasing processes.

The Search for the Natural Unity of Scientific Knowledge

In the nineteenth century it seems that all knowledge was based on mechanics—the elegant and harmonious system created by the genius of Isaac Newton, René Descartes, Francis Bacon, etc. The kinetic theory of gases and the theory of heat, it seemed at first, did not provide for any exceptions to the orderly system of mechanistic conceptions. What initially was ontologically presented as a chaos of molecules, was hypostatized as the epitome of order. Nineteenth-century physics brilliantly met all epistemical difficulties posed by the fundamentally stochastic nature of many phenomena including living systems—it simply ignored them and retreated farther into science's hard core.

In the late nineteenth century, this orderly picture collapsed. The well-defined boundaries among individual disciplines faded, and doubts appeared concerning many of the integrating ideas.[55] The crisis of physics, or more pointedly, a crisis of positive science, ensued. Edmund Husserl, in *The Crisis of European Sciences*, conjectured that:

> The European crisis has its roots in a misguided rationalism. But we must not take this to mean that rationality as such is evil or that it is of only subordinate significance for mankind's existence as a whole. Rationality, in that high and genuine sense of which alone we are speaking, the primordial Greek sense which in the classical period of Greek philosophy had become an ideal, still requires, to be sure, much clarification through self-reflection; but it is called in its mature form to guide [our] development. On the other hand we readily admit . . . that the stage of development of ratio represented by the rationalism of the Age of Enlightenment was a mistake, though certainly an understandable one.[56]

Rather than turn to a tortured analysis of misshapened Western rationality, we shall locate the "crisis" within a narrower framework and argue that it partially obtains from both the discovery of thermodynamics and the revision of the theory of matter according to particle physics. But it also led to neo-Kantian and phenomenological questioning of science's positivist epistemology. Moreover, it led to a number of attempts to resituate the hard core of the mechanical paradigm. The cause for the resulting chaos lay in the massive flows of new knowledge that assaulted the human mind from all directions. Sets of interacting relationships came to occupy the center of attention of such staggering complexity that, even armed with Newtonian mechanics, physicists were unable to understand an entity like an atom. Relativity took over in the field of physics, and, in microphysics, quantum mechanics appeared to offer answers.

The process of investigation in other sciences followed parallel pathways. Biology attempted to divest itself from its ad hoc life principle and tried to accommodate a more testable theory of life.[57] The laws of physics were found to be insufficient to explain the complexity and richness of interactions that take place in living organisms, and, thus, new principles had to be postulated—laws not of life forces but of integrated wholes. In view of parallel developments in physics, chemistry, biology, sociology, and economics, contemporary science became aware of "the science of organized complexity."[58] For a time the unified image of the world vanished and even ceased to concern scientists as disciplines were overwhelmed by the discoveries they were witnessing and by the specific obstacles that they confronted in their work. Social science, in particular, entrenched itself in its pursuit of facts. Facts, individual and isolated, rather than synthesizing theories, became the driving force of scientific research.

While the principles of thermodynamics presented a number of difficulties for biologists, the critical role of matter for dialectical materialist philosophers was compromised. Particular difficulty arose in connection with what came to be termed "the disappearance of matter."[59]

In an audacious effort to resuscitate mechanicalism's hard core, the crisis led to the adoption, perhaps first with Maxwell, of pure mathematical formalism. This prompted Hertz to write that Maxwell's theory consists merely of "Maxwell's equations.... There is no mechanical explanation, and there is no need of one." Hertz continued, "One cannot escape the feeling that these equations have an existence and an intelligence of their own, that they are wiser than we are, wiser even than their discoverers, that we get more out of them than was originally put there."[60]

> Just as Newton's laws of motion furnished scientists with the means for working with matter and force without explaining either, so Maxwell's equations have enabled scientists to accomplish wonders with electrical phenomena despite a woefully deficient understanding of their physical nature.[61]

In a similar fashion mathematized social science has been praised for purging devils, demons, and mystical forces by providing rational explanations of social phenomena. However, if understanding of social reality and the power to reason in real terms about a particular phenomenon are lacking, what is the nature of our grasp of reality? The amazing fact is that increasingly one of the central bodies of knowledge concerning the livelihood of man is almost entirely mathematical. Mathematical "laws" are the only means of probing, revealing, and mastering a class of phenomena in the real world.

Galileo had appealed to science to remove and discard all that was not quantifiable; yet there remained a material reality to his analysis. In probing the depths of matter, positivists moved one step beyond Galileo and sought a purely mathematically descriptive science. How similar was the pathway of economic analysis in replacing the substantive with merely tractable properties?

Consequently, we must now add that modern science is purging itself of the intuitive and real content, both of which appeal to the senses. In point of fact, it is increasingly engaged in a purely synthetic form of knowledge pertaining to ideal Platonic constructs, which are singularly mathematical in description. Many of the sciences have become rationalized fictions.[62]

These remarks serve to establish a contextual background and a glimpse of the philosophical dilemma central to that paradigmatic crisis addressed by a number of philosophers.[63] While the crisis prompted a trenchant neomechanicalism, it also led to discrete speculations on the role of energy in the dynamic of the livelihood of man.

The Energeticist School

It was in an unsettled political and philosophical climate that V.I. Lenin, both in seeking to interpret the philosophical meaning of the crisis of science, transmuted into a crisis of Marxism, and in criticizing those philosophers such as E. Mach and W. Ostwald, who either departed from dialectical materialism or casually neglected it, referred to the work of Abel Rey.[64] Lenin quoted Abel Rey at length.

> The criticisms of traditional mechanism made during the whole of the second half of the nineteenth century weakened the premise of the ontological reality of mechanism. On the basis of these criticisms a philosophical conception of physics was founded which became almost traditional in philosophy at the end of the nineteenth century. Science was nothing but a symbolic formula, a method of notation ... and since the methods of notation varied according to the schools, the conclusion was soon reached that only that was denoted which had been previously designed by man for notation. Science became a work of art for dilettantes, a work of art for utilitarians: views which could with legitimacy be generally interpreted as the negation of the possibility of science.... The collapse of traditional mechanism, or more precisely, the criticism to which it was subjected, led to the proposition that science itself had also collapsed. From the impossibility of adhering purely and simply to traditional mechanism it was inferred that science was impossible.[65]

Having presented Rey's analysis, Lenin notes that Rey classified the response to the crisis of physics in terms of three schools: the energeticist, the neomechanistic, and the critical.

It is to the energeticist school that we shall turn our attention, for it is from this school that there have gradually emerged a number of significant, albeit subterranean, developments in the history of economic thought. It may be forcefully argued that the paradigmatic crisis of mechanicalism was an important juncture for both economic thought and philosophy.[66] From its formative period at the turn of the century there began a critique of mechanicalism's hard core, which had come to form the center of conventional economic analysis. Interwoven with this critique there subsequently developed what has come to be known as a systems theoretical challenge to economic analysis. In the development of the systems theoretical paradigm the first step was taken in the direction of the exploration of the thermodynamic realities of the livelihood of man. Parenthetically, those who today are quick to embrace bioeconomics and ecological economics are, to a considerable extent, unwittingly reviving fragments of a lost paradigm.

Lenin referred at length to Rey and, in particular, to the energeticist school of the German chemist Wilhelm Ostwald and others, which: "[operates] with pure abstractions ... and seeks a purely abstract theory which will as far as possible eliminate the hypothesis of matter.... The notion of energy thus becomes the substructure of the new physics."[67] Lenin denunciated "energeticism," arguing after Boltzmann that motion cannot exist without matter. He rejected Ostwald's ontological proposition that energy rather than matter is the universal coordinate.[68]

It is to Wilhelm Ostwald's cosmological monism[69] that we shall briefly turn. From a 1895–96 edition of the journal *The Monist* we read that:

> Professor Wilhelm Ostwald, one of the most prominent chemists of Germany, and Professor at the University of Leipzig, delivered on September 20, 1895, ... a protest against the materialism of science.... [Ostwald claims that] there are processes which are not representable by mechanistic equations, and this much is certain that we must give up hope of interpreting the world as a mere play of atoms. Professor Ostwald proposes to replace mechanism by the energetic world-conception.... By reducing the laws of nature to analogous modes of an energy, [Ostwald] hopes to attain to a science that would be free from hypotheses. Professor Ostwald finds a substratum of energy redundant and believes that energy should, with the exception of time and space, be the sole magnitude for scientific equations.[70]

Ostwald, particularly in his *Energetische Grundlagen der Kulturwissenschaften*[71] (hereafter referred to as *Kulturwissenschaften*), attempted the task of building a bridge between the social and natural sciences using the concept of energy. It was his position that in physical, biological, and societal phenomena, the transformation of energy is invariably involved. The only thing that changes from one division to another is the way in which energy is transformed. Distinct from the conventions of his day, Ostwald considered that in society or culture, "crude" energy (*Rohenergie*) is transformed into useful energy (*Nutzenergie*). The greater the coefficient of useful energy obtained in such a transformation, the greater is the progress of culture.[72] *Kulturwissenschaften* was a grand synthesizing effort whose objective was the unity of scientific knowledge. However, Ostwald's was a one-eyed natural-scientific reductionism—a monism. Nonetheless, his ideas had a powerful influence on later sociothermodynamic analysis and the thermodynamic dimensions of the autopoiesis of social systems.

Even though he was an early contributor to the understanding of the role of energy in culture, Ostwald was, in fact, not the first. Evidence of the nineteenth century's mechanistic attitude to life and society is conspicuous in the "social physics" of H.C. Carey's 1858 publication *Principles of Social Science*, no less than it is in W.S. Jevons's *The Coal Question*.

In the first volume of Carey's *Principles* can be found the declaration: "The laws which govern matter in all its forms, whether that of coal, clay, iron, pebble stones, trees, oxen, horses, or men are the same."[73] Consistent with this mechanistic attitude is his theory that "man is the molecule of society"; and that association is only a variety of "the great law of molecular gravitation [by which] man tends of necessity to gravitate towards his fellow man . . . that gravitation is [in human societies], as everywhere else in the material world, in the direct ratio of the mass (of cities), and in the inverse ratio of the distance."[74]

On the basis of this "gravitational" proposition, Carey wrote that commerce is "a change of matter in place," whereas "production, mechanical and chemical, changes in the form of matter." Carey espoused mechanicalism as the template for economic analysis and sought to introduce the first principle of thermodynamics into that analysis.

> From the indestructibility of matter, as the physical premise, it obviously follows that what we term production and consumption are mere transformations of substance. [The] phenomenon is an alteration of matter in its quality, merely, without increase or diminution of its quantity. In every transition of matter from one condition to another, force is employed, or, as we say, consumed, and force is also evolved or produced. . . . Economic value is nothing but a kind of inertia; utility, an equivalent of mechanical momentum.[75]

Coauthor of the neoclassical school of economics, W.S. Jevons took as his point of departure Adam Smith's comment: "The progressive state is in reality the cheerful and the hearty state to all the different orders of society; the stationary state is dull; the declining melancholy." Jevons proceeded to hypothesize that the development of England, as a "progressive state," was principally a consequence of its originally ample coal basins in conjunction with the institution of free trade. Indeed, he speculated that, "[In] our Victorian age may we not owe indirectly to the lavish expenditure of our material energy far more than we readily conceive?"[76]

Moreover, in Jevons's analysis, Smith's dismal "stationary state" would ensue when England's coal deposits were exhausted, at which time free trade would work to the disadvantage of England.[77]

> At a future time . . . we shall have influences acting against us which are now acting strongly for us. We may even then retain no inconsiderable share of the world's trade, but it is impossible that we should go on expanding as we are now doing. Our motion must be reduced to rest, and it is to this change my attention is directed.[78]

Jevons's musings were in keeping with an emergent theme.

Upon reviewing Babbage's *On the Economy of the Machinery and Manufactures* in 1835, J.R. McCulloch had pointed to the importance for the success of Britain's manufacturing industry to its ample deposits of coal and raw materials for iron, brass, and steel.[79] Nassau Senior had earlier borrowed from Babbage a physical theory of production based on an "engineering perspective." Though Senior's analysis included a physical classification of production inputs (land and other agents provided by nature, raw materials, labor skills, and instruments of labor), it was seriously faulted insofar as the appropriate concept for treating energy was absent. Indeed Senior, like McCulloch, was puzzled about the classification of coal (energy), books, and seeds (information). Consequently, he assigned coal to the category "instruments of production," since it was not materially embodied in the final product like materials.[80]

Senior's physical approach to production was partially incorporated in J.S. Mill's theory of production.[81] However, Mill discounted the import of both Senior's physical classification and use of the conservation principle in his treatment of manufacturing. In response to Senior's criticism of the need to distinguish coal and raw materials embodied in physical output, Mill diffidently replied that although it was obviously correct to classify coal with materials, he wanted to "avoid a multiplication of classes [which were of] no scientific importance."[82]

Jevons, however, was of another opinion. Following the German chemist and agriculturalist Justus von Liebig's aphorism that "Civilization is the economy of power," Jevons wrote: "[Our] power is coal. It is the very economy of the use of coal that makes our industry what it is; and the more we render it efficient and economical, the more will our industry thrive, and our works of civilization grow."[83]

Generally informed of the considerable advances in the mechanical theory of the universe,[84] Jevons, like Carey, was apparently aware of the significance of the first law of thermodynamics—the conservation law—for the economy of man.

> These views lead us at once to look upon all machines and processes of manufacture as but the more or less efficient modes of transmuting and using energy. If we have energy in any one of its forms, as heat, light, chemical change, or mechanical motion, we can turn it, or may fairly hope to turn it, into any other of its forms.[85]

The first law became a maxim for Jevons, such that he spoke, for instance, of "coal-driven labor."[86]

These provocative comments notwithstanding, it is in his chapter on exports and imports that Jevons firmly establishes his thesis that coal is the principal material (energy) foundation for the efficiency of English manufactures. He wrote that whereas England had previously provided itself with its own raw materials, it now imports them. "The reversal of every other branch of trade is the work of coal, and the coal-trade cannot reverse itself."[87] In the context of free trade, Jevons wrote:

> One most peculiar advantage is the power which coal, skillfully used, places at our disposal. It is our last great resource—the one kind of wealth by the sufficient employment of which we might reverse every other trade, draw every other material from abroad until the kingdom was one immense Manchester.... But take away that resource, and our expectations from free trade must be a very minor character.[88]

In the conclusions to his substantive opus, *The Coal Question*, Jevons gives expression to what recent analysts have identified as an ecological analogy in economic thought. "My work is completed in pointing out the necessary results of our present rapid multiplication when brought into comparison with a fixed amount of material resources.... Are we wise in allowing the commerce of this country to rise beyond the point at which it can be long maintained?"[89]

Airing a societal, and decidedly substantive perspective, which was subsequently to vanish from his thought, Jevons went so far as to caution the further institutionalization of the price-making market.

> To say the simple truth, will it not appear evident, soon after the final adoption of free-trade principles, that our own resources are just those to which such principles ought to be applied last and most cautiously? To part in commerce with the surplus yearly interest of the soil may be unquestioned gain; but to disperse so lavishly the cream of our mineral wealth is to be spendthrifts of our capital—to part with that which can never be reproduced.
>
> After all, commerce is but the means to an end—the diffusion of civilization and wealth. To allow commerce to expand until the source of civilization is exhausted is like killing the goose to get the golden egg. Is the immediate creation of the greatest possible quantity of material wealth to be our only purpose? Have we not hereditary possessions in our just laws, our free and nobly developed constitutions, our rich literature and philosophy, incomparably above material wealth, and which we are beyond all things bound to maintain, improve, and hand down in safety to posterity? And do we accomplish this duty in encouraging a growth of industry which must prove unstable, and perhaps involve all things in its fall?[90]

While Jevons speculated on the fundamental instability of that economic system that seeks to produce and distribute the wealth of society in strict observance of market system coordinates, he was also alarmed by the possible long-term resource exhaustion that attaches thereto.

> If we lavishly and boldly push forward in the creation of our riches, both material and intellectual, it is hard to over-estimate the pitch of beneficial influence to which we may attain in the present. But the maintenance of such a position is physically impossible. We have to make the momentous choice between brief but true greatness and longer continued mediocrity.[91]

However interesting the contributions of Carey and Jevons, it was Wilhelm Ostwald's concept of "social energetics" that served as a stimulating point of departure for Russian Critical Marxism and for a number of developments that have reemerged in recent years.[92]

Ostwald's Social Energetics

While Jevons speculated upon the political economy of Great Britain's fossil fuel resources, Ostwald explored a monist synthesis marked by a functionalist perspective.

Methodological atomist, Ostwald's general proposition was that any event or social or historical phenomenon is nothing but a transformation of energy. He then asserts that society is merely an arrangement for the better utilization and more perfect transformation of *Rohenergie* into *Nutzenergie*. Moreover, he maintains that it is only in this connection that society in serving this purpose is justified. The instrumental role of the state, according to Ostwald, is to facilitate the better utilization of energy. Furthermore, when the state or society instead hinders this purpose, and lacks justification, it forfeits it purpose for existence. He held similar radical functionalist views on the role of wealth and money. Insofar as wealth and money are useful derivative representations of energy, their accumulation and circulation are purposeful. When their functionality is impaired, their reason for being is lost as well.

In a contemporary critique of Ostwald's thesis, John Grier Hisben wrote:

> The theory of "Energetics" so called, first propounded by Rankine some fifty years ago, has been revived recently in Germany. . . . [There] is no name more eminent, or one which is more closely identified with this novel movement of thought than that of Ostwald. In his lectures [he disclosed that] the mysteries of science and philosophy [are] made manifest in the universal solvent—the concept of energy.
>
> His may be styled a philosophy without hypothesis, for such is his claim, that the system which he offers is founded solely upon observed facts, and that these facts of themselves form a compact system which needs no metaphysical speculation whatever in its construction. He insists, moreover, that it is the physicist, and he alone, who is entitled to an opinion in matters philosophical; for he only is in possession of the facts, and facts alone have philosophical significance.[93]

Later in Hisben's critique he noted that Ostwald insists that:

> When reduced to their lowest terms, the traditional concepts of metaphysics, that of substance and that of causation, may be more adequately and precisely expressed as varied manifestations of the fundamental concept of energy. The concept of matter from this point of view becomes superfluous, for energy needs no substratum or vehicle to render it any more elemental in character, or

any more intelligible. Matter, consequently, gives place to energy, and with the passing of matter that most perplexing of all philosophical difficulties, the transition from physical to psychical phenomena, becomes immensely simplified.[94]

Hisben continues: "As Ostwald puts it, the concept of energy seems to be far more *geistig* than that of matter. It is possible to conceive more readily of psychical energy as a kind of transformed physical energy, than to conceive of the essential coordination of matter and of mind."[95] Here, then, is the crux of the philosophical difficulty that was to plague the dialectical materialist perspective, in particular, that embraced by Lenin. These arguments are more than mere historical curiosities; elements of Ostwaldian "social energetics" have in recent years been reasserted by interdisciplinary analysts.[96]

Frederick Copleston notes that, "For Ostwald energy was the one basic reality which, in a process of transformations, assumed various forms, including psychic energy, both unconscious and conscious."[97] Ostwald wrote of "energetics" or the thermodynamical process that:

> You cannot run the mill with the water that's gone by. . . . You have to have a fall of temperature to run any kind of heat engine. Every machine, every chemical and physical process, every living being, is leaking energy all the time, that is, transforming it into unavailable forms. That is the way we get our living.[98]

Indeed, consistent with this perspective, Lotka and Soddy later suggested that the livelihood of man may be considered as a heat engine in which heat is converted into motion only at the price of some irreversible waste and dissipation.[99]

Reflecting a position later present in the work of some systems ecologists, Ostwald wrote:

> To catch what we can of this stream of energy and to utilize it to the best advantage, is the aim of human endeavor, the measure of civilization. This is the function of the will of the individual and the duty of the leaders of men. Wealth in all ages consists essentially of the command of energy, whether counted by slave power, horse power, or kilowatt hours.[100]

Further elaborating the proposition that first appeared in *Kulturwissenschaft*, Ostwald, in "Natural Philosophy," wrote:[101]

> The objective characteristic of progress consists in improved methods for seizing and utilizing the raw energies of nature for human purpose. Thus it was a cultural act when a primitive man discovered that he could extend the radius of his muscle energy by taking a pole in his hand, and it was another cultural act when he could send his muscle energy a distance of many meters to the desired

point. The effect of the knife, the spear, the arrow, and of all other primitive implements can be called in each case a purposive transformation of energy. And at the other end of the scale of civilization the most abstract scientific discovery, by reason of its generalization and simplification, signifies a corresponding economy of energy for all the coming generations that may have anything to do with matter.[102]

In an indiscriminate reductionist generalization, Ostwald's notion of progress embraces the entire sweep of civilizational endeavor in his concept of economizing energy.

If we consider further that, according to the second principle, the free energy accessible to us can only decrease, but not increase, while the number of men whose existence depends directly on the consumption of a due amount of free energy is constantly on the increase, then we at once see the objective necessity of the development of civilization in that sense. His foresight puts man in a position to act culturally. But if we examine our present social order from this point of view, we realize with horror how barbarous it still is. Not only do murder and war destroy cultural values without substituting others in their place, not only do countless conflicts which take place between different nations and political organizations act anti-culturally, but so do also the conflicts between the various social classes of one nation, for they destroy quantities of free energy which are thus withdrawn from the total of real cultural values.[103]

Ostwald writes that the law of conservation of energy (the first law of thermodynamics) must serve as the foundation of all the natural sciences. In defending this position he notes that "the idea of matter as the real substratum of all natural phenomena and as endowed with weight and mass, has arisen from the paramount influence of Newton's theory of gravitation."[104] Now, however, it is necessary, according to Ostwald, to revise our knowledge in accordance with "modern energetics." His concept of energetics includes not only the first but also the second law of thermodynamics. He writes that:

[While] the first law of energetics ... under the conservation of its numerical value yields an equation for every case where one energy becomes transformed into another, the second principle which governs the relations of intensity of energy, answers the question whether and when a transformation of existing energies would take place. [Moreover,] every transformation of energy ... presupposes some difference of intensity. On the other hand, since everything that happens may be characterized as a transformation of energy of some kind or other, the presence of difference in intensity is the general assumption of each occurrence. These considerations are collected together as a whole in the second principle of energetics, of which the part relating to heat was discovered by Sadi Carnot as early as 1827. [In] order for something to happen there must be no compensated differences of intensity, and the occurrence will be in proportion to these differences.[105]

Insisting that energetics disposes of idealist materialism, for Ostwald energy is the sole universal generalization. "All phenomena," he wrote, "are reduced to properties and relations of energy, and especially matter; insofar as such a concept would at all prove useful, it is to be defined in terms of energetics."[106]

In order to drive the point home that all phenomena are subject to analysis in energetic terms, in *Kulturwissenschaft* Ostwald meditated on man's technological development. Reflecting upon what Alfred Lotka later referred to as man's exosomatic development, Ostwald analyzed the development of technologies in terms of energetics. Disregarding the institutional contexts or the political finalization of technology, he asserted that every tool is a "transformer of energy" whether it is animated by "physiological" or "inorganic" energies.[107] Thus, every tool is a piece of "capital" in the sense that it is a transformer of energy. His analysis speculated that physical capital represented an "accumulation of provisions for the times when they will not be directly procurable. [This] results, as is well known, in the foundation of capital."[108] Moreover, emphasizing merely organic needs, Ostwald formulated an energy theory of value-in-use and wrote:

> Value in general rests upon the transformation of energy. One and the same amount of energy measured numerically is of course not indifferent even for events of nature which do not permit valuation. On the contrary a given amount of energy is the more convertible the greater the differences of intensity with which it is affected with relation to its environment. The valuation of energy for man's purpose is determined in a similar, although somewhat more complicated way, by differences of intensity and the coefficients of transformation dependent on them. An amount of energy is the more valuable, the more completely it may be transformed for man's purposes. Thus a piece of coal and a piece of roasted meat may contain an equal amount of chemical energy while both have a very different value with regard to human purposes. This is because man cannot utilize by means of his digestive apparatus the chemical energy of coal, but can that of meat.[109]

Ostwald formulated his system of ethics on the basis of the "energy imperative."[110] His energy imperative gave expression to a concept of "efficiency," which he expressed as the ratio of work to means, of accomplishment to opportunity, and which can be made the measure of a man as well as a machine, since Ostwald includes all thoughts and feelings as forms of energy.[111] Kant's categorical ethical imperative, "Act that your conduct may be taken as a universal law," is, in Ostwald's opinion, neither as comprehensive nor as definite as the energy imperative, which though it includes ethical conduct, is not confined to it. According to Slosson's early reading of Ostwald:

> We call one automobile "good" and another "bad" if the former will carry us twice as far as the latter on the same amount of gasoline consumed. A "good" friend is one who helps us in our endeavors through judicious advice and without annoyance, while a "poor" friend only multiplies our difficulties; here

again goodness and badness are determined by the ratio of the total energy employed and the results obtained. It is this second principle of thermodynamics, the law of degradation and dissipation of energy, that prevents us from undoing the past, that gives significance to such phrases as "time flies" and "the world moves."[112]

The second law of thermodynamics, in Ostwald's analysis, is therefore of greater importance to philosophy and sociology than the first, the law of conservation and transmutation of energy. Ostwald's recognition of its significance gives to one-eyed functionalism a character decidedly different from the mechanicalism of the earlier part of the nineteenth century.[113]

Slosson notes that in contrast to Spencer's fundamental and paradoxical theory that evolution is a progress from homogeneity to heterogeneity—a concept grounded in the first principle of thermodynamics—of matter and energy, Ostwald's conception begins from the second law. In connection with the celebrated second law, Slosson writes:

> While we are sure [that statements of science about the general validity of this law] as applied to the physical world [hold], its application to human development may be doubted. It seems to me to hold good in this case also if it is applied with proper caution. The difficulty lies in the circumstance that we have no exact objective means of measuring homogeneity and heterogeneity in human affairs, and we can therefore not study any given system closely enough to draw a quantitative conclusion.[114]

To a certain extent Ostwald's "social energetics" obtained from his functionalist generalization of the role of the entropy law in society. It was a formulation that was extended surreptitiously into an agency theory of history. He asserted that humankind is in a state of development in which progress depends much less on the leadership of a few distinguished individuals than on a laboring collective. But "the *Actual*, that is, what acts on us, is energy alone."[115] Validation of this proposition was allegedly to be found in the proposition that great scientific discoveries were made simultaneously by independent investigators. For Ostwald this was an indication that different societies were evolving the requisite conditions for such discoveries. On the basis of these observations Ostwald came to the conclusion that the convergence of society demands that "mankind must strive for a thorough equalization in the conditions of existence of all men."[116] He went on to write that:

> It seems pretty certain that [an] increase of culture tends to diminish the differences between men. It equalizes not only the general standard of living, but attenuates also even the natural differences of sex and age. From this point of view I should look upon the accumulation of enormous wealth in the hands of a single man as indicating an imperfect state of culture.
>
> The property which has been described as an irresistible tendency toward

diffusion may also be observed in certain cases in man. In conscious beings such natural tendencies are accompanied by a certain feeling which we call will, and we are happy when we are allowed to act according to these tendencies or according to our will.[117]

Ostwald developed the view that human history was intimately linked to the growth in the availability of energy and the improvement in the efficiency with which it could be transformed. In some respects these views were not significantly different from some of his contemporaries.

Such was the ferment of the period that social energetics exercised Max Weber to write a review of Ostwald's *Energetic Foundations of the Science of Culture*.[118] One of Weber's first points was that Ostwald had excluded the material world. Thus, Weber anticipated later strictures against "energetic dogma." Ostwald defined cultural and civilizational advance as an increase in the availability of energy and the substitution of human energy by alternative forms. He also defined cultural progress in terms of increasing thermodynamic efficiency in energy use. Ostwald's point was that a greater availability of energy and a concomitant decrease in the share of human energy were signs of cultural progress.[119] On this issue, Weber cleverly pointed out that, in terms of calories expended, it was cheaper to weave a piece of cloth by hand than mechanically. Nevertheless, mechanical weaving was ostensibly a sign of cultural progress.

Weber took Ostwald to task in connection with his Comtean hierarchy of sciences. Ostwald had argued that "general" sciences occupied the lower steps of the "pyramid" of sciences, and these were to form the foundation for the less general sciences, those that occupied the higher steps. Weber warmed to his favorite topic, arguing that "basic" or "fundamental" concepts of general sciences played no part in economic or cultural theory. It was irrelevant to economics, he insisted, whether astronomy adopted the Copernican or the Ptolemaic system. Nor was the validity of economic theory, as a set of ideal-typical, hypothetical, theoretical propositions, dependent on the findings of the physics of energetics. The proposition that the eternal truths of economic theory could be sustained even if the law of conservation of energy was impugned was a decidedly curious feature in Weber's intellectuality,[120] for it represents a denial of the sociology of science, in particular the flagrantly emulative behavior that has characterized economic thought since its inception. Moreover, at a paradigmatic level of analysis, Weber's remarks on the relevance of Ostwald's central propositions are even less than germane. In the case of political economy, it was influenced both at the methodological and philosophical levels by the mechanical paradigm.

In the closing years of the nineteenth century and in the early twentieth century, Ostwald sparked a broad interest in energetics and "psychic energy." This encouraged L. Winiarsky's idiosyncratic attempt to render socialism as a natural science. Consistent with the thermodynamic understanding, Winiarsky wrote that energy has various forms and may be transformed from one to another, that is from potential to kinetic, and vice versa.[121] From this position, and while alluding to trophism, he conjectured that life itself is but a specific form of psychico-chemical energy and that all organisms, especially the human organism, are an embodiment of energy and the mechanisms for its transformation. From the second law of thermodynamics, he ventured that psychosocial phenomena proceed in accordance with the energy gradient, ceasing when the gradient is dissipated. From Sorokin's analysis of Winiarsky, we learn that it is essentially the difference in energy intensity between individuals and communities that accounts for the dramaturgy of human history.[122]

Proposing a kind of "energy-stages theory of development," Winiarsky remarked that

> Even in a primitive group, order, power, law and social control spontaneously appear; simply because the energy arising from its inequalities passes in the form of domination from a higher to a lower point, but never inversely. Since the radiation of energy proceeds in this way, there is a tendency toward the equalization of differing intensities; and this goes on until an equilibrium is reached in which there are no such differences; whereupon, according to the law of thermodynamics, all transformation stops.[123]

With Boltzmann's theory of *Warmtod* as a metaphor, Winiarsky pessimistically concluded that insofar as the universe is driven to a thermodynamic equilibrium, so shall the history of mankind be driven.

Just as Ostwald formulated a theory of money on the basis of energy, so Winiarsky developed a measure of economic energy.

> Biological energy is the central motor of social phenomena. Passing through a series of transformations in the forms of political, juridical, moral, esthetical, intellectual and religious phenomena; it eventually arrives at economic energy, which, being measured through money (gold), serves for the measurement of biological energy itself. Economic energy plays here the same role as heat energy in mechanics.... Gold is a general social equivalent, an incarnation and personification of bio-social energy. At the same time it is a general transformer: the greater part of material and immaterial values may be produced through corresponding money expenditures.[124]

Furthermore, he held that exploitation, oppression, class divisions, and such phenomena would disappear in accordance with the laws of thermodynamics, in such a manner that the outcome would be "social entropy," an equality among all people.[125]

7

Narodnik and Nihilist Dimensions: A Critical Kernel in Russian Marxism

Introductory Remarks

While it is possible, of course, to draw into the light the shadowy history of social energetic thought, the foregoing material is a sufficiently esoteric introduction to a no less concealed, but more palpable intellectual heritage that attaches to a systems theoretical critique of political economy. We will return in a later chapter to social energetics, for it was integral to the maturing of Russian Critical Marxism. In the following we shall turn to a more conventional appreciation of the roots of Russian Critical Marxism.

It should be said that in the further development of European socioeconomic thought, the battle of methods—*Methodenstriet*—marked a phase in the fragmentation of the paradigmatic hard core. This challenge, on the one hand, gave rise to the esoteric, descriptive formalism of the marginalists, and it signified a detour from substantive categories of economic analysis. On the other hand, it marked the beginning of a second, divergent, yet curiously buoyant, theme in political economy—holism. In this connection, and of particular importance, was the catalytic role of social energetics, for despite its hermetic theoretical constructs, it had an instrumental role in the synthesis of dialectical materialism and holism that was pivotal to a critique of political economy. This is not to say that reconstructed holism did not resonate with broader intellectual themes. It most certainly did, and our archaeological dig would be seriously remiss if we failed to trace these sometimes dissonant harmonies. The dissonant though luxuriant intellectuality we shall turn to is that situated in late-nineteenth-century Russia, for it is in the reckless cadence of its history that a paradigmatic critique of political economy matured and withered.

Our effort is not so ambitious as to essay a comprehensive reading of the syncretically interwoven harmonies and disharmonies of Russian philosophy.

Ours is a less ambitious project: to provide an unavoidably prejudiced sketch of Narodnik influences and nihilist strains on Russian Critical Marxism.

Narodnik Influences

In a curious turn, the Russia of today is captured by events and questions that resemble those of an earlier period. It seeks to answer once again the question posed by its double-eagle emblem: "Ought Russia to look West or East?" Today socioeconomic policy is engaged in a tumultuous search for an appropriate model of development. Should it be of an Anglo-American type, an East Asian type, or some other? Much of Russian nineteenth-century thought was occupied with questions of world outlook. Should it adopt a Westernizing or Slavophile mode? Must Russia follow Peter's path, or turn to a reconstructed Muscovite Russia? While the confused currents of that earlier debate may be historically distinct, they are not without significance for today's drama.

Chaadaev came out decidedly as a Westernizer, and his Westernism was a cry of patriotic anguish. He was the typical nineteenth-century Russian of the cultured upper class. Russian history presented itself to him as devoid of meaning and with no connecting links, belonging neither to the East nor to the West. Chaadaev considered Russia a lesson and a warning to other peoples. He could not reconcile himself to the fact that he was condemned to live in an uncultured society (today some Russians speak of an "uncivilized" society) in a despotic state that gripped an unenlightened people as in a vise. He spoke of the latent powers of the Russian people, powers that had not yet revealed themselves. For Chaadaev the Russian people had created nothing great in history, had fulfilled no great mission. But the Russians lack of accomplishments offered a fertile ground for their future. There was thus a great hope and faith in the future of the Russian people, a people who would be called to realize a great mission. Precisely on that latent power and backwardness, the Russian people of the nineteenth century would be called upon to solve problems that have been implacable for the West, burdened as it is by its own history. A "historylessness" Russia had the dubious advantage of backwardness.

In *A Madman's Apology*, Chaadaev expressed thoughts about Russian messianism. Judgment upon the past was one thing, hope for the future was quite another. Precisely in the strength of the latent power lying in Russia's immense untapped forces, the Russian people were called to articulate their own original word to the world, to fulfill their great mission. Colleague of Alexander Hertzen, the poet and thinker V.S. Pecherin, was prompted to write: "How sweet to hate one's own native land and eagerly to await its annihilation."[1] But these words of despair cloaked a love of Russia.

The basic Western influence, by which Russian nineteenth-century thought and culture were molded to a remarkable degree, was that of German romanticism and idealism. This did not mean a slavish imitation, but German thought was taken actively and reworked into a Russian type of thought. Thus, at the beginning of nineteenth century, Hegel was "Russified." Like the German romantics, Russian thought strove after wholeness and did so more consistently and radically than the romantics, who themselves lost wholeness. The wholeness of the Orthodox Christian East was set in opposition to the rationalist fragmentariness of the West. This became a fundamental theme rooted in the depths of Russian philosophy. Russian Marxist atheists assert wholeness and totality no less ardently than the Orthodox Slavophiles. The Russian Westernizers were influenced by Hegelianism, which to them was simply a totalitizing system of thought and life embracing absolutely everything. Hegel's doctrine of the rationality of actual fact, which in Hegel himself was entirely a matter of logic and meant the recognition of the fact that only the rational was authentically real, was in Russia a matter of the most painful experience.

The Russian Hegelians at first appreciated Hegel in a conservative way and interpreted his thought of the rationality of "actuality" to mean that one must reconcile oneself to one's actual environment and recognize reason in it. Russian romantic idealists of the 1840s escaped from actual social conditions into the world of thought, imagination, literature, and the reflected world of their ideas. But the identity of life and idea consists not only in the carrying over of life into idea but also in the carrying over of idea into life. A merely ideational relation to life makes actual conflict metaphysical. But in some this took the form of a crisis in Hegelianism. The left revolutionary Russian thought rejected Hegelianism until its Marxist praxiological reconstruction.

The Russian search for an integral outlook that would give an answer to all the questions of life united theoretical and practical reason and gave a philosophical basis to the social ideal. Integrated truth is both truth in the abstract and that truth that finds expression in justice. The unifying idea of wholeness was to be found in Marxism-Leninism, but also, as we shall see, in Russian Critical Marxism.

It was the Slavophiles who established the mission of Russia as distinct from that of the Cultural West.[2] The Slavophiles postulated that the Russian people had no gift for politics. They had a religious and spiritual vocation and merely wished to be free from political affairs in order to realize that vocation. Ostensibly the Slavophiles were therein expressing one of the poles of Russian consciousness, a characteristic trait of the intelligentsia of the nineteenth century and of much of Russian literature. The founders of that nationalism that was so characteristic of Russian nineteenth-century thought, the Slavophiles believed in the people, in justice that belonged to the people, and for them the people came first. The Slavophiles, as with the Narodniks, were ardent defenders of the commune, which they regarded as organic and as the original Russian structure of economic life among the peasantry. They were decided opponents of the ideas of Roman law on property. They did not regard property as sacred and absolute, rather "owners" of property were regarded as stewards of a common heritage.

They repudiated Western, bourgeois, capitalist civilization. And if they thought that the West was decaying, it was because it had taken the path of bourgeois civilization wherein the unity of life had been split asunder.

The meditative among the Slavophiles did not live in the present, which was abhorrent to them; they lived in the future, or in the past. Theirs was the dream of an ideal Russia before Peter's time whereas others, the Westernizers, dreamed of an ideal West. The more interesting type of Westernizer was he who made a Russian reconstruction of Western ideas. This theme was, in particular, characteristic of "Russified" French social thought. In Russia, if Hegel was taken up in a totalizing and maximalist fashion, so also were Saint-Simon, Comte, and Fourier. Postulated were three developmental stages for the realization of socialism: the stage of utopian socialism, Narodnik socialism, and Scientific or Marxian socialism.

Narodnik belief was weighted in favor of "the people," not society as a political entity, nor with the Hegelian state. There were two other principles that further underlay the foundation of Narodnik thought or socialism—the principle of the supremacy of human personality and the principle of the communal socialist organization of human society. Personality and people—these were two fundamental ideas of Russian Narodnik socialism expressed in the thought of Alexander Ivanovich Hertzen.[3]

Hertzen's fate is a subject of immense interest in the history of Russian cultural consciousness, the Russian national idea, and the Russian social idea. A Westernizer who passed through Hegelian and Feuerbachian thought, Hertzen was one among those Russian Westernizers who dreamed passionately of the West and idealized it. He came upon it in the atmosphere of the Revolution of 1848, and at first he was attracted by it and founded great hopes upon it. However, it was his fate to live through the bitter disillusionments that followed the Revolution of 1848 and among the Cultural West more generally. His passion for the West was typically Russian, as was his disillusionment with the Cultural West. Hertzen was dazzled, repulsed, and resentful of the pettiness of the West. Certainly this paradoxical humor is not bound to the Russia of Hertzen's time but is present today as well.

Hertzen, as distinct from other representatives of the political left, did not profess an optimistic theory of progress. On the contrary, he defended a pessimistic philosophy of history. He did not believe in the rationality and goodness of a historical process that moved toward the realization of higher good. He recognized the higher value of human personality, although it is crushed by the progress of history. Hertzen saw a greater expression of the principle of personality than in the European who had become a bourgeois. Among the Slavophiles, the principle of personality was combined with the principle of community. Thus, we must understand that the concept of personality is not a atomistic one; it refers not to a self-sufficient person as ideal, nor to an individualism that undermines the solidarity of community, but to one that affirms communal solidarity.

Living outside the grip of Russia itself, Hertzen became the founder of Narodnik socialism, which reached its highest development in the 1870s. To be a socialist in those days meant to demand economic reforms, to despise liberalism, and to regard the development of capitalist industry as the chief evil, because it destroyed the conception of the peasant/communal order of life as the highest type of collectivity.

He laid the foundation of the original Russian individualistic socialism, which was to be represented in the 1870s by N. Mikhailovsky. Socialist individualism is opposed to bourgeois individualism. The man of the Cultural West had a pettiness of mind and could not save the West from it. Hertzen believed that socialism could be brought into being more readily and with better results in Russia than in the West, and that it would not be bourgeois. Like many Narodniks he was opposed to a political revolution that might drive Russia into the bourgeois path of development.

It was precisely in Russia, in the Russian people, that there lay hidden the latent power to fashion a new and a better life, not petty and not bourgeois. Hertzen saw these potentialities in Russia, in the peasant commune. In the Russian peasant world was allegedly hidden the fertile possibility of bringing together the principle of personality and the principle of community and social life. Belief in the Russian people, in truth latent in the peasant, was for him the final anchor of salvation. Among the people was preserved the secret of the true life, a secret concealed from the governing cultured classes. Hertzen became one of the originators of Russian *narodnichestvo*.

Hertzen and the Narodnik socialists believed in a special path of progress for Russia, in its vocation to realize social justice better and earlier than the West. They believed it was possible for Russia to escape the horrors of capitalism. The Westernizing liberals thought that Russia must pass along the same road as Western Europe—an argument articulated in the centers of power today. The Narodniks repudiated politics; they thought that politics would push Russia along the trite Western road of development; they recognized the primacy of the social over the political. The subsequent atheism of the Russian revolutionary socialist and anarchist tendencies was Russian religiousness turned inside out, a Russian apocalyptic.

Once more pressed from the lips of the stoics and echoing in the public forum, the Greek meaning of the Apocalypse is a constant in that aspect of Russian culture that speaks to a world born anew. Today the birth pangs are not of socialism but of a questionable liberalism and nationalism. It is most important to note that the liberal tradition has always been weak in Russia and that we have never had a liberalism with moral authority or that gave any ethical inspiration. The authors of the liberal reforms have, of course, some significance, but their liberalism was exclusively practical and businesslike; they produced no theory whatever, a thing allegedly craved by the Russian intelligentsia.

Consciousness of the socioethical gulf between the intelligentsia and the people was fundamental to the meaning of the *narodnichestvo*. The Narodniks of the intelligentsia did not feel themselves an organic part of the people/community; the people were to be found outside them. The intelligentsia was not a function of the life of the people, it was broken off from that life and felt guilty in relation to the people. "The people" must be understood to mean the simple laboring people, and especially the peasantry.

This deep sense of socioethical-based guilt played an immense part in the social psychology of *narodnichestvo*. The intelligentsia was always in debt to the people and had to pay that debt. The culture that the intelligentsia accepted was built up at the people's expense, with their labor and social solidarity, and this laid a heavy responsibility on those who shared in that culture. The mystic/religious Narodniks (Dostoevsky and Tolstoy) believed that in the people a mystic/religious truth was hidden; those who were not mystic/religious and often antireligious (Hertzen and Bakunin) believed that in the people was hidden a social truth. The true man, the man who is not crushed by the sense of guilt, by the sin of exploiting his brothers, is the laboring man, the man of the people. Culture for its own sake is not a justification of life but is bought at the too heavy price of the enslavement of the people. *Narodnichestvo* was not infrequently hostile to culture, and in any case rebelled against too great a respect for it. *Narodnichestvo* of the socialist type had a much greater significance, for it saw the guilt of the cultured classes in this, that the whole of their life and culture was founded upon exploitation of the people's labor.

The Russian genius was keenly aware of its loneliness, its separation from the soil, its guilt, and cast itself down in order to stoop into contact with the soil and the people. Such was the sentiment of Tolstoy and Dostoevsky. What a difference there is in this respect between Tolstoy and Nietzsche! The general outlook on life of *narodnichestvo* had a flavor of the soil—it depended on the land. The Narodnik of the intelligentsia, on the other hand, had broken away from the land and desired to return to it. The Narodnik view of things held good only in a peasant, agricultural country. The general outlook of the people was collective, not individual. The people were a collective whole and with it the intelligentsia desired to unite, entering into its life.

Russian *narodnichestvo* was a product of the consciousness of the intelligentsia that maintained that their life could only find its justification in socioethical terms. To justify life solely in individualistic terms was an absurd product of the inorganic character of the Westernizing colonizing of Russian life. To the Russian mind what was important was not one's attitude toward the principle of property —an alien concept in the Russian mind—but one's attitude toward the integrity of community and the socioethical imperative that informed it.

In his search for an integral outlook, his quest for an integrated truth, the Narodnik sociologist N. Mikhailovsky distinguished the work of conscience from the work of honor. The work of conscience goes on among the privileged classes, the nobility, while the work of honor, the demand for the recognition of human worth, goes on among the people, the lower, the oppressed classes. The upper-class Narodniks were moved especially by motives of conscience, the lower-class Narodniks by motives of honor. An aversion for the bourgeoisie and a dread of the development of capitalism have always been distinctive of the Russian people. All the Narodniks idealized the peasant way of living; the peasant commune seemed to them an original product of Russian history, the ideal type or, as Mikhailovsky expressed it, the highest type on a low rung of development.[4] In the Narodnik doctrine the commune was only the reflection of Russian conditions of life; never mind that the Russian peasantry, living as they were in conditions of serfdom, were devoid of material means and the most elementary enlightenment.

The Narodniks believed in a path of development for Russia, in the possibility of escaping Western capitalism; they believed that the Russian people were predestined to solve social problems better and more quickly than the West. Among some Russian stoics, and in spite of (or because of) the calamity of its socioeconomy, this messianism shorn of much of its *narodnichestvo* survives to this day.

Unity of Science and Nihilist Strains

Marxism, a transplanted Western motif in nineteenth-century Russian intellectuality, was vigorously challenged but also complemented by other philosophic themes, themes that reinforced the thrust of the unity of science. Prominent among these was nihilism. By the end of the century, ebullient expectations, still a spirited issue in Marx's work, had succumbed to a host of disillusioned antirationalist trends associated with the terms *decadence, vitalism,* and *nihilism.* This intellectual mood, so pervasive in the final two decades of the last century, signaled a decisive historical rejection of the heritage of modernity. A formidable exponent, Friedrich Nietzsche, is often celebrated as the spiritual godfather of contemporary attempts to escape from the bad conscience of the Age of Enlightenment, the modernist-rationalist legacy that ceased to reflect critically on its own intellectual presuppositions.

In the narrow sense of the word, nihilism is an intellectual liberation movement. It is to be found in the concealed layers of Russian social movements, although nihilism in itself is not a social movement. "We are all nihilists [for we are situated in] . . . that apparent disorder that is in actuality the highest degree of bourgeois order," says Dostoevsky.[5] Bourgeois society is home to a consummate nihilism that does not efface old structures of value but subsumes them. Modes of honor and dignity do not die; instead, they are incorporated into the market, take on price tags, and gain a new life as commodities. Thus, any imaginable mode of human conduct becomes morally permissible the moment it becomes economically possible, that is, becomes "valuable." The Dadaist "anything goes" is viable if it pays. There is a strange intimacy, a sense of being caught in a vortex where all facts and values gyrate wildly, explode, are deconstructed and reconstructed; a basic uncertainty about what is basic, what is valuable, even what is real; a reddening of manic hopes in the midst of their radical negations. This is the meaning of modern nihilism.

Russian nihilism denied God, the soul, the spirit, ideas, standards, and the highest values. Nonetheless, nihilism must be recognized as a spiritual even a religious phenomenon. It grew up on the spiritual soil of orthodoxy. It is orthodox asceticism turned inside out, an asceticism without grace. At the base of Russian nihilism, when grasped in its essence and depth, lies the orthodox rejection of the world, its sense of the truth that "the whole world lieth in wickedness," the acknowledgment of the sinfulness of all riches and luxury, of all creative profusion in art and in thought. Like orthodox asceticism, nihilism was an individualist movement, but it was directed against the fullness and material richness of life.

To fulfill the rejection of the world, all its strength must be devoted to emancipating earthly man, emancipating the laboring people from their excessive suffering; to establishing conditions of happy life; to destroying superstition and prejudice, conventional standards, and lofty ideas, which enslave man and hinder his happiness. For the intellectual it meant destroying the old beliefs, social ethics no less than the Cultural West's Enlightenment prejudices.

Nihilism is a negative apocalyptic. It is a revolt against the injustices of history, against false civilization; it is a demand that history come to an end, and a new life, outside or above history, begin. Nihilism is a demand for nakedness, for the stripping from oneself of all the trappings of bourgeois culture, for the annihilation of all historical traditions, for the setting free of the natural man, upon whom there will no longer be fetters of any sort. It is a declaration of war against all historical traditions. Nihilism opposes "reason" and all the beliefs and prejudices of the past. The intellectual asceticism of nihilism finds expression in a radical materialism.

In Russia, materialism assumed an entirely different character from its Western form. Materialism was turned into a peculiar sort of dogmatic theology. In materialism there was nothing skeptical; it was a faith. The attitude of the Russian nihilists to science was idolatrous. Science, most particularly the natural sciences, became an object of faith. To sustain an alternative view was to be a moral suspect. Whereas earlier the idealists had been interested mainly in the humane sciences, philosophy, and aesthetics, the nihilists were chiefly interested in the natural sciences and political economy, and eventually these became the interests of the Russian Marxists.

The polyglot Nicolai Chernishevsky dominated the radical intelligentsia and penned the utopian novel *What Is to Be Done?* It became a catechism of Russian nihilism, a textbook of the Russian revolutionary intelligentsia. An ascetic book, and a novel depicting a socialist utopia, it was a sort of manual of the devout life for Russian nihilists.[6]

Chernishevsky was not, like many other Narodniks, an opponent of industrial development. But he posed the traditional problem for Russian nineteenth-century thought: "Can Russia escape capitalist development?" and answered it by saying that Russia could shorten the capitalist period to nothing and go straight on from the "lower forms" of economy to socialist economy—a project later attempted by Stalin. There was a strong ascetic motive in Chernishevsky's antiestheticism. The subservience of literature and art to social aims, an ethic of social utilitarianism, the subjection of the personality of the individual to the interests and requirements of society, were holistic images that populated the novel. Not dissimilar to Hertzen and later Mikhailovsky, Chernishevsky identified the interests of the people with the interests of human personality in general.

"The destroyer of aesthetics," was the nickname of Dimitry Pisarev, the chief exponent of Russian nihilism. A child of the nobility, Pisarev was mainly interested in the emancipation of the individual person, in his or her liberation from superstition and prejudice, the ties of family, traditional morals, and the conventions of life. Intellectual freedom held a central position for him, and he hoped to attain it by popularizing natural science. He preached a paradoxical materialism; on the one hand, he was naively convinced that materialism sets personality free, and on the other hand, he believed that it denies personality. If personality is entirely produced by environment, then it cannot possess freedom and independence of any sort. Pisarev wanted to produce a new type of human being, "the thinking realist," traits of which are to be found in Turgenev's creature Bazarov in *Fathers and Sons*. Factually, it was Turgenev who in describing his creature coined the term *nihilism*. The type of thinking realist preached by Pisarev produces traits completely different from those of the "superfluous people" depicted with irony by Dostoevsky, a type given over to daydreaming, with a feeble capacity for action.[7] The thinking realist was alien from all daydreaming and romanticism; he was the foe of all lofty ideas that had no relation to action and were not put into practice. His cult was that of work and labor. Pisarev recognized only the natural sciences and despised the humanities. The thinking realist was, of course, a foe of aesthetics and denied the independent significance of art. In that respect he demanded a stern asceticism, the subservience of art and literature to social aims. Pisarev was committed to a pogrom against aesthetics; he rejected the literary accomplishments of Pushkin and proposed that Russian novelists should write popular tracts on natural science. Had the program of Russian nihilism actually been realized to the full, the results for culture would have been more destructive than those it, in fact, later encountered.

Proclaiming a revolt against all beliefs, all abstract ideas, for the sake of the liberation of personality, the nihilists emptied it of its qualitative content, devastated its inner life, and denied it its right to creativeness. The nihilist principle of utilitarianism is in the highest degree unfavorable to the principle of personality; it subjects personality to utility, which holds sway tyrannically over personality.

In its thought and creative activity nihilist materialism displayed a violent asceticism, an intruded asceticism and poverty of thought.

For Nietzsche, during the transitional phase of the West, that is between the complete collapse of the old values and the emergence of the new values, Christian/social ethic–centered doctrines such as Marxism sought to stem the anarchic tide but dissipate themselves. For Nietzsche, Marxism was an "incomplete" nihilism that clung to decadent values. Nietzsche joined Dostoevsky in rejecting contemporary bourgeois civilization as decadent: "We moderns, with our anxious care for ourselves and love of our neighbor, with our virtues of work, of unpretentiousness, of fair play, of scientificality—acquisitive, economical, machine-minded—appear as a weak age."[8] Exploring the sources and meanings of nihilism, Nietzsche, in *The Will to Power* (especially in Book One), "European nihilism," considered modern politics and economics profoundly nihilistic in their own right. Nietzsche's aesthetic as "applied psychology," his disdain for all sentimentalism, and his contempt—shared by Kierkegaard and Heidegger—for "mass man" and the philistine complacencies of "average" living, is profoundly unsettling of the erstwhile faith in the bourgeois promise of concord and equilibrium. For Nietzsche it is a self-deceptive promise, for it becomes the vehicle of a self-punitive irony, a manic laughter at the frailty of humankind, a morbid fascination with the sheer incapacity of human beings to be even halfway decent, let alone to relish the aesthetic sublime honored by Herder and Hegel.[9]

While in the theory and practice of science, the paradigmatic crisis was a pivotal issue, for the mystic bourgeois modernity itself was devoid of meaning. But their secret—a secret they themselves denied—was that, behind their facade, they were a violently destructive ruling class. All the anarchic, unbridled, precipitant actions exalted by nihilism—actions that Dostoevsky and Turgenev ascribed to such cosmic traumas as the death of God—located in the seeming banal of everyday bourgeois life were also described by Marx in his famous description of capitalism in the *Communist Manifesto*. It furnishes the classic testimony of the incessant, dynamic process of development intrinsic to modernity. The dynamism of the social world offers the certain promise of happiness and of disaster.

> Constant revolutionizing of production, uninterrupted disturbance of all social conditions, everlasting uncertainty and agitation distinguish the bourgeois epoch from all earlier ones. All fixed fast-frozen relations, with their train of ancient and venerable prejudices and opinions, are swept away, all new-formed ones become antiquated before they can ossify. All that is solid melts into air, all that is holy is profaned, and man is at last compelled to face with sober senses, his real conditions of life, and his relations with his kind.[10]

The trauma was elaborated in a literary way by Dostoevsky in his *Notes from the Underground* and in *Crime and Punishment*. Modernity lapsed into a universe of nihilism in which theories float in a void, unanchored or secured to any moorings. A habitual pessimistic decadence pervades and insinuates a "meaninglessness" to history.

The philosophy of nihilism, the philosophy of Bazarov, hero of Turgenev's *Fathers and Sons*, dealt primarily with the values that encouraged a sweeping secularization of ethics and wisdom and an increasing dependence on science as a source of models for moral life and of instruments for practical existence. Untempered individualism was the backbone not only of Turgenev's creature but also of nihilist philosophy.

While some theorists looked for new types of social relations that would emancipate the individual from enslavement to anachronistic customs and invidious institutions, others argued that the individual must effect his own emancipation through his own actions—through relentless and continuous criticism of authority. The basis of the nihilist's moral ideal is the individual, self-liberated and freely given to his own passions and lusts for the purpose of exacting from life as many "rational" enjoyments as human nature can absorb. The nihilists joined Kant, radicalized the moral imperative, and contended that "when God is dead, everything is permitted."

That "God is dead," was a defining experience. It meant the collapse of the Platonic-Christian table of values which had allegedly given meaning to life. While the proposition announced the loss of the "old God," it also proclaimed the need for a new one. Nihilism voiced not only a "no" to the old values, but also a "yes" to new values to replace the dissolved ones. It yearned for the ascendance of a secular god to provide a new meaning and rank-ordering to human existence; for a "new god" was needed to preserve humanity from the engulfing crises of modernity. However, between the collapse of the old and the advent of the new, questionable doctrines would present themselves to stem the tide of irrationalism. As a counterweight, Cartesian reason was presented as disclosing a "rational god," and thereby power and knowledge acquired the transcendentality of the new god. The irrational meant that which was without proper limits, a flawed mode of intellectuality that might dangerously reflect other than instrumentalism and leave humanity to inhabit a world bereft of gods.

The emphasis on the instrumentality of knowledge was a central pillar of the nihilist value system. The notion of science for science's sake was attacked, to be replaced by the categorical utilitarian claim that the worth of science is measured by its practical utility and its contributions to the solution of social needs. Utilitarianism placed emphasis not only on the search for socially applicable knowledge but also on the professionalization of techniques and a division of labor involved in the processes of the appropriation of knowledge. It was also the point of departure in the search for the elevation of work in general and scholarly work in particular—to the level of a fundamental social value. In nihilist philosophy, work both creates and emancipates the individual; it is the nerve center of the processes involved in the formation of personality.

Whereas medieval Russians fled to a suprasensory heaven, modern Russians were asked to flee to "civilizational progress," where utilitarian values replaces Gestalt-giving ideas and where experiential development of the personality replaces pious creativity. But where the uninhibited development of personality is the leitmotif, might not such a society feel a sense of collective futility; the futility of a life which does not realize itself in an enduring subject.

Nihilists gave prominence to the vulgar materialist and productionist dictum that societies with a great respect for work occupy higher levels on the ladder of cultural achievement. Or, the more civilized a society is, the more precise and adequate are its skills for judging the true value of knowledge. It was by combining the criterion of utility in the appraisal of knowledge and rationality and the appropriation of knowledge that the nihilists elevated scientific knowledge to the level of a prime mover of modern civilization. Nihilist philosophy was a philosophy of scientism: To the nihilists, science was the very panacea for all social ills and the only sure path to a better/open society.[11] They subordinated moral and aesthetic values to the rigors of science. The values that they emphasized were actually values that created the intellectual and social atmosphere indispensable for the growth of modern science. The natural sciences ostensibly bring man into direct contact with nature and help him rise above the obscurantism of various moralistic theories and unfathomable metaphysics. Natural science was extolled as the only infallible guide to a healthier future. The world was inhabited by only one evil—ignorance—and only one way to salvation—science. In science was found not only a system of positive knowledge but also a programmatic attitude toward society and culture and an optimistic view of the future. They followed Comte's dictum that in the future the conflict between "the intellectual" and "the moral" would completely disappear by a full dissolution of the ethical imperative in scientific thought.

Nihilism arose at the time when the avant-garde of the intelligentsia were convinced that moral truths could no longer be accepted in their orthodox form, that a scientific worldview should fully replace the supernatural and mythical worldview, and that the full rejuvenation of society depended on the triumph of reason, science, and freedom. Like Comte, they believed in a gradual subordination of the aesthetic quality of the sentiment of ideal perfection to the scientific quality of the idea of real existence. Small wonder then that priority was given to the popularization of science over all other literary forms. Philosophy was relegated to the background; only that philosophical thought that was grounded in "science" was acceptable. Russian nihilism did not create these values; it merely brought them into sharper focus and codified them, concealed under the form of literary works and their criticism, for under the conditions of censorship it could not otherwise find expression.

The formula of atheist radical individualism is to be found Dostoevsky's Kiriloff of *The Possessed*, for whom "If there is no God, then I, Kiriloff, am God." In the novel, Kiriloff presents an irrefutable argument: God is that which gives meaning to human life and creates a difference between good and evil. "If there is no such God outside myself, then I myself am God, for I do these things." Kiriloff then resolves to actualize and realize his godhead by conquering the fear of death. Dostoevsky's images were not those distilled from his fertile imagining, for he, in fact, participated in a revolutionary group associated with Petrashevsky. The most extreme revolutionary tendency in Petrashevsky's group was represented by N. Speshnev, who apparently served Dostoevsky as a model when he drew the image of Stavrogin.[12] This "new man," this strict materialist, combined a denial of genuinely moral ideals with a frenzied hatred of society on account of its immorality. Thus, a theme in the Russian enlightened youth from 1860 onward achieved its embodiment in Bazarov.

In the coils of *The Possessed*, Dostoevsky sketches the Russian revolutionary movement in the second half of the nineteenth century, but some of the types he portrays deserve scrutiny. The Russian revolutionary movement included not only the heroic types but also people like Dostoevsky's Liputin, a petty provincial official, an envious, coarse despot, a miser and a usurer; and like Verkhovensky, a cheat, scoundrel, and murderer, who wanted to unite his few followers not by common ideals but by joint responsibility for the crimes committed. That such "socialists" did exist is witnessed by the activity of Sergei Nechaev.

A sinister and grim character, Nechaev was the founder of the revolutionary society called The Axe, or the People's Justice. He composed the *Revolutionary Catechism*, a document of unusual interest, unique of its kind. In this document is to be found the extreme expression of the principles of atheistic revolutionary asceticism. They are the rules by which the genuine revolutionary should be guided, his manual, as it were, of a spiritual life. For Nechaev "the revolutionary is the doomed man. He has no personal interests, business, feelings, connections, property, or even name. Everything in him is in the grip of the one exclusive interest, one thought, one passion, revolution."[13] The revolutionary has broken with civil order, with the civilized world, and with the morals of the world. He lives in this world in order to destroy it. He must not even love the sciences of this world. He knows one science only, the science of destruction. To the revolutionary everything is moral that serves the revolution. Nechaev's catechism is reminiscent of a grim degree of asceticism turned inside out and mixed with an extremist form of revolutionary ascetic denial of the world. According to Nechaev, the psychology of the revolutionary requires the rejection of the world and the meaning of personality lauded by Narodnik social thought.

Nechaev despised the masses and wanted to drag them forcibly to revolution. He alarmed everybody. Revolutionaries and socialists of all shades rejected him and found that he was, in fact, compromising the work of revolution and socialism. Even Bakunin repudiated Nechaev.

Despite his banishment, he sincerely believed that he was a socialist, which he understood in the following terms.

> To become a good socialist, one must reject all tender, soft feelings of kinship, friendship, love, gratitude, and even honor itself. . . . He is not a revolutionary who pities anything in this world. . . . A revolutionary knows only one science —the science of destruction and extermination. He lives in the world with this sole aim. To leave not one stone on another, as many ruins as possible, the extinction of most of the revolutionaries—that is the perspective. Poison, the knife, the noose—the revolution consecrates everything.[14]

In understanding Nechaev (and for that matter Stalin), we might bear in mind Dostoevsky's remarks from his *Notes from the House of the Dead*:

> Whoever has experienced the power, the complete ability, to humiliate another human being . . . with the most extreme humiliation, willy-nilly loses power over his own sensations. Tyranny is a habit, it has a capacity for development, it develops finally into a disease. I insist that the habit can dull and coarsen the very best man to the level of a beast. Blood and power are intoxicating. . . . The man and the citizen die within the tyrant forever; return to human dignity, to repentance, to regeneration, becomes almost impossible.[15]

It might be said that Nechaev anticipated the Bolshevik type. Indeed, his asceticism passed over into Dzerzhinsky, the founder and controller of the Cheka, for Dzerzhinsky was a fanatical despot who sanctioned every means in order to bring socialism into being.

Morally dedicated to treachery, Nechaev had his follower the student Ivanov assassinated on the suspicion that he was an agent provocateur and in order to strengthen party discipline. This ruthless act formed the basis of Dostoevsky's *The Possessed*, wherein he described the murder of Shatov. Dostoevsky revealed a great deal of truth. As a counterpoint to the consummate of scientific rationalism, that theme that descends to us from Dostoevsky in his probing of the limits of nihilism, is a certain remnant of revitalizing moralism. But even while Dostoevsky leads us in a deconstructivist style to empty despair, he clears the ground for a rehabilitation of morality.

The rationality of Turgenev's Bazarov, no less than Dostoevsky's Liputin, closely approximates that considered in Plato's *Republic* to be of the most inferior kind. It is this very ideal that one might detect in Turgenev's Bazarov. Indeed, Russian nihilist social philosophy rested on this inversion of Plato's rationality, that everything emanates from the individual, and everything returns to it, and that the individual needs no protection or guidance—he needs only science. Underlying nihilism's emphasis on unmitigated radical individualist values was a utopian belief that Russian society could find its way out of feudal darkness, sustained by oppressive law and petrified custom, only by a total and unrelenting attack on every existing institution, myth, and practice. To enter the stage of democracy and advanced civilization, Russia had first to produce individuals free of internal and external constraints. Throughout the nineteenth century, Russians of the intelligentsia were irresistibly and passionately drawn to socialism.

The nihilist's radical "emancipation of the individual," however, was not the only path to a higher stage of social development. Equally important was the intellectual development in the spirit of realism by means of acquiring knowledge free of superstitious belief in supernatural interference. Rationality—the cultivation of and reliance on man's rational faculties—was viewed as the only fountain of free thought, or critical realism. The true sentiment of the intelligentsia, then, was that "rationality," most realistically expressed in the laws of natural science, was the only realistic source of designs for a new society unencumbered by internal conflict. The worldview embedded in rationality and sustained by natural science provided the most reliable prospects for the emancipation of Russia from the gnawing effects of feudal institutions. Only "reason," engaged in the pursuit of science, can enrich intellectual and material culture. To the nihilists science stood for the categorical rejection of every kind of antirationalism.

Positivism, as a promise to describe the world with the sort of fidelity that is ostensibly the key to successful explanation and prediction for purposes of intervention and control, provided powerful arguments against all current efforts to consolidate idealistic philosophy as an ideological weapon of the autocratic system. Having given prominence to utilitarian intellectual elitism as the hallmark of advanced civilization, nihilist philosophy was the philosophy of scientism. Presented as an antidote for social ills and the only sure path to the good society, scientism more correctly reinforced the alienating and objectual dimensions of modern society. They were not the authors of instrumentalism and utilitarianism; they merely brought them into sharper focus and codified them. They showed that the libertarian movement of the Reform epoch had produced, among other effects, an intellectual climate favoring an intensive national concern with the development of science; the values that sparked the Russian intelligentsia in their search for a society of democratic institutions were the same values that created indispensable conditions for a versatile and accelerated development of scientific thought. In the process the nihilists subordinated moral and aesthetic values to science. They followed Comte's dictum and belief in the subordination of the aesthetic to the scientific and the prioritization of science over all other cultural modalities.

Following Comte and the materialist philosophers Moleschott, Buchner, and Vogt, some nihilists emphasized the unity of the sciences: They viewed the "moral" sciences as a mere extension of the natural sciences; they spoke not about sociology as a distinct science but about the application of the methods of natural science in the study of human history and social life. The natural sciences bring man into direct contact with nature and help him rise above the obscurantism of various moralistic theories and unfathomable metaphysical systems. Philosophy was relegated to the background; only that philosophical thought that was grounded in science was acceptable. Nihilists among the avant-garde of the Russian intelligentsia were convinced that "moral truths could no longer be accepted in their orthodox form," that a scientific worldview should fully replace "the supernatural and mythical worldview," and that the full rejuvenation of society depended on the triumph of "reason, science, and freedom."

In their efforts to establish an objective study of Russian society, the members of the intelligentsia had to reject the worldview of the masses as incompatible with all the basic truths of science, for the function of science is to dislodge the despotism of the government, the ignorance of the masses, and the quixotic ideal of "the coming dominance of Russia in the intellectual life of Europe."

Contrary to some Russian Marxists, the nihilists expressed the view that every search for an integrated social science must bypass history, because historians are partial interpreters of the national past; they search through the maze of documentary material to select and embellish events that illustrate their ideological biases. Statistics—the systematic collection and scrutiny of numerical data bearing on every aspect of social life—was for them the science with the most promise of evolving into a systematic and thorough analysis of social existence. Disregarding or ignoring post-positivist arguments latent in Marx and Nietzsche, their main argument was that the growth of the natural sciences is in itself the safest path to objective and comprehensive knowledge of society—knowledge of its present-day structure and its future evolution. The natural sciences do not handle social problems directly; they provide models for an objective analysis of social problems by an educated citizenry; they elucidate the place of man in nature; and they are the indices of social progress.

In an organic fusion of positivism and voluntarism, early Russian nihilists borrowed Saint-Simon's thought and concentrated on the discovery of inexorable natural laws of social development, elaborated social technologies, and sought those techniques that promised the rational mobilization of human effort. Together they might bring about the modernity project.

Narodnik socialism had spent itself by the 1880s, and the revolutionary movement could develop no further under its banner. The revolutionary intelligentsia were disillusioned with the peasantry and resolved to rely solely upon their own personal heroism. The murder of Alexander II not only failed to bring about the triumph of the revolutionary intelligentsia but also led to a strong reactionary movement among the public as well as in the government.

A Critical Kernel in Russian Marxism

While Russian Critical Marxism was subtly influenced by elements of a nihilist tradition in literature, other modes of intellectuality were also influential. Certainly the role of Narodnik thought and practice of which we spoke earlier was crucial to the maturing of Critical Marxism in its Russian edition.

As previously noted, the Narodniks felt that the communal practices of the village commune could be used as a framework or scaffolding for communal modernization. P.N. Tkachev, in 1875, wrote a letter to Engels about Russia's own particular line of development and about the special character of the coming

Russian revolution, to which it would be impossible simply to apply the principles of Marxism. Tkachev considered the absence of a developed bourgeois Russia's great advantage in facilitating the possibility of a social revolution. Like Lenin, Tkachev was an exponent of the theory of revolution.

His fundamental idea was the seizure of power by a revolutionary minority. This required the disorganization of the existing authority by terrorism. The masses, in Tkachev's opinion, are always ready for revolution, because they are only the material of which a revolutionary minority makes use. Revolutions are made but seldom prepared for. Tkachev did not recognize any sort of evolution. Revolution ought not to be preceded by propaganda and the education of the masses. A Russian revolution, he conceded, would not necessarily follow the Western pattern. Could Russia escape capitalist development and the rule of the bourgeoisie? Could Marxist theory be applied to Russia without taking account of any special path of development for Russia? These were two of the questions that penetrated the consciousness of Tkachev.

The illusions of a revolutionary Narodnik and the myth about the peasantry had collapsed. The people had not accepted a revolutionary intelligentsia. A new revolutionary myth was needed, one in accord with traditions of the Slavophile and Narodnik messianic and holistic traditions. Marxism presented itself.

On Russian soil, Marxism was originally the extreme expression of Russian Westernism. The first generation of Russian Marxists waged war in the first place on the old tendencies of the revolutionary intelligentsia, that is with the *narodnichestvo*, and succeeded in alienating itself and dealing itself an irreparable injury. Russian Marxism sought emancipation through the industrial development of Russia, which was the very thing that *narodnichestvo* had tried to avoid. Capitalist industry was to lead to the formation and development of the working class, which is the liberating class. The Marxists, therefore, were in favor of the proletariatization of the peasantry. The Narodniks had no desire to invest in such a project. The emerging proletariat was, for the Marxists, the only social force that could be relied on. It was necessary to develop the revolutionary class-consciousness of this proletariat; it was necessary to go, not to the peasantry that had rejected the revolutionary intelligentsia, but to the workmen in the factory. The Marxists wished to rely not so much on the revolutionary intelligentsia as on the social and economic conditions. The sorcerer's apprentices, the members of the revolutionary proletariat, were bound to wrest control of the productive forces from the Faustian-Frankensteinian bourgeoisie.

In accord with the intellectuality in which Russian Marxism arose, the Marxists from the beginning stressed the determinist and evolutionary elements of Marxism. Socialism was the progeny of economic necessity, of an inevitable development. They were interested in the actual economic development of Russia, not as a positive aim and a boon in itself, but because it was the arsenal that supplied them with the weapons for revolutionary conflict.

While today in some circles Russians passionately embrace "scientific capitalism," in an earlier period "scientific socialism" was an article of faith. But the solid hope that scientific socialism offers for the realization of a longed-for purpose is linked with industrial development, with the organization of a class of industrial workers. An exclusively agricultural and peasant country offers no such hope. Therefore, the first step for Russian Marxists was to overthrow the Narodnik worldview and to prove that in Russia capitalism was developing and must develop. The Marxists considered the Narodniks reactionaries who supported obsolete modes of production, while the Narodniks regarded the Marxists as confederates of capitalism and bound to contribute to its development.

Engels's developmentalism suggested that the Narodniks and Tkachev were un-Marxian in that they did not understand dialectical materialism and that Russia would necessarily have to pass from feudalism to capitalism to communism. Russia would have to emulate the modernity project of the Cultural West. For the path to communism could move only in a monodevelopmental line. In this connection Engels was a Menshevik! But Tkachev was right in his opposition to Engels, and his cogency was not the cogency of the *narodnichestvo* against Marxism but the historical rightness of the Bolsheviks against the Mensheviks, of Lenin against G.V. Georgii Plekhanov.[16]

Content with a deterministic reading of Marx's historical materialism, Plekhanov was opposed to a revolutionary socialist seizure of power, i.e., to the communist revolution in the course it actually took. The social revolution must be waited for. The liberation of the workers should be the work of the workers themselves, not of a revolutionary clique. The realization of socialism needed an increase in the number of workers and the development of their consciousness, and it presupposed a greater development of industry. What was needed above all was the revolutionizing of thought, not a cataclysmic upheaval.

But in his writings on Russia, Marx articulated his multilineal concept of history and clarified his nuanced divergence from Engelsism. He never indicated that Russia must, of necessity, pass through capitalism in order to achieve communism. While he may not have been a Menshevik, was Marx a Marxist-Leninist?

How is it possible to desire the growth of capitalism, to welcome this growth, and at the same time regard capitalism as an evil and a moral wrong against which every socialist is called to fight? This complicated question gives rise to moral conflict such that Nechaev could with certitude answer. The growth of capitalist industry in Russia presupposed the turning of the peasantry into a proletariat, depriving them of their means of production, i.e., reducing a considerable part of the nation to a condition of beggary. The question was answered by Lenin, who asserted the possibility of establishing socialism in Russia independently of the development of capitalism. In Bolshevist Marxism the proletariat ceased to be an empirical reality, for as an empirical reality the proletariat was a mere nothing; it was above all the idea of a proletariat that mattered, and those who became vehicles for the expression of this idea might be an insignificant minority. If this insignificant minority is entirely possessed by the gigantic idea of the proletariat, if its revolutionary will is stimulated, if it is well organized and disciplined, then it can work miracles; it can overpower the determinism that normally controls social life. And Lenin proved in practice that this is possible, bringing about the revolution in Marx's name but only tangentially in Marx's way.

In an 1877 letter to the editor of *Otyccestvenniye Zapisky*, Marx wrote that "one will never arrive there (an understanding of history) by the universal passport of a general historico-philosophical theory, the supreme virtue of which consists in being supra-historical."[17] In the same letter, Marx indicated that to interpret *Capital* as establishing the laws by which all societies of all time must develop was to misunderstand the work. *Capital*, Marx wrote, was not meant to be the "historico-philosophical theory of a Universal progress."[18] Four years later in a letter to Vera Zasoulich of the Freedom of Labor group, Marx reaffirmed that the rise of capitalism was "explicitly restricted to the countries of Western Europe."[19] In the Western movement the transformation of feudalism into capitalism was essentially the transformation of private property in land and agriculture. These were two separate cases, and each must be analyzed on its own terms. Thus, there was not one law of social development applicable to all societies, rather each society must be examined in terms of its own structure and in terms of the evolution of the individual structures opened to them.[20] Marx further indicated that "events strikingly analogous but taking place in different historic surroundings led to totally different results."[21]

Whereas Marx felt there were a variety of different ways of arriving at communism, Engels presented only one road to communism.[22] Engelsism led directly to the dialectical materialism of the Stalin era.[23] The validity of the dialectical laws of nature, the attempt to apply the same laws of social evolution, the belief that all societies must follow a unilinear and historically inevitable path of development were all present, as we have seen, in Engels and were only enlarged and magnified under Stalin.[24]

Plekhanov was already writing decisively and sharply against Tkachev in the 1880s. It has become customary to consider Plekhanov the father of Russian Marxism. According to James D. White, though there is a germ of truth in this belief, there is much that is illusory. Since Marxism belongs to the left Hegelian tradition, and as Plekhanov patently belonged to the Hegelian school, one is drawn to conclude that the Marxism identified with dialectical materialism was dominant in Russia.[25] Plekhanov, like many of the later Marxist Mensheviks, had no wish to recognize special paths of development for Russia. Engels did not understand the special character of Russia's path of development, however much Stalin tried to disguise this.

But the specious triumph of "historical inevitably" under Stalin also meant that it was Engelsism, i.e., Scientific Marxism, that was presented to the world as the genuine Marxism. During that era, what the world understood as Marxism was really Engelsism. History is only now beginning to retrace the steps by which this forgery was perpetuated. It was not Stalin who first distorted Marxism, nor Kautsky, nor Plekhanov. As we noted above, the first deviant from Marxism was Engels. And, thus it was Engelsism that laid the basis for the doctrinal materialistic idealism of Stalin and the subsequent neo-Marxist critique.

It is apparent that Marxism, during its nineteenth-century adolescence in Russia, was merely a set of occasionally complementary economic doctrines instead of a system of philosophy. Rather than the philosophical trend commonly associated with radical intelligentsia, nineteenth-century Russian Hegelianism was, in fact, the doctrine of the opposing camp. Assuming a sublime Platonic perspective, Hegel argued that the true unity between the individual and the common interest, its purest expression as the "Divine Idea as it exists on Earth," was the sole aim of the state.[26] With cavalier abandon, he epitomized the semifeudal Prussian state in his *Philosophy of History* of 1837. Consistent with this theme, the Russian historian and political philosopher Boris Nikoláyevich Chicherin fashioned right Hegelianism into a rationalization for Russian autocracy.[27] He extolled Hegel's state principle at the expense of popular representation. The Russian democratic movement was consequently more inclined to oppose Hegelianism than to adopt it.[28]

From 1893, however, the influence of Marxism was beginning to be felt among the students. The works of Engels and Plekhanov began to be read in student study circles, and in that year the leading light among the Narodniks, N.K. Mikhailovsky, came to Moscow and delivered a lecture accusing the Russian Marxists of being disciples of the tsarist minister Witte in their desire to encourage the extension of the capitalist system.

Nor, as we have seen, were the traditions of Russian Hegelianism without their influence. Pyotr Lávrovich Lavróv, philosopher and idealist, subscribed to a concept of imminence, an uninterrupted rise in critical consciousness of individuals accompanied by the emergent solidarity of society. The master armchair philosophers of the radical intelligentsia of the 1870s, Lavróv and Mikhailovsky, were defenders of what was called subjective sociology, that is to say, the point of view that sees it is necessary for sociology to assign moral value to phenomena. Lavróv and Mikhailovsky in their own way defended human personality without distinguishing it from the individual, and socialism to them, as to Hertzen, had an individualist character: The socialist organization of society is necessary to ensure a complete life for each individual. A society is well balanced if the interests of the majority may be identified with the ideals of the most conscious and progressive minority, i.e., the intelligentsia. This was a theme present in Lavróv's *Historical Letters*, a work written under the pseudonym of P.L. Mirtov.

In *Historical Letters*, Lavróv placed human consciousness at the very center of his system. Although he conceded there might lie outside this domain truths that consciousness could not comprehend, that was of little practical importance. Man could not help judging phenomena as they related to humankind.

Historical Letters became the moral catechism of the Narodnik intelligentsia of the 1870s. Lavróv gave expression to the theme of repentance, of the guilt of the cultured classes before the masses, and of their obligation to discharge their debt. He posed the traditional Russian question of the price of progress and culture. But the *narodnichestvo* of Lavróv and Mikhailovsky belongs to the type that regards itself as bound by the interests, but not necessarily the opinions, of the people. They thought that true enlightened opinions were to be found among the intelligentsia and not among the people. It was the duty of the intelligentsia to give the people knowledge, to serve the interests of the people and work for their freedom but to preserve its own independence in opinions and ideas.

In the 1870s there was a strong Narodnik movement that found expression in going to the people. This movement did not at first bear a revolutionary or political character. The Narodniks of the intelligentsia desired to merge themselves into the people, to enlighten the people, to serve the peasants in their daily need and interest. The ultimate failure of this "going to the people," in which so much self-denial and capacity for sacrifice, so much faith and hope, so much nobility were displayed, was, of course, due to the fact that they came up against government repression and persecution. This was not the only problem, for the tragedy of the Narodnik movement lay above all in that the people did not welcome the intelligentsia.

There were other elements of *Historical Letters* that might be considered. Subscribing to an ontological concept that was to be instrumental to the methodological individualists of the Vienna Circle, Lavróv held that beyond the realm of man the world was not an organized whole but a meaningless chaos, "nothing but simultaneous concatenations of facts, so minute and fractional that man could scarcely even approach them in all their particularity."[29] For Lavróv the order of the cosmos was speculative. It did not exist in nature, as such, but was imposed by man, whose scientific laws sought to find order in chaos. Order and meaning were noncontextual, they were the synthetic products of the human mind. This was a kind of existential phenomenology, a materialism and a material monist ontology that acknowledges an irreducible dualism of attributes. Physicalism therein is an indefensible philosophical position that is better replaced by a nonreductive materialist ontology.[30] Lavróv claimed that "the distinction between important and unimportant, the beneficial and the harmful, the good and the bad, are distinctions which exist only for man; they are quite alien to nature and to things in themselves."[31] From such propositions, to speak of objective historical laws was illusory. For him, as for the monists of the Vienna Circle (Ostwald, Mach, Avenarius, et al.), each historical event, each fragment of the historical process was unique and unrepeatable. It neither had meaning in and of itself, nor could it be revealed by a battery of interpretations. Any law constructed out of these entities must, Lavróv reasoned, be purely subjective interpretations imposed upon a subjective choice of events. For Lavróv this voluntarist subjectivity meant that man might construct his own laws in accordance with those ethical criteria and ideals that he wished to realize. Man could achieve whatever aims he chose simply by setting them and consciously striving toward them.[32] Lavróv's seems to have been an image of society distinguished by the disappearance of signifiers, the signs of modernity—production, meaning, reality, power, the social, and so forth. It is perceived to be a game with the vestiges of that which had been destroyed. Meaningfulness seems to obtain not from the contextual but from "textual," from differences within the "text" and with the structures and rules of signification responsible for the production of meaning. Relationships between signifiers and what they signify were conceptualized as strictly arbitrary, there being no "natural" links between the text and the world. His is a voluntarist theory of history, of the hyperreal, of the synchronic, and of the inertial, where one is in a kind of post-history devoid of meaning, a universe of nihilism in which theories float in a void, unanchored or secured to any moorings. Meaningfulness itself is fluid.

For the Nietzscheans, because all differences are of the same order, they continue to operate endlessly. While for Nietzsche all differences are of the same order, for the left Hegelians contradictions have a gradation of importance. In the Nietzschean scheme, power and knowledge acquire a de facto transcendental status, and "meaning" is constituted by an endless procession of differences that move beyond the historically specific to become universal mechanisms. Meaningfulness is, in the Nietzschean spirit, deemed a moment in the play of power, where agreement based on validity is merely a subterfuge for vested social interests. Thus, "it is not the supposed truth, but the powerfulness, the force of an argument that determines the truth."[33] We are assaulted by floating images maintaining no relationship with anything at all, where meaning becomes detachable. If validity claims are exclusively contextual, does not the important distinction between power and validity threaten to evaporate? Contexts become "contexts of domination" and thus potentially self-perpetuating.

If meaning is purely contextual, then its valorization is subsumed by power claims. Instead of being tied to the force of the better argument, meaning and justice are reduced to moments in a skeptical rhetoric. Philosophical discourse becomes an endless procession of oppositions in which each concept defines itself in the negative, that is, by not being another concept. It has been widely argued that knowledge should be seen as a social construct and that once we acknowledge this view it is appropriate to look for criteria according to which we can judge whether social theories are true or false. This becomes an analysis of the ways that meanings are negotiated within a discipline and displaces inquiry.[34] This approximates Rorty's view that we replace the conception of knowledge as accurate representation with a view of knowledge as "a matter of conversation and of social practice."[35] Knowledge once again assumes the dimension of justified belief wherein the task of philosophy is inertial, that of keeping the conversation going not of finding objective truth. In this sense philosophy becomes antifoundational, for it then involves abandoning the "desire to find 'foundations' to which one might cling, frameworks beyond which one must not stray."[36] Does this mean that thought remains imprisoned in its own philosophical framework and cannot escape? This insistence on the endless play of differences is an uncentered political practice that projects all contradictions as equally important. Have we not at this juncture become Orwell's pigs, for whom all arguments are equal but some are more equal than others? Moreover, it projects an extreme cynicism about emancipatory social action because it is seen as a chimerical goal not worth pursuing. If meaning is already inscribed in the structure of the sign system of which it is a part, then it is impossible for the system to progress and develop. So, we must be aware that each new signification is an advance, a variation on the pre-existing system. This scheme rejects the possibility of a philosophical escape from existing conditions. It degenerates into a cynicism about the possibility of change. But cannot cynicism and apathy create the space for new meaning and the possibility for social action? It was Hegel who focused on the contest between theory and narrative by criticizing Kant for elevating ideas to an a priori status when their true status was distinctly transient. And it was Marx who castigated the meta-narrative dwelt on by philosophers, arguing that there are no immobile absolutes, no spiritual beyonds, and that every absolute represented a mask justifying exploitation of humans by humans. Marx had argued that philosophical abstractions in themselves have no value or precise meaning. Thus in an age of declining political possibilities, Marxism appeared to offer some intellectual ammunition for Russian political philosophers and activists.

A habitual pessimistic decadence pervades and insinuates a meaning-less of history interpreted as "merely one damn thing after another," a mere pastiche of a historical past nostalgically reduced to a lost world. Even the metaphysical answer to the question, What is history?—that it is the "systematic exploration of the riddle of death, with a view to overcoming death"—is expunged from the consciousness of the stubbornly devout. To the structuralist, interpretive order was orchestrated, a conscious construction of the human mind.

A Keystone to Russian Critical Marxism

Clearly Russian Critical Marxism did not spring from philosophically barren ground. The luxuriant intellectuality of late-nineteenth-century Russia held within its compass *narodnichestvo* with its embrace of communal social ethics, nihilism with its negative apocalyptic, and Marxist thought; together these reinforced a native holism and later fused with the hermetic theoretical construct of social energetics. Russian Critical Marxism emerged in a challenging intellectual environment, but one that reinforced the thrust of the unity of science. This is not to say that a harmonious synthesis existed, for Narodnik thought was problematic for those who clenched Scientific Marxism with its triumphal historical inevitability. Nonetheless, these diverse elements were to prove instrumental to an immanent critique of political economy that sought to give an answer to all the questions of the livelihood of man.

Among those who contributed to the concept of the unity of nature and the role played by the energy nexus in critical thought was Alexander A. Bogdanov.[37] Bogdanov's intellectual and political biography is singularly difficult to reconstruct because of his long exclusion from the historical record in the Soviet Union. His exclusion from the record took place at a time before even the primary sources had been assembled to write the history of Social Democracy in Russia. The establishment of *Istpart*, the organization to collect and publish materials on the Russian revolutionary movement, occurred almost simultaneously with the republication of Lenin's *Materialism and Empirio-criticism* as part of a renewed offensive against Bogdanov and his ideas.[38] The suppression of material relating to Bogdanov was consequently incorporated into Soviet historical writing from its very inception. The history of Russian Social Democracy was also written from an explicitly Leninist point of view, ostensibly in terms of the development of Lenin's ideas, and as their vindication. Since Western historians also tend to focus their attention on Lenin, consequently histories of Social Democracy in Russia do not provide the historical context that the study of Bogdanov's ideas requires. It is the author's hope that the foregoing provides a modest foundation for Bogdanov's ideas.

As obscure as the record is, it is his extraordinary contribution that we claim corresponds not only to a cultural and systems theoretical critique of political economy but also to Critical Marxism. His sensitivity to cultural issues and his systems theoretical constructions were contiguous both to those of the Slavophile traditions of nihilism and *narodnichestvo* and to the Westernizing of Marxism and Engelsism. In this they were markedly distinct from Cartesian economics. A commitment to both better understand the present and invent an alternative future encourages us to explore the repressed knowledge identified with Bogdanov's "paradigm lost."

Let us turn briefly to his intellectual bibliography. Our intent is merely to acquaint the reader with the man in the succeeding scant paragraphs, not to exhaust the subject. The following, then, is in the nature of a prologue.

Bogdanov, a pseudonym for Alexander Aleksandrovich Malinovsky, was born in 1873 to the family of a public-school teacher. He graduated with high distinction from Tula gymnasium and immediately enrolled in Moscow University's Department of Natural Sciences. In 1894, he was exiled to Tula by the police authorities because of his participation in the student movement. Deeply involved in propaganda activities among the workers of a local weapons factory, he was at first a spokesman for populism but gradually transferred his allegiance to Marxism.

In the autumn of 1895, Bogdanov enrolled in the medical school of Kharkov University and immediately became active in local Social Democratic circles. Soon after graduation in 1899 he was sent to a Moscow prison for his participation in revolutionary circles and early in 1901 was exiled first to Kaluga and then to Vologda, where he remained until the end of 1903. While in exile, he worked for a while as a psychiatrist in Kuvshinov near Vologda. When, in 1903, the Social Democrats split into the Bolsheviks and the Mensheviks, Bogdanov, still in exile, joined the former.

In early 1904, Bogdanov went to Switzerland and was elected to several ranking positions in Bolshevik organizations, serving at the same time on the editorial boards of several newspapers. He returned to Russia in time to take part in the revolution of 1905 as a Bolshevik representative in the St. Petersburg Soviet of Worker's Deputies; he also edited *The New Life*, a Bolshevik journal published legally during "the days of freedom" at the end of 1905. He was arrested again, but instead of being sent to prison he was ordered to leave the country. Unknown to the police, he stayed for a while in Kuokkala, Finland, sharing a dacha with Lenin. He was selected to serve on the Central Committee of the Social Democratic Party in 1907, but his views on both revolutionary philosophy and current political tactics brought him into conflict with more orthodox Marxists. In 1907, he argued with his close friend Lenin: After the dissolution of the Second State Duma, Lenin thought it advisable for the Social Democrats to take part in the forthcoming elections for the Third Duma to assure themselves of contact with legal and semilegal labor organizations. Bogdanov, on the contrary, was the chief spokesman for the so-called Maximalist Group, which advocated a full boycott of the election and a total retreat into illegal activities.[39]

He insisted on the possibility of mounting a new armed uprising in 1907 and 1908, diverted party funds (his network was perhaps the chief fund-raiser) into revolutionary partisan operations, and opposed the Bolshevik participation in the new parliament. But Bogdanov's dream of an imminent upsurge of the proletarian offensive in the Russia of 1907 was ill-founded. By 1908 the reaction was in full swing, and tsarist authorities were in full command of the situation. Many members of the intelligentsia fell into a mood of post-revolutionary despondency and withdrawal. Some former revolutionary thinkers turned to religion and even to conservatism and nationalism. Those who clung to revolutionary political tactics and programs were either banished to the fringes of the Russian state or forced into emigration. Bogdanov was among the latter. The expatriate world of Russian revolutionaries—Geneva, London, Paris, Stuttgart—was a world of disappointed men and women who lashed one another with bitter recriminations and rancorous ideological disputes. The break that ensued was in the last analysis caused by a fundamental difference between the rigid Lenin and the polymath Bogdanov, whose personal proclivities toward revolutionary action could not be reconciled to the views of a self-appointed leader. Referring to Lenin, in his science fiction novel *Red Star*, Bogdanov made a fleeting reference to the Old Man of the Mountain, an invaluable, hardheaded, and somewhat inflexible revolutionary leader. The two men fell out over philosophical and tactical questions.

An enforced isolation from official Bolshevik activities led Bogdanov to broaden his participation in the work of various fringe groups of unorthodox Marxists; he was particularly close to persons, typified by Maxsim Gorky, whose holism contended that a political and economic revolution could be successful only if it were preceded by an ideological, or cultural, revolution. The recurrent theme of holism attracted the attention of the Russian socialist philosopher, who, though he appropriated selected dimensions of natural science methodology to the social sciences, was, as we shall see, of a circumspect intellect.

As for his intellectual career, his 1896 lectures delivered to various workers' circles were the basis for *A Short Course of Economic Science*. A comprehensive though not original survey of Marxist economics and sociology, the book reaffirmed the Marxist idea that political economy was the only social science approaching the methodological rigor of the natural sciences and that the analysis of social structure was its primary task. *A Short Course of Economic Science* was composed while he still thought of himself as a Narodnik. As we have seen, by the 1890s a great deal of common ground existed between Narodnik and Marxist thinkers in terms of social and economic theory.

Russian Marxism was less than a decade old when it first revealed a pronounced tendency to contribute its own creativity to the legacy of the German master. In the 1890s Peter Struve, the author of the Social Democrats' party program, initiated the Russian flirtation with the "revisionism" of Eduard Bernstein. By 1902, Struve and his followers (the later Vekhi group) bade farewell to the radicalism of their youth in exchange for a more amorphous social philosophy combining Kant's ethical teachings and elements of English liberalism.

In 1908, V.V. Vorovsky wrote of early Russian Marxism: "It was emasculated. It was divested of all its sociological content—its very essence, leaving it as a mere economic doctrine, which was discussed, evaluated and accepted (or rejected) exclusively as a system of political economy regardless of its connection with the entirety of its author's world outlook."[40]

Bogdanov's transition from Narodism to Social Democracy was one of gradual evolution. He did not enter the polemic between Narodniks and Social Democrats on behalf of either side. Unlike Plekhanov, Struve, and Lenin, he did not define his standpoint as a Marxist in terms of his rejection of points of Narodnik doctrine. It was this feature that set Bogdanov apart from other Russian Marxist writers and gave his thought its peculiar direction. Unlike most of his contemporaries, he did not yet address himself to Tkachev's question of Russia's future social and economic development or to whether Russia must inevitably pass through a capitalist stage. These problems mattered little in his writings. It is, of course, at first sight remarkable that Bogdanov did not contribute anything to the major discussion of his day. If, however, one takes Bogdanov at his word on how his first two books were written, the matter is easy to appreciate. The problem of Russia's path of development was one that, as we have seen, preoccupied the intelligentsia; it was of much less interest to the workers. The kind of instruction allegedly demanded by workers was on the evolution of society in general, on economics and science, in fact, on the areas covered by Bogdanov in his lectures. The attitude that Bogdanov shared with Narodnik doctrine was putting oneself at the disposal of the workers' movement, of going to the people, rather than dictating to them and deciding for them what they ought to study or how they ought to act. This was a characteristic simultaneously of Bogdanov's philosophy and his revolutionary practice. For to dictate to the workers, to presume to lead them in any direction, presupposed certain access to a foundational, an Archimedean point whereby the nature of knowledge in general obtained and from which the knowledge of absolute truths could reveal itself. Bogdanov strenuously denied this foundationalism. With a postpositivist flavor he wrote in *The Basic Elements of the Historical View of Nature* that "human knowledge has no access to unconditional and absolute truths." Therein Bogdanov expressed a concern about the role of science during a revolution, posing the question: Does knowledge lead to freedom, or is it just one more weapon in the hands of the oppressor? Bogdanov's literary hero Netti responds: "Thus far science is the weapon of our enemies. We will triumph when we have made it our weapon. . . . The proletariat must master it by changing it." Moreover, he argued that there was no such thing as absolute, unchanging truth, nor could there be, because whatever existed was in a constant state of change and interaction with its environment. The emphasis on the relativity of historical knowledge brought Bogdanov into conflict with Marxists, who claimed that the laws of historical development are absolute. For him historical change is universal, causal, and relative. "Change is universal in the sense that it applies to both nature and society with the same regularity—it is causal in the sense that it has no room for teleological explanations—it is relative."

In addition to a historical approach to economic problems, Bogdanov assimilated the philosophical viewpoint regrettably common to writers on primitive economic culture such as Lavrόv, which was positivism, that is, the rejection of metaphysics—the idea that an absolute truth about reality is possible, that a reality indeed exists. Bogdanov, like Comte himself, took the view that metaphysics was a historical product, that it had emerged at a given stage of social development, but that it would be overcome in the course of time with scientific advancement. On the basis of all that has gone before, he predicted that one can be certain of one thing—that progress in science will lead to greater unity in views on life and on the world than there is now, that it will not open any new chasms between animate and inanimate nature but will fill, fully or partly, those gaps in this sphere from which modern perception suffers. A main theme of Bogdanov's argument, indeed, was to point out the undenying unity and interdependence in all spheres of existence. To Bogdanov science is one and indivisible; therefore, sociology could rise to a scientific level only by operating on the basis of natural science models. He rejected the traditional view of philosophy as a discipline standing apart from and above science; he also argued that sociology should not be submerged in philosophy but should depend on its own substantive claims and methodological tools. At one time, he argued that the improvement in the scientific standards of sociology and other disciplines would lead to the demise of philosophy as a mode of inquiry and a body of knowledge. In *Knowledge from a Historical Point of View*, Bogdanov proposed a schema of concepts and propositions treating human society as an integral part of nature, subject to self-adjusting natural processes and precise scientific measurement. In *Essays in the Psychology of Society and Empirio-monism* he further advanced a set of propositions giving a firmer and more comprehensive footing to the notion of the unity of man and nature.

Bogdanov contended that during the first four decades of its existence, Marx's theory had helped explain a mass of historical developments and had not encountered serious opposition from other theories. Many able writers enriched it by helping it to expand its competence over new areas of sociological problems. However, history was not at a standstill; particularly in science many changes of revolutionary proportions raised serious questions that Marxist theory could not ignore. In particular the materialism articulated by Marx was identified with a philosophy that failed to grasp the significance of the achievements of physics.

He was no less concerned with technological and economistic determinism, which had arisen in the Marxian literature of the Second International. He considered the dialectic, narrowly interpreted, as a pitfall and refused to present it as a universal method or as the totality of the process of evolution. Indeed, he thought that the term "evolution" in Marx, as in Hegel, was unclear. It was this very problem that the Russian philosopher sought to address in the development of a general science of organization. His greatest work, the three-volume treatise *The Universal Organizational Science: Tektology*, represents a synthesis of a multifaceted yet unified thought. This is the work that undoubtedly has most to say to us.

Bogdanov found important points of correspondence with Marx's social theory, which can be categorized into two levels. The nature of these can be found in the first two themes of his proposed plan of study published in *Neue Zeit* by Kautsky in 1903. The first theme was to identify those qualities common to all forms of society, taking into account their historical aspect. The second was to identify the constituent elements of the internal structure of bourgeois society as a particular form.[41] In his endeavor, Bogdanov attempted to revise Marxian and Hegelian dialectics.[42] Such an undertaking was not inconsistent with certain historic themes in Russian social thought.

Bogdanov declared himself to be a positivist and used the positivist approach to metaphysics to expound the philosophical presuppositions of Marx's theory of commodity fetishism and explain to workers what had eluded many a philosopher. Bogdanov's positivism, however, was singularly distinct from the Comtean thematic mathematization of science.

Bogdanov was an important philosophical and political interpreter of social upheavals and the outbursts of scientific discoveries that marked the turn of the nineteenth century, and in view of the turbulent state of the former Soviet Union, his view may cast some light upon the future of "real socialism." The developments in science and technology, political and social practice, that were initiated in Bogdanov's time have, of course, proceeded apace in our century. Where the social cataclysms and the rapid pace of scientific and technological discoveries will finally lead few would be so foolhardy as to predict. This uncertainty is all the more reason for us to study the paradigm change taking place in science and society at the turn of the century, in order to gain a clear sense of our present bearings. Bogdanov, as an interpreter of these changes, can teach us much. His splendid edifice of thought, which has great intrinsic worth, commands the historicist's attention.

As we have noted, in the late nineteenth and early twentieth centuries the synthesis of natural scientific knowledge was confounded by a paradigmatic crisis. Today, insofar as there is a renewed search for a metascience and a reemerging awareness of the role of energy and the biospheric imperative in economic analysis, considerable advantage may be gained by an analysis of A.A. Bogdanov's early and fundamental contribution.[43]

8
Social Energetics: A Marxian Variant

Undoubtedly influenced by the Slavophile holism that infected Russian intellectuality, and having absorbed W. Ostwald's concept of social energetics, A.A. Bogdanov initially attempted to revise Marxism along biophysical lines. This constituted his particular historicism—a general theory of social dynamics synthesized with Darwinian evolutionary dynamics. Marking his entry into the philosophical arena in 1899, the year he ended his formal studies, Bogdanov published *The Fundamental Elements of the Historical Outlook on Nature*, a work influenced by Ostwald's *Philosophy of Nature*. Bogdanov's first work was followed, in 1901, by *Knowledge from a Historical Viewpoint*. In these works, he wanted to formulate a synthesis between the economic and social materialism of Marx and what Bogdanov considered to be the monism of the natural sciences.

Bogdanov was very much influenced during this time by the energeticism of Wilhelm Ostwald. He became intrigued by Ostwald's energetics and Le Chatelier's law of equilibrium in thermodynamics because they seemed to offer broad explanatory principles applicable to both social and physical phenomena. Similarly, he thought Darwin's and Spencer's bio-organismic theories suggested general principles of social change that could be viewed as a process of adaptation or of growth and differentiation.

The influence of Ostwald on Bogdanov is apparent in several of his comments. For instance, he speaks at length of the law of the conservation of energy, which he regards as the force common to all types of phenomena both physical and social. References to energy are encountered occasionally in *A Short Course of Economic Science*, where he speaks, for example, of the "expenditure of social labor energy." Susiluoto remarks that for Bogdanov the law of the preservation of energy guaranteed the continuity and measurability of phenomena. Following Ostwald's *Kulturwissenschaften* this law also applied to society, in which changes could be regarded as increases and decreases in energy.

Bogdanov used Ostwald's theory of energy as a model for a neo-Kantian theory of knowledge and an interpretation of the historical succession of social systems. The theory of energy rested on two pillars: the law of the conservation of energy and the pre-Heisenberg principle of the full measurability of natural processes. The law of the conservation of energy was the same as the law of the uniformity and continuity of natural processes; this is also expressed in the statement that in nature everything must issue from something else, that nothing in nature is *sui generis*. The energy orientation contributed to a major redefinition of "causality" as the key explanatory mechanism of the work of nature. Indeed, Bogdanov thought that the fundamental transformation of the meaning of causality was the most revolutionary development in nineteenth-century science. The classical law of causality considers cause and effect as discrete (and, therefore, static) phenomena set off from each other both quantitatively and qualitatively. The energy theory is concerned not with cause and effect as distinct phenomena but with the processes involved in causal sequences. It represents the last and decisive step in uprooting the static notion of nature. The basic contribution of the energy orientation, according to Bogdanov, is that it shifts the focus of scientific inquiry from ontological to functional aspects of nature: modern science no longer asks what nature and society are but how they work.

Reinforcing the concept of the unity of the sciences, the energy view justifies and makes mandatory the use of natural science models in the social sciences. In the social sciences, the energy approach is the same as the historical approach: it places the primary emphasis on the interaction of social processes, particularly on the relationship between technology and ideology, the two universal categories of social processes. Social processes are to human society what the transformation of energy is to nature in general: they depict the continuity and measurability of social change.

Bogdanov's sociological theory, at least as presented in *Knowledge from a Historical Point of View*, is both historical and monistic. It is historical inasmuch as it places the primary emphasis on the dynamics of social processes; it is monistic inasmuch as it interprets all phenomena of social dynamics as specific adaptations to increases and decreases in social energy and inasmuch as it operates on the assumption that human society manifests a spontaneous tendency—which it shares with organic nature—to eliminate internal contradictions and to strengthen harmonious relations. In his earlier sociological theory, Bogdanov was much closer to Comte's emphasis on social consensus than to Marx's emphasis on class warfare as the key to the mysteries of organized social life.

Bogdanov was concerned primarily with applying the energy approach to the study of the evolution of knowledge as an index of the evolution of human society: He equated the study of the socialization of knowledge with the study of the inner dynamics of social relations and the main lines of social progress. Knowledge, as the moving force of history, is not an epistemological but a sociological phenomenon. For Bogdanov an analysis of cooperative relations among social groups provided the basis for a study of general forms of knowledge. Characteristic for the entire society, an analysis of cooperation among and within individual groups provides, he argued, the basis for an inquiry into ideological tendencies. The history of human society, he noted, is the history of the growing complexity, depth, and precision of man's knowledge of the universe. The history of society is the continuous and accumulative socialization of knowledge —the gradual, but inexorable expansion of social experience. While the objectivity of physical elements does not have an epistemological basis, for all knowledge is individual—and therefore subjective—in origin, it has a sociological basis, for its regularity and validity stem exclusively from the fact that it is a product and a reflection of social organization.

Denigrating Ostwald's concept of energeticism on the rationale that obtains from his concept of matter, Lenin notes that:

> In the preface to his *Lectures on Natural Philosophy* [Ostwald] declares that he regards "as a great gain the simple and natural removal of the old difficulties in the way of uniting concepts of matter and mind by subordinating both to the concept of energy.". . . On page 394 of Ostwald's *Lectures* we read: "That all external events may be presented as processes between energies can be simply explained if our mental processes are themselves energetic and impose this property of theirs on all external phenomena." This is pure idealism: it is not our thought that reflects the transformation of energy in the external world, but the external world that reflects a "property" of our mind! . . . If the primary concept of energy is so defined as to embrace psychical phenomena, we have no longer the simple concept of energy understood and recognized in scientific circles.[1]

Affirming mechanicalism and opposing Ostwald, Lenin wrote that the transformation of energy is regarded by science as an objective process independent of the minds of men and of the experiences of humankind; that is to say, it is regarded materialistically. Any divergence from this position is a divergence from diamat, which he brands as idealist. Lenin writes on energetics that:

> Both materialism and idealism can be expressed in terms of "energetics" just as they can be expressed in terms of "experience," and the like. Energeticist physics is a source of new idealist attempts to conceive motion without matter —because the disintegration of particles of matter which hitherto had been accounted non-disintegrable and because of the discovery of hitherto unknown forms of material motion.[2]

Further, in connection with Lenin's understanding of energetics, he maintained that it serves philosophers as a mere pretext for renouncing materialism for idealism. Its ad hoc appeal is an aesthetic arising during a hiatus when "physicists have left the atom but have not yet arrived at the electron."[3]

Lenin once again defers to Abel Rey's analysis of the Maxwellian paradox and those who argue for social energetics when he writes:

> The abstract fictions of mathematics seem to have interposed a screen between physical reality and the manner in which the mathematicians understand the science of this reality.... Although they desire above all to be objective when they engage in physics; although they seek to find and retain a foothold in reality; they are haunted by old habits. So that even in the concepts of energetics, which had to be built more solidly and with fewer hypotheses than the old mechanism ... we are still dealing with theories of mathematicians.... The crisis in physics lies in the conquest of the realm of physics by the mathematical spirit. The progress of physics on the one hand, and the progress of mathematics on the other, led in the nineteenth century to a close amalgamation between these two sciences.[4]

Referring pointedly to the Maxwellian descriptive mathematical formulation that led to the alleged "disappearance of matter," to the idealization in science, and to the entire mathematical movement, Abel Rey maintained that theoretical physics had become mathematical physics, not as a branch of physics, but as an esoteric branch of mathematics.[5] Cultivated by mathematicians accustomed to abstract conceptualizations, the mathematician found himself cramped by concrete material and intractable elements. Accordingly, he tended to reduce them to abstractions of an entirely nonmaterial and conceptual manner, or to ignore them altogether. Concrete reality, as physical objective data, completely disappeared. What remained was only a formal representation of relations in terms of differential equations. Descriptive formalism everywhere replaced the real element. Thus, historically and by virtue of the mathematical form assumed by theoretical physics, the crisis of physics suggested a withdrawal from objective facts and concrete reality.[6] No less problematic was the lack of concreteness of the issues addressed by political economy.

But as early as 1883, the Ukrainian socialist Serhii Podolinsky, a friend of Lavróv, had, in fact, sought a reconstruction of political economy. Podolinsky, who "as a political thinker combined Marxist economics, a Ukrainian orientation on peasantry, i.e., a Narodnik, and Russian revolutionary populism," sought to invest Marxism with the basic principles of the natural sciences.[7] Pointedly, he added an energetic dimension to his populist Marxism. He was among the first to measure the output : input ratio in agriculture in energy terms, and his analysis led him to effectively scrutinize the economic process from a thermodynamic perspective.[8]

Podolinsky's thesis, that energy limits and governs the structure of human societies, was a tenuous elaboration of Marx's thought. For in *Capital*, Marx speculated on the role of energy in the economy: "What Lucretius says is self-evident: *nil posse creari de nihilo*, out of nothing, nothing can be created. Creation of value is transformation of labour-power into labour. Labour-power itself is energy transferred to a human organism by means of nourishing matter."[9]

Inspired by Marx's work, Podolinsky was concerned as to whether his energy analysis could be fitted into the Marxist framework. He used the laws of thermodynamics to analyze the flow of energy through agriculture and industrial production and wrote: "[The earth receives] incredible quantities of physical forces from the Sun which can then experience the most diverse transformations, and all physical and biological phenomena are expressions of such transformations.[10]

Keenly aware that he was in the line of succession to the Physiocrats and Carnot and Clausius, Podolinsky cited the former group's emphasis on nature as the source of wealth and the economic implications of the latter pair's discoveries. According to Kaufmann, Podolinsky, tried to reconcile the labor theory of value with a thermodynamic analysis of the economic process.[11] Credited with being the first to develop the concept of energy returns to energy input in different types of land use, Podolinsky attempted in a series of articles, to combine Marxist theory with an ecological approach. His principle was that a society was not viable unless energy return to human energy expenditure covers the energy cost of human labor. He placed emphasis on the basic ecological fact, which at first seemed to imply that since energy used by man (as food, as clothing, as warmth, etc.) came from nature and not from labor, that labor did not create value. This was his initial standpoint. He wrote:

> We have in front of us two parallel processes which together form the so-called circuit of life (*Kreislauf des Lebens*). Plants have the property of accumulating solar energy, but animals, when they feed on vegetable substances, transform a part of this saved energy into mechanical work and dissipate this energy into space. If the quantity of energy accumulated by plants is greater than that dispersed by animals, then stocks of energy appear, for instance, in the period when mineral coal was formed, during which vegetable life obviously was preponderant over animal life. If, on the contrary, animal life were preponderant, provision of energy would be quickly dispersed and animal life would have to go back to the limits determined by vegetable wealth. So, a certain equilibrium would have to build between the accumulation and the dissipation of energy.[12]

Interested in demonstrating that controlled energy supply increases human work, Podolinsky sought to develop his concept of the energy productivity of labor. Seeking to achieve a definition of "useful work" or "productive work" he utilized a biological metaphor. Plants, by themselves, have the quality of "accumulating," "keeping," "saving," and "retarding" the dissipation of energy, and this process is intensified by means of human work. "Work . . . is that kind of use of the mechanical and mental energy accumulated in the [human] organism which has as a consequence an increase in the general energy budget of the Earth's surface."[13] Labor then creates value, and this value is measured in energy terms. In other words, "useful" or "productive" work is that which makes a positive contribution in energy terms.[14]

While agricultural activity lends itself favorably to Podolinsky's definition of useful labor, he also considered that equally qualified were tailors, shoemakers, and builders. They, too, furnished "protection against the dissipation of energy into space."[15]

In conclusions transmitted to Friedrich Engels, Podolinsky stated that the socialist model was flawed because it assumed that "scientific socialism" would overcome all natural resource scarcities and enable unlimited material expansion. Podolinsky's biophysical analysis led him to conclude that ultimate limits to economic growth lay not in the shackles of the relations of production, but in physical and ecological laws.

With some knowledge of the elementary energetics of human physiology, Engels, in a note of 1875 (later included in *Dialectics*), refers to experiments that sought to determine the energy dissipation of the human body. Engels, however, believed that "economics should not be mixed up with physics."[16] On December 19, 1882, Engels wrote to Marx that Podolinsky had "discovered" the following facts, already well known: If the food intake of one person per day were equal to 10,000 kilocalories, the physical work done would be a fraction of this energy. This physical work would become economic work if employed in fixing solar energy, for instance in agricultural activity. In agriculture one would have to reckon, among energy inputs, the energy value of fertilizers and other auxiliary means, a difficult thing to compute. In industry, all energy accounting had to stop; it was extremely difficult to calculate in energy terms the costs of production. The wish to express economic relations in physical terms could not be carried out. All that Podolinsky had managed to show, wrote Engels to Marx on December 22, 1882, was the old story that all industrial producers have to live from the products of agriculture. From Podolinsky's analysis it became clear to Engels that "human labor is able to retain and prolong the action of the sun on the earth's surface beyond the time that it would take place without such labor."[17] However, Engels then asserted that "to seek to express economic relationships in terms of units of measure borrowed from physics [is] absolutely impossible."[18]

> My idea of the Podolinsky business is as follows. His real discovery is that human labor has the power of detaining solar energy on the earth's surface and permitting its activity longer than would be the case without it. . . . Podolinsky has strayed away from his very valuable discovery into mistaken paths because he was trying to find in natural science a new proof of the truth of socialism, and has therefore confused physics with economics.[19]

Podolinsky's article began by explaining the laws of energetics, quoting Clausius that although the energy of the universe was a constant, there was an irrevocable tendency toward the dissipation of energy.[20] "Entropy" referred to the quantity of energy that would no longer be transformed into other forms of energy. All physical and biological phenomena were expressions of the transformations of this energy. In March 1880, he had published an article against social Darwinism. Though he realized that the availability of energy was a crucial consideration for the increase (or decrease) of population, following Marx, he thought that the distribution of production was explained by the relations among social classes.

The Marxian doctrine that labor was the source of value for Podolinsky had to be reconciled with an energy analysis of the economic process. His initial position was based on the ecological fact that implied that since the energy used by man came from nature and not from the act of labor, then labor did not create value. Rather the role of labor was the increase in "the accumulation of energy on earth." "Work," he wrote, "is that kind of use of the mechanical and mental energy accumulated in the (human) organism which has as a consequence an increase in the general energy budget on the Earth's surface."[21] In this connection, Podolinsky considered that though agriculture was the principal activity that lent itself to such a definition, it extended to other activities as well. Insofar as human work has the capacity to increase the summary flow of energy:

> Humanity is a machine that not only turns heat and other physical forces into work but succeeds also in carrying out the inverse cycle, that is, it turns work into heat and other physical forces necessary to satisfy our needs, and, so to speak, with its own work turned into heat is able to heat its own boiler.[22]

He concluded that the energy viewpoint was compatible with the Marxian view that labor creates value. Energy accounting thus gave a scientific basis to the labor theory of value, a point that neither Marx nor Engels appreciated.

In his correspondence with Marx of April 8, 1880, Podolinsky wrote: "With particular impatience I wait for your opinion on my attempt to bring surplus labor [and implicitly surplus value] and the current physical theories into harmony."[23]

The Austrian Marxist Otto Jensen printed Engels's letters to Marx and Podolinsky and explained that in these letters Engels had anticipated a critique of social energetics before social energetics itself appeared on the scene.[24] For Engels, in a letter to Marx (December 19, 1882), commented that: "Podolinsky has completely forgotten that a man who works does not only incorporate present solar heat, he is rather a great squanderer of past solar heat. How we squander energy reserves, coal, minerals, forests and so on, you know better than I do."[25]

Although, on the one hand, Engels understood how a calculus of energy inputs and outputs could be established in hunting and in agricultural activities, even to the extent of remarking that the calculus would be difficult in agriculture because one should include the energetic value of fertilizers and other auxiliary means, he thought, on the other hand, that: "The energy value of a hammer, a screw, or a needle calculated according to the cost of production is an impossible quantity. In my opinion it is absolutely impossible to try and express economic relations in physical magnitudes."[26] Thus, he rejected a net energy analysis.

But Engels was not unaware of the development of thermodynamics. He wrote that:

> [For] almost two centuries heat was considered a special mysterious substance instead of a form of motion of ordinary matter. . . . Nevertheless, physics dominated by the caloric theory discovered a series of highly important laws of heat and cleared the way, particularly for Fourier and Sadi Carnot.[27]

That Engels appears to have kept himself abreast of numerous developments in the natural sciences is apparent in *Anti-Dühring* and later in *Dialectics*.[28] Though he had an understanding of the implications of the entropy law, it was a somewhat confused one. This is apparent when, in *Dialectics*, he writes:

> Clausius' second law . . . however it may be formulated, shows energy as lost, qualitatively if not quantitatively. *Entropy cannot be destroyed by natural means but it can certainly be created.* The world clock has to be wound up, then it goes on running until it arrives at a state of equilibrium from which only a miracle can set it going again. The energy expended in winding has disappeared, at least qualitatively, and can only be restored by an *impulse from outside*. Hence, an impulse from outside was necessary at the beginning also, hence, the quantity of motion, or energy, existing in the universe was not always the same, hence, energy must have been created. i.e. it must be creatable, and therefore destructible. *Ad absurdum!*[29]

Marx, though he rejected Podolinsky's analysis, was himself not unaware of the concept of "metabolism" between man and nature—a term he employs throughout *Capital*. For metabolism, Podolinsky substituted the phrase "circuit of life." His interest in scientific developments, in fact, led him to speculate on the chemical transformations that the human body experiences during a working day. Despite such speculations, Marx's dismissal of Podolinsky's "Marxian social energetics" marked a particular phase in the development of Marxist and Marxian thought.

Aside from Podolinsky, S. Suvorov, *Studies in the Philosophy of Marxism*, appears to have attempted a similar generalization.[30] From Lenin we learn that:

> In the gradation of the laws that regulate the world process, the particular and complex become reduced to the general and simple, and all of them are subordinate to the universal law of development—that law of the economy of forces. The essence of this law is that every system of forces is more capable of conservation and development the less its expenditure, the greater its accumulation and the more effectively expenditure serves accumulation. The forms of mobile equilibrium, which long ago evoked the idea of objective purposiveness (the solar system, the cycle of terrestrial phenomena, the process of life),

arise, and develop by virtue of the conservation and accumulation of the energy inherent in them—by virtue of their intrinsic economy. The law of economy of forces is the unifying and regulating principle of all development —inorganic, biological and social.[31]

In a footnote, Lenin adds: "It is characteristic that Suvorov calls the discovery of the law of conservation and transformation of energy, 'the establishment of the basic principles of energetics'."[32] Suvorov, like Podolinsky before him, and Bogdanov, sought to revise Marxism on the basis of social energetics; that is, on the basis of principles of thermodynamics. Suvorov sought to revise Marxism:

[by] establishing the fundamental law of social dynamics according to which the evolution of productive forces is the determining principle of all economic and social development. But the development of productive forces corresponds to the growth of productivity of labor, to the relative reduction in expenditure and increase in the accumulation of energy . . . this is the economic principle.[33]

The basis of both Marx's 1870 criticism of Lange and Lenin's criticism of Bogdanov's social energetics and Suvorov's law of economy principally derives from the attempt to employ biological metaphors in the social sciences. Lenin considered this reprehensible. Indeed, Lenin heaps vitriolic contempt on Bogdanov's works, saying that they were "indescribable bosh," that:

Such unspeakable nonsense is served up as Marxism! Can one imagine anything more sterile, lifeless and scholastic than this string of biological and energeticist terms that contribute nothing and can contribute nothing, in the sphere of the social sciences? . . . The only "Marxism" here is a repetition of an already known conclusion, and all the "new" proof of it, all this "social energetics" and "social selection" is a mere collection of words, a sheer mockery of Marxism.[34]

This pithy assessment was based on the premise that empirio-monism, as the social-science application of energetics, did not increase concrete knowledge of societal phenomena. It merely interpreted reality in a different way.[35] One might say that its practical value was not evident, or that it lacked instrumentalism.

Lenin was certainly not a lone critic of energetics. In connection with Ostwald's energeticism, V.I. Vernadsky, in a critique of what he viewed as the underlying vitalist complexion,[36] referred to it as an outgrowth of philosophical thought on the subject of the psychic processes. Central to this was the idea that living natural bodies possessed a peculiar vital force that differentiated the living from the dead. These notions were leaving the domain of modern science. However, new vitalistic notions, with their foundation not in scientific data but in philosophical concepts such as Driesch's "entelechy" or Ostwald's vital energy were emerging.[37]

9

The Phenomenological Marxism of Bogdanov

Machian Influences

The paradigmatic crisis of mechanicalism caused a number of authors to attempt neomechanical reconstructions and others, such as Ostwald, to seek a grand unity of science in principles of energy, extending to a socioenergetic theory of history. In particular, the efforts of Ostwald stimulated a number of economists to revise their thinking about the economic process. However, in some cases the early reconstruction of economic thought consistent with a thermodynamic paradigm came to be regarded as an unwarranted and malicious attack on the established mechanical paradigm, an attack on science and materialism. Clearly, the most interesting of the substantive contributions to this emerging paradigm arose in prerevolutionary Russia.

Bogdanov may have identified a vitalist dimension in Ostwald's concept and consequently sought to distance himself from Ostwald.[1] Copleston notes that: "[From] Ostwald's form of monism Bogdanov moved towards the empiriomonism or empirio-critism of Avenarius and Mach, according to which the sole adequate basis or source of knowledge, both prescientific and scientific, is constituted by 'pure experience,' which Mach conceived as reducible to sensations."[2]

Starting from his empirio-monist position, according to which the originally (ontologically specified) chaotic "elements of experience" can be arranged in many different ways, Bogdanov proceeded to a type of praxiology that gives the most general rule of practically organizing the elements of experience.[3]

According to Bogdanov, what we regard as the material world, nature, and the common world, is the product of collectively organized experience, insofar as it has a social basis. That is to say, the common world, as experienced, has been progressively formed in the course of human history out of the raw material of sensation. In addition, however, to the world that is basically the same for all, there are private phenomenological perspectives. That is to say, in addition to collectively organized experience there is organization in the form of ideas or concepts that differ from person to person and group to group.[4] It was with this notion that Lenin took great exception.

Copleston reflects that:

> [For] the Marxist, matter is the basic reality, this means that all reality falls within the sphere of experience, actual or possible. In fact, we can say that reality is experience. If, therefore, we accept the empirio-monism of Avenarius and Mach, it follows that reality is reducible to sensations, inasmuch as, according to empirio-monism, sensations are the ultimate data or elements of experience.[5]

Karl Kautsky, the leading German orthodox Marxist theorist of the period before the First World War, was asked by Lenin to express an opinion on the Russian Marxists' quarrel over Machism. Kautsky wrote that he deplored it. He was himself a dialectical materialist, yet, nonetheless, he speculated that Marxian social theory could be united with Machist philosophy.[6]

In discussing what he referred to as the excursions of the empirio-criticists into economic thought, and specifically Marxian thought, Lenin took aim first at Franz Blei and his work entitled *Die Metaphysik in der National-ökonomie* (Metaphysics in Political Economy), and then at Bogdanov. Blei, according to Lenin, considered Marx's theory as "unbiological," it knows nothing of "vital differences."[7] Lenin notes that once having framed his thesis within Marxist thought, Bogdanov, in his 1902 article *The Development of Life in Nature and Society*, attempted the unacceptable—to reformulate Marxism.

For Alexander Vucinich, the distinction between Lenin and Bogdanov is fundamental.[8] Lenin and Bogdanov subscribed to what they both termed philosophical monism. Lenin's monism was virtually ontological: It was based on the axiom of the material unity of the universe in its natural and sociocultural dimensions. His position may be interpreted as contiguous to the concept of the unity of scientific knowledge, but it lacked the phenomenological character of Bogdanov's. Bogdanov's monism is principally epistemological: It is based on the notion of the unity of knowledge, on the idea of "the continuity in the system of experience" and of the unity of "cognitive material" or "psychic and physical elements."[9]

Karl Ballestrem notes that the irreconcilable differences between Lenin and Bogdanov erupted into an open factional struggle, splitting the Bolsheviks into two bitterly fighting groups for years to come.[10]

The events of December 1905 led to Bogdanov's arrest. He was jailed in the summer of 1906 and while in prison wrote *Empirio-monism*. When he left prison, he sought to resume his collaborations with Lenin and presented him with a copy of this newest literary product. This time Lenin's reaction was even worse than earlier. "I sat down to a careful study of it," Lenin wrote in a letter to Gorky on February 25, 1908. Referring pointedly to Bogdanov's alleged betrayal of natural scientific materialism, Lenin noted that Bogdanov was first led astray by Ostwald's energetics and later by Mach's subjective idealism, and that it was under their influence that he wrote *Empirio-monism*.[11]

> On reading it through I lost my temper and was unusually furious: it became clearer than ever to me that he was moving along an arch-mistaken way, not a Marxist way. I wrote then "a declaration of love" to him, a short letter on philosophy to the length of three exercise books.[12]

Reserving for himself the construction of a monist viewpoint, Bogdanov, with justification, rejected the notion that he himself was a Machian empirio-critic. Indeed, in a rebuttal of Plekhanov, who had also rebuked him for becoming a "Machian," Bogdanov wrote:

> I cannot, however, acknowledge myself a "Machist" in philosophy. In the general philosophical conceptions, I took only one thing from Mach's general philosophical conception—the idea of neutrality of the elements of experience with respect to "physical" and "psychological" and the exclusive dependence of these characterizations on the interconnection of experience.[13] . . . Thus in all that follows, in the teaching of the genesis of physical and psychological experience, in the teachings of substitutions in the teaching concerning the "interferences" of completes . . . there is nothing in common between Mach and me. I am much less a "Machist" than [comrade] Beltov [a pseudonym for G. Plekhanov] is a "Holbachian" and I hope this does not prevent either of us from being a good Marxist.[14]

Believing that a monistic unity might be achieved on the basis of Mach's philosophy of neutral elements, Bogdanov noted first, the common ground in terms of which the physical and mental arose could be traced and explained in a historical fashion; and second, the seemingly distinct complexes, physical and mental, which, he argued, could be shown as interrelated through a reformulation of their causal connections. This process of creating a phenomenological and monist interpretation of empirio-criticism constitutes one aspect of Bogdanov's original contribution to philosophical thought and Russian Critical Marxism.

Contrary to the assertions of the empirio-critics (and even his own earlier thought), Bogdanov, with a thoroughly post-empiricist flourish, maintained the "objectivity" of reality is not simply given but is rather the result of an extended and practical history of man.

> It is necessary to understand reality as practice, taught Marx. But what is human practice? First of all, [it is] the struggle with the elementalness of nature, the process of subordination to man, i.e., production. This proceeds not according to individual but according to collective strengths, and thus the

practical nature of man is a social nature. In it one must seek explanations of every development of humankind, for the forms of his life and thought.... Marx considered reality from the point of view of social practice in its straightforward direct form, i.e., in the form of production.[15]

Copleston records that if, as Machians, we assume that the ultimate elements of experience are sensations, it is obvious that we customarily think that the world of experience would not have arisen without a process of organization.[16] J.D. White apprises that Bogdanov came to this understanding with the diluting of his Ostwaldian "energy" perspective. This marked an interesting phenomenological turn in Bogdanov's thought.

It was Plekhanov's and Lenin's violent polemic against Bogdanov that shaped to a great extent the future course of the philosophic thought of the Russian Marxists. Between 1908 and 1910 Plekhanov wrote over one hundred pages of refutation challenging Bogdanov's ties to the Marxist legacy. Despite Lenin's apparent sympathy for interdisciplinary pluralism, as found in the preface to the first edition of *Materialism and Empirio-Criticism* of 1909,[17] he wrote that a number of would-be Marxists had undertaken a campaign against the philosophy of Marxism. Indeed, Lenin found it necessary to determine "just what Marxism was so that one could distinguish Marxists from non-Marxists and force the latter either to change their opinions or to leave the party or at least the Bolshevik wing of it."[18] In *Materialism and Empirio-Criticism*, Lenin presented what he regarded as the "correct interpretation" of the philosophical views of Marx and Engels. He upheld their principle that all reality exists as a thing-in-itself and is subject to eternally valid laws.

According to Biggart and Yassour, "Lenin's *Materialism and Empirio-Criticism* was largely written as a refutation of Bogdanov's philosophical thought in an attempt to drive him out of the Party."[19] Lenin portrayed Bogdanov as a pawn of neo-Kantian epistemological idealism that sought to blur the differences between the infrastructure and the superstructure of human society. In *Materialism and Empirio-Criticism*, Lenin claimed that Bogdanov's "creativity" was little more than a rehash of earlier idealistic supporters of bourgeois society.[20] Lenin's ridicule of Bogdanov and other followers of Ostwald and Mach stemmed from their definition of matter, which did not repeat Plekhanov's homily.

Bogdanov charged that as represented by Marxism-Leninism, Plekhanov's homily advances the erroneous theory that knowledge is an Archimedean point, an absolute *epistemologica* (for it reflects the "objectively" existing external nature) and relative historically (for its depth and reliability are limited by the availability of instruments extending the power of sense organs). To Bogdanov, knowledge is relative both epistemologically (for its origin is essentially subjective) and historically. Lenin's absolutizing of knowledge was, in Bogdanov's eyes, the principal weakness of his *Materialism and Empirio-Criticism*.

Despite its Archimedean objectivism, *Materialism and Empirio-Criticism* became the keystone of disciplinary Marxism-Leninism, its epistemological objectivism, the Soviet theory of knowledge. In the short preface (dated September 2, 1920) to the second edition of *Materialism and Empirio-Criticism*, Lenin took particular exception to Bogdanov, whom he described as "imparting bourgeois and reactionary views."[21]

> As for Bogdanov's latest works which I have had no opportunity to examine, the appended article by V.I. Nevsky gives the necessary information. Comrade Nevsky, working not only as a propagandist, but as a worker in a party school, had ample opportunity to convince himself that under the guise of "proletarian culture" Bogdanov is introducing bourgeois and reactionary views.[22]

Shortly after the second edition of *Materialism and Empirio-Criticism* appeared, Lenin wrote to Nikolai Bukharin inviting him to comment. Unlike Lenin, Bukharin was not convinced of the noxious character of Bogdanov's ideas and quipped that in reiterating the charge that Bogdanov's empirio-monism was a form of idealism, Lenin's concerns were misplaced, for Bogdanov had moved beyond his epistemological discourse and was focusing on Tektology—a general organization theory.[23]

Later orthodox Soviet critics have been unanimous in their condemnation of Bogdanov. According to one such critic, Bogdanov's thought was extremely dangerous and had to be suppressed "because he stood head and shoulders above all the other revisionists and attempted to introduce systematically his revisionist views in philosophy, political economy, and sociology."[24] Lenin was apparently plagued by Bogdanov and his popularity. By 1920, the Bolsheviks were presented with a dilemma: They were unable to publish the works of one of the most prolific and influential Russian Marxists, Plekhanov, because of the latter's support for the Mensheviks, while the works of Plekhanov's and Lenin's philosophical adversary, Bogdanov, were regularly being published. Lenin was concerned that unless an "orthodox" version of Marxism was available to the educated public, Bogdanov's "heretical" edition of Marxism would impress itself upon the minds of the new regime. Indeed, the dissemination of Bogdanov's ideas was considered of sufficient importance to merit discussion in the Politburo where, on May 6, 1920, "Lenin circulated an indignant note on the proposed publication of a tenth edition of Bogdanov's *Short Course of Economic Science*: 'It would appear that there is no mention here of the 'Dictatorship of the proletariat'?!!!? And this is to be published by the State Publishing House?'"[25]

What was apparently emerging in Bogdanov's thought resembled what Merleau-Ponty later referred to as Western Marxism. However, Eastern Marxism, that is, the Marxism of Lenin, was synonymous with official and institutionalized party ideology of the "East" and "West" alike. Western Marxism might have started its career within the confines of party bureaucracies (i.e., Bogdanov's apprehensions preceded those of Lukács), but the incompatibility of that theory and the institutional contexts inevitably came to the fore. Western Marxism was characterized by the tension between theory and its institutionalization. But it was inextricably connected with phenomenology from its very origin even if in an unacknowledged way.[26]

It has already been suggested that the history of Russian Social Democracy was written from a Leninist point of view, one that set the ground for critique, vindication, and vilification. Focusing their attention on Lenin, Western historians too often do not provide the broader context that the study of Bogdanov's ideas demand.

> The Russian Marxists ridiculed the subjective sociology, and quite to their own detriment, entrenched themselves in a position proclaiming the existence of objective laws independent of human consciousness, overlooking the fact that Lavróv's views had much in common with those which Marx propounded. Victor Chernov was thus able to taunt his Social Democratic opponents with quotations from the *Theses on Feuerbach* upholding the anthropomorphic subjective principle.[27]

It is of more than antiquarian interest to note that that "school of thought which harmonized most in Russia with democracy, social transformation and the scientific outlook was positivism."[28] Bogdanov consequently was following a traditional philosophical trend in Russian thought in seeking a reconciliation of materialism and positivism.

The alleged father of Russian Marxism, George Valentinovich Plekhanov, formulated the thesis that matter is prior to spirit or mind or consciousness. For Lenin, materialism is essentially the doctrine that "matter, nature, being, the physical—is primary; and [that] spirit, consciousness, sensation, the psychical—is secondary."[29] The Soviet philosopher A.M. Deborin reasserted Plekhanov's and Lenin's proposition, saying that, "Matter is all that exists. Being from its very nature is of a material character."[30]

As V.I. Ivanovsky, a contributor to *Pravda* under Bogdanov's editorship, wrote:

> If anyone suggests that the connection of a scientific outlook with positivism undermines the recognition of matter as the ultimate basis of the world, he is sadly mistaken—simply because a scientific outlook does not demand such a recognition. The scientific outlook can be built not only on a materialist, but also an energeticist, an agnostic, a phenomenalist or various other bases.[31]

Lenin's line of argument principally derives from Engels's diamat. This philosophy upholds the existence of one single and absolute world substance, namely, matter, i.e., reality, per se, as it presents itself as an object of perception and scientific research. Consequently, all research that denies the centrality of the material nature is false. It follows then that the diamat is the only scientific

Weltanschauung, and every scientist is, consciously or unconsciously, a materialist in his method of research who accords priority to matter. Moreover, according to Lenin, since material substance by necessity exists in space and time, entities that have no existence in space and time, e.g., aesthetics and culture, are idealist illusions.

Though Nikolai Bukharin, an admirer of Bogdanov, tried to explain to Lenin that Bogdanov's formulation was distinct from a pure Machian interpretation, Lenin was unconvinced and interpreted *Empirio-monism* as a sort of solipsism:[32]

> We have seen that subjective idealism is the point of departure for and the fundamental principle of the empirio-criticist philosophy. The world is our sensation—this is the basic truth that they try to stamp out without success, using little words like "element" and theories like that of "independent series," "coordination," "interaction." This philosophy is absurd in that it ends up in solipsism, in recognizing the existence solely of the philosophizing individual. But our Russian disciples of Mach assure us that the accusation of solipsism against Mach is a matter of extreme subjectivism. This is what Bogdanov says in the preface to his Russian translation of Mach's Analysis of Sensations . . . and what the whole Machist confraternity repeats after him in all the keys.[33]

Bogdanov was persistently labeled a "Machist" despite the fact that his psycho-energetics and other doctrines make his views quite remote from "Machism."[34] In 1908 there was a complete break between Lenin and Bogdanov, and Lenin directed his *Materialism and Empirio-Criticism* mainly against Bogdanov.[35]

Lenin's specific criticism of Bogdanov obtained from the latter's alleged attempt to "refute materialism from the standpoint of recent and modern positivism and natural science."[36] Whereas Bogdanov stated that the Russian Marxists were at odds with contemporary scientific thought in general, "which demands an unlimited critique and rejects all absolutes in knowledge."[37]

The Austrian philosopher, leader of the early Vienna Circle, and antimetaphysical empiricist, Ernst Mach cultivated in the minds of some a nihilist nostalgia. Perhaps with the aid of Mach's worldview, Bogdanov thought that Marxism might be brought into harmony with the advancements in science and philosophy.[38] But let us better locate the argument by turning briefly to Ernst Mach.

Mach himself was neither an opponent nor explicitly a proponent of any school of political philosophy, but rather an untiring and erudite foe of metaphysics in all avenues of human thought. A professor of physics at the Charles University of Prague, and later professor of the History and Theory of Inductive Sciences at Vienna, Mach eschewed the very notion that his thoughts formed a coherent philosophical system. Yet his rules of thought and his reflections on the nature of the world—comments and discussions that introduced his major works on physics and optics—did give a particular, even if unsystematic, worldview. In conjunction with the writings of several contemporaries, such as the German philosopher Richard Avenarius, this worldview was soon dubbed Critical Empiricism. Its major premises can be taken from one of Mach's more famous works, *The Analysis of Sensations*.[39] In his approach, Mach proved himself to be a troubled phenomenalist, arguing that there are no "things-in-themselves" that, while remaining unchanged and unchangeable, somehow give rise to sensation.[40] Mach's approach seems to lead him toward solipsism, though he and Avenarius denied this.[41] For Mach, the belief in the reality of the *other* is not a problem for philosophy. Rational people are those who believe in the *other*. To question the existence of the *other* was deemed not merely problematic but irrational. Kantian reality is a "texture," a "tone" of certain cognitive experiences that points, in the last resort, not to the "thing-in-itself" but to the relation between the cognitor and that cognated, the signifier and the signified.[42]

Avenarius offered a second denial of solipsism by noting that the presence of the *other* formed an intrinsic part of the primeval experience of man. Indeed, the notion of reality, as a given common to all, arises from the expressions of the *other* toward the objective world. The *other* announces "the sun rises," and I, turning my head, perceive the sun above the horizon. Thus, the reality of the *other* precedes and forms the ground for my perception of the objective. To question the reality of the *other* is to question reality itself.[43] This is tantamount to postulating that reality is a social construction.

The writings of Mach and, to a lesser extent, Avenarius struck a responsive chord among some Russian Marxists in their struggle to keep abreast of current scientific thinking. A general movement of Russian empirio-criticism appeared in the early years of this century and included individuals such as Vladimir Bazarov, Pavel Yushkevich, N. Valentinov, I.A. Berman, and Aleksandr A. Bogdanov. While each attempted to further develop the ideas contained in the original, it was Bogdanov who accepted the challenge of harmonizing Marxism (historical monism) and "Machism" in pursuit of a praxis-oriented socialist theory consistent with the discoveries and changes of the current era.[44] This proved to be a point of entry for the development of a phenomenological Marxism.

Mach reduced phenomena to "experience," to sensations that are neither purely physical, nor purely mental, but neutral.[45] According to Lukács, Mach's subjective idealism expressed the "unknowability," indeed the nonexistence, the unthinkable nature of an objective reality independent of consciousness. This was the implicit Machian axiom. Knowledge, according to Mach, progresses historically, as newer and more efficient ways of generalizing experience are demanded and discovered. Bogdanov saw in Mach's proposition an instrument for inventing a Marxist epistemology that sought to reduce reality to commonly appreciated dimensions. Constrained by Plekhanov's and Lenin's ontological materialism, Bogdanov sought to make a distinction between the physical experiences of society and the mental experience, the experience of the individual.[46]

Mach and even Avenarius were products of the scientific institutes characteristic of the crisis of physics, in which critical thought and praxis had been separated, where logical positivism was considered to be the very apogee of contemplative philosophy. This artificial separation led Mach to reject explanation in favor of pure description, a rejection that precluded the empirio-critics from developing an adequate notion of causality as the explanatory connection between various elements of experience. However, this self-imposed refusal to explain, Bogdanov concluded, prevented the empirio-critics from constructing a monist system that would overcome the false dualism of objective and subjective complexes.

Insofar as Russian Marxism, or more precisely Engelsism, was regarded as a deterministic, economic, materialist doctrine, with even finalistic overtones, it was argued that it was incapable of producing a compelling epistemological system. More correctly, Marx's procedure was in a sense pre-epistemological. Indeed, it is worth recalling that, for Marx, the legitimate understanding of reality demands a pre-epistemological procedure seriously at variance with what reality would itself seem to sanction were abstractive recapitulation the basis for legitimate truth claims, and given the idea of a separate and distinct theory of knowledge, that is, epistemology. For this reason epistemology was problematic for Marx, for it champions a problematic correspondence theory of the truth and an atomism, contrary to Marx's holism. For Marx, it separates thought from reality and in the process legislates the former as a fictive "idealism." No less does it condemn essentialism and noncorrespondential materialism as relics of a prescientific era. Thus it was, in fact, not that Marxism was epistemologically barren, but that an epistemology was at variance with Marx's procedure. Peter Struve (1952) and the "Legal Marxists" nonetheless argued that Marx and Engels had provided an exposition of historical materialism, but their theory lacked a purely philosophical basis. The resolution for this alleged problematique was sought outside Marxism. And it was Struve who argued that a critical philosophical reappraisal might be provided by the German neo-Kantians.

Referring to Bogdanov's epistemological contribution, Valentinov wrote that, "[T]he injection of empirio-criticism into Marxism seemed to me a task of paramount importance. Empirio-criticism would give Marxism the epistemological foundation it lacked and would permit the elimination ... of its weak aspects, while even further consolidating its strong one."[47]

The empirio-criticists were not materialists insofar as materialism postulates an ontological assertion about the existence of something that cannot be concretely experienced. Consequently, empirio-criticism succumbed to metaphysics. Bogdanov sought to place empirio-criticism and diamat alongside each other as philosophies unsuited to the present. For Bogdanov, Marx, and Mach were more than obsolete thinkers; they were serious competitors as well.[48] The view that Bogdanov held of himself has been confirmed in a recent study by Jensen. This study demonstrates that empirio-monism goes beyond Marx and Mach since it attempts "to end the division of knowledge into philosophy and science ... and to bring knowledge back to unity."[49] For Bogdanov, this unity can ultimately be achieved within an organizational paradigm.

Curiously, to Bogdanov empirio-criticism was not a rejection of ontological materialism but its revival. Materialism, he maintained, had lost its original meaning, the concept of matter having shed its sensuous nature and turned into a vague abstraction. In other words, Bogdanov was reaffirming the Kantian critique of reason and in the process acknowledged that Hume and the empiricists were the forerunners of Mach's empirio-monism and his own empirio-criticism.

Bogdanov refused to accept empirio-monism in its Machian form. For him, the writings of Mach and Avenarius reflected the bourgeois nature of European thought and society. Empirio-monism, he argued, was oriented toward shallow contemplation not praxis, toward a pure description of the world as it is, not toward changing it.[50]

The empirio-monists, said Bogdanov, would have us believe that they have arrived at a proper concept of reality for contemporary man and an equally proper way of orienting him in that reality that corresponds to "experience." This experience has nothing whatever in common with the traditional concepts of reality, whether materialist or idealist. It replaces matter and idea as primary being.[51] While experience is comprised at once of things and mental representations. Both things and representations are composed of the same parts or "elements." Experience is not divided into separate realms but is a homogeneous whole. Further, the empirio-critic purports to reject all possibility of things-in-themselves either as the cause of experience or as that which experience reflects. Thus, experience is in no way "material" or "ideal" in the usual sense of these terms.[52]

Despite a heavy dependence on natural science models, Bogdanov recognized that sociology, dealing with unique problems in logic and methodology, is quite distinct from physics. The problem facing sociology is how to reduce the unlimited complexity of concrete social situations and divergent influences to simple conceptions capable of scientific treatment. Without a reduction of the multitude of complex observations to limited simple notions, the sociologist can describe the universe of his inquiry, but he cannot explain it. To be a scientist, he must resort to an abstract method that, in turn, has two characteristics: It is deductive, for it draws general conclusions by testing and verifying hypotheses; it is historical, for it concentrates on social processes dominated by discernible "tendencies." Bogdanov noted that the basic task of the abstract method is to detect the tendencies of social processes that reveal regularities of scientific import. Because empirio-criticism considers all elements from the simple to the most complex homogeneous, no matter how diverse they appear, they all may be related to one another, or, rather, they all have relationships to one another that may be discovered with time. This permits the empirio-critic to raise the prospect of depicting the character, bonds, and dependencies of reality as an integrated whole without dividing it into separate realms such as matter, mind, or inorganic nature, life, etc. And, it is this feature that admits the possibility of the unity of scientific knowledge. With this, the empirio-critical doctrine of experience and its elements purports to be monistic and, as such, superior to other doctrines that regard reality as divided, hierarchical, or of different orders, with some primary and others manifestations of the primary.[53]

The objective is nothing but a manifestation of social experience, i.e., what is organized from the social viewpoint, namely, the "physical." Experience that is organized in an individual manner, on the other hand, is the "psychic." These two halves of intersubjective analysis, the social experiential and the psychical, are juxtaposed. What we have here are two different phases in the organization of human experience. Juxtaposing "physical" experience to "psychic" experience, Bogdanov sought to show that the realm of physical experience consistently represents the more advanced stage of organization and that the psychic is derivative thereof. "The psychic is experience organized individually, the physical is experience organized socially. The second type is one of the results of the development of the first."[54] Physical objects, according to Bogdanov, belonged to collective experience, whereas psychical objects figuratively belonged to the individual.[55] Bogdanov's guiding principle was "collective human practice," which is the whole system of experience, i.e., the system of human labor. The meaning of this practice consists in organizing nature in accord with human needs. And individual experience, without social character, is the immaterial world. Labor activity has a social nature—it elaborates the "organizational" forms, the concepts, the norms, the ideas, i.e., the "spiritual realm." Experience is the sole reality, the sole source of knowledge. According to Avenarius, "Reality is a complete experience," an "assemblage of *I and non-I*."[56] Finally, experience of the outside world reduces to human sensation; the physical and the psychic, therefore, differ strictly and solely according to the "models of their relations." Experience is the reverberation of reality and of real relations in human consciousness. Bogdanov admits the primacy of nature—a primacy based on the "chaotic dispersion of elements" that are perceived. Sensations provide the possibility of psychic experience, which, in his eyes, corresponds to the physical world; hence, psychic experience is the basis of our physical experience, which is our knowledge of the "real." The law of causality is, like other laws, a cognitive abstraction, created by thought as a way of harmonizing experience. The notion of experience is completely overturned when one attributes objective reality to matter as does Lenin (as well as Deborin, Plekhanov, and others who were faithful to Engels's notions). It is the view of Avenarius that our experience does not impose any necessity on us; i.e., there are no immutable laws of nature. Lenin accused Avenarius and Mach of going back to Humean skepticism.

> Objectivity cannot be based on individual experience; ... the foundation of objectivity has to be found in collective experience. We call objective experiential data, the vital experience of which is identical for us and for other men, data that grounds in a consistent manner our activity, and on which, we are convinced, other men should also base themselves if they want to avoid contradiction.[57]

The epistemological and sociological views of Bogdanov, which paved the way for general theory of organization—Tektology—as first tendered in his *Empirio-monism*, were later elaborated in the *Philosophy of Living Experience*.

While banishing Ostwald into the intellectual hinterlands (but never abandoning him), Bogdanov was imbued with the images in the "scientific philosophy" of Ernst Mach and Richard Avenarius, with whom he was united not by common scientific interests but by a complementary epistemology. He named his new philosophical system "empirio-monism" and defined it as a synthesis of Mach's and Avenarius's theory of knowledge and Marx's theory of social history. Empirio-monism repudiated the mechanistic alignment in science as an ideology grounded in the custom-bound organization of social labor in the seventeenth century. Empirio-monism, like positivistic philosophies of Mach and Avenarius, demands that philosophers and scientists renounce their traditional concern with the "explanations" of mechanically intertwined phenomena and instead emphasize the "description" of pure forms of experience, which are reducible to mathematical description.[58]

Bogdanov accepted Mach's theory that knowledge is a form of social adaptation aiming at the purest description of experience within the maximum economy of thought. He also accepted Mach's view that the elements of experience (colors, sensations of hardness, heat, and cold, etc.) are identical for both the physical and psychical realms. But Mach's empirio-criticism does not completely overcome the Cartesian dualism of mind and matter, since it assumes different causes and laws for the psychical and physical. Bogdanov attempts to overcome this dualism by considering the psychical and the physical as different modes of organization of the same experience. The psychical is individually organized experience, and the physical, socially organized experience; the former may be understood subjectively and the latter objectively. For Bogdanov, "The objective character of the physical world is due to its existence, not only for me personally, but for all, it has the same significance for everybody as it has for me . . . on the other hand, the subjective element in experience is that which has no universality and has meaning only for one or more individuals."[59] The physical world, in effect, represents experience that is socially or scientifically organized. The only reality we can know, Bogdanov conjectures, is that reflected in human experience.

Physical elements are derived from psychical elements by a "collective synchronization," that is, by a long distillation of generalized wisdom from personal experience. They are objective, for they have a common meaning for human groups; they make up socially functional knowledge, which is accepted and integrated through interpersonal communication. Psychical elements, on the other hand, are individually organized experience, that is, experience cast within the limits of personal life. In brief, psychical elements make up the experience that is dependent on the "individual subject"; physical elements make up the experience that is dependent on the "collective subject." The social scientist, according to Bogdanov, must be guided by the axiom that the "social milieu" (as a system of communication) is the major link between man as "the individual world of experience" and the universe as a total experience. Both psychical and physical elements are historical; both are products of long historical developments characterized by improvements and enrichments in the bonds that give human experience a structured form. The institutionalized system of social relations is the structural core of both society and personality. Here the purpose of language, art, science, and ideology is to organize that experience by means of cognitive models that range from words and concepts to scientific theories, myths, religious symbols, and artistic creations. But where do these models come from? Bogdanov maintains that "thought takes its forms, in the final analysis, from social practice."[60]

However, empirio-monism does not resolve the question of objectivity by majority vote. Bogdanov himself makes this quite clear when he writes:

> In the history of thought ... objectivity was sometimes on the side of one man against the rest of humankind. For example, in Copernicus' time the objective astronomical reality existed only for him, while hundreds of millions of people were mistaken in this regard.... Copernicus alone embraced the accumulated astronomical experience up to that time in its entirety and was able to organize it harmoniously with the methods which corresponded to the level achieved by the collective efforts of humankind; other people possessed only parts and fragments of this experience, so that it remained unorganized in all its fullness.[61]

In *Empirio-monism*, Bogdanov maintained that the key to knowledge lay in the principles of its organization, not in a search for "reality" or "essence." Neither materialism nor idealism, therefore, was an appropriate or useful epistemological position. Bogdanov regards empirio-criticism, as developed by Avenarius and Mach, as the highest expression of speculative philosophy. But precisely because empirio-criticism is speculative and unpractical, it is an unsuitable praxiological guide to the transformation of society. For Bogdanov, as for Marx, philosophy must base its methods and conclusions on actual social and laboring practices in order to transform society and emancipate huhumankind. To this end, Bogdanov bases his philosophical approach on the practices of labor and adopts a new mode of causality as the starting point for his epistemology.

Causation was understood by nineteenth-century science to be controlled by rigid and necessary laws. Every effect was thought to be predetermined by a specific cause: the cause α would, under the same conditions, always produce its corresponding effect β. Bogdanov revised this mechanical, deterministic model of causality, challenging economism in the process, by introducing human labor as a new factor. Human forethought and technical skill now entered the picture and helped control and guide the causal sequence. The effect β was no longer rigidly determined by its antecedent α, but was the result of human planning and labor. Moreover, the cause α was converted into the effect β in the same way that the energy of coal or flowing water is converted into the work of machines. In general terms, a cause produces an effect in the same way that one force used in production is changed into another. While this meant that the forces of nature can be harnessed by man and, with the proper technology, directed toward the solution of a particular problem, it also meant that the future was not pregiven but was being invented in the present. Adopting an Ostwaldian appreciation, Bogdanov asserted that man is able to change the world and invent his future by "systematic and planned . . . transformation of energy."

Though he followed the path of Mach and Avenarius in denying the Cartesian dualism, Bogdanov believed that they had not gone far enough in explaining the existence of two different realms of experience, the subjective and the objective. Bogdanov attempted to unite these realms in *Empirio-monism*, by deriving the physical world from "socially organized experience" and the mental world from "individually organized experience." The two worlds revealed two different "biological-organizational tendencies."

Why, asked Bogdanov, do people differ so radically about the second realm, the sphere of individually organized values? The answer, he thought, was that people are torn apart by conflicts that derive from differences in class, race, sex, language, or nationality, by specialization arising from technical knowledge, and by invidious relations of dominance and subordination of all kinds. If these conflicts were overcome, he continued, a new consciousness would emerge, as a result of which people would be in much greater agreement about values than ever before.

Empirio-monism rejects the mechanistic orientation in science as an ideology rooted in the custom-bound organization of social labor and disciplinary thought of the seventeenth century. Defining empirio-monism as both an ideology of the productive groups of modern society and a philosophy fully congruent with natural science, Bogdanov was convinced that it could be the source of the most practical and socially useful knowledge. However, empirio-monism was considered by some to be too philosophical, too involved in arguments over the ontological primacy of "matter" or "spirit" to meet the technical needs of modern society. Nonetheless, Bogdanov maintained that empirio-monism could be applied to man's ceaseless search for gradual improvements in production techniques. Placing the main emphasis on technical forms of social adaptation, Bogdanov argued that every ideology and every change in social forms ultimately derives from the technical process. Ideology, "the entire sphere of social life outside the technical process," is wholly derived from technology. The term *technology*, according to him, denotes not the material equipment of a society but the organization and utilization of knowledge related to external nature. Techniques are reducible to knowledge, the very essence of human social existence and the primary matrix of social relations. Science is the single most powerful component of the technical process, and it, too, is responsive to accumulative technical needs. Every scientific advance he regarded as originating in the sphere of man's direct relations to nature, that is, to the sphere of technical experience.

The ideology of the new technical intelligentsia, elaborated by the new philosophy, was a response to the historical need for rapid technological advancement; it minimizes the role of "sacred values" in industrial work and encourages continuous search for practical inventions. The new philosophy and the ideology of technical intelligentsia were similar in yet another respect: Both rejected the notion that scientific laws have independent existence. Instead, they regard scientific laws as transitional products of the human mind—special methods for meeting the challenge of practical social needs. Giving expression to what among American institutionalists is termed the "Veblenian dichotomy," Bogdanov noted that whereas technological innovations are always progressive, for they are based on a continuous accumulation of practical experience, ideological adaptations too often are regressive. Archaic, though powerful ideologies, particularly in class-structured societies, often inhibit both historically necessary ideological adjustments and the timely application of new technical discoveries. Technical progress creates the dynamic conditions for social change, but ideology determines the static conditions that regulate and modify technical innovations. Though of a secondary character, ideological elements play a vital role in organizing the "material" and the "conditions" of social development.

For Bogdanov science is the epitome of the modern age, the bridge between technical and ideological processes. It encompasses both practical knowledge and theoretical thought. The rapidly expanding institutional base of science, for Bogdanov, was the most powerful force forging the theoretical (ideology) and the practical (technology) unity of scientific knowledge. He constantly emphasized the accelerated growth of secular knowledge as the quintessence of modern civilization. The growth of productive social forces and the resultant expansion of man's control over nature were expressions of scientific knowledge.

Bogdanov's empirio-monistic theory of society sustained a nuanced Marxism, accepting some of its more salient points while casually incorporating aspects at variance with Marx's Marxism. It recognizes the "socio-economic formations" as stages in the "natural history" of social systems; it accepts in principle the Marxian view on the relationship of the infrastructure to the superstructure of major social activities; and it places strong emphasis on strain and stress in social dynamics generated by the accumulative growth of material culture. Bogdanov claimed that he considered his concept of "technical process" identical to the Marxian notion of "social relations in production." Indeed, he recognized Marx as the founder of modern sociology and emphasized particularly the scientific usefulness of the Marxian concept of social structure and the Marxian claim that the social existence of men determines their consciousness.

The whole of the Marx-Mach, Lenin-Bogdanov controversy perhaps reflected the pathological state of a small party, led by a combative talent intolerant of opposition and frustrated because his organization, cut off from its home base, was melting away from lack of accomplishment. It was in this environment that Lenin replied to Bogdanov indicating that to think philosophic idealism would disappear if individual consciousness were replaced with socially organized experience is to imagine that capitalism itself would disappear when the individual capitalist is replaced by a publicly held corporation.

Counterpoising Plekhanov, who referred to Bogdanov's studies as a categorical denial of materialism, Bogdanov presented his own theory of the evolution of philosophy and ideology as follows:

1. Ideological forms are adjustments that organize social life; more precisely, they organize the technological process (either directly or indirectly).

2. The evolution of ideology is marked by the existence of the need for organizational adjustments of the social process and possesses the materials needed for this.

3. As to the survival of ideological forms, they are therefore dependent on the degree of harmony with which they organize, in the real world, the content of social labor.

Bogdanov admits no authoritarian absolutism in the name of any truth of whatever kind. Every truth (and every error), like every ideology, possesses a historical and therefore transitory character. Truth is objective to the extent that it possesses a general validity for the life of a society and represents a force that is adequate and organizational. In contrast, it has been argued that Plekhanov and Lenin had returned to eighteenth-century materialism, with respect to the Archimedean idea of an absolute truth and the concept of matter as thing-in-itself. This latter point, Bogdanov argued, is compatible neither with Marx nor with Engels, both of whom solved the question of the thing-in-itself in accord with post-Kantian thought.

Bogdanov completely neglected the Kantian notion of a thing-in-itself, since he regarded it as a useless multiplication of entities that "attempts to explain the known by the unknown, what is accessible by what is unexperienced and inexperienceable."[62] Bogdanov's epistemology also led him to deny the objectivity of space, time, classical causality, and absolute truth. Truth, for Bogdanov, is nothing more than an instrument for organizing human experience and is valid only within the time and space of a particular society and era.

A Response to the Crisis of Russian Marxism

To some thinkers it became increasingly clear that not only was mechanicalism confronted with crisis, but so too was Marxism. As an alternative to the growing sclerosis of the doctrinal Marxism of the Second International, and possibly as a result of his exposure to Machian philosophy, Bogdanov authored a phenomenological Marxism.

The earliest documented efforts at a synthesis of Marxism and phenomenology go back some years before Herbert Marcuse's efforts.[63] Goldmann correctly argues that the crucial rapprochement between phenomenology and Marxism may be situated much earlier than even Lukács's early works, such as *The Theory of the Novel*. While it can be situated at the juncture of the three themes of German academic thought of the period, important for our purposes is the Russian contribution. According to Goldmann, the vigor of Lukács's Marxism in *History and Class Consciousness* consists in the unambiguous advance the work makes by substituting the phenomenological idea of the atemporal meaningful structure with the Marxist concept of meaningful structure, which is both dynamic and temporal, based on the idea of the totality.[64]

As evincing as Lukács contribution was to phenomenological Marxism, there is evidence of its origins in the revisionism of A.A. Bogdanov. It can be argued that the primary aim of Bogdanov's work was to deconstruct the theoretical and political sclerosis of Marxism associated with its Russian epigones. He cautioned that the "socialist ideal" could not simply be equated with Marxist ideology and adopted a somewhat irreverent attitude toward the "Holy Scriptures of Marx and Engels." Although he frequently expressed admiration for Marx's theories, he refused to accept Marxism as a body of prescribed thought. Rejecting absolutism in favor of relativism, he wrote: "Marx succeeded in establishing the foundation for the new social science and new historical philosophy. It is conceivable that all of science and all of philosophy will acquire a new appearance in the hands of the proletariat because different conditions in life engender different ways of perceiving and understanding nature." Thus, it was important to avoid both "ideological haughtiness" and "ideological slavery." Culture, he argued, should strive toward liberation from all "eternal truths."

Was it not ironic that leaders such as Plekhanov and Lenin subscribed to Marxism as the embodiment of unequivocal and eternal truths when, at the same time, Marxism was a "teaching that radically denies all absolute and eternal truths?" Ever critical, Bogdanov charged that Lenin's thinking had more to do with faith than with Marx's "scientific laws." Lenin based his arguments not on reason but on an appeal to higher authority. The very notion of eternal truths was a "fetishism"; to Bogdanov, all truth was historically and culturally conditioned —that is, relative. All too often, ideas, norms, and values were ossified in the form of dogma, becoming symbolism without content. In this sense, ideology bolstered "theoretical conservatism" and invidious authoritarianism.

Bogdanov's embryonic phenomenological Marxism appreciated the simultaneous paradigmatic crises of mechanicalism, of capitalism, and of human existence therein. But at the level of theory it was an appreciation of the degeneration of Marxism into a doctrine as a function of its fixity. To the extent that history conditions theory, the sanctification of doctrinal Marxism to the plane of metaphysics revealed it to be an ideological remnant, tolerably useful for appreciating a historical phase, but of increasingly dubious value. Furthermore, in disallowing qualifications and theoretical reconstructions, doctrinal Marxism assumed merely symbolic formality lacking intersubjectivity. Too often it was resigned to no more than a set of hackneyed cliches. Yet it is this "strength" that made doctrinal Marxism instrumental to the bureaucracy that was to institutionalize it. It became a valued constant of an occult intellectuality.

The "phenomenological" qualification appended to Marxism, far from being a mere philosophical afterthought, is the conceptual otherness of a determinate sociohistorical problem: the need to develop a critical approach to social reality to appreciate and inform the historical process according to a genuinely humanistic project. While phenomenological Marxism is a response to the crisis of Marxism and mechanicalism, its task is nothing less than the radical reconstitution of Marxism itself.

Phenomenology is understood as a critical inquiry into the mediations of the experiential universe and the operations that inform them. Thus, it is to be expected that the crisis of Marxism—its frozen articulation of abstract categories that no longer meaningfully disclose social reality but instead cover it with an opaque veil of ideas—necessitates a phenomenological reconstitution. For Bogdanov, new content could be expressed only in new forms (phenomenological Marxism) dialectically related to older forms (classical Marxism). By seeing Marxism as the outcome of phenomenology and phenomenology as a moment of Marxism, is it possible to attain any reconciliation that simultaneously produces a relevant phenomenology and a nondoctrinal Marxism? Marxism can be a warranted historical mediation only insofar as it is able to articulate concretely and give praxiological meaning to social reality. A dialectical perspective sees phenomenology as a moment of Marxism and Marxism as the logical outcome of phenomenology. To this extent, Marxism and phenomenology are not distinct but merely distinguishable moments of the same broad perspective.

Phenomenology was viewed as a redirection of attention not to abstractions but to the *Lebenswelt* of lived experience.[65] Its principal purpose is to study the phenomena, or appearances, of human experience while attempting to suspend all consideration of their objective reality or subjective association. The phenomena examined are those experienced in various acts of contextually "informed" consciousness, mainly cognitive or perceptual acts, but also such acts as valuation and aesthetic appreciation. It is the tracing of all mediation to the human and organizational operations that constitute reality. To the extent that the human operations to which phenomenology reduces all mediations are themselves historical, they take place within a context preconditioned by the sedimentations of the past, which equally affect all the subjects caught in it—hence, the intersubjective character of every subjectivity. Thus, phenomenological analysis unavoidably ends up in Marxism as class analysis, which explains different kinds of consciousness in terms of class (authority/organizational) position. It is important to note that it was Bogdanov's phenomenological Marxism that paved the way for Bogdanov's Tektology.

Phenomenological Marxism can be preliminarily described as that approach that constantly reduces all theoretical constructs—including Marxism itself—to their living context in order to guarantee the adequacy of the concept not only to the object it claims to apprehend but also to the goals it seeks to attain. In fact, its point of departure is the rejection of the theory of reflection, central to "doctrinal" Marxists but actually an untenable remnant of positivism. Bogdanov recognized that Marxism was in need of an autocritique, a critical reflection upon itself. This is the task of phenomenology.

What does it mean to claim that a concept "reflects" the reality to which it refers? Concept and object are qualitatively different; there is not and cannot be any necessary connection between the two. If there were, then not only would absolute knowledge be possible, but it would have long ago been attained. The problem of knowledge is much more complicated. The attempt to determine reality metaphysically ends up in Kantianism and Hegelianism as soon as it is realized that the apprehended object can never be apprehended in its very being —which is fundamentally preconceptual—and that what is eventually apprehended is a set of projected categories that claim to describe the object. Kantianism is the realization that our intellectual relationship to reality is always mediated by these categories, which, as such, constitute an impregnable shield protecting it from our grasp. Thus, according to Kantianism, the "materialist" theory of reflection is a crude form of objective idealism unaware that the very materiality of its object is constituted by projected categories subsequently appreciated as independent of the subject doing the projecting. Hegelianism is the further realization that the projective process is both necessary and partial such that the Kantian thing-in-itself becomes superfluous, and absolute knowledge— in terms of which the partial conception appears as partial and whose very partiality presupposes a totality of which it is a part—turns out to be an unavoidable consequence. The difference between Marxist and idealist philosophy does not concern the metaphysical quandary whether consciousness precedes matter or vice versa. The difference is between a dynamic, creative philosophy that explains man's making of himself by making the object, on the one hand, and contemplative philosophies that counterpoise an abstract subject to an abstract object, both equally inert, on the other hand.

As the autoconsciousness of bourgeois society, Marxism is a creative and not a contemplative philosophy.[66] Ostensibly, bourgeois philosophy is contemplative precisely to the extent that it is the world outlook of a class that does not produce but passively consumes what other classes produce for it. Thus, the philosophy of bourgeois consciousness is neither idealism nor irrationalism, but objectivism, according to which subject and object passively confront each other as full-fledged, ready-made, metaphysical entities. Thus, in mechanical materialism it lays its hopes on a preconstituted material world, and in idealism it relies on a system of ideas. Marxist philosophy, not concerned merely with reflecting the world but with changing it, reconstitutes the world not only physically but also conceptually/theoretically. The relation between concept/theory and object is not one of reflection or symmetry but one of adequacy. To the extent that the concept/theory is qualitatively different from the reality it apprehends and to the extent that it is necessarily partial in its depiction, the criterion of truth cannot be correspondence between concept/theory and object; rather, it must be the correspondence between the concept/theory and the fulfillment of the goal for which the concept/theory was originally devised.

Since the concept/theory cannot reflect reality, it is not attached to reality;[67] the concept/theory must be created. Furthermore, since an infinite number of possible partial concepts/theories can be created to describe the same object—at least to the extent that the object is determined by the totality of the relationships into which it enters—the criterion determining the character of the unavoidable partiality of the concept/theory is always a function of a social situation with its own needs and problems. In other words, the process of concept/theory production should not be seen as at all different from the process of commodity production. Thus, it is possible to talk about all knowledge, including science, as class-determined. If the concept bears not a necessary but only a historically contingent relation to the object, and if that relation is determined by a certain teleology inextricably connected with a certain social situation (class), then all knowledge is the result of a certain mode of social production and, consequently, is subject to the same dialectic described by Marx in *Capital.*

The structural symmetry between commodity production and concept/theory production can be roughly described as follows: The crisis of capitalist society consists in the fact that whereas man makes himself through labor, under capitalist conditions of production he destroys himself in the process. The subject making the object through labor makes himself as a creative subject; but under capitalism the object is taken away from the subject, and, to the extent that the object embodies his subjectivity, capitalism deprives the subject of his subjectivity and his humanity. Further, since under capitalism all decisions are made by the organizers of the means of production, the subject is reduced to the level of an object that, however, must remain minimally a subject so that he can continue producing. Thus, alienation results: the original producing subject is reduced to the level of an object to be appropriated into the labor market just like any other commodity, while the object he originally produced, in becoming capital, has become the abstract subject.

Essentially, the crisis of capitalism can be described as follows: The capitalist productive system originally developed to satisfy human needs (even if, from the beginning, these needs were not really universal but only particular, i.e., those of the rising bourgeoisie). However, with the reversal of subject and object, the productive system became counterproductive to its original goal. No longer connected with the producing subject, collapsed into the object-become-subject, the original goal of satisfying human needs is completely forgotten. This process may be described as one of rationality embodying both means and ends: when technological rationality becomes its own criterion, atomic destruction and Nazi barbarism face no significant opposition. Far from being a departure from bourgeois rationality, such atrocities are its logical outcome. The subject-reduced-to-object faces a seemingly self-determined and independently given rationality within which he can fit only as a mere object determined by that very same technological (Promethean) rationality.

No less a process takes place in the case of knowledge. In a similar manner it can be argued that science narrowly defined presents theorizing as an activity undistinguished from the observation and ultimately as bound to it by its support for correspondence requirements. Consequently, disciplined observation replaces both critical theory and practical reason in knowledgeable society. Such a science makes observation more than merely a necessary condition for social and political practice, it becomes sufficient for knowing and a metaphor for action.

The crisis of the sciences (intellectuality) consists in the alienation of the scientist into a robot characterized by what Husserl called the naturalistic outlook: the subject's failure to see anything but what the conceptual constructs he himself has created allow him to see. Thus, not only does he fail to see the preconceptual reality presupposed by his scientific constructs, whose primacy is a necessary condition to it, but he also loses sight of the original telos that functioned as the criterion in constructing those categories. To the extent that means make sense only in relation to the end in terms of which they are means, once the end disappears those means lose their meaning; and, although the resulting scientific system exhibits a high degree of rationality, its foundation is precisely a thoroughgoing irrationality because there is no longer a telos to give it any meaning.[68] This process not only produces the atomic bomb and bacteriological warfare as allegedly "neutral" results, it also prevents science from making any progress, since science does not and cannot thematicize the original abstractive process that produces the mathematizable forms that are alone susceptible to tractable scientific treatment. To the extent that this abstractive level is not penetrated by science and remains its outer limit, a science that has lost sight of the subject can never explain the circularity of its own objective methodology. Thus, it becomes possible to talk about class science, since the original telos, which has long been forgotten but which nonetheless permeates all of science, was, and had to be, grounded in a social situation that gave it relevance, its pretended universality notwithstanding. Since the universal can concretely present itself only in the form of a particular, concrete universality is not the denial of particularity but its affirmation. Thus, science was from the very beginning bourgeois science. Yet, to the extent that the bourgeoisie claimed to be the universal class, its science sought to be universal, and the crisis of science is inextricably connected with the crisis of bourgeois society.

Moreover, the same process applies to Marxism, which originally put itself forth not as dogmatic metaphysics but as a specific type of consciousness developed in a unique historical era to perform an equally specific social goal: the overcoming of class societies and the installation of a new social order with classless—and therefore universal—aims. Marxism is not the empirical consciousness of the proletariat since, as a result of alienation, such a consciousness necessarily reflects the ideology of the ruling class. Rather, Marxism is the objective consciousness that the proletariat ought to have once it becomes fully constituted as a class for itself as well as in itself.

Chernishevsky's insistence in *What Is to Be Done?* on the need to bring revolutionary consciousness through the party to the working class from outside that class stems from "something wanting" in Marxist philosophy: a premature totalization of the capitalist mode of production. Lenin took the voluntarist road in the face of Bernstein's, and initially Bogdanov's, social democratic reformism because the trade unions and their political organs did not make a qualitative turn and become revolutionary organizations. To the extent that trade unions demands met with partial success, they became stable organizations effectively mediating the class struggle and freezing working-class consciousness at the level of reformism. Thus, at the close of the nineteenth century it became evident that Marxism, as it had been developed by Marx and Engels, was not entirely adequate. Because of the new lease on life given to capitalism, Marxism ceased to be the self-consciousness of the proletariat and became a separate doctrine. For Bernstein it was an objective science; for Bogdanov it was a science in need of updating; and for Stalin it turned into a fixed metaphysics.

To the extent that Marxism was a premature totalization, i.e., it allegedly failed to address the cultural dimension, according to Bogdanov, it took a pre-revolutionary situation as a revolutionary one. A new critical Marxism adequate to concrete realities must start out by reconstituting first and foremost the ontological presuppositions, i.e., notion of class. And this is precisely what Bogdanov sought in referring to "organization."

In speaking of phenomenological Marxism, we would be seriously amiss if we did not refer to Bogdanov's contemporary, Edmund Husserl, with other than a passing remark. The founder of twentieth-century phenomenology, Husserl intended to develop a philosophical method that was devoid of all presuppositions and that would describe phenomena by focusing exclusively on them, to the exclusion of all questions of their causal origins and their status outside the act of consciousness itself. His aim was to discover the essential structures and relationships of the phenomena as well as the acts of consciousness in which the phenomena appeared and to do this by as faithful an exploration as possible, uncluttered by ontological or cultural presuppositions. Husserl's idea of a "presuppositionless" science amounted to rejecting all antecedent commitments to theories of knowledge, both those formally developed as philosophical systems and those that pervade our ordinary thinking. Originally he intended by this suspension, or bracketing, of extraneous commitments to go beyond the duality of choices between idealism and realism, to "the things themselves." This suspension of all reference to the reality of the thing experienced left the philosopher with nothing but the socially informed experience itself. Here the line between idealism and phenomenology became blurred, although the suspension of belief in the reality of an object of consciousness is not the same thing as denying that it exists. Rather, consciousness, he asserted, is dependent upon the objects it considers. With its stress on the things themselves, phenomenology seemed to remedy the scandal of Hegelian Marxism, i.e., its inability to relate to the existing state of affairs.[69]

It can be shown that certain notions developed by Husserl in his later writings can be extremely useful in the reconstitution of Marxism, i.e., in the development of fundamental categories of analysis that can deal adequately with present sociohistorical realities.[70] Husserl's critique of science centers on the failure of science to change reality; instead, according to Husserl, it has occluded reality with its categories, checkmating man as the historical agent and reducing him to the level of a passive object operating among similar objects. In fact, Husserl's analysis of science is a paradigmatic analysis of any knowledge whatsoever, including Marxism. Whereas Marx "materialized" Hegel—stood him on his head—critical or phenomenological Marxism sought to "materialize" Husserl by interpreting the base as the *Lebenswelt* and the worker as transcendental subjectivity. Only by doing so was it possible to vindicate the need for revolution and the quest for a qualitatively different way of life.

The *Lebenswelt* is that domain of experience that is both precategorical and categorical. It includes our relation to reality as such—ostensibly free from any conceptual/theoretical mediation, the array of concepts/theories we use to articulate reality, and the conceptualized/theorized reality resulting from apprehending reality through concept/theory. Far from being a passive process, perception is itself a form of labor—the very process of perception exhibits the structure of labor. It involves the preconceptual/pretheoretical apprehension of reality, the sorting out of concepts/theories needed to abstract certain crucial features of that reality, and the conceptualizing/theorizing of those features of reality deemed relevant, i.e., determined as essential in relation to some telos itself given to us as needed in the *Lebenswelt*. It is inappropriate to identify the *Lebenswelt* with the "empirical" or the "common sense" world, since doing so ends up occluding precisely the crucial dialectic that makes the notion fruitful and relevant. The *Lebenswelt* does include the empirical and the common sense world, but it also encompasses much more. Although it is true that ordinary perception involves the mere identification of preconceptual/pretheoretical entities through conceptual/theoretical structures, this is not all that takes place or can take place. The *Lebenswelt* is also the domain in which concepts/theories are invented and historical projects are formulated. Although most experience is of the mundane type whereby precategorical content is mechanically synthesized with pregiven conceptual/theoretical forms (in fact, as recent developments in optics indicate, the identification is between the concept/theory and its projection, which is substituted for the precategorical reality it seems to be grasping), this mundane experience is parasitic to the original constitutive experience that generated the conceptual/theoretical repertory. It is only a moment of the whole, but it ends up being considered as the whole itself. Husserl tried to uncover the transcendental subjectivity that generated these concepts/theories and that is constantly repressed in mundane experience, i.e., the alienated experience of everyday life under certain sociohistorical conditions. However, he was unable to draw the revolutionary conclusions implicit in his own analysis, and he thus ended up identifying the crisis as first and foremost a philosophical crisis resolvable through a philosophical solution: the new phenomenology.

According to the Marx of *The Economic and Philosophic Manuscripts*, revolution is necessitated not just by material or even by cultural deprivation but, more important, by dehumanization; under capitalism men and women (both capitalist and proletarian) are limited to mundane experience, i.e., to a nonhuman level of existence.[71] The character of work continually forces the worker into the role of a transcendental subject who not only mundanely transposes pregiven categories into a pregiven reality but also transforms that pregiven reality and, in laboring, is constantly faced with the limitations of the given categories. Thus, he constantly, and for the most part unwittingly, functions as a transcendental subject. The worker, as a worker, must function as a transcendental subject while presenting himself at all times as a passive, manipulatable, object-like thing. Communist society is not—as doctrinal Marxism assumes—a streamlined and more efficient version of present society, projecting into every worker the lifestyle of the capitalist. Instead, communist society must be a qualitatively different society, in which every subject can be a real subject in a genuinely intersubjective society. Thus, as Bogdanov was to stress, revolution cannot mean simply a change from private to collective management; that would leave everyday life unchanged and, as such, would be utterly irrelevant.[72] Revolution must be interpreted, first and foremost, as a qualitative change in this everyday life through which fragmented workers become subjects consciously (politically) engaged in determining their destiny (concretely, not through vanguardist-bureaucratic party representatives).

Doctrinal Marxism, relating to Marxism not as a living philosophy of human self-becoming but as a fixed metaphysics, can only conceive of the new society in the abstract. Thus, it regarded socialism as practically attained once collective ownership of the means of production had been attained. However, collective ownership is only a means to the attainment of a qualitatively superior humanity. If the means no longer attains the end, the means must be changed. Unfortunately, reified Marxism had, with the Second International, been reduced to an abstract formalism in which the dialectical tension between means and ends had collapsed in the facticity of an instrumental rationality utterly concerned with technological efficiency. It could not penetrate the living reality it obscured, and thus it threatened to perpetuate the very alienation it sought to redress. Thus, Bogdanov was concerned with the prospects of the Soviet worker who would be threatened, atomized, depoliticized, and alienated.

This is why phenomenological Marxism (re)interprets the base-superstructure distinction. The base is not simply the domain of production—which can be easily understood in a mechanistic way as the physical means of production—but the sphere of teleological human activity. The superstructure is not the ideological reflection of the base but rather the domain of cultural and socioethical objectifications. A qualitative change of the base and superstructure (revolution) could not, therefore, be identified with either industrialization or collectivization of the means of production but had to be seen as a radical change in the quality of life. This means that what had to change was not only the mode of production (the abolishment of the private ownership of the means of production) but also the way we relate to ourselves and others. As we shall see, Bogdanov understood that for Marx the change in the mode of production made sense only to the extent that it was a precondition of a qualitative change in the lifestyle. Revolution, therefore, could only mean a qualitatively different life. The technological and productive paraphernalia entered only to the extent that it was necessary to this end. An alienated Marxism neglected this means-ends dialectic and considered socialism as a realized project once private property had been abolished and industrialization carried out, without perceiving that it might be possible to realize what were thought to be the means and without at the same time necessarily guaranteeing the attainment of the ends.

This interpretation of economy, base, superstructure, and revolution also led Bogdanov to a reinterpretation of the very notion of class, with all its organizational and political consequences. If revolution is first and foremost a qualitative change of everyday life for the entire society, and revolutionary consciousness—as well as bourgeois consciousness—is a function of a certain socioeconomic situation that informs one's lifestyle, then the criterion for class membership is a function not of the relationship to the means of production, but of the quality of life that results from that relationship.

In Bogdanov's interpretation, everyday consciousness obtains from the individuation of society's organizational tendencies.[73] Based on his organizational paradigm, a political phenomenology of formal organizations, distinct from the Weberian tradition, sought to integrate the disparity between Marxian approaches to macrosocietal issues and sociologies of consciousness in microsettings. The first approach focuses on the real structures of society, the second on the social construction of reality. Such linkage might occur from two directions: scaling Marxism down to the level of organizational practice, and scaling microsociologies up to the level of organizational structure. For the first of these tasks, special tools were synthesized from the various traditions and used to reinterpret Marx's category of labor as a kind of *Lebenspraxis* of everyday organizational life. For instance, the theory of alienation is often put forward as the Marxist contribution to microsociology. The Marxian tradition is, of course, largely macro, especially in its classical concerns with economy, state, imperialism, revolution, and long-term social change. A strategy for the development of a possible integrative frame combining the micro and macro foci of social reality

—theory, practice, and consciousness—within the context of holism was initiated under diverse influences. The integration consists of the macro level necessarily providing the content of the microlevel phenomenon of consciousness and the micro level providing the reality of the macrolevel phenomena. The discussion unveiled important commonalities in the specification of these concepts/theories. They were delineated as moments of a global whole of social existence that pervade man-in-the-world as a social being and as an actor interacting with other men. As moments, they are in a coevolutionary relationship, one of interpenetration and mutual implication. The main result is that they are elements of a single whole indicating a further criterion for support of the enterprise toward an integration of micro and macro levels of social reality, since keeping them apart would result in grasping them only as reified rather than actual presentations.

Rationality intercontextually coevolves to legitimize actions that have already occurred. This contradicts previous notions of rationality claiming that actors were rational and purposive behavior resulted in both planned and accidental consequences. Thus "rationality," "legitimacy," and "authority" are social structures of consciousness as well as features of everyday settings; as such their construction was reinterpreted phenomenologically as the praxiological foundations of organizational life, the organizing out of which organizations are constituted.

Phenomenological Marxism is an approach that seeks to reduce theoretical constructs—including Marxism—to their "lived" context in order to guarantee the adequacy of the concept/theory to the "reality" it apprehends. To accomplish this demand necessarily meant the rejection of the theory of reflection. It sought to reunify theory and praxis through the rediscovery of labor as *Lebenspraxis* as central to the *Lebenswelt* of everyday organizational life, and also through the unification of scientific knowledge.[74] Thus it bore the marks of an Althusserian interactionist theory-as-practice argument and presented revolution as necessarily involving all the activities of everyday life, as fundamentally a cultural phenomenon.[75] This at once distanced it from the appreciation of the paradigmatic crisis as subordinated to the economy and infused it with the cultural nexus. Embracing an aesthetic and cultural approach was oppositional to methodological approaches that entailed socioeconomic reductionism of cultural phenomena or the intrusions of the natural sciences in the human-cultural domain. This presents Marxism as the historically valid mediation that concretely articulates and informs social reality, while phenomenology is the tracing of all mediations to the human operations that constituted them. The crisis in reified Marxism necessitated a phenomenological reconstitution, in which new content is expressed in novel forms (phenomenological Marxism) dialectically related to previous forms (classical Marxism). Similarly, Bogdanov's phenomenological analysis revised Marxism as the class analysis that explains consciousness in terms of class position and labor, and expressed in more general organizational modes of analysis.

While repeatedly using the standard Marxist class categories, such as bourgeoisie and proletariat, Bogdanov apparently did not accept the doctrinal practice of treating these classes in themselves as the subjects of history. Neither did he see classes as mere bearers of social structure. For Bogdanov, classes are not rigorously defined as aggregates of economic interests. They represent collective responses to changes in the organization of society wherein they are provided with (and/or denied) opportunities for development as a whole. Their capacity to respond to these opportunities depends on their ability to propose solutions to problems that are in the interests of social culture as a whole.

While giving a central place to the questions of class, class alliances, and class struggle, Bogdanov departs from classical versions of Marxism in that he does not think that politics is an arena that simply reflects already unified collective political identities or already constituted forms of struggle. Politics for him is not a dependent sphere. It is where forces and relations, in the economy, in society, in culture, have to be actively worked on to produce particular forms of power, forms of domination. This conception of politics is fundamentally contingent, fundamentally open ended. Reducing the proletariat to merely its economic dimension distorts the entire history of its political development. While the proletariat plays a key historical role, it is not a role that can be understood in narrow economic terms, for classes are as much cultural as economic institutions.

Bogdanov's phenomenological Marxism was an approach that sought to appreciate all theoretical constructs—including Marxism—in terms of their organizational, lived context in order to guarantee the adequacy of the concept/theory to the object it apprehends and the goal it seeks. Its point of departure from orthodox Marxism occurs with its rejection of the theory of reflection. A critical Marxism adequate for contemporary issues reformulated the notion of class to embrace new appreciations of everyday life; the concept/theory of the economy to (re)incorporate the formerly differentiated spheres of leisure, education, culture, etc.; and the idea of revolution to involve all the activities of everyday life. Phenomenological Marxism was thought to serve as the basis for a theoretical critique of the Marxism of the Second International and of the Marxism of Lenin. Moreover, it might be argued that phenomenology emerged in Marxism neither with the collapse of the liberal market economies in the 1930s, nor with the post–World War II alleged failure of structuralism; rather, its roots may be found in the early genetic structuralism of Bogdanov, an early response to the paradigmatic crisis of mechanicalism and Marxism.

Rival Concepts of Dialectical Materialism

There is little question that Lenin and Bogdanov discerned a nuanced reality. Both looked at the same revolutionary scene in Russia but perceived dissimilar problems and potential. Lenin, with his Marxist perspective, saw class conflict and centers of power that others, to their detriment, neglected. Bogdanov, with his phenomenological Marxism, saw elements of exploitation and alienation to which Lenin was blind. Through a long stream of publications, Bogdanov at least drew Lenin's attention to other dilemmas and other realities. If Lenin ignored them or refuted them, that was a choice. Out of their dialogue came two different attempts at social alchemy and cultural change. Ultimately, two visions of socialism emerged, the phenomenological Marxist alternative being the threat and the appeal of Bogdanovism.[76] In contrast to Lenin, Bogdanov focused on changes in both private property and authority relations as essential to socialism; together they would make possible "new comradely relations" as well as a genuinely classless society. It was too facile, argued Bogdanov, to consider socialism the negation of capitalism in terms of private ownership; alienation and even exploitation could continue unless there were an additional, and explicit, change in relations of authority. Bogdanov in essence not only offered a more dynamic definition of socialism than Lenin but also drew attention to sources of alienation that Marx had not foreseen—namely, those of a political and cultural nature that perpetuated invidious relations despite a change in the economic base. Precisely for these reasons, Bogdanov attempted to cast a wide net in social transformation, encompassing collectivist organization of labor, aesthetic creativity, or political behavior.[77]

> Scholars have not hesitated to label Bogdanov "Lenin's rival" and Bogdanovism the "second strongest ideology . . . among the former revolutionaries after 1917." Articles from the 1920s frequently juxtaposed the "materialistic-dialectic Lenin" with the "tektologist Bogdanov." One author spoke of the dangers of Bogdanov's influence, arguing that "a decisive battle against Bogdanovism is . . . the most important task of Lenin's theory. Not without reason were the basic philosophical writings of Lenin himself dedicated towards this task."[78]

It appears that Lenin's understanding of materialism was in accordance with both Newtonian mechanics and a strain of economism present in the Second International edition of Marxism. "Some authors," writes Sochor, "find in [Leninism] a distinct strain of economism, that is to say, an undue emphasis on economic factors and the development of productive forces to the detriment of social and cultural factors."[79] He inveighs against those modern scientists who question materialism, arguing that while they may be good physicists, they are bad philosophers. When faced with the assertion that in modern physics "matter is disappearing," Lenin retorted that, on the one hand, the philosophical concept of matter was not affected by the historically changing views of physicists on the structure of matter; on the other hand, what was called the "disappearance of matter" had nothing to do with the basic materialist doctrine, that "matter is prior to mind." This simply means that, what was once taken to be an ontological absolute, is known to be a property only in certain states, in that it is a relative and not an absolute property. For Lenin, matter is a philosophical/ontological category serving to designate an objective reality that is given to man in his sensations, which copy it, photograph it, reflect it, and which exist independent of the sensations. But Lenin's reflection theory has been accused of making no contribution at all to a better understanding of the problem. Perception, it has been argued, is not a "copy" of the real object; it is not something new that is created "inside of us"; it is neither cause nor effect; it is a functional relation that in no way affects the existence of the object that is perceived.[80]

Lenin took the view that it was not materialism in general that had become untenable but only its traditional mechanical form. Mechanics, for centuries a total explanation of the world, had been reduced by the progress of natural science to a mere moment of knowledge, indeed a mere moment of the physical world itself.[81] "The sole property of matter, with whose recognition philosophical materialism is bound up, is the property of being an objective reality, of existing outside our mind," wrote Lenin.[82] Whereas Engels wrote, "The fundamental forms of all being are space and time; being outside of time is just as much an absurdity as being outside of space,"[83] Lenin asserted that, "There is nothing in the world but matter in motion, and matter cannot move save in space and time alone."[84] Axelrod-the-Orthodox was convinced that what Lenin calls materialism was nothing less than a form of naive realism. For Lenin, Engels's *Anti-Dühring* was central to Marxist philosophy, and anyone who departed from it was mistaken on the most essential points. Lenin was apparently interested in philosophy for the sole objective of forcing the "enemies" of Marxist philosophy back into the trenches. Some critics insist that the philosophy Lenin learned from Engels seems vulgar and naive when compared with the philosophy of Marx. But it was from this naivete that the individual would be subordinated to the organization—a position that in a different context enabled totalizing Taylorism (Stakhanovites) to emerge.

Lenin takes as point of departure the identity of the physical moment and the psychic moment, something that materialists do not do. For, if materialism took the identity of the physical and the psychic as fundamental, empirio-criticism would have to do the same. According to Bazarov, Lenin's materialism is a "transcendental materialism" that puts all its hope in a sort of Kantian thing-in-itself, as if the object was given to us in a causal nexus as phenomenon.

Lossky notes that the philosopher Byhovsky defined matter as that "which acting upon our sense organs produce sensations; matter is objective reality, given to us in sensation ... our knowledge of it originates through the senses."[85] Deferring to Lenin and his followers, Lossky notes that the dialectical materialist's understanding of matter is, in part, facilitated by their contention that a definition by nature is a means of subsuming one concept to a more inclusive generic one. Since matter is the most fundamental of categories, Byhovsky writes:

> [Matter] cannot be defined *per genus et differentiam* since matter is all that exists, the most general conception, the genus of all genera. All that exists is some aspect of matter, but matter itself cannot be defined as a particular instance of some genus. For the same reason it is impossible to indicate the specific difference of matter. If matter is all that exists, it is unthinkable to seek

for the characteristics that distinguish it from something else, since that something else could only be nonexistence, i.e., it could not exist.[86]

In pursuit of the profound distinction that dialectical materialists make between their position and that adopted by mechanicalists, Lossky defers to Byhovsky, for whom a mechanist contradiction is mechanical; it is the contradiction of conflicting things, or of mutually opposed forces. On the basis of a mechanistic interpretation of motion, the phenomenon of contradiction can only be external and not internal. On the basis of his definition of a "unity" as an integral whole, Byhovsky maintains that contradiction is not contained and does not occur in a unity. Being a unity implies that there is no inner necessary connection between its elements. The theory of equilibrium, according to Byhovsky, is an instance of a methodology underpinned by the substitution of the mechanical principle of conflict between forces moving in opposite direction for the dialectical principle of unity of opposites.[87]

For Bogdanov, the Machist attempt to create a new worldview was only a semantic exercise. Diamat, on the other hand, is regarded as a worldview, significantly and substantially new. Marx's attempt to break away from past philosophy is portrayed as successful in so many respects as to place diamat close to the solution of philosophy. It is Bogdanov's notion that a complete break is necessary in searching out the solution, which requires him to retire both Marx and Mach. Where empirio-criticism is but a refinement of ordinary materialism, diamat is a step beyond both materialism in particular and past thought in general.[88]

Hegel had, according to Bogdanov, marked an enormous advance in systematized knowledge.[89] Bogdanov looked with favor on Hegel's attempt to work out the laws of the dialectic pursuant to establishing them as a universal method of explanation and view of process. On the basis of this new and broader method, he noted, Hegel was able to create "the fullest and most structured system of knowledge to his time."[90]

Turning from Hegel, for Bogdanov, Feuerbach's singular contribution was not the fact that he had attempted to create some sort of diamat; it lay, rather, in his attempt to turn philosophy away from self-developing idea toward a concern for self-developing social man.[91] Feuerbach's attack on the idealist substitution and individualism of dialectical idealism was a crucial first step toward an active worldview. Feuerbach had begun the search for concepts of man and the world that Marx would later establish.[92]

As Bogdanov indicated in his critique of Feuerbach, one had to seek the essence of world activity and man in the labor collective in order to overcome fully the limitations of idealist substitution and individualism. Marx, Bogdanov said, took the experience of the proletariat as his starting point rather than that of the family or the individual. This taught him that the essence of world activity was human activity in the broadest sense, that is, "collective practice" or "living collective labor."[93]

Bogdanov held that the center of Marx's thought was human activity rather than some sort of primary matter, as the term *diamat* is usually meant to designate. Marx's thought must be understood as the opposite of idealism. Where "idealism" deals with the activity of thought or ideas, Marx's "materialism" deals with concrete human labor activity.[94] "Matter," for Marx, was not primarily physical substance, but concrete reality in all its aspects, both physical and psychical. In this way it was an opposite of "idea" or "spirit."[95]

Both Hegel and Marx defined the dialectic as "development through opposition."[96] But whereas Hegel had focused on the struggle of ideal contradictions, Marx concerned himself wholly with the struggle of such real concrete opposites as man and nature, the bourgeoisie and the proletariat, etc. In his dialectic, said Bogdanov, Marx dealt with processes "not logical, but material, i.e. real."[97] Marx's dialectic, Bogdanov suggested, was fundamentally determined by his view of social man and the world process as human labor activity. Although Marx called his doctrine materialism, its central concept is not matter, but practice, activity, and live labor.[98] Marx's dialectic was materialistic in the same manner as the rest of his thought; it was antithetical to its "idealist" predecessors.[99]

Bogdanov considered diamat a "truly active worldview" and for that, distinct from any before it. In other words, Marx met one of the most important criteria Bogdanov set down for the contemporary philosophy; that is, he created a worldview that bore an active relationship to life. Similarly, Bogdanov found that, nonetheless, this worldview had a serious flaw; its method of explanation and view of the world-process (diamat) was inappropriate to it. Bogdanov deemed Marx's dialectic unreal and in particular ways a vestige of Hegelian idealism. The problem with the Marxist formulation lay in moving the dialectic into the realm of inorganic (less organized) nature. Engels attempted to apply the concept of negation to the world in general.[100] For Bogdanov, a truly active worldview must have a truly universal appreciation of process, a truly universal method of explanation, and its concepts of dialectics must express the "logic of reality" only in the respects in which that logic is actually dialectical.[101]

But Bogdanov also considered diamat as a worldview to be learned from and transcended. For Bogdanov, Marx said much that was true about the character of society, economics, philosophy, and the flow of history, which must be taken as part of the picture of present reality. Where he was wrong, said Bogdanov, he had to be challenged. "Getting beyond Marx," for Bogdanov, meant beginning in those places where Marx had been correct about reality and proceeding to search for a concept of process and universal explanation that those starting points implied. The key to that search was a critique of Marx's dialectic.[102] Bogdanov viewed history as a process primarily motivated by the struggle against nature and the resulting technical and scientific advance, with various organizing adjustments being, as a rule, developed in order to facilitate and ensure further progress.[103]

Bogdanov accused Marx of dealing with "development" rather than "organizational processes," stating that the first term was indefinite and relatively "unscientific" compared to the second. "Development," he said, was usually applied "in the sense of complicating some kind of complex, real or abstract."[104] Development might mean growth of order or organization. Alternatively, the term may be applied to all processes without regard to progress or regress in organization.[105] Bogdanov argued that dialectics should properly apply only to processes moving from lower to higher forms of organization. But this interpretation meant that disjunctive crises were problematic.

> [The] basic concept of dialectic with Marx, as with Hegel, did not achieve full clarity and completeness; and thanks to this the ... application of the dialectical method becomes imprecise and vague, arbitrariness creeps into its scheme, not only the limits of the dialectical remain undetermined, but sometimes its very meaning is grossly distorted.[106]

In his discussion of Engels's dialectics (on the basis of *Anti-Dühring*), Bogdanov noted that Engels had applied Hegel's law of dialectics to real phenomena and that the result was a series of misrepresentations of fact. Consequently, in Bogdanov's eyes, Engels's dialectic in *Anti-Dühring* was contaminated by idealism.[107]

Bogdanov discerned the major mistake of dialectical materialism in "that it does not explain or clarify the dialectic. And, were it to do so, it would cease to be itself and become another paradigm of understanding of the world."[108] "As we can see, here the dialectic is nothing other than an organizational process proceeding by the path of contradiction or, what is the same thing, by the path of struggle of different tendencies."[109]

According to Bogdanov, the "organizational" understanding of the dialectic makes it clear that the Hegelian dialectic is not at all something universal and that it cannot be a general method of knowledge. It is a partial case of organized processes, which can be reached in other ways.[110] Bogdanov defines dialectic as the "organizational process, taking the path of the conflict of opposing tendencies."[111] He notes that this notion of the dialectic does not fully agree with Marx's developmentism.[112]

> In reality any developing form contains opposing or "contending" forces. Their quantitative relationship is continuously changing depending on the entire sum total of internal and external conditions. Until the quantitative preponderance is maintained on one side, the form is preserved; but the more it is reduced, the weaker becomes systemic stability. The moment quantitative preponderance is destroyed, systemic stability disappears also; then the "quantity is transformed into quality," and there occurs a sharp transformation of the form in question in the guise of upheavals, revolutions—that which we call by the general name of "crisis." The form "negates" and passes into its opposite "antithesis." In antithesis there also appears an internal "contradiction," it develops in an analogous way and leads to the "negation of the negation" or "synthesis," which though formally similar with the "thesis" is enriched by the new content, or perfected in comparison to the "thesis."[113]

Bogdanov conceived organization and social change in a non-Hegelian dialectical manner, as proceeding until a state of equilibrium is attained between various factors involved.

> The organism is at war with its environment, continuously transferring to it the energy it expends and equally continuously drawing energy from it; so long as these two processes continue more or less in balance it remains "the same," and becomes different "something else" insofar as one of them gains predominance over the other.[114]

G. Kline writes that Bogdanov "like Hegel [and unlike Lenin] saw synthesis and harmony as more permanent and productive than opposition and conflict."[115] The corresponding equilibrium can be, and is, disturbed by external factors. The process of organization then begins again, until a new equilibrium is attained, which is disturbed in its turn. This proposition on equilibrium was generally adopted by Nikolai I. Bukharin in his *Historical Materialism*. Indeed, Vucinich advises that Bogdanov's ideas carried a strong influence, and his theory of "moving equilibrium" in the development of society found a way into N.I. Bukharin's widely noted work on Marxist functionalist sociology.[116] This will be discussed in the next chapter.

In Bogdanov's analysis the conflict of opposites thus occurs *between* entities —an entity being a product of organization—not *within* entities. The Marxist objection is that the "true" concept of dialectic, as conceived by Hegel and interpreted by Marx, Plekhanov, and Lenin in a materialist context, is that of an "immanent" dialectic, of a conflict of opposites within a given entity. In a given society, for example, there is an internal conflict of opposites, the class struggle. It is not simply a case of conflict between different societies. The dialectical movement, as conceived by Bogdanov and those who adopted the same point of view, was analogous to the idea of the transmission of motion or energy from body to body in the mechanical paradigm. Whereas for the Marxist, the dialectic expresses the autodynamism of matter.

The question whether the dialectic should be conceived as occurring *between* or *among* things or whether it should be conceived as essential, immanent, and necessary in things-in-themselves, constituting, so to speak, "the inner life of an entity," may seem to be a matter of purely academic interest for those who are prepared to postulate a dialectical movement apart from the movement of thought. However, for the orthodox Marxist this is not the case. For the materialist conception of history is bound up with the idea of a dialectical movement that operates not only between organized wholes but also within them. Capitalist society, for example, is said to generate its opposite—the proletariat; it gives rise to what is destined to negate it. For an orthodox Marxist, an understanding of the dialectic is essential for understanding the movement of history and is a condition for intelligent and successful revolutionary action.[117] Indeed, history for Marx was synonymous with the autogenesis of the species being of man through its own activity—through its autopoiesis. While, as previously pointed out, Bogdanov's concept of dialectics possessed non-Hegelian dimensions, he, nonetheless, followed Marx in elaborating the autopoietic dimensions of history. But whereas the dialectic of Hegel and Lenin may be understood as closed, even deterministic, systems, Bogdanov's non-Hegelian dialectics is in essence a theory of open self-reproducing or autopoietic systems! This is an important distinction between Marx's and Bogdanov's theory of history.[118]

Zenkovsky comments that Bogdanov departed from Marx, asserting that "the concept of dialectic has not yet achieved full clarity and completeness." Joravsky notes that Marx's and Engels's customary definition of dialectics corresponded to a "science of the general laws of motion and development of nature, human society and thought."[119] In effect, one can argue that this picture of dialectics as the queen science restores what Engels rejected: "a special science dealing with the great totality of things and our knowledge of things," provided the "great totality" is conceived as processes rather than fixed things.[120] Zenkovsky remarks that in Marx's dialectic the concern is with development, whereas Bogdanov places primary emphasis on the "creative modification of being"—the process of organization. From this idea grew his philosophy of Tektology, i.e., a theory of processes of organization and the creative modification of being. Tektology, Bogdanov asserts, as a doctrine of "practical mastery" of the "potentialities" in existence, "lies wholly in practice."[121] According to Bogdanov, the dialectical character of life is not that the "organism contradicts itself—being simultaneously 'the same' and 'not the same'; the organism makes itself 'not the same' in the struggle with the environment."[122] This is the essential deviation from the dialectics of Marx and of Lenin. Bogdanov rejects the cardinal concept of Marxist dialectic—that of the "self-movement of matter." For Bogdanov, "dialectic is not something universal; it is a special case of the process of organization, which may also take other forms."[123] Dialectics "is an organizational process which proceeds through contradictions. No matter how we state this, it is obvious that dialectics is not something universal, . . . it cannot be a general method of knowledge. It is a special case of organizational processes"[124] that proceeds by means of the struggle of various or "opposite" tendencies. The struggle is that of two real forces vying for predominance, and the process goes on from a lower level of organization to a higher one.[125] Engels, he said, had nothing to say about this in the *Anti-Dühring*.[126] Little wonder that Bogdanov was prosecuted by Lenin in *Materialism and Empirio-Criticism*.

In reference to *Anti-Dühring*, Bogdanov commented that:

> Engels . . . uncovered only the contradiction between two concepts . . . and not a contradiction between real forces or tendencies. But a contradiction of two concepts is only an ideal contradiction, existing only in thought; to reduce physical fact to it . . . means to go over to the point of view of idealism, to return to the dialectic of Hegel.[127]

According to Bogdanov, the contradiction in a process of movement exists between a body and its environment. Both are forces bearing some relation to one another. Movement is a type of organizational process that begins when the body and its environment cease to be in a state of rest ("equilibrium") vis-à-vis one another, which proceeds in the form of a struggle of the two forces and ends when a new state is achieved.[128]

For Engels, as for Hegel, negation meant the development of antithesis out of thesis. But a real negation, a real antithesis, is something that stands outside of and in opposition to something else. Bogdanov rejected the notion that a definite negation could be assigned to, let alone be found within, each component of the real world. The logic of the real world did not correspond to the logic of ideas in this regard.[129] According to Bogdanov, Engels (and by implication, Lenin) had lost the possibility of explaining "the transformation of quantity into quality" by his insistence on considering change in ideal terms.[130] He explained that real changes in quality occurred in the following manner:

> If one or another process—the movement of a body, the life of an organism, the development of a society—is defined as the struggle of two opposed forces, then as long as one force predominates, the process goes in that direction. When the other force grows and becomes equal to the first, then the whole character of the process changes, its quality changes.[131]

The "developmental dialectic" was inexact and without proper bounds. In other words, it was so broad as to render it meaningless.[132] The basic flaw in the Marxian developmental dialectic lay in the attempt to apply laws governing ideal processes to real phenomena. In so doing, the logic of ideas obscured the logic of reality. Bogdanov did not deny the usefulness of such concepts as "contradiction," "negation," and "transformation of quantity into quality"; but, as with the notion of dialectic itself, he felt that these concepts had a real character that could not be reconciled with the logic of ideas.[133] The result of applying idealist laws of the dialectic to the real world was not another form of dialectical idealism. It was a "materialist" philosophy that failed to find for itself an appropriate universal method of explanation.[134] Marx had failed, so Bogdanov maintained, to create a concept of the dialectic compatible with his own active worldview.

> Elements of the dialectic may be found almost everywhere, but life and movement are not exhausted by them. Philosophy must, consequently, conceive of its task in the broadest and most general form: [it must be] to research the bonds of the world process in order to discover all possible ways and means of organization. Such is the basic notion of Empirio-monism.[136]

The correct view of the dialectic, Bogdanov concluded after a nine-page critique of Engels, is to understand it as:

> An organizing process proceeding by the path of struggle [to an] opposite tendency. Does this coincide with the understanding of Marx obviously not completely? There [in Marx] the affair proceeds with the respect to development and not concerning the organizing process.[136]

Consequently, the core concept of the dialectic in Marx, as in Hegel, departs from correspondentialism and fails to achieve finality, and for this reason the dialectial procedure lacks the precision and specificity more usually associated with the scientific method.[137] This, however, does not mean that the notion of dialectical causality should be entirely rejected, but merely transmuted.

> Life is actually dialectic but not in the sense that an organism contradicts itself, being simultaneously "there" and "not there." No, the essence is otherwise; the organism is struggling with its environment; it uninterruptedly surrenders its energies to it ... and uninterruptedly assimilates energy from it; it remains "there" in so far as these two processes approach approximate equilibrium; it becomes otherwise, "not-there" in so far as one of these predominates over the other.[138]

For Bogdanov, the "contradictions" of the dialectic operate not within a given form of being but between a being and its environment:

> A body always moves in some environment, i.e., in spatial relations with other things. This environment renders resistance to it, an opposing to the mechanical energy of transference. This opposition can be great or small depending upon the environment, be it water, solid etc., but it exists and gradually destroys the force of movement. While the force exceeds it, motion continues. At a certain moment there is equilibrium and the body stops. . . . Here we have not only "contradiction" or more accurately counter-action—a term much better suited for a materialistic dialectic; here there is even the transition from quantitative change to qualitative [change].[139]

Bogdanov argued that the inorganic world exhibits many organizational processes that could be described "tektologically."[140] He considered his own "organizational dialectic" to be compatible with Marx's materialism, his view of man and the world.[141]

Bogdanov suggested that the "movement" of reality has a universal character, that there is a real "law" or set of "laws" that, after the fashion of the "unreal" Hegelian or Marxian dialectics, govern and explain all processes.[142] For Bogdanov, an organizational process is one that moves from lower to higher degrees of complexity and order; such a process may be dialectical in character, but the dialectical process is only a partial case. The task of philosophy, then, is to seek out all possible ways and means of organization.[143] This was the project that Bogdanov set for himself and that he addressed in the three volumes of *The Universal Organizational Science: Tektology*.

10

From Phenomenology to Tektology

The Systems Practice of Bogdanov

We may, with Kant, Hegel, and Marx as our early guides to totality theory, speak of systems practice; for this is the praxis-orientation of practical reason. "By 'the practical,'" wrote Kant, "I mean everything that is possible through freedom."[1] The philosophy of praxis is the philosophical effort to come to terms with the problem of practical reason expressed in the question, How can we rationally determine and justify the norms of action contained in recommendations or plans for action? Systems practice must go beyond the actual state of the philosophy praxis and develop practicable ways of mediation between the divergent requirements of argumentation (on the part of the involved) and democratic participation (on the part of the affected).[2] Systems practice should not misunderstand itself as a guarantor of socially rational decision making; it cannot, and need not, "monologically" justify the social acceptability of its designs.[3]

> Reason is impelled by a tendency of its nature to venture to the utmost limits of all knowledge, and not to be satisfied save through the completion of its course in a self-subsistent systematic whole. Is this endeavour the outcome merely of the speculative interest of reason? Must we not regard it as having its source exclusively in the practical interests of reason?[4]

While the purpose of theoretical reason is to mediate disputed claims regarding the empirical validity of theoretical propositions (hypotheses), the intent of practical reason is the mediation of disputed claims concerning the normative validity of practical propositions (assertions of norms, recommendations for action). Moreover, it is the task of practical reason to mediate the societal acceptability of disputed value premises or life-practical consequences of actions with respect to the consequences of all those affected in the satisfaction of their needs.[5] In both cases, a decision is to be informed by "the peculiarly unforced force of the better argument"[6] rather than resorting to power or deception. The challenge to practical reason, thus, consists in using noninvidious action reasonably, that is, in determining the ends and means of one's actions "with reason."

In practice, subjectively functional action tends to produce consequences that affect individuals not involved in the underlying decision. Their way of being affected need not correspond to their standards of value; the action in question may appear "irrational" or unreasonable to them. Hence, any action the consequences of which are constrained to those involved—in one word, any action that is not strictly "private"—sees itself faced with the question, How can the involved claim rationality for their action even though not all the affected may benefit or agree with the costs imposed upon them, and some may seriously be harmed? Or, How can conflicts of interest among the involved and the affected be resolved "with reason," i.e., by argumentative processes of consensus-formation rather than by resort to power and deception?

Rationality that meets the import of this question is what philosophers of praxis call practical reason. Practical reason cannot be reduced to or derived from alleged "value-neutral" theoretical-functional reason but must be grounded in a critically reflected, socioethically informed interest. For Kant, "an interest is that by which reason becomes practical—that is, a cause determining the will."[7] In addition to the two conditions constitutive of the functional concept of rationality, practical reason requires that the standards of value of all the affected—be they involved or not—converge. And since the group of those actually or potentially affected can never be delimited in advance with certainty, this condition entails the requirement of the generalizability of the standards of value ("norms") underlying the action in question.

But how can we ever justify the generalizability of empirical observations or normative assertions to universally valid statements? Even according to Bogdanov's phenomenology there are no nomological "laws," that is, no principle allowing us to generalize observational to theoretical statements. In this connection, the problem of induction has become the fundamental philosophical problem of empiricism. Moreover, since there is allegedly no principle (despite the rhetoric of positive economics to the contrary) that would permit us to universalize subjective valuations to generally binding transhistorical norms of action (moral "laws"), the problem of practical reason is a central concern of the philosophy of praxis.

There are, of course, essential differences between the two basic dimensions of reason. These have to do with the fact that theoretical reason is committed to producing "objective" knowledge about some segment of the phenomenal world, whereas practical reason seeks to secure socioethically justified consensus about norms mediating interpersonal relationships of the *Lebenswelt*.[8] That is to say, theoretical reason is bound to "observe" the "laws" that effectively govern the phenomenal world of experience (*Lebenswelt*), while practical reason is free to determine the laws that—according to its own judgment—ought to govern our social world of human relationships.[9] Practical reason—the praxis-oriented mediation of the *Lebenswelt*—is the emancipating reason that informs, or rather should inform, institution building.

However, political economy has long neglected Kant's and Marx's injunction that practical reason cannot be reduced to (or derived from) "value-neutral" theoretical-functional reason but must be grounded in a critically reflected socioethically informed interest. We shall need both the idea of practical reason as a critical standard against which to examine the instrumental rationality that our decision-making tools may produce and the systems idea as a critical reminder to reflect on those implications of our designs that reach beyond the limited context of the application that we are able to consider for all practical purposes, i.e., their whole-systems implications. Any philosophy of praxis must take into account Marx's treatise on the critical significance and, indeed, unavoidability and centrality of the idea of totality (systems).

It is within the context of totality and practical reason that the Marxian interpretation of society may be characterized by five hierarchically oriented components:

1. forces of production,
2. relations of production,
3. the legal and political superstructure,
4. ideology, and
5. forms of social consciousness.

The process and change in the higher strata of the social order are evinced by processes and changes in the lower ones. Notably, "morality, religion, metaphysics, and all the rest of ideology as well as the forms of consciousness corresponding to these" are social constructs.[10] Rather than indicating a determinative linkage, Marx, in the preface to his *Contribution to the Critique of Political Economy*,[11] chose the less definitive term *correspond* and referred to the legal and political superstructures that "rise" from the relations of production and in turn are held to "correspond" to a definite "stage in the development" of the material productive forces.[12] The legal and political superstructure, ideology, and forms of social consciousness, what Marx referred to as the "general process of social, political and intellectual life," are "conditioned" by the "mode of production of material life," understood as both forces and relations of production.[13]

The primary line of influence is presumed to be from productive forces to production relations, and from relations to superstructure, ideology, and social consciousness in general, although the converse causation and mutual causation is not denied.

Bogdanov formulated in *A Short Course of Economic Science* a form of positivist "stages theory" that shares a number of points with Marx. Lenin praised Bogdanov's clear and correct presentation of political economy as a science concerned with the historical development of social relations in production and distribution. Indeed, Bogdanov follows Marx in an uninhibited manner and on the whole faithfully. He provided a rather differentiated enumeration of the epochs of social development: (1) primitive tribal communism, patriarchal tribal organization of society, ancient slavery, feudal society, petit bourgeois society, commodity capitalism, industrial capitalism; (2) manufacture, industrial capitalism; (3) mechanical production, socialist society. Each epoch is a context within which he sought to appreciate:

1. the relations between society and nature, i.e., above all, the level of technology;
2. the relations of production and distribution within society;
3. characteristics of social psychology; and
4. tendencies of development.[14]

Based on the notion of the unity of the sciences, the energy view, according to Bogdanov, justifies and warrants the use of the natural science models in understanding these four relations. In the social sciences, the (Ostwaldian) social energetic approach, Bogdanov argued, is ostensibly the same as the historical approach: it places the emphasis on the interaction of social processes, particularly on the relationship between technology and ideology, two categories of social processes. Social processes are to human society what the transformation of energy is to nature in general: they depict the continuity and measurability of social change. His sociological theory, at least as formulated in *Knowledge from a Historical Point of View*, is both historical and monistic. It is historical inasmuch as it places the primary emphasis on the dynamics of social processes; it is monistic inasmuch as it interprets all phenomena of social dynamics as specific adaptations to increases and decreases in social energy and inasmuch as it operates on the assumption that human society manifests a spontaneous tendency—which it shares with organic nature—to eliminate internal contradictions and to strengthen harmonious relations.[15]

Bogdanov's praxiology had diverse coevolving components: forces of production that he appreciated in terms of social energetics and technology, metaphysics, fetishism, social consciousness, and the ideology-culture nexus. It is important to note that his metascience of praxis—Tektology—was the integral resolution of these three elements and was thus systems practice–oriented. That is, it both embraced the idea of practical reason as a critical standard against which to examine instrumentalities and was a pioneer of the systems idea.

In the further elaboration of these ideas, we shall first turn to aspects of the role of social energetics and technology in Bogdanov's systems practice. Thereafter, we shall turn to some remarks on social consciousness, and thence to the role of ideology and culture.

Forces of Production: Technology and Social Energetics

In *The Philosophy of Living Experience*, Bogdanov affirmed Marxian praxiology and optimistically speculated that the proletariat would realize the active relationship of man to the world and in recognizing it, would act on not only the possibility but the necessity of changing it. This realization is at once a reflection of the way in which machine production itself changes the world and a reaffirmation of Ostwaldian thinking. For according to Bogdanov, the outcome and essence of machine production is "the systematic transformation of efforts, or, in scientific and exact terms, the transformation of energy."[16]

Expressing a view offered by a number of earlier philosophers, Bogdanov noted that machine production changes the world by turning the physical, chemical, and electrical forces of nature into one another after the manner in which natural forces are turned into mechanical forces of production.[17] Such a view is not inconsistent with that of some Marxians, whose concept of forces of production can be understood to comprise all of physical technology. Marx usually employs the term to mean the sum total of tools, instruments, and machines available in a society, plus all sources of energy that move these implements: steam, water, coal, animal, and human power. With the term *forces of production* Marx brings together under a single concept the instruments, energy, and labor involved in the active effort of individuals to change material reality to suit their needs.[18] Unequivocally, the domain of *Capital* is political economy and, Marx's insistence that "political economy is not technology" notwithstanding,[19] a primary role for productive forces; for capitalism's imminent demise and transcendence is explained by Marx, not by relations of production per se, but by a germinating, essential disequilibrium between institutional adaptability and technological progressivity or, in Marxian terms, a growing conflict between forces of production and relations of production. In other words, the basic contradictions of capitalism emanate from its institutional structure, from the "internal" logic of the system of production and political relations.

Whereas earlier philosophers of progress sanctioned the advance of technology on the basis of religious and moral imperatives, today, though technology remains a means to "make everyone happy," a means by which people consciously exploit natural resources and orient natural processes to serve human ends, it can no longer be considered as benign. Bogdanov argued that throughout history changes in technology have been of profound importance to social change. Undoubtedly, the most popular representation of Marx's assessment of the technology-institution nexus is the widely acknowledged "fundamentalist" interpretation.

At once contesting the utopian belief in the neutrality of technology and giving expression to the above-noted fundamentalist correlation is Marx's controversial remark in *The Poverty of Philosophy*: "In acquiring new productive forces men change their mode of production; and in changing their mode of production, in changing their way of earning their living, they change all their social relations. The hand-mill gives you society with the feudal lord; the steam-mill, society with the industrial capitalist."[20]

In *Grundrisse*, Marx speaks of a time when systematic automation will be developed to the point that direct human labor power will be a source of wealth.

The preconditions will be created by capitalism itself. Ostensibly, it will be an age of the true mastery of nature, a post-scarcity age, when men can turn from alienating and dehumanizing labor to the free use of leisure in the pursuit of the sciences and arts.

To Marx's hand-mill aphorism Engels later added:

> The men who in the seventeenth and eighteenth centuries laboured to create the steam engine had no idea that they were preparing the instrument which more than any other was to revolutionize social relations throughout the world. Especially in Europe, by concentrating wealth in the hands of a minority and dispossessing the huge majority, this instrument was destined at first to give social and political domination to the bourgeoisie, but later, to give rise to a class struggle.[21]

Marx's memorable, though allegedly inaccurate, aphorism has remained a succinct précis of technological determinism.[22] Langdon Winner reservedly supports a technologically determinist view of Marx, describing him as having "isolated the primary independent variable in all of history"—technology.[23] Such a view is also present in Kostas Axelos's Heideggerian interpretation. Axelos asserts that alienation is in the very character of productionist *techné*, as it has gone on historically from the beginning until the present. Having so defined alienation, he then cynically contends that technology in its whole history is itself endemically characterized by alienation. Axelos writes:

> In Marx's eyes, a labourious development, that of the forces of human history, has alienated man from his being, from the products of his labour, from his true nature, and from the world in its totality, and all this to the point where his true social nature is lost for the sake of a technicist civilization.[24]

According to Axelos, Marx's allegedly technicist attitude in *Poverty of Philosophy* is reinforced by his assertion that:

> What characterizes the division of labour in the automatic workshop is that labour has there completely lost its specialized character. But the moment every special development stops, the need for universality, the tendency toward an integral development of the individual begins to be felt. The automatic workshop wipes out specialists and craft-idiocy.[25]

In Marx's *Poverty of Philosophy* there is, of course, the above aphorism. But shortly thereafter Marx states that all relations "co-exist simultaneously and support one another."[26] Moreover,

> In the social production of their existence, men inevitably enter into definite relations, which are dependent on their will, namely relations of production appropriate to a given stage in the development of their material forces of production. The totality of these relations of production constitutes the eco-

nomic structure of society, the real foundation, on which arises the legal and political superstructure and to which correspond definite forms of social consciousness.... At a certain stage of development, the material productive forces of society come into conflict with the existing relations of production.[27]

In *Grundrisse*, Marx states that production, distribution, exchange, and consumption "all form members of a totality, distinctions within a unity.... Mutual interaction takes place between the different moments. This is the case with every organic whole."[28] The following passage from *Capital* also suggests codetermination: "The specific economic form, in which unpaid surplus-labor is pumped out of direct producers, determines the relationship of rulers and ruled, as it grows directly out of production itself, and in turn, reacts upon it as a determining element."[29]

For Bogdanov, this feature of machine production generated a new perspective on the world and, subsequently, on complex mutual causality. The new view was that, for the labor collective, "every process in the world is the possible source of every other process. The practical synthesis of phenomena, the practical unity of nature," he said, "is expressed in this perspective."[30]

By placing the main emphasis on technical forms of social adaptation, Bogdanov shared the utopian's dream of an Athens without slaves and argued that every ideology and every change in social forms ultimately derives from the technical process.[31] The term *technology*, according to Bogdanov, denotes not merely the material equipment of a society but the organization and utilization of knowledge related to external nature.[32]

Bogdanov, considering his theorizing contiguous to that of Marx, recognized that social processes were part of a historical development. However, unlike Marx and Engels, he linked the study of societies with a quasi-Darwinist perspective. He sought to reformulate historical materialism in the terms of energeticism, "social selection, adaptation to a social environment, social equilibrium, and harmony."[33] That Bogdanov sought to revise Marxism according to a natural scientific, energeticist, and phenomenological program was considered by Lenin an affront to the doctrine of materialism. However, the venerable father of Russian Marxism, Plekhanov, indicated that "energeticism" was a form of materialism.

Bogdanov considered Darwinian adaptation the key process revealing the regularities of biological change. In his view, social selection (a nonreductionist transposition of Spencer's "natural selection") was the principal technique for changing social needs as defined by practical reason. It was the main mechanism of adaptation.

Bogdanov wrote:

> Social adaptation, an extension of natural adaptation, holds the key for a full understanding of the historical nature of social phenomena. Its basic operative

mechanism is social selection, which produces either positive results, when it creates the forms of adaptation that add to the intensity and plasticity of social life; or negative results, when it brings forth the forms of adjustment that reduce both the quality and the intensity of social energy. While positive selection produces social progress, negative selection produces social regress.[34]

By "social selection" it should be understood that Bogdanov was, in fact, referring to instituted modes of social integration. Capitalism constituted a mode of social selection based on invidious metaphysical criteria, whereas Bogdanov's socialism was a mode of selection based on broader criteria.

The idea of progress, a dominant theme of classical sociology, was deeply rooted in Bogdanov's system of social thought. To him social progress was an extension of natural progress: Just as natural progress is measured by the expansion of living energy and by the diversification of the forms of life, so social progress is indicated by the expansion of social energy and the growing division of social labor, the former contributing to the "fullness of social life" and the latter to social harmony. Again, just as social progress is an extension of natural progress, so sociology is metaphorically an extension of biology.

Bogdanov's voluminous writing is part of a tireless search for a general science of society whose function, according to Bogdanov, is to enrich the store of knowledge helping man to find his place in nature and society. Of all scientific questions, the most important is the one concerned with the main line of social development and the basic indices of social progress.

In Book 3 of *Empirio-monism*, Bogdanov wrote:

> We can formulate the fundamental connection between energetics and social selection as follows: Every act of social selection represents an increase or decrease of the energy of the social complex concerned. In the former case we have "positive selection," in the latter "negative selection." ... The rapid growth of the productive forces of capitalist society is undoubtedly an increase in the energy of the social whole ... but the disharmonious character of this process leads to its culmination in a "crisis," in a vast waste of productive forces, in a sharp decrease of energy: positive selection is replaced by negative selection.[35]

For the young Bogdanov, energy represented the practical relationship of society to nature, of human activity to that which resists it. It was neither substance nor idea, but the factual outcome of the relationship between work and its object.[36] The transformation of energy, Bogdanov said in *The Philosophy of Living Experience*, refers to the creation and change wrought by active, human effort on nature:[37] "to see energy in the processes of nature means to look at those processes from the perspective of their possible labor exploitation by man."[38] As late as 1920, he wrote: "Man is able to change the world by systematic and planned transformation of energy."[39]

But he felt that "where ever at all possible the principle of selection should give its place to a higher general energetic principle." In nature, the development of animal species was regulated by a struggle for survival; whereas in society, struggle and adaptive cooperation reached its highest level in the collective. Moreover, transcending Darwinian modes of selection the evolution of consciousness and knowledge in society became the informative power of development. Bogdanov advised that society's ability to adapt to nature depended on its ability to obtain, process, and generalize information.[40]

In turning to the meaning and role of information, Bogdanov was departing from the reductionism of Ostwald's "social energetics." He did not deny the similarities between the first law of thermodynamics and his broader concept. But he argued that the law was unsuitable for inclusion in a "labor world view," since it was based on an abstract and "fetishistic" concept of energy.[41] N.I. Bukharin, following Engels, argued: "It would be truly monstrous to suppose that, let us say, the law of the conservation of energy makes the law of labor value."[42] According to Bogdanov, all exponents of the second law of thermodynamics saw "energy" as primary substance, as a Kantian thing-in-itself, or as a pure useful fiction. The first view, he said, considers energy as something apart from man and outside any direct relationship to labor activity. In the second, energy exists only in thought and not in fact. In both views, it is taken to be an absolute. This was not energy from "the labor point of view."[43]

In Bogdanov's subsequently revised analytical framework, energy and social energetics were a second-order construct. For while social energetics was an important contribution to social dynamics, it was not the informative one. The concept of organization subordinated that of energy, while the function it performed remained the same, i.e., to establish the unity of all aspects of nature and human activity, or, in the metaphor that Bogdanov repeated in Tektology, "to fill in the chasms between animate and inanimate nature."

Social Consciousness, Ideology, and Culture

Critical Marxism in Eastern Europe has been interpreted as a response to bureaucratic Stalinism and has a tradition appropriated from Western Marxists, represented by Georg Lukács, Antonio Gramsci, and later members of the Frankfurt School.[44] Not only must we discard remnant liberal, Cold War interpretations that present Stalinism as an inevitable consequence of Marxism, so, too, must we dispose of Marxist apologies, which dismiss it as merely a "Russian accident" rationalized ostensibly in terms of backwardness. While this concedes the possibility of an unambiguous continuity between Stalinism and "Scientific Marxism,"[45] it also admits Russian variants of Critical Marxism, for an authentic and cogent critique is evident in the works of Bogdanov.

We casually use the term *culture* to refer to the "higher" arts as opposed to popular or everyday practice. Culture is often used to signify that which is "superstructural" as opposed to that which is the "base." But we also use the term culture to signify that which is "symbolic" as opposed to that which is "material." These various binary distinctions are not comparable, although they all seem to point in the direction of the vintage philosophical distinction between the "ideal" and the "real," or between the Cartesian duality of "mind" and "body."

While Marxist aesthetics is argued to have come of age in the writing of the Critical Marxism of Lukács, Korsch, Brecht, Bloch, and the Frankfurt School, it was anticipated by Bogdanov.[46] Their work went well beyond the scattered observations of Marx and Engels on cultural questions and was a major advance over the doctrinal theories of Plekhanov and others of the Second International. It can be plausibly argued that Critical Marxism has enriched cultural theory more than economic or political theory. Hegelian and non-Hegelian Marxists alike have recognized that the problem of "cultural hegemony," as Gramsci called it, was key to understanding the resilience of capitalism.[47] Furthermore, Bogdanov appreciated that a purely "scientific" materialist theory gives little indication of the potential advantages of socialism beyond the possible abolition of economic exploitation. A study of Bogdanov's work goes a long way to refute the sophist notion that an interest in "subjective factors" was the preserve of Western Marxism. Whatever the reasons for the Leninist, and eventually Stalinist, outcome, as we have seen, it cannot be attributed to a lack of alternative formulations. Pointedly, Bogdanov provided a synthetic cultural critique within the Russian context, which in Western Marxism is more usually associated with the recently rediscovered works of Antonio Gramsci.

Marx had contended that the short-run conflict between labor and capital over the division of industrial income would inevitably lead to a long-run struggle between capitalism and socialism; therefore, a society could not in the long run be both democratic and capitalistic. Whether this proposition is, in fact, supported by history is problematic and raises the question of how an exploitative society can gain the consent of the exploited, a condition that Bogdanov and later Gramsci explored. It must be noted that Bogdanov's concept of cultural hegemony, while undoubtedly a central pillar in his political thought and a major contribution to Russian Critical Marxist theory, cannot be fully grasped without taking into account his other concepts.

In the political platform of the *Vpered* group, with which Bogdanov was affiliated, "general cultural hegemony" was the necessary complement to "political hegemony." He viewed the development of a political culture less as an instrument for securing political legitimacy than as a process of establishing moral and intellectual leadership in the new society, that is, as a cultural rather than a political hegemony. Bogdanov repeated at every available opportunity the need for the proletariat to believe in itself, not in seemingly unapproachable authorities, be they intellectuals or other purveyors of an "absolute truth."

Convinced that a ruling class dominates other classes by a synthesis of state-orchestrated violence and consent secured through the exercise of moral and intellectual leadership, Bogdanov maintained that national leadership could be achieved only by gaining the consent of other classes and social grounds through creating a system of alliances and continually adapting it to changing conditions. The building of alliances is central to the concept of hegemony.

In the Vpered platform, there was a specific call to achieve cultural hegemony alongside political hegemony because "political forms an organic whole with the other aspects of ideological life of society"; the socialist ideal included both "political and cultural liberation." Effectively, Bogdanov distinguished between the political institutions comprising and associated with the state and the nexus of cultural relations of society distinct from the economic structures as well as from the state.

In one of the best-known passages of Gramsci's *Prison Notebooks* he compared civil society to a system of fortresses and earthworks standing behind the state: civil society had become far more complex in advanced capitalist countries than it was in tsarist Russia before 1917, when society was ostensibly dominated by the state, and the ruling class relied much more on force and much less on hegemony, than was the case in the West. Thus, in Russia, he contended, a frontal attack, a "war of movement" could succeed, but in the West a different revolutionary strategy was required, a "war of position." However, Bogdanov maintained that the Russian revolutionary strategy required the construction of a proletarian culture, in Gramsci's terms, a "war of position."[48]

Indeed, Vpered's platform contended that Bolshevism should be not only a political movement but also a sociocultural movement. Socialism would be possible only when the proletariat developed its own intellectual and moral awareness—its own cultural hegemony—which could be counterpoised to the "old cultural world" and would provide a consensual basis for human interaction. The necessary precondition for Bolshevik victory was the creation of a proletarian culture "within the framework of present-day society," a culture that was "stronger and more structured than the culture of the declining bourgeois classes." For cultural hegemony to be achieved, institutional props were required. In this connection, the party, for Bogdanov, was not merely an instrument for seizing power; it was also the nucleus of the new society. A strong, well-disciplined, well-organized "vanguard party" was necessary but not sufficient, for the party should be considered a means, not an end. In his words: "For the conscious political activist, the power of his party is one of his main ends or goals." What was needed were mutual ties and solidarity among the workers, thereby creating, in embryonic form, the "comradely relations" of the future socialist society. For Bogdanov, loyalty to the proletariat and to socialism was not the same as reverence of the party. "A conscious comradely organization of the working class in the present and a socialist organization of all of society in the future—these are different moments of one and the same process, different degrees of one and the same phenomenon."[49]

Bogdanov detected in the party's internal relations a reinforcement of the habits of passive submission and weakness of initiative already instilled by the capitalist production process and its attendant culture. Admittedly, a certain amount of "authoritarian discipline," of blind adherence to leaders, and of centralization was an inevitable result of class struggle.[50] All the more reason, Bogdanov contended, to counteract the authoritarian tendency by promoting areas of collectivism and comradely relations. Were there not other vehicles? He feared the danger that the party and its members would reconstitute themselves as a new class, despite the revolution and the avowed goal of a classless society. Hence, the achievement of socialism would become ever more remote.

Consistent with Hertzen's earlier concerns, Bogdanov claimed that trade unions were governed by the rules of capitalist society, that trade unions could not become the instrument for a radical renovation of society. He complained that trade unions were permeated with bourgeois fetishisms, such as private property, bourgeois individualism, legalism, and morality; they acted on the basis of competition within the market and on the basis of compromise within the political arena. In other words, the "fetish character" that Marx attributed to economic objects in the epoch of commodity production is only a particular, modified case of the general fate of the cultural nexus. The English and American trade unions, for example, understood organization as a collection of individuals, not a collectivity, as far as Bogdanov was concerned. They reflected the existing culture rather than fostering new attitudes and values. Consequently, Bogdanov argued, they could not serve as adequate transitional forms for the construction of socialism. While Lukács was sympathetic to syndicalist currents in the proletarian movement, like Bogdanov he was hostile to trade unions and, in his early years, to electoral activity; he was largely insistent on the primacy of workers' councils or soviets as the basic organizational form of the revolutionary movement.[51]

Bogdanov's qualms about the conservatism of labor unions prompted him to look elsewhere, to *Proletkul't*.[52] Together with some former members of the Tula study group, Bogdanov and his adherents believed the party should predominate in the political sphere, the workers' councils in the economic sphere, and the Proletariat Culture movement (Proletkul't) in the cultural sphere. The central assumption underlying this tripart arrangement was that the "cultural front" was a warranted area of effort and concern, consistent and coevolving with the political and economic fronts. This is consonant with his conviction that cultural change was an essential, and overlooked, component of the transition to socialism.

Socialism would only be an accomplished fact, Bogdanov warned, when the proletariat would be able to oppose the metaphysics of the "old cultural world" with its own political force, its economic plan, and its "new world of culture, with its new, higher methods."

The theory of the collapse of capitalism on which the Second International settled was based on a mechanistic conception of Marx's thought. It assumed the proletarian revolution as both a necessary and inevitable consequence of the development of economic contradictions of the capitalist mode of production. Nonetheless, the emphasis on a cultural dimension of revolutionary praxis, with its stress on education and the emancipatory power of reason, was a common theme among the left. For them the project of a cultural revolution was totalizing. A central theme of this revolt was its contraposition of *Kultur* and *Gemeinschaft* with *Zivilization* and *Gesellschaft*, the former concepts suggesting the sought-after natural, face-to-face community that would truly meet man's socioethical imperative and creative needs, the latter concepts defining the existing "society"—mechanized, alienated, and destructive of the essential vitality of fullness of human life.[53] For Lukács, cultural revolution was no aesthetic ersatz for political and economic revolution; it was not a museum putsch, nor a bit of theatrical scandal. These gambits leave culture in the ghetto to which capitalism condemns it. Cultural revolution is far more impatient, more totalizing, less easily satisfied than mere politico-economic revolution. It entails not only the *Aufhebung* of the relations of production but also the transformation of all commodified relationships and where commodities have become the epicenter of social life. The meaning of the cultural transformation of society, above all, is the end of the domination of the economy over the totality of life. The new social order means the Aufhebung of the economy as autojustified.

Marx developed a highly particular conception of socialism as the self-emancipation of the working class: "The emancipation of the working class must be achieved by the working class itself."[54] This involves, in the first instance, a specific claim about the agency of socialist transformation: the exploited class in capitalist society, collectivized by the very conditions of production it experiences, has the practical interest and capacity and will develop the organization and consciousness required to inaugurate a classless society. At the same time, however, Marx's conception of socialism implies a particular view of the process of self-transformation. "The proletarian movement," he wrote, "is the self-conscious independent movement of the immense majority, in the interest of the immense majority."[55] This view of socialist revolution informs Marx's analysis of the Paris Commune of 1871, with its concentration on the dismantling of the bureaucratic state machine by the working people of Paris and its replacement by organs of popular self-government. In Red Vienna, the Paris Commune experiences provided a model for Otto Bauer. But importantly, Bauer placed considerable emphasis on the role of culture. Max Adler's insistence on the socialist mission of the working class to raise the cultural level of society above the commercial ethic of the bourgeoisie was shared by Karl Polanyi.[56]

Role of the Intelligentsia

A central problem in Marxism is that of the transformation of the proletariat. This is a problem that agitated Lenin and Bogdanov, but also Gramsci. It stemmed from a host of arrested questions posed by Marx. Since consciousness was at the core of Marx's thought, how precisely would the proletariat acquire it? Would this be a spontaneous process? Would the proletariat require assistance? These questions raise the issue of the mediation in Marxism's agency theory of history. Marx viewed the closing of this gap largely as a spontaneous and necessary process, as a by-product of changes in the economic base of society, reinforced and crystallized by revolutionary struggle.[57] He appears to deliberately sidestep the question of the revolutionary practice that will turn a mere fragment of a person into a fully developed individual. Others see "a leap of faith" in Marx's assertion that the proletariat would successfully undertake the construction of the socialist order.

Lenin was more than dubious about the spontaneous transformation of the proletariat. Neither the "school of capitalism" nor the revolutionary struggle produced a sufficiently altered proletariat. Left to its own efforts, Lenin lamented, the proletariat developed only a "trade-union consciousness."[58] Spontaneity "overwhelms" consciousness and introduces myopic arguments that "a kopeck added to the ruble [is] worth more than Socialism and politics."[59] Lenin appears to have been visited by the ghost of Hertzen, whose earlier critique of the labor movements of the West centered on the issue of emancipatory consciousness.

For Lenin, since working-class consciousness did not arise of its own accord, the proletariat would have to look to "professional mediators" for assistance. History needed a helping hand in overcoming the hiatus between the existing and the projected proletariat. The necessary consciousness could, Lenin argued, be provided by the mediating and vanguard role of the party. The professional revolutionaries were the vanguard of the working class, composed of the allegedly most "conscious elements" from among the workers and sympathetic "bourgeois intellectuals." They would assume the leadership of the proletariat and mediate the "spontaneous awakening of the masses."

Bogdanov readily accepted the premise that spontaneity alone did not transform the proletariat, but well aware of the failed history of the nihilists, he objected to Lenin's solution, which superimposed bourgeois intellectuality on the workers' movement. While he acknowledged that bourgeois intellectuality rendered a service to the proletariat, he hastened to add that intellectuals who genuinely adopted the workers' point of view were as rare as "white crows." More usually, intellectuals imparted their own petulant "individualist" habits of thought and behavior within working-class organizations, since communalism and equality were not integral to their culture. Bogdanov views the intellectual as an individual who belonged to no particular social class and, being confined to one particular professional specialization, was the supreme example of fragmentation, the furthest removed from the community of huhumankind and the real world.[60] Consequently, the intellectuals' view of the world contrasted with the ostensibly "collectivist" and "monist" outlook of the workers. Though they rendered service to the proletariat, they also imparted potentially metaphysical habits of thought and work, such as their unease with discipline and with the equality essential to workers' organizations. Bogdanov considered the outlook of the intelligentsia as one characterized by a metaphysical perspective, one incapable of achieving harmony either with itself or with the peasants or proletariat. Unlike Lenin, who maintained that the proletariat received its socialist consciousness from the intelligentsia, Bogdanov was convinced that the most urgent task following the revolution was to purge all traces of invidious thought.

The notion that the proletariat was an autonomous entity and had no need of disciplined guidance from a vanguard party was a constant among adherents of the Proletkul't movement. No less was it an issue, after 1920, with the Worker's Opposition, which argued that the influence of the intelligentsia threatened the revolution with degeneration. Consequently, Bogdanov contended that the proletariat should not place its trust in outside classes but should cultivate from among its own an authentic social consciousness. For Bogdanov, the liberation of labor is a matter for labor. Neither could he ignore the failed history of the intelligentsia's mediation, for neither the Narodnik nor the nihilist efforts had proved successful. Here Bogdanov can be seen returning to the earlier themes of Hertzen and Mikhailovsky, themes that were more widely appreciated. Bertolt Brecht, for instance, speaks of the "type of intellectual revolutionary of whom the proletarian revolutionary is suspicious: this is the type who expects a thoroughgoing improvement from the revolution. In no sense standing under unbearable pressure, but freely selecting and choosing what is better, he opts for revolution."[61] Demanding only a "thorough-going improvement," let alone demanding less, enables one to accept virtually anything, such as accepting the state bureaucracy of the Soviet Union as a proletarian revolutionary regime.

Stirred by these misgivings, Bogdanov counseled the working class to "verify everyone and everything in its own mind, with its general class consciousness." The liberation of the workers, to be genuine, had to be "a matter for the workers themselves."[62] Here Bogdanov reaffirms Marx's praxis-oriented convention of self-conscious action. Socialist intellectuality should originate in the working class. They should be, in Gramsci's terms, "organic intellectuals."[63]

Gramsci hoped that intellectuals who were expressly nurtured from within the ranks of the working class would play an innovative and leading role but at the same time would "remain in contact" with the masses, "to become, as it were, the whalebone in the corset."[64] What Gramsci envisaged was some form of interaction between "spontaneity" and "conscious leadership" that had to be "educated, directed, purged of extraneous contaminations" by the more conscious elements, by the intellectuals.[65]

Gramsci's and Bogdanov's solutions to the problem of social consciousness implied a rather lengthy and protracted societal transformative process. Lenin's solution, on the other hand, suggested a shortcut to the consciousness-raising process. The substitution of party for class as the motive force of revolution was Lenin's most distinctive innovation in revolutionary theory and practice. It was not without a manipulative and elitist connotation. Social consciousness was attenuated and came to denote "any willingness on the part of the workers to follow the commands of the party." After the October Revolution, "The original mission of the vanguard, that of raising the masses to consciousness, tended to be forgotten because of the more immediate problem of keeping the party in power."[66]

On the basis of his experience in workers' circles in Tula, Bogdanov felt that socialism would elude the workers unless a change in attitudes and in authority relations took place, particularly in the workshop, but also in other spheres of social life. Moreover, he believed that advanced technology could transform relations of production, creating conditions that would eliminate the gap between the ordinary worker and the engineer and give rise to a "new consciousness." These developments would lay the groundwork for a "new comradely discipline" activated by the "will of the collective" and governed by considerations of competence rather than invidious power relations.[67] But he was not convinced that the "new consciousness" would be born without a midwife. If anything, he argued that cultural change lagged behind technological change and posed obstacles to the complete transformation of an emergent class. The proletariat was still guided by "ideological remnants," unquestioned common sense appreciations from the past, and by attitudes suited to bourgeois metaphysics rather than the proletariat. For Bogdanov, ideology was not just an instrument of domination or a set of false beliefs but a terrain of struggle, the site on which the dominant ideology was constructed, and also terrain of resistance to that ideology. These included, among others, individualism, authoritarianism, competitiveness, and divisiveness—all fetishisms that had to be purged if the proletariat were truly to be liberated.[68] Bogdanov obliquely suggested that ideology is effective insofar as it succeeds in binding an alliance of diverse social forces. The proletarian movement had to build up a new alliance of social forces cemented by an ideology—a new common sense—expressing proletarian values in ways that are related to its needs and experiences. For Bogdanov, as for Gramsci, a class cannot be hegemonic if it confines itself to its own immediate material interests as a class. It must take into account the range of popular issues that do not have a narrow class character and that give rise in many cases to significant social movements. The hegemonic class is the one that succeeds in combining interests stemming from these issues with its own interests so as to achieve national leadership. In order to attain hegemony, the proletariat had to make its interests the interests of other groups as well; it had to become a "universal" class. The revolution, by transforming the relations of consciousness and social being, art, and social organization and the crisis of form and content that exists under capitalism, would restore the essential unity and wholeness of culture, for the aesthetic and social-political (or "life") moments are inextricably linked.

Metaphysics and Fetishism

With a somewhat Comtean appreciation of metaphysics, Bogdanov expounded the philosophical presuppositions of Marx's theory of commodity fetishism.[69] Bogdanov, for instance, regarded the problematique of the value of commodities as a species of metaphysics. Value was a quality imposed on commodities by a society at a certain stage of its development, but one that at previous and later stages could be seen to have been created by the collective consent of society and that could be dispensed with by the same means.[70] It might be argued that Bogdanov subscribed to an institutionalist's theory of value. This at once confronts marginalist and costs theories of value and situates Bogdanov's theory as approximate to that of Marx. But, according to Bogdanov:

> [Whoever] possesses a commodity, be it the producer or some other person, it does not matter, the commodity can be sold for the value attached to it. Hence, nothing is easier than to conclude that the value, the capacity to be sold for a certain sum of money, is a quality of the commodity itself, a quality independent of men, of society—in effect a natural quality of the commodity.[71]

Bogdanov implied that the very existence of the capitalist system was founded on a metaphysical view of the world, wherein commodity fetishism was necessary in order that there might be value. In this connection, Bogdanov was one of the very few Russian Marxists to examine the implications of this aspect of Marx's theory and to consider the question of social perception or social psychology that made possible commodity fetishism and other varieties of metaphysical thinking.[72] Already in his textbook on political economy, Bogdanov indicated what his future line of enquiry would be. There he wrote:

> But what follows from this? Fetishism is not only an expression of the impotence of the perceptive faculty, but also its resignation from further struggle. Perception stops short at fetishism. Therefore, the development of human relations cannot be completed consciously where these relations are perceived in a fetishised way. The process can take place only spontaneously.... But spontaneous development is inevitably associated with mass suffering and takes place extremely gradually. This is the way that the development of exchange relations took place.[73]

Concerned with the negative influences of fetishes and idols as much as he was with the positive contributions of science, Bogdanov regarded bourgeois life as steeped in fetishism and idolatry, guiding behavior and filling in the gaps in our knowledge. The entire economic existence of the bourgeoisie is permeated by the fetish of exchange value, that which interprets the working relations among men as quantities of things. Indeed, the "fetish character" that Marx attributed to economic objects in the epoch of commodity production is but a particular modified case of the general fate of bourgeois culture. The most decisive feature of capitalist society is that economic life ceases to be a means to social life; economic "life," autojustified, placed itself at the center, the goal of all social activity. "Everything ceases to be valuable for itself or by virtue of its inner (e.g., artistic, aesthetic) value; a thing has value only as a ware bought and sold on the market."[74] No esoteric analysis is needed to show how destructive this has been of culture. Just as man's independence from the worries of subsistence (the unrestricted use of his powers as autojustified) is allegedly the human and social precondition for culture, so all that culture offers can possess real cultural value only when it is valuable for itself. As a result of commodification, the novel, the sensational, and the conspicuous elements assume an importance irrespective of whether or not they enhance or detract from the aesthetic value of the product. Central in Bogdanov's social thought is not economic welfare narrowly defined, but culture. The social upheaval caused by capitalist industrialization was not simply the material impoverishment of the workers but also the disruption of the ethical culture to which they belonged and through which they defined their identity. Bogdanov recognized that economic institutions had an impact on people's cultural self-understanding. He advocated an alternative organization of industrial production, one that expressed human respect and encouraged cooperation, values out of which the workers could define their lives.

The cultural crisis, which attends capitalist industrialization, is itself a moment in the larger crisis and is symptomatic of the fundamental inability of the bourgeois class to perceive the social basis of its own existence. Capitalist industrialization, Bogdanov argued, worsens the situation by tearing the individual from a social base. For the artist, his works, and the public are subsumed in market relations. For Bogdanov, genuine art requires a "sensual-naive immediacy," and precisely this is liquidated by capitalism, which transforms all of social life into abstract, reified appearances. Moreover, the entire legal and moral existence, he argued, is under the influence of idols—of juridical and ethical norms that are presented to members of society not as expressions of their own real relations but as fully independent forces, exercising pressure on people and demanding strict adherence to them. In the metaphysics of political economy the "laws" of the market were/are viewed, not as social constructs, but fetishized as natural phenomena independent of social reality. Society was allegedly governed by the dynamics of the market and in turn dominated by natural laws. Inclined by some force akin to gravity, trade would flow, creating a pool of goods organized in markets. Money would appear, and all things would be drawn into the whirl of wealth-generating, price-making exchanges. In such circumstances neither political, religious, nor ideological strivings to change the course of the economic system were deemed effectual. However, polytheism was not expunged from modern society; it has only been twisted and somewhat weakened. From a vivid religious form it has been transformed into a pale metaphysical form. Theoretical knowledge about the real meaning of these idols and fetishes is still limited; even those to whom this knowledge is available find it almost impossible to rid their everyday activities of a subconscious fetishistic influence. Scientific knowledge did not destroy fetishism but merely reduced its power.

Fetishism and idolatry are social facts. They are expressions of accumulated cultural experience and hence are the captive of power. Although they reflect both the state of technical progress and the basic principles of social bonds, they are, for Bogdanov, merely substitutes for knowledge; they are strongest in the areas of social behavior in which science has not asserted itself. But they also find their way into science and philosophy when these serve as expressions of class ideologies, particularly in the case of political economy.

The atomistic thing-in-itself is ostensibly the cornerstone of both the Kantian theory of knowledge and Newtonian mechanics. However, in both cases it is a fetish, for it is merely an expression of the search for absolutes, a search sociologically congruent with the authoritative character of the earlier social structures. Post-positivist thought has rejected both epistemological objectivism (the knowability of the Kantian thing-in-itself) and ontological materialism (as embodied in Newtonian science) and has identified itself with a new ideology that has substituted relativism for absolutism in epistemology and particularism for absolutist universalism in social and political relations. Not the cognitive impenetrability of the thing-in-itself, but the diachronic dynamic of interacting forces of nature and society is the guiding idea of modern science and socialist society.

Proletarian Culture

To ease the birth pangs of a new society it was essential for Bogdanov to elaborate a new outlook that would be free of metaphysics and fetishism; it would be the outlook appropriate to a socialist society, and, indeed, he argued, socialism would be impossible without it. This was a position held by Bogdanov consistently in later years, and in 1917 he predicted that, insofar as metaphysical thinking prevailed, any attempt to create a socialist society was doomed to failure. Revolution could not mean simply the substitution of one form of oppression for another. A new society free of exploitation and oppression needed a new subject—the social individual in Marxian, and no less so in Narodnik, thought. Thus, revolution had to penetrate every feature of everyday life, down to the very structure of personality. A keen observer of the revolution, its excesses and deficiencies, Bogdanov rejected all invitations to rejoin the Bolshevik Party after the October Revolution.

Of course, Russia was transformed in 1917 by the Soviet revolution. Yet this proved to be a fleeting moment of the proletarian perspective on history. For in the aftermath of that moment, with the recognition that history, even in the USSR, was not going to go that way, Bogdanov had to confront the failure of that moment, the fact that such a moment, having passed, would never return in its old form. Bogdanov here came face to face with the revolutionary character of history itself. He had to face the incapacity of the Bolsheviks to hegemonize their initial success. Here was a historic defeat of the revolutionary project, a new historical conjuncture, and a moment that Stalin was able to dominate.

Bogdanov was attuned to the notion of difference to specificity of a historical conjuncture: how different forces come together conjuncturally to create the terrain on which a different politics constitutes itself. That is the intuition drawn from his Tektology that Bogdanov offers us about the nature of political life. And, parenthetically, helping us to understand the implosion of the USSR, he gives not the tools with which to solve the puzzle but the means with which to ask the right kinds of questions about the politics of the axial years 1989 and 1991.

From his appreciation of metaphysics, Bogdanov considered the narrow materialist concept of a socialist revolution to be unduly restrictive. It was reduced to a "revolution of property, a change of rulers," whereas, in fact, the revolution should be perceived as "a creative revolution of world culture, with spontaneous education and struggle of social forms replaced by conscious creation—a matter of a new class logic, new methods of unifying forces, new methods of thinking."[75]

Bogdanov's discussion of private property, for example, illuminated its more elusive dimensions and suggested another perspective on the inner workings of society. Not everything was as cut and dried as Marx's understanding of exploitation, with enemies (i.e., large owners of private property) standing out in bas relief; cultural factors contributed to the perpetuation of a given system and complicated or sometimes muted the line of exploitation. Bogdanov's views, however perceptive, implied that revolution might not be the panacea that the Bolsheviks had anticipated.[76]

Of course, this position differed from that of Marxians, who contended that bourgeois industrial society was prerequisite to the realization of reason and freedom. This realization was necessarily forestalled by the capitalistic mode of organization. Full maturity of the productive forces, man's mastery over nature, and a material wealth sufficient to furnish the rudimentary needs of society at the attained cultural level were prerequisite to socialism. However, in spite of this substantive link between capitalist productivity and socialist freedom, Marx, and Lenin after him, unlike Bogdanov, thought that only a revolution and a revolutionary social class could accomplish the transition. For in this transition, far more was involved than the liberation and rational utilization of the productive forces—namely, the liberation of man himself, abolition of his enslavement to the instruments of his labor, and thereby the complete transvaluation of all prevailing values. These new principles and values could be realized only by a class that was free from the old and repressive principles and metaphysical values, whose existence embodied the very negation of the capitalist system and therefore the historical possibility of opposing and overcoming this system. Marx's idea of the proletariat as the subject/object of history, as the absolute negation of capitalist society, telescopes in one notion the relation between the preconditions and the realization of freedom. The former can be accomplished only if undertaken and sustained by free individuals—free from the needs and interests of domination and repression. Only this would turn quantity into quality and establish a different nonalienated society—the determinate negation of capitalism.

Although Bogdanov also followed the general Marxist succession of development, he introduced a note of caution: The route to socialism could be diverted by decline, degeneration, and stagnation. "The history of the ancient world," noted Bogdanov, "shows that human society may sometimes regress, decline, and even decay; the history of primitive man and also that of several isolated Eastern societies shows the possibility of a long period of stagnation. For this reason, from a strictly scientific point of view, the transition to new forms must be accepted conditionally."[77]

Whereas Bogdanov explicitly called for a transformation in the mode of organization of society (in its culture as distinct from its property relations) as an additional vehicle for man's escape from alienation, without such reorganization society might lapse into a fetishistic authoritarian existence. Marcuse later remarked that unless the revolution itself progresses with practical reason, i.e., through freedom, the need for domination and repression would be carried over into the new society, and the fateful separation between the "immediate" and the "true" interests of the individuals would be almost inevitable. The individuals would become the objects of their own liberation, and freedom would be a matter of administration and decree. Marcuse, evidently influenced by the rise of the fascism of central Europe and Stalinism, reasoned as Bogdanov had that "progress" might come to mean progressive repression, and the "delay" in freedom would threaten to become self-propelling and self-perpetuating.[78]

The depth of the cultural reversal Bogdanov aimed for was profound, a reversal of the ground rules of the settlement of the social alliances that underpinned it and the values that made it popular. (We do not mean the attitudes and values of the intelligentsia, the ideas of the people who simply, in everyday life, have to calculate how to survive, how to look after those who are closest to them.)

Emboldened by their own intellectuality, Marxists naively thought that the world would collapse as the result of a logical contradiction; this is the illusion of the intellectual, that ideology must be coherent, every bit of it fitting together like a philosophical investigation. Consequently, when the Marxist theorists spoke about the crisis of capitalism, they naively saw capitalism disintegrating and socialism marching in and taking over. They failed to appreciate that the disruption of the normal functioning of the old economic, social, cultural order provides the opportunity to reorganize it in new ways, to restructure and refashion, to modernize and move ahead. Thus, the elimination of class distinction, Bogdanov reasoned, could not be achieved merely through violent revolutions and the abolition of private ownership rights but had to be supplemented through a nihilist going-to-the-people education of the members of society in organizational skills. To this end, in the years 1908 to 1914, Bogdanov and his associates retreated to Italy, to Bologna and the island of Capri, where Gorky had been living since 1906. There they founded a party school for workers. Bogdanov and Gorky together with Lunacharsky, Skvortsov-Stepanov, and Trotsky, all of whom were estranged from Lenin's party, taught there.[79] It was in this environment that Bogdanov advanced the erstwhile idea that the intelligentsia should play merely an auxiliary, mediating role rather than a leading role in the workers' movement and that the object of educating the workers was eventually to make them completely independent of the intelligentsia.[80] This idea formed the basis for the party schools and was given theoretical expression in Bogdanov's philosophical works. In opposition to Bogdanov's schools, Lenin together with Zinoviev organized his own studio outside Paris at Longjumeau.

Bogdanov's idea behind the party schools was to develop independent ideologues from within the proletariat itself. And it was in this effort that Bogdanov's ideas provided an entry for Gramsci's concept of the "organic intellectual." Between 1909 and 1911, the two party schools organized by Bogdanov operated in Bologna and Capri, and it is not improbable that something of Bogdanov's work was probably known in Italian party circles. Perhaps it was not entirely coincidental that at the Socialist Youth Congress held in Bologna, Tasca, 1919, Gramsci's early mentor in the socialist party, appeared as an ardent advocate of a program of culture and education for the working class.[81]

The party schools program consisted of a series of lecture courses intended to provide workers with at least a smattering of knowledge in several fields (e.g., political economy, history, literature), as well as instruction in organizational skills. An active member of the Socialist (later Communist) Academy of Sciences, Bogdanov together with Lunacharsky established after the October Revolution the Proletariat Culture movement (Proletkul't), an organization dedicated to advancing "the fourth form of labor movement: the creative role of the workers' class in culture and ideology."[82] The academy was an organization concerned primarily with elaborating the theoretical legacy of the fathers of Marxism and with training new cadres of social scientists in the spirit of historical materialism.

Proletkul't was a mass organization of 400,000 members, with its own administrative apparatus, factory cells, and a network of study circles. Its manifest purpose was to revolutionize the cultural sphere as a complement to changes being undertaken in the political and economic spheres. The study circles, the most prominent aspect of Proletkul't, attempted to inaugurate a new aesthetic created by the workers themselves.

To those who argued that the proletariat was too oppressed and too burdened with physical work to take on the additional task of creating a "proletarian culture," Bogdanov retorted, "And if [proletarian culture] were beyond one's strength, the working class would have nothing to count on, except the transition from one enslavement to another, that is, from under the yoke of capitalists to the yoke of engineers and the educated."[83]

The central issue was the very process of creating products of proletarian culture. The methods of work were designed to foster desired characteristics, such as collectivism in place of individualism and universalism rather than narrow specialization. Proletkul't adherents fervently believed that art contained cognitive as well as aesthetic functions and that by engaging in artistic endeavors, workers would begin to develop initiative, originality, and creativity. Moreover, they hoped that the worker-artists would break free of the elitist notion that certain types of activities, epitomized by the bourgeois arts, were reserved for intellectuals. Proletkul't sought to instill a new self-assurance in workers. Eventually all of past culture would be submitted to a critical review, and a new proletarian culture, encompassing philosophy, arts, and sciences, would emerge.

Unlike Lenin, Bogdanov, from his Tula period, was active in workers' circles. He thereby gained an appreciation of their objective needs and desires, but also their range of abilities and limitations. Consequently, he felt that workers were, in fact, capable of engaging independently in creative, scholarly, and ideological work, a view that essentially contradicted Lenin's more doctrinal position on social consciousness and ideology.

Employing biological metaphors, maintaining that ideology, as a social selection mechanism, played a function parallel to that of a brain in an organism, Bogdanov adopted what he considered to be the two most fundamental ideas of Marx—namely, that the task of philosophers is not only to interpret the world but also to change it and that social consciousness is determined by social existence.[84]

Bogdanov claimed that it was not until 1859 that the first decisive step was made in the search for a scientific study of the structure and dynamics of human society. In that year, Marx published *A Contribution to the Critique of Political Economy*, in which he set down the guiding ideas for a general scientific theory of society. Bogdanov thought that an introductory statement might present the essence of scientific sociology:

> In the social production which men carry on they enter into definite relations which are indispensable and independent of their will; these relations of production correspond to a definite stage of development of their material powers of production. The sum total of these relations of production constitutes the economic structure of society—the real foundation, on which rise legal and political superstructures and to which correspond definite forms of social consciousness. The mode of production in material life determines the general character of the social, political, and spiritual processes of life. It is not the consciousness of men which determines their existence, but on the contrary, their social existence determines their consciousness. At a certain stage of their development, the material forces of production in society come in conflict with the existing relations of production, or—what is but a legal expression of the

same thing—with the property relations within which they had been at work before. From forms of development of the forces of production these relations turn into their fetters. Then comes the period of social revolution. With the change of the economic foundation the entire immense superstructure is more or less rapidly transformed.[85]

Bogdanov expressed Marx's argument in more plebeian terms: "To help develop consciousness in a given class means to develop the very foundations of its organization, to participate in the formation of that brain which should control the mighty body."[86]

We have shown that social forms belong to the comprehensive genus—biological adaptations. But we have not thereby defined the province of social forms; for a definition, not only the genus, but also the species must be established. . . . In their struggle for existence men can unite only with the help of consciousness: without consciousness there can be no intercourse. Hence, social life in all its manifestations is a consciously psychical life. Sociality is inseparable from consciousness. Social being and social consciousness are, in the exact meaning of these terms, identical.[87]

This interpretation of Marx and Engels, who in *German Ideology* had written that "social being determines social consciousness," did not meet with Lenin's understanding. Without equivocation, Lenin retorted that:

Social being and social consciousness are not identical, just as being in general and consciousness in general are not identical. From that fact that in their intercourse men act as conscious beings, it does not follow at all that social consciousness is identical with social being. . . . Social being reflects social consciousness, that is Marx's teaching.[88]

From his appreciation of consciousness, Bogdanov considered Marxist ideology the starting, not the definitive, point in the development of proletarian culture. Marx, he wrote, succeeded in establishing the foundation for the new social science and the new historical philosophy. It was conceivable that all of science and all of philosophy would acquire a new appearance in the hands of the proletariat because different conditions of life engender different means of perceiving and understanding nature.[89] While Marx had objected to Hegel's idea that philosophical activity, i.e., culture, was prior to material production, Bogdanov was drawn to a nuanced interpretation of Hegel's proposition.

The course of history, for Bogdanov, was determined neither by the forces of production nor philosophic reflection, but was shaped by a confluence of both. Bogdanov's historicism suggested that change in the sphere of culture and the environment were concomitant with modes of organization and governance. Culture in its variant forms—whether language, knowledge, customs, or aesthetics —had an internal structure, an implicit organizational character for the utilization of use-values.[90] In Bogdanov's words, "Any product of 'spiritual' creativity—a scientific theory, a poetic work, a system of legal or moral norms—has its own 'architecture,' and represents a subdivided totality of parts."[91] In a similar manner, he viewed ideologies as modes of social integration that are conditioned by the modes of production and the productive relationships within a given society. Unlike Marx, he did not consider ideology merely as the "superstructure" of the productive relationships within a society. For Bogdanov, ideologies "also organize a certain content, are determined by it and adapted to it." With similar reasoning he wondered why Marxism treats law as part of the superstructure when, in reality, it is a basic and codified norm in the articulation of the social organization of production. The concept of ideology, law, and culture as the basic elements in the articulation of society and the mode of production evidently situated Bogdanov within an institutional school of political economy.

For Bogdanov, ideology is a salient force in society entrusted with the task of organizing experience into structured knowledge. Although "vital," ideology is not "primary" in social causation; for every change of structural significance ostensibly has its origin in technology rather than ideology. Bogdanov admitted that ideology could play a constraining and disorganizing role as well as an organizing role. Anticipating Gramsci's later contribution, Bogdanov argued that a society could achieve coherence and integration even when there were classes and social groups hostile to one another, provided it shared a common language and "a sum of common concepts."[92] In capitalist society, for example, a reigning ideology, the (false) "culture of individualism" served as a common denominator for its members.[93] "A plurality of human beings and events becomes a meaningful totality through culture. Culture assigns a vital and shared meaning to the most diverse facts of life, thus guaranteeing their uniform interpretation within a practical worldview."[94] But, he maintained, there is one thing that no ideology can achieve: it cannot be a prime mover of social change.

A central element of proletarian and total or cultural revolution was the liberation from fetishisms—metaphysical distortions of reality—that dominated human beings, such as passive submission to authority, the illusions of the independent "I," and preoccupation with private property. Such fetishisms constrained social consciousness and served to support an invidious disciplinary system of organization.

Bogdanov complained that the "place and function" of ideology in the "system of life" was barely appreciated. There was a common thread to "speech, cognition, art, customs, law, rules of propriety, and morals," namely, that they "regulated and controlled all of the practical life of society." In other words, culture had an "organizational function," and unless the proletariat devised its own "organizational tools," it would not gain independence and self-mastery.[95] Bogdanov's later formulation of a general theory of organization—Tektology—was purported to be the "organizational tool" that sought not merely to capture the historical monist perspective but also to articulate his phenomenological and cultural perspectives.

We obliquely implied above that there is an intriguing parallel between Bogdanov's and Gramcsi's thought. Through the factory councils, Gramsci hoped to develop the managerial skills of the workers and to instill a new "producer's mentality." Indeed, Gramsci's Taylorist productionism is evident in his designation of the factory as "the cell of a new state" and in his vision of a Promethean communist society "organized on the model of a large engineering works."[96] Though not without a technicist dimension, Bogdanov aimed at something broader and more illusive in the Proletkul't study circles—the creation of an authentic proletarian culture, the development of multidimensional capabilities and interests of the workers.

The emphasis was on self-realizing practice, with the organizations mediating this process. With a Narodnik's emphasis on personality, Bogdanov stressed an explicit cultural-educational program because he perceived culture as a vital source of influence on a person's constitution, not merely an embellishment or subsidiary phenomenon. The whole point of education was not to accumulate bourgeois encyclopedic knowledge, the possession of which legislates politically correct socialization by reproducing civil society as a social engineering project, but to achieve consciousness and realization of the self.

Similarly, Gramsci wrote that culture is "organization, discipline of one's inner self, a coming to terms with one's own personality; it is the attainment of a higher awareness, with the aid of which one succeeds in understanding one's own historical value, one's own function in life, one's own rights and obligations."[97]

Bogdanov and Lenin were consistently at loggerheads on the alleged necessity and feasibility of a "new world of culture," debating this point before and after the revolution. For Bogdanov crises erupt, not only in the political domain and the traditional areas of industrial and economic life, not simply in the class struggle, but in a wide series of polemic debates about fundamental moral and intellectual questions on a whole range of issues that do not necessarily, in the first instance, appear to be articulated with politics, in the narrow sense, at all. Correspondingly, Bogdanov understood that the occupancy of power was not simply about commanding the apparatuses of the state. However, Lenin was undaunted in his belief that the seizure of state power was the single most important goal for the proletariat; all other considerations were subservient to this goal. Anything that distracted the proletariat from this central concern was considered a waste of time. He expressed annoyance and impatience when "pedagogics were confused with questions of politics and organization." Workers had to be raised to the level of intellectuals "in regard to party activity," but in other respects, it was "not so easy and not so imperative." The appropriate cultural task was to "assist every capable worker to become a professional agitator, organizer, propagandist, literature distributor."[98] Ever the pragmatist, Lenin called for a "cultural revolution" when he realized that workers woefully lacked the skills and knowledge to build socialism after the takeover of power.

That Proletkul't was dismantled is, in fact, less surprising than its inception under Lenin's regime. Proletkul't's conspicuous but brief experiment was cut short by Lenin in 1921, perhaps, in part, because of continuing mistrust of Bogdanov, and partly because Lenin considered it frivolous in the face of more pressing needs. As early as May 1919 Lenin had participated in an overt campaign against Bogdanov and Proletkul't. On May 6, 1919, at the First Congress on Extra-Mural Education, Lenin had displayed the extent of his concern that Bogdanovist ideas might acquire influence among the left-intelligentsia, castigating "bourgeois intellectuals who very often regard the new type of workers' and peasants' educational institutions as the most convenient field for testing their individual theories in philosophy and culture and in which, very often, the most absurd ideas were hailed as something new, and the supernatural and incongruous were offered as purely proletarian art and proletarian culture." On May 19 he had excoriated "those who are now shouting about 'consumers' or 'soldiers' communism, who look down upon others with contempt and imagine that they are superior to the Bolshevik Communists." Counterpoising his own economistic conception of revolution to that of Bogdanov and borrowing a term from Bogdanov's own intellectual lexicon, he stressed the importance that he attached to the "fundamental, elementary, and extremely simple task of organization, and said that is why I am so strongly opposed to all these intellectual fads and 'proletarian cultures.' As opposed to these fads I advocate the ABC of organization. Distribute grain and coal in such a way as to take care of every *pud*—this is the object of proletarian discipline . . . the fundamental task of proletarian culture, of proletarian organization."[99] Heightening Lenin's anxiety was the August 14, 1920, announcement that an international arm of Proletkul't had been constituted.

> On 17 August Lenin inquired of the Deputy Commissar for Education M.N. Pokrovsky, during a meeting of Sovnarkom: "(1) What is the legal status of the Proletkul't? (2) Who is in charge of it? and (3) How are they appointed? (4) What else is there of importance to be known about the status and role of the Proletkul't and the results of its work?"[100]

Nikolai Bukharin had considerable sympathy with Bogdanov's project and in 1918 had welcomed the foundation of the Proletkul't as a "laboratory for the creation of a purely proletarian culture."[101] According to Biggart, Bukharin endorsed the cultural iconoclasm of the more radical members of the Proletkul't, while rejecting Proletkul't's interest in complete autonomy from the state.[102] Though ultimately unsuccessful, he defended it against the encroachment of the state centralizers of the Moscow soviet and of the Commissariat of Education. And when the Commissariat subordinated Proletkul't to its domain, Bogdanov retired.[103]

The doctrinal Marxist views failed to recognize that the "success" of the Russian Revolution resulted from political intervention at a historical juncture that, according to the view of the Second International, could never bring about a socialist outcome. Gramsci himself mistakenly celebrated the Bolshevik Revolution as a "revolution against Karl Marx's *Capital*."[104] The corresponding type of political theorizing that linked all historical changes to a mechanistic relation between forces of production and the social relations of production had with Bogdanov become severely discredited.[105] Concerned with the economistic interpretations of Marx's thought that pervaded the Second International, Bogdanov did not see them as abstract or academic problems but, on the contrary, as problems deeply embedded in political practice. They would prove to be the root causes of the massive defeats suffered by German, Austrian, Hungarian, and Italian antisystemic movements in the years after World War I. The crushing defeat of socialist movements in Europe and the consequent support working-class groups gave to fascism and Nazism pointed to the failure of Scientific Marxism as an adequate appreciation of the political realities of the time.

Within Lenin's framework, socialism proceeded in a series of stages, with specific tasks allocated to each stage. There was a clear demarcation point between capitalism and the transition to socialism that consisted of the seizure of power. The transitional period was, in fact, predicated on the seizure of power. Other prerequisites to socialism, such as a high level of economic development and a mature working class, could be fulfilled during the transitional period—a project undertaken with disastrous consequences by Stalin.

To Bogdanov socialism could be accomplished not in a series of discrete stages, but over a continuum. The seizure of power was one political moment in a lengthy process of revolutionary change. By implication, therefore, the transition to socialism had its genesis under capitalism, and the socialist revolution was the culmination of all the morphotransformations preceding it. He stressed that the cultural revolution could not consist mainly of an acquisition of skills and knowledge after the fact; rather, the cultural revolution meant a thorough revamping of bourgeois culture and a step-by-step creation of a new proletarian culture. In Bogdanov's words, "socialist development will be crowned with socialist revolution."[106]

Recognizing that the thrust of Bolshevik activists was on acquiring power as a goal and that thinking about what real socialism might mean was neglected,[107] Bogdanov was convinced that the development of a new ideology was a goal and a necessary complement to Lenin's efforts at delegitimation of the tsarist and later Kerensky regimes. As the revolutionary momentum developed, hoped Marx, workers would succeed in throwing off their false consciousness; for the ideology that served the interests of the ruling class could no longer hoodwink people into submission. The main cultural prerequisite to revolution, therefore, is delegitimation.

Class consciousness, the recognition of the allegedly historical mission of the proletariat, while supposedly necessary to win the battle, was insufficient. More than "merely" a war against Marx's capitalism, class consciousness also demanded the creation of new elements in the proletariat itself: the development of a socialist proletariat culture.

Bogdanov protested that the socialist effort would be undermined if goals were compartmentalized and some were relegated to a distant future. This was a problem that originated in Marx's own analysis. Bogdanov wrote: "According to the old concept [of the 1850s] ... socialism first conquers and then is implemented; up to its victory, it is not a reality, it does not exist, it is simply the 'ultimate goal.' "[108] Consequently, Bogdanov advocated the furtherance of socialist cultural prerequisites prior to the seizure of power. As he pointed out, between the realm of necessity and the realm of freedom lay "not a leap, but a difficult path."[109] For socialism was not simply a question of a "massive outburst of will" or "winning the battle"[110] but an organizational process of historical development. On this point Bogdanov came perilously close to the social democrat Bernstein.

A German socialist and a personal friend of Marx and Engels, Eduard Bernstein shifted attention from a cataclysmic episode associated with the revolutionary seizure of power to a nonviolent, evolutionary series of measures. He believed that the new society could not be introduced ready-made by decree, but had to build on elements initiated under capitalism. He argued that socialists should exploit concrete opportunities for betterment through the workers' increased power at the ballot box, through vigorous trade union activity, and through cooperation with other democratic forces. Orthodox Marxists launched a barrage of criticisms at Bernstein, caustically referring to him as a social democrat. They argued that he underestimated the revolutionary moment and suggested a complacent policy. He was bitterly attacked by Lenin, who held that the workers' liberation would come only with the violent overthrow of the existing order. Bogdanov was also accused of minimizing or ignoring the inevitability of revolutionary struggle and of "qualitative leaps."

Though the comparison of Bernstein and Bogdanov should not be overdrawn, they both emphasized socialist transformation as a process more than a spectacular event and a process that begins under capitalism. Both sought to reinterpret Marxist doctrine in the light of fresh advances made in economic thought. Bernstein advocated a gradual reform of capitalism, while Bogdanov promoted a gradual implementation of the cultural prerequisites to socialism. To Bogdanov, the destructive aspect of revolution, the violent overthrow of the bourgeois state, was unavoidable; the point was that it had to be accompanied by a creative aspect, the building of the proletarian state. Revolution was, in the fullest sense, a cultural process of creative destruction.

Bogdanov recognized that the conquest of power was itself not a panacea. Unless the ascendant class was fully prepared for its new role, the seizure of power could prove to be a retrogressive act.[111] Even leadership under the communist party, and seizure of power by the communist party, would not necessarily guarantee a new socialist order. Similarly, for Gramsci the worst possible scenario could occur, with the revolution "degenerating pathetically into a new parliament of schemers, talkers, and irresponsibles."[112]

It was for this reason that preliminary constructive work had to be initiated under capitalism. Bogdanov noted that the struggle against capitalism could not merely be equated with the struggle for socialism. The former was largely confined to the political arena, while the latter involved the "creation of new elements of socialism in the proletariat itself, in its internal relations, and in its conditions of everyday life."[113]

Marx anticipated a working-class revolution, because in his view the proletariat represented the absolute negation of the bourgeois order. The accumulation of capital destined the workers to increasing social and material misery. However, if the proletariat is not necessarily the negation of capitalism, as Bogdanov was speculating, then it is no longer qualitatively different from any other class and hence no longer capable of creating a qualitatively different society.

Bogdanov was at odds with Lenin on how the revolution was to be effected. His dispute with orthodox Marxism over the issue of class interests was grounded in his rejection of economism. Attentive to the broader realms of human interest, including science, philosophy, art, and morals, for Bogdanov the theory of class interests was evidently inadequate. His views were not without a certain tradition in Russian sociology.

Contesting narrow economism, "Class interests," wrote Tugan-Baranovsky, "are not a criterion of goodness, of truth or of beauty. Human history is something infinitely higher than a mere struggle by social groups for the [material] means of life."[114] Arguing that man's history is related to every social activity, Tugan-Baranovsky rejected what he understood as the economistic formulae of Feuerbach, Marx, and Engels to reduce ethics, art, and spirituality, that is, culture, to a utilitarian level. He concluded that the class struggle could not be viewed as determining, nor as strictly coordinating, the economic coordinates of history. Those Marxists who sought to reduce the broader realm to a utilitarian level did so in order to preserve the monistic integrity of their system. Convinced they were proceeding from false premises, Tugan-Baranovsky concluded that the facts of history would prove them wrong.[115] Perhaps it has!

Bogdanov, while believing that in fastening upon class conflict as a key to explaining social strife Marxism was a great liberating force, saw class difference as only one of several sources of social struggle. To him, any relationship of domination and subordination, whether based on sex, race, class, nationality, or possession of technical knowledge, was also appropriate for criticism within a broader philosophy of praxis. Bogdanov's theory of the social dynamic differs from Marxist orthodoxy. While he recognized the role of "contradiction" in socioeconomic divisions, Bogdanov relegated class contradictions to a more balanced role in his philosophy. This axial proposition was precisely one on which Western Critical Marxism later turned.

Bogdanov's distinctive formulation of the social dynamic is sufficiently interesting to justify, at this point, a review within the context provided by social consciousness, ideology, and culture. Insofar as Gramsci's concept of social change is today of resurgent interest, let us then turn to Bogdanov's appreciation.[116]

Organization and Social Class Dynamics

Bogdanov's theory of social-class dynamics differs from orthodox Marxist theory. While he recognized the role of "contradiction" in socioeconomic divisions that shelter antagonistic social classes, as a rule Bogdanov relegated the dialectics of historical materialism to a lesser role in his philosophy. He thought that both Hegel and Marx, by offering an imprecise formulation of dialectics, had invited arbitrary interpretations.

As Spencer before him, Bogdanov devoted much attention to functional details of the process of social integration and differentiation. In his opinion, organizational adaptations were the most important processes of integration, operating in both technological and ideological domains wherein normative constraints are significant. He argued that the more advanced a society is, the more it depends on ideology as a reigning ingredient of the various forms of organizational adaptation.

Habituated and normative forms, i.e., institutionalized modes, of organizational adaptation reduce contradictions in social life by limiting particular functions that, if left uncurbed, would create disharmony and conflict. Their origin is in primordial customs, the ancestor of customary law, morality, and positive law. Bogdanov warned that normative forms—whether expressed in customs and values or in law—have a tendency to become a "sacred tradition," an "absolute duty," or "pure justice" by detaching themselves from the concrete needs and interests of the members of society. The more "absolute" moral precepts and values are, the more removed they are from the reality of society. Somewhat restrained optimism about the future of society led Bogdanov to believe that invidious or coercive institutions would eventually lose their raison d'etre and cease to exist. He made no effort to document his statement that the more advanced a society is, the less it depends on the invidious forms of social organizational adaptation. Parenthetically, this notion is suspiciously similar to the Marxian "withering away of the state." Normative forms are analogous to the inhibitory functions of the central nervous system. He admitted, however, that the analogy is imperfect, for it compares not two equally complex phenomena but a "whole" (society) with particular parts of an organism.

Devoting much attention to the processes of social differentiation, particularly to stratification, and noting that the study of society as "a living whole with a single orientation in the selection of social forms" is the most important task of sociological scholarship, Bogdanov readily admitted, in his *Essays in Tektology* that this approach is correct only up to a certain point. To do a thorough job, a student of social structure must also investigate the components of society that enjoy relative independence. The division of labor in society inevitably leads to the formation of groups with independent criteria for selecting and incorporating social innovations. In his analysis of social differentiation stimulated by the division of labor, Bogdanov was concerned particularly with the emergence, evolution, and sociological attributes of social classes. The division of labor in society does not by itself lead to the formation of classes: as long as differences induced by the division of labor do not threaten the fundamental unity of society, they are not social-class ingredients. In this situation, the processes of social selection lead to a harmonization of relations between social "fragments" by working out common organizing principles. But when the emphasis on differences and contradictions is so great that individual social components evolve their own organizing principles, ideologies emerge. Without ideologies there are no true social classes. Although the material base of social classes is in the technical process, they are organized by ideology. The technical process is the dynamic factor of social selection and adaptation, the motive force of social evolution; the ideological process is the static factor of social selection and adaptation that "limits, regulates, and organizes" the products of social evolution. It is of interest to note that Gramsci's latter critique of economism, while situated within the politics of the Italian workers' movement,[117] argued, in a manner little distinguished from Bogdanov's, that the place of social class in Marxist theoretical discourse had been primarily a conceptual rather than a subjective identity.[118] What constitutes a class must be defined in a practical sense and in organizational terms.[119] This is not to say that Bogdanov radically departed from Marx, for Marx does seem to approach the organizational phenomenon of the separation of ownership from direct control in volume 3 of *Capital.*

> The capitalist mode of production has brought matters to a point where the work of supervision, entirely divorced from the ownership of capital, is always readily obtainable. It has, therefore, come to be useless for the capitalist to perform it himself. . . . The wages of management both for the commercial and industrial manager are completely isolated from the profits of enterprise in the cooperative factories of labourers, *as well as in capitalist stock companies.* . . . Stock companies in general . . . have an increasing tendency to separate this work of management from the ownership of capital. . . . [The creation of stock companies brings about the] transformation of the actually functioning capitalist into a mere manager, administrator of other people's capital, and of the owner of capital into a mere owner, a mere money-capitalist.[120]

It is somewhat apparent, from this reading, that already for Marx the function of owning capital was becoming extraneous to the organization of capitalism itself. Nonetheless, Marx defined class in terms of whether one owned or worked the means of production. He never revised the definition to suggest that if one managed the means of production—that is, organized them—one was in a different class than if one owned them or worked them. It was Bogdanov, not Marx, who seized upon the social implications of the distinction—the separation of ownership and the organization of production.

Bogdanov's insight was a shared one. Lukács was to later note that social and cultural forms are shaped by the fact that:

> [The] main economic tendency of capitalism is ... objectification of production, its separation from the personality of the producers. Through the capitalist economy an objective-abstract force, capital, becomes the real producer and capital has no organic relation to those who happen to own it; indeed it is often utterly superfluous whether or not the owners are personalities at all (e.g., joint stock companies).[121]

Bogdanov's appreciation of bureaucracy bore similarities to later editions of Bukharin's and Trotsky's work, but Bogdanov's was methodologically distinct. That is, it was grounded in his Tektological approach. He became aware that something new was happening under advanced capitalism—something that could not be explained within Marx's "old categories"; classes existed for reasons other than strictly economic ones. Bogdanov recognized the importance of gradations of authority positions and was appreciative of the separation of ownership and control. He critically argued that the existence of social classes is due not to a distorted distribution of ownership rights in society but rather to the possession of organizational experience by individuals in a given society. Thus, the ruling class in a social system is composed of organizers of production who are not necessarily the owners of the means of production. The elimination of class distinction in society, therefore, could be achieved not through vanguardist-led revolution and the abolition of private ownership but rather through education of members of society in organizational skills.[122]

The emergence of social class distinctions was no longer strictly the result of the division of labor and private property; instead, in Bogdanov's framework, it was the result of the separation of the custodians and carriers of ideology, knowledge, and experience, that is, organizers, who on the strength of these factors safeguard for themselves their position in production. This point of view, he insisted, was contrary to the one gained from Marx.

Consequently, he distanced himself from the Marxian position, further abstracting the notion by often replacing the concept (and term) "class" with that of "organization." Rather than merely tendering unconnected adaptations of Marxism, Bogdanov's ideas on ideology, classes, and revolution offered an integrated and singular conceptualization of society and social dynamics. Seeking to combine the alleged "conflict model" of Marxism with his own general theory of organization, he was keenly interested in the integrating and disintegrating agents that bound society together and dissolved it.[123]

Clearly Bogdanov's point of departure was that classes must be distinguished not according to categories of wealth but according to the "position of people in production."[124]

> According to Bogdanov, a society, as a system, consists of an aggregate of people interrelated on a functional basis. Their common link is production relations, or, as Bogdanov put it, social-labor relations. Production itself, he maintained, should be distinguished in its technical, economic and ideological dimensions.[125]

With the growth of production and division of labor, a distinct organizing function arises; in fact, noted Bogdanov, "Organizing labor represents historically the earliest form of complex (skilled) labor."[126] Further technological progress fragments society into classes, based on relations of authority-subordination, and into social groups, based on relations of specialization.[127] With the further development of technology, the role of the worker in the system of production changes, and this change facilitates a breaking away from the stranglehold of ideology. Tentatively at first, the workers question separate elements of ideology, such as the concept of property. As class struggle ensues, the questioning becomes more generalized, encompassing all existing norms.

Bogdanov's class concept proved to be particularly perceptive. He foresaw that the rapid development of technology and communication, as well as "the growing complexity of organizational functions," would create the demand for people directly engaged in organization. A curious phenomenon arose as a result —the growth of what Bogdanov called a "bourgeois technical intelligentsia," which, quite distinct from the classical capitalists, exercised considerable control over the means of production but did not own them. This stratum, Bogdanov noted, displayed "special class tendencies" because of the organizational function it performed and the authority positions it occupied. Since the salaries of these "managers" were not exposed to the ordinary "norms of exploitation," the managers developed vested interests in capital, even though they were not capitalists themselves, in the usual sense of the term.[128]

Bogdanov's blinkered critics hammered away at the point that class analysis could not be supplanted by organizational (tektological) analysis; nor could sources of exploitation be explained by authority relations.[129]

There is yet a further dimension. By helping to bring about the "blurring of boundaries," technology is actively changing the nature of property and class relations. Consequently, we are increasingly obliged to think about the political and ideological functions of various types of people on the basis not of the property they own but of what they know and the organizational skills they exercise. Here we find elements of both a renaissance and an anticipation of a contemporary genre. Bogdanov was speaking of one of the premises of traditional technocratic theory—a theme present in Plato's *Republic* and in Galbraith, among others—the supremacy of intellectual elites (symbolic analysts) over property and the eclipse of entrepreneurial capitalism.[130]

Despite external similarities, each type of class formation has a distinct origin and unique social attributes. In the so-called archaic type, one anchored in the patriarchal nature-bound economic processes, the organizing power of the masters grew gradually until it covered the total existence of slaves. The bond between the master and the slave was fixed, that is, it could not be broken by the will of the state. The dependence of the slave on the will of the master was total and irrevocable. The working man was transformed into a tool of production. The extreme exploitation of slaves by their masters ostensibly brought about the process of the decline of the social system built upon the institution of slavery. Technical progress came to an end. Slave ideology did not develop beyond an embryonic state, and class struggle was absent. Bogdanov further argues that degeneration of both classes culminated in the disorganization and destruction of the entire system of social relations.

The capitalist class system, according to Bogdanov, originated in the petit bourgeois organization of production. The entrepreneur controlled only a part of the worker's existence—the working day. The bond between the entrepreneur and the worker was flexible, contractual. The corresponding type of class development led to a progressive transformation of the amorphous mass of workers into a collectivity able to respond to the constantly expanding organizational role of entrepreneurs. Explosive technical progress, characteristic of this type of class development, stimulated an equally mercuric development of antagonistic class ideologies and an irreconcilable class warfare. For Bogdanov, the real source of modern class struggle is in the differential attitudes of the two classes toward technical progress: While the bourgeoisie views technical progress as a vehicle for widening the scope of the exploitation of the working class, the latter sees in it a way to a qualitative, that is, a revolutionary, change in social structure. Every revolution has a "motive force" and an "organizing force": irreconcilable contradictions in the social organization of production and class ideologies are the "motive force"; class consciousness is the "organizing force." There is no "genetic continuity" and stability in the composition of individual economic collectivities or social classes, for in a capitalist system there are neither kinship nor personal bonds for a stable class organization. In capitalist society social classes are subject to change faster than in any other type of society. The dynamism of the capitalist world offers a certain promise of happiness and of disaster.

The motion is open-ended, the revolutionary kernel springs alive from the system's deepest imperatives. In the first part of the *Communist Manifesto*, Marx lays out the polarities that shape and animate bourgeois culture: the theme of insatiable desires and drives, permanent revolution, ceaseless development, relentless creation and renewal in every sphere of life; and its radical antithesis, the theme of nihilism, insatiable destruction, the shattering and swallowing up of life, and the darkness of the abyss. Visions of radiant joy and bleak despair are juxtaposed to an array of cosmic and apocalyptic visions. On the one hand, we feel ourselves charged with a vitality that heightens our whole sense of being—and are simultaneously seized by shocks and convulsions that threaten at every instant to annihilate us. Marx shows how these dualities give structure to the everyday life by the drives and pressures of capitalism.

> The bourgeoisie cannot exist without constantly revolutionizing the instruments of production, and with them the relations of production, and with them the relations of society.... Constant revolutionizing of production, uninter-

rupted disturbance of all social relations, everlasting uncertainty and agitation, distinguish the bourgeois epoch from all earlier ones.[131]

Marx's pithy observation on capitalism unfolds:

> All fixed, fast-frozen relations, with their train of ancient and venerable prejudices and opinions, are swept away, all new-formed ones become antiquated before they can ossify. All that is solid melts into air, all that is holy is profaned, and men at last are forced to face . . . the real conditions of their lives and their relations with their fellow men.[132]

Social classes, Bogdanov noted, are not only specific groups based on distinct positions in the organization of production but also clearly demarcated subcultures. Since each class has a unique source of experience, many "common" concepts have in reality different meanings. The class status affects and shapes the entire process of cognition. The meaning of such notions as "idealism," "ideal," and "progress" varies from one social class to another. "The bourgeoisie sees regress in everything in which its ideological adversaries see a high point of progress."

But there exist two different definitions of progress: one definition is objective, dynamic, and scientific; the other is subjective, static, and metaphysical. The objective definition regards social evolution as a process leading to a "complete" and "fully harmonious" social existence; the subjective definition views progress in terms of the particularistic values of individual groups or classes. The objective definition views progress as infinite; the subjective depicts progress as a finite realization of the ideals of individual groups or classes. The objective sees progress as a derivation from the socioeconomic infrastructure of society; to it, morality, as a derivative force, cannot account for social progress. The subjective presents progress in moral terms and treats morality as a quality irreducible to the material conditions of life; it operates on the assumption that moral obligation is the propelling force of social progress. The objective view of progress is causal: it recognizes no predetermined and transcendental goals and views social life as a product of causally explained activities of infrastructural forces. The subjective view of progress is teleological: it regards the course of history as a gradual realization of a final goal that determines the main lines of social change.

The function of the sociologist, according to Bogdanov, is not merely to formulate a scientific definition of progress but also to examine and combat pseudoscientific notions of progress. He recognizes, however, that, despite its unscientific qualities, the subjective definition of progress must be recognized as an important component of social reality inasmuch as it reflects the thinking and the sentiments of various segments of the population and inasmuch as it reflects elements of dissonance in the interrelations of the vital components of the social structure. The task of the sociologist is to establish the magnitude of discrepancies between the objective and subjective interpretations of progress in specific societies. The sociologist must not overlook the possibility of a congruence of objective and subjective notions of progress that takes place when group "ideals" concur with "real processes"—when the "ideal" is "an expression, even though a partial one, of historical development." The classes that are unhampered by a narrowness of vision can produce, in due course, a historical and objective notion of progress. They can both comprehend the historical nature of the ideals of progress and give them an abstract formulation. Such an ideal, expressed by a leading European thinker, i.e., Marx, is universal cooperation for universal development. Bogdanov wrote that, "Progress means an increase in the fullness and harmony of conscious human life."[133]

While sharing the view that the bourgeoisie and the proletariat were the two pivotal classes of modern society, Bogdanov placed considerable emphasis on the fact that between the two class extremes there is "an infinite number of transitions, nuances, and combinations."

In a manner somewhat consistent with Thorstein Veblen, Bogdanov was very careful in distinguishing the relations between the proletariat and the bourgeoisie from those between the proletariat and the "technical intelligentsia," the bourgeoisie's organizing arm in the process of production. The first relationship is dominated by conflict, the second by cooperation. The first relationship is primarily that of one social class to another; the second relationship is primarily that of one professional group to another. Accordingly, the proletariat's role in the production process is only partly connected with its social-class identification. While the gap separating the proletariat from the bourgeoisie as two social classes is steadily growing wider, the gap between the proletariat and the "technical intelligentsia" as two professional groups is steadily shrinking. Marxist sociologists placed primary emphasis on the conflict between the proletariat and the bourgeoisie; Bogdanov stressed the expanding community of interests of the workers and the "technical intelligentsia." Already in the last century the work of manual labor was becoming increasingly organizational and intellectual and had begun to resemble the work of the "technical intelligentsia."[134]

Bogdanov believed that a new society, dominated by the proletariat, would eventually arise, but he was convinced that the proletariat could emerge victorious only by absorbing the progressive traditions of the bourgeoisie and the technical intelligentsia. In fact, he regarded the gradual eradication of the differences in the acquisition, modernization, and dissemination of technical and scientific knowledge as the main factor in the dynamics of social-class relations.[135] The proletariat, according to him, is a product of the material and nonmaterial culture of the modern industrial society. He wrote:

> The proletariat has learned and will learn from bourgeois classes—in this lies one of the sources of its strength. The greatest ideologue of the working class [Marx] understood this from the very beginning. The economic science of bourgeois classes, the dialectical method of Hegel's bourgeois philosophy, the

realism of bourgeois materialism, and the critique of capitalist social relations presented mainly by petty-bourgeois utopians—all these Marx incorporated, in a transmuted form, into the basic material of the new [proletarian] ideology. This synthesis contained no eclecticism and no compromises with the bourgeois worldview.[136]

Instead of dialectics, Bogdanov stressed "moving equilibrium" as the basic process in the development of nature and society. All components of a society are engaged in a constant search for an equilibrium in their interaction and their relations to the total natural and social environment.[137] In capitalist society, Bogdanov argued, the equilibration of interacting—and contending—social forces is achieved with the help of "external norms," that is, the institutional structures generated and enforced by the state, rather than with the help of "internal norms," that is, the norms generated by society itself and applied without resort to institutionalized coercion. The future society, the society unencumbered by "external norms" and invidious institutions, would come about as a result of the gradual but inexorable growth of technology rather than by revolutionary political action. Technology alone can create the prerequisite conditions for the growth of social cooperation and for the full elimination of social-class conflict.

Bogdanov conceptualized a world in which conflict is overshadowed by a general harmony, or complementarity, of universal processes and all change is essentially gradual, though he viewed conflict as an indispensable step in the growth of cooperation. Social harmony, he said, is a reconciliation, rather than the nonexistence, of social contradictions. Cooperation, not less than freedom and equality, is a cultural value that can emerge only in societies that have experienced suppression and inequality.

The heroic optimism of the Marxist self-transformation of the proletariat was a process neither spontaneous nor untroubled. As a Hegelian, Bogdanov recognized the importance of mediation in history but acknowledged the role of intellectuals rather than the state as mediators of the new socialist totalization, bridging the gap between the old society and the new. Socialism was to be realized not by a leap but by a hazardous path.[138] While recognizing the cultural prerequisites of revolution, Bogdanov was offering a different conceptualization of the very process of revolution. Revolution was not a bit of theater, a dramatic performance, or the sublime synthesis of contradictions of capitalism, it was a multilayered process of culture building. This view was one shared by Lukács, for whom the economic determinism of economistic Marxism was a mistaken universalization of the unique, and regrettable, situation of capitalism.

Indeed, Lukács's *History and Class Consciousness*[139] reflects the intellectual impact of M. Weber and G. Simmel in rejecting a deterministic Marxism founded on economics and stressing the autonomous action of the proletariat.[140] According to Lukács, dialectical materialism interprets history in terms of the false consciousness of acting human beings in relation to their own actions. For Lukács only two classes have the chance to dominate the whole of capitalist society, the bourgeoisie and the proletariat, and only the proletariat can achieve an accurate understanding of the whole of society. In fact, he went so far as to challenge the priority of economics during the prerevolutionary period as well, arguing that "the culture of the capitalist epoch had collapsed in itself and prior to the occurrence of economic and political breakdown."[141] He defined culture as "the ensemble of valuable products and abilities which are dispensable in relation to the immediate maintenance of life."[142] And he claimed that with the onset of the revolution, the importance of culture increased even more dramatically: "During capitalism every ideological movement was only the 'superstructure' of the revolutionary process which ultimately led to the collapse of capitalism. Now in the proletarian dictatorship, this relationship is reversed."[143] One of Lukács's primary goals in the short-lived Bela Kun–led Hungarian Soviet Republic (August 1919) was the democratization of culture, which, to be sure, did not mean toleration of all varieties of cultural expression.[144] In an expression of romantic anticapitalism he asserted that the "new culture" that was being created would end the rule of civil society, the division of labor, and the primacy of the economy over man. It would restore the conditions that had generated "the greatness of old cultures (Greek, Renaissance)," which "consisted in the fact that ideology and production were in harmony; the products of culture could organically develop out of the soil of social being."[145] Lukács stressed revolutionary culturalism over revolutionary economics and politics, but he also suggested a movement away from it in his linking of a "new culture" with the triumph of the proletariat. To Lukács the *is* and the *ought* would merge once the subject of history, the proletariat, objectified its ethical principles in the concrete mores of communist society. Recognizing itself in the world it had created, it would no longer be subjected to the moral alienation plaguing bourgeois culture.

Bogdanov prescribed cultural transformation as an indispensable and instrumental component of the proletarian revolution. The University of the Proletariat would issue "leaders of the proletariat," who would fulfill the role of Diderot and the Encyclopaedists by preparing a proletarian encyclopedia that would reflect social consciousness. They would examine the unstated ontological dimensions and micropolitics of power in all spheres of knowledge, making revisions and changes as appropriate, to ensure compliance with the workers' class point of view, much the same way, he assumed, the bourgeois class had.[146]

While asserting the class-bound status of knowledge, Gramsci defended a Marxism that was methodologically continuous with the natural sciences. The dichotomy between the *Geisteswissenschaften* and the *Naturwissenschaften*, which was fundamental for Lukács, was rejected by Gramsci and Bogdanov. And again like Bogdanov, Gramsci assimilated the methods of the natural sciences to those of the "cultural sciences." Scientific objectivity, he claimed, was not the correspondence of an external reality to man's conception of it. The "objective," he asserted, always means "humanly objective," which can be held to correspond exactly to the "historically subjective." In other words, the objective means "universal subjective."

For both Bogdanov and Gramsci prime importance was attached to establishing the link between theory and practice lost in the economistic interpretations of Marx's thought and to formulating an interpretation of historical materialism that would relocate it as a vector of practical reason and as a mode of intention in the course of the historical process.[147] Seeking a renewal of theory and practice, Gramsci turned to elaborate a concept of civil society, while Bogdanov turned to his metatheoretical edifice, Tektology.

In Hegel, civil society is the reign of dissoluteness, misery, and physical and ethical corruption and must be mediated, regulated, dominated, and annulled by the superior order of the state. This meaning that Hegel attributes to civil society, which differs from the philosophers of natural law (Locke to Rousseau), makes it a pre-Marxist concept in that it is the antithesis of primitive society, no longer the reign of natural order.

Hegel's conception of civil society encompasses "not only the sphere of economic relations and the formation of social classes, but also the administration of justice as well as the organization of the police force and the corporations."[148] In Marx and Engels, however, civil society encompasses the whole of prestate social life. It is a moment in the development of the economic relations that precedes and shapes the political sphere, constituting one of the two terms of the antithesis, society-state.

> Civil society embraces the whole material intercourse of individuals within a definite stage of the development of the productive forces. It embraces the whole commercial and industrial life of a given stage, and insofar, transcends the State and the Nation, though on the other hand, again, it must assert itself in its foreign relations as nationality and inwardly must organize itself as state.[149]

For Gramsci, civil society includes "not the whole complex of material relations, of commercial and industrial life, but the whole ideological-cultural relations, of spiritual and intellectual life."[150] Gramsci conceives civil society to be the theater of all history. It is within the framework of civil society that a historical juncture arises, for hegemony is the conjunctive moment between objective conditions and the actual domination of a leading group. This theme was plumbed by Gramsci in his *Prison Notebooks*.[151]

Gramsci's concern was to identify not only the objective material but also the ideological conditions necessary for hegemony. The failed German, Austrian, Hungarian, and Italian antisystemic movements posed some very serious challenges to understanding the nature and role of politics and ideology in the historical process. Gramsci saw hegemony as the key element of political thought. Therefore, the formation of the concept of hegemony was extremely important in his work. Initially he embraced Leninist principles, but eventually he developed his own concept of hegemony, which he elaborated at some length in his *Prison Notebooks*.[152] Both Bogdanov and Gramsci conceived of their ideas not as a supplement to historical materialism but as a basis for a new interpretation of historical materialism.[153] While Bogdanov, having rejected a narrowly defined class-bound determinist analysis, appreciated that the proletariat might not be the dialectic negation of the bourgeoisie, Gramsci's concept of ideology rejected both epiphenomenalism and social class reductionism. Both appreciated ideology as a quasi-independent factor in the maintenance of state power.

Gramsci was convinced that the proletariat had to secure hegemony, that is, it had to assert "moral and intellectual leadership," prior to the seizure of power. The working class could not be expected to play a role in history without creating its own *Weltanschauung*, without first establishing its claim to be a ruling class in the political, cultural, and ethical fields. For Gramsci, as for Bogdanov, the basic problem of revolution was not political insurrection but "how to make a hitherto subaltern class believe itself a potential ruling class and credible as such to other classes."[154]

A successful hegemony is one that is able to create a "collective national-popular will," and for this to occur, the dominant class must be capable of articulating its hegemonic principle by absorbing all the national popular ideological elements. It is only then, Gramsci contends, that the dominant class can appear as representative of the proletarian interest. In the creation of a "national-popular will," the dominant class is able to transform the class character of ideological elements by enunciating a hegemonic principle that differs from the one to which they are presently articulated.

Thus, Gramsci's hegemony meant something quite distinct from Lenin's dictatorship of the proletariat.[155] Rather than a relationship based largely on one-dimensional power, it involved a consensual relationship, with a minimum use of force. Gramsci went far beyond Lenin in seeing hegemony as a political and cultural predominance of the working class and its party aimed at securing the "spontaneous" adherence of other groups, an adherence obtained through a process of raising social consciousness by persuasion and education.

Culture, and therein ideology, for Bogdanov and Gramsci was recognized as the battlefield, the terrain of the struggle, since men's and women's acquisition of consciousness does not come about individually, but through the intermediary of the ideological terrain where hegemonic principles confront each other. It is, therefore, through ideology that subjects are created and through ideology rooted in the economic conditions of life that they act.

The concept of ideology as practice is articulated in Bogdanov's notion of ideology as a mode of organization. In this theory, hegemony is achieved through the establishment of an organic link connecting civil society and political society. Thus, political society effectively represents the interests of the hegemonic class that resorts to the hegemonic apparatuses of society, i.e., schools, churches, and propaganda, to organize and direct social groups by securing consent to their leadership.

Gramsci proposed a concept of hegemony as a condition in which a fundamental social class attains predominance over other social classes, with their tacit or explicit consent, through its being able to gain agreement with an organic ideology. An organic ideology is able to organize social groups and direct them throughout all their organizing activities. The class that carries out this transformation is able to reinforce its power over society by virtue of its decisive function in the nucleus of economic activities. Once the ruling class obtains the consent of society, it becomes the hegemonic class. That is when the dominant class forges a cultural and ideological link between the economic, political, intellectual, and moral aims; it becomes the hegemonic class, and the social formation constitutes a "historical bloc"—a coalition of oppressed groups.[156] On an intellectual and moral plane the hegemonic class is able to diffuse throughout society a conception of the world that obscures the very nature and character of class domination. Other classes accept and consent to it as a "natural" or "common sense" view of the world, thus engendering a new type of social integration.

Social integration appears through the concept of "hegemonic apparatuses," which are the instruments for the exercise of hegemony and through which organic intellectuals become organizers. Organic intellectuals are the agents or mediators of praxis. They are the custodians and conveyors of organic ideologies and seek to realize moral and intellectual reform. This role of intellectuals at the levels of both class organizations (political parties) and the hegemonic apparatuses is crucial for maintaining class hegemony as well as the emergence of counter-hegemonic forms of class struggle.

A member of the Russian intelligentsia, Bogdanov had sustained the nihilist's principle of going-to-the-people. This was a theme, as we have seen, present in Gramsci, whose organic intellectuals included not only scholars and artists but also administrators who could be either traditional or organic in character, according to how well they linked to the economic realm.[157]

For Gramsci, the Platonic guardians of the post-revolutionary state should not be those ruled by party bureaucrats. One of the basic tenets of Marx, as well as Hegel, is that the subject makes itself in and through making the object: a leadership operating as a manipulative bureaucracy can only make itself into a Machiavellian bureaucracy! Instead, the "educators" of a new hegemonic totality were to be the organic intellectuals, the vanguard of the coming cultural community. In the literature on Gramsci, there has been considerable debate over whether this mediation should be understood as "external" or "internal" to the working class.[158] If the former, then Gramsci, like Bogdanov, would be open to Korsch's charge against Lenin, Kautsky, and Luxemburg, that he wanted to bring class consciousness to the proletariat from without. If "internal," he risked regressing to the belief that proletarian praxis autonomously generated its own theory.[159] In this connection, Gramsci wrote: "Every social group, coming into existence on the original terrain of an essential function in the world of economic production, creates together with itself, organically, one or more strata of intellectuals which give it homogeneity and an awareness of its own function not only in the economic, but also in the social and political fields."[160] In contrast to Lenin, Bogdanov and Gramsci arrived at the idea that the working class could foster intellectualism from within its ranks; it would retain the characteristics of an internalized force rather than being superimposed from without.

Gramsci's concept of "ideological hegemony" is one of manufactured consent.[161] The ideological hegemony of the ruling classes is received by the masses as common sense, i.e., the market economy is presented as a natural phenomenon, which blinds them to their actual lived experience. Hegemony persists because there are procedures, such as elections, collective bargaining, and the courts, through which conflicts can be resolved and whose outcome is not predetermined; in consequence, the state has a semiautonomous existence and can influence conditions under capitalism to favor the interests of labor in specific cases. This makes the realization of capitalist interests a precondition for the realization of other interests. A posteriori consent is reproduced by the system's indulging the interests of various groups on an occasional basis; wage earners continue to consent to the system because it continues to meet some of their interests.[162]

In a manner similar to that of Bogdanov and Gramsci, Herbert Marcuse claimed that movements in advanced nations are a drift toward "bourgeois rights." In Marcuse's view, the capitalist system has succeeded in "channeling antagonisms in such a way that it can manipulate them." Both materially and ideologically, "the very classes which were once the absolute negation of the capitalist system are now more and more integrated into it."[163] In *One-Dimensional Man*, Marcuse regards "integrated man" as one in society without opposition. Both the proletariat and the bourgeois "no longer appear as agents of historical transformation."[164] Capital's principal antagonists, with Marcuse, are united in an "overriding interest in preservation and improvement of the institutional *status quo*."[165] This condition arises, according to Marcuse, because technological development transcends the capitalist mode of production and creates a totalitarian productive apparatus that determines not only the socially needed occupations, skills, and attitudes but also individual needs and aspirations.[166]

Marcuse, consistent with the "double movement" hypothesis in Karl Polanyi's *The Great Transformation*, remarked that:

> The most advanced areas of industrial society exhibit throughout ... two features: a trend toward consummation of technological rationality, and intensive efforts to contain this trend within the established institutions. Here is the internal contradiction of this civilization: the irrational element in its rationality.... The industrial society which makes technology and science its own, is organized for the ever-more-effective domination of man and nature,

for the ever-more-effective utilization of its resources. It becomes irrational when the successes of these efforts open new dimensions of human realization.[167]

For Marcuse, the world is a mean and cursed place, insofar as the proletariat, instead of overthrowing the system, has been seduced by "bourgeois" aspirations. In his view, Marxism has proved no match for the resilience of capitalism and its capacity to absorb the history-making potentialities of the working class and turn them to its own advantage.

Gramsci's central concept of "hegemony" sought to address precisely this issue and has been understood to imply the slow, progressive education of the population to socialism through an essentially democratic process of enlightenment.[168] It was in this connection that he insisted on the centrality of culture for socialism. Like Bogdanov, he stressed the role of intellectuals in building a new cultural hegemony. But for Bogdanov socialism was not something that could be achieved on behalf of the working class by some magnanimous group acting in its name, whether Stalinist "vanguard" or social-democratic parliamentarians. In this regard Bogdanov was a close adherent to Marx's self-emancipation principle.

Gramsci's hope and Bogdanov's aspiration were for a proletariat that would cultivate its own organic intelligentsia, one that would be the mediator of its revolutionary struggle and the herald of a new hegemony.[169] But Gramsci appreciated that in the period of transition certain traditional intellectuals, exemplified by Marx and Engels themselves, would make common cause with the working class. Before his turn to the Leninist party as the "modern prince," as the collective intellectual, Gramsci went through a fervent period of support for the workers' councils as the legitimate organizational form for the proletariat.[170]

"All men are intellectuals," Gramsci contended, "but not all men have in society the function of intellectuals."[171] The nebulous distinction between intellectuals and nonintellectuals was thus a historical construct that would disappear with the achievement of socialism. Even before that event, intellectuals were not to assume total control over the revolutionary struggle, for "the popular element 'feels,' but does not always know or understand; the intellectual element 'knows,' but does not always understand and in particular does not always feel."[172] Intellectuals must, therefore, integrate their knowledge with the passions of the masses in order to avoid becoming a caste or priesthood. They must form an "intellectual-moral bloc" with the populace.[173] Resembling Bogdanov's concerns, Gramsci's reflections on the role of the intellectuals were also based on the assumption that converted traditional and organic intellectuals would come together in a less exclusively vanguardist party. "That all members of a political party should be regarded as intellectuals," he wrote, "is an affirmation that can easily lend itself to mockery and caricature. But if one thinks about it nothing could be more exact.... What matters is the function, which is directive and organizational, i.e., educative and intellectual."[174]

But when the Italian councils were undermined by a combination of nationwide socialist ambivalence and the successful maneuverings of the Turin capitalists, led by Gino Olivetti, Gramsci turned his attention to the building of a vanguardist political party on the Leninist model. He then naively relied on an idealized version of the communist party to act as both the organizer of production and the creator of a new hegemony. Because Gramsci so closely identified the communist party with the organic intellectuals—even though it was the party that had denounced Korsch and Lukács in 1924 precisely for their intellectualism—there was no place in his theory for the unattached, yet critical, intellectuals. Believing that the party was the central mediator of the proletariat's drive for totalization, he failed to see how external to the consciousness of the working class it could become, especially when communism came to power, and concomitantly, how vital a role might still be played by critical bourgeois intellectuals who did not pretend to be organic. But Bogdanov saw firsthand how the party intelligentsia was detaching itself from the people, not going-to-the-people but "distancing-itself-from-the-people." In a short article on the subject of the intelligentsia, Bogdanov wrote:

> Being unable to find a unifying point of view on the basis of life itself, people start looking for it outside life. Some have their heads in the beyond, in the world of mysticism and metaphysics, others in the "logical" world of empty formal abstractions. And, of course, all that goes there is lost to life.[175]

Though Bogdanov had high hopes for socialism, his views were not without some cynicism. This, no doubt, reflected his anxiety with the entrenched attitudes he found among some leaders. A critical observer of emergent Bolshevism, he was troubled by the relatively easy encroachment of despotism. From his critical reflections on the trespass, he was concerned even more that cultural change was the crucial dimension of revolution, the *sine qua non* for socialism.

In the years from 1913 to 1919 in particular, when Gramsci grew active in the Italian socialist party and became involved in the struggles of the Turin proletariat, the idealist roots of his Marxism were most apparent.[176] This period invites a comparison with Lukács's "revolutionary culturist" phase.[177] Gramsci insisted on the centrality of culture for socialism. It was during this, his *Ordine Nuovo* period, when he emphasized cultural-educational work, that Gramsci was closest to a Bogdanovite position.[178] Dismissing the reduction of the superstructure to a projection/reflection of the socioeconomic base, he invoked the notion of a cultural totality. Nor was this posture unique to Gramsci. Lukács's philosophical idealism and aestheticism amounted to a revolt against the primacy of the (economic) base, an attempt at the level of philosophy and culture in the strict sense to liberate human subjectivity and spiritual creativity from abstract-objectified fetters.[179]

Gramsci regarded socialism not merely as a series of discrete stages identified with specific tasks of economic development from capitalism to socialism but as a continuum, his views converging with those of Bogdanov. Convinced of the multidimensionality of the struggle for socialism, both theorists focused on the preconditions for socialism as much as on the preconditions for the appropriation of power itself. Demonstrating a faculty that escaped Lenin, Gramsci wrote: "A historical act can only be performed by 'collective man,' and this presupposes the attainment of a 'cultural-social' unity through which a multiplicity of dispersed wills, with heterogeneous aims, are welded together with a single aim, on the basis of an equal and common perception of the world."[180] With Cicero and Marx as his guides, Gramsci noted: "No society sets itself tasks for whose accomplishment the necessary and sufficient conditions do not either already exist or are not at least beginning to emerge and develop."[181]

Gramsci became a "Bogdanovite" insofar as he looked beyond the seizure of power to discern the elements of a "complete revolution." Both Bogdanov and Gramsci were dissatisfied with narrow materialist conceptualizations of socialism that stressed public ownership of the means of production and the dictatorship of the proletariat. They searched for a more dynamic conceptualization, one that penetrated to the core of socialism, and they thought they found their answer in the cultural realm.

Directing their attention to cultivating new modes of thought and behavior, believing these were the essential criteria of socialism, they realized the hiatus between the existing proletariat and the projected "new man" of the socialist order would not be overcome by a single blow at the moment of revolution and could be bridged only by a process of actively sponsored cultural change. Thus, a cultural revolution was the necessary complement to political and economic revolution.

For both Gramsci and Bogdanov the appropriation of power was but a political moment in an otherwise lengthy transition to socialism. Instrumental to socialism's success was the conscious cultivation of embryonic elements prior to the political event. Bogdanov realized the need for vigilance after the event as well.

The organization Worker's Truth, led by Bogdanov, managed to attract intellectuals who analyzed the way the party was performing in the early 1920s. They drew the conclusion that the consciousness of the working class had to be fostered in order to radically change the structure of the party and its methods. The group denounced the way the working class was oppressed by the party bureaucracy and the substitution of the power of the bureaucracy for that of the working class.

For Bogdanov, a bureaucrat was not simply a government functionary who sits in an office and directs certain affairs. A bureaucrat was a privileged functionary, cut off from real life, from the people, from the needs and interests of common folk. Bureaucrats and the *nomenklatura* were interested in their jobs as positions to be preserved and improved, not as tasks to be done. They would knowingly do something functionally unnecessary or even harmful to the people if it would preserve their positions. Careerism and subservience, red tape and protocol were their constant companions.

For Marx:

> Bureaucracy considers itself the ultimate purpose of the state. . . . The higher circles rely on the lower in everything involving a knowledge of particulars; the lower circles trust the upper in everything involving an understanding of the universal, and thus they lead each other into delusions. . . . The universal spirit of bureaucracy is mystery, sacrament. Observance of this sacrament is ensured from within by hierarchal organization, and with relation to the outside world by its closed corporative character. Authority is therefore the criterion of knowledge, and the deification of authority is its manner of thought.[182]

Max Weber, for instance, despaired of socialism. In his eyes, it would merely complete, in the economic order, that which had already happened in the political order. Socialization of the means of production, he conjectured, would merely subject economic life to the bureaucratic management of the state. The role of the state would become totalizing, with bureaucratic socialism yielding a new form of serfdom.

As though fearful of pushing his logic further, Bogdanov only hinted at this potential tragic outcome of the revolution. But in various forms it became perhaps his most serious private fear, offsetting to some extent his public rhetoric that exploitation of the working class was impossible in a "workers' state." His was a concern with the emergence of a bourgeoisified *nomenklatura*. Later, Lenin, too, articulated concern: "Our state right now," he wrote, "is such that the whole organized proletariat must defend itself against it." He continued: "The trade unions cannot lose such a basic function as non-class 'economic struggle,' in the sense of struggle against bureaucratic perversions in the Soviet apparatus, in the sense of protecting the maternal and spiritual interests of the toiling masses by ways and means not available to that apparatus."[183]

Development of the vanguardist party into a new kind of exploitative bureaucratic state was a source of personal disquietude for Bogdanov, as a "petit bourgeois degeneration" overcame the Bolshevik left. Lenin was aware of the issue and in a resolution adopted in 1921 remarked: "A situation is gradually taking shape in which one can 'rise in the world,' make a career for oneself, get a bit of power, only by entering the service of the Soviet regime."[184] In the left's economic programs Bogdanov professed to see an institutionalization of the official "arbitrariness" of War Communism and the rise of "privileged Communist groups"—a new state of *chinovniki*—indifferent to the needs of the masses and enjoying "absolute immunity" from social accountability. A rebirth of alienation came to concern him more than the fate of the urban masses alone: programs that plunder the countryside would lead, he predicted, not to a classless socialist society but to "the eternal reign of the proletariat" and "its degeneration into a real exploiter class" in relation to the peasantry.

Thus, the mission of Worker's Truth was to organize the working class not only to give it class consciousness but also to lead it to claim the power that belonged to it. In its overt opposition to economistic appreciations of man and socialism-communism, Bogdanov's "left-wing communist" organization offered the beginnings of a critique of the Bolshevik perspective and program. It was the expression of opposition to the "reified" conception of socialism-communism that was surfacing in the Soviet Union. For socialism-communism was entering a new stage in the structural development of society; it was being institutionalized not as a qualitative break with the capitalist system of production but as something other. In its opposition Worker's Truth was a self-determining praxis of the working class. Among the points in the organization's program was freedom of action for the socialist parties and freedom of discussion and elections of the new Soviets in the factories. These elements of the program evoked a widespread response among the disenchanted populace, suffering as they were from material shortages. The result was a widespread strike movement.

Like Proletkul't before it, by September 1923, the organization had been neutralized, for confronted by it and other groups the party admitted the necessity of resorting to coercion in order to subdue what was labeled as subversive.

> Instead of superseding the hired-labor relationship that is the fundamental characteristic from which all the other deformations of bourgeois political society originate, socialism in its Stalinist phase of development evolved new forms of this very relationship. The problem of economic and thereby political alienation, far from ceasing to exist, has thus become socialism's real and vital problem.[185]

Historical experience indicates that socialism is not immune from distorting possibilities, for "real socialism" was pursued on the basis of various social modalities that in themselves represent forms of alienation. Bogdanov recognized that the problem of alienation was of historical, continuing, and vital significance to cultural renovation under socialism.

While according priority to the concept of alienation present in the yet-to-be-discovered *Manuscripts of 1844*, Bogdanov sought to extend the analysis. Often reacting against a "deterministic Marxism," in a manner later present among West European Marxists, an inquiring, and admittedly maverick, mind led Bogdanov to detect significant dimensions missing from Marx's analysis. Some of Bogdanov's ideas on human liberation and alienation, for example, were closer to the "early Marx," the one of the *Economic and Philosophic Manuscripts of 1844*. Indeed, White draws a comparison between Bogdanov's "Sobiranie cheloveka" and Marx's *Manuscripts of 1844*. He points out that Bogdanov's article, published in *Pravda*, April 1904, was written two decades before the *Manuscripts* was discovered.[186]

> Bogdanov's main contribution to Pravda, an article entitled *The Community of Man*, affords an excellent example of how close his version of empirio-criti-

cism came to the early Marx.... The basic argument is that the metaphysical approach to philosophy is a product of man's fragmentation. At the dawn of man's existence, when life was extremely simple, man shared all experience with his fellows in their primitive society, so that one person was barely differentiated from the rest; they acted and thought as a group, in harmony with each other and with the natural forces which surrounded them. The conception "I" could not exist. But with the division of society into specialized groups and the accumulation of different experience by them, society lost its natural unity and individuality made its appearance.[187]

According to Marx, the history of human society is a process of the self-realization of the true consciousness of man. He wrote: "It is not the consciousness of men that determines their social being, but, on the contrary, their social being that determines their development."[188] Whereas Marx sees the absence of man and his alienation as produced through the subjectivization of the principle of property, Bogdanov sought to locate the essence in the concept of organization.

With his feet firmly planted in the Russian intellectual and cultural traditions, Bogdanov retained a point of contact with Hertzen's Narodnik socialism, its principle of the supremacy of the human personality. Bogdanov dealt extensively with the problem of the "fragmentation of personality" as a source of alienation in industrial bourgeois society. He maintained that in the bourgeois society, subjectivity and the world, the soul and action, spirit and nature, feeling and reason, form and content are torn asunder; art is ripped from the totality of social life, and the possibility of a culture that is immediately linked to social being rapidly diminishes. He advanced a theory according to which the fragmentation of personality was more typical of the early stage of industrial civilization than of the advanced stage. The technology of early industry emphasized strict specialization in production equipment and mechanical processes. This emphasis "crippled the body and the soul of the worker" by narrowing the range of his experienced competence, intellectual endeavor, and social identification. Modern industrial production emphasizes "the knowledge of general methods" rather than "the familiarity with infinite details." It replaces fragmented work assignments with participation in complex systems of the technological process, a prelude to the coming full automation of industrial production. For Bogdanov the unity of science as a "systematization of techniques" triumphs over the diversity of rigid specialization. While the early industrial technology reflected the fragmented nature of empirical science, the modern industrial technology reflects the integrated nature of theoretical science. The acute awareness of the unifying patterns of various types of work and the advanced scientific level of production offer the worker a broader scope of experience, responsibility, and intellectual involvement and, thereby, a new and higher integration of cultural values—and of personality. While Marx saw in the economic organization of modern industrial production the main source of the alienation of the worker, Bogdanov saw in modern technological advances, and in modern science, a new condition contributing to the realization of the "wholeness" of personality.

The self-estrangement of man, the perception of a pseudo-reality, is legitimated and perpetuated through the offices of the price-making market system, in which social phenomena are universally represented as thing-like, leaving no foothold for the individual, and in which man is entrapped in a condition of self-estrangement. Unlike Hegel, Marx did not define alienation as a timeless universal condition. Rather, having located it precisely in the context of the market economy, he optimistically pointed to a resolution of man's alienated state in a foreseeable social context, namely, socialism. Marx expected that creator and artifact would be reunited when man transcended capitalism. In doctrinal Marxism, alienation is a direct result of economic relations such that, once private ownership of the means of production is replaced by state ownership, it becomes a logical impossibility. But alienation is first and foremost the result of the exercise of invidious authority, and capitalist exploitation is only one of many possible forms of alienation. Thus, removing capitalist exploitation is no guarantee that domination is abolished. This perspective, however, was not shared by all Marxian analysts. An increasingly cynical socialist, Bogdanov did not share in doctrinal Marxism's optimism. Although he did not argue against Marx's thesis, he clearly implied that the technological base of personality integration is more fundamental than the economic base of personality fragmentation.

> The task of socialism [is] to overcome those forms of human existence which create the alienated man; the dissolution of the alienated forms of man's social life becomes the central problem of socialism. If the problem of socialism is not comprehended in these terms, the result may be the evolution of political forms into paroxysms of dehumanization.[189]

For Lenin, however, the question of alienation was not so much unimportant as irrelevant in a socialist society. "He did not direct his attention to the work process itself as a source of alienation."[190] The socialist revolution and revolutionary authority have often been regarded as sufficient guarantee that man would be liberated not only from the hired-labor relationship but also from all other forms of alienation. For Lenin the problem of alienation thus became "superfluous." Lukács adhered to Lenin's position and considered false and irrational the argument that insofar as socialism was developing further the material forces of production (mechanization, Taylorism, etc.), it too was unable to solve the conflict between culture and civilization.[191] For Lukács, the point of departure was that market principles should no longer prescribe attitudes and behavior. As Lukács confidently remarked in an early work, "When economic life is organized in the direction of socialism, those elements which previously were accouterments at best now come to the fore: the inner and outer life of man is dominated by human and no longer by economic motives and impulses."[192] He maintained that the laws of political economy would no longer be applicable to a socialist idea and states: "Liberation from capitalism means liberation from the rule of the economy."[193] This was a denominational constant.

In agreement with Nikolai Bukharin, Lukács maintained that political economy—"a system without a subject ... an anarchistically constructed society of commodity producers"[194]—and its categories of analysis were not applicable to post-capitalist organized society.[195] Marxism employed a "dialectical-historical" methodology: categories and economics laws discussed by Marx related only to capitalist commodity production and not to the late-capitalist formulation. Bukharin explained:

> As soon as we take an organized economy, all the basic *problems* of political economy disappear: problems of value, price, profit, and the like. Here "relations between people" are not expressed in "relations between things" and social economy is regulated not by the blind forces of the market and competition, but consciously by a ... plan. Therefore here there can be a certain descriptive system, on the one hand, and a system of norms, on the other. But there can be no place for a science studying "the blind laws of the market" since there will be no market. Thus the ends of capitalist commodity society will be the end of political economy.[196]

In his *Essays on Tektology* Bogdanov wrote:

> In political economy many important questions are resolved incorrectly or remain unsolved, because of the inability of specialists to adopt the organizational point of view. A vivid example is the theory concerning the laws of exchange. The notion of "marginal utility," which rules over the old official science, originates from principles which can be frankly called "anti-organizational." It takes as its basis the subjective relationship of a separate man to his individual needs; the individual psychics with its fluctuating valuations of useful things. Meanwhile, the exchange of goods is an expression of the organizational relations among people in a society; it is a system of production; and the activity of separate psychics with its subjective valuations reduces to an adjustment of a given individual with his economy to the objective, independent conditions of social organization. But none of the subjective valuations can change even that price of merchandise for the individual which he finds at a given moment in the market, not to speak of the technical conditions of production of the merchandise, which constitute one of the most permanent moments in the determination of prices.[197]

In contrast to Lenin, Bogdanov focused on changes in both private property and authority relations as essential to real socialism; together they would make possible new comradely relations as well as genuinely classless society. It was too facile, argued Bogdanov, to consider socialism the negation of capitalism in terms of private ownership; alienation and even exploitation could continue unless there were an additional, and explicit, change in authority relations. Bogdanov, in essence, not only offered a more practical/cynical understanding of socialism than Lenin but also drew attention to sources of alienation that Marx had not foreseen and that doctrinal interpreters rejected—namely, those of a political and cultural nature that perpetuated invidious authority relations despite a change in the economic base. Precisely for these reasons, Bogdanov attempted to cast a wide net in social transformation, encompassing collectivist organization of labor, aesthetic creativity, and political behavior.[198]

As fiercely as Marcuse, Bogdanov railed against fragmentation and one-dimensionality and sought ways to "integrate" man in technified society.[199] His prescient assessment of the multidimensional threats of corporatism have, with Ivan Illich, been elaborated. Illich writes that:

> Society can be destroyed when further growth of mass production renders the milieu hostile, when it extinguishes the free use of the natural abilities of society's members, when it isolates people from each other and locks them into a man-made shell, when it undermines the texture of community by promoting extreme social polarization and splintering specialization, or when cancerous acceleration enforces social change at a rate that rules out legal, cultural, and political precedents as formal guidelines to present behavior. Corporate endeavors which thus threaten society cannot be tolerated. At this point it becomes irrelevant whether an enterprise is nominally owned by individuals, corporations or the state, because no form of management can make such fundamental destruction serve a social purpose.[200]

Bogdanov's vision of socialism meant the liberation of the individual from invidious norms and the veil of abstract obligations. Returning to the concept of personality, he noted that the "splintering of man" through authoritarianism and specialization would be succeeded by the "integration of man" and his multifaceted cultural development. Such a transformation would be possible once the contradictory nature and spontaneity of societal development gave way to organization and planning. In the new society, without competition and class struggle, the "psychology of disconnectedness" would be replaced by the recognition of the self as "an integral part of the whole."[201]

The threat was that organizational relations could perpetuate classes, i.e., authority situations, together with exploitation, even if property relations were altered. Advances in technology, social development, and science, Bogdanov argued, might eventually overcome the self-estrangement of man; however, so long as society remained fragmented, i.e., not a unitary whole, false consciousness would continue to exist.[202] "Workers were subordinate not only to capitalists, who had organizational power, but also to engineers and managers who had derived power and expertise.... Only when technological progress outstripped the organizational function, and the latter no longer corresponded to the system of production, 'surmised Bogdanov,' would class conflict ensue."[203]

Bogdanov, having supplanted orthodox Marxian "relations of production" with his organizational (Tektological) view, questioned whether exploitation and alienation could continue even if the base were transformed, i.e., even were socialism instituted. Might not a change in the ownership of the means of production be insufficient to secure a classless society and socialism? Could it be comfortably assumed that collectivized enterprises controlled by workers materially transformed the social, cultural, and intellectual status of workers to a significant degree? Could factories, mines, and large-scale agricultural enterprises become domains of freedom by reason of their operations being managed by workers' collectives? Despite Bogdanov's espousal of worker collectivism, a view that prompted at least one analyst to label him a syndicalist, his position on workers' control is not entirely clear. He did not, for example, condone the type of workers' control that had sprung up during War Communism, because of its parochialism and inbuilt competitiveness. Lenin's decree of November 14, 1917, on factory committees, reported Bogdanov, had the "unexpected consequence" of destroying the solidarity of the working class. Factory committees were drawn into "the sphere of competition," where every committee was compelled "to fight for the interests of its own enterprise, its own labor force, against those of other enterprises." Allegedly, Bogdanov's attitude was typical of that of the left opposition, who supported workers' control but not "anarcho-syndicalism." He shared with Hertzen the view that anarcho-syndicalism was an example of the individualism long associated with the trade unionism of Western Europe. The question of whether by eliminating capitalistic economic exploitation Soviet socialism had actually eliminated social domination was moot. By removing "class rule," had it also removed invidious hierarchical organizational rule?

The question was spurned by Lenin:

> Our opponents told us repeatedly that we were rash in undertaking to implant socialism in an insufficiently cultured country. But they were misled by our having started from the opposite end to that prescribed by theory . . . because in our country the political and social revolution preceded the cultural revolution, that very cultural revolution which nevertheless now confronts us.[204]

The reasoning on this position was that cultural transformation could begin only after the political revolution had been secured and had thereby reduced the available alternatives to society. This posture—a "war of maneuver"—contrasted with Gramsci's culturalist concept of a "war of position." This argues for a protracted struggle during which the proletariat develops the cultural, ideological, economic, and political means to challenge the superstructure.[205]

As we have seen, many of Gramsci's ideas are more approximate to those of Bogdanov than to Lenin. They perceived similar problems in the process of revolutionary change and offered comparable solutions. The parallel between these two philosophers of praxis challenges the commonly held assumption that there was a chasm separating Russian Marxism and its allegedly more creative Western variant. In this connection Western Critical Marxism constitutes a continuing dialogue with Leninism and a challenge to its premises; in many ways, it is the Lenin-Bogdanov debate on a grand scale.

11

Tektology: The Metascience of Praxis

Introductory Remarks: A Philosophy of Praxis

The perspective of nature as a unitary and dynamic system of systems reasserted itself as a result of the convergence of some germinal ideas in the natural sciences at the end of the nineteenth century: the notion of omnipresent energy (atomic theory, field theory, the conservation of energy); the notion of the creation and evolution of forms of living energy (evolutionary theory); and the notion of the continuity of energy and life. In this perspective every thing and every event is a thermodynamic process or nexus of processes defined by its location in a web of trophic and quasi-trophic interconnections with other natural and artificial ecosystems. Late-nineteenth-century concepts of nature converged on this unitary evolutionary view. They emphasized the physical unity of nature and acknowledged the fact of the biological and ecological unity in the broad sense of physical nature.

Indeed, the concept of the unity of science was present in the thought of Marx, who in his *Economic and Philosophical Manuscripts* wrote: "Natural science will in time incorporate into itself the science of man, just as the science of man will incorporate into itself natural science: there will be one science."[1] Nor can one disregard the contribution of Friedrich Engels, who implored Marxism to renew itself. There was a detectable theme in nineteenth-century Marxist philosophy, which was the acquisition of positivist attributes. However, the term "positivism" must be understood in a very broad sense; it implies the search for a "scientific" philosophy, a science-based instrumentalism and was often limited to a synthesis of scientific generalizations. Without doubt, there is more interest here in a "scientific worldview" than in philosophy. A conviction that all existence is scientifically comprehensible, a fetishization of formal methods, and the heroic view that science is the creative and unshakable foundation of these inquiries was ubiquitous.[2]

But positivism, as an attempt to subordinate philosophy to science, had little success anywhere in Europe among philosophers *par excellence*. Nonetheless, positivism was intoxicating for those bent on a unity of science, and they drank greedily from the heady brew. This phenomenon was widespread in Europe at the time of Ernst Mach, in particular, and in Russia it was strikingly expressed, especially among natural scientists.[3]

Mach's search for a unity of scientific knowledge was well founded in the critical thought of the Marxian tradition. In a contemporary reconstructive effort Frolov writes:

> The integral science of man will therefore be a synthesis of many specialized sciences, both natural and social, that study man from different angles. This was foreseen by Marx, who believed that science's ideal future state would be one in which natural science will . . . incorporate into itself natural science: there will be one science.[4]

Affirming Marx's and Engels's postures, Bogdanov believed that the fundamental trend of human thought was toward a "scientific monism" that constituted a unity of scientific knowledge. First, the idealist, both finalist and vitalist, monisms, whose interest was to subject nature to a crude level of production and to subject exploited producers to the will of the organizers of production; then, the speculative monisms of metaphysical philosophies, which attempted to surmount the inadequacies of nascent science. These were the past stages of human thought. Following a Comtean thesis, the time had come, he believed, to construct a synthesizing monism.

As we have seen, Bogdanov took the view that bourgeois science was a historical product, that it had emerged at a given stage of social development, but that it would be transcended in the course of time with scientific advancement.[5] However, J.D. White, in his philosophical review of Bogdanov, has remarked that in the latter's *Short Course of Economic Science* he assimilated a positivist philosophical viewpoint, that is, the rejection of metaphysics—the idea that absolute truth about reality is possible.[6] Bogdanov's volume on philosophy, *The Basic Elements of the Historical Outlook on Nature*, was influenced not only by Ostwaldian energetics but also by other systems of thought, including the tradition of holism present in much of Russian intellectuality, as well as a quest for a unity of scientific thought. With his further understanding of the metaphysical and analytical limitations of social energetics, he sought, in Tektology, a more general theory.

The term *tektologia* originates from the Greek root *ag*, which also gave rise to numerous other words, such as *teklon* (builder), *taksis* (order), *tekhne* (trade, arts), and *teknon* (child). Despite the heterogeneity of these notions, they nonetheless contain the concept of an organizational process. As a physician, political economist, and ideologist, Bogdanov was struck by the systemic analogies between living systems and societies and between scientific and social organizations and processes. For this reason, he named his metascientific system tektologia.

The German Darwinist Ernst Haeckel used this word before Bogdanov, but only in relation to the laws of organization of living beings. Haeckel's use of the term denoted a study of the regulatory processes and the organization of all systems, a "general natural science." Vucinich notes that: "Bogdanov borrowed the term 'Tektology' from Ernst Haeckel, who used it to designate a branch of morphology dealing with the organism as a complex system of morphons of various orders."[7] While the term was provided by Haeckel, the Marxian variant was garnished by Bogdanov's phenomenological and culturalist appreciations. Already politically ostracized, perhaps Bogdanov did not overtly claim that Tektology was anything new. To the contrary, he presented it as essentially a projection of Marx's thought consistent with the traditions of practical theory.

Following Marx's praxiology, Bogdanov contended that the ultimate intent of Tektology is not merely to describe the overall structure of the social world but to produce reliable information for reshaping it.[8] Thus, Bogdanov did not neglect the praxis-orientation of the activity of organization. His voluminous writing remains part of a tireless search for a metascience of society. The function of science, according to him, is to enrich the store of knowledge helping man to coevolve with the biosphere.

Bogdanov's organizational theory marked a radical departure from Marxist doctrine. While in Marxist thought "dialectical materialism" is a universal law of change in nature and society, in Bogdanov's tektological view it is only a small component of a more universal dialectic of organizational processes.[9] Having tried to adapt the empirio-monism of Mach for use within Marxism and presenting it as a development of Marxist theory, he went on to outline a general science of organization—Tektology—emphasizing its practical aspect and its function of changing the world.[10] Russian orthodox Marxists of the day were fearful that Tektology was an attempt by Bogdanov to replace the philosophy of Marx. It appeared to them that by the creation of the universal organizational metascience its author wanted to challenge Marxism by positing Tektology as a proxy Marxism.

Zenkovsky writes that:

> Bogdanov's inspiration or, if you will, intuition is defined by two basic Marxian propositions. On the one hand, he accepts the Marxist interpretation of the Hegelian doctrine that the "mystery" of being is revealed only in history. On the other hand, he accepts the "philosophy of the act" . . . which is intended not so much to "explain" the world as to "change" it (Marx's formula), i.e., to intervene in it creatively. In neither of these propositions does Bogdanov deviate from the foundations of Marxism.[11]

Just as Bogdanov's phenomenology and empirio-monism were contiguous to his previous studies in the "historical view of nature" and in the philosophy and sociology of knowledge, so his work on Tektology was a partial synthesis of these. Despite a basic continuity in the evolution of his thought, it should be stressed that, while empirio-monism was concerned mainly with the philosophical foundations of a general theory of society, Tektology hinted of positivism and was presented as a "general natural science," a kind of metascience.

Foreign in its universality to the traditions of scientific thought, the idea of general theory of organization was fully understood by only a handful of men and did not therefore spread. Partially, this was due to the fact that Bogdanov addressed earlier the questions of philosophy, and Tektology was therefore perceived by many, philosophers in particular, as a new philosophical system, despite the fact that the author of Tektology considered it to be a universal natural science and repeatedly protested against the enveloping confusion over the universal organizational science and Marxist philosophy.[12]

While subscribing to an empirio-monist organic theory of society, Bogdanov first thought in terms of the primacy of human individuals over society. As in the case of Podolinsky, the energetic view was literally intertwined with strains of Narodnik "collectivism." He had, therefore, to offer some explanation of why individuals formed societies. The Ostwaldian hypothesis first offered by Bogdanov was the conservation of energy; more could be achieved, and there was a better chance of survival if individuals acted in concert. Energy, by analogy, was held to play the same unifying role in the rest of the animate and inanimate world.[13] However, by 1904, Bogdanov returned to the Marxian conclusion, one that Durkheim would later express. Human society, he maintained, existed prior to individuals; collectivism was the natural human condition, and individualism was a historical product concomitant to the "metaphysical outlook." This proved to be an important factor in Bogdanov's decision to search for new general societal models consistent with Marx's philosophy of praxis. Bogdanov acknowledged Hegel and Marx as precursors to what he termed "today's formulation of the question." And that question was: What was the most politic way to organize some complex of elements, real or ideal? Bogdanov came down solidly in favor of Marx's philosophy of praxis, integral to which was materiality.

The philosophical distinctions between the "ideal" and the "real" and between the "mind" and the "body" have given rise, broadly speaking, to two Western philosophical narratives. Those who have promoted the primacy of the ideal or of the mind have tended to argue that the distinction points to an ontological reality, and that the ideal or the mind is more important or nobler or in some way superior to the real or the body. Those, like Marx, who have promoted the primacy of the real, i.e., the material, or the body did not, however, take the inverse position. Instead, they tended to argue that the real-ideal and mind-body distinctions are false dualities. Bogdanov, taking his cue from Marx, also argued that the dualities are false, for the very concept of the ideal or the mind is an ideological obfuscations intended to shroud the everyday experience.

"No doctrine, no system among those which existed before Marx was 'philosophy'," wrote Bogdanov, "in such a strict and full meaning of this word as is historical materialism. None had reached such a unity of views on cognition and life, none had opened up such endless opportunities for actively harmonizing cognition and life. In the teaching of Marx, philosophy for the first time found itself, its place within nature and society, instead of above and beyond them."[14]

A number of theorists have argued that central to Marx's Marxism was an examination of the development of socioeconomic formations as a process of natural history, and not without good reason.[15] It was, however, not his goal to apply the skeleton of natural science to an investigation of societal phenomena. As we have already seen, this challenge was seized by Engels, who, in *Dialectics of Nature*, devoted considerable time and effort to exhibiting that Marxism also met the criteria of the natural science of its time.

Bogdanov contended that, during the first four decades of its existence, Marx's philosophy had helped explain "a mass of historical developments" and had not encountered serious opposition from other theories. However, he thought that both Hegel and Marx, by offering an imprecise formulation of dialectics, had invited arbitrary interpretations.

Prat notes that in his *Philosophy of Living Experience*, Bogdanov critiqued the dialectical ideas of Engels, and by casual extension those of Marx, and reinterpreted the Hegelian idea as the rupture of an initial stability establishing a new dynamic balance.[16] Bogdanov wrote:

> Losing from view this vital and real meaning of the dialectic, Engels and Marx lost the possibility of explaining the transition from quantity to quality. After our research, such an explanation becomes very simple. If a given process—the motion of a body, the life of an organism, the development of society—is defined by the conflict of two opposing forces, then as long as one prevails quantitatively—even by only a little—the process goes to that direction. As soon as the other force, growing, is equal to the first, the whole character of the process—its "quality"—changes; either it ceases or, going further, it overcomes the second force, reversing the direction; in either case, our senses tell us that there is before us something "qualitatively" other.[17]

The idea of a "universal organizational science" is really bound up with the revision of the dialectic (in particular in Engels's version), which we find in Bogdanov's earlier works. His dialectic differed from both Hegel's and Marx's. On the one hand, Hegel's dialectic assumed idealist dimensions in which history was patterned on the metaphysical process of being. Marx, on the other hand, detached dialectic from this idealist base. In his work, according to Marcuse:

> The negativity of reality becomes a historical condition. It becomes a social condition associated with a particular historical form of society. The totality which the Marxian dialectic approaches is the totality of class society, and the negativity which underlies its contradictions and shapes its every content is the negativity of class relations.[18]

Marxism needed further elaboration and development. Since history was not at a standstill, philosophical thought was challenged to take into account recent scientific discoveries and theories. Particularly in natural science, many changes of revolutionary proportions had presented themselves. Bogdanov numbered among these Darwin's theory of evolution, for it raised serious questions that historical monism, i.e., Marxist theory, could no longer ignore.[19] "Although the theory of historical monism did not cease to be true in its basic claims, it was no longer satisfactory."[20]

The Marxist philosophy of praxis, noted Bogdanov, was very much in need of establishing closer relations with new scientific theories of morphotransformation (particularly Darwinian). After forty years of existence, Marxist sociology continued to imitate the natural sciences, even though these dealt with phenomena that were "essentially homogeneous, simpler, and more general."[21]

The alleged flaw in Marx's sociology could be attributed to his reputed failure to appreciate the stream of evolutionary ideas emanating from Darwinism and positivist thought. Analyzing society as distinct from the global processes and laws of nature, Bogdanov stressed that Marxism had neglected to account for the consequential dependence of sociology on biology.[22] Bogdanov's argument, thus, cautiously anticipated that of some contemporary social ecologists and evolutionary economists.

Perhaps for reasons of "political correctness," Bogdanov presented his metascience of praxis not as constituting a paradigmatic change but rather as displaying a continuity with Marxism's hard core. For in the process of writing *Grundrisse* and *Capital*, Marx had developed a critical/dialectic, essentialist logico-procedural means of research. The dialectic as procedure, formulated by him, was formalized when the traditional methods of classical science predominated. Bogdanov acknowledged that while Marx and Engels had many perspicacious ideas that could be further developed, their procedure, borrowed from Aristotle, Kant, and Hegel, has been considered, rather than a universal ontology or theory of knowledge, a needlessly cryptic variation on the banal notion that opposing forces can sometimes produce motion and change.[23] The ideas of the classics of Marxism and the materialist dialectics exerted a profound influence on the inception and content of Tektology. Dialectical materialism was to Bogdanov a near truth that had been made an erroneous dogma by Lenin and his followers.

Bogdanov regarded the evolutionary schemata already present in the works of Hegel, Marx, and Engels, and in Spencer's social evolutionary perspectives, as the major precursors of Tektology. He believed, however, that these antecedents were too specialized and fell short of the universal overarching organizational viewpoint of Tektology, of its formalization of both the practical and theoretical organizational methods of man and the elemental methods of nature. In Tektology, all these methods "explain and illuminate one another; in the absence of such an integral approach the solution of the question of organization is impossible, because a part torn from the whole can neither be made the whole, nor understood apart from the whole."[24] Indeed, from his phenomenological viewpoint Bogdanov wrote:

> Theoretical philosophy strove to discover a unity of experience in the form of some universal explanation. It wanted to paint an harmonious and intelligible picture of the world. Its tendency is contemplation. For Tektology the unity of experience is not "discovered," but actively created by organizational means: "philosophers wanted to explain the world, but the main point is to change it" said the great precursor of organizational science, Karl Marx. The explanation of organizational forms and methods by Tektology is directed not to a contemplation of their unity, but to a practical mastery over them.
>
> The entire content of human life has unfolded before us and it is now possible to sum up. The old teacher of scientific socialism, Engels, expressed it by a formula: production of people, production of things, and production of ideas. The concept of organizing action is hidden in the term "production." We shall, therefore, make this formula more precise: *organization of the external forces of nature, organization of human forces, and organization of experience.* . . . humankind has no other activity except organizational activity, there being no other problems except organizational problems.[25]

From Bogdanov's empirio-monistic paradigm there emerged a grand hierarchical evolutionary image tainted with Comtean positivism and not dissimilar to the more recent perspectives of E. Jantsch and E. Laszlo.[26]

According to Bogdanov's phenomenology, the world appears in consciousness as "an endless stream of organizing activities," meaning an infinite series of levels of organized experience integrally and continuously related to one another. Since each successive level is more organized, it is "higher" than the one preceding it. At the highest level, that of "the human collective," the endless stream is pushed ever farther along by collective will acting in response to collective need.[27]

In Bogdanov's grand evolutionary image the lowest possible level of organization is that which he variously calls "the primal world environment," "the elemental universe," and "ether with its electrical and light waves." On this level the world is a chaotic mass of elements with next to no organization at all. If organization is defined in terms of resistance to activity, then the chaos of elements offers infinitely little resistance. This level represents the lower limit of organized experience, and man, of course, cannot possibly think about it in any real way.[28]

The second of the four levels is that of inorganic nature "with its internal atomic and inter-atomic energies." On this level, said Bogdanov, we find the elements of experience organized into stable complexes and those complexes organized in a relatively simple way.[29] From an analysis of *Philosophy of Living Experience*, we learn that at the third level, that of life, there is a much higher degree of organization of complexes. What distinguishes the organization of life from that of inorganic nature is that its complexes, i.e., its life forms, are self-perpetuating in the sense of autopoiesis, while inorganic complexes are not reconstituted by their own activity.[30] Of itself, life shows a series of varying degrees of organization, from the simplest cells to the human organism. Parallel to this series we find a series of psychical complexes, from those peculiar to micro-organisms to the psyches of individual men. This is the level of subjective, individually organized experience.[31]

The fourth level is that of the human collective, "a multi-million part system composed of individuals in social relation to one another." On this level, life not only perpetuates itself but also expands and reconstructs the world. This socially constructed and still-to-be constructed world, this realm of the conquering forces of labor and thought, this kingdom of socially organized elements of the universe, is the most grandiose and complete manifestation of life that we know.[32] Bogdanov tells us: "Such is our picture of the world: an uninterrupted series of forms of the organization of elements, developing in struggle and eternal action, without a beginning in the past, without an end in the future."[33]

Bogdanov, writes Utechin, on the basis of a historical process, identified a phase in man's development as the fourth and final stage, in which:

> Collective self-sufficient economy and the fusion of personal lives into one colossal whole, harmonious in the relations of its parts, [would systematically group] all elements for one common struggle—the struggle against the endless spontaneity of nature.... An enormous mass of creative activity, spontaneous and conscious, is necessary in order to solve this task. It demands the forces not of man, but of humankind—and only in working at this task does humankind as such emerge. All ideological forms, including philosophy and the sciences, merge at this stage into one universal organizational science necessary for the great task of harmonizing the efforts of humankind.[34]

It was in the context of Bogdanov's grand evolutionary synthesis that Tektology was presented as systems theory–based methodological appreciation.

Tektology is characterized, first and foremost, by its organizational point of view. Ostensibly, any scientific question can be posited and solved as a tektological problem, which is to say, a problem involving the internal organization of a system and its relationship to its environment. Tektology is, in Bogdanov's words, "capable of yielding new results and leading to new statements of the most diverse questions of cognition." Old problems, posited within the framework of the specialized sciences, can now be restated and explained within a tektological framework, which is what Bogdanov does in his own phenomenological reconsideration of human experience and science. His studies of ideology and culture are an example of such restatements and explanations.

In Bogdanov's usage, Tektology is a metascience dealing with processes that regulate the organization of all systems of natural and social phenomena. From his appreciation of thermodynamics and the life process he assumed there was an incessant process of organization-disorganization—that all human activities consisted of a temporal ordering, sorting, and organizing.[35] The "task of Tektology" was to systematize those activities. He contended that all the universal aspects of both society and nature could be revealed by studying the laws of organization. Individual sciences deal with the particular aspects of the universal theory of organization: mathematics, for example, studies "all kinds of complexes in a state of equilibrium." Tektology was a synthetic appreciation of the accumulated knowledge of specialized disciplines. It "combines the abstract symbolism of mathematics with the experimental character of the natural sciences."[36] He conceded, however, that since all natural phenomena cannot be treated on the same level of generality, the scope and nature of the procedure varies from science to science.

Tektology's alleged universality obtains from its embrace of the entire world of lived experience, for it assumes that the organization of human experience reflects the organization of the universe—that human thought is as tektological as the rest of nature. It is empirical inasmuch as it considers human experience the only source of scientific knowledge. Yet it is primarily a sociohistorical science, for human society and the exercise of practical reason is the central problem of emancipatory scientific inquiry. Thus, Bogdanov's main goal was to formulate a metascience of praxis that would guide the architectonic process of institutional building and that with practical reason would promote societal coherence and prevent cataclysmic change in any of life's major processes. As a Marxist he believed this to be possible only under a system of collective labor and collectivized means of production, but he also believed that Marx's praxiology had to be updated by means of contemporary scientific and organizational discoveries, but no less the advance of culture in the broad sense.

The complex theory of organization, which he devised and revised in the 1910s, has often been cited as an early version of cybernetics and a transition from the reductionism of both mechanicalism and social energetics to systems thinking.[37] It is a monistic systems theoretical approach inasmuch as it assumes the operation of the analogous structural principles at every level of reality. This distinguishes it from dialectical materialism, which, according to Bogdanov, is a "non-monistic" theory, insofar as it claims that nature and society are qualitatively different realities governed by different sets of laws.

Tektology may be understood as the synthesis of two convergent and ostensibly complementary lines of thought: one, methodological, the other, philosophical. The methodological approach attempts to understand complex systems from static, dynamic, and dialectical perspectives. It considers organic and social systems from the viewpoint of homeostasis and dynamic equilibria. Tektology moreover tries to explain morphotransformation—sudden structural and functional change—in nature and society.

The theory of dynamic equilibrium, which Bogdanov proposed as early as 1899, caused him to adopt a different dialectic from that of Marx and Engels.

Marx, in expounding his theory of reproduction, used the term *equilibrium*, but in doing so noted that although commodity production created the possibility for a normal course of reproduction on both a simple and expanded scale, "these conditions turned into an equal number of possibilities for crisis, since on the basis of the spontaneous pattern of this production, this equilibrium is itself an accident."[38] In Bogdanov's dialectic, a system's assimilation and disassimilation of energy (metabolism) create contradictions between the system and its environment. These contradictions disturb the relative equilibrium of the system and disappear only when a new equilibrium is achieved. The new equilibrium, however, need not necessarily be the result of "the struggle of opposites," as maintained by Marx, Engels, and Lenin. Such an equilibrium can often be attained in social organizations through the cooperation of its members.

In developing his concept of Tektology, Bogdanov tried to find through metaphors and models the organizational principles that would unite under one paradigmatic scheme "the most disparate phenomena" in the organic and inorganic worlds. Tektology, to Bogdanov, was a metascience both of nature and of society, a unifying monism that would allow human beings torn apart by strife to find a common language. And, since the sources of strife were larger than the merely economic, the common language must be larger than traditional Marxism, although it would include Marxism as a special case. It was a metascience of praxis.

For Bogdanov, Tektology represents a metascience of praxis, a further elaboration of the Marxian philosophy of praxis. It is of importance to note that from Bogdanov's conceptualization of Tektology there emerged an understanding of hierarchical systems and finalities as well as corresponding cybernetic categories of analysis in its holistic construction. Implicit in Bogdanov's analysis is an integrative and dynamic model, a model that has only in the last decade come to the attention of economic analysts.[39] His willfully repressed contribution was a major advance in the emerging concept of cybernetic economic analysis and modern coevolutionary political economy.

Dimensions in Tektology

While philosophy had been Bogdanov's greatest intellectual interest prior to 1910, his concern shifted thereafter to science. The last eighteen years of his career in print were devoted primarily to the study of the "science" of organization. It was in this area that he was at his most ambitious and original. The years 1913 to 1922 saw the appearance of three volumes attempting to create a "universal science of organization." Bogdanov viewed this synthesis construction as the science of sciences—a "metascience"—demanded by the development of automated production and the rise of the proletariat.[40] One may assume that the theory of Tektology, on which Bogdanov worked while writing a recondite work of science fiction, *Engineer Menni*, was envisioned as a tool for the organization not only of science (as a kind of metascience) but also for the organization and solution of human problems as raised by rapid scientific, technical, technological, and informational advances. Jensen writes that Bogdanov anticipated that the science of Tektology would facilitate the analysis of divisive problems, but he had not yet reached the point in his thought where he could feel confident that it would.[41]

Bello remarks that in Tektology—organization—scientific and social aspects of reality and philosophy are basically identical.[42] Bogdanov's position was that while traditional science had discovered the organizational character of nature, it lacked the necessary amplitude to deal with the whole of reality. The organizational experience of the bourgeois world was reductionist. For Bogdanov it reflected and was reinforced by a bourgeois science that was the product of thei Industrial Revolution and the division of labor. The diversification of sciences was, for Bogdanov, the necessary outcome. Specialization is convenient when it is moderate; it had produced and still produces numerous advances. However, many undesirable effects are also produced: inconsistency and complexity in the use of language, divergence of methods, etc. For Bogdanov, the culminating point in the struggle involving analysis-synthesis, or specialization-organization, could be reached in the proletarian society; therein a unity of scientific knowledge could be achieved.

The "universal organizational science" was not widely acclaimed in itself. Nonetheless, from 1922 to Bogdanov's death, work after work on organizational science appeared. As late as 1926, Bogdanov showed an optimism for the project that could have only come from significant support among Soviet intellectuals. Later his work on organization came to be praised as an important beginning to Russian research in cybernetics.[43]

The culmination of Bogdanov's philosophical work was his *The Universal Science of Organization: Tektology*. The first part of this work appeared in 1912 in St. Petersburg. With the February 1917 Revolution in Russia and its potential for an enormous transformation of society, Bogdanov declared, "The time for Tektology has come."[44] In 1922, a complete Russian edition in three volumes was published in Berlin. Also in Berlin, two volumes of a German edition appeared in 1926 and 1928.

Gorelik has commented that little is known about Tektology in the Western world. Even such authoritative and related works on the subject as Ludwig von Bertalanffy's *General Systems Theory*, and in particular, the section of that book dealing with the "History of Systems Theory," make no reference to Bogdanov and his Tektology. Because of its historical value and its continued relevance to contemporary critical thought, Bogdanov's Tektology can no longer be ignored and omitted through ignorance from the world literature on the subject of organization theory and systems,[45] nor can its contribution to the paradigmatic challenge to political economy be ignored.[46]

In this connection, Takhazhdian makes it clear that Bogdanov was not the first to venture down this pathway. Blauberg augurs that there is incontrovertible evidence that Bogdanov was following a tradition other than merely that of the Narodniks. Takhazhdian writes that:

> An interest in evolving the general principles of systems and structural research may well be called a major tradition in Soviet science. The literature on the subject has dealt in sufficient detail with the fundamental features of A. Bogdanov's Tektology, in which an attempt was made to formulate the general structural principles of organization.[47]

Among Bogdanov's forerunners were N. Belov and E. Fyodorov. Takhazhdian records that, in an article published in 1911, Belov, physician and physiologist, formulated the principle of negative feedback.[48] Moreover, Takhazhdian notes that Bogdanov was the first to indicate the close kinship between that discovery and the idea of cybernetics. Belov set forth his circular causal relation as follows: "The mechanism of the organism is probably based on principles of reverse structure. That principle can be explained as follows: all organs and tissues are in such an interrelation that if organ or tissue A affects organ or tissue B enhancing its life activity, it then affects A in return."[49]

Characteristically, according to Takhazhdian, this kind of interaction, which Belov called "parallel-intersecting," was not considered by him as pertaining to physiology alone, but as a manifestation of a general law—"the law of closed spaces"—operating in the sphere of mechanical, physical, chemical, biological, and other phenomena, a universal law for all organized natural formations. Takhazhdian further remarks:

> What is most important to us is the fact that, in evolving the principle of negative feedback, he proceeded from the idea of the organism as a dynamic integral system in which all organic functions are so closely intertwined that any change in one of them leads of necessity to a change in others, those changes being controlled by a definite mechanism which allows the organism as a whole to maintain its existence in conditions of a non-stable environment.
>
> The organism lives in constant conditions of an equilibrium of little stability. Therein lies its salvation. If the equilibrium were stable, i.e., if the organism always functioned within one and the same condition, it could not adapt itself with the necessary ease to the introduction of an exohoromone or in general to changes in the environment. These external variety would upset the internal stable equilibrium and the organism could perish. The presence of equilibrium and of a constant balancing enables the organism to adapt itself to new phenomena.[50]

The Russian crystallographer E. Fyodorov has been characterized by Takhazhdian as yet another precursor of Bogdanov's Tektology. In particular, Takhazhdian notes that Fyodorov speculated on the universality of Le Chatelier's principle. In Fyodorov's opinion that principle reveals the "general mechanism of counteraction to external influences," whose operation can be seen not only in the sphere of physical chemistry but also in all other fields of reality, including biology and psychical and social phenomena.

In Fyodorov's opinion:

> The general line of perfection in nature does not coincide with enhanced adaptability. Thus, life-stability is linked not with adaptability but with the capacity for adaptation. This is an expression of the law of perfectionism in biology, which characterizes the dynamic aspect of life phenomena. A more detailed formulation of this law runs as follows: The future belongs to what is less orderly but possesses that which in the highest degree ensures greater orderliness, i.e., is marked by life mobility. At any given moment, these elements are suppressed by orderly and adapted elements. In life, however, there takes place a constant process of the destruction of the latter and the advancement of the mobile elements of new and superior orderliness which, under the pressure of progressive life, perish in their turn, yielding place to even higher orderliness.[51]

This understanding, though apparent in Bogdanov's theory of equilibrium and later in Bukharin's adaptation thereof, was years later identified in the works of Norbert Wiener.[52] Wiener wrote that:

> We have ... seen that certain organisms, such as man, tend for a time to maintain and often even to increase the level of their organization, as a local enclave in the general stream of increasing entropy, of increasing chaos and de-differentiation. Life is an island here and now in a dying world. The process by which we living beings resist the general stream of corruption and decay is known as homeostasis ... [a system of] negative feedback mechanisms that we may find exemplified in mechanical automata.
> It is the pattern maintained by this homeostasis, which is the touchstone of our personal identity.... We are but whirlpools in a river of ever-flowing water. We are not stuff that abides, but patterns that perpetuate themselves.[53]

The bold attempt by Bogdanov "to gather together and harmoniously integrate the fragmented organizational experience of mankind"[54] has a strong appeal to contemporary theorists and philosophers who seek to unify scientific thought.[55] The need for a synthesis stems primarily from the growing attempts to tackle problems whose solutions lie within different and often far removed fields of specialization. The attempt by Bogdanov to provide just such a synthesis, therefore, should attract more than passing attention from contemporary system theorists.[56]

As a physician and a political theorist, Bogdanov was struck by the systemic analogies between living systems and social systems, between scientific and social organizations and processes. His principal objective was the theorization of a metascience of organization that would permit regulative mechanisms to preserve stability and prevent cataclysmic change in any of life's major processes—including the livelihood of man, i.e., the economic process.

In developing his concept of Tektology Bogdanov tried to find through structural analogies and models the organizational principles that would unite under one conceptual scheme "the most disparate phenomena" in the organic and inorganic worlds.[57] Vucinich asserts that in Bogdanov's usage Tektology is a metascience dealing with processes that regulate the organization of all systems of natural and social phenomena.

Bogdanov contended that all the universal aspects of both society and nature can be revealed by studying the laws of organization. As conceived tektologically, the organizational approach is both structural and functional. Its object of analysis is both the physical world and the world of ideas. It is structural, for all systems are systemic—that is, they have structures—it relies on a structural view of natural and social systems; it considers a natural or social system as fundamentally irreducible. According to Bogdanov, the more a system differs from the sum total of its component parts, the higher is the level of its organization. He asserts that there are a priori structures of transcendental subjectivity that can be apodictically known—structures of transcendental subjectivity that ground both our scientific objective knowledge and the pregiven *Lebenswelt* of everyday experience. Structuralism can also be understood in a wider sense as an approach to social explanation that has methodological, sociological, and historical dimensions, all of which logically and conceptually reinforce each other. This reinforcement is a crucial component in making possible scientific explanation. Systems were to be studied as synchronic structures, as a unity whose individual parts function relationally. The organizational approach is functional inasmuch as it is concerned with continuous changes of an adaptive and selective nature. Tektology studies not only the differentiation and convergence of existing forms but also the forces contributing to the maintenance of intra- and inter-system equilibria. Bogdanov stresses "moving equilibrium" as an area of inquiry in which the structural and functional aspects of organization are only two different sides of the same reality.[58] His mechanism of organization is dominated by "motion" and equilibrium; while orthodox Marxists treat equilibria as specific states of motion, Bogdanov views motion as a specific expression of equilibrium.[59]

For Bogdanov, general organizational theory or Tektology was a unifying concept that would allow human beings torn apart by strife to find a common language.[60] There is in Tektology a reorientation of thought on the introduction of the concept of "system" as the center of a new scientific paradigm (in contrast to the analytic, mechanistic, linear-causal paradigm of political economy). As with many scientific theories of broad scope, Tektology has its metascientific or epistemological aspects. The concept of organization or system constitutes a new paradigm, or a "new philosophy of nature," contrasting with the social Darwinian "blind laws of nature" of the mechanistic paradigm.

Bogdanov called for the application of "bi-regulation" and a degree of organization in his "universal organizational science." This would embrace the biological and social worlds in the way in which mathematics permitted the formalization of classical mechanics.[61] Bogdanov expanded on this when he wrote:

> It is easy to note that there is a special correlation and a deep kinship between mathematics and Tektology. The laws of mathematics do not refer to this or that field of the phenomena of nature, as laws of other special sciences do, but to all and any phenomena, and only from the point of view of their magnitudes; it is, in its own way as universal as Tektology.[62]

The main objective of Tektology, therefore, is to systematize the fragmented knowledge of organizational methods acquired by man in various fields of human endeavor so that these can be studied and developed in a planned fashion. For Bogdanov:

> Tektology must clarify the modes of organization that are perceived to exist in nature and human activity; then it must generalize and systematize these modes; further it must explain them, that is, propose abstract schemes of their tendencies and laws; finally, based on these schemes, determine the direction of organizational methods and their role in the universal process. This general plan is similar to the plan of any natural science; but the objective of Tektology is basically different. Tektology deals with organizational experiences not of this or that specialized field, but all of these fields together. In other words, Tektology embraces the subject matter of all the other sciences and of all the human experience giving rise to these sciences, but only from the aspect of method, that is, it is interested only in the modes of organization of this subject matter.[63]

All objects that exist, he wrote, can be distinguished in terms of the degree of their organization. Consequently, the key to understanding the world is organizational analysis. For "no matter how different the various elements of the universe—electrons, atoms, things, people, ideas, planets, stars—and regardless of the considerable differences in their combinations, it is possible to establish a small number of general methods by which any of these elements joins with another."[64] Together these concepts of organization, according to Bogdanov, are applicable to all systems wherever they appear in nature or society.

Bogdanov wrote:

> If organizational methods were different in different fields, if, for example, the organization of things, that is technology, had little in common with the methods or organization of people, that is, economic or the organization of experience, that is, the universe of ideas, then mastery over them would not be facilitated by a mere labeling of all of them as organizational. It is quite a different story, if after investigation it turns out that it is possible to establish between them a connection, kinship, and place them under common laws. Then the study of that connection and those laws would permit man to gain mastery over those methods and to develop them in a planned fashion; such a

study would become one of the most powerful instruments of any practice or theory.⁶⁵

In line with his concept of universality of the organizing factor, Bogdanov also argued, among other things, that: (1) Ideology is nothing more than an instrument for organizing social consciousness, and "truth" is an organized form of individual and social experience. The facticity of something is, thus, socially conditioned and therefore admits institutionally fashioned possibilities. (2) Phenomenologically, the existence of social classes is not due to the distribution of ownership rights in society but arises because of the possession of organizational experience by individuals in a given society. Thus, the ruling class in a social system is composed of organizers of production who are not necessarily the owners of the means of production. Committed to the Narodnik principle of going-to-the-people, for Bogdanov the elimination of social-class distinctions could be brought about through the education of society in organizational skills.

In connection with this last point a contemporary context is provided by the hotly debated issue of the efficacy of privatization, for instance, in the former Eastern Bloc economies and in the former Soviet Union. It is, moreover, of analytical interest for those engaged in the increasingly elaborated Coasian hierarchy versus market dialogue.⁶⁶

Tektology: Basic Concepts and Methods

Basically, Bogdanov's world is that of structural-functional changes. Retaining vestiges of Ostwald's social energetics, Bogdanov indicated that in this world only the differences in energy tensions result in changes and reactions; only these differences have a practical meaning. Therefore, activities (actions, forces), resistances (reactions) to these activities, and their various combinations are the primary elements of Tektology. The notions of activity and resistance are not independent but are mutually related concepts. The strength of resistance, for example, cannot be determined without reference to the opposing activities. Such a determination can be made only in terms of the "quantity of energy" that must be expended by the opposing activities to overcome the resistance in question. The combinations of actions and reactions result in three basic types of complexes (systems): organized, disorganized, and neutral.

Although the concept of organization replaced that of energy in Bogdanov's system, it absorbed the function performed thereby and sustained an interest in establishing the unity of all aspects of nature and human activity, or, in the metaphor that Bogdanov repeated in *Tektology*, "to fill the chasms between animate and inanimate nature."⁶⁷

Reasserting the original Aristotelian systems problem,⁶⁸ Bogdanov noted that entities on higher levels of organization possess properties that are greater than the sum of their parts. An organized complex, or a system, is defined as a complex in which the whole is greater than the sum of its parts. This does not happen "because new activities are created by a combination of existing activities, but because the activities on hand are combined more successfully than the resistances opposing these actions."[69] Disorganized complexes are complexes where the whole, in practice, is smaller than the sum of the parts. Neutral complexes are complexes characterized by the equality of organizing and disorganizing activities.[70] "All human activity is organizing or disorganizing. This means that any human activity, whether it is technical, social, cognitive or artistic, can be considered as some material of organizational experience and be explored from the organizational point of view."[71]

All phenomena and human activity, then, can be profitably studied from this point of view. Tektology calls for the study of "any system from the point of view of both the relationships among all of its parts and the relationship between it as a whole and its environment, i.e., all external systems."[72]

Bogdanov holds that in order to comprehend the creative and destructive forces in nature and society it is necessary to understand the mechanisms of creation, regulation, and destruction of systems. For him the "mechanical side of life" is simply all that has been explained. "Mechanism . . . is nothing more than understood and explained organization."[73] Organization, as a universal attribute of nature and society, operates, according to Bogdanov's Tektology, through regulative and formative mechanisms.

Tektology and the Formulating Mechanism

In all his activities man basically joins and separates some elements on hand. The act of joining always precedes the act of separation. "Therefore, the primary moment of begetting changes, appearance, destruction, and development of organizational forms, or the base of formulating tektological mechanism is the joining of complexes."[74] Bogdanov denotes this by the term *conjunction*. The ubiquity of conjunction can be observed everywhere. "It is cooperation and any other social contact, for example, speech and connection of concepts into ideas, and the meeting of images and aspirations in the field of consciousness, and the fusion of metals and electrical discharge between two bodies, and an exchange of goods between enterprises."[75]

The results of conjunction can be tektologically different. At one extreme, activities of one complex may be combined with synergetic activities of another complex in complete cooperation. At the other extreme, the activities of one complex may be totally opposed to the activities of another complex. In normal situations, complexes fall between these two extremes and are combined in such a way that their activities partially join and partially oppose one another. The result of the combination of specific activities or resistances accompanying conjunction, Bogdanov calls the *analytical sum*. Normally, some organizational activities are wasted in structured complexes forming a part of a chain connection, which he denotes by the term *linkage*. The creation of common links and linkages in complexes is accomplished by means of "ingression," that is, insertion of facilitating devices between any two complexes that are united. Ingression is a general form of a chain connection; it is, Bogdanov argues, inherent in all organizational processes. Gorelik writes that:

> "Ingression," the exchange of elements between interacting complexes, is the mechanism involved in the creation of systems. Established systems are "regulated" by various universal forms of selection. These forms also explain the stability of systems, their convergencies and divergencies, differentiation and integration, and their structural transformations.[76]

For the basic form of disorganization, Bogdanov uses the term *disingression* the meaning of which is opposite to that of ingression. He describes the operation of ingression and disingression in the following way:

> In ingression, activities, which were not previously connected, are joined together in such a way as to create a linkage of connecting complexes. In disingression, these activities mutually paralyze one another, leading to the appearance of a "boundary," that is, separateness. Until these activities are completely paralyzed, the boundary does not exist: the complexes are in a state of partial disingression. Disingression is always admixed with some ingression since there cannot be any conjunction of complexes without some expenditure of effort in the form of mutual resistances.[77]

A breach in tektological boundaries between any two complexes generally is the start of conjunction—that is, creation of new systems. Bogdanov calls this breach an organizational crisis of a given complex. In some respects his formulation corresponds to a theory of organizational change through functional differentiation, which in turn corresponds to an autopoietic reconstruction of a system, which admits the possibility of a quantum transformation. He also distinguishes between two types of crises:

(1) "Crisis C," or conjunctive crisis, arising out of a breach in existing tektological boundaries and leading to the creation of new systems, transformations, appearance of new links, partial or full disingression; and

(2) "Crisis D," or disjunctive crisis, which leads to the creation of new tektological boundaries.[78]

Anticipating the relatively recent neofunctionalist literature on homeostatic analysis, Bogdanov argued that an organizational crisis manifests itself in a breach of the existing systemic equilibrium and at the same time constitutes a process of organizational transition to a new equilibrium. In sum, therefore, "conjunctive, ingression, linkage, disingression, boundary, and crises C and D, these are the basic concepts for formulating tektological mechanisms."[79]

In tracing the origins of World War I, Bogdanov offered a combination of "conventional" Marxist appreciations and a number of prescient remarks. From the conventional view he held that the war erupted as a result of an explosive combination of the "struggle of monopolies" and the "competitive progress of armaments." Capitalists, in an effort to save themselves, wrote Bogdanov, adopt an increasingly reactionary ideology, combining nationalism, clericalism, and militarism.[80] However, from his theory of Tektology, he was led to a kind of modified Hilferding insight in which the military industry, strongly encouraged by finance capital, provided a defense of the international markets and formed a "colossal supplementary market" in order to avert internal crisis. Heavy industry benefited by this turn of events, expanding its share in the economy, "and together with it, the influence of corresponding groups of capitalists in the politics of the governments," thereby accelerating the growth of militarism. This expansion of what might be called a military-industrial complex explained, from Bogdanov's point of view, why the latest crisis of capitalism took the form of war. Previously, such crises were peaceful, because they were largely the result of the overproduction of commodities. Now, however, the situation could be described only as "a system of armed peace." The world war was a "crisis of overproduction, not only of things but also of organized human forces—organized precisely in the form of militarism peculiar to that society."[81]

Lenin, as you will recall, seized on Ludendorf's German wartime economy as an example of the most advanced stage of capitalism. During the war, state intervention in the economy increased enormously, with certain sectors falling directly under state control. To Lenin, this intervention meant the emergence of "state capitalism" on the world scene, its "most concrete example" to be found in Germany. Among the positive features he perceived were "large-scale capitalist engineering" and "planned state organization" of the German economy.[82] "State monopoly," claimed Lenin, "is a complete material preparation for socialism, the threshold of socialism, a rung on the ladder of history between which and the rung called socialism there are no intermediate rungs."[83]

Lenin's concept of state capitalism was, to some extent, grounded on Rudolf Hilferding's earlier analysis. Hilferding sought to address the ambiguities that attach to state capitalism and wrote:

> Once the state becomes the exclusive owner of all means of production, the functioning of a capitalist economy is rendered impossible by destruction of the mechanism which keeps the life-blood of such a system circulating. A capitalist economy is a market economy. Prices, which result from competition among capitalist owners (it is this competition that "in the last instance" gives rise to the law of value), determine what and how much is produced, what fraction of the profit is accumulated, and in what particular branches of production this accumulation occurs. They also determine how in an economy that has to overcome crises again and again, proportionate relations among various branches of production are reestablished whether in the case of simple or expanded reproduction.[84]

After the war, Bogdanov conceded that the role of the state seemed more permanent than he had envisaged. He maintained that it was still "an open question" whether state capitalism was the highest form of capitalism.[85]

Tektology and the Regulating Mechanism

Next, Bogdanov considers questions concerning the Spencerian "fate of forms which have appeared—their preservation, consolidation, diffusion or their decline and destruction,"[86] that is, questions of the regulating tektological mechanism.[87] At the base of the regulating mechanism lies the general concept of selection—natural and artificial. Artificial selection corresponds to culturally mediated and specifically institutional norms. In general, the regulative mechanism accounts for the maintenance or preservation of the stability of such systems as a social class, an organism, or a planet. It also helps maintain the continuity of natural and social development and avoids cataclysmic changes.[88] Selection, the most universal tool of the regulative mechanism, is subject to growing specialization in both nature and society. One of the basic tasks of Tektology is to reduce the multitude of selective processes to a small number of fundamental categories.

In the scheme of selection, there are three components: the object of selection, the act of selection, and the criteria of selection. Selection is "conservative" when it produces "static results," which contribute to the maintenance of a "stable equilibrium." It is "progressive" when it produces "dynamic results," which evoke changes in the existing—or bring forth new—organizational forces. It is "positive" when it leads to a greater heterogeneity of elements and an increased complexity of internal relations; and it is "negative" when it leads to a growing homogeneity of elements and reduced complexity of ties between them.[89]

Bogdanov wrote that: "In the industrial capitalistic system of production under conditions of positive selection so-called 'prosperity' has created definite properties; these properties are sharply replaced by others with the approach of an 'industrial crisis,' and the sign of selection . . . becomes negative."[90]

Living systems and automatic machines are dynamically structured complexes in which "bi-regulators" provide for the maintenance of order.[91] Commentators on Bogdanov, such as Jensen and Susiluoto, have pointed repeatedly to the apparent prefiguring here of the concept of cybernetic feedback.[92] Bogdanov considered the "law of disingression" to have "tremendous practical and theoretical significance." He believed it showed that ideas, norms, and political institutions, all "disingressive complexes for the stable organization of vital activities of society," have an in-built tendency toward rigidity, or ossification. Although internal changes are important for the evolution of a system, Bogdanov maintained, the real impetus for change comes from the environment, which affects both the internal structure of the system and the relationship between it and the environment. At the same time, each disturbance of the equilibrium creates pressure to establish a new equilibrium. Bogdanov's was a homeostatic open system—a single-looped or first-order system—with a moving or dynamic equilibrium and a bi-regulator—a double-looped or second-order system—to provide for the adaptive maintenance of order.[93] In Bogdanov's words, "The bi-regulator is a system for which there is no need of an external regulator; the system regulates itself."[94]

Bogdanov's conception of equilibrium was a central one. In the context of the economic process it *did not* refer to the temporary equality of supply and demand but was employed in the context of the Marxian model of reproduction to indicate conditions under which reproduction could be sustained. This is a far cry from the concept of equilibrium found among mainstream economic texts. In the first place equilibrium is treated as a condition for the normal organization of distribution and exchange for different social formations. "Exchange by the value of labor is the norm of living equilibrium," he wrote in *Essays in Tektology*. This norm in commodity production acts "only as a spontaneous tendency" brought about with constant infractions and only in "the epoch of collectivism becomes the principle of the scientific and conscious organization of society." The necessity of an equilibrium is regarded as critical for sustainable proportionality in the economy, and, in this regard, the basic difference in the mechanism for achieving equilibrium is emphasized—whereas under capitalism it is attained through spontaneous fluctuations, under the conditions of a collectivist regime it obtains from the planned organization of the economy.

Bogdanov's Counterpart: Nikolai Bukharin

Whereas Bogdanov emphasized organizational concepts and rejected the narrow interpretation of dialectical materialism, Bukharin sought to reconcile the Bogdanovian concept of equilibrium with the dialectics of Marx and Engels. Indeed, according to Prat, Bukharin took from Bogdanov the theory of equilibrium.[95] Bukharin had used the concepts of regulation and equilibrium in his critique of the marginal utility school. But it was only in the *Theory of Historical Materialism* that he justified his theory of equilibrium from a Marxist standpoint. Let us punctuate our presentation of Bogdanov's thought and turn to his counterpart Nikolai I. Bukharin.

Bukharin followed the acrimonious philosophical dispute between Lenin and Bogdanov from Moscow (Lenin and Bogdanov were in exile in Europe). That he was Bogdanovian in spirit was not surprising. His work *Economics of the Transition Period*, and more particularly *Historical Materialism*, showed Bogdanov's enduring influence on his intellectual development. Alongside Bogdanov, Bukharin has also been regarded as one of the founders of systems thinking, though there are a variety of opinions concerning the philosophical and epistemological positions of the two.[96] Bukharin was not, however, a sycophantic disciple, as his party enemies were to argue. Though he admired and was influenced by Bogdanov's creative capacity within the framework of Marxist ideas, he accepted with reservation some of the older theorist's phenomenological arguments. Theirs was a similarity of intellectual temperament.[97] Like Bogdanov, the mature Bukharin was a "seeking Marxist," refusing to regard Marxism as a closed, immutable doctrine and Marx as an Old Testament prophet. He was alert both to its inadequacies and to the accomplishments of rival thought. Both scholars regarded Marxism as an open-ended body of thought, vulnerable and receptive to new intellectual currents. Both believed it legitimate to refer to the work of non-Marxists. Bogdanov's declaration, "The tradition of Marx-Engels must be dear to us not in its letter but in its spirit," was echoed by Bukharin on page 1 of the preface to *Historical Materialism*. "It would be strange," he wrote, "if Marxist theory eternally stood still."

In his remarks on Bukharin's *Historical Materialism*, Lenin repeatedly reacted critically to borrowings of the tektological vocabulary, calling it "organizational gibberish." Indeed, still reveling in the possibility of a worldwide socialist revolution, Bukharin thought it possible to take over Tektology as a metascience of methods for organizing that new world. He concluded that with its adoption the barrier between the natural and the social sciences would be abolished. However, distinct from Bogdanov's reference image, Bukharin was tinged with positivism, for he asserted that in both nature and society, causality was subject to similar sets of objective laws over which we could not exercise our will.[98] It was his subscription to tektological terminology that Lenin considered to be the reason for the allegedly idealistic mistakes Bukharin made in his work. Nonetheless, Lenin seems to have been favorably disposed to *Historical Materialism* and referred to it as an excellent work.

Upon Bukharin, Lenin conferred the sobriquet "the darling of the Party." "I wish to say a few words about Bukharin," wrote Lenin. "He is in my opinion, the most outstanding [figure] . . . and the following must be borne in mind about [him]: Bukharin is not only a most valuable and major theorist of the party; he is also rightly considered the favorite of the whole party, but his theoretical views can be classified as fully Marxist only with great reserve, for there is something scholastic about him (he has never made a study of dialectics, and, I think, never fully understood it).''[99] With characteristic maliciousness, Stalin pointed out that Bukharin's theory of equilibrium had nothing to do with Marxism.

In what is widely regarded as his major work, *Historical Materialism*, Bukharin assured his readers in the introductory pages that though he intended to depart from the usual treatment of the subject, he remained faithful to the tradition of the most orthodox, materialist, and revolutionary understanding of Marx. Like Bogdanov, however, he sought to systematize and to introduce "innovations" into Marxist tenets. Both he and Bogdanov attempted to reconcile Marxism with scientific advances of the period. But whereas Bogdanov sought to revise Marxism initially on the basis of social energetics, and later on the basis of his general theory of organization, Bukharin sought to modernize it in light of the achievements of Western sociology.

Cohen, repeating the injunctions hurled against Bukharin, writes that Bukharin subscribed to a "mechanistic understanding of Marxist dialectics," which he located within the context of his general theory of equilibrium.[100] According to Bukharin, the theory of equilibrium was a general "formulation of the laws of motion of material systems."[101] While historical materialism "is not political economy, nor is it history; it is the general theory of society and the laws of its evolution, i.e., sociology."[102]

As we earlier noted, Marx was convinced that having overthrown Hegel's metaphysical understanding, he had rendered dialectics rigorously materialistic and consequently confined himself to its application to history. Engels took it upon himself to extend and systematize a nuanced variant of the dialectic in history, nature, and human thought. He attempted this in *Anti-Dühring* and in *Dialectics of Nature*, and in so doing he laid the groundwork for an universalistic doctrine of dialectical materialism.[103] However, according to Cohen, Bukharin turned his back on Engels's interpretation by stating that Marx and Engels "liberated the dialectic from its mystic husk in action," but it retains "the teleological flavor inevitably connected with the Hegelian formulation, which rests on the self-movement of 'Spirit.'"[104]

For Bukharin all that remained was to give a "theoretical-systematic exposition" of the dialectical method. "This," he believed, was "given by the theory of equilibrium."[105] Bukharin felt he analyzed equilibrium in a dialectical way and referred to the process of development as occasioned by "first, the state of equilibrium, second, the disruption of this equilibrium, third, the restoration of the equilibrium on a new basis. Then the story is repeated from the beginning. As a whole what we have here is the process of movement, the basis of which is the development of internal contradictions."[106]

At the heart of *Historical Materialism* is his contention that dialectics and social change are explained by equilibrium theory. Accordingly, the dialectic (or dynamic) point of view, is that all things, material and social, are in motion and that motion derives from internal conflict or contradiction. Within this context it was conjectured that any system, again material or social, tends toward a state of equilibrium (analogous to adaptation in biology).[107]

> In other words, the world consists of forces, acting in many ways, opposing each other. These forces are balanced for a moment in exceptional cases only. We then have a state of "rest," i.e., their actual "conflict" is concealed. But if we change only one of these forces, immediately the "internal contradictions" will be revealed, equilibrium will be disturbed, and if a new equilibrium is again established, it well be on a new basis, i.e., with a new combination of forces, etc. It follows that the "conflict," the "contradiction," i.e., the antagonism of forces acting in various directions, determines the motion of the system.[108]

According to Bukharin, Heraclitus, in ancient times, and Hegel, in the modern epoch, argue not only that there is in the world constant motion, constant change, but also that "changes are produced by constant internal contradictions, internal struggle."[109] By locating the source of motion in the conflict of forces and not in "self-development," Bukharin believed that he had purged Hegel's triad of its idealist elements.

The exhibition of Hegelian dialectics in terms of equilibrium was pivotal to Bukharin's analysis. Bogdanov, however, regarded the attempt to present Hegel's triad within the auspices of equilibrium as methodologically doubtful. Some ten years prior to Bukharin's equilibrium-centered revision of Hegel's thought, Bogdanov wrote:

> As to the logic of denial which forms triads, it is suitable in total only for dialectics of idealistic concepts, but not for the real dialectics of the universe. The suitability of the "triads" to many real phenomena is the result of their application to selected experiences: when attention is devoted to the moment when this struggle has ended, a formal similarity between these two stages of equilibrium is inevitably obtained, and the intervening period of struggle can even be arbitrarily called a period of negation.[110]

Every system, Bukharin argued, is involved in two stages of equilibrium: internal and external. The first refers to the relationship between different components within a system, the second to the entire system in its relationship with its environment. In neither case is there ever an "absolute, unchanging equilibrium." It is always "in flux"—a dynamic or moving equilibrium. It is for this reason, parenthetically, that Bukharin's general theory of equilibrium is analogous to a theory of persistent nonequilibrium.

In common with Tektology, the "Theory of Historical Materialism" tendered the proposition that man belonged to nature. "[Society] is unthinkable without its environment," that is, nature. Society adapts itself to nature, strives toward equilibrium with it, by extracting energy from it through the process of production. The key to Bukharin's theory is the relationship between internal and external equilibrium: "The internal structure of the system must change together with the relation existing between the system and its environment."[111]

It becomes apparent that basic to Bukharin's philosophical outlook is the notion of interaction between the system and the environment:

> Any object—a stone, a living being, human society, etc.—can be taken as a whole, made up of parts (elements) connected one with the other. In other words, this whole can be seen as a system. And no system exists in a vacuum; it is surrounded by other natural objects which, relative to it, can be called the environment.[112]

According to Bukharin, and following Bogdanov, "the internal (structural) equilibrium is a magnitude which depends on the external equilibrium (is a 'function' of this external equilibrium)."[113] Prat notes that this position was resolutely criticized in the USSR. It seemed to revise the dialectical materialist notion that the source of motion is to be found in internal contradictions. However, the counterpoising of "internal" and "external" contradiction assumes a philosophical position that contradicts the essentialist appreciation of dialectical materialism.[114]

The dialectic governing the production of surplus value described by Marxist economics emphasizes the struggle between labor and capitalists, economic classes defined by their relation to the means of production. Both capital and labor are produced within the economy, and so the dialectic governing the extraction of surplus value described by Marxist economists is confined to forces within the economy.[115] This goes to the very heart of the debate in Marxist agency theory of history.

An organizational and biophysical analysis of production complements the Marxist analysis of distribution because it allows researchers to include the environment in the dialectic governing the appropriation of surplus value.[116] Adding some degree of confusion to his own analysis, Marx disregarded the history-making energy and material flux throughout the economy and stated that the one-way flow of natural resources did not have a historical dimension:

> But just as in the beginning, the only participants in the labor-process were man and the earth, which latter exists independently of man, so even now we still employ in the process many means of production, provided directly by nature, that do not represent any combinations of natural substances with human labor. . . . [It] is the everlasting condition imposed on human existence, and therefore is independent of every social phase of its existence or rather is common to every such phase. It was therefore not necessary to represent our laborer in connection with other laborers: man and his labor on one side, Nature and its materials on the other suffices.[117]

Instead, a diachronic tektological analysis affirms nature's substantive role in the socioeconomic process. It is a dynamic factor in the dialectic governing the appropriation of surplus value.

It is worth noting that Bogdanov's dialectic incorporated biophysical elements, i.e., energy (as did Bukharin's), and only later organization. However, this dialectic was attacked on the basis of the principle that it was subject to forces of change external to the system in question. In other words, it was a nonessentialist, i.e., non-Marxian, dialectic.

Marx wrote:

> The simple circulation of commodities—selling in order to buy—is a means of carrying out a purpose unconnected with circulation, namely the appropriation of use-values, the satisfaction of wants. The circulation of money as capital is, on the contrary, an end in itself, for the expansion of values takes place only

within this constantly renewed movement. The circulation of capital has therefore no limits.[118]

The environment's role in economic production is part of the dialectic that governs the production of surplus value. As high levels of economic/entropic activity deplete high-quality fuels and other natural resources, fewer goods and services can be produced. This tends to intensify the struggle over surplus value.

Dialectic analysis focuses on the process of change instead of stasis. Change is the focus of analysis because a system contains important contradictions that prevent stable equilibria from emerging.

In *Historical Materialism*, Bukharin seems to have visualized the ultimate unity of science in a sort of Ostwaldian energetics, which, in the particular case of human society, would calculate the absorption of energy from nonhuman nature by the "living machines," and whose organization in society would be derived from their spatial distribution in the productive process.[119] This itself was determined by the "non-living machines" at which they labored.[120]

This theoretical reference image expresses Bukharin's conceptualization of historical materialism. It systematizes socioeconomic development. Socioeconomic equilibrium (homeostasis) is unceasingly being displaced and can be restored either by "a gradual adaptation of the various elements in the social whole (evolution)"; or by "violent upheaval (revolution)." Insofar as the envelope of homeostasis, primarily the relations of production, as embodied in the classes directly participating in production, is sufficiently broad and resilient, evolution occurs. In this manner capitalism allegedly progressed through its several historical stages. However, when the forces of production swell to a point where they come into conflict with "the fundamental web of these productive forces, i.e., property relations," revolution becomes a possibility admitting the possibility of a new envelope of production relations.[121]

Copleston comments that Bukharin used the language of dialectical materialism, speaking of, for example, "internal contradictions." He also asserted the dialectical law of the transformation of quantity into quality.[122] A process of gradual development or evolution is the preparation for a leap, a sudden change, which in human society takes the form of a revolution. The final phase of the dialectic was the theory of sudden changes. It was this phase that Bogdanov classified as "Crisis C": the conjunctive crisis.

Bukharin followed Hegel's analysis in *Wissenschaft der Logik* and Engels's assessment in *Anti-Dühring*.[123] Hegel wrote: "The alteration of existence involves not only a transition from one proportion to another, but also a transition, by a sudden leap, into a quantitatively, and, on the other hand, also qualitatively different thing; an interruption of the gradual process, differing qualitatively from the preceding, the former, state."[124]

Engels followed Hegel's lead: "According to [the law of the transformation of quantity into quality] all processes of development are punctuated by what Engels (following Hegel) called 'nodes,' at which change is both accelerated and deepened. Hegel and Engels used the illustration of the boiling and freezing of water."[125]

Both Hegel's and Engels's point of departure was a description of what has come to be known as the "Bernard Instability."[126] Engels greeted the theorem of the "nodal line" of quantitative relationships with enthusiasm, since this appeared to allow the real process to be conceived as simultaneously continuous and discrete.[127] On the basis of the preceding perspectives Bukharin added that the transformation of quantity into quality was one of the fundamental laws in the motion of matter: "[It] may be traced literally at every step both in nature and society."[128] Bukharin fortified his argument by referring to evidence of cataclysmic events in nature and mentioned De Vries's mutation theory. Departing from natural phenomena and pointing to the English Revolution, the French Revolution, and the Revolution of 1848, Bukharin remarks that revolution is a natural social phenomenon that "bourgeois scholars" attempt to deny. Bukharin quotes Plekhanov: "The violent changes presuppose a preceding evolution, and the gradual changes lead to violent changes. These are two necessary factors in a single process."[129]

It is of parenthetic interest to note that Bukharin, in his admonishment of "bourgeois scholars,"[130] remarks that insofar as Marx is perceived as an evolutionist, his views are respected.[131] However, insofar as Marx espouses revolutionary ideology, i.e., radical structural (institutional) transformations, Marxian theory is rejected.

Despite his albeit brief comments on cataclysmic transformation, according to his critics (notably Lenin), Bukharin did not understand the dialectical process of matter, the immanent character of matter that by its autodynamism is "self-actuating." He conceived the motion of an entity as resulting from an impulse coming from outside it. As with Bogdanov, it was on the basis of his understanding of dialectics that Bukharin's critics assailed him as an idealist, for it admitted the possibility of the theory of the "First Mover."

As a Marxist, Bukharin accented instances when social conflicts are in the foreground. However, like Bogdanov (and for that matter Goethe), he also understood that elements of harmony and "moments of cooperation" normally prevail.[132] Following Bogdanov's tektological concept of integration, he was convinced that conflict and struggle could be treated as an imbalance in the system.[133] However, it was only equating conflict with contradiction that allowed Bukharin to make the claim that Hegel himself could be presented as a theoretician of equilibrium: "Hegel observed this characteristic of motion and expressed it in the following manner: he called the original condition the thesis, the disturbance of equilibrium the antithesis, [and] the reestablishment of equilibrium."[134] The distinguishing characteristic of Bukharin's sociological theory and its practical implications was that equilibrium presupposes social harmony, while orthodox Marxism postulates social conflict.[135]

The aim of socialism, the development of and the emancipation of man, was the same as the self-realization of man in the process of production. This was a truth that Bukharin thought the left (Marxists) had neglected: "Preobrazhensky sees the contradictions but does not see the unity of the national economy, he sees the struggle but he does not see the collaboration." Social "unity" implied a significant degree of class harmony or collaboration, which for Bukharin meant that the proletariat and the peasantry were united in an economic collaboration in which even the new bourgeoisie could participate "within limits" and perform a "socially useful function."[136] Ostensibly, economic class collaboration prevailed over, or at least tempered, the disruptive aspects of class struggle.[137]

While Lenin was apparently favorably disposed to *Historical Materialism*, others were less generous. These others interpreted the theory of equilibrium idiosyncratically and suggested that it advocated equilibrium between the private-capitalist and socialist sectors of the Soviet national economy. For Preobrazhensky economic equilibrium and social equilibrium were incompatible. In their desire to ridicule Bogdanov's thought, Lenin's successors seized on the theory of equilibrium as a symbol of anti-Soviet activity: "This false 'theory of equilibrium' has been extensively used by the Trotskyites and right-wing restorationists in order to bolster their counter-revolutionary ideas."[138]

Stalin struck at the "theory of equilibrium," claiming it had the aim of supporting the individual peasant economy, of arming the kulak elements with a "new" theoretical weapon in their struggle against the collective farms and of discrediting the collective farms.[139]

The principal criticism of Bukharin's sociological theory and its political economic connotations was its functionalism: that homeostasis presupposes social harmony, while conventionally interpreted Marxism argues for the preponderance of social disharmony. Similar arguments may be found in Jürgen Habermas's recent criticisms of the structural-functionalist school of sociology. Western sociologists, who depart from the Parsonian systems approach, have argued that functionalism, with its homeostatic equilibrium concept, is unable to accommodate real endogenous change and therefore puts a premium on harmonious stability. They have suggested that equilibrium implies a normative (conservative) orientation, which regards disequilibrating elements as abnormal and pathological.

It is questionable whether Bukharin's theory of equilibrium really could account for endogenous change. In the last analysis, and as reflected in his treatment of technology, he made internal equilibrium dependent on the interrelations between society and nature. The impetus of pervasive change, technology, that which mediated between man and nature, was, however, made exogenous to the system.[140] According to Bukharin, it is the relation between a system, such as society, and its physical environment—an external contradiction—that is a decisive and basic factor.

Society is viewed "as a huge working mechanism, with many subdivisions of the divided social labor." Production relations are "the labor coordination of people (seen as 'living machines') in space and in time." He acknowledged that: "The productive forces determine social development because they express the interrelation between society ... and its environment. ... And the interrelation between environment and system is the quantity which determines, in the last analysis, the movement of any system."[141]

We may say of a system that it is in a state of equilibrium when it cannot of itself, i.e., without appropriating energy from its environment, emerge from this state. If forces are at work on a body, compensating each other, that body is in a state of equilibrium; an increase or decrease in one of these forces will disturb the equilibrium. Note that the forces involved are located outside of the system itself. This admits the possibility of a theory of history—a historical materialism —that departs from Marx's essentialism.

Tektology and the Theory of the Economy as a Metabolic System

The metaphoric appreciation, by Bogdanov, of the economic process as a form of metabolism and the economy as an open system, though consistent with a theme in Marx's *German Ideology* and *Capital*, was critically reinforced by his incorporation of thermodynamics. Bogdanov's contribution is a reference image only recently reconstructed in the literature. As we shall presently see, Bukharin also made a notable, though neglected, contribution to this very contemporary reference image.

By means of the selection mechanism, organizations—perceived by Bogdanov as open systems—disassimilate and assimilate low-entropy matter-energy from the environment and thus, in effect, are regulated by it. In cases where a relative equality exists between the two processes, there is a preservation of an organizational complex in the form of a dynamic equilibrium. For a continued preservation of a complex, however, a simple dynamic equilibrium is not sufficient. "Only growth in activities, preponderance of assimilation, that is growth of activities of a complex at the expense of its environment insures the preservation of that complex."[142]

Similarly, the dynamic element of disassimilation "can be represented as a diminution in the activities of a complex, their absorption by the environment."[143] The preponderance of assimilation over disassimilation is defined by Bogdanov as "positive progressive selection." The contrary situation—that is, preponderance of disassimilation over assimilation—is defined as "negative progressive selection."[144] Acts of selection consist of various processes of conjunction and disingression. The two processes occur in parallel. For example, positive progressive selection by some complex leads to the growth of its energies by assimilation of low entropy from the environment. The act of assimilation is a conjunctive act, but assimilated activities must be torn away from those complexes of the environment to which they belonged; tearing off presupposes disingression.

Ludwig von Bertalanffy years later provided the open-system steady-state analogy already explicit in Bogdanov's *Essays in Tektology*, writing: "We may ... summarize anabolic and catabolic processes as 'assimilation' and 'dissimilation,' respectively, and consider, as a first approximation, the steady state as a balance of 'assimilation' and 'dissimilation.' "[145]

Considering the role of positive and negative selection, it can be said that together they embrace the entire dynamics of this evolution:

> Positive selection by making a system more complex and increasing its variety supplies for it the ever-growing quantities of material from the environment; negative selection by simplifying the material, removing from it all that is volatile, discordant, antagonistic, introducing into its connections homogeneity and coordination, brings order and systematization to this material. Both these processes complement each other and spontaneously organize the universe.[146]

Bogdanov wrote that it follows that "the regulating mechanism of selection is not something separate from formulating tektological mechanisms, but only their definite combination."[147] There are definite limits to progressive selection. Bogdanov apprises that:

> The strength of an organization lies in precise coordination of its parts, in strict correspondence of various mutually connected functions. This coordination is maintained through constant growth in tektological variety, but not without bounds.... There comes a moment when the parts of the whole become too differentiated in their organization and their resistance to surrounding environment weakens. This leads sooner or later to disorganization.[148]

Systemic disorganization culminates in either of the two states: the complex in question disintegrates completely, or it changes in such a way that its preservation is provisionally assured. The latter is achieved by means of a process that Bogdanov calls "contra-differentiation of parts," meaning the reverse of systemic differentiation.[149] Contra-differentiation limits or completely removes disorganizing influences of systemic contradictions by creating new linkages through what Bogdanov describes as a conjunctive process of affected parts that thereby attenuates systemic collapse. At the base of this process again lie the mechanisms of selection. Positive selection, by making a system more complex and increasing its variety, produces for the system more material, i.e., low entropy, from the environment. Negative selection, by simplifying this material, removes from the system all that is discordant and noxious. Thus, both positive and negative selection play crucial roles in the preservation and development of organizational complexes.

Bukharin's Contribution to Open Systems Analysis

While bearing a resemblance to Bogdanov's, Bukharin's theory of equilibrium was also analytically similar to that of his contemporary A.J. Lotka, whose energy systems analysis for ecological systems depicted conditions of succession, climax, or the steady-state. In fact, Bukharin, in defining stable and unstable equilibria, specifically employed energy and ecological analogies together with the principle of conservation and feedback concepts. He then proceeded to generalize them.[150] Bukharin wrote:

> An existing society presumes "a certain equilibrium" between its three major social elements—things, persons, and ideas. This is internal equilibrium. But "society is unthinkable without its environment," which is nature. Society adapts itself to nature, strives toward equilibrium with it, by extracting energy from it. This is achieved through the process of social production. In the process of adaptation, society develops "an artificial system of organs," which Bukharin calls technology and which constitutes "a precise material indicator of the relation between society and nature." ... The productive forces determine social development because they express the inter-relation between society ... and its environment. ... And the inter-relation between environment and system is the quantity which determines, in the last analysis, the movement of any system.[151]

Bukharin formulated a metabolic and ecologically oriented theory of open-system dynamics, locating these propositions within the context of economic reproduction and his general theory of equilibrium. Similar to Ostwald's, but also W.S. Jevons's, proposition, Bukharin asserted that a society grew when it extracted more energy from nature than it put back in.[152] He wrote:

> Human society ... has had to abstract material energy from external nature; without these loans it could not exist. Society best adapts itself to nature by abstracting (and appropriating to itself) more energy from nature; only by increasing this quantity of energy does society succeed in growing. The ... abstraction of energy from nature is a material process. ... This material process of "metabolism" between society and nature is the fundamental relation between environment and system, between "external conditions" and human society.[153]

The basic theoretical elements for an "ecological Marxism" were present in such formulations between society and nature in terms of human ecology. Pointedly referring to economic reproduction, Bukharin noted:

> The metabolism between man and nature consists ... in the transfer of material energy from external nature to society; the expenditure of human energy (production) is an extraction of energy from nature, energy which is to be added to society (distribution of products between the members of society) and appropriated by society (consumption); this appropriation is the basis for further expenditure.[154]

However, Bukharin's system was characterized by dynamic equilibrium with a negative feedback and was one that could have stabilized its functioning at some lower level of energy consumption.[155] It becomes relatively clear that for Bukharin the role of feedback mechanisms is to regulate (in the sense of Bogdanov's "negative selection") the tendency toward disorganization. In other words, to produce a temporary and local reversal of the normal direction of entropy. Parenthetically, this concept figures in Norbert Wiener's later formulation of cybernetics, and in Schrödinger's and Bertalanffy's notion of living systems and was more recently adapted by R. Passet and Y. Tamanoi to the analysis of economic systems.

In economies of the "stagnant type," Bukharin noted:

> If the relation between society and nature remains the same, i.e., if society extracts from nature, by the process of production, precisely as much energy as it consumes, the contradiction between society and nature will again be reproduced in the former shape; the society will mark time, and there results a state of stable equilibrium.[156]

Expressing himself in a manner not unlike the patriarch of social energetics, Wilhelm Ostwald, Bukharin concluded that a growing society is one that extracts from nature more energy than it can consume.[157] However, unlike Ostwald, Bukharin located his reductionist analysis within a dialectical context. "The distinction," he wrote, "between society and nature will be in each case reproduced on a new and higher basis, a basis on which society will increase and develop."[158] Such a society-nature relationship forms a new equilibrium of an unstable character "with a positive indication."[159] Unstable equilibrium with "negative indication" (a declining system) was described in similar contexts.

Bukharin was insistent that the capitalist world economy and imperialism laid the foundations for a socialist order. Thus, "The growth of world market connections proceeds apace, tying up various sections of the world economy into one strong knot, bringing ever closer to each other hitherto 'nationally' and economically isolated regions, creating an ever broader base for the world socialist economy."[160] These concepts may have prefigured in Bukharin's appreciation of the world dynamic.

Consistent with Lenin, Bukharin argued that the processes of centralization and organization had created a strong tendency toward "transforming the entire national economy into one gigantic combined enterprise under the tutelage of the financial kings and the capitalist state, an enterprise which monopolizes the national market and forms the prerequisite for an organized socialist economy."[161]

Of no less significance were his conclusions wherein he notes that "the process of subjugating nature to man's domination on an unprecedented scale begins to choke the capitalist grip."[162] Bukharin's article, "The World Economy and Imperialism," first appeared in the Bolshevik journal *Kommunist* in 1915. His was an attempt to interpret the disparate effects of finance capital in terms of the interrelation between the world economy and national economies. He treated the relationship of the national economies to the world economy as an organic one, as the relationship of parts to the whole, as subsystems of a total organization. This allowed Bukharin to explain the increasing integration and interdependence of national economies and at the same time to explain conflict in terms of the divergent interests of the national units of which the world economy was composed.

This organic or organizational approach to the question of the world economy was ostensibly Bukharin's main contribution to socialist writings on imperialism. In this respect as well he was likely influenced by Bogdanov's writings.

Whereas Stepanov shared Hilferding's conviction that finance capital had prepared the foundations of a socialist order, Bogdanov believed socialism to imply the complete reconstruction of all existing cultural and economic relationships. The construction of socialism on any other basis was, for Bogdanov, "opportunistic culturalism."[163] He saw socialism as emerging with the development of technology, science, and the growth of collectivism among all sections of humanity. It was something that could not be achieved in the short term.

Quite simply Bukharin departed from a strict Marxian interpretation. Effectively, he supplemented the dialectic of class conflict with the dialectic of man and the biosphere.

> The equilibrium between the system and the environment will in each case be established on the basis of the extinction of a portion of this system. The contradiction will be reestablished on a new basis, with a negative indication. Or, in the case of society, let us assume that the relation between it and nature has been altered in such a manner that society is obliged to consume more and more and obtain less and less.... New equilibrium will here be established in each case on a lowered basis, by reason of the destruction of a portion of society. We are now dealing with a declining society, a disappearing system, in other words, with a motion having a negative indication.[164]

In Bukharin's analysis the imperative was viability; that is, the preservation at a certain level of the reciprocal relationship between an organism and its environment.[165] According to Bukharin, the physical equivalent of the concept of biological adaptation was dynamic equilibrium.

Unlike Bogdanov's tektological perspective, Bukharin's analysis of growth, equilibrium, and the breakdown of systems was a one-sided interpretation in which they were presented Ostwaldian style as a function of the quantity of energy.[166] Moreover, Bukharin did not pay any attention at all to a conception that an increase in energy also meant growth in the potential for destruction.[167] While cognizant of the first law of thermodynamics, Bukharin seemed to have neglected the second law—the entropy law. Nonetheless, he elaborated upon Bogdanov's concept of open systems prior to Ludwig von Bertalanffy's contribution of 1932. Indeed, Bukharin's conception is evident in his theory of equilibrium.

It is quite clear that the internal structure of the system (its internal equilibrium) must change together with the relation existing between the system and its environment. The latter relations [are] the decisive factor; for the entire situation of the system, the fundamental forms of its motion (decline, prosperity, or stagnation) are determined by this relation only.[168]

This conceptual stance was critical to Bukharin's transition from dialectical to historical materialism and to the cybernetics of social governance. "The task which became the central one was that of pinpointing the 'contradiction' between society and nature, and that mediating link through which the interaction between society and nature was channeled."[169]

However, the equilibrium that endured between the system and its environment determined which relations were feasible and prevailing in the social system itself. In the analysis of social phenomena, Susiluoto senses that Bogdanov and Bukharin, though referring to the role of energy as important, regarded technology as the principal dynamic. Without doubt, Bukharin's "external formulation" led to the notion that technology played a definitive role in the evolution of society. The combinations of social technology of labor were the deciding factor in the combinations and relations between men.[170] Bukharin remarked that:

Human society in its technology constitutes an artificial system of organs which also are its direct, immediate and active adaptation to nature (it may be stated parenthetically that this renders superfluous a direct bodily adaptation of man to nature; even as compared with the gorilla, man is a weak creature; in his struggle with nature he does not "interpose" his jaws, but a system of machines). When viewed from this point of view, the question leads us to the same conclusion: the technological system of society serves as a precise material indicator of the relation between man and society.... We may therefore definitely state that the system of social instruments of labor, i.e., the technology of a certain society, is a precise material indicator of the relation between society and nature.[171]

In the process of production, society develops "an artificial system of organs," which Bukharin calls technology and which constitutes "a precise material indicator of the relation between society and nature." Thus, the fundamentalist causative thesis that machines make history received an unequivocal support in Bukharin's *Historical Materialism*. Bukharin wrote: "The historical mode of production, i.e., the form of society, is determined by the development of the productive forces, i.e., the development of technology."[172] Lukács, a leading opponent of technicist and mechanical interpretations of Marx, criticized Bukharin's *Historical Materialism*, noting that, "Technique is a part, a moment, naturally of great importance, of the social productive forces, but it is neither simply identical with them, nor ... the final or absolute moment of the changes in these forces."[173] It is by identifying social technology with productive forces

They continue by noting: "This order must have a tendency to self-maintenance, which is generally expressed in the concept of equilibrium."[182]

Equilibrium is defined as the self-maintenance of order, regularity, and nonrandomness or interdependence among variables.[183] Criticisms of Parsons's equilibrium concept have mostly been from conflict theorists who feared that the concept inhibited the study of conflict and change, rather than from a concern with measuring the state of the system.[184]

As Canon noted, the word *equilibrium* had even by 1932 come to have a fairly exact meaning, a meaning limited to closed systems only.[185] Since biological organisms and social systems are open systems, a concept reserved for closed systems will not suffice.[186] Thus, Canon coined the term *homeostasis* to apply only to open systems.[187] Referring to equilibrium in open systems, i.e., homeostasis, Bailey notes: "This can only mean that all cases of homeostasis are also cases of equilibrium, but that not all cases of equilibrium need be homeostasis."[188]

Equilibrium, as defined in closed systems, departs substantially from the definition of Parsons and Shils.[189] Equilibrium is a single, unique, and nonarbitrary state, and rather than being a state of interdependence among system parts, as defined by a departure from randomness, it is rather a state of complete randomness associated with high entropy. In other words, it is, more or less, the opposite of the concept as defined by Parsons and Shils. It represents not maximum integration or maximum consensus, but rather a lack of integration, consensus, order, or organization. The goal of the concerted process of social action is not solely or even usually the establishment and self-maintenance of a state of equilibrium or maximum disorder but is usually the establishment of a state of nonequilibrium.

Bukharin was something of a structural functionalist.[190] Describing equilibrium in terms similar to those used to describe Canon's concept of homeostasis, he wrote: "If the disturbance of equilibrium is of short duration and the body returns to its former position, the equilibrium is termed stable; if this does not ensue, the equilibrium is unstable."[191]

Evidently, Bogdanov and Bukharin were strongly influenced by the natural sciences and energetics of their time, but no less influenced by sociological discourse. The result of this was a number of points of comparison, which extended into details, between their theories. The types of equilibrium set forth by Bukharin were surprisingly close to Bogdanov's concepts of organizing, disorganizing, and neutral processes. Bogdanov's organizing process corresponds to Bukharin's positive equilibrium in flux (the growth process of the system). The disorganizing process corresponds to negative equilibrium in flux. Finally, the neutral state corresponds to stable equilibrium.[192] Moreover, whereas Bogdanov refers to "positive" and "negative selection," Bukharin speaks of "positive" and "negative indications." Both terms are analytically synonymous to the cybernetics of positive and negative feedback.

("the combinations of instruments of labor") and by making internal structure a function of an external equilibrium that Bukharin is able, despite his pluralistic analysis of social development, to preserve monistic causality in economic determinism. More generally, Lukács sought to demonstrate how human-social relations, conscious activity, and the dialectic of social being and consciousness vanish from Bukharin's work.

Although equilibrium theory, general systems analysis, and structural-functionalism vary in their focus and stress different dimensions, they all display a preoccupation with self-regulation.[174] Hence, what is being debated is whether society is characterized by order and integration or by conflict and coercion.[175]

While the concept of equilibrium has a long history in sociology and notably one prominently associated first with Emile Durkheim and then with Talcott Parsons, sociology's recourse to functionalism has engendered a fusillade of criticism.[176] For sociology's task, as Durkheim made clear, is to help normalize the social division of labor in order to create a society characterized by functional order and occupational recognition. But to normalize the division of labor is to guarantee sociology's place in it at the same time that the new solidarity fully realizes capitalism rather than negating it. To speak of a new individualism that would permit industrial society to survive without accepting the alternatives of either bourgeois negative individualism or revolutionary disorder is to seek the actualization of all that is potentially good (e.g., fungible, useful) in the existing society and the destruction of all that is dysfunctional.

The critics charge that the equilibrium concept, by emphasizing self-maintenance and a return to a particular state if disturbed, implies an emphasis on the maintenance of the status quo. This, they say, makes the approach inherently conservative and de-emphasizes analysis of conflict and change.[177] In an early criticism, Sorokin charged that the equilibrium concept was unsuitable for the analysis of social change and concluded that the concept of equilibrium was "either inapplicable at the most [or] useless . . . in the study of socio-cultural phenomena."[178]

The concept of equilibrium, as used by Parsons, is allegedly deficient both sociologically and from an idiosyncratically defined systems point of view. One problem is the unnecessary linking of the equilibrium concept with the notion of societal integration, insofar as integration implies consensus over conflict.[179] Moreover, the concept of equilibrium was borrowed from thermodynamics, but as used in functionalism it ironically has a meaning basically the opposite of its meaning in its classical application.[180]

Referring to equilibrium, Parsons and Shils write:

> The most general and fundamental property of a system is the interdependence of parts or variables. Interdependence consists in the existence of determinate relationships among the parts or variables as contrasted with randomness of variability. In other words, interdependence is *order* in the relationship among the components which enter into a system.[181]

Tektology and Open Systems

Milan Zeleny suggests that Bogdanov's Tektology included the concept of an open system as a complex that can maintain itself only at the expense of its environment, i.e., that all living systems, including the economy, are open systems.[193] Bertalanffy was to later employ this concept and conceive of a living organism as a specific form of the movement of matter. "We must conceive living beings as systems of a specific type, as systems of elements in mutual dynamic interaction, and discover the laws that govern the pattern of parts and processes." This conception, later developed in Bertalanffy's biophysics of open systems and general system theory, according to Kamarýt,[194] approaches the dialectical concept of change. It emphasizes the structural similarity as well as the specificity of phenomena, including the specificity of biological forms of the movement of matter.

Kamarýt maintains that this was already emphasized by Engels in the second half of the nineteenth century. For instance, Engels made a number of methodological and, in his time, valuable statements. He characterized life as a dynamic process, as a specific mode of existence of "protein" substances whose fundamental property is the continual exchange of matter with the environment. It is the continuous regeneration of chemical particles that potentially contains all higher forms and properties of life.[195]

However, Bogdanov's two basic modes of interaction, that is, positive progressive selection and negative progressive selection, are more than merely progressive (increasing) and regressive (decreasing) processes. Gorelik and Zeleny assert that these processes were critical elements in Bogdanov's organizational dynamic. Positive selection contributes to increased complexity and internal heterogeneity through the assimilation of useful ambients from the environment. The negative selection facilitates the disassimilation of all that is volatile, discordant, and noxiant to the system, resulting in a state of increasing homogeneity, order, and coordination. For Bogdanov, positive selection is characterized by the growth in the heterogeneity of internal relationships of a system that eventually leads to a decrease in systemic structural stability.[196] This happens because positive selection adds new structural contradictions to any existing contradictions, so that the whole system is weakened.

Negative selection is allegedly accompanied by the growth of homogeneity in internal systemic relationships and increases systemic structural stability. In this case, negative selection progressively disassimilates the least stable elements, connections, and groupings that hinder the internal organization of the system in question. This results in the whole system becoming structurally more integrated.[197] For this reason, if negative selection is arrested short of the disintegration of a given system and is replaced by positive selection, the whole system may be raised in a synergetic manner to a higher level of organization.

Positive selection adds new contradictions and enriches the system's organization while weakening the whole from a structural viewpoint. Negative selection removes the weakest links, simplifies the organization, and leads to a greater structural stability.[198] Apparently, Bogdanov recognized quite early that it is the interaction between organization and structure that sustains the system's self-production, that is, its autopoiesis.[199]

Another concept introduced by Bogdanov is that of an organizational (systemic) integration. The more powerful that integration, the more resilient the system becomes (i.e., the more capable of forming new links, regrouping its structure, and adapting to environmental perturbations). The weaker the forces of integration, the more "skeletal" the system becomes (i.e., more durable, less vulnerable, less adaptive, but more autonomous). Gorelik notes that in this connection Bogdanov's negative selection was a key concept. Negative selection manifests itself more intensively in "diffused" systems; that is, systems whose frontiers expand in various directions. In "fused" (solid) systems, both positive and negative selection are less intensive.[200] This finding, according to Gorelik, provides an answer to the question, Which structures, fused or diffused, are more favorable to the preservation and development of systems? It turns out that under conditions of negative selection, fused structures are more favorable to systemic preservation and development than are diffused structures; and, under conditions of positive selection, diffused structures are better. Following Bogdanov, Gorelik speculates that centralized management is to be preferred to the decentralization of management for the preservation and development of social systems in "hard times," i.e., during the reign of negative selection processes. However, under the conditions of positive selection, prevailing during periods of "good times," Gorelik considers decentralized management to be more favorable to systemic preservation and development.[201]

Consistent with Gorelik's analysis, Zeleny accords to Bogdanov the notion that in favorable environments the resilient part tends to grow faster through positive selection and is limited by the "skeletal" part. In unfavorable environments the skeletal part is strengthened through negative selection and protects the resilient part. Both tendencies ensure the harmonious survival of the whole.[202] Indeed, Bogdanov challenges us "to gather together and harmoniously integrate the fragmented organizational experience of humankind."[203] While Tektology was presented as a general theory of organization, it was not without a pragmatic dimension.

12

Tektology and Soviet Planning

Tektology should have been enthusiastically embraced by Bogdanov's contemporaries, particularly by the proponents of Soviet "scientific planning," whose needs it was in part developed to serve. And, in many respects, which we will examine herein, it did. But despite theoretical advances proposed by Bogdanov and through partial practical efforts, the Bolsheviks survived the civil war not by planning but by various other means, including "shock methods."

Shock methods consisted of selecting a certain number of critical enterprises and giving them preferential treatment in the provision of materials, fuel, and food rations. It was hoped that reviving a small number of vital plants, even at the expense of the rest, would ensure a sufficient flow of production to satisfy the most pressing national needs. The shock factories were to act as "growth poles," stimulating upstream and downstream development. The system worked poorly. Uncontrollable political pressures worked to expand the list of favored enterprises to the point that shock factories were no better off than others. Perverse effects were also registered. Some shock factories experienced greater privation than others. As a method it failed to address the needs of the economy as a whole, since remedying one bottleneck only served to expose another in a different sector.[1]

Embodying the policy choices of a theoretically informed political will and social action, the formulation of Soviet planning in the early 1920s was of considerable ideological importance to the Bolshevik's self-description. It was from the search for alternative methods that Bogdanov's tektologically informed approach to planning gained adherents, for economic planning was central to the claim that by abolishing private property and the marketplace, socialism would create a rational system for the distribution of wealth in society. Planning was to replace the anarchy of the markets. We must ask ourselves: What role did Bogdanov's Tektology play?

In January 1921, Bogdanov proposed a system of planning to a conference on Scientific Organization of Labor and Production Processes.[2] Later again, lecturing at a Moscow trade union club, in April of 1921, Bogdanov addressed the topic of planning and from his Tektology proposed three "laws." These were: the law of the weak link, i.e., law of the minimum; the law of chain linkage; and the law of proportionality.[3] The obvious idea that a chain cannot be stronger than its weakest link was often pointed out during this discussion. The point was doubtless driven home by the discovery that voluntaristic shock methods only compounded shortages of resources. The existence of links, including feedback relations, determines certain proportions in the economy. The possible expansion of production of some goods necessarily depended on the most scarce input factor.

The statistician Strumilin, concerned with methodological issues, asserted that a plan would be rational only if it obtained the "maximum coefficient of utilization" of all available resources; that, in turn, required concentrating production in the most efficient enterprises.[4] But insofar as the ruble could not be used to calculate value, since it was all but worthless, and prewar economic proportions had been disrupted by war and revolution, others were inspired to propose new systems of measuring the inputs and outputs of production. They worked out imaginative calculations of the types and intensity of labor used in production, the forms and flow of energy expended as measured in calories, and even conducted related field research. Lacking a comprehensive medium for measuring cost plans, and inspired by the practical possibilities of Ostwaldian social energetics, they proposed schemes of moneyless accounting relying on labor units or energy units or combinations of both.

Bogdanov, for instance, proposed that a national plan be based on that nonfinancial or real factor input that was in shortest supply and on which the rest of the economy was therefore dependent; of the four factors of production, food, labor, equipment, and materials, materials were most lacking and should be the medium of planning. This crudely corresponded to Bogdanov's "law of the minimum." For each unit of each kind of material distributed to producers, the plan would specify an end-use. These uses would further be classified by priority. From a plan that appropriately determined the flow of all material inputs to users, production targets could then be derived for each branch and ultimately be calculated for individual enterprises within each branch. The concept of weak links enabled the theorists to contemplate the problem of reconciling priorities for growth with the "interconnectedness" of the parts of the economy. The weak links in the chain could be used as a form of information in guiding planners about the first-order needs of the economy. Translated into a ranked set of priorities, and applied consistently by all structures in the system, they could direct productive resources "rationally" to the areas of greatest need.

The systemness, that is the interdependence, of all the elements of the economy was the second proposition of Bogdanov. He carried the chain metaphor further, calling it a "chain-linkage," which can be rendered, not too anachronistically, as "feedback." Bogdanov noted that the relationship among the economy's sectors was dynamic not static. Each link in the chain had both backward- and forward-leading linkages (feedback), except for the first and last links. The last was the sector of final demand, the first that of the basic elements of production. The rest supplied inputs to the next link and received as inputs the outputs of the preceding link. Parenthetically, it must be noted that whereas in his general theory of organization, Bogdanov (and no less, Bukharin) appreciated the embeddedness of the economy in the biosphere, this open systems intuition did not initially penetrate the first-generation Soviet planning model. Nonetheless, from a rather restricted and banal point arose a methodological advance of considerable importance. A plan could not simply specify the desired output targets of critical sector or sectors that served to satisfy final demand. Rather, growth targets had to be consistent with the fulfillment of the input needs of other sectors. Moreover, targets had to be calculated iteratively for all parts of the economy, first by calculating backward from the sector taken as the leading link (be it an estimate of the population's consumption needs or the material requirements of a bottleneck area) all the inputs needed to meet the target, then the inputs required by the sectors producing those goods, and so on back to the beginning of the chain; then, the process had to be repeated from the other direction to ensure that the needs determined by the plan were consistent with the resources available to the economy.

From his tektological perspective, Bogdanov called for a form of synoptic planning: the centralization of direction and decentralization of management; for a distinction between a central plan and production programs. The former set overall goals for the economy, the latter were to be set at the branch level and for individual enterprises. This point disturbed some of the Bolsheviks who associated centralized economic power with the mobilizing approach used in commanding and moving resources for war. They complained that these schemes for planning paid insufficient attention to the need for central power. While Lenin accepted the ideal of synoptic planning, he rejected the idea of planning backward from a projected figure for future final demand and balancing the anticipated output targets for all sectors with the figures calculated for input needs of each sector.

The starting point of Bogdanov's planning method was the calculation of final requirements of the population. To meet those requirements, consumer goods had to be produced, and this meant the use of producer goods, whose production, in turn, demanded other producer goods. Hence, the elaboration of the plan was a synoptic iterative procedure. Though not referring to the term *input-output* coefficients, Bogdanov insisted that for the output of a product, calculated inputs of certain other products are needed. This was an important contribution to the elaboration of the formal methodology underlying input-output analysis. Bogdanov's appreciation of the synoptic iterative procedure thus constituted the missing link between the ambiguities of Quesnay's *Tableau Economique* and Marx's own interpretation in volume 2 of *Capital* and the so-called balance method identified with Bazarov, Groman, and other Gosplan leaders of the 1920s, including Bukharin.

Cohen writes, "Official Bolshevism in 1925–27 was largely Bukharinist; the party was following Bukharin's road to socialism.... From 1926 onward, he, almost alone, shaped official Bolshevik understanding of the outside world, of international capitalism and revolution."[5] He was, moreover, a proponent of Bogdanov's philosophy of planning.

For Bogdanov, planned economic development had to also respect his third principle: proportionality (balance). In the second part of *The Universal Organizational Science: Tektology* he discusses Le Chatelier's principle: "If any change of conditions is imposed on a system in equilibrium, then the system will alter in such a way as to counteract the imposed change."[6] He argues that this principle has a universal tektological character. That a dynamic model based on conditions of economic equilibrium could be derived from volume 2 of Marx's *Capital* was not a unique point of view. Occasionally, it was even acknowledged obliquely by Bogdanov's opponents. What was more easily denounced as un-Marxist was Bogdanov's and later Bukharin's extrapolation of this concept into a grand model capturing not only economic and social phenomena but socioenergetic ones as well.

Turning his attention specifically to economic problems, in his *A Short Course of Economic Science* (chapter 10), Bogdanov argues that the equilibrium of social economy is possible when through distribution each of its elements receives all the necessary means for carrying out its social productive function. From this law of distribution and from the existence of feedback linkage between the branches of the economy, he postulated the necessity of a certain proportionality in the economy as a condition for systemic equilibrium. Proportionality referred to the acknowledgment of dynamic, i.e., moving, equilibrium, the fact that each sector in the economy had a constituting, constitutive, and integral relationship to the whole. However, the whole to which he addressed his attention curiously excluded other than narrow economic considerations. To draw up a single economic plan it was first necessary to take account of how the various branches of the economy related one to another. The calculation of the proportion would determine the "norm of equilibrium," the point of departure for further consideration. This, in turn, would determine the priorities for projects to reconstruct the economy's various sectors. The parameters of corresponding relationships could be altered by changes in the structure of the economy or by technological and even environmental dynamics. These parameters could be expressed quantitatively as coefficients or input norms for each consuming sector in the plan.

In building a model of the Soviet economy, Bazarov took the Bogdanovian conception of equilibrium as his point of departure and distinguished two different types of equilibrium. Mechanical equilibrium was characterized by the immutability of all the component parts and connections of the system, while dynamic equilibrium maintained the correspondence between the components of the system, all the dimensions of which changed simultaneously. Incorporating Bogdanov's and Bukharin's economy-environment systemic considerations into his second-generation formulation, Bazarov argued that the concept of moving equilibrium supposed a constant metabolism and energy between the given system and the environment.[7]

The problem of the balanced nature of economic growth was closely connected with discussions on genetic and teleological approaches to planning. The terms themselves—the genetic and teleological approaches—were introduced by Bogdanov's advocate Bazarov. He regarded his contribution as an attempt to apply constructive models for "investigating the existence of structural forms or organizational connections of universal validity."[8] According to the genetic approach, an appraisal of the emerging and possible tendencies (appreciated as scenarios) in the economy ought to serve as the basis of forward planning. With the teleological approach, the accent was placed on directive planning associated with the establishment and accomplishment of set objectives. Groman spoke of Bogdanov's regulative norms and considered the aim of the reconstruction process to be the attainment of a number of proportions of state coefficients.[9] Thus, environmental feedback considerations were once again neglected.

In connection with the law of proportionality, Bogdanov had himself formulated a corollary, the law of labor expenses. Here he deferred, perhaps for reasons of political correctness, to Marx's letter to Kugelmann:

> The volume of products corresponding to the various needs calls for various and quantitatively determined amounts of total social labor.... This necessity for the division of social labor in definite proportions cannot be eliminated by the specific form of social production; it can only alter its form of appearance. ... And the form in which this proportional division of labor manifests itself in a condition of society in which the interconnection of social labor exists in the form of the private exchange of the individual products of labor, is precisely the exchange value of these products.[10]

Ostensibly valid for all economic formations (i.e., institutional contexts for the livelihood of man), the "economic law" regulates the proportions of the economy that in the specific case of commodity production manifests itself as the law of value.

Speaking to this law of labor expenses, Bogdanov noted that under both capitalism and socialism labor expenses were a regulator, but in transitional socialist contexts they would exert influence in a more systematic way. This treatment was used by Bogdanov to argue that political economy had a historical and cultural character that could not be casually set aside. And this concept was axial in the early planning debates in the Soviet Union.

For Bukharin regulation was an omnipresent phenomenon. Consequently, he understood the functioning of the economy as a kind of regulative cybernetic system.[11] For him, as for Bogdanov, the law of value functioned as a kind of regulative mechanism in capitalist society. He selected as his point of departure Rudolf Stammler's distinction between *Naturwissenschaften* and *Zweckwissenschaften*, that is, between natural sciences and goal-oriented sciences. Stammler advised that it would make no sense to speak of a society at all without conscious regulation and guidance. While Stammler envisaged cybernetics in the traditional nineteenth-century context of society, Bukharin referred specifically to the anarchic development of commodity-economy under capitalism. In post-capitalist society, after the anarchic phase of the revolution, the return of society to equilibrium would no longer be one of "blind regulation," i.e., markets, but one of consciously planned guidance.[12] The recognition of the necessity for economic equilibrium was a major theme among some Soviet economists of the 1920s. But it was also, for perhaps doctrinal reasons, a source of bitter controversy. Seeking to defuse the controversy, Bukharin, in 1928, noted that in the transitional phase:

> One could construct, by analogy with the second volume of *Capital*, reproduction schemes, i.e., set out the conditions for the sound combination of different spheres of production and consumption and different spheres of production among themselves, or, in other words, conditions for moving economic equilibrium. . . . Herein consists the task of elaborating a national economic plan, which more and more approximates to the balance of the whole economy.[13]

For Bogdanov and Bukharin alike, equilibrium was connected with the law of labor expenses, which regulated the proportions of the economy. From Bogdanov's argument about the necessity of maintaining definite proportions in the economy, Bukharin came to the conclusion: "If any branch of industry does not systematically receive back the costs of production plus a certain additional sum . . . which is able to serve as a source of expanded production, then it will either remain at the same level, or it will regress."[14] From both theoretical and practical perspectives obtained the necessity of a balanced development of all sectors of the economy.

As Bogdanov before him, Bukharin argued, "Marx already gives hint of such a formulation (the doctrine of equilibrium between the various branches of production and the theory of labor value based thereon etc.)."[15] The concept of equilibrium and the corresponding concept of proportionality did not refer to the temporary equality of supply and demand but were employed in the context of the Marxian model of economic reproduction to indicate the conditions under which reproduction could be sustained, a usage distant from the concept found in Walrasian economics. There is a mistaken view that Bogdanov's and Bukharin's concepts of proportionality and equilibrium were Walrasian in nature. This misreading has led to an extravagant anticipatory interpretation and an exaggeration of the cogency of Bukharin's ideas. It is causally interpreted as a premonition of subsequent versions of market socialism.

In May 1920, Bukharin's *Economics of the Transition Period* was published. Lenin made a careful reading of the book, inserting annotations in the margins; many of his comments were critical, but on the whole he appraised the book as "splendid" and wrote about the "superb qualities of this outstanding book."[16] Bukharin's *Economics* was a generalization of the policy of "war communism," which Bukharin at that time regarded not as a temporary policy in wartime but as a basic method for transforming a capitalist society into a socialist one. No one in the Bolshevik party, Bukharin included, had foreseen the introduction of the New Economic Policy (NEP), which turned out to be a much more reasonable policy, and under the conditions in Russia from 1920 to 1922, the only possible transitional policy. Thus, *Economics* soon became obsolete and was never reprinted.

Much of Bukharin's appeal obtains from the fallacious belief that he stood for the principles of the market, which was bound up with his sensibility about economic proportionality and interlinkages or balances in the economy that the NEP had introduced. It may well be this misappreciation that contributed to the somewhat favorable reception of Bukharin's ideas among some Western interpreters.

Bukharin's appropriation of the Bogdanovian concepts of equilibrium, balance, and proportionality, in contrast with the alleged voluntarism of his opponents, is recklessly presented as evidence for the belief that he subscribed to market principles. The problem of the balanced character of economic growth was connected with the discussions on the correct approach to economic planning, but also with social and, importantly, environmental equilibrium.

In 1928, Bukharin proposed that the Soviet government purchase light industrial goods and grain from abroad rather than resort to extraordinary voluntarist measures. Problematic as that might have been, under the conditions it would have been the lesser evil. The Rights—a political grouping with whom Bukharin was allegedly associated—were justified in pointing out that the development of light industry had been slighted. Though it was without doubt necessary to maintain a priority for department I of the economy, department II should have been developed more rapidly, for it could have provided the goods demanded both in urban centers and in rural regions and possibly thereby the financial means for the government's projects.

While a number of Bolsheviks treated the NEP as primarily a tactical or strategic maneuver, Bukharin took a different approach:

> NEP . . . is not only a strategic retreat but also the solution to a major problem of social organization, or more specifically, a problem of the relationship between the spheres of production that we must rationalize and those that we cannot rationalize. We will say frankly: we attempt to take on the task of organizing everything—even organizing the peasantry and the millions of small producers. . . . From the standpoint of economic rationality this is madness.[17]

In the years 1928 to 1929, Bukharin was sure that the NEP, as the party's basic line in economic policy, had not yet been exhausted, that there was still room in the Soviet economy for the development not only of socialist enterprises but also of certain elements of entrepreneurial capitalism. The Rights were opposed to forced and hasty collectivization, whose only result could be a decline in agricultural production, an aggravation of the problem of food supplies, and a disruption of export plans. The Rights also had good reason to oppose "gigatomania" in industrial construction and excessive capital expenditures that often made no sense economically. Only in the more distant future would the development of socialism result in the elimination of the bourgeoisified NEPman sector and the exploitative kulak farm. Bukharin felt, however (and, until 1928 Stalin supported him in this view), that the urban and rural capitalist elements would be squeezed out basically by economic, not by administrative, dispossession—that is, as a result of competition in which the socialist sector would gain the upper hand over the capitalist sector by proving itself more efficient economically.

In connection with administrative procedures, Bukharin grasped that there was something beyond the political hegemony that Lenin and Stalin had secured. He worried about a possible degeneration of the body politic and the rise of a "new class" composed of NEPmen, specialists, and, most distressingly, of the party itself. The theoretical pretext was provided by "the scholar," who provided Stalin with the conjectural basis for the policy of forced collectivization.

Preobrazhenzky, the scholar in question and author of the so-called law of primitive socialist accumulation, proposed that the socialist sector of the economy be accomplished by "alienating" the part of the product created by the peasantry—a policy that Bukharin charged jeopardized the alliance (balance) of the workers and the peasantry. In *The New Economics*, Preobrazhenzky advanced the thesis that in the period of transition to socialism, two laws were in operation: The spontaneous law of value operated to the extent that the private economy existed, and the law of primitive social accumulation operated in that the state was compelled, if it were to survive, to implement a policy of unequal exchange with the private sector.[18] The government's pricing policy, which preserved terms of trade that were favorable to the peasants, carried the danger that the excess rural demand would lead to a divergence between state wholesale prices and the prices charged to the peasants by the private middlemen, with a loss of profits going to the state. If market forces were allowed to operate freely, Preobrazhensky argued, prices would rise to eliminate excess demand. Such a market equilibrium would not, as Bukharin naively believed, entail equal exchange. What was called for, argued Preobrazhensky, was a policy of unequal exchange, consciously implemented by the state, whereby state prices were raised to market-clearing levels, thus attracting the additional profits into the state sector.[19] Preobrazhensky's call for unequal exchange and the exploitation of the peasants was evidence, for Bukharin, not only of his disregard for the worker-peasant alliance but also of his disregard for the need to maintain balance and proportionality in the economy. Bukharin argued that the gradual elimination of the law of value would be accompanied by its transformation into an objective law of proportional labor outlays. The two were, according to Bukharin, historically specific forms of a more basic law common to all societies, according to which labor must be distributed in definite proportions in all societies.

Bukharin charged that Preobrazhenzky disregarded the need to maintain balance and proportionality in the economy. Bukharin's insistence on the need to maintain certain definite proportions between the different sectors of the economy would be violated by Preobrazhenzky's proposals.[20] Preobrazhenzky argued that this was necessary to accumulate the means necessary for industrialization.[21] Indeed, he viewed the economic situation as one of inadequate industrial capacity, whereas Bukharin's assessment was that the weakness of the Soviet economy lay in the narrowness of the peasant's demand for consumer goods.[22] This was the binding constraint on the pace of industrialization, a constraint that had equally plagued economic development in tsarist times. Bukharin wrote:

> The growth of our economy and the indisputable growth of socialism are accompanied by unique crises. Notwithstanding the decisive difference between the laws of our development and the laws of capitalist society, these crises "repeat" those of capitalism as if in a concave mirror: in both cases there is a disproportion between production and consumption. In our case this relation is turned "upside down" (they have overproduction, whereas we have a goods famine; there demand on the part of the masses falls short of supply, whereas here demand is in excess of supply).[23]

The implication was a program of proportional industrial investment and a pricing policy designed to expand peasant demand. A situation in which demand was in excess of production, for Bukharin, would reflect "the fact that society is really making the transition to socialism, and that the growth of consumption is the immediate driving force of economic development."[24] A "goods famine," however, was not a characteristic feature of the Soviet economy, though Bukharin insisted it could arise from planning errors. Thus, he was resistant to the view that a goods famine was characteristic of the economy. Modeling his reference image after the experiences of the American economy, he argued for the expansion of the home market for consumer goods.[25] Tarbuck writes:

> Bukharin's basic approach was what could be termed increasing the surplus by accelerating the turnover of capital; which included a policy of lowering prices for industrially produced consumer goods. This would provide the incentive for the peasants to produce the necessary agricultural produce, particularly the grain which would feed the towns and for export. Such a policy would be seen to benefit both town and country and hence to lessen the tensions and contradictions within the system as a whole.[26]

Preobrazhenzky's policies, and those of Tugan-Baranovsky, it was hypothesized, would lead to a crisis of oversupply of consumer goods in relation to the demand. In a kind of textual debate, Tugan-Baranovsky, like Bogdanov and Bukharin, grounded himself in Marx's reproduction schemes of *Capital* (volume 2) and argued that even an absolute contraction in the market for consumption goods, brought about by the replacement of workers by machines (i.e., the rising organic composition of capital), need not lead to a condition of disproportionality, as it would be possible to coordinate such a contraction by an expansion of the market for the means of production. As accumulation proceeded, the output of department I would comprise a growing share in the total output.

In his critique of Tugan-Baranovsky, Bukharin argued that such a program would lead to excessive (disproportionate) growth of the means of production and that, with a time lag, it would engender an overproduction of consumer goods.[27] Though he accepted that in terms of values there would be an increase in the means of production compared with the means of consumption over time, he did not accept that the proportions between the departments could alter over time. Since under the objective conditions the mass market for consumer goods was the peasantry, Soviet industrialization, he argued, demanded that the purchasing power of the peasants, i.e., the agricultural sector, grow in proportion with the growth of output of the industrial sector. In what was basically a closed economy, excessive growth of the means of production harbored the danger of a subsequent overproduction of consumer goods. Consequently, the capacity of the market for consumer goods determined the permissible rate of expansion of production. The corresponding pattern of proportional growth required, in Bukharin's view, that exchange between the two sectors be equal exchange. Those proposals that called for a more rapid expansion of the industrial sector over the agricultural sector he condemned as "Tuganism."[28] Preobrazhensky's proposals violated these conditions because the unequal exchange that he proposed meant that the industrial sector would grow more quickly than the private peasant sector, and the consequence of this, in Bukharin's view, was that a sales crisis would eventually develop. For Bukharin, the policy of intervening to maintain relative prices that were favorable to the peasant was required by objective economic conditions and was not an effort at "wrecking" or a compromise involving a lower rate of industrial growth than was technically possible. Nor did it represent a market-orientation in Bukharin's thought.

Preobrazhensky came to the same conclusion as Tugan-Baranovsky: Given an increasing organic composition of capital, proportionality could be maintained only by a gradual transfer of capital from department II to department I, which meant that the latter had to grow more rapidly than the former.[29] For Preobrazhensky, as for Tugan-Baranovsky, the view of Bukharin, that proportionality required that the demand for consumer goods grow in line with output as a whole, was invalid. The implication of this for the Soviet economy was that if industrialization was to be based on a rising technological level, as Preobrazhensky claimed, then it would be necessary, in order to avoid an overproduction of consumer goods, for the department I industries to grow more quickly than department II and for the industrial sector as a whole to grow more quickly than agriculture. To this Bukharin retorted:

> We think that the formula which calls for maximum investment in heavy industry is not quite correct, or rather quite incorrect. If we must put the main emphasis on the development of heavy industry, then we must still combine

this development with a corresponding development of light industry, which has a more rapid turnover, which realizes profits more rapidly, and which repays those sums expended on them much sooner. We must, I repeat, strive for the most favorable combination.[30]

From the Bogdanovian concept of equilibrium, Bazarov came to the conclusion that the Hungarian economist J. Kornai would address sixty years later, that a characteristic feature of the Soviet economy was its tendency toward imbalanced development: "The tendency towards relative underproduction must be recognized to be just as characteristic of our social system as the tendency to overproduction is for capitalism."[31]

Although the first five-year plan itself was directed toward a balanced growth of the economy, during the course of its fulfillment a number of difficulties arose. The shortage of consumer goods and the fact that the purchase price for grain did not cover the expenses of its production led in 1928 to a reduction in grain sales by the peasants. To ensure grain procurements the methods of the War Communism period were employed. A leading group in the party and government, led by Bukharin, opposed this turn of events; they were labeled right-wing deviationists and after a bitter struggle were defeated. As a result of the curtailment of the NEP, the so-called command-bureaucratic system of managing the economy arose.

Moreover, command methods in management corresponded to voluntarist economic theorizing. The notion of unbalanced growth came to dominate. Thus not only did Bukharin and Bazarov come under attack—Bazarov and Groman were arrested on the charge of "wrecking activities"—but also Bogdanov's theories were again berated. P. Vyshinsky recited Lenin's earlier invective: "With Bazarov we have the full set of tektological gibberish—organizational linkages, structural forms, universal applicability . . . quantitative analysis etc., models."[32] Bogdanov's Tektology, his theory of equilibrium, and those associated with early Soviet planning methodologies were labeled wreckers, right-wing opportunists, and counter-revolutionary Trotskyists.

Whereas Preobrazhenzky and Tugan-Baranovsky had formulated this transformation to socialism in narrow economic terms consistent with the NEP, i.e., through pricing policy, Stalin reformulated it in coercive political terms. Stalin, in his policies toward the peasantry, adopted Trotskyist conceptions of "primitive socialist accumulation," along with Zinoviev's and Kamenev's proposals for excessive taxation of the well-to-do strata in the countryside, while substantially broadening and deepening these proposals and conceptions. It was logical for Stalin to bring in many prominent former Left oppositionists to carry out his new policy. Clearly Bukharin was confronting what Bogdanov had feared, namely, that the origins of a class could be linked to political authority gradations as well as economic ones.[33]

In 1923, Bukharin had already tied the economic irrationality of War Communism to bureaucratic overcentralization. "We will say frankly: we attempted to take on the task of organizing everything—even organizing the peasantry and the millions of small producers.... From the standpoint of economic rationality this was madness."[34] Bukharin now believed that there were severe limitations on what the proletariat could and should try to organize:

> Taking too much on itself, it has to create a colossal administrative apparatus. To fulfill the economic functions of the small producers, small peasants, etc. it requires too many employees and administrators. The attempt to replace all these small figures with state *chinovniki*—call them what you want, in fact they are state *chinovniki*—gives birth to such a colossal apparatus that the expenditure for its maintenance proves to be incomparably more significant than the unproductive costs which derive from the anarchistic condition of small production; as a result, this entire form of management, the entire economic apparatus of the proletariat state, does not facilitate, but only impedes the development of the forces of production. In reality it flows into the direct opposite of what was intended, and therefore iron necessity compels that it be broken.... If the proletariat itself does not do this, then other forces will overthrow it.[35]

For Bukharin economic planning meant the rational use of resources to achieve desired goals; the plan had therefore to be based on scientific calculation and objective statistics, not "doing whatever you please" or "acrobatic *salto mortale*." Second, planning seeks to eliminate from economic development the anarchy and crises (disequilibrium) inherent in capitalism; the plan must therefore foster and operate within "conditions of dynamic economic equilibrium," defining and adhering to "correct proportions" throughout the whole economy, taking into account and providing for reserves, and "leveling down to bottlenecks." Third, planning, especially in a backward agrarian society, must be provisional, allowing for the "very significant elements of incalculable spontaneity" among the vagaries of harvests and the market; it cannot be one hundred percent planning or "a five-year bible." Finally, the planning process must in every respect avoid "over-centralization" or "over-bureaucratization." The negative ramifications of a wrong decision in such circumstances "may be no less than the costs of capitalist anarchy"; and, by eradicating flexibility and initiative from below, it leads to "economic arteriosclerosis," to "a thousand small and large stupidities" and what Bukharin termed "organized mismanagement."[36] Instead:

> Centralization has its limits and it is necessary to give subordinate agencies a certain independence. They should be independent and responsible within prescribed limits. Directives from the center should be confined to formulating the task in general terms; the specific working out is the business of lower agencies, which act in accordance with actual conditions of life."[37]

The *idée fixe* of Bolshevism, the class struggle, in Bukharin's analysis and following Bogdanov's, was forsaken. The nexus of class dominance with legal ownership of property would later hamper the critiques of neo-Marxists for decades. Like Bogdanov before him, Bukharin cautioned against "a new ruling class" based not only on the juridical rights that attach to property but also on authority and privilege—what Bogdanov referred to as "organizational" forces. While Bukharin had in his earlier study of capitalism, *The Economic Theory of the Leisure Class*, ignored the problem of "the managerial class" and of "power without property," he now saw that "an exploiting organizational class could emerge on the basis of nationalized property.... His discussion was prompted by the 'different élite' theories of Bogdanov."[38]

Bogdanov long had argued that the ruling class in any given society is the group that organizes the culture and economy, whether or not it actually owns the means of production. For him the essential source of exploitation lay in the relationship between organizer and organized. Bukharin's contention that "the difference between technician and worker" cannot be eliminated within a capitalist society was directed against Bogdanov's conclusion that until the proletariat ripened into a capable organizing class, socialist revolution was premature.[39]

In *Pravda*, June 30, 1929, Nikolai Bukharin published a seemingly routine exercise in Marxist polemic. It was a long review of a book by a German theorist, Hermann Bente, in which a Weberian description had been advanced of the increasing bureaucratization of modern economy, and the postulate suggested that the bureaucratization of industrial societies was the dominant social trend.[40] Bukharin noted that "The latest forms taken by capitalism, the deep internal and structural changes they reveal, and above all, the sharply rising trend toward state capitalism pose a number of new problems."[41]

Bukharin, drawn to heterodox notions about the possible convergence of modern societies, was forced to employ an Aesopian vocabulary and wrote: "The Soviet reader may be startled to find a certain formal resemblance between some of the organizational problems posed and solved by Bente and the problems raised and settled in Soviet practice." And though Bukharin then hastens to muffle this dangerous observation, it is clear that he has made two major points that the attentive reader was likely to grasp: (1) that in modern society there may be forms of bureaucratic degeneration that are not limited to capitalism and indeed are characteristic of industrial societies; (2) that many of the harsh descriptions Bente offers of the "organized mismanagement" of advanced capitalism also apply to Stalinist collectivism.[42]

> It may be said that contemporary state capitalism in the advanced capitalist countries stands in the same relationship to the state capitalism of 1914–1918 as the present system of the growing socialist economy in the U.S.S.R., with its planning in key areas, does to the economy of military communism.
>
> The reasons for bureaucratic centralization are the complexity and the enormous size of economic enterprises, which makes direct personal supervision impossible. At the same time, the longer the chain of command, the more difficult it is to set the entire machine in motion. Consequently, past a certain point, it is better to renounce the advantages of absolutely autonomous admin-

istration and to replace the artificial links by live ones, i.e., directives by men. Life is varied, and responses to it must be varied, too. . . . Directives from the center should be confined to stating the problem in general terms, and specific action should be worked out by the subordinate agencies, which operate in accordance with, and in response to, actual conditions.[43]

In the September 30, 1928, edition of *Pravda* Bukharin released his article "Notes of an Economist," which criticized many of Stalin's economic policies, reserving for particular criticism Stalin's forced pace of industrialization. Bukharin proposed an extensive program for overcoming the country's economic difficulties through developing and modernizing the NEP. He spoke out against a new "revolution," advocating restrictions on the kulaks, development of cooperatives, and a more equitable and balanced pricing policy. While defending the principle of economic planning, he opposed "hypertrophied planning," since not everything could be foreseen in a plan. He recapitulated his argument that industrial planning had to keep pace with agricultural development and take into account the Soviet Union's available resources. Industrialization could not be accomplished at the expense of agricultural production, he asserted, stressing that the rate of industrialization should be realistic. Though formally directed against Trotskyism, in fact, he was directing his outrage against Stalin's economic policies.[44]

Earlier, in April of 1928, at the plenum of the Central Committee and the Central Control Commission, Bukharin's position had been seriously threatened. During these meetings Bukharin had accused Stalin of undermining the NEP and of establishing "monstrously one-sided" relations with the peasantry that were destroying the social and economic equilibrium between the working class and the peasantry. Bukharin insisted that such a policy was a surrender to Trotskyism. While supporting efforts at rapid industrialization, Bukharin warned that without a balanced development of agriculture and industry, industrialization was bound to fail. He further accused Stalin of creating a bureaucratic state, of robbing the peasants, and he condemned Stalin's "theory of the permanent revolution"[45] as the USSR advanced toward socialism:

> This peculiar theory takes the bare fact that an intensification of the class struggle is now taking place and elevates it into some sort of inevitable law of our development. According to this strange theory, it would seem that the further we advance toward socialism, the more difficulties will pile up and the sharper the class struggle will become, and at the very gates of socialism we apparently will either have to start a civil war or, perishing from hunger, lay down our bones to die.[46]

The criticism to which Bogdanov's Tektology was subjected had dire consequences not only for economic theory, for the adoption in practice of unbalanced voluntaristic methods led to the irrational use of economic resources, the results of which are clear.

13

Techno-utopia: An Athens Without Slaves

A plaintive constant in much of the history of Western philosophy is a whispering nostalgia for an antiquity lost. Eurocentric philosophers and technocrats alike are haunted by dreams of an Athens without slaves.

In a celebrated passage of *Capital*, Marx reintroduces an Aristotelian concept, instilling it with a more flexible though not transcended notion, for there is still a sphere of necessity and a sphere of freedom. The latter begins only where labor that is determined by necessity and mundane considerations ceases. Marx regarded "necessity," "need," and "external purposes" (*ussere Zweckmässigkeit*) as being of the same order: they are determinations that the subject does not sovereignly derive from his own being and therefore are negations of his sovereignty. The realm of freedom begins only "beyond the realm of necessity" and merges with that development of human energy that is an end in itself: with the pursuit of the Good, the Beautiful, and the True. The important difference with Aristotle is that the unfolding of freedom in Marx no longer presupposes that the burden of necessity should be shouldered by an unfree social strata. The machine has taken the place of the slaves, and the "associated producers" organize themselves so as to reduce the necessary labor time to a minimum, so that everyone can work, though only a little, and that everyone, alongside work, can engage in activities that are an end in themselves.

It seems that, according to Bogdanov, the role of institutions is to contain and neutralize conflict. In the architectonics of institutionalizing conflict situations, some degrees of freedom are lost. In particular it may require that we forego technically feasible developments, even certain lines of inquiry where the likely application is incompatible with the maintenance of other higher norms and freedoms. Bogdanov was prescient in his views on this matter.

In his work of science fiction *Red Star*, Bogdanov spoke of the replacement of fetishisms by a "reign of science"—that is, "the purity and clearness of knowledge and the emancipation of the mind from all the fruits of mysticism and metaphysics." Lenin shared with him a fervent belief in the virtues of science and technology. They both anticipated positive consequences from technological progress. For Lenin, it meant a spur to economic development; for Bogdanov, it implied an impetus for cultural development. Advanced technology would bring about a change in sociolabor relations, surmised Bogdanov; the change, in turn, would stimulate cultural transformation. With this, Lenin had no quarrel. The difference between Lenin and Bogdanov was that the latter typically emphasized the cultural dimension, and the former dismissed it as not being immediately relevant. By disregarding the sociocultural formation of the working class in the production process, Lenin ended up with a view of the factory as a place where things alone are produced, ignoring that relations between people are produced and reproduced there and extend their influence beyond the factory gates.

But, however much he pinned his hopes for socialism on technological advance, Bogdanov did not simply endorse narrow cultural values based strictly on a scientific-technological ethos.[1] Unlike Lenin, he focused on the structural changes occurring under capitalism and tried to investigate which accompanying cultural changes would be conducive to socialism. If Marx was right, that the new develops within the womb of the old, why not try to identify the new features? Consistent with this line of thinking, Bogdanov predicated cultural change as prior to the transformation of the production process. He assumed that at least embryonic elements of a "proletarian culture" would manifest themselves under conditions of scientific and technological advance, especially increasing automation.

Science and technology, he argued, were not value free and should be submitted to a review from the proletarian point of view. Similarly, he promoted the removal of barriers between scientists and the public to make science accessible to all. This corresponds to what has been called a "re-inverted" mode of the development of knowledge and runs counter to the conservatism of Durkheim's functional differentiation.

Capitalism allegedly performed a useful function in transforming "the initial vagrant proletariat into a factory or workshop proletariat," confessed Bogdanov.[2] Sustaining in his science fiction a millennial view apparent in Marx, Bogdanov believed that technology could create the prerequisite conditions for the growth of social cooperation and a full elimination of social-class conflict. Indeed, it was the "historical mission" of the period of manufacturing "to create a machine out of a man." This formative process, maintained Bogdanov, was both painful and necessary; it laid down the preconditions for industrial production. With increasing mechanization, workers gradually became less of an addition to the machine and more its master. They learned to regulate and control, and they developed initiative and judgment; the most specialized, boring, and detailed tasks, meanwhile, were transferred to the "iron slave."

And yet, as we shall see, science and technology were also sources of deep apprehension.³ Automation by itself could not produce a complete transformation of either the work situation or the worker. Bogdanov advanced several reasons for this shortcoming. First, he believed that under capitalism, automation was introduced only to the degree that it proved profitable to the capitalist. Second, he perceived a considerable and continuing discrepancy between the occupation of an "ordinary worker" and that of an engineer: "The former is only technically conscious while the latter has a scientific character; the former requires ... a general understanding of mechanics, disciplined attention, and intelligence; the latter a refined, precise, scientific-technical knowledge."⁴ Only under full automation, thought Bogdanov, would the level of skill and knowledge of the "ordinary worker" be raised sufficiently to transcend the division between worker and engineer. The role of the engineer as a leader over a group of workers would remain, but it would no longer be qualitatively different from that of a worker. In fact, the content of all labor would become similar, involving mostly the regulation and control of highly specialized machines. The result, he argued, would be a change in attitude toward work: "The worker who is at once organizer and executor ... cannot but regard his labor positively—that is ... as an indispensable, natural, normal, and, to some extent, agreeable part of his existence."⁵

Third, Bogdanov assumed that the merging of the organizational and executive functions could be achieved once labor relations were based on collectivism rather than on authoritarianism. Under capitalism, workers formed a "comradely collective of executors," not organizers; they did not participate in organizational decisions. This restriction, a serious one, could be removed only by a change "in the whole system of economic relations," thereby promoting full participation.

In short, he forecast a post-capitalist system that differed significantly from its predecessor. The division of labor would be transformed and would lose its significance; in its place, labor mobility would predominate. By this statement, Bogdanov meant not only that the place of work would be changed but that "the function of 'organizer' would be interchanged with that of 'executor' and vice versa." This interchanging would allow for a narrowing of the gap between worker and manager, remove the psychological distinctions between them, and knit, from common experiences, a common culture. More important, avowed Bogdanov, the nature of authority relations would change; it would be based on competence rather than blind subordination to power. Bogdanov's vision was a shared one.⁶

The industrialization of Russia in the 1890s and the accompanying growth of various technologies had opened broad vistas for techno-utopian speculation. The works of August Bebel, Friederich Engels, and Karl Kautsky, with their exaltation of the technologizing of everyday life, captured the imagination of Russian socialists who were looking for the ultimate purpose of revolution to inspire themselves and their followers—a dream of a golden future in which men and women could work and study in total freedom, harmony, and community, liberated from the backwardness, poverty, and greed that tormented their lives. In this sense, techno-utopia was seen by Bogdanov as a weapon in the arsenal of revolution, a snapshot of man's possible future that would bedazzle the worker and inspire him more deeply than could the arid words of polemical party propaganda. However, the revolutionary euphoria that had seized so many thinkers and writers in the years 1905 to 1907 and produced so many apocalyptic visions and assorted dreams of an imminent *New Jerusalem* also permeated the spirit of Bogdanov and endowed his social vision with a sense of immediacy and hope.

The systematization of the productive process was a main focus of Bogdanov's techno-utopia. Factories are operated by electrical power and fully automated. "Moving equilibrium" is maintained by data-retrieval machinery in all enterprises. Data on stockpiles and inventories, production rates, and labor needs according to specialty are channeled into a Central Institute of Statistics, which collates and computes the information and sends it where it is needed.

Both Lenin and Bogdanov admired Taylorism as the latest achievement in capitalist organization and efficiency, despite their condemnation of its exploitative side. To Marxists, capitalism embodied all things evil, but it allegedly created the necessary preconditions for socialism. The tension present in this proposition was accentuated under the circumstances of underdevelopment in Russia. Should capitalist possibilities be embraced or rejected? Lenin, in *Development of Capitalism (1896–98)*, argued that capitalism should be welcomed. In post-1917 USSR the question became more complex. Given that the capitalist stage was unevenly developed and had produced only incomplete preconditions for socialism, what was the ideologically correct attitude? For Lenin, socialists under the dictatorship of the proletariat were not simply replacing the capitalists. And for him the political and economic equation had been fundamentally altered. But had the function of capitalism been played out? To the extent that Lenin conveyed an ideological message on Taylorism, it was a contradictory one. Taylorism was exploitative, but it was at the same time a useful mechanism for increasing productivity and instilling efficiency. As early as 1914 he contended that Taylorism was at once a way of extracting the last ounce of sweat from the worker and of securing "an enormous gain in labor productivity."[7]

Of particular interest is Lenin's suggestion that Taylorism was not entirely successful because it was "confined to each factory" and ignored the "distribution of labor in society as a whole." In other words, it was not so much the inherent methods and principles of Taylorism that Lenin rejected as it was their use and application. He implied further that socialists would make better use of the instrument devised by capitalists. "The Taylor system—without its initiators knowing or wishing it—is preparing the time when the proletariat will take over all social production and appoint its workers' committees for the purpose of properly distributing and rationalizing all social labor."[8] Thus, to Lenin, Taylorism was linked with the general advance of capitalism, which was positively interpreted since it paved the way for socialism. The essential question for Lenin became a political one: Who would control and use Taylorism? Lenin argued that workers, within the framework of the dictatorship of the proletariat, were in a unique position to take advantage of capitalist workmanship. "For the first time after a century of labor for others," wrote Lenin, "there is the possibility of working for oneself, and with the work based on all the achievements of the latest technology and culture."[9]

Bogdanov was perhaps more circumspect. Although he maintained that capitalism was the necessary precondition for socialism, he was not convinced that the adoption of bourgeois science, technology, and culture was the central task during the period of the transition to socialism. Rather, he argued that the theoretical premises would have to be reworked and a proletarian science and culture consciously developed. This effort, and not political control, would ultimately secure the transition to socialism. Thus, in modern terms, Bogdanov was asserting that the "achievements of capitalism" were not value free and required a fundamental alteration before they could serve workers' interests. A central distinction between Bogdanov and Lenin was over the cultural dimensions of technique.

More particularly, Bogdanov argued that Taylorism was based on the "correct idea" of studying scientifically the movements of workers in order to find the best means for carrying out a task. It was geared toward the exceptional rather than the average worker. This orientation meant selecting the very best people and training them to perform "gigantic tasks," while discarding the rest as loafers and idlers. But was this selection process really good for the system as a whole? queried Bogdanov. And would not a worker "sink into torpor fulfilling day after day, hour after hour, a fully mechanical job under a strict, uninterrupted, one could say penal, surveillance?"[10] Moreover, it was a mistake to think, he asserted, that this stupefaction of the worker harmed only the individual; in fact, it ran counter to machine production. It was important, stressed Bogdanov, to foster the attitudes and behavior patterns that were conducive to socialism.[11]

Though he celebrated machine production, Bogdanov feared and hated the system of capitalist production that made human beings appendages to machinery. For if ever there was going to be a change in attitudes, there had to be some counterpart to the factory atmosphere, "a socialism here and now," where creativity and initiative, rather than hierarchy and discipline, were emphasized. Bogdanov, thus, fought against Taylorists (the Stakhanovites)—particularly Alexie Gastev, founder of the Central Labor Institute and perhaps the greatest proponent of the man-the-machine mentality. Planning, productivity, labor discipline, and recruitment, all problems of development industry outlined in Bogdanov's techno-utopia, became issues of heated debate among Soviet planners of the 1920s and 1930s.

Gastev was a prominent figure in the development and popularization of

Soviet ideas concerning "scientific management" and the rationalization of labor.[12] Committed to the notion that through science the Russian culture could be reformed, Gastev's aim was nothing less than its transformation. But his ideas owed as much to American industrial engineers and capitalists such as Frederick W. Taylor as they did to Marx and Engels. In his romantic vision of industrialism men and machines merged, whereas technology was perceived as merely an extension of the human body—as an exosomatic appendage. This reference model allegedly permitted labor to acquire the speed and efficiency of their creations, the nerves of steel and muscles of iron.

Gastev's project did not arise in nonpartisan ways but rather obtained from Lenin's mechanistic appreciation of organization. Here emerged a particular view of the role and function of the structure of state and its economic organizations. In its entirety it was to be patterned on the structure of a "huge machine . . . functioning with clock-like precision."[13] To ensure that state organizations did indeed function like a clock, Lenin laid down five general principles of management, encapsulated in the following:

1. Primacy of political approach to the solution of all economic problems. This is considered to be a necessary condition for the preservation of the supremacy of the proletariat as represented by the communist party.

2. Planned development of the national economy.

3. Democratic centralism, involving the planning and direction of the entire economic life of the country from a single center with participation by local organs.

4. Existence of a uniform accounting and information system providing requisite data inputs into economic planning and a control model.

5. Injection of a motive power into the system in the form of incentives, comradely discipline, and, if necessary, even some compulsion.

In order to perfect his economic machine, Lenin strongly advocated the adoption of Taylor's "scientific management" methods, which were sweeping North America and Europe. As a result, extensive studies and experimentation in this area, known in the Soviet Union under the name of "scientific organization of labor" (*nauchnaya organi truda*), were initiated in the early 1920s.

After Lenin's death the study of variants of Taylorism and organization management problems decreased considerably and ceased almost completely toward the end of the 1930s. The main reason for this appears in the Soviet acceptance of enormous environmental, social, economic, and organizational costs as a price for rapid economic development. Possible benefits that could arise from theoretical studies of organization were considered remote and thus of little value in the solution of the practical problems of the day. What has been important throughout Soviet history is the industrialization of the country as fast as possible with apparently little regard for material cost. Principles of management that were suggested by Lenin were considered to be for the job in hand.

Implementation of the Leninist-Taylorist principles of management has over the years been in the creation of a highly problematic economic apparatus in the Soviet Union. However, as contemporary events demonstrate, the actual functioning of this organization in the country has not been as smooth as was originally envisaged by its creator, nor as totalitarian as its opponents claimed. The dilemma among conservative elements in the Soviet economic administration remains how to maintain centralized control on a national scale for political guidance and economic planning without at the same time stifling decentralized decisions and organizational innovations needed to sustain the economy.

Gastev's program was not without support from the highest levels. During a plenary session of the Supreme Council of the National Economy on April 1, 1918, force of circumstances prompted Lenin to remark: "In the decree, we must definitely speak of the introduction of the Taylor System, in other words, of using all scientific method of labor which this system advances. Without this, it will be impossible to raise productivity, and without that we will not usher in socialism."[14] In "The Immediate Tasks of the Soviet Government," Lenin wrote:

> The Taylor system, the last word of capitalism in this respect, like all capitalist progress, is a combination of the subtle brutality of bourgeois exploitation and a number of its greatest scientific achievements in the field of analyzing mechanical motions during work, the elimination of superfluous and awkward motions, the working out of correct methods of work, the introduction of the best system of accounting and control, etc. The Soviet Republic must at all costs adopt all that is valuable in the achievements of science and technology in this field. The possibility of building socialism will be determined precisely by our success in combining the Soviet government and the Soviet organization of administration with the modern achievements of capitalism. We must organize in Russia the study and teaching of the Taylor system and systematically try it out and adapt it to our purposes.[15]

Soviet Taylorism was an image of Russian socialist culture at odds with Bogdanov's vision of socialism. Engaged in his ascetic enterprise, Gastev sneered at Bogdanov's cautionary vision and adamantly expressed the view, in the official organ of Proletkul't, that bookishness and confident generalities were entirely inappropriate. In his view, to comprehend the new culture and psychology of the proletariat that was being manufactured, "It is necessary to be a kind of engineer; it is necessary to be an experienced social constructor and to take one's scientific methods not from general presuppositions regarding the development of productive forces, but from a most exact molecular analysis of the new production, which has brought into existence the contemporary proletariat."[16] Mechanization and standardization, Gastev argued, were proceeding to eliminate both unskilled labor and creative forms of labor. Both in the world of socialism and capitalism an undifferentiated invidious industrial structure was being institutionalized. Machines, from being managed, will become managers. Those laborers whose work was standardized and devoid of any subjective dimension were, according to Gastev's characterization, embracing "proletarian psychology" and the new culture of the proletariat. "The methodical, constantly growing precision of work ... imparts to proletarian psychology a special alertness full of distrust for every kind of human feeling, trusting only the instrument, the apparatus, the machine."[17] Gastev forecast a society that would boast of "striking anonymity," its common norms and rhythms pervading life and shaping the new proletarian culture. Workers, mechanized and standardized like cogs in a vast machine, will cultivate a proletarian psychology of anonymity. Advocating nothing less than the Americanization of Soviet industry, a messianic Gastev imagined a "new America," a nation of "self-colonizers" turning themselves into human machines.[18]

Certainly Gastev's crass anti-intellectual and anti-humanist specter of the socialist future was repugnant to Bogdanov. Gastev, like so many others, bore the scarrings of Pisarev's nihilism. Gastev's pronouncements on culture made a mockery of the concept of "proletarian culture." Bogdanov admonished him for equating work habits and production behavior with culture. "Proletarian life is a whole," comprised of various dimensions, not just work; it was wrong "to break off one piece, even if it is very important, basic."[19] Gastev's image of the future society recalled and anticipated "industrial militarism," rather than workers' collectivism. Almost ten years later, at Gastev's zenith, similar criticisms were echoed. One critic conceded that Lenin himself had tied the cultural revolution to the technological revolution (e.g., his statements on electrification) but affirmed that only a "vulgarization of Marxism" could assume a direct relationship between technology and culture. Moreover, the culture that Gastev described was merely a "culture of muscles," not a "culture of the mind"; hence it could not encompass proletarian culture.[20]

Bogdanov argued that Gastev overemphasized the industrial mobilization and the militarization of industry that characterized the Western societies and economies of the World War I period. For Bogdanov, this phenomenon was atypical and not a harbinger of the future. He argued that Gastev mistook the exceptional and abnormal circumstances as the norm and projected them into the future. Gastev believed that at its particular stage of industrialism the Russian economy demanded increased specialization and inequality, which attended a further division of labor. Concentrating his attention on the standardization of function and neglecting the vital processes of planning and regulating, Gastev's mechanization of the proletariat was denaturing and little different from the loathsome German ultraconservative theorist Ernst Junger's celebrated dehumanizing techno-euphoria. For to deprive the proletariat of all creativity meant the militarization of labor and the reduction of a community of workers to mere barracklike existence.

> The world of the machine, the world of the mechanism, the world of industrial urbanism is creating its own collective bonds, is giving birth to its own types

of people, whom we must accept just as we accept the machine, and not beat our heads against the gears. We must introduce some corrective factors into its yoke of iron discipline; but history urgently demands of us to pose, not these small problems of the protection of personality by society, but rather a bold design of human psychology in reliance upon such a historical factor as machine production.[21]

Junger described the emerging technological man as a new man who rages toward the fulfillment of the nihilist typus. For Junger, the age of world wars marked the beginning of the new age of total mobilization in which nation-states would vie for planetary domination, unlimited power for the calculating, planning, and molding of all things. His was a celebration of a society in which it would be understood that "technology and nature are not opposites," that technology is "the embodiment of an icy will," a society in which class antagonisms would be in a community committed to realizing the Nietzschean will to power given visible form by the machinery of mass production.[22] Junger's image was that of a technological-industrial firestorm, the totalizing process of modern technology. The essence of modern technology was nothing technical; instead, the essential was the fact that humanity had been gripped by Nietzsche's irresistible will to dominate, which expressed itself in the guise of machine technology. He believed that humanity would be redeemed only if it submitted itself to the nihilistic claim of the technological will-to-power. European culture should submit to the inexorable historical process of technological totalization, a self-empowering process that has no "purpose" beyond its own expansion. Technology is but an expression of a transcendent force that has no purpose external to its goal—a period of repose characterized by totalization, total organization, total planning, and total control. For Junger, technified society was the nihilistic technological era wherein the ordinary worker either would learn to participate willingly as a mere cog in the natural technological order—or would perish. In surrendering to this goal, so Junger wrote, the worker develops cultic symbols of technology that replace traditional religions. The achievement of this goal, however, required a period of instability and nihilism: the planetary technological totalitarianism. This was the *Anfang* of the Cultural West, a submission to the technological *Gestalt* meant the rediscovery of the mystical Being of "Greek antiquity." By the total objectification of his self, Junger's worker sought to attain an entirely detached perspective. Devoid of bourgeois individuality, he achieves his specious "freedom" by surrendering to the higher power working through him. Thus, Junger's creature, the technological man, approached Nietzsche's "last man."

Expressing a view consistent with his aesthetic, Bogdanov believed that specialization and, with it, inequality could be largely overcome by raising the cultural life of the masses. In this regard Bogdanov shared with Lukács the view that in "the proletarian society, specialization loses not only its class character but also its alien character in relation to the essence of human life."[23]

If the goal of the new society consisted in the enhancement of mere satisfaction, of man's well-being, none of the functional changes would enter the picture; that is, their meaning would be scarcely noticeable. In this case the task of the proletarian state could be fulfilled in the organization of production and distribution; economic life—with quite different aims, of course would continue to dominate the human principle. ... Actually, however, in reaching this point the proletarian state has only established the indispensable preconditions for the achievement of its goals. Humanity must still struggle for their realization.[24]

Bogdanov's reference image of industrialism was inimical to Gastev's proletariat-as-automaton or to Junger's technocratic idol. Rebelling against Gastev's technological nihilism, Bogdanov shared Lukács's image of a different collective, where the individual might be able to realize his individuality.

The proletarian collective is distinguished and defined by a special organizational bond, known as *comradely cooperation*. This kind of cooperation in which the roles of organizing and fulfilling are not divided but are combined among the general mass workers, so that there is no authority by force of unreasoning subordination but a common will which decides, and a participation of each in the fulfillment of the common task. Where work demands the direct supervision of an individual person, there will emerge, instead of authority and force, a comradely recognition of competence; and he who in one endeavor was the instructor may then in another follow the directions of a comrade whom he had just been supervising: the organizer and executor change places frequently.[25]

Is technological man Janus-faced, the harbinger of a new era of Western history, or the final representative of the Cultural West's denouement?[26] Bogdanov's critique of Gastev's man-as-machine was an assessment later presented by others, including Herbert Marcuse in his *One-Dimensional Man*. Following a Heidegger-like theme, he noted that technology penetrates all spheres of modern industrial society; scientific and technological progress creates specific thinking and behavior characteristic of "one-dimensional" man typified by commodity fetishism within the fiction of commensurability.[27] Marcuse reaches this conclusion on the basis of his understanding of technological rationality. In *One-Dimensional Man*, subtitled *Studies in the Ideology of Advanced Industrial Society*, Marcuse writes that: "In the medium of technology, culture, politics and the economy merge into an omnipresent system which swallows up or repulses all alternatives. ... Technological rationality has become political rationality."[28]

Bogdanov drew a picture of a society heavily influenced by his systems thinking. Distinct from Gastev's cultic technocratic image, to Bogdanov a socialist economy meant progressive rationalization of the parts and organization of the whole as not to be equated with political intervention or state control. Ultimately, and in keeping with his systems thinking, he envisaged socialism as a "self-regulating system."[29] Indeed, for Bogdanov a genuine socialist society was both self-regulating and harmonious. Although the organizational function in a system would remain, it would be substantially altered once it was founded on a "general and all-embracing organization of labor." That is, the regulating mechanism would not be the "old authoritarian centralism" but "scientific centralism." Most of the functions would be performed by a "gigantic statistical bureau based on exact calculation for the purpose of distributing labor power and instruments of labor."[30]

14

Dystopian Warnings

In constructing his socialist techno-utopia, Bogdanov was not indifferent to the dangers of collectivism and advanced technology projected by some of the dystopian fantasizers. Nor were his science fiction tales the only foreboding statements on the threats incipient in industrialism. Chernishevsky's utopian novel, *What Is to Be Done?*, that catechism of Russian nihilism, had presented an ascetic socialist utopia that, nonetheless, awkwardly embraced industrialization. With this, Chernishevsky established a genre. L.B. Afansev's *Journey to Mars* bore a warning against industrialization, whether capitalist or socialist, and Bogdanov may well have had some dark warnings in mind as he set out to describe the self-adjusting world on Mars in his science fiction novel *Red Star*. Indeed, he was acutely aware of the dreadful sociocultural consequences of a premature revolution in a backward society. But a deep-seated belief in the rational power of "systems" prevented him from descending into the depths of social pessimism—a feeling that enveloped many thinkers after the failure of the 1905 revolution.

In their preface to the translation of *Red Star*, Graham and Stites offer a careful study of Bogdanov's life and writings. They show that he was a sincere, albeit idiosyncratic, Marxist who was committed to the construction of socialism.[1] The key to Bogdanov's philosophy is his substitution of tripart Marxian dialectic with "process of organization." His main goal was the formulation of a metascience of organization that would permit regulative mechanisms to preserve stability and prevent cataclysmic change in any of life's major processes. He wanted to replace the "spontaneous" processes of change in nature and human life with a "conscious" intervention in existence.[2] However, unlike some utopian socialist philosophers, he believed that even after socialism had been successfully created, civilization would be plagued by a whole series of problems, which we would now probably recognize as problems of "technified societies." For if a triumphant socialism should someday flow through the floodgates that the bourgeoisie cast open, what dreadful impulses might flow in along with it, or in its wake? It is easy to imagine how a society committed to the free development of each and all might develop its own distinctive varieties of nihilism. Indeed, a socialist nihilism might turn out to be far more explosive and disintegrative than its bourgeois precursor—though also more daring and original—because, while capitalism cuts the infinite possibilities of modern life with the limits of the bottom line, socialism might launch the liberated self into immense unknown human spaces with no limits at all.

In his 1908 novel *Red Star* Bogdanov referred to the possibility of a socialist state surrounded and beleaguered by capitalist states. "It is difficult to foresee the outcome of these conflicts," says the novel's hero, Sterni, "but in those instances where socialism prevails and triumphs, its character will be deeply perverted and for a long time to come by years of encirclement, unavoidable terror and militarism, and the barbarian patriotism that is their inevitable consequence. This socialism will be a far cry from our own."

The foreboding of his fictional technified society turned out to be those issues central to the critique presented by K. Polanyi, H. Marcuse, and J. Habermas, among others. A central problem common to these analyses was how to organize the socioeconomy of modern technological society in a manner that would make technified production subordinate to man's societal and cultural needs and aspirations; how to "re-embed" the economy in society; how to institute a sociopolitico-ethical order in which personal responsibility of man for his fellow man, and man for his physical environment, could supersede the purely economic imperative and impersonal technocracies.

Indeed, Bogdanov's novels are filled with a foreboding image of perverted socialism, evoking elements of an antecedent Orwellian dystopia. Though committed to socialism, Bogdanov appreciated the multiple problems facing a socialist state. He expressed concern about the rise of dangerous technologies, so dangerous they would have to be removed from populated areas. He spoke of an exploding population whose rapid growth would trigger food shortages and decade-long famines. Natural resources were likely to be exhausted, including the radioactive matter that would become the principal source of energy. He spoke presciently of ecological degradation and of the dangers of technically advanced medical practices, which in prolonging human life presented moral and ethical issues for science and humanity. Expressing his views on early Soviet Russia, Bogdanov noted in a poem that it was not socialism but life "that wretchedly gropes on in vain / Toward happiness, seeking to be free."

In real life, in early 1928, some of the events described in Bogdanov's utopian novels seemed to be coming true in Stalinist Soviet Union. Throughout the twenties and thirties the Soviet Union was the only socialist country, while the imperialist powers were very much masters of the world situation. The Soviet population was sure that a life-and-death struggle was not only inevitable but imminent. Espionage and subversive activities by Europeans, and especially fascists, were stepped up in those years. Added to this was the presence of counter-revolutionary organizations. Small and disorganized as these organizations were, together with the tension of the international situation they contributed to a spy mania. It was in this atmosphere that the secret police announced that it had discovered a counter-revolutionary conspiracy among the engineers of the coal mines in the Ukraine. Fifty-three engineers and technicians were brought to court under accusations punishable by death. Bogdanov must have seen in the looming Shakhty trial the grotesque and growing perversion of the socialist ideals present in his novels.[3] Indeed, as Stalin tightened his grip over the Soviet Union, it became ever more difficult for intellectuals like Bogdanov to retain their faith in Soviet socialism.[4] He must have been haunted by the words he put into the mouth of the character Sterni years earlier, for Sterni had maintained that even if socialism begins to develop, it could be deeply perverted and turn toward militarism.

In *Engineer Menni*, Bogdanov explored the dark side of technified culture. He discerned, albeit ambiguously, a potentially threatening fusion of technology and authoritarianism celebrated by Ernst Junger. Bogdanov brought a cultural revolutionary critique of reification perspectives to bear on specific developments in the Third International and the Soviet Union. Much of his analysis focused on the elements that recreate a political elite and authority structures, whether they be new, i.e., noneconomic, forms of power or an invidious rigid value structure. He addressed the growth of a "soulless bureaucratism" and the triumph of the organizational apparatus over "revolutionary will" within the communist party of the Soviet Union. He noted that among alienation's various manifestations the most serious was due to a growing rift separating the "ordinary citizen" from an elite of economic and political decision makers, from technical experts and from a bureaucratized administrative apparatus needed for regulation of an increasingly technified social fabric. After all, bureaucratization offers above all the possibility for carrying out specialized instrumentalities according to purely objective considerations. The "objective" discharge of business primarily means a discharge of business according to calculable rules and with little regard for person. "Without regard for person" was the watchword of all pursuits of naked economic interests whether situated in capitalist or socialist contexts.

Searching for an understanding of some of the problems that agitated the likes of Marcuse and Habermas, Bogdanov clearly viewed the growth of science and technology as the most potent force of the emerging era. He was convinced their growth would be brought under control by incorporation into a new socialist value system. This view resembles Habermas's solution of accepting technology while proposing to subdue its "negative consequences" through a new "institutional framework" of "symbolic interaction." However, once having thereby "revolutionized rationality," Habermas, unlike Bogdanov, impugns his own argument by saying: "The structure of scientific-technical progress would be conserved, and only the governing values would be changed."[5]

Speaking through the character Netti, a proletarian engineer and Pisarev-like "thinking realist," in *Engineer Menni* Bogdanov addressed the sociology of science and wrote:

> I have studied several disciplines.... As I studied I came to the following conclusion. Modern science is just like the society that has created it: powerful, but splintered, and extravagant with its resources. Because of this fragmentation the individual branches of science have developed separately and lost all vital connection with each other. This has given rise to all manner of deformities, sterile artificialities, and confusion. The same phenomena and notions have dozens of different names in the various disciplines and are studied in each branch as though they were something novel. Each branch has its special language which is the privilege of the initiated and serves to exclude everyone else. Many difficulties derive from the fact that science has become divorced from life and labor, forgotten its origin and lost sight of its purpose. For this reason it busies itself with pseudoproblems and often beats about the bush trying to answer simple questions. I have noticed all this, and my opinion of contemporary science is as follows. Such as it is today it is worthless to the working class both because it is too difficult and because it is inadequate. The proletariat must master it by changing it. In the hands of the workers it must become much simpler, more harmonious and vital. Its fragmentation must be overcome, it must be brought closer to the labor that is its primary source. This is an enormous task.... As always, the first steps will be taken in isolation, but eventually men will join forces. The mission cannot be accomplished in a single generation, but each step on the way will contribute to liberation.[6]

Once again through the character of Netti, Bogdanov sought to present in a popular format the foundations of Tektology. He sought to simplify and unify scientific methods, and to this end he studied and compared the most disparate approaches applied by man in his learning and labor. Finally, he arrived at the following conclusion: No matter how different the various elements of the universe—electrons, atoms, things, people, ideas, planets, stars—and regardless of the considerable differences in their combinations, it is possible to establish a small number of general methods by which any of these elements join with another, both in spontaneous natural processes and in human activity. Thus, when the time came for the radical reformation of the entire social order, even the most serious difficulties of the new organization could be overcome systematically. Just as natural science had earlier served as a tool of scientific technique, now Tektology became a tool in the scientific construction of social life as a whole.

Zenkovsky, among others, speculates that Bogdanov was influenced on these issues by the Aristotelian philosopher N.F. Fyodorov, whose critique of contemporary society was, without doubt, stimulating to Bogdanov. Fyodorov wrote: "At the present the problem is to find, at last, the lost meaning of life, to understand the purpose for which man exists, and to order life in conformity with it. Then all the confusion and meaningless of contemporary life will disappear of itself."[7]

In the introductory pages of *The Philosophy of the Common Task*, Fyodorov, like Bogdanov, offered a critique that in some respects echoed contemporary critical commentaries on technified society. Fyodorov wrote, "Science, which was formerly the handmaiden of theology, has now become a handmaiden of commerce." To this he added:

> Science is under the yoke of manufacturers and merchants.... The scientists themselves bear this yoke willingly and prize the opportunity to advise and collaborate with businessmen. At the present time everything serves war; there is no discovery which military men have not studied with a view to its military applications.... Man has apparently done all the evil he could, both to nature (attrition, devastation, depredation) and to other men.... The very arteries of communication serve only for strategy or commerce, for war or profiteering.[8]

Consistent with Fyodorov, Bogdanov was brilliantly prescient in sketching out issues that would confront all industrialized nations two generations after he conceived them: the dangers of atomic energy, the problems of preserving the environment, the dilemmas of biomedical ethics, and the shortage of natural resources and food.[9] Indeed, according to Bogdanov, humankind would create such a fearful "machinery for the transformation of energy" that in order to avoid destruction people would have to establish a social system based on rational organization.[10] Moreover, he believed that nature was far more problematic than the class conflict. Intuitively, he anticipated the dangers of the technological civilization on the biosphere. Pointedly, he contemplated that only after the proletarian revolution had been successful and had eliminated struggles among human beings would they see that a more daunting battle lay ahead: the struggle of a united humanity to avoid being overwhelmed by the by-products of its own technological successes.[11] He argued that technical progress was bound to make concrete plans for the organization of the "state of the future" rapidly obsolete.

15
Dystopia Realized

On April 7, 1928, the day after a special plenum of the Central Committee of the Communist Party had been called by Stalin to consider the Shakhty conspiracy, Bogdanov conducted an experiment on himself that as a physician, he well knew was likely to be fatal. He exchanged his own blood with that of a young student who was suffering from both malaria and tuberculosis. He continued making detailed observations even as he lay dying. The fatal experiment was, according to Jensen, part of a search for immortality.[1] N.F. Fyodorov, a well-read librarian, was particularly fascinated by the Christian concept of resurrection and everlasting life. Lossky writes that Fyodorov formulated the notion that "man's duty is to enter the path of supramoralism, to realize a synthesis of theoretical and practical reason and to become the reason of the Universe. Through knowledge and action man must transform all the forces of nature . . . into instruments and organs of huhumankind. Having learned to control nature huhumankind will be able to overcome death."[2] Utechin asserts that Bogdanov's philosophy was permeated by the idea of overcoming nature's entropic effect on the human body—a notion derived from Fyodorovist strains in Russian philosophy.

Graham and Stites provide a less romantic and eccentric interpretation of Bogdanov's death, casting him in the role of Leonid, the hero of his novel *Red Star*, for whom "The new life is inaccessible to me, while I do not want the old one, to which I no longer belong either intellectually or emotionally." Political events, i.e., conspiracy trials and authoritarianism, that he mused about in his utopian/dystopian novels in early 1928 were in Stalin's Soviet Union of 1928 becoming a traumatic reality. Depressed by the emerging prospects, A.A. Bogdanov may have conducted his experiment knowing full well its inevitable outcome.

Bukharin published a moving eulogy to this man who had "played an enormous role in the development of our party and in the development of social thought in Russia."[3] He praised Bogdanov for his intellectual breadth and influence and as a man of courage and revolutionary boldness but also as a victim of the times.

335

During the period 1924–29 Bukharin played a central role in Soviet politics and sustained his position as a leading party theorist. In 1926, he was one of Stalin's collaborators in the struggle against Trotsky, Zinoviev, and Kamenev. But in July of 1928, as the defeated leader of the Right opposition, Bukharin told his former opponent Kamenev that Stalin was a "Genghis Kahn" who "will cut our throats."[4] Within two years Bukharin was denounced as the leader of the "Rightist deviation" and a "falsifier of Marxism," and in 1929 he was ejected from the Politburo.

In his speech "The Right Deviation in the CPSU(B)," for example, Stalin said:

> In Bukharin's theses it was stated that the fight against Social Democracy is one of the fundamental tasks of the sections of the Comintern. That of course is true. But it is not enough. In order that the fight against Social Democracy be carried on successfully, a special stress must be placed on fighting the so-called "Left" wing of Social Democracy, that "Left" wing which, by playing with "Left" phrases and thus adroitly deceiving the workers, is retarding their mass defection from Social Democracy.[5]

In understanding Stalin, we might bear in mind Dostoevsky's remarks from his *Notes from the House of the Dead*; they are well worth repeating:

> Whoever has experienced the power, the complete ability, to humiliate another human being ... with the most extreme humiliation, willy-nilly loses power over his own sensations. Tyranny is a habit, it has a capacity for development, it develops finally into a disease. I insist that the habit can dull and coarsen the very best man to the level of a beast. Blood and power are intoxicating.... The man and the citizen die within the tyrant forever; return to human dignity, to repentance, to regeneration, becomes almost impossible.[6]

In polemicizing against Bukharin and his group, Stalin and his supporters often made crude use of the method of vulgar sociologism, alien to Marxism. This method consists, in particular, in the linking of almost any cultural phenomenon or political statement with the political moods or interests of one or another class.

Just as Lenin and his circle had perceived Bogdanov's philosophy as a significant threat, so Bukharin's platform in 1928–29 was thought preferable to Stalin's among not only the broad masses of working people but also the urban and rural capitalist elements. Stalin and his supporters immediately branded Bukharin as a "defender of the capitalist elements," "exponent of the ideology of the kulaks," and "a transmission belt for kulak influences within the party."[7] With such a vulgar sociological approach it would have been possible to call Lenin a "defender of kulak-capitalist elements" in 1921–22 because of the introduction of the NEP. It is worth noting that these assessments of Bukharin were not without a lasting influence on the "history" of the party, or the appreciation of Bukharin in the West.

Although he had remained a Politburo member, after the April 1929 Central Committee plenum an intensive campaign was launched against the "Right deviationists," with criticism particularly directed at Bukharin. In November of that year, at the Central Committee plenum, Rykov read a written statement from Bukharin, Tomsky, and himself, stating that the "group of three" unconditionally stood for the general party line and disagreed with the majority of the Central Committee only in regard to certain methods of implementing this line. The group noted in their statement, "In general, very positive results have been achieved on the rails of the accepted party method of conducting the general line." They declared, "The disagreements between us and the majority of the Central Committee have been eliminated."[8] It was during the November plenum that Bukharin was removed from the Politburo, and thereafter he, together with Rykov and Tomsky, submitted an acknowledgment of their so-called mistakes. And while the Sixteenth Party Congress of January 1934 elected Bukharin to the Central Committee, with the Seventeenth Congress he was demoted to the rank of a candidate member of the Central Committee. During this Congress, Bukharin finally capitulated completely to Stalin. His lengthy speech included the following statements:

> It is clear that the "Rights," of whom I was one, had a different political line, a line opposed to the all-out socialist offensive, opposed to the attack by storm on the capitalist elements that our party was beginning. It is clear that this line proposed a different pace of development, that it was in fact opposed to accelerated industrialization, that it was opposed to . . . the liquidation of the kulaks as a class, that it was opposed to the reorganization of small peasant agriculture . . . that it was opposed to the entire new stage of a broad socialist offensive, completely failing to understand the historical necessity of that offensive and drawing political conclusions that could not have been interpreted in any way other than as anti-Leninist. . . . It is clear, further, that the victory of this deviation inevitably would have unleashed a third force and that it would have weakened the position of the working class in the extreme. . . . It would have led to intervention before we were ready . . . and, consequently, to the restoration of capitalism as the combined result of the aggravated domestic and international situation. . . . It is clear, further, that Comrade Stalin was completely right when he brilliantly applied Marxist-Leninist dialectics to thoroughly smash a whole series of theoretical postulates advanced by the Right deviation and formulated mostly by myself.[9]

It is difficult to imagine that Bukharin was altogether sincere in his remarks. But in the face of the fascist threat he may have felt it necessary to put aside "family disputes" and rally around the existing leadership—that is, Stalin.

As late as 1935 Bukharin was assailed in the magazine *Bolshevik* as a "right capitulator," who had allegedly wanted the Soviet Union to renounce industrialization and the collectivization of agriculture and to grant unlimited freedom to private capitalist interests. In March of 1937, then an editor of *Izvestiia*, he was accused of being a Trotskyite and expelled from the party. Finally, in March of 1938, at the last public trial of the Great Purge, together with twenty other prominent old Bolsheviks, he was tried, found guilty of high treason, condemned to death, and executed.[10]

A full fifty years after his execution for treason, sabotage, and terrorism, Bukharin was vindicated. The trial was formally condemned by the Supreme Soviet as a gross violation of socialist legality, based on falsifications and illegally obtained confessions. Whether or not Bukharin's early philosophical contributions on biophysical economics, let alone his political and philosophical tracts, will be resurrected remains an issue.

16
Concluding Remarks

For two centuries, economic thought has sought to reveal the truths of the livelihood of man from the traditions dominated by classical liberalism, with its conception of atomism rather than holism and of individualistic rationality rather than systems rationality. Its atomistic approach has sometimes been reflected in misplaced concreteness, in a failure to consider the wider contexts of economic action. The multiplying threats to the global biosphere, however, suggest that such an approach is increasingly problematic.

The paradigmatic, epistemological, and methodological controversies touched upon herein may remind one of Plato's allegory of the cave. The central idea, that economic analysis is imprisoned in "truth statements," "facts," or worlds that it invented, has proved to be a recondite theme in social thought. It is explored in Fyodor Dostoevsky's *Crime and Punishment* and in Franz Kafka's brooding narratives. The ideas expressed in these works draw upon a history of social thought whose compass includes Plato.

Plato was among the first to intellectualize the predicament of huhumankind as a prisoner of its thought and action. His allegory of the cave, found in Book 7 of the *Republic*, provides an evocative image that has inspired many to explore the ambiguous relationship between illusion and reality. Plato initiated the subjectivist turn in the "history of truth." While his appreciation of truth was that of unconcealment (*altheia*), it was also the presencing of ideas that were unconcealed and made available to the conscious self. In his allegory, he depicted the education necessary for a person to be transformed in such a way that he or she could encounter things in their unconcealed whole, in their truth.

With Plato, humanity took on the role of the viewer. What was stressed was the right way of "seeing." The stages that marked one's journey from the darkness of the cave toward the sunlight involved the correctness of vision and the correct correspondence between the outward appearance and perception of that appearance. In no less a manner did Aristotle perceive truth as the disclosure or unconcealment of the hidden and as correctness of perception. Consequently, he promoted the shift toward the notion of truth as the right correspondence between assertion and concrete reality. Aristotelian thought informed Medieval Christian theology, which offered knowledge not about entities but the personal salvation of the immortal soul. Truth came to be associated with "right believer" and falsity with "heresy" and "unbelief." The Greek concept of disclosure of the concealed, which with Aristotle governed the essence of *techné*, was transformed following the Enlightenment into a calculatingly self-directed and increasingly hegemonic rationality. This change in the notion of truth was compelling for modern thought.

The works of various critical theorists have developed new attacks on the basic problem, linking the idea that huhumankind becomes imprisoned by its images, ideas, and ideologies and with the need for a radical critique of this situation. While this has entered the literature of social psychology, it is essential to critical theory, which builds from the idea that while society creates its reality, it does so in confining and alienating ways. In this sense, the image of the psychic prison radicalizes many ideas pertaining not only to culture, suggesting that the enactments, accomplishments, semiotics, and semantics that shape the life-world often serve micro- and macropolitical purposes but also economic thought.

The history of economic thought itself reveals that its theories are "inventions" rather than "discoveries" and that the inventions that are acclaimed are usually those attuned to the dominant interest of the period.[1] They are not without invidious micro- and macropolitical dimensions.

Within the epic domain of positive economics there is a continued adherence to a nonscientific epistemology encouraged by mathematization. Many economists have adopted the view that formal, or mathematical, proofs are sufficient, rather than being necessary, to establish the validity of a theory. It is not unusual for theorists to set up their models in such a way that the postulated behavior runs counter to all that is known about actual economic performances without this seriously impugning either the argument or the theorist's reputation. Economics has become characterized by its fragmentary approach, by its loss of totality, and by its problematic "ontological substratum"; and the more formally intricate economics becomes, the more it isolates itself epistemologically and methodologically, the more resolutely it turns its back on the problems of its own sphere of influence, the more it suffers from Sorokin's "quantiphrenia."

The objection is not with the mathematical formalization of economics, rather it is the fetishistic misuse that has been made of formalization—in particular, the way it has been used to give a pseudoscientific facade to a body of theory. It is also formalism, whether in words or statistics or mathematics, that creates the false scientific hopes that the blackboard is all we need.[2] "The way the mathematical rhetoric has been transformed into economic rhetoric has been to define the economic problem as dealing with a certain kind of (easily manipulable) mathematics."[3] This results in the neglect of any comparable consideration of values, and indeed to the determination of ends by default. It is technique that determines not only the means but also the ends themselves. Consequently, "much of economic theorizing consists not . . . of forming explicit hypotheses about situations and testing them, but of investigating economic models."[4] It is a speculative and arcane endeavor where what finally counts is not the quality of the work produced but the continued existence and promotion of the profession. Any question raised about quality would surely be considered a form of treason or self-sabotage. It is entirely possible for a student to be graduated from a narrow, discipline-centered academic institute in almost total ignorance of the traditions of his or her craft and, for that matter, with only a superficial knowledge of the literature.

We must remind ourselves that the purpose of theory, at least in economics, is not to explain what actually happens under observable conditions but rather to determine, logically, the conditions that must be satisfied if a certain goal is to be satisfied.[5] We must return to a lost tradition of practical reason and praxiology. The problems of economics are not problems of rhetoric: they are not about the art of probing what people believe they ought to believe.[6] With these remarks, we fear we may have overstepped the bounds of diplomacy. But the intent is not to condemn economics as a pseudoscientific pursuit but to suggest that this phenomenen itself is instrumental to the dialectic of paradigm change in economic thought.

To clarify the existence of a historic rupture in the community of political economists, we have contended that economic thought, and in particular Marxian thought, confronted in the latter part of the nineteenth century a crisis of science. Critical Marxian thought emerged with a revolutionary innovation, a paradigm shift. But it was a paradigm lost in epochal convulsions.

Let us briefly review our thesis.

We contended that in the historic development of economic thought from the feudal to the modern epochs, we can identify the waxing and waning of broad themes and a titanic clash between two forms of rationality. From the Enlightenment two paradigms presented themselves: an upstart mechanicalism and the renovated vestiges of Aristotelian holism. Whereas Anglo-American economic thought aligned itself with methodological individualism, holistic appreciations populated much of German thought. But fixing its attention upon mechanicalism was the first step toward creating a paradigm and an important victory for Cartesian method.

With mechanicalism, both the philosophical and methodological underpinnings of economic thought were revolutionized. Philosophically, it retreated from the remnants of the Platonic-Aristotelian praxiological constitution, while analytically its reference image adjoined mechanics. Political economy was appreciated as more closely associated with mechanical systems, systems that seek their justification and coherence in their own equilibrium. The economy was no longer seen to be embedded in culture, society, and polity, and ultimately in nature, rather the economic system was differentiated from, and determinant of, social relations. Holism, practical reason, and praxiology were expunged from mainstream economic thought in its bid to become a science. This constituted a complete inversion of tradition. Two cultures coalesced, and knowledge was fragmented into two opposed modes of inquiry.

Economic science in the late nineteenth century sought to reinforce its authenticity as a science. It sought to be viewed as a science of no less prestige than celestial mechanics. The mechanical paradigm proved irresistible. It was simple, predictable, and above all it worked. There was an order to things, and that order could be ascertained with mathematical precision and scientific observation. Few nineteenth-century scientists escaped the compulsion to reduce, to quantify, and to mathematize. Today conventional economic thought remains in the grip of the machine model of reality, which constitutes the received paradigm.

Refuting holism, the Newtonian universe was represented by man as a huge mechanism that had been wound up once and for all time. Many theorists saw it as the basis of all knowledge. Life was discussed, from this point of view, as being merely a special kind of mechanical motion.

But with the advance of rational mechanics, the philosophical criticism of science gradually became harsher and more penetrating. Importantly, mechanicalism was not being criticized for its limitations but for its ontological presuppositions. A rival knowledge grounded on holism was reinforced within variants of German Idealism. Even while the Darwinian perspective of the evolution of life was developing, from the physical sciences and from industry there was a growing awareness that Newton's laws of motion did not provide for a complete understanding of physical phenomena. In particular, the rigorous principles of thermodynamics were found to be alien to the Newtonian world. Consequently, both in biology and in evolution theory, the second principle of thermodynamics presented a major obstacle to the understanding of life and the livelihood of man. This, in turn, led to a monist effort to synthesize the unity of scientific knowledge, to a philosophy of history that supplemented Marx's categories with that of dialectics of energy and organization. Pointedly, it meant the reassertion of the Aristotelian systems problematique and the collapse of the Laplacean prototype for political economic thought.

It signified the beginning of a paradigmatic challenge to political economy. This challenge, on the one hand, gave rise to the "marginalist revolution," in truth a fortification of the "hard core" of the mechanical paradigm, and to substantive categories of economic analysis. On the other hand, it marked the beginning of a reemergent holistic theme in political economy.

While more conventional appreciations of the Enlightenment have with good reason emphasized its positivist and mechanicalist thrust, a countercurrent was also apparent in Enlightenment thought that was to provide the philosophical grounding for the "knights of totality." "Totality" or "holism" has enjoyed a privileged and nostalgic place in the intellectual discourse of the Cultural West. Referring to the instrumental contributions of Montesquieu, Rousseau, Kant,

Hegel, and Vico, we related that it was in the tradition defined by these philosophers that Marx grounded himself. Indeed, the concept of totality has been at the center of the grand narrative that is Marxism. And it is here that we found a compass to help us traverse the vast and largely uncharted intellectual territory that is Russian Critical Marxism.

Although totality has been of enormous importance for Western Critical Marxists, other key concepts such as social energetics, praxis, phenomenology, and genetic structuralism were identified as central in the early Russian Critical Marxist tradition, and in some cases curiously absent from Western Marxism. But each of these taken in isolation would not be sufficient to give us a complete view of the topography of Russian Critical Marxism. Threading our way through tangled analyses of how these concepts were analytically engaged by Russian Critical Marxists, it is apparent that they come together in a grand, and historically contingent, synthesis.

Russian Critical Marxism and systems thinking was a synthetic invention that absorbed elements of Narodnism and nihilism in addition to the contributions of German Idealism. And while it was a response to the crisis of science, it also constituted a reaction to the timeworn economistic determinism of Scientific Marxism. Moreover, its cultural dimension anticipated and possibly informed Western Marxism.

The cosmological monism expressed by members of the Vienna Circle and the concepts of *Kulturwissenschaften* and social energetics exerted a powerful influence on the revision of Marxism, and also on Anglo-American appreciations of political economy. However, the paradigmatic challenge contingent to thermodynamics appreciations of the livelihood of man came to be regarded as an unwarranted and malicious attack on the received mechanical paradigm, an attack on science in general and materialism in particular. The most interesting of the substantive contributions to this emerging paradigm arose in prerevolutionary Russia and are identified with the philosopher, translator of *Capital*, and challenger to Lenin, Alexandr A. Bogdanov.

Standing head and shoulders above the other "revisionists," Bogdanov attempted to introduce systematically his critical views in philosophy, political economy, and sociology. Although he grounded himself on, and expressed admiration for, Marx's theories, he refused to accept the scientific interpretation of Marxism. An active member of the Socialist Academy of Sciences, he was among the founding members of the Proletariat Culture movement, an organization dedicated to advancing the labor movement and the creative role of the workers' class in culture and ideology. It is this that connects him with the aestheticization and cultural modalities of Critical Marxism later associated with Gramsci and Lukács.

Bogdanov was an idiosyncratic Marxist committed to the construction of socialism. Following Marx's dictum, Bogdanov contended that the intent of Tektology was not merely to describe the structure of the social world but to produce reliable information for changing it. In developing his praxiological Tektology, Bogdanov tried to find through genetic structural analogies and metaphors the organizational principles that would unite under one conceptual scheme "the most disparate phenomena" in the organic and inorganic worlds. This cybernetic and open systems approach apparent in Bogdanov's and Bukharin's thought was later identified in the West with the contributions of Norbert Wiener and Ludwig von Bertalanffy. Alien in its universality to the scientific thinking of even today, the idea of a general theory of organization was fully understood by only a handful of men and officially repressed. A subterranean knowledge, it became a paradigm lost in the annals of the history of economic thought.

Though committed to socialism, Bogdanov appreciated the manifold problems confronting a socialist state. He anticipated the possibility of a socialist state surrounded and beleaguered by capitalist states, and were socialism to prevail in such circumstances, a perverted edition, shorn of its possibilities, would lie in rot. He expressed concern about the rise of dangerous technologies, an exploding population whose growth would trigger food shortages and famines, and the depletion of natural resources. He discerned, albeit ambiguously, Stalin's embrace of a technocratic craze, a potentially threatening fusion of technology with authoritarianism. Nonetheless, pledged to the socialist project, both methodologically and philosophically, he contributed to the early Soviet planning, influencing Bazarov, Bukharin, and Groman.

Insofar as N.I. Bukharin is a well-recognized and amply documented political figure, our treatment of him concerned itself more with his critical appreciations of Marxism and his contribution to systems thinking. It, nonetheless, proved inconsiderate to appreciate his contribution isolated from his political life. A "seeking Marxist" and the "the darling of the Party," Nikolai I. Bukharin, alongside Bogdanov, has been regarded as one of the founders of Russian Critical Marxism and systems thinking.

Historical Materialism, among Bukharin's later works, showed Bogdanov's substantial influence on his intellectual development. He was not, however, Bogdanov's disciple, as his party enemies were later to argue. Though not repudiating Bogdanov, he did not accept *in toto* the older theorist's philosophical arguments but rather admired and was influenced by his capacity for creative innovation within the framework of Marxist ideas. The mature Bukharin refused to regard Marxism as a closed, immutable system and was sensitive both to its inadequacies and to the accomplishments of rival modes of intellectuality. Indeed, Bukharin attempted to reconcile Marxism with intellectual and scientific advances of the period. Whereas Bogdanov sought to revise Marxism initially on the basis of social energetics and phenomenology, and later on the basis of his general theory of organization, Bukharin sought to modernize it in light of the achievements of Western sociology.

Incorporating into his work the Bogdanovian concept of equilibrium, Bukharin came under a sustained attack. In their desire to slander Bogdanov,

Stalinists seized on the theory of equilibrium as a deviant symbol of anti-Soviet thought. That a growth model based on conditions of economic equilibrium could be derived from volume 2 of *Capital* did nothing to propitiate Scientific Marxism.

Bukharin's singular contribution to Russian Critical Marxism obtains from his lasting ecological contributions. In defining stable and unstable equilibrium, he employed energy and ecological analogies together with the principle of conservation and feedback concepts. For Bukharin the role of negentropic feedback mechanisms was central in the regulation of the general tendency toward disorganization. In other words, to produce a temporary and local reversal of the normal direction of entropy. This appreciation predates Norbert Wiener's formulation of cybernetics and Schrödinger's and Bertalanffy's theory of living systems. As we have seen, in *Imperialism and the World Economy*, Bukharin regarded the subjugation of nature under global capitalism as part of the contradictions of capital. Effectively, Bukharin supplemented the history-making Marxian dialectic of class conflict with the broader dialectic of man and the biosphere. He formulated a metabolic and ecologically oriented theory of open-system synergetics and located these propositions within the analytical context of economic reproduction.

Distinct from Walrasian general equilibrium, Bukharin's was a general "formulation of the laws of motion of material systems." Every system, he argued, is involved in two stages of equilibrium: internal and external. The first referred to the relationship between different components within a system, the second to the entire system in its relationship with its environment. In neither case is there ever an "absolute, unchanging equilibrium." It is always "in flux"—a dynamic or moving equilibrium. For Bukharin, it is the relation between a system, such as society, and its environment—an external contradiction—that is a decisive and basic factor.

For Bukharin "society is unthinkable without its [physical] environment." It adapts itself to nature and strives toward equilibrium with it by extracting energy from it. Presenting an argument comparable to the environmental-economic sustainability debate of the late 1980s, he asserted that a society grew when it extracted more energy from nature than it put back in. Following Marx's lead he referred to this energy flux as a metabolic life-sustaining relation between society and nature, between "external conditions" and human society. It is a relation mediated by an artificial system of organs. If society extracts from nature precisely as much energy as it consumes, the contradiction between society and nature will be reproduced; society will mark time, and a state of stable equilibrium results.

In the conclusions of his *Imperialism and the World Economy* the basic theoretical elements for an ecologically centered Critical Marxism were present in such formulations. Thus, the *idée fixe* of Bolshevism, the class struggle, in Bukharin's analysis was complemented. The nexus of class dominance with legal ownership of property would later hamper the critiques of neo-Marxists who sought to reduce environmental issues to property relations.

Bukharin was one of a small circle who cautioned against "a new ruling class" founded on privileged access to and the exercise of authority and privilege—what Bogdanov referred to as "organizational" forces. While Bukharin had in his earlier studies of capitalism glanced over the problem of "the managerial class" and of "power without property," later he realized that an exploiting organizational class could emerge on the basis of nationalized property. His discussion was prompted by the "different élite" theories of Bogdanov. Bukharin was not merely an appreciative disciple of Bogdanov, for Bukhardin was adroitly critical of the introduction of phenomenological dimensions that were ostensibly inconsistent with Marxism.

The narrow political hegemony secured by the party festered a degeneration of the body politic, the emergence of technocrats, and a distressingly vicious parochialism within the party itself. The crises emergent in the Soviet Union were neither structurally nor analytically distinct from those of capitalism, for in both systems an "economic arteriosclerosis" manifest itself, creating disproportions between production and consumption. Indeed, when appreciated from the organizational (tektological) analytic framework, the strong family resemblance between capitalism and socialism was conspicuous. Opposed to the hypertrophied and needlessly centralized edition of planning, Bukharin defended economic planning in principle.

Written from a covertly Leninist point of view, much of the history of Russian Social Democracy was first presented as a celebration and later as a vindication of Leninism. Since Western historians also tended to focus, with cultlike attention, on Lenin, the histories of Russian Social Democracy do not yet provide the historical context that the study of the Russian Critical Marxist's ideas demands. In its own small way this volume has sought to redress this lingering deficiency.

Our interest in Bogdanov was not scholastic. We appropriated him for ourselves in our own way. Reading Bogdanov has fertilized our imagination, transformed our way of thinking. Certainly, appropriating him does not license us to read him any way that suits us, uncontrolled by a respect for the distinctive grain and formation of his thought. Our "reading" was neither willful nor arbitrary, precisely because that would be contrary to our purposes.

Bogdanov retunes our intellectual ear to the historically specific and distinct register in which his concepts first sounded. It is from him that we can learn to understand and practice the discipline imposed by an unswerving attention to the peculiarities and unevenness of national cultural development.

Bogdanov made it possible for us to read Marx again in a new way, that is, to go on "thinking" face to face with the realities of the modern world from a position somewhere within the legacy of Marx's thought—the legacy of Marx's thought, that is, not as a quasi-religious body of dogma but as a living, developing, constantly renewable stream of ideas.

From his boldness and independence of mind, Bogdanov came to "inhabit" Marx's ideas, not as a straitjacket that confined and hobbled his imagination, but as a framework that liberated his mind, set it free, put it to work. Those fed on a diet of so-called Marxist writing in which the explicator is mindful of the quasi-religious character of a task and allows only for the occasional free-range movement of textual emendation were annoyed with Bogdanov's Critical Marxism. Clearly, the freedom and freshness of Bogdanov's writing was revolutionary in its impact.

The notion of the production and transformation of paradigms as a cultural terrain that all ideologies must encounter and negotiate with and to the logic of which they must conform if they are to become historically organic changed the thinking of a whole generation on these questions.

Bogdanov's ideas help us to cut through the arid wastes of an abstract definitional debate about ideology, to look at the cultural logic and forms of practical reasoning where everyday interests take shape and where the historic struggle to create the forms of a new culture is engaged. Nothing is so calculated to destroy the simple-minded notion of ideology as "correct thoughts" parachuted into the empty heads of waiting proto-revolutionary subjects as Bogdanov's stubborn attendance to the real, living textures of everyday life, thought, and culture that circumscribe the historical effectivity of even the most coherent and persuasive of philosophies.

We do not claim that, in any simple way, Bogdanov has the answers or holds the key to our present troubles; we do believe that we must "think" through our problems in a Bogdanovian way. We must not use Bogdanov, as we have for so long abused Marx, like an Old Testament prophet who, at the correct moment, will offer us the consoling and appropriate quotation. We cannot pluck up this Russian from his specific and unique political formation and transport him to the end of the twentieth century and ask him to solve our problems for us, especially since the whole thrust of his thinking was to refuse this easy transfer of generalizations from one conjuncture, nation, or epoch to another. But it is by trying to understand Bogdanov that we have come to have some glimmer of an understanding of the profound transformation that is now under way in both the Western and Eastern European societies under the aegis of the "new Right"—the moment of reconstruction in the very moment of destruction.

While there remain ontological barriers to the *Nachkonstruktion* of a paradigm lost, the adoption of a critical systems appreciation is helpful in illuminating the deficiencies of the orthodox approach and in suggesting directions for future research. For example, the elements of the authentic critical systems approach outlined above may prove useful in developing criteria for evaluating the relative advantages and disadvantages of planning and market mechanisms, as well as the performance potential of their combination. Although such an approach is vastly underdeveloped in its application to economics, modern systems thinking, which has effectively merged with cybernetics, control theory, and information theory, does explicitly deal with the issues of information and uncertainty and relates them to system and structure.

Importantly, a *Nachkonstruktion* raises the issue of the relationship between the socioeconomic system and its environment, including, most importantly, the biosphere upon which all life depends. This also constitutes a challenge to the indulgent complacency that has too long characterized economic thought.

More generally, a paradigmatic *Nachkonstruktion* may supply even further leads to a progressive reconstitution of economics on post-Ricardian foundations, with the inclusion of the evolutionary processes governing the formation and adaptation of preferences and technology within the economic system as a whole.

Notably, a paradigmatic *Nachkonstruktion* encourages interdisciplinary enquiry and the erosion of the often artificial and hardened barricades between the social sciences. It has become fashionable for economists either to ignore other social sciences or to colonize them with positivist methods. But as with all colonial conquests, in some respects it is not simply the oppressed but also the oppressor who loses out.

The legacy left by the agonizingly flawed, yet admirably heroic, efforts of the early Russian Critical Marxists and systems thinkers to see things as a whole cannot be disregarded. The questions they asked continue to be the right ones, even if the answers they offered were not. To give up the quest that they began is to resign ourselves to a destiny that everything that makes us human should compel us to resist.

If economic science is to have an emancipatory interest, it must reach beyond technical issues and formalizable pseudo-problems by questioning the social pressures and institutional contexts that today inform the research agenda. These conditions are neither immutable nor ineluctable, for we create and reinforce them in everyday decisions. The organization of our scientific and professional institutions reflects our social and political priorities. Should we allow the socio-institutional causes of economistic thinking to persist? Or should we strive for a paradigmatic change that could initiate enlightened, socially informed, and humanistic practices? The inability of economic science to form an opinion on such matters is symptomatic of its intellectual malaise and the crisis of political economy.

A paradigmatic *Nachkonstruktion*, critical systems thinking bears the character of a promise of the future, a potentiality rather than actuality.

Notes

Introduction

1. Kenneth M. Stokes, *Critique of Economic Reason.*
2. Edgar Morin, *La Methode. I, La Nature de la Nature.*
3. See Johann P. Aranson, "Perspectives and Problems of Critical Marxism in Eastern Europe," parts 1 and 2. Also see: Alvin Gouldner, *The Two Marxisms. Contradictions and Anomalies in the Development of Theory*; Barry Smart, "Phenomenological Marxism and Critical Theory"; Martin Jay, "For Gouldner: Reflections on an Outlaw Marxist"; Vladimir Tismananue, "Critical Marxism and Eastern Europe"; Jeffrey Herf, "Technology, Reification and Romanticism"; Paul Piccone, "Phenomenological Marxism."
4. May notes that in a comparative analysis of Hegel's and Marx's concepts of the master-slave relation, Hegel's account was more psychologically grounded insofar as he took into primary consideration such factors as desires, need for recognition (thymos), and fear of death. This contrasts with Marx's macrosocial appreciation (J.A. May, "The Master-Slave Relation in Hegel's 'Phenomenology of Spirit' and in the Early Marx: A Study in One Aspect of the Philosophical Foundations of Marxism").
5. Janos Kornai, *Anti-Equilibrium: On Economic Systems Theory and the Tasks of Research.*
6. F.E. Emery, *Systems Thinking*, 10.

Chapter 1

1. J.K. Galbraith, *American Capitalism: The Concept of Countervailing Power*, 17.
2. Stephen Gudeman, *Economics as Culture.*
3. Hugh Emy, "Michael Pusey's Economic Rationalism in Canberra."
4. Fritzjof Capra, *The Turning Point. Science, Society, and the Rising Culture*, 194–95.
5. Michel Foucault, *Discipline and Punish*, 27.
6. Michel Foucault, "Truth and Power."
7. Karl Polanyi, *Primitive, Archaic, and Modern Economies: Essays of Karl Polanyi.*
8. Ibid.
9. Mitchell in Yngve Ramstad, "Reasonable Value Versus Instrumental Value, 762.
10. Paul K. Feyerabend, "On the Critique of Scientific Reason," 137.
11. Rationality, however, is institutionally defined and more closely approximates a

means for legitimating an ongoing project. This critical perspective, though a central issue, lies discretely beyond the narrow purview defined in this work. But in this connection, see Stokes, *Critique of Economic Reason* and *The Empire of Reason*.

12. Mark Blaug, "Kuhn Versus Lakatos, or Paradigms Versus Research Programmes in the History of Economics."

13. Bruce Caldwell, *Beyond Positivism: Economic Methodology in the Twentieth Century*, 68.

14. Feyerabend in Caldwell, *Beyond Positivism*, 68; also see Ernst Gellner, "The Rational Mystic."

15. Vilfredo Pareto, *Manual of Political Economy*, 120.

16. "The uncertainty principle of quantum theory also refutes the classical idea of objectivity—the idea that the world has a definite state of existence independent of our observing it" (Morris Kline, *Mathematics and the Search for Knowledge*, 191).

17. Kuhn in Feyerabend, "On the Critique of Scientific Reason," 24.

18. Caldwell, *Beyond Positivism*, 68.

19. See Paul Feyerabend, *Against Method: Outline of an Anarchistic Theory of Knowledge*; also see Ermanno Bencivenga, "Theories and Practices."

20. See Alfred S. Eichner, "Why Economics Is Not Yet a Science."

21. See Feyerabend, *Against Method*.

22. See J.W. Grove, "The Intellectual Revolt Against Science"; William Newton-Smith, "Is Science Rational?"; Lawrence Richard Carleton, "Problems, Methodology, and Outlaw Science"; and William J. Broad, "Paul Feyerabend: Science and the Anarchist."

23. Thomas Kuhn, *The Structure of Scientific Revolutions*, 182.

24. Joseph A. Schumpeter, *History of Economic Analysis*, 45–46.

25. Leo Festinger, *A Theory of Cognitive Dissonance*.

26. Donald N. McCloskey, "The Rhetoric of Economics," 493–94.

27. The process of consciously building socially legitimated and viable institutions infused with new and relevant meaning is referred to as social architecture. The term *architectonik* restores the original Greek meaning of *architectoniki*, which referred more to institutional than to physical building. The new adaptive institutions required involve a paradigm shift. In this connection the further development of the Classical branch of political economy continues to be relevant.

28. Karl Popper, *The Logic of Scientific Discovery*, chapter 1; Blaug, "Kuhn Versus Lakatos."

29. In January 1993, MIT economist Paul Krugman, in a disregard for decorum, condemned the Clinton administration's appointments of Laura D'Andrea Tyson as chief economic advisor and Robert Reich as labor secretary. Krugman suspected an "effort to disenfranchise professional economists [in favor of] pop internationalists."

30. Nancy J. Nersessian, "The Roots of Epistemological 'Anarchy.'"

31. Feyerabend, *Against Method*.

32. See Paul K. Feyerabend, "Democracy, Elitism, and Scientific Method"; J. Curthoys, W. Suchting, and Paul K. Feyerabend, "Feyerabend's Discourse Against Method: A Marxist Critique."

33. Ludwig Wittgenstein, "Remarks on Frazer's Golden Bough."

34. Antonio Gramsci's concept of "historic bloc," situated in the broader notion of hegemony, while originally appreciated in nation-state and more recently international relations contexts, may, nonetheless, be analytically useful in the domain of the philosophy of science. Normal science is hegemonic science. See Carole Counihan, "Antonio Gramsci and Social Science"; Antonio Gramsci, *Selections from Prison Notebooks*; and Valeriano Ramos, Jr., "The Concepts of Ideology, Hegemony, and Organic Intellectuals in Gramsci's Marxism."

35. Karel Kosik, *Dialectics of the Concrete.*
36. Pitirim Sorokin, *Fads and Foibles in Modern Sociology.* See Stokes, *The Empire of Reason.*

Chapter 2

1. Marshall Clagett, *The History of Science.*
2. Alexandre Koyre, *Galileo Studies*; Jacob Bronowski, *The Common Sense of Science*; Marshall Clagett, *Greek Science in Antiquity.*
3. In H.G. Dick, *Selected Writings of Francis Bacon*, n.p.
4. N.N. Moiseev, "The Unity of Natural Scientific Knowledge."
5. Cicero, Marcus Tullius, *Works: Cicero in Twenty-Eight Volumes*, n.v., n.p.
6. David Hume, *Enquiry Concerning Human Understanding*, n.p.
7. Bertrand Russell, "On the Notion of Cause," in *Proceedings of the Aristotelian Society*, vol. 13, n.p.
8. Denis Diderot, *D'Alembert's Dream*; E.J. Dijksterhuis, *The Mechanization of the World Picture.*
9. This is not to say that Marx was, in fact, a doctrinaire economic determinist, for as some of his carefully crafted correspondence indicates, his was a nuanced position. See Karl Marx, "Letter to Vera Zasoulich."
10. In the construction of his ideal republic, Plato appreciated the disharmony introduced with the emergence of agencies that subordinate political life and the privileged position of ultimate norms for merely organic unity of a community. Referring to an association that issues from the interdependence of individual need giving expression to a division of labor and commerce patterned after different talents of its members, Plato condemns it as a City of Pigs, a community better suited to animals than citizens. Although the organic unity of such a community might provide for the survival of its members, its organizing principle is utterly indifferent to the hierarchy of norms that contributes to the just society and the good life. What unites its members is simply the volition to satisfy their particular desires by pursuing whatever needs and occupations may complement those of others. Each participant aims at his own welfare, and no one aims at the common benefit that could result from their complementary occupations. This subordinates the community to blind avarice, disregards the virtues of the good life, and leaves a fevered state where the divisions cultivate cravings for riches and disparities in wealth that gnaw on its own unity. It is a city without merit.
11. The economy is an instituted process of interaction serving the culturally defined material needs without which society could not persist. The two levels on which it is constituted—the interaction of man and nature and the institutionalization of that process—represent fundamental inseparable elements of the substantive economy.

Chapter 3

1. Robert M. Unger, *Knowledge and Politics*, 125.
2. Georg Lukács, *History and Class Consciousness*, 198.
3. Karl Marx and Friederich Engels, "Manifesto of the Communist Party," 343.
4. Lukács, *History and Class Consciousness*, 27.
5. Jan Smuts, *Holism and Evolution.*
6. Martin Heidegger, *What Is a Thing.*
7. An anticipatory reading of ancient Greek thought, useful though it may be, is not to suggest a chauvinist Eurocentrism. Eurocentrism is a culturalist phenomenon that assumes

the existence of irreducibly distinct cultural invariants that inform the historical paths of different peoples. While other Eastern philosophies are neglected, Arab-Islamic philosophy is treated in Eurocentric reckonings as if it had no other function than to transmit the Greek heritage to the Renaissance world. In the Eurocentric myth, Greece is presented as the mother of rational philosophy, while the "Orient" never succeeded in advancing beyond metaphysics. The myth and tyranny of Greek ancestry performs an essential cultural function. If our presentation reflects a Hellenic nostalgia, it merely reflects the regrettably limited scope of the author's knowledge of non-European sources.

8. Aristotle, *The Politics,* 1253a.
9. Ibid.
10. Aristotle, *Topics,* 150a, 15–21, 634–36.
11. John Bednarz, Jr., "Complexity and Intersubjectivity: Towards the Theory of Niklas Luhmann," 56.
12. In John Morrall, *Political Thought in Medieval Times,* 29.
13. Kenneth M. Stokes, *Man and the Biosphere: Toward a Coevolutionary Political Economy.*
14. M. Berman, *All That Is Solid Melts Into Air: The Experience of Modernity.*
15. Karl Marx, *Grundrisse: Foundations of the Critique of Political Economy.*
16. While Hume accepted Descartes's contention that sense experience cannot provide certain grounds for our belief in an external world of object, the most any individual is warranted to say with certainty is that he or she presently has such and such a sense impression.
17. Reductionism, from a methodological point of view, refers to the tendency to "look down" from the whole to the parts, to work through "analysis" to explain the properties and the behavior of an entity as a result of the properties and the behavior of its components. Symmetrically, we can say, again from a methodological viewpoint, that systems theory means "looking up" from the parts to the whole, to proceed by "synthesis," to consider the properties and the behavior of the components as being always due to an effect of the properties and the behavior of the whole. However, for positivistic science, Beings in their totalities simply do not exist. This is primarily because all Beings are reduced to their smallest component parts. In this essentially methodological process, Being is destroyed. The analyst can, of course, reduce uncertainty and ambiguity once he denotes himself to the detailed study of a small sector, limited in space and time, that is, once he forgets the system as a whole, which then becomes a vague environment. However, what can be readily elucidated and freed of ambiguity becomes of quite secondary interest because the essential has been eliminated, that is, the self-organizational complexity that attaches to Being (Edgar Morin, "Complexity," 572).
18. G. Angyal, *The Foundations for a Science of Personality.*
19. Unger, *Knowledge and Politics,* 48.
20. Ernst Cassirer, *The Philosophy of the Environment,* 13–14.
21. Vico is sometimes omitted from the Enlightenment when it is narrowly defined.
22. Giambattista Vico, *The New Science,* 36.
23. Note that poiesis, artful revealing, was distinct from techne. The latter is translated as a "skilled making." The word meant a knowing and careful producing, a drawing forth, and an artistic disclosure of things. It referred to an authentic or artful producing, bringing into the arena of accessibility and letting it present itself. To "pro-duce" something means "to lead forth" (*pro-ducere*), to release it so that it can manifest itself and linger in presence in its own way. Techne could be interpreted as involving poiesis, a producing or bringing forth of something. These aspects of techne involved intimate knowing of what things are. "Skilled making" was possible only because the artisan was gifted with the

techne to disclose the entity as a whole and to care for the thing to be made. It is techne that enables us to be at home with things, to understand what things are. The disclosure of works of art makes possible the productive disclosure of things within the world. Techne involves a particular kind of knowing, an unconcealment and disclosedness revealing what does not yet show itself and does not yet stand forth.

24. Karl Marx, "The Eighteenth Brumaire of Louis Bonaparte,"in *The Marx-Engels Reader*, R.C. Tucker, ed., 97.

25. The Marxian "making" of history, insofar as it obtains from Vico and is a distant echo of Aristotelian holism, suggests a quaver of the aesthetic. The aesthetic creation of history is possible only when man is free. Unfree man is condemned to "make" a history not freely chosen. Aesthetic creating is poetic; it is a process of poiesis, a revealing or undisclosure of the hidden essence.

26. Louis Althusser, *Politics and History: Montesquieu, Rousseau, Hegel and Marx*.

27. Stokes, *Man and the Biosphere*.

28. *Immanuel Kant's Critique of Pure Reason*. For Kant's remarks on totality, refer to the section titled "Methodology," part 3.

29. Attila Agh, "Totality Theory and System Theory," 120.

30. Ernst Cassirer, *The Question of Jean-Jacques Rousseau*.

31. J.-J. Rousseau, *Emile*.

32. J.-J. Rousseau, *The Social Contract*, 32.

33. Quoted in Lucio Colletti, *From Rousseau to Lenin: Studies in Ideology and Society*, 173.

34. J.L. Talmon, *The Origins of Totalitarian Democracy*.

35. Ernst Troeltsch sought to combine Kant's universal imperative with an appreciation of the dynamic of moral consciousness. Absolute morality must exist, he held, only through the belief that absolute morality must realize itself through persons in history, not in institutionalized value systems. Kant's imperative is then fulfilled in an "ontology of personality." See Benjamin A. Reist, *Toward a Theology of Involvement: The Thought of Ernst Troeltsch*.

36. By "the practical," wrote I. Kant, "I mean everything that is possible through freedom" (Kant, *Critique of Pure Reason*, 828). Practical reason is not goal-oriented and manipulative but a hermeneutic knowledge of appropriate norms for social action. Theoretical reason is bound to "observe" the "laws" that effectively govern the phenomenal world of experience, while practical reason is free to determine the laws that—according to its own judgment—ought to govern our social world of intercontextual relationships. While the purpose of theoretical reason is to mediate disputed claims regarding the empirical validity of theoretical propositions (hypotheses), the intent of practical reason is the mediation of disputed claims concerning the normative validity of practical propositions (assertions of norms, recommendations for action). Moreover, it is the task of practical reason to decide upon the societal acceptability of disputed value premises or life-practical consequences of actions with respect to the consequences of all those affected in the satisfaction of their needs. (See Werner Ulrich, "Systems Thinking, Systems Practice and Practical Philosophy: A Program of Research," 140.) Social knowledge directed by practical reason strives for consensus as to the ethical values and goals of a just society. In this connection, practical philosophy is the philosophical effort to come to terms with the problem of practical reason expressed in the question: How can we rationally determine and justify the norms of action contained in recommendations or plans for action? Moreover, practical reason cannot be reduced to, or derived from, alleged "value-neutral" instrumental reason but must be grounded in a critically reflected interest. For Kant "an 'interest' is that by which reason becomes practical—that is, a cause determining the will" (I. Kant, *Groundwork of the Metaphysic of Morals*, 122n).

37. I. Kant, "Idea for a Universal History with Cosmopolitan Intent," in *The Philosophy of Kant,* 119.
38. Lucien Goldman, *Immanuel Kant,* 36.
39. Ibid., 105.
40. Kline, *Mathematics and the Search for Knowledge.*
41. Herman L.F. von Helmholtz, *Popular Scientific Lectures.*
42. Kline, *Mathematics and the Search for Knowledge.*
43. René Passet, *Economic Systems and Living Systems.*
44. Pierre-Simon de Laplace, *A Philosophical Essay on Probabilities,* n.p.
45. Passet, *Economic Systems and Living Systems*; also see Mark Blaug, *The Methodology of Economics: Or How Economists Explain.*
46. G.W.F. Hegel, *The Phenomenology of the Spirit,* 11.
47. G.W.F. Hegel, *The Philosophy of History,* 104.
48. There has been a long-standing debate over the extent of Hegel's religiosity. Georg Lukács, in *The Young Hegel,* argued for Hegel's radical humanism, as did Walter Kaufmann in *Hegel: A Reinterpretation.*
49. Agh, "Totality Theory and System Theory," 121, 122.
50. One ominous implication of this is a theodicy in which conspicuous evil could in the end be seen as part of a larger good. Heidegger, for instance, regarded the technological epoch as both exceedingly dangerous and hopeful, since the new beginning could arise, he contended, only from a period of darkness and despair. Heidegger's cautious and unrepentant endorsement of the Nazi party, with its corporate policy of messianic terrorism, serves as perhaps the most graphic illustration of such a theodicy.
51. Hegel as quoted in Georg Lukács, *The Ontology of Social Being: Hegel's False and His Genuine Ontology,* 68.
52. Hegel, *Philosophy of History,* 104
53. In Leo Rauch, ed., *Hegel and the Human Spirit: A Translation of the Jena Lectures.*
54. The concept underlying "recognition" was not invented by Hegel. It is as old as Western political philosophy itself and refers to a thoroughly familiar part of the human personality. Over the millennia, there has been no consistent word used to refer to the psychological phenomenon of the "desire for recognition": Plato spoke of "thymos" or "spiritedness," Machiavelli of man's desire for glory, Hobbes of his pride or vainglory, Rousseau of his *amour propre,* Hegel of recognition.

The most articulate champion of thymos in modern times, and the prophet of its revival, was Friedrich Nietzsche, the godfather of present-day relativism and nihilism. Nietzsche's doctrine of the "will to power" can also be understood one-dimensionally as the effort to reassert the primacy of thymos as against desire and reason and to undo the damage that modern liberalism had done to man's pride and self-assertiveness. For Nietzsche, the very essence of man was neither his desire nor his reason, but his thymos. Thymos, or the alleged desire for recognition, is thus the seat of Nietzschean "values." There is here a powerful psychological component to the historical thesis based on the Greek term *thymos.* In the classical Greek the word means rage, or lust (for food or drink), and is a quality associated with animals. With Plato it has a more specific meaning akin to respect. Socrates did not believe that courage and public-spiritedness could arise out of a calculation of self-interest (recall his commentary on the City of Pigs). Rather, they must be rooted in thymos, in the just pride of the guardian class in themselves and their own city, and in their potentially irrational anger against those who threaten it. Thus for Socrates, thymos was an innately political virtue necessary for the survival of any political community, because it is the basis on which private man is drawn out from the selfish life of desire and made to look toward the common good. But Socrates also believed that thymos has the capability to destroy political communities as well as to cement them together.

But this once again popular invocation of thymos is not only psychologically deficit in a Freudian sense, it is forced. For even granting that there is a thymotic instinct, like other instincts—smiling, eating, touching, and so forth—it takes on meaning only in a social context. Moreover, what constitutes acceptable dignity or recognition varies from historical period to period, and from one society to another: what is tolerable in one place and time is not in another. Thymos is a social construct: there can be no meaningful invocation of thymos if it does not take into account the socialization of people into groups and collectivities.

55. Parenthetically, once appropriated by Scientific Marxism, the contingency of personal totalization upon global totalization, for some theorists, meant the theoretical impossibility of socialism in one country.

56. Agh, "Totality Theory and System Theory," 121.
57. Bednarz, "Complexity and Intersubjectivity," 56.
58. See Karl Marx, *The Poverty of Philosophy*.
59. Engels in Agh, "Totality Theory and System Theory," 124.
60. Marx, *Grundrisse*, 100.
61. Agh, "Totality Theory and System Theory," 124.
62. Arguing a contrary position, Joachim Israel maintains that Marx's method was that of methodological individualism. However, this argument is ostensibly constructed on the basis of a narrow textual analysis. (See Joachim Israel, "The Principle of Methodological Individualism and Marxian Epistemology.")
63. In Agh, "Totality Theory and System Theory," 124.
64. Marx, *Grundrisse*, 265.
65. Karl Marx to Heinrich Marx, November 10, 1837, in D.R. Kelley, "The Metaphysics of Law: An Essay on the Very Young Marx," 355.
66. Karl Marx, *Writings of the Young Marx on Philosophy and Society*, 356–57.
67. The bourgeois transit from partial rationality to irrationality was at the center of Georg Lukács's *The Destruction of Reason*.
68. Agh, "Totality Theory and System Theory," 127.
69. Karl Marx, *The Economic and Philosophic Manuscripts of 1844*, 159.
70. Karl Marx and Friederich Engels, *The German Ideology*, 28, 99–100.
71. Karl Marx, *Capital: A Critique of Political Economy* 3:250.
72. Marx and Engels, *The German Ideology*, 28.
73. Ibid., 125.
74. Karl Marx and Friederich Engels, *Selected Works*, 134. Note that the phrase "Critical Criticism" refers to Hegel and the Young Hegelians.
75. Marx, *Capital* 1:82n. In the first volume of *Capital* Marx explored the relationship between technological means of production and society and argued that social relations molded technology, rather than vice versa, as has often been assumed in discussions of Marxism. It was on this basis that Georg Lukács, for instance, challenged determinist claims about Marx's view of technology (Donald MacKenzie, "Marx and the Machine," 473–503).
76. Karl Marx, "Correspondence to Friederich Engels" (December 7, 1867), in *Marx and Engels Collected Works* 31:404.
77. Marx, *The Poverty of Philosophy*, 228.
78. Like all its predecessors the capitalist mode of production proceeds under definite material conditions, which are, however, simultaneously the bearers of definite social relations entered into by individuals in the process of reproducing their life. Those conditions, like these relations, are, on the one hand, prerequisites, and on the other hand,

results and creations of the capitalist process of production; they are produced and reproduced by it (Marx, *Capital*).

Marx wrote: "The result we arrive at, is not that production, distribution, exchange and consumption are identical, but that they are all elements of a totality, distinctions within a unity. Production predominates ... from it, the process continually recommences ... but there is interaction between the various elements. This is the case in every organic whole" (Marx, *Grundrisse*, 99–100).

79. Karl Marx and Friederich Engels, *Critique of the Gotha Programme: A Contribution to the Critique of the Social-democratic Draft Programme of 1891*, 331.

80. See the correspondence of Engels to Bloch 1890 and Engels to Schmidt 1890, as found in K. Marx and F. Engels, *Selected Correspondence*.

81. The French philosopher Maurice Godelier notes that: "Marx ... in posing that the structure is not to be confused with the visible relationships, but that it explains their hidden logic, is clearly a forerunner of the modern structuralist movement" (Maurice Godelier, "Systems, Structure and Contradiction in Das Kapital"; also see Donald McQuarie and Terry Amburgey, "Marx and Modern Systems Theory," 12).

82. See correspondence of Engels to Bloch 1890, in Tucker, *Marx-Engels Reader*, 760–62.

Chapter 4

1. Erwin Laszlo, *Evolution: The Grand Synthesis*.
2. See Kenneth M. Stokes, "The Marx-Engels Conception of Darwin's Theory."
3. See Karl Marx and Friederich Engels, "Wage Labour and Capital" in *Selected Works* 1:191.
4. Karl Marx, *Pre-Capitalist Economic Formation*, 81.
5. Ibid., 132
6. Norman Levine, "Marxism and Engelism: Two Differing Views of History," 220.
7. Marx, "The Eighteenth Brumaire of Louis Bonaparte," in Tucker, *Marx-Engels Reader*, 595.
8. Alfred Schmidt, *The Concept of Nature in Marx*, 61.
9. See Marx, "Critique of the Hegelian Dialectic and Philosophy as a Whole," in *Philosophic Manuscripts of 1844*, 170.
10. Levine, "Marxism and Engelism," 221. In connection with productionism let us note that conventionally, the Greek term *techne* is understood as a "skilled making" of the sort that anticipated the amazing production process of industrial technology. The rise of modern science was intrinsically linked to the transformation of substance from hypokeimenon to human subject. For the Greeks, *hypokeimenon* meant "substance" in the sense of that which lies forth as the ground and gathers the various aspects of an entity. Hypokeimenon was the essence of things. Living substance meant that which "actualized" itself, in the sense of bringing itself forth into presence. These aspects of techne involved an intimate knowledge of the hypokeimenon. Skilled making was possible only because the artisan was gifted with the techne to disclose the entity as a whole and to care for the thing to be made. It is the techne that enables us to be at home with things, to understand things in their totality. We postulate that it is in this essentialist sense that Marx appreciated one aspect of the primacy of production.
11. Schmidt, *The Concept of Nature in Marx*, 16–17.
12. Though Engels wrote *Anti-Dühring*, he never completed *Dialectics*. Begun in 1885, when he had to set aside his work on the subject in order to complete *Capital* (Marx died in 1883 with only the first volume published), Engels's *Dialectics* remained an assortment of loose notes (David Joravsky, *Soviet Marxism and Natural Science: 1917–1932*, 10).

13. Ibid.
14. Schmidt, *The Concept of Nature in Marx*, 51.
15. Friederich Engels, "Socialism: Utopian and Scientific," in Marx and Engels, *Selected Works* 1:143; see also Marx, *Pre-Capitalist Economic Formation*, 29.
16. Hegel's idealist philosophy of nature gained its bad reputation precisely through the alleged artificialities, empty constructs, and curiosities contained in it. In the case of Engels, the same constructions had a still more repellent effect (Schmidt, *The Concept of Nature in Marx*, 18).
17. Jack Mendelson, "On Engel's Metaphysical Dialectics: A Foundation of Orthodox 'Marxism'," 67.
18. G.W.F. Hegel, *The Phenomenology of the Mind*, 220.
19. "Modern natural science has had to take over from philosophy the principle of the indestructibility of motion, it cannot any longer exist without this principle. But the motion of matter is not merely crude mechanical motion, mere change of place, it is heat and light and magnetic stress, chemical combination and dissociation, life, and finally consciousness. The indestructibility of motion cannot be merely quantitative, it must also be conceived qualitatively; matter whose purely mechanical change of place includes indeed the possibility under favourable conditions of being transformed into heat, electricity, chemical action, of life, but which is not capable of producing these conditions from out of itself, such matter has forfeited motion; motion which has lost the capacity of being transformed into the various forms appropriate to it may indeed still have dynamis but no longer energia, and so has become partially destroyed. Both, however, are unthinkable" (Friederich Engels, *Dialectics of Nature*, 21).
20. In Levine, "Marxism and Engelism," 225.
21. Friederich Engels, *Anti-Dühring: Herr Eugen Dühring's Revolution in Science*, 133.
22. Engels, *Dialectics of Nature*, 38.
23. Engels, *Anti-Dühring*, 16.
24. Ibid., 62.
25. Ibid., 70.
26. The force of Engels's argument is apparent in the writings of the Soviet scientist and philosopher, V.I. Vernadsky, who, in 1945, wrote of man's biophysical and evolutionary linkage with nature. "In everyday life one used to speak of man as an individual, living and moving freely about our planet, freely building up his history. Until recently historians and the students of the humanities ... consciously failed to reckon with the natural laws of the biosphere. Basically man cannot be separated from it; it is only now that this indissolubility begins to appear and in precise terms before us. He is geologically active, connected with its material and energetic structure. Actually no living organism exists on earth in a state of freedom. All organisms are connected indissolubly and uninterruptedly, first of all through nutrition and respiration, with the circumambient material and energetic medium" (Vladimir Vernadsky, "Problems of Biogeochemistry: The Fundamental Matter-Energy Difference Between the Living and the Inert Natural Bodies of the Biosphere," 84).

"humankind taken as a whole is becoming a mighty geological force. There arises the problem of the reconstruction of the biosphere in the interests of freely thinking humanity as a single totality. This new state of the biosphere, which we approach without our noticing it, is the noösphere" (ibid., 489).

The view has been expressed that Friederich Engels's view of nature was at variance with Marx's interpretation. Concepts like objectification, affirmation, reappropriation, and alienation with which Marx wrestled throughout his life, it has been argued are not to be found in Engels's works (Levine, "Marxism and Engelism," 224). Rather than the interdependence of man and nature, Engels was primarily concerned with discovering the essence of the external world, its fundamental substance and laws. (See Zbigniew A. Jordan, *The Evolution of Dialectical Materialism*, for a comparison of Marx's and Engels's interpretation of nature.) Others, however, disputing Henri Lefebvre's critical remarks in *Dialectical Materialism*, have found in *Anti-Dühring* places where Engels fluently explains his conception of alienation (Bozidar Debenjak, "Engels and the Problem of Alienation," 45).

27. Engels, *Dialectics of Nature*, 26. Italics added.
28. Ibid., 144.
29. Mendelson, "On Engels's Metaphysical Dialectics," 69.
30. Ibid.
31. Tucker, *The Marx-Engels Reader*, 90–91, Marx's emphasis.
32. In Richard Adamik, "Marx, Engels, and Dühring."
33. See Engels's "Essays on Feuerbach" in Engels, *Dialectics of Nature*.
34. Mendelson, "On Engels's Metaphysical Dialectics," 69.
35. Engels, *Dialectics of Nature*, 205. By moving dialectics from mind to matter and by attempting to remove Hegelian mysticism from dialectics, Engels argued that the "dialectics of the mind is only a reflection of the forms of motion in the real world, both of nature and of history" (ibid., 203).

Once the distinction between natural and social regularities was blurred, Engels could no longer grasp the different relations of natural science and critical social theory to laws and practice. He developed a precritical epistemology in which the active role of subject was again lost sight of. In accord with his metaphysical presuppositions Engels could only conceive of ideas in a naively realistic way—as "images" or "copies" derived from the true reality, nature and society (Mendelson, "On Engels's Metaphysical Dialectics," 70).

Engels also spoke of dialectical thought as the "conscious reflex" of the dialectical movement of the "real world." This reflection or copy theory of knowledge was later to be elaborated by Lenin and then codified as the official epistemology of Soviet Marxism. It cuts off knowledge from its mediation through the synthetic activities of the subject and reduces it to a passive and uncritical reproduction of a separate object undergoing a law-governed evolutionary process (ibid.). However, insofar as this accusation of a copy theory is true, Engels was not consistent in this attitude and shared an inconsistency with Marx. Engels had already agreed with Marx on the profound difference between human and natural science and the crucial difference between the two centered around production (John L. Stanley and Ernst Zimmerman, "On the Alleged Differences Between Marx and Engels," 238).

For Engels motion was the binding element of nature. If this binding element consists in mere motion, and the mind merely reflects that motion (copy theory), both motion and mind would simply be randomly represented, and history would be no more than a series of accidents or contingencies that simply change the direction and flow of motion in unpredictable ways. In such a case science could not overcome alienation but could merely represent it in already discovered empirical phenomena; nature could not be brought under human control but could merely be analyzed and depicted post facto. However, as Marx expressed it, "All science would be superfluous if the outward appearance and essence of things directly coincided" (*Capital* 3:817). Therefore, some inner connection beyond mere motion had to be sought, and Marx and Engels found that inner connection in dialectics (Stanley and Zimmerman, "On the Alleged Differences," 239).

36. Engels, *Dialectics of Nature*, Appendix 1, 320; also see Schmidt, *The Concept of Nature in Marx*, 78.
37. Marx and Engels, *Collected Works* 11:373–74.
38. Engels, *Anti-Dühring*.

39. Ibid., 77. This argument for the autodynamism of the social and material worlds was critical to Soviet arguments against Pareto's theory of equilibrium.
40. Mendelson, "On Engels's Metaphysical Dialectics," 67.
41. Engels, *Dialectics of Nature*, 43.
42. Marx, *Capital* 1:169.
43. Mendelson, "On Engels's Metaphysical Dialectics," 69. Lukács expressed the opinion that there can be no question of a dialectic of external nature, independent of man, because all the essential moments of a dialectic would in that case be absent. Expressing these views in *History and Class Consciousness* (24, n6), Lukács wrote: "The misunderstandings that arise from Engels's dialectics can in the main be put down to the fact that Engels—following Hegel's mistaken lead—extended the method to apply also to nature. However, the crucial determinants of dialectics—the interaction of subject and object, the unity of theory and practice, the historical changes in the reality underlying the categories as the root cause of changes in thought, etc.—are absent from our knowledge of nature."
44. In Joravsky, *Soviet Marxism and Natural Science*, 9.
45. Schmidt, *The Concept of Nature in Marx*, 195.
46. Terrel Carver, "Marx, Engels and Scholarship." Also see Stanley and Zimmerman, "On the Alleged Differences."
47. Schmidt, *On Marx's Concept of Nature*, 60.
48. Ibid., 191.
49. See Engels's work titled "Die Lage Englands, I, Das 18 Jahrhundert," as found in Marx and Engels, *Collected Works*, 551.
50. Engels, *Dialectics of Nature*, 238.
51. See Engels's article titled "Ludwig Feuerbach and the End of Classical German Philosophy," in Levine "Marxism and Engelism," 225.
52. Mendelson, "On Engels's Metaphysical Dialectics," 68. In other words, it displays general systems theoretical tendencies.
53. Levine, "Marxism and Engelism," 228.
54. Quoted in ibid.
55. See Engels's article titled "Socialism: Utopian and Scientific," in Marx and Engels, *Selected Works*, vol. 1, 386.
56. Henri Lefebvre, *Dialectical Materialism*, 19.
57. Levine, "Marxism and Engelism," 228.
58. Terrel Carver, "Marx, Engels and Scholarship," 256. In the 1870s and 1880s Engels was not merely responding to the revival of idealism. He was not merely trying to defend Marxism or materialism in general from the renaissance of subjectivist philosophy. He was, rather, building on themes present in his 1858 correspondence (Levine, "Marxism and Engelism," 227).
59. On July 14, 1858, Engels wrote to Marx and reflected therein on Hegel's Philosophy of Nature (Marx and Engels, *Selected Correspondence* 2:113). In that letter he noted that in the realm of physics there was the discovery of the correlation of forces, the law that under certain conditions mechanical motion would be changed into heat, and then heat into light, etc., as noted by Grove in 1838 (Levine, "Marxism and Engelism," 228).
60. Ibid.
61. Friederich Engels, *The Origin of the Family, Private Property, and the State*.
62. Ibid., 19.
63. Levine, "Marxism and Engelism," 232.
64. Erwin Ban, "Engels als Theoretiker."
65. It is, then, paradoxical that the Stalinists would also profess to be in favor of political struggle and revolution, for were socialism inevitable or fated, why bother to struggle?
66. See Marx and Engels, *Selected Correspondence*, 208, 496, 500, 503.

Chapter 5

1. Engels's understanding of the second law of thermodynamics was clearly partial. He wrote: "The heat radiating in space must necessarily be able to convert itself into some other form of motion; and that in that new form it can immediately be reconcentrated and reactivated. In this way we are free of one main obstacle to dead suns being re-converted into incandescent nebulae" (Engels, *Dialectics of Nature*). Implied by this argument is that dialectical materialism with its immanent transformation of matter—the transformation of the quantitative into the qualitative—can contravene the second law.

2. This is not to say that Marx and Engels were unaware of the then emerging and speculative theory of social energetics, for in their personal correspondence they were sufficiently stimulated to note the contributions of the Ukrainian Serhii Podolinsky.

3. Gramsci, *Prison Notebooks*.

4. Roisin McDonough, "Ideology as False Consciousness: Lukács."

5. Russell Jacoby, "The Inception of Western Marxism: Karl Korsch and the Politics of Philosophy."

6. Karl Kautsky, *The Class Struggle*, 125.

7. Perhaps among the most influential Marxist theoreticians of imperialism in the years before World War I was Rudolf Hilferding with his study *Das Finanzkapital*, which appeared in 1910. It was conceived as an extension of Marx's ideas to modern economic developments. For Hilferding, the internationalization of finance capital was an important factor in equalizing the level of economic development throughout the world. It was one of the positive developments in the recent evolution of capital with which Hilferding was particularly concerned, for to him it appeared that modern capitalism was evolving in a direction that would make the emergence of socialism a distinct possibility. The concentration of the economy had put central planning and control within easy reach. The fact that industry was controlled by the banks meant that a single bank could "exercise control over the whole of social production" (Hilferding, *Das Finanzkapital*, 218).

8. It is, nonetheless, necessary to remark that Lenin's fight for an authoritative vanguardist party and program was based on the need to organize a confused movement. "Politics," he wrote, "cannot be separated mechanically from organization" (speech concluding the Eleventh Congress of the Russian Communist Party, quoted in John R. Ehrenberg, "Lenin and the Politics of Organization"). The demands of organization replaced theory and ideology as the leading problem with which Russian Marxism had to deal.

Chapter 6

1. René Descartes, *Discourse on Method and the Meditations of Descartes*.

2. Jeremy Rifkin and Ted Howard, *Entropy: A New worldview*.

3. Adam Smith, *Wealth of Nations*, 270.

4. Baron Jean-Joseph Baptiste Fourier, *The Analytical Theory of Heat*; Joseph Grattan-Guinness, *Joseph Fourier 1768–1830*; Ilya Prigogine and Isabella Stengers, *Order Out of Chaos: Man's New Dialogue with Nature*.

5. Prigogine and Stengers, *Order Out of Chaos*.

6. Clagett, *Greek Science in Antiquity*; Andrew Meldrum, *Eighteenth Century Revolution in Science: The First Phase*; Prigogine and Stengers, *Order Out of Chaos*.

7. Meldrum, *Eighteenth Century Revolution in Science*; Prigogine and Stengers, *Order Out of Chaos*.

8. Kline, *Mathematics and the Search for Knowledge*.

9. Naftali Prat, "Diamat and Contemporary Biology," 199.
10. Kline, *Mathematics and the Search for Knowledge.*
11. James P. Joule, *Scientific Papers.*
12. Prigogine and Stengers, *Order Out of Chaos.*
13. Howard T. Odum and Elisabeth C. Odum, *Energy Basis for Man and Nature*; Passet, *Economic Systems and Living Systems*; Yoshiro Tamanoi, Atsushi Tsuchida, and Takeshi Murota. "Towards an Entropic Theory of Economy and Ecology: Beyond the Mechanistic Equilibrium Approach."
14. Nicholas Georgescu-Roegen, *Energy and Economic Myths: Institutional and Analytical Economic Essays.*
15. Sadi N.L. Carnot, *Memoir on the Motive Power of Heat.*
16. In mechanics a process is said to be reversible if, and only if, it can follow an identical course phase by phase in the reverse order.
17. The laws of thermodynamics can be briefly stated as follows. First law: The principle of conservation of matter and energy states that energy can be neither created nor destroyed, only transformed. Another common formulation is "the energy of the universe is constant." The first law of thermodynamics was clearly formalized in 1847 by von Helmholtz, in his essay on the preservation of force.

Second law: A popular statement of this law is the principle that heat flows from hot to cold; it is connected to such common-sense observations as the fact that lakes do not freeze by themselves in the middle of summer. There are also formal definitions, such as, "the entropy of the universe is always increasing," or, the equivalent formulation that entropy of a closed thermodynamic system must also increase.

For an exposition of the thermodynamic laws the reference image is that of an hourglass, an isolated system that can exchange neither energy nor matter with the outside. If the stuff inside the hourglass represents matter-energy, the simple fact that the hourglass is completely sealed expresses the first law of thermodynamics, the conservation law. As in any hourglass, including that which is the universe, the stuff pours down continuously from the upper to the lower half. However, two important features must be distinguished between our ordinary hourglass and the universe.

First, as the matter-energy within pours down, it changes, and it undergoes qualitative change. So long as it is in the upper portion, it represents available matter-energy, that is, it has a potential, a form that can be used by human beings, as well as by any living organism. When it reaches the lower half, the matter-energy loses this property; it becomes unavailable.

Second, the hourglass (universe) cannot be turned upside down, which means that the available matter-energy of an isolated system is continuously and irrevocably degraded into the unavailable state. We are reminded that the concept of entropy is, at bottom, a relative index of the amount of unavailable energy. The last statement constitutes a simpler as well as a more telling formulation of the second law of thermodynamics than found elsewhere.

18. Rudolf J.E. Clausius, *Reflections on the Motive Power of Fire by Sadi Carnot; and Other Papers on the Second Law of Thermodynamics.*
19. Prigogine and Stengers, *Order Out of Chaos.*
20. That the universe tends toward a final state of thermal equilibrium was Boltzmann's *Warmtod* (heat death).
21. This universal condition represents the ultimate manifestation of Boltzmann's "ordering principle." See Ludwig Boltzmann, *Der zweite Hauptsatz der mechanischen Wärmtheorie* and *Theoretical Physics and Philosophical Problems.*
22. T.H. Huxley, *Evolution and Ethics and Other Essays.*
23. Both Hegel's and Maxwell's concept may be understood as points of bifurcation in the sense of René Thom's catastrophe theory. In connection with Maxwell see R. Campbell Lewis and William Garnett, *The Life of James Clerk Maxwell: With a Selection*

from his Correspondence and Occasional Writings and a Sketch of His Contribution to Science. London: Macmillan and Co., 1882.

24. Kline, *Mathematics and the Search for Knowledge.*
25. Ibid.
26. H. Poincaré, *Value of Science.*
27. Ibid.
28. Boltzmann, *Theoretical Physics and Philosophical Problems*; Engelbert Broda, *Ludwig Boltzmann: Man, Physicist, Philosopher.*
29. Werner Heisenberg, "The Representation of Nature in Contemporary Physics."
30. According to Georgescu-Roegen, "The entire edifice of statistical theory rests on the general assumption that the relation between any sample and the parent population is homomorphic to that produced by a random mechanism. Most econometricians have assumed all along ... that all economic data fulfill this condition and yet no justification other than verbalism has been offered in support of this position" (*Energy and Economic Myths*, 261).
31. Kenneth E. Boulding, *A Primer on Social Dynamics*, 193.
32. Anatol Rapoport, "Methodology in the Physical, Biological and Social Sciences."
33. Sir Arthur Stanley Eddington, *Fundamental Theory.*
34. J. Monod, *From Biology to Ethics,* 19.
35. Aleksandr I. Oparin, *Chemical Origin of Life.*
36. Prigogine and Stengers, *Order Out of Chaos.*
37. According to Schlipp, Albert Einstein considered the laws of thermodynamics to be least likely ever to be overthrown. He wrote: "A theory is more impressive the greater [the] simplicity of its premises, the ... different kinds of things it relates and the more extended is its area of applicability. Therefore the deep impression which classical thermodynamics made upon me. It is the only physical theory of universal content concerning which I am convinced that, within the framework of the applicability of its basic concepts, it will never be overthrown" (P.A. Schlipp, ed., *Albert Einstein: Philosopher Scientist*, vol. 7).
38. Only later did evolution theory include geospheric phenomena. (See Alfred J. Lotka "Biased Evolution"; Erwin Schrödinger, *What Is Life? and Other Scientific Essays.*
39. For a long time other important physicists, such as Bohr and Pauli, held the view that the happenings of nature were subject only to probabilistic interpretation, while Planck, Einstein, and Schrödinger, among others, adhered to the classical mechanical conceptions of causality and determinism. It then comes as no surprise that Schrödinger's thermodynamical interpretation of living systems was predicated on causal and deterministic grounds.
40. Alfred J. Lotka, *Elements of Mathematical Biology, Elements of Physical Biology.*
41. This position was assumed by Karl Pearson, who argued that an observer traveling away from the earth at a speed greater than light would view events on our planet in their reverse order (Lotka, *Elements of Mathematical Biology*, 24; Ilya Prigogine, *Introduction to Thermodynamics of Irreversible Processes*). (That the speed of light cannot be exceeded in no way undermines Pearson's argument.) The core of the argument is that evolution is relativistic: any movie film may be projected either "forward" or "backward." How can we, given this apparent duality of Time, ascertain which is the right way? However, the more serious fault is that it fails to explain the concept of "forward" and "backward." In other words, assuming that we are presented with individual unconnected frames, how can we splice them in the correct order? If we cannot, there is no Time at all in nature (G.A.Y. Gunter, ed., *Bergson and the Evolution of Physics*; Ilya Prigogine, *From Being to Becoming: Time and Complexity in the Physical Sciences*).

While the principles that attach to material and energy transformations are critical to our understanding of natural and artificial processes, the second law of thermodynamics is special in another way as well. It is the merit of classical thermodynamics to have clarified the problem of Time in relation to nature.

Nowhere is the entropy law more important than in the determination of Time. Saint Augustine once wrote, "I know what Time is, if no one asks me, but if I try to explain it to one who asks, I no longer know" (Eddington, *Fundamental Theory*, 127). All known laws of physics, except this one, are invariant under Time reversal; that is, they would not change if Time were to "flow backward." Actually, without a Time's arrow even the concept of mechanical reversibility loses all meaning. It then behooves those claiming that evolution is a relativistic concept to demonstrate how, if there is no irrevocable process in Nature, one can make sense of ordinary temporal laws.

In classical physics, Time can go in either direction. Because Newtonian physics is based on relatively simple closed mechanical systems, every change of matter in motion must be theoretically reversible. For example, imagine a film of billiard balls colliding with each other. Even when the film is projected in reverse the sequence of events makes sense, so long as we are dealing with simple mechanical motion. In the Newtonian sense, Time can be represented equally well as either positive or negative.

The point of departure is the observation, which numerous philosophers including Friederich Engels have insisted upon (Engels, *Dialectics of Nature*, 26), that the world is in a process of becoming. We are immersed in a world of Heraclitean flux and are experiencing a world that is always changing around us—an experience that may be explained by the unfolding of the second law of thermodynamics. We experience the passage of time with a succession of events unfolding one after another. Prigogine notes that it is to the merit of classical thermodynamics to have clarified the problem of Time in relation to Nature (Prigogine and Stengers, *Order Out of Chaos*).

If the stream of consciousness moves only "forward," the corresponding attribute must reflect an irrevocable process. With every event there is a transformation and a corresponding dissipation of matter-energy, and thus an increase in entropy. It is with this dissipation of matter-energy that we experience the passage of time. The forward direction of Time is a function of the irreversible change in entropy (ibid.). Prigogine argues that it is Time that reflects the change in energy from available to unavailable. To say that the world is running out of available matter-energy is to say that the world is running out of Time. Or, in the words of Sir Arthur Eddington, "Entropy is Time's arrow" (A.J. Ayer, *Language, Truth, and Logic*, 57–58). Boltzmann's *Warmtod*, long identified with universal thermodynamic equilibrium, refers to the cessation of all events; with *Warmtod* "real" Time stops. However, Vernadsky has noted that, "Physico-chemical processes creating a living natural body in the biosphere are not reversible in time. This may be the result of a peculiar state of space-time having a substratum corresponding to a Non-Euclidean geometry" (Vernadsky, "Problems of Biogeochemistry," 508).

42. Schrödinger, *What Is Life?*

43. As a possible direction of escaping from this gloomy image, discussions focused on the so-called Maxwell demon, which was said to be able to act as a sorter between high- and low-speed molecules so as to reduce entropy in isolated systems (C.W. Francis Everitt, *James Clerk Maxwell: Physicist and Natural Philosopher*; David Keith Chalmers MacDonald, *Faraday, Maxwell, and Kelvin*). A variety of thought experiments on this issue were reviewed, and it was concluded that the demon generates more entropy than is reduced. Though a number of variations of the story exist, the conclusions are unanimous; every effort to find an exception to the entropy law failed. Nonetheless, some obscurity remains, in particular, the apparent paradox of living systems (Paul I. Medow, "J. Robin's 'Culture and Technology: Fusion or Collison': An Extended Summary").

44. Max Planck, "The Unity of the Physical Universe," 16.

45. The deterministic point of view was so firmly held that philosophers applied it to

actions of human beings as a part of Nature. Ideas, volitions, and actions are necessary effects of matter acting on matter. The human will is determined by external physical and physiological causes. Hobbes explained apparent free will in this way: Events from without act on our sense organs, and these press on our brains. Motions within the brain produce what we call appetites, delights, or fears, but these feelings are not more than the presence of such motions. When appetite and aversion jostle each other, there is a physical state called deliberation. One motion prevails, and we say that we have exercised free will. However, no choice is really made by the individual. We are conscious of the result but unconscious of the process that determined it. There is no free will. It is a meaningless conjunction of words. The will is bound fast in the actions of matter.

46. Meldrum, *Eighteenth Century Revolution in Science*.
47. Prigogine and Stengers, *Order Out of Chaos*.
48. Ludwig von Bertalanffy, "The Theory of Open Systems in Physics and Biology" and *Problems of Life*.
49. Prigogine and Stengers, *Order Out of Chaos*.
50. Among structuralists the analogous arguments have only recently begun to penetrate their appreciation of international political economy.
51. By ignoring the truths of the entropy law determinist and statistical mechanics provided the illusion that Time was autonomous, independent of the workings of Nature. This alienation of Time from Nature began with Descartes's suggestion that the world is organized in such a way that there is a total separation between man and Nature.
52. In Emily Herman Bergson, *Eucken and Bergson: Their Significance for Christian Thought*. See Gunter, *Bergson and the Evolution of Physics*.
53. Schrödinger, *What Is Life?*
54. It was Fourier's heat propagation that Carnot identified as a possible cause of power losses in a heat engine. Carnot's cycle, no longer the ideal but the "real" cycle, became the point of convergence of two universalities of the nineteenth century—energy conservation and heat propagation. The combination of these two discoveries led William Thompson to formulate his new principle: the existence in nature of a universal tendency toward an equilibrium identified with the degradation of mechanical energy, i.e., the celebrated second law of thermodynamics. Thompson stated them forcefully in his treatise "On the Universal Tendency in Nature to the Dissipation of Mechanical Energy" (Silvanus P. Thompson, *The Life of Lord Kelvin*; Andrew Gray, *Lord Kelvin: An Account of His Scientific Life and Work*; P.M. Harman, *Wranglers and Physicists: Studies on Cambridge Physics*; Prigogine and Stengers, *Order Out of Chaos*).
55. Nicholas Georgescu-Roegen, *The Entropy Law and the Economic Process*; Moiseev, "The Unity of Natural Scientific Knowledge."

One might, for instance, refer to the nineteenth-century debate pertaining to alternate forms of rationality that challenged Euclid's geometry and that in the 1930s was generalized and analyzed in terms of Gödel's theorem.

56. Edmund Husserl, *The Crisis of European Sciences and Transcendental Phenomenology*, 290.
57. H.L. Bergson, *Introduction to Metaphysics*.
58. Warren Weaver, "Science and Complexity."
59. In particular, the difficulty developed in connection with the formulation of a mechanical model of propagation of electromagnetic waves. Despite Herculean efforts to determine physically what an electric field and a magnetic field were, scientists were unsuccessful (Kline, *Mathematics and the Search for Knowledge*, 143).

Our ignorance about the physical nature of electromagnetic waves disturbed many of the principal creators of the theory, Helmholtz and Lord Kelvin among them. What was lacking was a mechanical theory of ether. Maxwell, in proving that electromagnetic waves travel at the speed of light, also concluded that these waves travel in ether. Since Newton's time ether had been the accepted medium in which light moved. Because the waves move with enormous speed, the ether must be highly rigid, for the more rigid a body, the faster waves travel through it. However, if ether pervades space, it must be completely transparent and the planets must be able to move through it without frictional losses. Moreover, ether cannot be touched, smelled, or isolated from other substances. Such a medium is physically incredible.

60. Hertz in Kline, *Mathematics and the Search for Knowledge,* 144. Hertz's comments are no less appropriate to V. Pareto's equations of a man-less world of economic calculations.

61. Ibid., 146.
62. Ibid., 199.
63. Poincaré, *Value of Science,* 171.
64. Abel Rey, *The Physical Theory of the Modern Physicists.*
65. Abel Rey as quoted in Vladimir I. Lenin, *Collected Works* 14:256.
66. Mooney writes that what Teilhard de Chardin was searching for was a synthesis of knowledge, which neither science nor philosophy had yet achieved, and this involved him in a criticism of both—the first for being too specialized, the second for losing contact with the physical world (Christopher F.J. Mooney, "Teilhard de Chardin and Modern Philosophy"). Science, he said, has excluded from its consideration that which is proper to man, his power to think and to reflect, and has consequently been speaking about an inhuman and truncated world. Philosophy, on the other hand, while concentrating on man, has ignored man's relationship to matter and has tended to construct an a priori and purely deductive knowledge starting from abstract principles and ideas.

"Teilhard's solution to this dilemma . . . was to widen the range of pure science. We have knowledge of man on the fringe of the universe, but still no science of the universe including man as such. Present day physics . . . as yet makes no place for thought" (ibid., 68).

67. Lenin, *Collected Works* 14:257.
68. Joravsky, *Soviet Marxism and Natural Science,* 2.
69. By a monistic philosophy we are given to understand a unitary conception of the world based solely on scientific knowledge acquired by reason and through critical experience.
70. See *The Monist,* vol. 6.
71. Wilhelm Ostwald, *Energetische Grundlagen der Kulturwissenschaften.*
72. Ostwald's coefficient is analytically similar to Alfred Lotka's formulation of the Maximum Power Principle and as reformulated by H. Odum.
73. Henry Charles Carey, *Principles of Social Science,* 62.
74. Ibid., 41–42.
75. Ibid., 61.
76. W.S. Jevons, *The Coal Question: An Inquiry Concerning the Progress of the Nations,* 456.
77. Ibid., x.
78. Ibid., xxxi.
79. J.R. McCulloch, "Philosophy of Manufacturers," 455–60.
80. Paul Christensen, "The Materials-Energy Foundations of Classical Theory," 79.
81. See John Stuart Mill, *Principles of Political Economy.*
82. Ibid., 34–35.
83. Jevons, *The Coal Question,* 142.
84. Jevons wrote: "It has been rendered apparent that the universe, from a material point of view, is one great manifestation of a constant aggregate energy. The motion of

falling bodies, the motions of magnetic or electric attractions, the unseen agitation of heat, the vibration of light, and even the molecular changes of chemical action, and even the mysterious life-motions of plants and animals, all are but the several modes of greater or lesser motion" (ibid., 162).

85. Ibid.
86. Ibid., 287.
87. Ibid.
88. Ibid.
89. Ibid., 455.
90. Ibid.
91. Ibid., 460.
92. "We need and are irresistibly being led," wrote Teilhard de Chardin, " to create by means of and beyond all physics, all biology and all psychology, a science of human energetics" (Pierre Teilhard de Chardin, *The Phenomenon of Man,* 311).
93. John Grier Hisben, "The Theory of Energetics and Its Philosophical Bearings," 321.
94. Ibid.
95. Ibid., 322.
96. Howard T. Odum, *Environment, Power, and Society* and *Systems Ecology: An Introduction*; Odum and Odum, *Energy Basis for Man and Nature.*
97. Frederick C. Copleston, *Philosophy in Russia: From Herzen to Lenin and Berdyaev*, 285.
98. In Edwin E. Slosson, *Major Prophets of Today,* 199. Implicit in Ostwald's social energetics is the notion of life as a "heat engine." This same concept was later asserted by the economist F. Soddy, and more recently by Y. Tamanoi and R. Passet.
99. Alfred J. Lotka, *Elements of Mathematical Biology, Elements of Physical Biology*; Frederick Soddy, *Cartesian Economics: The Bearing of Physical Science Upon State Stewardship*; Tamanoi et al., "Towards an Entropic Theory of Economy."
100. Ibid., 201.
101. Dimensions of Ostwald's are to be found in "Natural Philosophy" in Slosson's *Major Prophets of Today.*
102. Ibid., 201.
103. Ibid.
104. Wilhelm Ostwald, "The Modern Theory of Energetics," 481, 484.
105. Ibid., 506–7.
106. Ibid., 488.
107. Ibid., 511.
108. Ibid., 513.
109. Ibid.
110. Wilhelm Ostwald, "Der Energetische Imperativ."
111. Slosson, *Major Prophets of Today*, 206.
112. Ibid., 207.
113. Ibid.
114. Ibid., 208.
115. Ostwald in ibid., 209.
116. Ostwald, "Natural Philosophy," in ibid., 201.
117. In ibid., 227–28.
118. Max Weber, *Energetische Kulturtheoriem.*
119. J. Martinez-Alier, *Ecological Economics: Energy, Environment and Society*, 188.
120. Ibid., 189.
121. L. Winiarsky, "L'energie sociale et ses mensurations."

122. Pitirim Sorokin, *Contemporary Sociological Theories Through the First Quarter of the Twentieth Century*, 25.
123. Winiarsky, as quoted in Pitirim Sorokin, *Contemporary Sociological Theories*, 27.
124. Ibid., 27–28.
125. From L. Winiarsky, "La Method mathematique dans la sociologie et dans l'economie," as quoted in ibid., 23–29.

Chapter 7

1. In Nicholas Berdyaev, *The Origin of Russian Communism*, 27.
2. In what follows I will use the term Cultural West as descriptive of a nuanced reading of the European modernity project. Importantly, the term is not hostaged to the territorially defined West but extends beyond its shores.
3. It would be perilous to argue that the notion of the primacy of "the people" was something unique to Slavophile thought. For there were and are parallels with some aspects of Central European thought. In this connection one might refer to points of correspondence with Karl Polanyi's concept of the "reality of society." See Kenneth M. Stokes, "Social Ethics and Reflections on Socio-Economic Transition."
4. Mikhailovsky in Berdyaev, *The Origin of Russian Communism*, 61.
5. Dostoevsky in ibid., 45.
6. Not without reason did Marx make a study of Russian in order to read Chernishevsky.
7. "We have little sense of personal dignity, of necessary egoism. . . . Are there many Russians who have discovered what their real activity is? . . . It's then that what is known as dreaminess arises in characters who are eager for activity. And do you know what a Petersburg dreamer is, gentlemen? . . .

"In the streets he walks, with a drooping head, paying little attention to his surroundings . . . but if he does notice something, even the most ordinary trifle, the most insignificant fact assumes a fantastic coloring in his mind. Indeed, his mind seems attuned to perceive the fantastic elements in everything.

"These gentlemen are no good at all in the civil service, though they sometimes get a job" (Fyodor Dostoevsky, *Petersburg News*).
8. F. Nietzsche, *Twilight of the Idols and the Antichrist*, 91.
9. The profound unrest that obtains from Nietzsche's Buddhist will-to-will in Western metaphysics and technological nihilism for Heidegger reduced humanity to the status of an animal with infinite craving.
10. Marx and Engels, "Manifesto of the Communist Party," in *Collected Works* 6:487.
11. The correspondence of the nihilist's philosophy bears a striking resemblance to that expressed by Karl Popper in *The Open Society and Its Enemies*.
12. Dostoevsky was a member of the Fourierist and left-wing Hegelian-oriented Petrashevsky circle, which held its meetings at the St. Petersburg home of Michael Butaschevich-Petrashevsky. The gatherings ended tragically. All its members were arrested, and twenty-one were condemned to death, commuted to penal servitude. Among them was Dostoevsky.
13. Sergei Nechaev in Michael Bukunin, *Social-politscher Briefweschel mit Alexander Hersen and Orgarëv*, 63.
14. Sergei Nechaev in Roy Medvedev, *Let History Judge: The Origins and Consequences of Stalinism*, 597.
15. Fyodor Dostoevsky, *Collected Works*, vol. 3, 596, 597.
16. The split among the Russian social democrats, that is between the Bolsheviks and the Mensheviks, began with the Congress of the Social Democratic Party, which took

place in London in 1903. At that Congress the Bolsheviks received a quantitative "majority," the Mensheviks a "minority" of votes. In 1917 Plekhanov was to support the Mensheviks.

17. Marx and Engels, *Selected Correspondence*, 355.
18. Ibid., 352.
19. Marx, "Letter to Vera Zasoulich," 278.
20. Levine, "Marxism and Engelism," 237.
21. Marx and Engels, *Selected Correspondence*, 355.
22. Levine, "Marxism and Engelism," 239.
23. See N.I. Bukharin, *Historical Materialism: A System of Sociology*.
24. Levine, "Marxism and Engelism," 239.
25. James D. White, "The First Pravda and the Russian Marxist Tradition," 184.
26. G.W.F. Hegel, *The Philosophy of Right*.
27. Boris Chicherin, in his *Essays in the History of Russian Law* and *Property and the State*, in particular showed his adherence to Hegelianism, treating the state as the supreme coordinator and expression of community life and national spirit. (See Michael T. Florinsky, ed., *Encyclopedia of Russia and the Soviet Union*.)
28. White, "The First Pravda," 185.
29. Peter Lavróv, *Historical Letters*, 104.
30. In this connection Martin Heidegger's *Being and Time* may be interpreted as an existentialist attempt at a nonreductive materialist ontology.
31. Lavróv, *Historical Letters*, 102.
32. White, "The First Pravda," 187.
33. Manfred Frank, *What Is Neostructuralism?* 82.
34. E. Roy Weintraub, "Methodology Doesn't Matter, but the History of Thought Might," 263–79.
35. Richard Rorty, *Philosophy and the Mirror of Nature*, 171.
36. Ibid., 315.
37. Karl G. Ballestrem, "Lenin and Bogdanov"; George Gorelik, "Reemergence of Bogdanov's Tektology in Soviet Studies of Organization" and "Bogdanov's Tektology: Its Nature, Development and Influence"; Kenneth M. Jensen, *Beyond Marx and Mach: Alexander Bogdanov's Philosophy of Living Experience*; Ilmari Susiluoto, *The Origins and Development of Systems Thinking in the Soviet Union: Political and Philosophical Controversies from Bogdanov and Bukharin to Present-Day Reevaluations*.
38. John Biggart, "Bukharin and the Origins of the 'Proletarian Culture' Debate," 232.
39. At this time, Bogdanov maintained that political revolution was a necessary precondition of socialism. This is the so-called Maximalist position.
40. V.V. Vorovsky as quoted in White, "The First Pravda," 184.
41. Karl Kautsky, "Ein Brief uber Marx und Mach."
42. It is of particular interest to note that if ecology is concerned with the interactions of two or more living systems in a natural environment with the interfaces between systems, then dialectics as "the science of universal interconnections" is a general systems science that embraces not only ecology but also the economy of man.

It is intriguing to note that while both ecology and economics derive from the same Greek root, *oikos*, meaning "household," this etymology notwithstanding, these sciences have shared little with respect to methodology and their scope of analysis. There exist salient similarities between biology and economic science, and, far from being superficial, these analogies are profoundly rooted in the fact that the ultimate subject matter of biology and economic science is one, vis-à-vis the life process.

That economics and ecology may be related is by no means a new idea. The historical roots of the perspective can be traced back to the eighteenth-century conceptions of the

Physiocrats. William Petty's dictum that nature is the mother and labor is the father of wealth provides an even earlier source. Though the trail is largely lost with the advent of the Mechanical paradigm and the neoclassical branch of economics, Alfred Marshall, one of the founding fathers of neoclassical economics, believed that the Darwinian concept of natural selection represented an important economic principle and that "in the later stages of economics, when we are approaching nearly to the conditions of life, biological analogies are to be preferred to mechanical ones" (Alfred Marshall, *Principles of Economics*, 771).

The economist J.A. Hobson noted in 1929: "[All] serviceable organic activities consume tissue and expend energy, the biological costs of the services they render. Though this economy may not correspond in close quantitative fashion to the pleasure and pain economy or to any conscious evaluation, it must be taken as the groundwork for that conscious valuation. For most economic purposes we are well advised to prefer the organic test to any other test of welfare, bearing in mind that many organic costs do not register themselves easily or adequately in terms of conscious pain or disutility, while organic gains are not always interpreted in conscious enjoyment." Unfortunately, these seminal conceptions of economic processes closely integrated into the larger economy of nature were overwhelmed by the penetration of narrower Darwinian concepts.

43. See Stokes, *Man and the Biosphere.*

Chapter 8

1. Lenin, *Collected Works* 14:271–72.
2. Ibid., 373.
3. Ibid., 285.
4. Ibid.
5. Ibid., 307–8.
6. Ibid., 232.
7. Roman Serbyn, "In Defense of an Independent Ukrainian Socialist Movement: Three Letters from Serhii Podolinsky to Valerian Smirnov," 7.
8. Serhii Podolinsky, "Menschliche Arbeit und Einheit der Kraft."
9. Marx, *Capital* 1:215.
10. Podolinsky, "Menschliche Arbeit," 414.
11. R. Kaufmann, "Biophysical and Marxist Economics: Learning from Each Other," 91.
12. Podolinsky, "Menschliche Arbeit," 420.
13. Ibid., 422.
14. Kaufmann, "Biophysical and Marxist Economics."
15. Podolinsky, "Menschliche Arbeit."
16. Martinez-Alier, *Ecological Economics,* 208.
17. Engels to Marx on December 22, 1882, in Marx and Engels, *Collected Works.*
18. Ibid.
19. Ibid.
20. S. Podolinsky, "Le socialisme et la theorie de Darwin."
21. Podolinsky, "Menschliche Arbeit," 422.
22. Ibid., 453.
23. Podolinsky in Martinez-Alier, *Ecological Economics,* 62.
24. Otto Jensen, *Marxismus und Naturewissenschaft: Gedenkschrifts zum Todestage des Naturwissenschaftlers Friederich Engels, mit Beitragen von F. Engels, Gustav Echstein und Friederich Adler,* 13.
25. Marx and Engels, *Selected Correspondence.*
26. Engels to Marx, December 19, 1882, in Marx and Engels, *Collected Works,* vol. 20, 133–35.

27. Engels, *Origin of the Family*, 48.

28. In 1885 Engels explained that "a knowledge of mathematics and natural science is essential to a conception of nature which is dialectical and at the same time materialist. Marx was well versed in mathematics, but we could only partially, intermittently and sporadically keep up with the natural sciences" (from Engels's "Anti-Dühring" as found in Joravsky, *Soviet Marxism and Natural Science*, 6).

29. Ibid.

30. S. Suvorov, *Studies in the Philosophy of Marxism*.

31. Lenin, *Collected Works* 14:331–32.

32. Ibid., 332n.

33. Ibid., 333.

34. Ibid., 327–28.

35. Susiluoto, *The Origins and Development of Systems Thinking*, 121.

36. In this connection, years later Teilhard de Chardin wrote that "to make room for thought in the World, I have had to 'interiorize' matter; to imagine an energetics of mind; to conceive a noögenesis rising upstream against the flow of entropy; to provide evolution with a direction, and critical points" (*The Phenomenon of Man*, 318).

Mooney notes that Teilhard's theory of "critical points is extremely important . . . these always mark a profound change in nature by which something totally new is produced" (Mooney, "Teilhard de Chardin and Modern Philosophy," 76).

37. Vernadsky "Problems of Biogeochemistry," 509.

Chapter 9

1. Ostwald reflected that, "Matter is merely a form of thought. . . . Away with matter, I will build a world without it. . . . The Actual, that is, what acts upon us is energy alone" (Ostwald in Slosson, *Major Prophets of Today*, 209).

2. Copleston, *Philosophy in Russia*, 285. The Austrian philosopher and scientist Ernst Mach was one of the most profound thinkers in nineteenth-century physics, and while he was largely responsible for providing the impetus to Albert Einstein's formulation of relativistic physics, he also had considerable influence in inductive philosophy among members of the Vienna Circle.

3. Ballestrem, "Lenin and Bogdanov," 292.

4. Copleston, *Philosophy in Russia*, 286.

5. Ibid.

6. Kautsky, "Ein Brief uber Marx und Mach," 452.

7. Lenin, *Collected Works* 14:318.

8. Alexander Vucinich, *Social Thought in Tsarist Russia: The Quest for a General Science of Society, 1861–1917*.

9. A.A. Bogdanov, *Filosophia zhivogo opyta*, 216 (hereafter cited as *Philosophy of Living Experience*).

10. Ballestrem, "Lenin and Bogdanov," 291.

11. A.A. Bogdanov, *Empirio-monism*, vol. 1, 7; Lenin, *Collected Works* 14:50–51.

12. Ballestrem, "Lenin and Bogdanov," 288.

13. V.V. Zenkovsky, *A History of Russian Philosophy*, 742.

14. Bogdanov, *Empirio-monism*, vol. 2, xii; also found in Michael M. Boll, "From Empiriocriticism to Empiriomonism: The Marxist Phenomenology of Aleksandr Bogdanov," 46.

15. A.A. Bogdanov as quoted in Boll, "From Empiriocriticism to Empiriomonism," 46.

16. Copleston, *Philosophy in Russia*, 286.

17. Lenin wrote: "It is common knowledge that a powerful current flowed from natu-

ral to social science not only in Petty's time, but in Marx's as well. And this current remains just as powerful, if not more so, in the twentieth century as well" (Lenin, *Collected Works* 20:196).

18. J.T. Blackmore, *Ernst Mach*, 240–1.
19. Avraham Yassour, "Lenin and Bogdanov: Protagonists in the 'Bolshevik Center,'" 31; see Biggart, "Bukharin and Proletarian Culture," 232.
20. Boll, "From Empiriocriticism to Empiriomonism," 57.
21. A month before the Second Congress of Proletkul't, Lenin brought forth a second edition of *Materialism and Empirio-Criticism*, explaining in a new preface that he did not have time to bring it up to date, but that an appendix by V.I. Nevsky did the job for him. Nevsky's essay, "Dialectical Materialism and the Philosophy of the Dead Reaction," was a reply to Bogdanov's *Philosophy of Living Experience*, which had just appeared in a second edition (Joravsky, *Soviet Marxism and Natural Science*, 86).
22. Ibid., 31.
23. Biggart, "Bukharin and Proletarian Culture," 232.
24. S. Gonikman, "Teorija obscestva i teorija klassov Bogdanova," 27 (hereafter cited as "Bogdanov's Theory of Society and Classes").
25. Lenin in Biggart, "Bukharin and Proletarian Culture," 231.
26. See Maurice Merleau-Ponty, *Adventures of the Dialectic*.
27. White, "The First Pravda," 187.
28. Ibid., 185.
29. Lenin, *Collected Works*, 146.
30. A.M. Deborin, "Hegel and Dialectical Materialism," xli.
31. V.I. Ivanovsky, "Chto takoe 'positivizm' i 'idealizm' "; also found in White, "The First Pravda," 192.
32. Lenin, *Collected Works* 12:384–85. Even before the revolution Bukharin had been influenced by the writings of Bogdanov. In an autobiography written for the encyclopedia Granat he confessed that at the time of the struggle between the Leninist and Bogdanovist subfactions of the Russian Social Democratic Labor Party he had "felt a certain heretical [sic] attraction towards Empirio-criticism which led [him] to read everything that had appeared on the subject in Russian" ("Autobiographical Sketch of 1927–29," in G. Haupt and J.-J. Marie, *Makers of the Russian Revolution*, 33).
33. Lenin, *Materialism and Empirio-Criticism*, 157.
34. Nikolay Valentinov, *Encounters with Lenin*, 258.
35. Ibid., 236.
36. Lenin, *Collected Works* 14:22.
37. Bogdanov, *Philosophy of Living Experience*, 260.
38. Boll, "From Empiriocriticism to Empiriomonism," 41.
39. Ibid., 41–42.
40. Ibid., 43.
41. Ibid.
42. Ibid.
43. Ibid., 44.
44. Ibid.
45. Jürgen Habermas, *Knowledge and Human Interests*, 81–84.
46. Lukács, *Destruction of Reason*, 413d; White, "The First Pravda," 194.
47. Valentinov, *Encounters with Lenin*, 226.
48. Jensen, *Beyond Marx and Mach*, 67.
49. Bogdanov in ibid., 167.
50. Boll, "From Empiriocriticism to Empiriomonism," 45.
51. Bogdanov, *Philosophy of Living Experience*, 174–75.

52. Ibid., 175; also found in Jensen, *Beyond Marx and Mach*, 71.
53. Jensen, *Beyond Marx and Mach*, 73.
54. Bogdanov, *Empirio-monism*, 1:184.
55. Copleston, *Philosophy in Russia*, 262.
56. Avenarius in Yassour, "Lenin and Bogdanov," 26.
57. Bogdanov, *Empirio-monism* 1:25–26.
58. Bogdanov, *Philosophy of Living Experience*, 214.
59. A.A. Bogdanov, *Vseobshchaia Organizatsionnaia Nauka: Tektologia* 1:25 (hereafter cited as *Tektology*).
60. Bogdanov, *Philosophy of Living Experience*, 229.
61. Bogdanov, *Empirio-monism*, 222.
62. A.A. Bogdanov, "Matter and Thing-in-itself," 403.
63. Herbert Marcuse, "Beitrag zu einer Phanomenologie der historischen Materialismus."
64. Lukács sought to dialectically articulate a dynamic Marxism free of the metaphysical shackles of scientism and positivism. He did so by vindicating the Hegelian heritage of Marxism and uncompromisingly approaching every problem in terms of the totality. His whole effort, however, was fundamentally vitiated by objective idealism, since it did not deal with the concrete realities of the time but substituted for them a set of highly articulate categories lifted *tout court* from Marx's works. But this prevented Lukács from dealing with real historical forces and led him into political dead ends entailed by his uncritically accepted Marxist categories.

The problem with Lukács's book was that despite all its materialist rhetorical, it operated entirely with an idealistic dialectic that brilliantly articulated Marxist categories transposed lock, stock, and barrel from Marx without, however, retaining their grounding in sociohistorical reality, i.e., their materiality.

Lukács had reproached Engels for attempting a dialectics of nature: "It is of first importance to realize that the [dialectical] method is limited here to the realm of history and society. The misunderstandings that arise from Engels's account of dialectics can in the main be put down to the fact that Engels—following Hegel's mistaken lead—extended the method to apply also to nature. However, the crucial determinants of dialectics —the interaction of subject and object, the unity of theory and practice, the historical changes in the reality underlying the categories as the root cause of changes in thought, etc.—are absent from our knowledge of change" (Lukács, *History and Class Consciousness*, 24).

The real shortcomings were clearly pointed out by Gramsci, who wrote: "It seems that Lukács asserts that one can only speak of the dialectic for the history of man but not for nature.... If his assertion presupposes a dualism between nature and man, he is wrong, because he falls into a view of nature proper to religion, Greco-Christian philosophy, and also idealism, which in reality does not manage to unite man and nature and relate them together other than verbally. But if human history should also be conceived as the history of nature (also through the history of science), how can the dialectic be separated from nature? Perhaps Lukács... has fallen... into a form of idealism" (Antonio Gramsci, *Il Materialismo Storico e la Filosofia di Benedetto Croce*, 145).

65. Following Husserl and Marcuse, the term *Lebenswelt* is a familiar one to phenomenological discourse, but it was not in Bogdanov's lexicon. Nonetheless, we shall employ it here.

66. To speak of self-consciousness in connection with society is, of course, problematic, for where is the "self" in society? Marxists, including Lukács, in referring to the consciousness of society, assert that the proletariat has the possibility for consciousness of itself. It is here, then, that the self resides. The philosophy of proletarian consciousness, or

to use Gramsci's phrase "the philosophy of praxis," is then purported to be Marxism.

67. Marx, *Capital* 1:74.

68. Jürgen Habermas, "Knowledge and Interest."

69. See Lukács, *History and Class Consciousness.*

70. While this was a project of Maurice Merleau-Ponty, who referred to "world-referring structures of perception," we maintain that it was already present in Bogdanov's work. See Merleau-Ponty, *Adventures of the Dialectic.*

71. Marx, *Philosophic Manuscripts of 1844.*

72. This proposition is very contemporary. See Agnes Heller, "The Marxian Theory of Revolution and the Revolution of Everyday Life."

73. Bogdanov's phenomenological Marxism may be seen to coincide not only with that of Edmund Husserl but also with that of Maurice Merleau-Ponty. Whereas Bogdanov appreciated the organizational informing of social reality, and while Merleau-Ponty's phenomenology began with a structuralist perspective, it culminated in a view of social reality as institutional in character. Unlike Husserl, Merleau-Ponty focused on the world-referring structures of perception rather than the internal organization of consciousness. His phenomenology is unique in that he explicitly affirms the reality of the world external to consciousness; thus, much of his philosophy consists of a refutation of certain idealistic suppositions. While Bogdanov appears to have argued that organizational phenomena serve the context for meaningful action and as axial between the Self and the Other, and here corresponds to Husserl, Merleau-Ponty referred to institutions. For Bogdanov the reference image of society is structural and organizational, while Merleau-Ponty's latter reference image is that society is a network of rule-governed institutions. Bearing a similarity to Bogdanov, Merleau-Ponty in *Adventures of the Dialectic* argued that history was irreducibly plural and that no single movement, not even Marxism, could be regarded as the exclusive agency of historical progress.

74. Smart, "Phenomenological Marxism and Critical Theory."

75. See Heller, "The Marxist Theory of Revolution."

76. Zenovia A. Sochor, *Revolution and Culture: The Bogdanov-Lenin Controversy,* 20.

77. Bogdanov drew a picture of a society heavily influenced by his systems thinking. To Bogdanov a socialist economy meant progressive rationalization of the parts and organization of the whole as was not to be equated with political intervention or state control. Ultimately, and in keeping with his systems thinking, he envisaged socialism as a "self-regulating system" (ibid., 87). Indeed, for Bogdanov a genuine socialist society was both self-regulating and harmonious. Although the organizational function in a system would remain, it would be substantially altered once it was founded on a "general and all-embracing organization of labour." That is, the regulating mechanism would be not the "old authoritarian centralism" but "scientific centralism." Most of the functions would be performed by a "gigantic statistical bureau based on exact calculation for the purpose of distributing labour power and instruments of labour" (A.A. Bogdanov, *A Short Course of Economic Science,* 383).

78. Sochor, *Revolution and Culture,* 13.

79. Ibid., 17.

80. Efforts at a synthesis of Marxism and phenomenology have assumed as their point of departure the rejection of Lenin's reflection theory.

81. Schmidt, *The Concept of Nature in Marx,* 64.

82. Lenin, *Materialism and Empirio-Criticism,* 267.

83. Engels, *Anti-Dühring,* 39.

84. Lenin in N.U. Lossky, *History of Russian Philosophy,* 348.

85. Ibid.

86. Ibid., 349.

87. Ibid., 351.
88. Jensen, *Beyond Marx and Mach*, 88.
89. The actual origin of dialectics lies in the ancient Greek formulation; it lay in conversation, in discussion and dispute. The dialectic, strictly speaking, is the art of quarreling. In this sense persons discuss the best means to achieve some end. Each states his opinion, each defends his opinion by reference to what is likely to occur if his method is followed, and finally a compromise is reached.
90. Bogdanov, *Philosophy of Living Experience*, 231–22.
91. Ibid., 234–35.
92. Ibid., 238.
93. Ibid.
94. Ibid.
95. Ibid.
96. Ibid., 241.
97. Ibid.
98. Ibid., 238.
99. Ibid., 241.
100. Boll, "From Empiriocriticism to Empiriomonism," 54.
101. Jensen, *Beyond Marx and Mach*, 89.
102. Ibid., 89–90.
103. I.V. Utechin, "Philosophy and Society: Alexander Bogdanov," 122.
104. Bogdanov, *Philosophy of Living Experience*, 241.
105. Ibid., 242.
106. Ibid., 180.
107. Jensen, *Beyond Marx and Mach*, 104.
108. Bogdanov, *Philosophy of Living Experience*, 261.
109. Bogdanov as quoted in Boll, "From Empiriocriticism to Empiriomonism," 54.
110. Prat, "Diamat and Contemporary Biology," 200. Bogdanov's view on Hegelian dialectics differs from Howard Parsons's conviction, in which he asserts that dialectics is the most encompassing of science.
111. Bogdanov, *Philosophy of Living Experience*, 242.
112. Prat, "Diamat and Contemporary Biology," 196.
113. Bogdanov, *Tektology*, 511–12.
114. Bogdanov, *Philosophy of Living Experience*, 253.
115. G.L. Kline, "Bogdanov, Alexandr Aleksandrovich," 331.
116. Prat, "Diamat and Contemporary Biology," 197; Vucinich, *Social Thought in Tsarist Russia*, 208.
117. Copleston, *Philosophy in Russia*, 287–88.
118. For an appreciation of the open systems dimensions of Marx's work, refer to Stokes, *Man and the Biosphere*.
119. See Engels, *Anti-Dühring*, 155; Jürgen Habermas (*Legitimation Crisis*) argues that while the early Marx saw socialism as appropriating the productive potential of the Enlightenment's philosophical tradition and translating it into reality, Engels anticipated the replacement of the whole of philosophy with science.
120. Joravsky, *Soviet Marxism and Natural Science*, 6.
121. Bogdanov, *Tektology*, 10.
122. Bogdanov, *Philosophy of Living Experience*, 24.
123. Ibid., 216f. For an orthodox Marxist, an understanding of the dialectic is essential for understanding the movement of history and is a condition for intelligent and successful revolutionary action. (See Copleston, *Philosophy in Russia*, 287–88.) However, as previously pointed out, Bogdanov's concept of dialectics was distinctly non-Hegelian.

Whereas Hegel's, Marx's, and Lenin's dialectics may be understood as closed, even social sciences cannot be undertaken with the aid of these concepts. Nothing is easier than to tack an energeticist or biologico-sociologist label onto such phenomena as crises, revolutions, the class struggle, and so forth; but neither is there anything more sterile, more scholastic, and lifeless than such an occupation (Lenin, *Collected Works* 14:328).

124. In Susiluoto, *Origins and Development of Systems Thinking,* 123.
125. Jensen, *Beyond Marx and Mach,* 94.
126. Bogdanov, *Philosophy of Living Experience,* 243.
127. Ibid., 243-44.
128. Ibid., 245.
129. Ibid., 250.
130. Ibid., 248.
131. Ibid.
132. Ibid., 242.
133. Ibid., 252-54.
134. Ibid., 254.
135. Ibid., 241.
136. Bogdanov as quoted in Boll, "From Empiriocriticism to Empiriomonism," 55.
137. Boll, "From Empiriocriticism to Empiriomonism," 55.
138. Ibid.
139. Ibid.
140. Bogdanov, *Philosophy of Living Experience,* 219.
141. Jensen, *Beyond Marx and Mach,* 107.
142. Ibid., 113.
143. Ibid.

Chapter 10

1. Kant, *Critique of Pure Reason,* 828.
2. Democracy means the popular determination of public and social policy. In language now familiar here, democracy means that no one shall be denied on invidious grounds the right and opportunity to participate in the recreation of community.

A democratic order does not mean that people are unrestrained or that laws are unenforced; it means that the restraints are self-imposed, directly or indirectly, and therefore are more likely to be observed. It means that the community at large has ultimate discretion over the rules, codes, laws, and constraints that organize its experience. In large communities, such discretion is accomplished through the principle and institutions of representation. The principles of representation must reflect or be consistent with the foregoing delineation of democratic determination of policy. And the institutions of representation must function effectively to assure responsiveness of representatives and their accountability to their constituencies.

The foregoing is intended to divorce the idea of democracy from a variety of uses that distort or contradict its basic meaning. Examples include pluralistic democracy, constitutional democracy, plebiscitary democracy, democratic centralism, and the like. Each of these, although in strikingly diverse ways, wholly or partially locates decision power with an elite fragment of the community.

Pluralistic democracy means brokerage and compromise among competing economic interest group(s), with the most powerful such groups constituting an influential elite. Constitutional democracy involves the creation of constitutional limitations on, and brakes in, the exercise of popular choice, leaving control with the elite who set the limitations. Plebiscitary democracy provides a vehicle through which the masses may emotionally proclaim and demonstrate their continued deference to a ruling elite. Democratic centralism is V.I. Lenin's caption for the literal dictatorship of the ruling elitist vanguard on the alleged behalf of the proletariat. All such modifiers then subvert the meaning of democracy, of popular sovereignty, and mask elitist rule with legitimacy commonly associated with democratic governance.

3. Peter B. Checkland, *Systems Thinking, Systems Practice.*
4. Kant, *Critique of Pure Reason*, 825.
5. Ulrich, "Systems Thinking, Systems Practice," 140.
6. Jürgen Habermas, "What Does a Crisis Mean Today? Legitimation Problems in Late Capitalism," 240.
7. Kant, *Groundwork of the Metaphysic of Morals*, 122n.
8. See Jürgen Habermas, *Communication and the Evolution of Society*, 63ff.
9. This difference explains why "facts," i.e., empirical statements, cannot be shown to be valid ("true") without reference to some objectified aspects of the phenomenal world, whereas "norms" or practical statements can be established as valid ("right") by their mere intersubjective assertion (Ulrich, "Systems Thinking, Systems Practice," 141).
10. Marx and Engels, *German Ideology*, 50.
11. Karl Marx, "Preface to a Contribution to a Critique of Political Economy," in Marx and Engels, *Selected Works*, vol. 1.
12. Ibid., 20.
13. Ibid., 20–21.
14. Ballestrem, "Lenin and Bogdanov," 303.
15. Bogdanov in Vucinich, *Social Thought in Tsarist Russia*, 212.
16. Bogdanov, *Philosophy of Living Experience*, 268–69.
17. Ibid.
18. Langdon Winner, *Autonomous Technology: Technics-out-of-Control as a Theme in Political Thought*, 78.
19. Marx, *Grundrisse*, 86.
20. Marx, *The Poverty of Philosophy*, 109.
21. Friederich Engels, "The Part Played by Labour in the Transition from Ape to Man."
22. Marc Bloch's work suggests that feudal lords actually tried to suppress hand mills, preferring centralized water milling with its greater potential for the exacting of feudal dues. See Marc Bloch, "Advent and Triumph of the Water Mill," 136–68. Robert Heilbroner's 1967 paper, "Do Machines Make History?" is headed by the above "handmill" quotation, and Heilbroner identified "the Marxian paradigm" with the fundamentalist view of technological determinism.
23. Winner, *Autonomous Technology*, 79.
24. Kostas Axelos, *Alienation, Praxis and Techne in the Thought of Karl Marx*, 17.
25. Marx, *The Poverty of Philosophy*, 144.
26. Marx, "Preface," in Marx and Engels, *Selected Works*, vol. 1, 20–21.
27. Marx, "Preface" to *A Contribution to the Critique of Political Economy*, 20–21.
28. Marx, *Grundrisse*, 99–100.
29. Marx, *Capital* 3:791; John E. Elliot, "Institutionalism as an Approach to Political Economy," 91–97
30. Bogdanov, *Philosophy of Living Experience*, 269.
31. Vucinich, *Social Thought in Tsarist Russia*, 219.
32. A.A. Bogdanov, *Iz psikhologii obshchestva (stat'i 1901–1904)*, 77 (hereafter cited as *From the Psychology of Society*).
33. Ballestrem, "Lenin and Bogdanov," 303.
34. Bogdanov, *From the Psychology of Society*. 51.

35. Bogdanov in Lenin, *Collected Works* 14:327.
36. Jensen, *Beyond Marx and Mach,* 122.
37. Bogdanov, *Philosophy of Living Experience.*
38. Jensen, *Beyond Marx and Mach,* 271.
39. Ibid., 209.
40. Susiluoto, *Origins and Development of Systems Thinking,* 42.
41. Jensen, *Beyond Marx and Mach,* 122.
42. N.I. Bukharin, *Ataka: Sbornik teoretischeskikh,* 150.
43. Bogdanov, *Philosophy of Living Experience,* 270–71.
44. V. Tismananue, "Critical Marxism and Eastern Europe." In East Germany, contrastingly, both reform communism and Marxist dissent have been weaker movements; the alleged neo-Leninism of Rudolf Bahro and the inverted Leninism of Gyorgy Konrad and Ivan Szelenyi both focus on "actually existing socialism," but in conceptually implausible ways. The theories, which emerged in Hungary in the 1960s and 1970s, also represent forms of reform communism.
45. Alvin W. Gouldner, "Stalinism: A Study of Internal Colonialism."
46. At the Fifth Congress of the Third International in 1924, the works of Lukács, Korsch, and others were officially condemned by Zinoviev, who was speaking for the Comintern Executive. An underlying thrust of the attack was that these "idealist deviationists" were all "professors," "intellectuals" (see excerpts from Zinoviev's speech found in Morris Watnick, "Relativism and Class Consciousness," 146).
47. Plekhanov and Axelrod were the first to employ the term *hegemony,* and Gramsci later adopted it.
48. Bogdanov's position shared a contradiction present in Austro-Marxism, the contradiction between a passive defensive political strategy and an active institutional strategy, a strategic distinction characterized by Gramsci's "war of position" and "war of maneuver."
49. A.A. Bogdanov, "Sotsializm v nastoiashchem," 68.
50. It was only with the appearance of R. Hilferding's *Finanzkapital* and its subsequent popularization that socialism came to be thought of as a centrally regulated planned economic system. Of course, the conception of socialism that Hilferding penned was attributed to Marx.
51. Georg Lukács, "The Old Culture and the New."
52. Proletkul't, though originally a nationally constituted organization, created an international arm. It was announced in *Izvestiia,* on August 14, 1920, that at a post-congress meeting of delegates to the Second Congress of the Comintern, a Provisional International Bureau of the Proletkul't had been formed under the presidency of Lunacharsky and secretary-generalship of Valerian Lebedev-Polyansky.
53. Lukács, "The Old Culture and the New."
54. Marx and Engels, *Collected Works* 24:269.
55. Ibid., 6:495.
56. Anson Rabinbach, *The Crisis of Austrian Socialism: From Red Vienna to Civil War, 1927–1934,* 63, 65.
57. See Robert C. Tucker, *The Marxian Revolutionary Idea.*
58. V.I. Lenin, *What Is to Be Done?* 32–33.
59. Ibid.
60. James D. White, "Early Soviet Historical Interpretation of the Russian Revolution 1918–24," 346.
61. Bertolt Brecht, *Gesammelte Werke* 20:64.
62. A.A. Bogdanov, "Proletariat v bor'be za sotsializm."
63. See Gramsci, "The Intellectuals," in *Prison Notebooks,* 5–25.

64. Ibid., 340.
65. Gramsci, "Intellectuals," 9–24, and "The Modern Prince," in *Prison Notebooks*, 198–99.
66. Alfred G. Meyer, *Leninism*, 55–56.
67. Bogdanov, *A Short Course*, 383.
68. A.A. Bogdanov, "Elementy proletarskoj kul'tury v razvitii rabocego klassa," 52,72.
69. Bogdanov, *Philosophy of Living Experience*, 983–88.
70. James D. White, "Bogdanov in Tula," 50.
71. Bogdanov, *A Short Course*, 125.
72. Bukharin suspected that Bogdanov had, like Western European sociologists, "psychologized" the human side of the mode of production and that his phenomenological empirio-criticism was distinctly non-Marxian. Bukharin sought to correct this allegedly mistaken view. Censuring the role of the psychological, he wrote: "The system of these relationships [i.e., labor relations] is as 'psychical' as a system of planets together with their sun. Determinateness of place at each chronological point—that is what makes the system a system." But in a curious turn, he later acknowledged the importance of psychology, ideologies, morality, and customs. They hold society together: they "coordinate men's actions and keep them within certain bounds, thus preventing society from disintegrating" (in Stephen F. Cohen, "Marxist Theory and Bolshevik Policy," 45).
73. Bogdanov, *A Short Course*, 67.
74. Lukács, "The Old Culture and the New."
75. Bogdanov, *Philosophy of Living Experience*, 100–101.
76. Sochor, *Revolution and Culture*, 63.
77. Bogdanov, *A Short Course*, 378.
78. Herbert Marcuse, *Eros and Civilization: A Philosophical Inquiry into Freud*, 434–35.
79. I.I. Skvortsov-Stepanov collaborated with Bogdanov in the Russian translation of Marx's *Capital*. His translation of Hilferding's *Finanzkapital* prefigured in his own theory of imperialism, a theory antecedent to Bukharin's and Lenin's.
80. For Antonio Gramsci, who allegedly followed much of Bogdanov's theorizing, philosophy was not only that of philosophers but also that of the masses. For Gramsci the role of the (socialist) party is to spawn "organic" intellectuals who, through constant engagement with the masses, formulate a worldview that reflects their experience and permits its transformation. (See Gramsci, *Prison Notebooks*, and Counihan, "Antonio Gramsci and Social Science.")
81. A specific point of contact between Proletkul't and Tasca took place in 1920, when an Italian delegation attended a meeting in Moscow, immediately after the Second Comintern Congress, to establish an International Bureau of Proletkul't. Moreover, Gramsci lived in Moscow between May 1922 and December 1923 and was undoubtedly exposed to some of the intellectual climate and dialogue within the Bolshevik party. Whether Gramsci, in fact, read any of Bogdanov's works, we are as yet uncertain.
82. The other "forms" covered politics, economy, and management. He left the Proletkul't in 1921, when by becoming a "cultural organ" of the Bolshevik party, it lost the last vestiges of autonomy.
83. Sochor, *Revolution and Culture*, 186.
84. Gorelik, "Bogdanov's Tektology," 46.
85. Bogdanov, *A Short Course*, n.p.
86. A.A. Bogdanov, "Programma kul'tury"; and also in Sochor, *Revolution and Culture*, 30.
87. Bogdanov in Lenin, *Collected Works* 14:322.
88. Ibid., 323.

89. Ostensibly, Bogdanov was suggesting that his metascience—Tektology—could accommodate precisely the unity of bourgeois sciences and a philosophy of praxis.

90. The homogenization of these use values by their submission to a generalized exchange value thus tended to homogenize culture itself.

91. A.A. Bogdanov, *Tektologia*, as found in Sochor, *Revolution and Culture*, 70.

92. A.A. Bogdanov, *Nauka ob obshchestvennom soznanii* (hereafter cited as *Social Consciousness*); and also in Sochor, *Revolution and Culture*, 71.

93. Ibid.

94. The concept of culture (as opposed to the concept of civilization) ostensibly comprises the ensemble of valuable products and abilities that are dispensable in relation to the immediate maintenance of life. Moreover, one can speak of culture in its apparent isolation from other social phenomena, for when we correctly grasp the culture of any period, we grasp with it the root of the whole development of the period, just as we do when we begin with an analysis of the economic relations.

95. Bogdanov, "Programma kul'tury," 54–56, 62–63.

96. "The Factory Council," in *Antonio Gramsci, Selections from Political Writings 1910–20*, 263.

97. Gramsci, "Socialism and Culture," in *Political Writings*, 11.

98. Lenin, *What Is to Be Done?* 122–23.

99. Lenin, *Collected Works*, vol. 36, 335–38. Italics in the original.

100. Biggart, "Bukharin and Proletarian Culture," 232.

101. Bukharin in ibid., 230.

102. Ibid.

103. In 1924 Trotsky described Bukharin as having been the Proletkul't's "protector" (ibid.).

104. Gramsci, "The Revolution Against 'Capital'," in *Political Writings*, 34.

105. Though in view of the collapse of the USSR one cannot but pose the indiscreet question whether Bogdanov's interpretation was not correct after all.

106. Bogdanov, "Ideal i put," 102–3.

107. Beyond theorizing, some Marxists actually made a virtue out of refusing to think about the future. Theirs was the ontologicalization of the present, an abstention from a more than furtive anticipation of historical time and the meaning of the future. The socialist party, argued Kautsky, could make positive propositions only for the existing social order. Suggestions that went beyond that could not deal with facts, but had to proceed from suppositions; they were regarded as fantasies and dreams.

108. Bogdanov, "Ideal i put," 100–101.

109. Bogdanov, "Programma kul'tury," 74.

110. Ibid., 72.

111. Bogdanov, *From the Psychology of Society*, 90–91.

112. Gramsci, "Conquest of the State," in *Political Writings*, 78.

113. Bogdanov, "Sotsializm v nastoiashchem," 68.

114. Tugan-Baranovsky, *The Theoretical Basis of Marxism*, 82.

115. Julius F. Hecker, *Russian Sociology: A Contribution to the History of Sociological Thought and Theory*, 234.

116. See Stephen Gill, ed., *Gramsci, Historical Materialism, and International Relations*.

117. Frank R. Annunziato, "Gramsci's Theory of Trade Unionism."

118. Gramsci, *Prison Notebooks*.

119. John Rosenthal, "Who Practices Hegemony? Class Division and the Subject of Politics."

120. Marx, *Capital* 3:386, 387–88 (emphasis added), 487.

121. Georg Lukács, *Soziologie des modernen Dramas*, 665–66.
122. *Large Soviet Encyclopedia* 6:589–80.
123. Sochor, *Revolution and Culture*.
124. A.A. Bogdanov, "Iz slovariia inostrannykh slov: Klass," *Pravda* (March 17, 1913): 1–2.
125. Sochor, *Revolution and Culture*, 57; Bogdanov's functionalism corresponds to that of both Ostwald and Spencer.
126. Bogdanov, *A Short Course*, 32.
127. Sochor, *Revolution and Culture*, 63.
128. Bogdanov, *A Short Course*, 38.
129. Sochor, *Revolution and Culture*, 66.
130. John Kenneth Galbraith, *The New Industrial State*; Jean Meynaud, *Technocracy*; Carl Mitchem and Robert Mackey, eds., *Philosophy and Technology: Readings in the Philosophical Problems of Technocracy*.
131. Marx and Engels, "Manifesto of the Communist Party," in *Marx-Engels Reader*, ed. R.C. Tucker, 476.
132. Ibid.
133. Bogdanov as quoted in Utechin, "Philosophy and Society," 121.
134. Ibid.
135. Bogdanov in Vucinich, *Social Thought in Tsarist Russia*, 225.
136. It is worth noting that Bogdanov's Tektology was intended to play a significant role not only in accomplishing this eradication but also in providing an alternative synthesis.
137. A.A. Bogdanov, *Novyi mir (stat'i 1904–1905)*, 15.
138. No less a difficult path must be tread by a society that now seeks to reverse seventy years of "socialism."
139. Lukács, *History and Class Consciousness*. In the 1967 preface Lukács offered an autocritique, referring to it as a deviation.
140. Georg Simmel, with whom Lukács studied and by whom he was deeply influenced, had raised the phenomenon of alienation and the loss of man's being and spirit in his objectified creations to the level of a theory of "the great tragedy of culture" (Simmel, *The Philosophy of Money*, chapter 6).
141. Lukács, "The Old Culture and the New," 4.
142. Ibid.
143. In Bela Kopeczi, "Lukács in 1919," 13. This was written when Lukács was minister of education in Bela Kun's short-lived revolutionary government. His revolutionary culturism was most clearly expressed in his essay "The Old Culture and the New," first published in Hungarian in *Internationale* on June 15, 1919, and then in Germany in the ultra-left journal *Kommunismus* on November 7, 1920.
144. Kopeczi, "Lukács in 1919."
145. Ibid., 10.
146. Bogdanov, *Philosophy of Living Experience*, 13.
147. Chantal Mouffe, "Gramsci Today."
148. Cited in Norberto Bobbio, "Gramsci and the Conception of Civil Society."
149. Marx and Engels cited in ibid.
150. Gramsci cited in ibid., 30.
151. Gramsci, *Prison Notebooks*.
152. Ibid.
153. Joseph A. Woolcock, "Politics, Ideology and Hegemony in Gramsci's Theory."
154. E.J. Hobsbawm, "The Great Gramsci," 42.
155. Marx, as has often been noted, said virtually nothing of the post-revolutionary political process. Engels spoke late in his life of the "dictatorship of the proletariat." It was

Lenin who, in August of 1917, elaborated a theory of such a "dictatorship," in his "State and Revolution."

156. The term *historical bloc* was used to denote unities of nature and spirit, superstructure and substructure, and subjective and objective moments of the historical process. But as with much of Gramsci's terminology, it had several meanings. It was also used to refer to a counterhegemonic group seeking to circumvent the privileging of one dimension of totality over another.

157. Ramos, "The Concepts," 34.

158. Paul Piccone, for example, contends that Gramsci meant an "internal mediator" (Paul Piccone, "Gramsci's Hegelian Marxism," 35).

159. Jerome Karabel, "Revolutionary Contradictions: Antonio Gramsci and the Problem of Intellectuals."

160. Gramsci, "The Intellectuals," in *Prison Notebooks*, 5.

161. Ibid.

162. Adam Przeworski, "Material Bases of Consent: Economics and Politics in a Hegemonic System."

163. Herbert Marcuse, *One-Dimensional Man*, 40.

164. Ibid., xv.

165. Ibid.

166. On this point Marcuse differs from Weber, who regarded the bourgeoisie and not the proletariat as the organizers—the social engineers for "liberating" man.

167. Ibid., 17.

168. For a discussion of the Gramsci legacy refer to A.B. Davidson, "The Varying Seasons of Gramscian Studies."

169. The concept of the intellectual was a nuanced one. The organic intellectual had emerged directly out of the class whose consciousness the intellectuals helped articulate; the latter had once been organic, but the traditional assumed a certain autonomy in relation to the class of their origin.

170. In the long section of the *Prison Notebooks* entitled "The Modern Prince," Gramsci attempted to trace the lineage of the communist party through Jacobinism to Machiavelli's *Prince*. With virtually no reference to the councils, which he had championed in 1919 and 1920 when he was explicitly anti-Jacobin, he defended the party as the proclaimer and organizer of an intellectual and moral reform.

171. Gramsci, *Prison Notebooks*, 9.

172. Ibid., 418.

173. Ibid., 332–33.

174. Ibid., 16.

175. Bogdanov as quoted in White, "The First Pravda," 198.

176. In the 1919–20 period of mass strikes and occupied factories, the so-called *bienno rosso,* Gramsci and his collaborators, Angelo Tasca, Umberto Terracini, and Palmiro Togliatti, turned their newly founded journal *L'Ordine Nuovo* into the major organ of the council movement centered in Turin (Franklin Adler, "Factory Councils, Gramsci and the Industrialists"). In opposition to the trade unions, which the syndicalists supported, and the party, which the parliamentary revisionists defended, only the councils truly prefigured a social order beyond capitalism: "The Factory Council is the model of the proletarian State. All the problems inherent in the organization of the proletarian State are inherent in the organization of the Council. In the one, as in the other, the concept of citizen gives way to the concept of comrade. Collaboration in effective and useful production develops solidarity and multiplies bonds of affection and fraternity. Everyone is indispensable, everyone is at his post, and everyone has a function and a post.... Whereas in the union, workers' solidarity was developed in struggle against capitalism in

suffering and sacrifice, in the Council this solidarity is a positive, permanent entity that is embodied in even the most trivial moments of industrial production. It is a joyous awareness of being an organic whole, a homogeneous and compact system which, through useful work and the disinterested production of social wealth, asserts its sovereignty and realizes its power and its freedom to create history" (Gramsci, *Political Writings*, 100).

177. Alastair Davidson calls it Gramsci's period of "cultural messianism" (see "Gramsci and Lenin, 1917–1922," 127).

178. Following the collapse of the Turin uprising in 1920, Gramsci edged nearer to a Leninist position, with a new appreciation of Lenin's stress on the party.

179. Lukács repeats both Hegel's and Marx's idea that philosophy originates out of alienated existence and is the ideal expression of the impulse to abolish alienation by actualizing philosophy.

180. Gramsci, "The Study of Philosophy," in *Prison Notebooks*, 349.
181. Gramsci, "Modern Prince," in ibid., 177.
182. Marx and Engels, *Collected Works* 1:271–72.
183. Lenin, *Collected Works* 42:297.
184. *Pravda*, July 27, 1921.
185. Predrag Vranicki, "Socialism and the Problem of Alienation," 281.
186. See White, "The First Pravda," 195–96.
187. Ibid., 195.
188. Marx, "Preface," in Marx and Engels, *Selected Works* 1:362–64.
189. Bogdanov in Vranicki, "Socialism and the Problem of Alienation," 280.
190. Sochor, *Revolution and Culture*, 116.
191. Lukács, *Destruction of Reason*, 596.
192. Lukács, "The Old Culture and the New."
193. Ibid., 22.
194. Ibid., 31. An economy integrated through commodity exchanges and commodity production is understood to be a commodity economy. Exclusively within the integrative context of a habitually recurring system of price-making exchanges do use-values assume the form of commodities. Insofar as use-values are not originally commodities, they must be "commoditized." That is, they must be coerced into the form of commodities, through the commodification of labor itself (Polanyi, *The Livelihood of Man*). Whereas elements of a commodity economy may exist in precapitalist and Habermas's "post-capitalist" societies, to a greater or lesser extent, they never serve to integrate the whole of economic organization of society. In precapitalist economy, according to Polanyi, they remain a partial and subsidiary activity embedded within societal norms. The role of the commodity economy in post-capitalist economy remains an area of speculation.

Political economy, by which conventional Marxists mean a systematic enquiry into the properties specific and peculiar to a commodity economy, does not directly study the general norms of economic life, that is, the biophysical foundation of society. Political economy so defined excludes the materially substantive dimensions of the livelihood of man.

195. For two years prior to World War I, Nikolai Bukharin lived in Vienna, where he wrote *The Economic Theory of the Leisure Class*. Originally published in 1919, the work was intended as a critique of political economy. In it Bukharin sought to address what he considered to be the sterility of the Austrian marginal utility school, and principally the work of the antisocialist Eugen von Böhm-Bawerk.

Bukharin wrote: "The success of the 'new' theories is therefore based on the altered condition of the social psychology and not at all on their logical perfection. One of the reasons for hostility to the theory of labor value on the part of the bourgeoisie is surely to be found in the latter's opposition to socialism" (Bukharin, *Economic Theory of the Leisure Class*, 175n).

"The methodological differences between Karl Marx and Böhm-Bawerk may be summarized ... as follows: objectivism-subjectivism, an historical standpoint, the point of view of production—the point of view of consumption" (ibid., 19).

Bukharin considered that the Austrian marginalist school had two defects: (1) that it described capitalism in a static state; and (2) that it lacked a sociological basis (Eugen von Böhm-Bawerk, *Capital and Interest: A Critical History of Economical Theory*).

196. Bukharin, "Ekonomika perekhodnogo perioda," in Stephen F. Cohen, *Bukharin and the Bolshevik Revolution: A Political Biography 1888–1938*, 93.
197. A.A. Bogdanov, *Essays in Tektology*, 50.
198. Sochor, *Revolution and Culture*, 209.
199. Ibid., 232.
200. Ivan Illich, *Tools for Conviviality*, xxiii.
201. Bogdanov, "Tseli i normy," in Sochor, *Revolution and Culture*, 197. Sochor writes that "however much he pinned his hopes for socialism on technological advance, Bogdanov did not simply endorse cultural values based on a scientific-technological ethos (p. 233). To be sure, his record was somewhat ambivalent. He came precipitously close to subjecting values to "the logic of rationality" (the scientifically best way to do things) in his norms of expediency. Furthermore, although he was genuinely concerned to free the individual from the constraints of "coercive norms and abstract obligations," he proceeded to dissolve the emancipated individual in an impersonal social collective.
202. White, "The First Pravda," 196.
203. Bogdanov in Sochor, *Revolution and Culture*, 65.
204. Lenin, "On Cooperation," January 6, 1923, in *Selected Works*, 695.
205. A "war of maneuver" corresponds with a frontal attack on the state, whereas a "war of position" corresponds to a protracted struggle (Gramsci, "State and Civil Society," in *Prison Notebooks*, 229–39). But strategically more is implied, for the seizure of the state machinery represented only a partial victory, a partial increase in power. It also presented a constraint on action and a decrease in power, since holding power meant being constrained to act within the interstate system—a problematic situation for those calling for a world revolution.

Chapter 11

1. Marx, *Philosophic Manuscripts of 1844*, 143.
2. Zenkovsky, *A History of Russian Philosophy*, 706.
3. Ibid., 720; Habermas, *Knowledge and Human Interests*, 81.
4. Ivan Frolov, *Man-Science-Humanism: A New Synthesis*, 8.
5. Habermas, *Knowledge and Human Interests*, 72.
6. Bogdanov, *A Short Course*, 50.
7. Vucinich, *Social Thought in Tsarist Russia*, 226.
8. A.A. Bogdanov, *Socializm nauki*, 102–4.
9. Bogdanov, *Philosophy of Living Experience*, 207–8. Murray Bookchin regards the dialectical nature of the ecological outlook, an outlook that stresses differentiation, inner development, and unity in diversity, as obvious to anyone who is familiar with Hegel's writings (see *Toward an Ecological Society*, 272). Even the language of ecology and dialectical philosophy overlaps to a remarkable degree. Apparently unaware of the wider implications of Bogdanov's Tektology, Bookchin notes that ecology more closely realizes Marx's vision of science as dialectics than any other science today, including Marx's own cherished realm of political economy. "Ecology," he writes, "could be said to enjoy this unique eminence because it provides the basis, both socially and biologically, for a devas-

tating critique of hierarchical society as a whole, while providing guidelines for a viable, harmonized future utopia" (ibid.).
10. Copleston, *Philosophy in Russia,* 286.
11. Zenkovsky, *History of Russian Philosophy,* 742.
12. A.L. Takhazhdian, "Tektologia: Istoriya i Problemy."
13. It is worth noting that this theme was in recent years reconstructed by the American ecologist Howard Odum, as found in his *Systems Ecology.*
14. Bogdanov, *From the Psychology of Society,* 275.
15. Marx observed, "Natural science will ... incorporate into itself the science of man, just as the science of man will incorporate into itself natural science: there will be one science" (Marx, *The Economic and Philosophic Manuscripts of 1844,* in *The Marx-Engels Reader,* ed. R.C. Tucker, 91).
16. Prat, "Diamat and Contemporary Biology," 196.
17. Bogdanov, *Philosophy of Living Experience,* 249.
18. Marcuse, *One-Dimensional Man,* 314.
19. This is somewhat unusual, for in the correspondence of Marx and Engels, as well as in Engels's *Dialectics of Nature,* there are numerous references to Darwin's theory.
20. Bogdanov, *From the Psychology of Society,* 40.
21. Ibid., 42.
22. Vucinich, *Social Thought in Tsarist Russia,* 216.
23. It is neither fair nor sound to label Marx's procedure a regression to premodern forms of thought, as Karl Popper and Frederick Hayek have done. Moreover, Popper's effort to link Marx's thought to totalitarianism parades a consummate ignorance of Marx's analysis of the development of capitalism. See Karl Popper, *The Poverty of Historicism*; and Frederick Hayek, *The Counter-Revolution of Science.*
24. Bogdanov, *Essays in Tektology,* 61.
25. Ibid., 61, 3. Italics in the original.
26. Erich Jantsch and Conrad H. Waddington, eds., *Evolution and Consciousness: Human Systems in Transition*; Laszlo, *Evolution.*
27. Bogdanov, *Philosophy of Living Experience,* 307.
28. Ibid.
29. Ibid.
30. F.G. Varela, H.R. Maturana, and R. Uribe, "Autopoiesis: The Organization of Living Systems, Its Characterization and a Model"; Humberto R. Maturana, "Autopoiesis: Reproduction, Heredity and Evolution."
31. Bogdanov, *Philosophy of Living Experience,* 308.
32. Ibid.
33. Ibid., 309.
34. Bogdanov as quoted in Utechin, "Philosophy and Society," 122. Susiluoto comments that Ferdinand-Bronislaw Trentowski had published in 1843 a work entitled "On the Relationship between Philosophy and Cybernetics or the Art of Governing People." On the basis of this discriminating image one is led to speculate on Bogdanov's concept of cybernetics and the livelihood of man. The question begs asking: Was Bogdanov the first economic cybernetician? (Susiluoto, *Origins and Development of Systems Thinking,* 20).
35. Utechin, "Philosophy and Society." Two things should be noted here: (1) that the organizational-disorganizational perspective is not "productionist" in the sense of Heidegger, and (2) the concept of production is reformulated as a thermodynamic phenomenon—a temporal sorting of low entropy and high entropy, within an institutional setting that guides appropriational movements.
36. Bogdanov in Vucinich, *Social Thought in Tsarist Russia,* 226.
37. Systems thinking, as understood through Kant's writings, refers to the totality of

relevant conditions on which theoretical or practical judgments depend, including basic metaphysical, ethical, political, and ideological a priori judgments. But the contemporary way of presenting systems thinking is to regard it as an interdisciplinary effort to "capture" different strands of knowledge and worldviews through a process of horizontal integration. "Vertical" systems thinking has become the hallmark of reductionist systems thinking. It is perhaps the latter that characterized Bogdanov's tektological effort.

38. Marx, *Capital*, vol. 2.

39. Felix Geyer and Johannes van der Zouwen, *Sociocybernetic Paradoxes: Observation, Control and Evolution of Self-steering Systems*; Stokes, *Man and the Biosphere*.

40. Jensen, *Beyond Marx and Mach*, 10.

41. Ibid., 375.

42. Ralph Bello, "The Systems Approach: A. Bogdanov and L. von Bertalanffy," 137.

43. N.N. Moiseev notes that the term *cybernetics* derives from the Greek term *kibernos* and refers to an object of regulation containing persons, for example, a city or a district. This understanding, Moiseev writes, was a common one in the nineteenth century. Whereas a system, though it may be an object of regulation, is not necessarily a kibernos. The same system with a human association is a kibernos (Moiseev, "Man's Coevolution with the Biosphere: Cybernetic Aspects," 22).

44. Bogdanov, *Tektologia* as found in Sochor, *Revolution and Culture*, 45.

45. Gorelik, "Reemergence of Bogdanov's Tektology," 345.

46. Curiously, Western analysts have, to a large extent, replicated the general Soviet approach to Bogdanov, that is, they have rehabilitated the Bogdanov of systems thinking but not the one of cultural revolution. Without question, there is an appreciable amount of continuity in Bogdanov's work, and some of his propositions on revolution and culture were derived from his systems thinking (Sochor, *Revolution and Culture*, 11–12).

47. Takhazhdian, "Tektologia," n.d.

48. N. Belov, *The Structure of Internal Secretion in Organs and Their Significance in Present-Day Biology*.

49. Belov in Takhazhdian, "Tekologia," 94–95.

50. Ibid.

51. E. Fyodorov, "Perfectionism"; also found in I. Blauberg, "The History of Science and the Systems Approach," 97.

52. Norbert Wiener, *Cybernetics: Or Control and Communication in the Animal and Machine*.

53. Ibid., n.p.

54. Bogdanov, *Essays in Tektology*, 9.

55. Boulding, *Primer on Social Dynamics*; Laszlo, *Evolution*.

56. Gorelik, "Reemergence of Bogdanov's Tektology," 347.

57. A.A. Bogdanov, *Red Star: The First Bolshevik Utopia*, 245.

58. Bogdanov's theory of moving equilibrium shows much similarity with Ludwig von Bertalanffy's theory of "open systems" insofar as both extend the Le Chatelier principle to all dynamic systems. Indeed, Bogdanov explicitly generalized Le Chatelier's principle (*Essays in Tektology*, 54–55). Vucinich concurs that, Tektology, as a general theory, covers not only cybernetic principles, that is, the principles of information systems, but also the "hierarchical orders" in the relations between systems and the principles depicting the origin and disintegration of systems (*Social Thought in Tsarist Russia*, 230).

59. In Vucinich, *Social Thought in Tsarist Russia*, 226–27.

60. Ibid.

61. Ibid.

62. Bogdanov, *Essays in Tektology*, 46.

63. Ibid., 82.

64. Bogdanov, *Red Star*, 245.
65. Bogdanov in White, "Bogdanov in Tula," 6.
66. Oliver E. Williamson, *Markets and Hierarchies: Analysis and Antitrust Implications* and *The Economic Institutions of Capitalism*; Ronald Coase, "The Nature of the Firm."
67. Bogdanov, *Essays in Tektology*, 22.
68. However, the Aristotelian proposition that the whole is greater than the sum of the parts is also logically vulnerable since it refers only to the quantitative aspect and presents the whole as a sort of remainder from the enumeration of the parts. Blauberg advises, "The solution to the problem is to say that the whole has new traits and properties, not present in the parts and resulting from the interaction of these parts" (Prat, "Diamat and Contemporary Biology").
69. Bogdanov, *Essays in Tektology*, 71.
70. Gorelik, "Reemergence of Bogdanov's Tektology," 348.
71. Bogdanov, *Essays in Tektology*, 90.
72. Ibid., 300–301.
73. Ibid., 51.
74. Ibid., 100.
75. Ibid.
76. Gorelik, "Reemergence of Bogdanov's Tektology," 40.
77. Bogdanov, *Tektology*, 121.
78. Ibid., 350.
79. Ibid., 147.
80. Bogdanov, *Social Consciousness*, 174–75; also found in Sochor, *Revolution and Culture*, 71.
81. Bogdanov in Sochor, *Revolution and Culture*, 85.
82. See Lenin's "Impending Catastrophe and How to Combat It," September 1917, in *Collected Works* 25:358–59.
83. Ibid. Meanwhile, we have learned, as Bogdanov predicted, that even a well-functioning planning bureaucracy with scientific control of the production of goods and services is not a sufficient condition for realizing the associated material and intellectual productive forces in the interest of the enjoyment and freedom of an emancipated society. For Marx did not reckon on the possible emergence at every level of a discrepancy between scientific control of the material conditions of life and a democratic decision-making process. This is the philosophical reason that socialists never anticipated the authoritarian welfare state, where social wealth is relatively guaranteed while political freedom is excluded (Jürgen Habermas, *Toward a Rational Society: Student Protest, Science and Politics*, 58).

Erich Fromm has expressed a number of disagreements concerning Marx's sociological and economic thinking. They refer mainly to the fact that Marx failed to see the degree to which capitalism was capable of modifying itself and thus satisfying the economic needs of industrialized nations, his failure to see clearly enough the dangers of bureaucratization and centralization and to envisage the authoritarian system that could emerge as alternatives to socialism (E. Fromm, *Man May Prevail: An Inquiry into the Facts and Fictions of Foreign Policy*, ix). This interpretation is difficult to reconcile with Karl Marx's views as expressed in *A Contribution to the Critique of Hegel's "Philosophy of Right"*: "As far as the individual bureaucrat is concerned, the end of the state becomes his private end: a pursuit of higher posts, the building of his career. In the first place, he considers his real life to be purely material, for the spirit of his life has its separate existence in the bureaucracy. Thus the bureaucrat must make life as materialistic as possible. . . . Real knowledge appears to be devoid of content just as real life appears to be

dead, for this imaginary knowledge and life pass for what is real and essential."
84. Hilferding, *Finanzkapital*, 322.
85. A.A. Bogdanov, "Nachal'nyi kurs politicheskoi ekonomii"; also in Sochor, *Revolution and Culture*, 86.
86. Sochor, *Revolution and Culture*, 86.
87. Gorelik, "Reemergence of Bogdanov's Tektology," 351.
88. This somewhat innocuous remark refers to what is known in the contemporary literature as the "epistemological break" offered by the "second cybernetics." M. Maruyama has shown that processes of mutual causation are characterized, respectively, by deviation amplifying and deviation neutralizing interactions. These relations are typically identified in discussions of cybernetics (M. Maruyama, "The Second Cybernetics: Deviation Amplifying Mutual Causal Processes").
89. Bogdanov in Vucinich, *Social Thought in Tsarist Russia*, 227–28.
90. Bogdanov, *Essays in Tektology*, 84.
91. Ibid., 164.
92. Bogdanov, *Red Star*, 245; Jensen, *Beyond Marx and Mach*; Susiluoto, *Origins and Development of Systems Thinking*.
93. The idea of single- and double-looped regulatory systems is present in G. Bateson's work. In particular, see *Steps to an Ecology of Mind*.
94. Bogdanov, *Essays in Tektology*, 211–19, 325.
95. Prat, "Diamat and Contemporary Biology," 197.
96. Ibid.; Copleston, *Philosophy in Russia*.
97. Cohen regards the interesting intellectual kinship between Bogdanov and Bukharin as having been distorted by the commonplace view that Bukharin was Bogdanov's disciple ("Marxist Theory and Bolshevik Policy," 55).
98. Susiluoto, *Origins and Development of Systems Thinking*, 80, 97.
99. Lenin, December 26, 1922, in *Collected Works*, 35: n.p.
100. Many pseudoscientific struggles erupted at the beginning of the 1930s. Prominent among them were the "Bogdanovian mechanistic theories" of Bukharin. And in almost every case insignificant differences in phraseology were elevated "to principled heights." In the tiniest phraseological inaccuracies someone would try to find enemy influences; in the guise of "revolutionary vigilance" narrow-minded sectarians cultivated intolerance and viciousness.
101. Susiluoto, *Origins and Development of Systems Thinking*, 81.
102. Bukharin, *Historical Materialism*, xii–xv.
103. Cohen, "Marxist Theory and Bolshevik Policy," 51.
104. Ibid.
105. Ibid., 52.
106. Bukharin, *Historical Materialism*, 77.
107. Ibid.
108. Ibid.
109. Ibid., 72.
110. Bogdanov in Bukharin, *Historical Materialism*, 100.
111. Ibid., 74, 78, 79, 239–41.
112. Ibid., 75.
113. Ibid., 79.
114. Prat, "Diamat and Contemporary Biology," 197.
115. Kaufmann, "Biophysical and Marxist Economics," 96.
116. Ibid., 97.
117. Marx, *Capital* 1:184.
118. Ibid., 151–52.

119. Joravsky, *Soviet Marxism and Natural Science*.
120. Ibid., 101.
121. Bukharin, *Historical Materialism*, 78, 79.
122. Copleston, *Philosophy in Russia*, 319.
123. Bukharin, *Historical Materialism*, 79.
124. Ibid., 80.
125. James P. Scanlan, *Marxism in the USSR: A Critical Survey of Current Soviet Thought*, 103. In this connection, see Engels, *Anti-Dühring*, 59, 151.
126. Scanlan, *Marxism in the USSR*, 103, Prigogine and Stengers, *Order Out of Chaos*.
127. Schmidt, *The Concept of Nature in Marx*, 189.
128. Bukharin, *Historical Materialism*, 80. It is of particular interest to note that among the most recent neo-Schumpeterian theories of innovation is one put forward by Gerald Silverberg ("Embodied Technical Progress in a Dynamic Economic Model: The Self-Organization Paradigm," 192–208). Silverberg's point of departure is Prigogine's and Stenger's (*Order Out of Chaos*) theory of dissipative systems, systems that display what Hegel and Bukharin (*Historical Materialism*) described as characterized by sudden transformation from quantity to quality.
129. Bukharin, *Historical Materialism*, 82.
130. The one-sidedness of Werner Sombart, whom Bukharin mentions as being among the class of bourgeois scholars, is once again apparent in Kenneth E. Boulding's emphatic remarks (in *Evolutionary Economics*) that dialectical processes are not evolutionary ones.
131. Bukharin, *Historical Materialism*, 83n.
132. Cohen, "Marxist Theory and Bolshevik Policy," 56.
133. Bukharin, *Historical Materialism*, 76.
134. Ibid., 74.
135. Cohen, "Marxist Theory and Bolshevik Policy," 59.
136. See Bukharin, in *Pravda* (July 7, 1926), 3.
137. Cohen, *Bukharin and the Bolshevik Revolution*, 199.
138. *Pravda*, October 1, 1951. In Valentinov, *Encounters with Lenin*, 259.
139. Valentinov, *Encounters with Lenin*, 259.
140. Ibid., 60.
141. Bukharin, *Historical Materialism*, chapters 5, 6.
142. Ibid., 160.
143. Ibid., 161.
144. Bogdanov, *Essays in Tektology*, 82.
145. Ludwig von Bertalanffy, *General Systems Theory: Foundations, Development, Applications*, 123.
146. Bogdanov, *Essays in Tektology*, 176–77.
147. Ibid., 166.
148. Ibid., 248.
149. Ibid., 254.
150. Ibid., 76–77. In the 1940s the Austrian physicist Erwin Schrödinger, and much more recently, R. Passet and Y. Tamanoi, among others, referred to the energy feedback loop identified in the work of Bukharin.
151. Bukharin, *Historical Materialism*, chapters 5, 6.
152. Ibid., 85.
153. Ibid., 107–8.
154. Ibid., 110.
155. Susiluoto, *Origins and Development of Systems Thinking*, 85.

156. Bukharin, *Historical Materialism*, 76.
157. Ibid., 77.
158. Ibid.
159. Ibid.; Susiluoto remarks that Bukharin's use of the terms *positive indication* and *negative indication* are analytically equivalent to both Bogdanov's "positive" and "negative" selection and the concepts of positive and negative feedback.
160. N.I. Bukharin, "Mirovaya ekonomika i imperializm," 11.
161. Ibid., 23.
162. N.I. Bukharin, *Imperialism and the World Economy*, 168.
163. A.A. Bogdanov, *Kommunist*, 1918, No. 3, 19–20.
164. Bukharin, *Imperialism and the World Economy*, 77.
165. N.I. Bukharin, *Selected Writings on the State and the Transition to Socialism*, 81.
166. From an analysis of the more recent edition of social energetics, for instance, present in the works of H. Odum, R. Costanza, and K. Boulding, one detects similar one-sidedness.
167. Susiluoto remarks that such an interpretation tended to make his system of thinking devoid of concrete applications. Bogdanov's system, by contrast, was genuinely open. It had points of application in medicine, biology, technology, planning, and economics. Bogdanov's Tektology led to a social activism in which human creativity was emphasized. Bukharin was a mechanist who saw human activity as being subject to the iron laws of equilibrium in nature (Susiluoto, *Origins and Development of Systems Thinking*, 100).
168. Bukharin, *Historical Materialism*, 85–86.
169. Ibid., 86.
170. Susiluoto, *Origins and Development of Systems Thinking*, 89.
171. Bukharin, *Historical Materialism*, 116, 123.
172. Ibid., 124.
173. Georg Lukács, "Technology and Social Relations."
174. Systems analysis is based on the premise that decomposing an organization into its various components or parts makes for easier solution, resolution, or dissolution of problems. However, dissecting an organizational issue or problem into its basic elements can obliterate relationships between the parts and the performance of the whole. In contrast, systems thinking requires that an organization as a whole be considered in managerial planning. Its perspective is holistic in that insights and understandings relative to the entire organization, its environment, and their interrelationships are required.
175. Sochor, *Revolution and Culture*, 49.
176. See T. Parsons and E.A. Shils, eds., *Toward a General Theory of Action*.
177. In the case of the revisionist Marxists, Bogdanov and Bukharin, their concept of equilibrium admitted revolutionary bifurcations and thus, in part, avoided the charge of conservatism. See Gouldner, *The Coming Crisis*; I.L. Horowitz, "Consensus, Conflict and Cooperation: A Sociological Inventory."
178. P.A. Sorokin, *Social and Cultural Dynamics*, 693; Kenneth Bailey, "Beyond Functionalism: Toward a Nonequilibrium Analysis of Complex Social Systems," 2.
179. Bailey, "Beyond Functionalism," 3; see also Talcott Parsons, *The Social System*, 109, 6n.
180. Bailey, "Beyond Functionalism," 3; and Bertalanffy, *General Systems Theory*, 39, 40n.
181. Parsons, *The Social System*, 107.
182. Ibid.
183. Bailey "Beyond Functionalism," 4.
184. Ibid., 7.
185. W.B. Canon, "Organization for Physiological Homeostasis."

186. Bailey, "Beyond Functionalism," 8.
187. Canon, "Organization for Physiological Homeostasis."
188. Bailey, "Beyond Functionalism," 8–9.
189. Parsons, *The Social System*, 107.
190. The Seventh World Congress of Sociology in Varna, Bulgaria, in 1970 revealed a rapprochement between Eastern and Western sociology. Soviet political sociologist F. Burlatskii expressed interest in incorporating into Marxism the systems theory, the political-cultural approach, and Parsonian functionalism. Polish sociologist A. Zdrawomyslow considered the emergence of a Marxist functionalism as a great theoretical advance. (See J.W. Freiberg, "Sociology and the Ruling Class.")
191. Bukharin, *Historical Materialism*, 74.
192. Susiluoto, *Origins and Development of Systems Thinking*, 98.
193. Milan Zeleny, "Spontaneous Social Orders."
194. Jan Kamaryt, "From Science to Metascience and Philosophy: Dialectical Perspectives in the Development of Ludwig von Bertalanffy's Theoretical Work," 78.
195. Ibid.
196. Bogdanov, *Essays in Tektology*, 87, 221; Gorelik, "Reemergence of Bogdanov's Tektology," 6.
197. Bogdanov, *Essays in Tektology*, 88, 221.
198. Ibid., 221.
199. Milan Zeleny, ed., *Autopoiesis, Dissipative Structures, and Spontaneous Social Orders*, 33.
200. Bogdanov, *Essays in Tektology*, 205–10.
201. Gorelik, "Reemergence of Bogdanov's Tektology," 7.
202. Zeleny, *Autopoiesis*, 33.
203. Bogdanov, *Essays in Tektology*, 9.

Chapter 12

1. It is of parenthetic interest to note that in the restructuring of the Russian economy since the dissolution of the Soviet Union, "shock methods" are once again being selectively employed with not dissimilar effects to those experienced in the early 1920s.
2. A.A. Bogdanov, "Organizatsionnaya nauki i khozyaistvennaya planomernost."
3. A.A. Bogdanov, "Organizatsionnye printsipy edinogo khozyaistvennogo plana," 40–45.
4. S. Strumilin, "K khozyaistvennomu planu na 1921–22 g," 10
5. Cohen, *Bukharin and the Bolshevik Revolution*, 215.
6. Bogdanov, *Tektology*, vol. 2, 100.
7. V.A. Bazarov, *Kapitalisticheskie tsikly i vosstanovitel'nyi protsess khozyaistva SSSR*, 61.
8. Ibid., 3.
9. In Soviet historiography the adherents of the genetic approach are customarily presented as opponents of structural transformations in the economy, and consequently as opponents of industrialization.
10. Marx to Kugelmann July 11, 1868, Marx and Engels, *Collected Works* 32:460–61.
11. Bukharin, *Economic Theory of the Leisure Class*, 26.
12. Bukharin, *Selected Writings on the State*, 93.
13. N.I. Bukharin, *Izbrannye proizvedeniya*, 395–96.
14. Ibid., 405.
15. Bukharin, *Historical Materialism*, 75.

16. V.I. Lenin, "Zamechaniia na knigu N. Bukharina," 54.

17. N.I. Bukharin, *Fourth World Congress of the Comintern: Selected Materials*, 75.

18. Marx had dealt at length with the process of appropriating noncapitalist means of production, as well as with the transformation of the peasants into a capitalist proletariat. Indeed, volume 1 of *Capital* is devoted to describing the origin of the English proletariat.

19. G. Preobrazhensky, *The New Economics*, 167.

20. The concept of proportionality between agrarian and industrial processes figured prominently in Kautsky. For according to Kautsky, the advent of imperialism was the product of highly developed capitalism, the impulse of an industrialized capitalist nation to acquire and annex an increasing amount of agrarian area. The impulse was to be explained by the interchange between agriculture and industry in modern capitalist society. These two sectors of the economy had to work in concert in order to maintain an equilibrium between the means of production and the means of consumption. An imbalance between the two resulted in an industrial crisis (Karl Kautsky, "Der Imperialismus," 908–9).

21. This process would also accelerate the proletarianization of the peasantry, thereby allegedly "accelerating" the historical process necessary for the accomplishment of socialism—an accomplishment claimed by Stalin for the Soviet Union in 1936. But for practical purposes the effect of proletarianization was factually little different from the experience of enclosures in England, that is, the institutional commodification of land and labor. Karl Polanyi detailed the instituting of the economic process, referring at length to the British circumstances and, in particular, to the role of the Speenhamland Act and its repeal by the parliament of 1834. In effect, this had the effect of formally dispossessing peasants and creating thereby a labor market. The labor market did not mature "organically," but was instituted. Polanyi writes: "By interest and inclination it fell to the landlord of England to protect the lives of the common people from the onrush of the Industrial Revolution. Speenhamland was a moat erected in defense of the traditional rural organization, when the turmoil of change was sweeping the countryside, and, incidentally, making agriculture a precarious industry. In their natural reluctance to bow to the needs of the manufacturing towns, the squires were the first to make a stand in what proved to be a century's losing fight. Yet their resistance was not in vain; it averted ruin for several generations and allowed time for almost complete readjustment. Over a critical span of forty years it retarded economic progress, and when, in 1834, the Reform Parliament abolished Speenhamland, the landlords shifted their resistance to the factory laws. The church and the manor were now rousing the people against the mill owner, whose predominance would make the cry for cheap food irresistible, and thus, indirectly, threaten to sap rents and tithes" (Polanyi, *The Great Transformation*, 165).

22. It is worth noting that much of so-called development economics and, in particular, elements of this argument were replicated years later and associated with dependency theory and debates thereof. For a brief overview, see James L. Dietz, "Dependency Theory: A Review Article."

23. Bukharin, *Selected Writings on the State*, 305.

24. Ibid., 307.

25. Ibid., 309.

26. K.J. Tarbuck, *Bukharin's Theory of Equilibrium*. 143.

27. See N. I. Bukharin, "Imperialism and the Accumulation of Capital," in K.J. Tarbuck, *Rosa Luxemburg and Nikolai Bukharin*, 206.

28. The "proportionality debate" between Preobrazhensky, Tugan-Baranovsky, and Bukharin had pronounced implications. The industrial goods–producing sector of the former Soviet Union became autojustified; that is, it operated in an autonomous manner more or less detached from serving final consumer demand.

29. G. Preobrazhensky, "The Problem of Economic Equilibrium Under Concrete Capitalism and in the Soviet System," 98–99.
30. In Cohen, *Bukharin and the Bolshevik Revolution*, 245.
31. Bazarov, *Kapitalisticheskie*, 99.
32. P. Vyshinsky, "Obrazchik vreditel'skoi filosofii (bazarovshchina)," 135.
33. Sochor, *Revolution and Culture*, 221.
34. Bukharin in Roy Medvedev, *Let History Judge: The Origins and Consequences of Stalinism*, 188.
35. Cohen, *Bukharin and the Bolshevik Revolution*, 140.
36. Bukharin, "Organized Mismanagement in Modern Society."
37. Cohen, *Bukharin and the Bolshevik Revolution*, 319.
38. Ibid., 143.
39. See Bukharin, *Ataka*, 227, *Proletarskaia revoliutsiia i kult'tura*, 47–7, and *Historical Materialism*, 310–11. He did not, however, challenge the older thinker's redefinition of class (Cohen, *Bukharin and the Bolshevik Revolution*, 144).
40. Bukharin, "Organized Mismanagement in Modern Society," 226. According to Stephen Cohen, in Bukharin's opinion Max Weber was the most outstanding of all non-Marxist social scientists ("Marxist Theory and Bolshevik Policy," 47).
41. Bukharin, *Pravda*, June 30, 1929.
42. Bukharin, "Organized Mismanagement in Modern Society," 227.
43. Ibid., 227–28, 233.
44. At the October 8 Politburo meeting, the publication of Bukharin's article was condemned for having been published without the Central Committee's knowledge.
45. J.V. Stalin, "The Question of Permanent Revolution," 19. Stalin's "theory of permanent revolution" situates itself within his "stages theory" wherein there were allegedly three transitional stages of post-bourgeois rule: a post-revolutionary government, i.e., the dictatorship of the proletariat; a socialist state; and a communist state. A somewhat ambiguous issue was whether in a post-revolutionary state the class struggle continued. It was this continuing struggle that Stalin's theory of permanent revolution ostensibly sought to address. This is not to suggest that other reasons did not exist. Stalin was effectively arguing that even after the accomplishment of the dictatorship of the proletariat and economic transformation, i.e., the abolition of private ownership of the means of production, the revolution was still far from complete. For Stalin revolution was not an event, but a process.

It is worth noting that Mao Tse-tung in his speech to the Work Conference of the Central Committee at Peitaiho in August 1962, "Long Live . . . ," endorsed a nearly identical position, which he used as a justification for the Cultural Revolution.

Parenthetically, it is perhaps worth noting that Georg Lukács in speaking of the necessity of a cultural revolution employed Stalin's device and linked the phase of the dictatorship of the proletariat with "the high point of the class struggle" (Lukács, "The Old Culture and the New").

46. Roy Medvedev, *Let History Judge: The Origins and Consequences of Stalinism*, 202.

Chapter 13

1. Sochor, *Revolution and Culture*, 233.
2. Bogdanov, *A Short Course*, n.p.
3. Vucinich, *Social Thought in Tsarist Russia*, 225.
4. Bogdanov, *A Short Course*, n.p.
5. Ibid.

6. A.A. Bogdanov, "O proletarskoi kul'ture 1904–1924," Mosow, 1925.
7. V.I. Lenin, "The Taylor System—Man's Enslavement by the Machine," March 13, 1914, in Lenin, *Collected Works* 20:153.
8. Ibid.
9. Ibid.
10. Bogdanov, "O proletarskoi kul'ture 1904–1924," Mosow, 1925.
11. Bogdanov in Kendall E. Bailes, "Alexei Gastev and the Soviet Controversy over Taylorism, 1918–24."
12. The Taylorist expression "scientific management" underwent a politicized transliteration to Russian rendered as "scientific organization of work" (*nauchnaya organizatsiya truda*) and abbreviated to NOT.
13. Lenin, *Collected Works* 36:7.
14. Lenin in Bailes, "Alexei Gastev," 373–94.
15. Lenin, "The Immediate Tasks of the Soviet Government," in V.I. Lenin, *Selected Works* 2:327.
16. Alexei Gastev, "O tendentsiyakh proletarskoi kult'tury," in Bailes, "Alexei Gastev," 377.
17. Ibid., 378.
18. Ibid., 385.
19. Bogdanov in Bailes, "Alexei Gastev," 379.
20. Ibid., 380.
21. Ibid., 384.
22. Ernst Junger in Michael Zimmerman, *Heidegger's Confrontation with Modernity*, chapter 3.
23. Lukács, "The Old Culture and the New."
24. Ibid.
25. A.A. Bogdanov, "O proletarskoi kul'ture," in Bailes, "Alexei Gastev," 380.
26. Stokes, *Empire of Reason*.
27. For Marcuse, and undoubtedly for Bogdanov, fetishism is understood as the mystification of the substantive reality of society. It is the quintessential character of commodity economy, repudiating social relations and substituting the practical fiction of reified commoditized man interacting with commoditized man in their economic affairs.
28. Marcuse, *One-Dimensional Man*, xvi.
29. Bogdanov, *Red Star*, 87.
30. Bogdanov, *A Short Course*, 383.

Chapter 14

1. Bogdanov, *Red Star*, 243.
2. Ibid., 24; Bogdanov's caution against Darwinist interpretations, with their emphasis on phenotypical selection and genotypical mutation, has, in the recent work of J. Salk, been reproached as "anti-evolutionary" in the age of high technology.
3. Abated by the voluntarist slogan "There is no fortress which Bolsheviks cannot storm," an assault was launched on the old, predominately noncommunist, intelligentsia group that had previously been tolerated and even favored because of their skills. The Shakhty Trial was part of the so-called Cultural Revolution of the late 1920s—a revolution directed and manipulated from above and charged by a rhetoric of acute class war and utopian visions.
4. As early as September 1923, Bogdanov was briefly detained after his arrest by agents acting for the people's commissar of internal affairs, Stalin. This action was allegedly in connection with the mandate of a party commission investigating the internal party situation.

5. Jürgen Habermas, *The Theory of Communicative Action*, n.p.; and see Habermas, *Toward a Rational Society*.
6. Bogdanov, "Engineer Menni" in *Red Star*, 187.
7. N.F. Fyodorov, *Filosofiya obschechevo dela*; also in Zenkovsky, *History of Russian Philosophy*, 589.
8. Fyodorov quoted in Zenkovsky, *History of Russian Philosophy*, 589.
9. Bogdanov, "Engineer Menni" in *Red Star*, 187.
10. Susiluoto, *Origins and Development of Systems Thinking*, 98.
11. Bogdanov, *Red Star*, 243.

Chapter 15

1. Jensen, *Beyond Marx and Mach*, 2.
2. Lossky, *History of Russian Philosophy*, 77.
3. N.I. Bukharin, "A.A. Bogdanov"; also in Cohen, *Bukharin and the Bolshevik Revolution*, 15.
4. "Bukharin-Kamenev Meeting," appendix A, in L.D. Trotsky, *The Challenge of the Left Opposition (1928–29)*, 377–83.
5. J.V. Stalin, *Works* 2:21–2.
6. Dostoevsky, *Collected Works* 3:596, 597.
7. In Medvedev, *Let History Judge*, 205.
8. Ibid., 206.
9. Samnadyatyi s'exd VKP(b). *Stenografisheskii otchet* (seventeenth party congress: stenographic record), 124–25.
10. The device of the purge had been a method of continuous party purification. Soon after the October Revolution the Eighth Party Congress ordered a re-registration of the entire party membership to weed out the unworthy—those who had joined the party in the flush of victory. However, the decade of the 1930s was marked by a series of purges culminating in the Great Purge of 1936–38. Of 139 members elected to the Central Committee by the Seventeenth Party Congress, 98 were shot; of 1,966 delegates attending the Congress, 1,108 were subsequently charged with committing antirevolutionary crimes and were arrested. Approximately 36 percent of the members, 850,000, were removed from the party roster.

Chapter 16

1. I. Bernard Cohen, *Revolution in Science*.
2. Donald N. McCloskey, "Has Formalization in Economics Gone Too Far?" 12.
3. Ibid., 9.
4. Ibid., 11.
5. Eichner, "Why Economics Is Not Yet a Science," 517.
6. Rhetoric is exploring thought by conversation. It is the art of discovering warrantable beliefs and improving those beliefs in shared discourse. It is "the art of probing what men believe they ought to believe, rather than proving what is true according to abstract methods; it is the art of discovering good reasons and finding what really warrants assent. On the eve of the Cartesian revolution the French philosopher . . . Peter Ramus, brought to completion a medieval tendency to relegate rhetoric to mere eloquence, leaving logic in charge of reason" (McCloskey, "The Rhetoric of Economics," 483).

Bibliography

Adamik, Richard. "Marx, Engels and Dühring." *Journal of the History of Ideas* 35 (1974).
Adler, Franklin. "Factory Councils, Gramsci and the Industrialists." *Telos* 31 (Spring 1977).
Agh, Attila. "Totality Theory and System Theory." *Problems of the Science of Sciences* 5 (1975–76): 119–30.
Althusser, Louis. *Politics and History: Montesquieu, Rousseau, Hegel and Marx*. Trans. by B. Brewster. London, 1959.
Angyal, G. *The Foundations for a Science of Personality*. New York: Viking Press, 1941.
Annunziato, Frank R. "Gramsci's Theory of Trade Unionism." *Rethinking Marxism* 1, 2 (Summer 1988): 142–64.
Aranson, Johann P. "Perspectives and Problems of Critical Marxism in Eastern Europe," Part 1, *Thesis Eleven* 4 (1982): 68–95; Part 2, *Thesis Eleven* 5–6 (1982): 215–45.
Aristotle. *The Politics*. Trans. by Carnes Lord. Chicago: University of Chicago Press, 1984.
————. *Topics*. Trans. by E.S. Foster. Cambridge, Mass.: Harvard University Press, 1966.
Axelos, Kostas. *Alienation, Praxis and Techne in the Thought of Karl Marx*. Trans. by Ronald Bruzina. Austin: University of Texas Press, 1976.
Ayer, A.J. *Language, Truth, and Logic*. New York: V. Gollancz, 1946.
Bailes, Kendall E. "Alexei Gastev and the Soviet Controversy over Taylorism, 1918–24." *Soviet Studies* 29, no. 3 (July 1977): 373–94.
Bailey, Kenneth. "Beyond Functionalism: Toward a Nonequilibrium Analysis of Complex Social Systems." *British Journal of Sociology* 35, no. 1 (1984): 1–18.
Ballestrem, Karl G. "Lenin and Bogdanov." *Studies in Soviet Thought* 9 (1969): 283–310.
Ban, Erwin. "Engels als Theoretiker." *Kommunismus* 1, no. 45 (3 December 1920): 1595–1605.
Bateson, Gregory. *Steps to an Ecology of Mind*. New York: Ballantine Books, 1972.
Bazarov, V.A. *Kapitalisticheskie tsikly i vosstanovitel'nyi protsess khozyaistva SSSR*. Moscow-Leningrad, 1927.
Bednarz, John, Jr. "Complexity and Intersubjectivity: Towards the Theory of Niklas Luhmann." *Human Studies* 7 (1984): 55–69.
Bejin, Andre. "Differenciation, Complexification, Evolution des Societes" (Differentiation, increasing complexity, and the evolution of societies). *Communications* 22 (1974): 109–18.

Bello, Ralph. "The Systems Approach: A. Bogdanov and L. von Bertalanffy." *Studies in Soviet Thought* 30 (1985): 131–47.
Belov, N. *The Structure of Internal Secretion in Organs and Their Significance in Present-Day Biology*. Novoye v meditsine, 1901.
Belykh, A.A. "A Note on the Origins of Input-Output Analysis and the Contribution of the Early Soviet Economists: Chayanov, Bogdanov, and Kritsman." *Soviet Studies* 41, no. 3 (July 1989): 426–29.
Bencivenga, Ermanno. "Theories and Practices." *Monist* 70, no. 2 (April 1987): 212–22.
Bergson, Emily Herman. *Eucken and Bergson: Their Significance for Christian Thought*. London: J. Clarke, 1912.
Bergson, H.L. *Introduction to Metaphysics*. Ed. and trans. by Thomas Anderson Goudge. New York: Bobbs-Merill, 1955.
Berman, M. *All That Is Solid Melts Into Air: The Experience of Modernity*. London: Verso, 1983.
Bertalanffy, L.v. *General Systems Theory: Foundations, Development, Applications*. New York: Braziller, 1968.
———. *Problems of Life*. New York: John Wiley, 1952.
———. "The Theory of Open Systems in Physics and Biology." *Science* 111 (1950): 23–29.
Biggart, John. "Bukharin and the Origins of the 'Proletarian Culture' Debate." *Soviet Studies* 31, no. 2 (April 1987).
Blackmore, J.T. *Ernst Mach*. Berkeley: University of California Press, 1972.
Blackstock, Paul, ed. *Russian Menace to Europe*. Glencoe, Ill.: Free Press, 1952.
Blauberg, I.V. "The History of Science and the Systems Approach." *Social Sciences* 8, no. 3 (1977): 90–100.
Blauberg, I.V.; Sadovsky, V.M.; and Yudin, E.G. *Systems Theory: Philosophical and Methodological Problems*. Moscow: Progress Publishers, 1977.
Blaug, Mark. "Kuhn Versus Lakatos, or Paradigms Versus Research Programmes in the History of Economics." In *Paradigms & Revolutions*, ed. Gary Gutting, 137–59. Notre Dame, Ind.: University of Notre Dame Press, 1980.
———. *The Methodology of Economics: Or How Economists Explain*. Cambridge: Cambridge University Press, 1980.
Blei, Franz. *Die Metaphysik in der Nationalökonomie* (Metaphysics in political economy), n.p., n.d.
Bloch, Marc. "Advent and Triumph of the Water Mill." In *Land and Work in Medieval Europe*. London, 1967.
Bobbio, Norberto. "Gramsci and the Conception of Civil Society." In *Gramsci and Marxist Theory*, ed. C. Mouffe. London: Routledge and Kegan Paul, 1979.
Bogdanov, A.A. "Autobiography." In *Makers of the Russian Revolution*, Georges Haupt and Jean-Jacques Marie, trans. C.I.P. Ferdinand and D.M. Idenos, 286–89. Ithaca, N.Y.: Cornell University Press, 1974.
———. *Bor'ba za zhizniesposobnost'* (The struggle for viability). Moscow, 1927.
———. "The Community of Man." *Pravda*. April 1904.
———. *The Development of Life in Nature and Society*. 1902.
———. "Elementy proletarskoj kul'tury v razvitii rabocego klassa." Moscow, 1920.
———. *Empirio-monism*, 3 vols. Moscow, 1904–1906.
———. *Essays in Tektology*, trans. George Gorelik. Seaside, Calif.: Intersystems, 1980.
———. *Filosofiia zhivogo opyta* (The philosophy of living experience). St. Petersburg, 1913.
———. "Ideal i put," n.p., n.d.
———. "Ideal poznaniya." *Voprosy Filosofi i Psikhologii* 2 (1913): 983–88.

———. *Iz psikhologii obshchestva (stat'i 1901–1904)* (From the psychology of society), St. Petersburg, 1904.
———. "Iz slovariia inostrannykh slov: Klass," *Pravda*. March 17, 1913.
———. "Matter and Thing-in-itself." In *Russian Philosophy III*, trans. G.L. Kline. Chicago: Quadrangle Books, 1965.
———. "Nachal'nyi kurs politicheskoi ekonomii." Karkov, U.S.S.R., 1923.
———. *Nauka ob obshchestvennom soznanii* (The science about social consciousness). Moscow, 1914.
———. *Novyi mir (stat'i 1904–1905)*, Moscow, 1905.
———. "O proletarskoi kul'ture 1904–1924," Moscow, 1925.
———. *Ocherki Organizationnoi Nauki* (Essays in organizational science). Samara, U.S.S.R., 1921.
———. "Organizacionnye principy social'noj techniki i ekonimiki." *Vestnik socialisticeskoj ackademii* 4 (1923): 272–84.
———. "Organizatsionnaya nauki i khozyaistvennaya planomernost." *Trudy Pervoi Vserossiiskoi Initsiativnoi Konferentsii po nauchnoi organizatsii truda u prozvodstva*. (Conference proceedings), vol. 1. Moscow, 1921.
———."Organizatsionnye printsipy edinogo khozyaistvennogo plana." *Vestnik truda*, no. 4/5/6 (1921): 40–45.
———. *Osnovnye elementy istoricheskogo vzgliada na prirodu* (The fundamental elements of the historical outlook on nature). St. Petersburg, 1899.
———. *Poznanie s istoricheskoi tochki zreniia* (Knowledge from a historical point of view). St. Petersburg, 1901.
———. "Programma kul'tury." In A.A. Bogdanov, *Voprosy sotsializma*. Moscow, 1918.
———. "Proletariat v bor'be za sotsializm," n.p., n.d.
———. *Red Star: The First Bolshevik Utopia*, ed. L.R. Graham and R. Stites, trans. Charles Rougle. Bloomington: Indiana University Press, 1984.
———. *A Short Course of Economic Science*, trans. J. Fineberg. London: Labour Publishing, 1923. Originally published as *Kratkij kurs ekonomicheskoi nauka* (1897).
———. "Sobiranie cheloveka," *Pravda*. April 1904.
———. *Socializm nauki* (The socialism of science). Moscow, 1918.
———. "Sotsializm v nastoiashchem." *Vpered*, n.p., n.d.
———. *Vseobshchaia Organizatsionnaia Nauka: Tektologia* (The universal science of organization: tektology). vol. 1, St. Petersburg, 1912; vol. 2, Moscow, 1917; vol. 3, Moscow: Izdatelstvo A. I. Grschebina, 1922.
Böhm-Bawerk, Eugen von. *Capital and Interest: A Critical History of Economical Theory*, trans. William Smart. London: Macmillan, 1890.
Bohr, Neils Henrik David. *Atomic Physics and Human Knowledge*. New York: John Wiley, 1958.
Boll, Michael M. "From Empiriocriticism to Empiriomonism: The Marxist Phenomenology of Aleksandr Bogdanov." *SEER* 59, no. 1 (January 1981).
Boltzmann, Ludwig. *Theoretical Physics and Philosophical Problems*, ed. Brian McGuinness. Dordrecht: D. Reidel, 1974.
———. *Der zweite Hauptsatz der mechanischen Wärmtheorie*. Vienna: Gerold, 1886.
Bookchin, Murray. *Toward an Ecological Society*. Montreal: Black Rose Books, 1980.
Boudon, Raymond and Bourricaud, Francois. "Herbert Spencer ou l'oublie"(On rereading Herbert Spencer). *Revue francaise de Sociologie* 25, no. 3 (July–Sept. 1984): 343–51.
Boulding, Kenneth E. *Ecodynamics: A New Theory of Societal Evolution*. London: Sage View Press, 1978.
———. *Evolutionary Economics*. London: Sage View Press, 1981.
———. *A Primer on Social Dynamics*. New York: Free Press, 1970.

Brecht, Bertolt. *Drums in the Night*, trans. John Willett. London: Methuen, 1970.
―――. *Gesammelte Werke.* 24 vols. Frankfurt, 1967.
Broad, William J. "Paul Feyerabend: Science and the Anarchist." *Science* 206, no. 4418 (November 2, 1979): 534–37.
Broda, Engelbert. *Ludwig Boltzmann: Man, Physicist, Philosopher.* Woodbridge, Conn.: Ox Bow Press, 1983.
Bronowski, Jacob. *The Common Sense of Science.* Harmondsworth, Middlesex: Penguin, 1960.
Bukharin, Nikolai I. "A.A. Bogdanov," *Pravda* (April 8, 1928).
―――. *Ataka: Sbornik teoretischeskikh*, 2nd ed. Moscow, 1924.
―――. *The Economic Theory of the Leisure Class.* New York: Greenwood Press, 1968.
―――. *Ekonimika perakhodnogo perioda* (The economics of the transition period). Moscow, 1920.
―――. *Fourth World Congress of the Comintern: Selected Materials.* Moscow-Petrograd, 1923.
―――. *Historical Materialism: A System of Sociology.* New York: International, 1925.
―――. *Imperialism and the World Economy.* London: Merlin Press, 1972.
―――. *Izbrannye proizvedeniya.* Moscow, 1928.
―――. "Notes of an Economist," *Pravda* (September 30, 1928).
―――. "Organized Mismanagement in Modern Society," trans. Valerie Rosen. In *Essential Works of Socialism*, ed. I. Howe. New Haven: Yale University Press, 1986.
―――. *Politischeskoe zaveshchanie Lenina.* Moscow, 1929.
―――. *Proletarskaia revoliutsiia i kult'tura.* Petrograd, 1923.
―――. *Selected Writings on the State and the Transition to Socialism*, trans. and ed. Richard Day. Armonk, N.Y.: M.E. Sharpe, 1982.
―――. *Teoriia istoricheskogo materializma; populiaryni uchebnik marksistskoi sotsiologii* (The theory of historical materialism; a popular textbook of Marxist sociology). Moscow, 1921.
―――. "Vestnik sotsialisticheskoi akademii," 3 (1923).
―――. "The World Economy and Imperialism," *Kommunist*, 1915.
Bukunrin, Michael. *Social-politscher Briefweschel mit Alexander Hersen und Orgarëv*, n.p., n.d.
Burke, James. *The Day the Universe Changed.* Toronto: Little, Brown, 1985.
Caldwell, Bruce. *Beyond Positivism: Economic Methodology in the Twentieth Century.* London: George Allen and Unwin, 1982.
Canon, W.B. "Organization for Physiological Homeostasis." *Physiological Reviews* 9 (1929): 399–431.
Capra, Fritzjof. *The Turning Point: Science, Society and the Rising Culture.* New York: Bantam, 1982.
Carey, Henry Charles. *Principles of Social Science.* Philadelphia: Lippincott, 1858.
Carleton, Lawrence Richard. "Problems, Methodology, and Outlaw Science." *Philosophy of the Social Sciences* 12, no. 2 (June 1982): 143–51.
Carnot, Sadi N.L. *Memoir on the Motive Power of Heat*, ed. B.P.E. Clapeyron. New York: Dover, 1960.
Carver, Terrel. "Marx, Engels and Scholarship." *Political Studies* 32 (1984): 249–56.
Cassirer, Ernst. *The Philosophy of the Environment*, trans. F.C.A. Koelin and J.P. Pettegrove. Boston, 1964.
―――. *The Question of Jean-Jacques Rousseau.* trans. P. Gay. Bloomington, 1963.
Chaadaev, Peter. *The Major Works of Peter Chaadaev*, trans. R.T. McNally. Notre Dame, Indiana: 1969.

Checkland, P. B. *Systems Thinking, Systems Practice.* New York: John Wiley, 1981.
Chernishevsky, N.G. *What Is to Be Done? Tales About New People,* trans. B.R. Tucker. New York, 1961.
Chicherin. *Essays in the History of Russian Law,* n.p., 1858.
———. *Property and the State,* n.p., 1882–83.
Christensen, Paul. "The Materials-Energy Foundations of Classical Theory." In R. Costanza and H. Daly, eds., "Ecological Economics." Special issue of the review *Ecological Modelling* 38 (1987).
Clagett, Marshall. *Greek Science in Antiquity.* New York: Abelard-Schumann, 1955.
———. *The History of Science.* Madison: University of Wisconsin Press, 1969.
Clausius, Rudolf Julius Emmanuel. *Reflections on the Motive Power of Fire by Sadi Carnot; and Other Papers on the Second Law of Thermodynamics.* New York: Dover, 1960.
Coase, Ronald. "The Nature of the Firm." *Economica* 4 (November 1937).
Cohen, I. Bernard. *Revolution in Science.* Cambridge, Mass.: Harvard University Press, 1985.
Cohen, Stephen F. *Bukharin and the Bolshevik Revolution: A Political Biography 1888–1938.* New York: Alfred A. Knopf, 1973.
———. "Marxist Theory and Bolshevik Policy." *Political Science Quarterly* 85, no. 1 (1970).
Colletti, Lucio. *From Rousseau to Lenin: Studies in Ideology and Society.* London: New Left Review, 1972.
Comte, Auguste. *Cours de philosophie positive.* ed. M. Serres. Paris: Hermann, 1975.
Copleston, Frederick C. *Philosophy in Russia: From Herzen to Lenin and Berdyaev.* Paris: University of Notre Dame, Search Press, 1986.
Costanza, R. and Daly, H., eds. *Ecological Modelling* 38 (1987).
Counihan, Carole. "Antonio Gramsci and Social Science." *Dialectical Anthropology* 11, no. 1 (1986): 3–9.
Curthoys, J.; Suchting, W.; and Feyerabend, Paul K. "Feyerabend's Discourse Against Method: A Marxist Critique." *Inquiry* 20, nos. 2–3 (Summer 1977): 243–371.
Davidson, A.B. "The Varying Seasons of Gramscian Studies." *Political Studies* 20, no. 4 (December 1972).
Davidson, Alastair. "Gramsci and Lenin, 1917–1922." In *The Socialist Register,* ed. Ralph Miliband and John Saville. London, 1974.
Day, R.B. *N.I. Bukharin, Selected Writings on the State and the Transition to Socialism.* New York, 1982.
Debenjak, Bozidar. "Engels and the Problem of Alienation." *Social Praxis* 3, nos. 1–2 (1975): 45–62.
Deborin, A.M. "Hegel and Dialectical Materialism." Introductory article in the translation of *Hegel's Collected Works,* vol. 1, 2nd ed. Moscow, 1929.
Descartes, René. *Discourse on Method and the Meditations of Descartes,* trans. F.E. Sutcliffe. Harmondsworth, England: Penguin, 1968.
Dewey, John. *The Quest for Certainty: A Study of the Relation of Knowledge and Action.* New York: Minton, Balch, and Company, 1929.
Diderot, Denis. *D'Alembert's Dream.* Harmondsworth, England: Penguin, 1976.
Dietz, James L. "Dependency Theory: A Review Article." *Journal of Economic Issues* 14, no. 3 (September 1980): 751–58.
Dijksterhuis, E.J. *The Mechanization of the World Picture.* New York: Oxford University Press, 1961.
Domb, C. *Clerk Maxwell and Modern Science: Six Commemorative Lectures.* London: University of London, Athlone Press, 1963.

Dostoevsky, Fyodor. *Complete Collected Works* (Polnoe sobranie sochinenii), 30 vols. Moscow, 1956.
Duncan, D. *Life and Letters of Herbert Spencer.* New York: Appleton, n.d.
Eddington, Sir Arthur Stanley. *Fundamental Theory*, ed. E. Whittaker. Cambridge, England: University Press, 1948.
Ehrenberg, John R. "Lenin and the Politics of Organization." *Science and Society* 43, no. 1 (Spring 1979): 70–86.
Eichner, Alfred S. "Why Economics Is Not Yet a Science." *Journal of Economic Issues* 27, no. 2 (June 1983): 507–20.
Elliot, John E. "Institutionalism as an Approach to Political Economy." *Journal of Economic Issues* 12 (March 1986): 91–114.
Emery, F.E., ed. *Systems Thinking.* Harmondsworth, Middlesex: Penguin, 1981.
Emy, Hugh. "Michael Pusey's Economic Rationalism in Canberra." *Quadrant* 36 (1992): 59–60.
Engels, Friederich. *Anti-Dühring: Herr Eugen Dühring's Revolution in Science*, ed. C.P. Dutt, trans. Emile Burns. New York: International, 1966.
———. *Dialectics of Nature*, trans. Clemens Dutt, 2nd rev. ed. Moscow: Progress, 1954.
———. *The Origin of the Family, Private Property, and the State*, ed. L.H. Morgan. New York: Pathfinder Press, 1972.
———. "The Part Played by Labour in the Transition from Ape to Man." *Die Neue Zeit* 2, no. 44 (1895–96).
———. "Socialism: Utopian and Scientific." In K. Marx and F. Engels, *Selected Works*, ed. I.B. Lasker. Moscow: Foreign Language Publishing House, 1946–49.
Erlich, A. *The Soviet Industrialization Debate.* Cambridge, Mass.: Harvard University Press, 1960.
Everitt, C.W. Francis. *James Clerk Maxwell: Physicist and Natural Philosopher.* New York: Scribner's, 1975.
Festinger, Leo. *A Theory of Cognitive Dissonance.* Stanford, Calif.: Stanford University Press, 1957.
Feyerabend, Paul K. *Against Method: Outline of an Anarchistic Theory of Knowledge.* London: Verso, 1978.
———. "Democracy, Elitism, and Scientific Method." *Inquiry* 23, no. 1 (March 1980): 3–18.
———. "On the Critique of Scientific Reason." In *Essays in Memory of Imre Lakatos*, ed. R.S. Cohen et al. Dordrecht, Holland: D. Reidel, 1976.
Filtzer, Donald A., ed. *The Crisis of Soviet Industrialization.* White Plains, N.Y.: M.E. Sharpe, 1979.
Florinsky, Michael T., ed. *Encyclopedia of Russia and the Soviet Union.* Toronto: McGraw Hill, 1961.
Foucault, Michel. *Discipline and Punish.* London, 1977.
———. "Truth and Power." In *The Foucault Reader*, ed. Paul Rabinow. New York: Pantheon, 1984.
Fourier, Baron Jean Baptiste Joseph. *The Analytical Theory of Heat*, trans. Alexander Freeman. New York: Dover, 1955.
Frank, Manfred. *What Is Neostructuralism?* trans. Sabine Wilke and Richard Gray. Minneapolis: University of Minneapolis Press, 1987.
Freiberg, J.W. "Sociology and the Ruling Class." *Insurgent Sociologist* 3, no. 4 (Summer 1973): 12–26.
Frolov, Ivan. *Man-Science-Humanism: A New Synthesis.* Moscow: Progress, 1986.
Fromm, Erich. *Man May Prevail: An Inquiry into the Facts and Fictions of Foreign Policy.* Garden City, N.Y.: Doubleday, 1961.

Fyodorov, E. "Perfectionism." *Transactions of the St. Petersburg Biological Laboratory*, vol. 8, 2, St. Petersburg, 1906.
Fyodorov, N.F. *Filosofiya obschechevo dela* (The philosophy of the common task). Harbin, China: 1930.
Galbraith, John Kenneth. *American Capitalism: The Concept of Countervailing Power*. Boston: Houghton Mifflin, 1956.
———. *The New Industrial State*. New York: New American Library, 1968.
Gellner, Ernst. "The Rational Mystic." *The New Republic* 208, no. 16 (April 19, 1993).
Georgescu-Roegen, Nicholas. *Energy and Economic Myths: Institutional and Analytical Economic Essays*. Toronto: Pergamon Press, 1976.
———. *The Entropy Law and the Economic Process*. Cambridge, Mass.: Harvard University Press, 1971.
Gerth, H.H., and Mills, C. Wright, eds. *From Max Weber: Essays in Sociology*. New York: Galaxy, 1958.
Geyer, Felix and Zouwen, Johannes van der. *Sociocybernetic Paradoxes: Observation, Control and Evolution of Self-steering Systems*. Beverly Hills, Calif.: Sage, 1986.
Gill, Stephen, ed. *Gramsci, Historical Materialism, and International Relations*. Cambridge: Cambridge University Press, 1993.
Godelier, Maurice. "Systems, Structure and Contradiction in Das Kapital." In *Introduction to Structuralism*, ed. M. Lane. New York: Basic Books, 1970.
Goldmann, Lucien. "Socialism and Humanism," in *Socialist Humanism*, ed. Erich Fromm. Garden City, N.Y.: Doubleday & Company, 1965.
———. *Immanuel Kant*, trans. R. Black. London: New Left Books, 1971.
Gonikman, S. "Teorija obscestva i teorija klassov Bogdanova." (Bogdanov's theory of society and classes). *Poa' Znamenem Marxisma* 12 (1929): 27–62.
Gorelik, George. "Bogdanov's Tektology: Its Nature, Development and Influence." *Studies in Soviet Thought* 26 (1983): 39–47.
———. "Reemergence of Bogdanov's Tektology in Soviet Studies of Organization." *Academy of Management Journal* 18, no. 2 (June 1975).
Gould, George M. "Some Questions of Psychic-Physics." *The Monist* 5 (1895).
Gouldner, Alvin W. *The Coming Crisis of Western Sociology*. New York: Basic Books, 1970.
———. "Stalinism: A Study of Internal Colonialism." *Telos* 34 (Winter 1977–78): 5–48.
———. *The Two Marxisms. Contradictions and Anomalies in the Development of Theory*. New York: Macmillan Press, 1980.
Graham, L.R. and Stites, R., eds. *Red Star: The First Bolshevik Utopia*, trans. Charles Rougle. Bloomington: Indiana University Press, 1984.
Gramsci, Antonio. *Antonio Gramsci, Selections from Political Writings (1910–20)*, ed. Quintin Hoare. London: Lawrence and Wishart, 1977.
———. *Collected Works*. Turin, 1948.
———. *Il Materialismo Storico e la Filosofia di Benedetto Croce* (Historical materialism and the philosophy of Benedetto Croce). In Antonio Gramsci, *Collected Works*. Turin, 1948.
———. *Selections from Prison Notebooks*, ed. Quintin Hoare and Geoffrey Nowell Smith. New York: International, 1971.
Grattan-Guinness, Joseph. *Joseph Fourier 1768–1830*. Cambridge, Mass.: MIT Press, 1972.
Gray, Andrew. *Lord Kelvin: An Account of His Scientific Life and Work*. London: J.M. Dent, 1908.
Grove, J.W. "The Intellectual Revolt Against Science." *Skeptical Inquirer* 13, no. 1 (Fall 1988): 70–75.

Gudeman, Stephen. *Economics as Culture*. London: Routledge and Kegan Paul, 1986.
Gunter, G.A.Y., ed. *Bergson and the Evolution of Physics*. Knoxville: University of Tennessee Press, 1977.
Habermas, Jürgen. *Communication and the Evolution of Society*, trans. Thomas McCarthy. Boston: Beacon Press, 1979.
———. *Knowledge and Human Interests*. Boston: Beacon Press, 1972.
———. "Knowledge and Interest." *Inquiry* 3 (Winter, 1966): 285–300.
———. *Legitimation Crisis*. Boston: Beacon Press, 1975.
———. *Toward a Rational Society: Student Protest, Science and Politics*, trans. K.J. Shapiro. Boston: Beacon Press, 1970.
———. "What Does a Crisis Mean Today? Legitimation Problems in Late Capitalism." *Merkur* (April–May 1973).
Harman, P.M. *Wranglers and Physicists: Studies on Cambridge Physics*. Manchester, England: Manchester University Press, 1943.
Haupt, George and Marie, Jean-Jacques, eds. *Makers of the Russian Revolution*, trans. C.I.P. Ferdinand and D.M. Idenos. Ithaca, N.Y.: Cornell University Press, 1974.
Hayek, Frederick. *The Counter-Revolution of Science*. Chicago: Free Press, 1955.
Hecker, Julius F. *Russian Sociology: A Contribution to the History of Sociological Thought and Theory*. New York: Columbia University Press, 1915.
Hegel, Georg Wilhelm Friedrich. *Hegel and the Human Spirit: A Translation of the Jena Lectures*, ed. L. Rauch. Detroit: Wayne State University Press, 1983.
———. *The Phenomenology of the Mind*, trans. U.B. Baille. New York: Harper & Row, 1967.
———. *The Phenomenology of the Spirit*, trans. A.V. Miller. Oxford, 1979.
———. *The Philosophy of History*, trans. J. Sibree. New York: Dover, 1956.
———. *The Philosophy of Right*. Oxford: Clarendon, 1958.
———. *Wissenschaft der Logik* (Hegel's science of logic). London: Allen & Unwin, 1969.
Heidegger, Martin. *Being and Time*, trans. J. Macquarrie and E. Robinson. New York: Harper & Row, 1962.
———. *What Is a Thing*. South Bend, Ind.: Gateway, 1967.
Heilbroner, Robert. "Do Machines Make History?" *Technology and Culture* 25, no. 3 (1967).
Heisenberg, Werner. "The Representation of Nature in Contemporary Physics." *Daedalus* 87 (1958): 95–108.
Heller, Agnes. "The Marxian Theory of Revolution and the Revolution of Everyday Life." *Telos* 6 (Fall 1970): 212–23.
Helmholtz, Herman L.F. von. *Popular Scientific Lectures*. New York: Dover, 1962.
Henderson, L.J. *Blood*. New Haven, Conn.: Yale University Press, 1928.
Herf, Jeffrey. "Technology, Reification and Romanticism." *New German Critique* 12 (Fall 1977): 175–91.
Hilferding, Rudolf. *Das Finanzkapital*. Vienna, 1923.
Hilferding, Rudolf and von Bortkiewicz, Ladislaus, eds. *Karl Marx and the Close of his System*. New York: A.M. Kelley, 1966.
Hisben, John Grier. "The Theory of Energetics and Its Philosophical Bearings." *The Monist* 13, no. 3 (1903).
Hobsbawm, E.J. "The Great Gramsci." *New York Review of Books* 4 (April 1974).
Horowitz, I.L. "Consensus, Conflict and Cooperation: A Sociological Inventory." *Social Forces* 41 (1962): 177–88.
Howe, Irving, ed. *Essential Works of Socialism*. New Haven, Conn.: Yale University Press, 1986.

Hunt, E.K. "The Importance of Veblen for Contemporary Marxists." *Journal of Economic Issues* 13 (March 1979).
Husserl, Edmund. *The Crisis of European Sciences and Transcendental Phenomenology.* Evanston, Ill.: Northwestern University Press, 1970.
Huxley, T.H. *Evolution and Ethics and Other Essays.* London: Macmillan, 1894.
Illich, Ivan. *The Right to Useful Unemployment.* Boston: Marion Boyers, 1978.
———. *Tools for Conviviality.* New York: Harper & Row, 1973.
Israel, Joachim. "The Principle of Methodological Individualism and Marxian Epistemology." *Acta Sociologica* 14, no. 3 (1971).
Ivanosky, V.I. "Chto takoe 'positivizm' i 'idealizm', *Pravda* (March 1904).
Jacoby, Russell. "The Inception of Western Marxism: Karl Korsch and the Politics of Philosophy." *Canadian Journal of Political and Social Theory* 3, no. 3 (Fall 1979): 5–23.
Jantsch, Erich and Waddington, Conrad H., eds. *Evolution and Consciousness: Human Systems in Transition.* Toronto: Addison-Wesley, 1976.
Jay, Martin. "For Gouldner: Reflections on an Outlaw Marxist." *Theory and Society* 11, no. 6 (November 1982): 759–78.
Jensen, Kenneth M. *Beyond Marx and Mach: Alexander Bogdanov's Philosophy of Living Experience.* Boston: D. Reidel, 1978.
Jensen, Otto. *Marxismus und Naturewissenschaft: Gedenkschrifts zum 30. Todestage des Naturwissenschaftlers Friederich Engels, mit Beitragen von F. Engels, Gustav Echstein und Friederich Adler.* Berlin: Verlagess des Allegemieinen Deutschen Gewerschtfbundes, 1925.
Jevons, W.S. *The Coal Question: An Inquiry Concerning the Progress of the Nations*, ed. A.W. Flux. New York: A.M. Kelley, 1965.
Joravsky, David. *Soviet Marxism and Natural Science: 1917–1932.* New York: Columbia University Press, 1961.
Jordan, Zbigniew A. *The Evolution of Dialectical Materialism.* New York: St. Martin's Press, 1967.
Joule, James P. *Scientific Papers*, ed. W. Scoresby. London: Dawsons of Pall Mall, 1963.
Kamaŕyt, Jan. "From Science to Metascience and Philosophy: Dialectical Perspectives in the Development of Ludwig von Bertalanffy's Theoretical Work." In *Unity Through Diversity: A Festschrift for Ludwig von Bertalanffy*, part 1, ed. William Gray and Nicholas D. Rizzo. New York: Gordon and Beach Science, 1973.
Kamshilov, Mikhail Mikhailovich. *Evolution of the Biosphere*, trans. Minna Brodskaya. Moscow: Mir, 1976
Kant, Immanuel. *Groundwork of the Metaphysic of Morals.* New York: Harper Torchbooks, 1964.
———. "Idea for a Universal History with Cosmopolitan Intent." In *The Philosophy of Kant*, ed. Carl J. Friedrich. New York: Modern Library, 1949.
———. *Immanuel Kant's Critique of Pure Reason*, trans. N.K. Smith. New York: St. Martin's Press, 1929.
Karabel, Jerome. "Revolutionary Contradictions: Antonio Gramsci and the Problem of Intellectuals." *Politics and Society* 6, no. 2 (1976).
Karsten, Siegfried G. "Dialectics and the Evolution of Economic Thought." *History of Political Economy* 12, no. 2 (1971).
Kaufmann, R. "Biophysical and Marxist Economics: Learning from Each Other." In R. Costanza and H. Daly, eds., "Ecological Economics." Special issue of the review *Ecological Modelling* 38 (1987).
Kaufmann, Walter. *Hegel: A Reinterpretation.* Notre Dame, Ind.: University of Notre Dame Press, 1978.

Kautsky, Karl. "Ein Brief uber Marx und Mach." *Der Kampf* 10 (1909).
———. *The Class Struggle*. New York: Norton, 1971.
———. "Der Imperialismus." *Die Neue Zeit* 32 (1914).
Kelley, D.R. "The Metaphysics of Law: An Essay on the Very Young Marx." *American Historical Review* 83, no. 2 (April 1978).
Kennedy, James Gettier. *Herbert Spencer*. Boston: Twayne, 1978.
Kline, G.L. "Bogdanov, Alexandr Aleksandrovich." In *The Encyclopedia of Philosophy*. New York: Macmillan, 1967.
Kline, Morris. *Mathematics and the Search for Knowledge*. New York: Oxford University Press, 1985.
Kommunist. 1915, 1918.
Knight, Frank. "The German Science in the Romantic Period." In *The Emergence of Science in Western Europe*, ed. Maurice Crossland. London: Macmillan, 1975.
Konstantinov, F.V. *The Fundamentals of Marxist-Leninist Philosophy*, trans. R. Daglish. Moscow, 1982.
Kopeczi, Bela. "Lukács in 1919." *New Hungarian Quarterly* 20, no. 75 (Autumn 1979).
Kornai, Janos. *Anti-Equilibrium: On Economic Systems Theory and the Tasks of Research*. Amsterdam: North-Holland, 1971.
Kosik, Karel. *Dialectics of the Concrete*. Dordrecht: D. Reidel, 1976.
Koyre, Alexandre. *Galileo Studies*, trans. John Mepham. Hassocks: Harvester Press, 1978.
Kretzschmar, Herman. *Max Planck als Philosoph*. Basel: E. Reinhardt, 1967.
Kubik, Wlodzimierz. "Socjologia Herberta Spencera"(The sociology of Herbert Spencer). *Przeglad Socjologiczny* 29 (1977): 339–48.
Kuhn, Thomas. *The Structure of Scientific Revolutions*. Chicago: University of Chicago Press, 1970.
Kunczik, Michael. "Elemente der Modernen Systemtheorie im Soziologischen Werk von Herbert Spencer" (Elements of modern systems theory in the sociological work of Herbert Spencer). *Kolner Zeitschrift fur Soziologie und Sozialpsychologie* 35, no. 3 (September 1983): 438–61.
Labedz, L., ed. *Revisionism: Essays on the History of Marxist Ideas*. New York: Praeger, 1962.
Large Soviet Encyclopedia (Bolshaya sovetskaya entsiklopediya), vol. 6 (1930): 589–90.
Laszlo, Erwin. *Evolution: The Grand Synthesis*. Boston: Shambhala, 1987
Lavróv, Peter. *Historical Letters*, trans. James P. Scanlan. California, 1967.
Lefebvre, Henri. *Dialectical Materialism*, trans. John Sturrock. London: Jonathan Cape, 1968.
Lenin, Vladimir I. *Collected Works*, 47 vols. Moscow: Foreign Languages Publishing House, 1960–80.
———. *Development of Capitalism (1896–98)*. Moscow: Progress, 1967.
———. "The Immediate Tasks of the Soviet Government." *Izvestiia* (April 28, 1918). In *V.I. Lenin Selected Works*, 2 vols. Moscow, 1947.
———. "Impending Catastrophe and How to Combat It." September 1917. In Lenin, *Collected Works* 25:358–59.
———. *Materialism and Empiro-Criticism*. Moscow: Progress, 1967.
———. *Selected Works*. 1 vol. New York: International, 1971.
———. "State and Revolution." In *Marx Engels Marxism*, ed. by V.I. Lenin. Moscow: Foreign Languages Publishing House, 1947: 341–63.
———. *What Is to Be Done?* New York: International, 1929.
———. "Zamechaniia na knigu N. Bukharina." In *Ekonomika perekhodnogo perioda*. Moscow-Leningrad, 1931.

Levine, Norman. "Marxism and Engelism: Two Differing Views of History." *Journal of the History of the Behavioral Sciences* 9 (July 1973).
Lewis, R. Campbell and Garnett, William. *The Life of James Clerk Maxwell: With a Selection from his Correspondence and Occasional Writings and a Sketch of His Contribution to Science.* London: Macmillan and Co., 1882.
Lewontin, R. and Levins, R. "The Problems of Lysenkoism." In *The Radicalization of Science,* ed. H. Rose and S. Rose. New York: Macmillan, 1976.
Linder, Marc. *Reification and the Consciousness of the Critics of Political Economy: Studies in the Development of Marx's Theory of Value.* Copenhagen: Rhodos, 1975.
Lossky, N.U. *History of Russian Philosophy.* New York: International, 1951.
Lotka, Alfred J. "Biased Evolution." *Harpers Monthly Magazine* (May 1924): 755–66.
―――. *Elements of Mathematical Biology, Elements of Physical Biology.* New York: Dover, 1956.
Luhmann, Niklas. *The Differentiation of Society,* trans. Stephen Holmes and Charles Larmore. New York: Columbia University Press, 1982.
Lukács, Georg. *The Destruction of Reason.* London: Merlin, 1980.
―――. *History and Class Consciousness.* Cambridge, Mass.: MIT Press, 1971.
―――. "The Old Culture and the New." *Telos* 5 (Spring 1970).
―――. *The Ontology of Social Being: Hegel's False and His Genuine Ontology,* trans. David Fernbach. London, 1978.
―――. *Soziologie des modernen Dramas.*
―――. "Technology and Social Relations." *New Left Review,* no. 39 (September/October 1966).
―――. *The Young Hegel.* London: Merlin, 1975.
Mach, Ernst. *The Analysis of Sensations.* n.p., n.d.
McCloskey, Donald N. "Has Formalization in Economics Gone Too Far?" *Methodus* 3, no. 1 (June 1991).
―――. "The Rhetoric of Economics." *Journal of Economic Literature* 21 (June 1983).
McCulloch, J.R. "Philosophy of Manufacturers." *Edinburgh Review* 61 [1835] 1984: 453–72.
MacDonald, David Keith Chalmers. *Faraday, Maxwell, and Kelvin.* Garden City, N.Y.: Anchor Books, 1964.
McDonough, Roisin. "Ideology as False Consciousness: Lukács." *Working Papers in Cultural Studies,* 10 (1977): 33–44.
MacKenzie, Donald. "Marx and the Machine." *Technology and Culture* 25, no. 3 (July 1984): 473–503.
McQuarie, Donald and Amburgey, Terry. "Marx and Modern Systems Theory." *Social Science Quarterly* 59, no. 1 (1978): 3–19.
Marcuse, Herbert. "Beitrag zu einer Phanomenologie der historischen Materialismus." *Philosophische Hefte* 1 (July 1928): 45–68. In *Telos* 4 (Fall 1969): 3–34.
―――. *Eros and Civilization: A Philosophical Inquiry into Freud.* Boston: Beacon Press, 1955.
―――. *One-Dimensional Man.* Boston: Beacon Press, 1968.
―――. "Socialism in the Developed Countries." *International Socialist Journal* 2, no. 8 (April 1965).
Markus, Gyrgy. "The Soul and Life: The Young Lukács and the Problem of Culture." *Telos* 32 (Summer 1977).
Martinez-Alier, J. *Ecological Economics: Energy, Environment and Society.* Oxford: Basil Blackwell, 1987.
Maruyama, M. "The Second Cybernetics: Deviation Amplifying Mutual Causal Processes." *American Scientist* 51 (1963): 164–79.

Marx, Karl. *Capital: A Critique of Political Economy*, 3 vols. Moscow: Progress, 1977.
———. *A Contribution to the Critique of Hegel's "Philosophy of Right,"* trans. Annette Jolin and Josephy O'Malley. Cambridge: Cambridge University Press, 1970.
———. *Contribution to the Critique of Political Economy*. New York: International, 1970.
———. *The Economic and Philosophic Manuscripts of 1844*, ed. Dirk J. Struik. New York: International, 1964.
———. *Grundrisse: Foundations of the Critique of Political Economy*. New York: Random House, 1973.
———. "Letter to Vera Zasoulich." In *Russian Menace to Europe*, ed. Paul Blackstock. Glencoe, Ill.: Free Press, 1952.
———. *The Poverty of Philosophy*. New York: International, 1963.
———. *Pre-Capitalist Economic Formation*, trans. J. Cohen. New York: International, 1966.
———. "Preface to a Contribution to a Critique of Political Economy." In K. Marx and F. Engels, *Selected Works*, vol. 1. Moscow: Foreign Languages Publishing House, 1955.
———. *Theories of Surplus Value: Part II*. Moscow: Progress, 1963.
———. *Writings of the Young Marx on Philosophy and Society*, ed. L. Easton and K. Gudatt. New York, 1967.
Marx, Karl and Engels, Friederich. *Critique of the Gotha Programme: A Contribution to the Critique of the Social-democratic Draft Programme of 1891*. Moscow: Foreign Languages Publishing House, 1959.
———. *The German Ideology*, ed. C.J. Arthur. New York: International, 1970.
———. "Manifesto of the Communist Party." In *The Marx-Engels Reader*, 2nd ed., ed. Robert Tucker. New York: W.W. Norton, 1978.
———. *Marx and Engels Collected Works*, 40 vols. New York: International, 1975–87.
———. *Selected Correspondence*, trans. Dora Torr. New York: International, 1942.
———. *Selected Works*, second English ed., 2 vols., ed. I.B. Lasker. Moscow: Foreign Languages Publishing House, 1946–49.
Maturana, Humberto R. "Autopoiesis: Reproduction, Heredity and Evolution." In *Autopoiesis, Dissipative Structures, and Spontaneous Social Orders*, ed. M. Zeleny. Boulder, Col.: Westview Press, 1980.
May, J.A. "The Master-Slave Relation in Hegel's 'Phenomenology of Spirit' and in the Early Marx: A Study in One Aspect of the Philosophical Foundations of Marxism." *Current Perspectives in Social Theory* 5 (1984): 225–66.
Medow, Paul I. "J. Robin's 'Culture and Technology: Fusion or Collison': An Extended Summary." Research Memorandum of 10 May 1985, Economic Research and Systems Planning Group, Stong College, York University, Toronto.
Medvedev, Roy. *Let History Judge: The Origins and Consequences of Stalinism*. New York: Columbia University Press, 1989.
Meldrum, Andrew. *Eighteenth Century Revolution in Science: The First Phase*. Calcutta: Longmans, Green, 1930.
Mendelson, Jack. "On Engel's Metaphysical Dialectics: A Foundation of Orthodox 'Marxism'." *Dialectical Anthropology* 4, no. 1 (March 1979): 65–73.
Merleau-Ponty, Maurice. *Adventures of the Dialectic* (Les adventures de la dialectique). Evanston, Ill.: Northwestern University Press, 1973.
———. "Le Marxisme 'Occidental'." *Telos* 6 (Fall 1970): 140–61.
Meyer, Alfred G. *Leninism*. New York: Praeger, 1957.
Meynaud, Jean. *Technocracy*, trans. Paul Barnes. London: Faber and Faber, 1968.
Mill, John Stuart. *Principles of Political Economy*, ed., with an introduction by D. Winch. Baltimore, Md.: Penguin Books, 1970.
Mitchem, Carl and Mackey, Robert, eds. *Philosophy and Technology: Readings in the Philosophical Problems of Technocracy*. New York: Free Press, 1972.

Moiseev. N.N. "Man's Coevolution with the Biosphere: Cybernetic Aspects." Research Memorandum of 2 September 1982, Economic Research and Systems Planning Group, Stong College, York University, Toronto.

———. "The Unity of Natural Scientific Knowledge." Research Memorandum of 1 September 1977, Economic Research and Systems Planning Group, Stong College, York University, Toronto.

Monod, J. *From Biology to Ethics*. San Diego, Calif.: Salk Institute for Biological Studies, 1969.

Mooney, Christopher F.J. "Teilhard de Chardin and Modern Philosophy." *Social Research: An International Quarterly* 34, no. 1 (Spring 1967).

Morin, Edgar. "Complexity." *International Social Science Journal* 26, no. 4 (1974): 555–82.

———. *La Methode. I, La Nature de la Nature*. Paris: Seuil, 1977.

Morrall, John. *Political Thought in Medieval Times*. London: Hutchinson University Library; 1971.

Mouffe, Chantal. "Gramsci Today." In *Gramsci and Marxist Theory*, ed. C. Mouffe. London: Routledge and Kegan Paul, 1979.

———. ed. *Gramsci and Marxist Theory*. London: Routledge and Kegan Paul, 1979.

Nersessian, Nancy J. "The Roots of Epistemological 'Anarchy.'" *Inquiry* 22, no. 4 (Winter 1979): 423–40.

Nevsky, V. "Dialectical Materialism and the Philosophy of the Dead Reaction." Appendix in V.I. Lenin, *Materialism and Empirio-Criticism*, 329–36. New York: International, 1927.

Newton-Smith, William. "Is Science Rational?" *Social Science Information / Information sur les Sciences Sociales* 19, no. 3 (June 1980): 469–99.

Nietzsche, F. *Twilight of the Idols and the Antichrist*. Harmondsworth, Middlesex, 1968.

Odum, Howard T. *Environment, Power, and Society*. New York: Wiley-Interscience, 1971.

———. *Systems Ecology: An Introduction*. New York: John Wiley, 1983.

Odum, Howard T. and Odum, Elisabeth C. *Energy Basis for Man and Nature*. New York: McGraw-Hill, 1976

Offer, John. "Retrospective Reviews: A Spencer Trio Recalled: Social Statics, First Principles and The Man Versus the State." *Sociology* 19, no. 4 (November 1985): 665–79.

Oparin, Aleksandr I. *Chemical Origin of Life*. Springfield, Ill.: C.C. Thomas, 1964.

Ostwald, Wilhelm. *Energetische Grundlagen der Kulturwissenschaften*. Leipzig: W. Klinkhardt, 1909.

———. "Der Energetische Imperativ." *Annals de Philosophie Natural* 10 (1905).

———. *Lectures on Natural Philosophy*, n.p., n.d.

———. "The Modern Theory of Energetics." *The Monist* 17 (1907).

Pareto, Vilfredo. "Mathematical Economics." *International Economics Papers*, no. 5 (1955).

Parsons, Talcott. "An Outline of the Social System." In *Theories of Society*, ed. T. Parsons, E.A. Shils, K.D. Naegle, and J.R. Pitts. Glencoe, Ill.: Free Press, 1974.

———. *The Social System*. Glencoe, Ill.: Free Press, 1951.

Parsons, T. and Shils, E.A., eds. *Toward a General Theory of Action*. New York: Harper & Row, 1951.

Passet, René. *Economic Systems and Living Systems*. Paris: Payot, 1979.

Piccone, Paul. "Gramsci's Hegelian Marxism." *Political Theory* 2, no. 1 (February 1974).

———. "Phenomenological Marxism." *Telos* 9 (Fall 1971): 3–31.

Planck, Max. "The Unity of the Physical Universe." In *A Survey of Physics: A Collection of Lectures and Essays*, ed. M. Planck. New York: Dutton, 1925.

Plato. *Republic*, trans. G.M.A. Grube. Indianapolis: Hackett, 1974.

Podolinsky, Serhii. "Menschliche Arbeit und Einheit der Kraft." *Die Neue Zeit* 1 (September 1883).

———. "Le socialisme et la theorie de Darwin." *Revue Socialiste* (March 1880).

Poincaré, H. *Value of Science*. New York: Dover, 1958.
Polanyi, Karl. *The Great Transformation*. Boston: Beacon Press, 1956.
———. *The Livelihood of Man*, ed. Harry Pearson. New York: Academic Press, 1974.
———. *Primitive, Archaic, and Modern Economies: Essays of Karl Polanyi*, ed. George Dalton. Boston: Beacon Press, 1968.
Popper, Karl. *The Logic of Scientific Discovery*. New York: Harper & Row, 1959.
———. *The Open Society and Its Enemies*. London: Routledge and Kegan Paul, 1966.
———. *The Poverty of Historicism*. London: Routledge, 1957.
Prat, Naftali. "Diamat and Contemporary Biology." *Studies in Soviet Thought* 21 (1980).
Pravda. June 1904; March 17, 1913; July 27, 1921; July 7, 1926; April 8,1928; June 30, 1929; October 1, 1951.
Preobrazhensky, G. *The New Economics*, trans. Brian Pearce. Oxford, 1965.
———. "The Problem of Economic Equilibrium Under Concrete Capitalism and in the Soviet System." In *The Crisis of Soviet Industrialization*, ed. D.A. Filtzer, 98–99. White Plains, N.Y.: M.E. Sharpe, 1978.
Price, Don K. *The Scientific Estate*. Cambridge, Mass.: Harvard University Press, 1965.
Prigogine, Ilya. *From Being to Becoming: Time and Complexity in the Physical Sciences*. San Francisco: W.H. Freeman, 1980.
———. *Introduction to Thermodynamics of Irreversible Processes*. New York: Interscience, 1968.
Prigogine, Ilya and Stengers, Isabella. *Order Out of Chaos: Man's New Dialogue with Nature*. New York: Bantam Books, 1984.
Przeworski, Adam. "Material Bases of Consent: Economics and Politics in a Hegemonic System." *Political Power and Social Theory* 1 (1980): 21–66.
Rabinbach, Anson. *The Crisis of Austrian Socialism: From Red Vienna to Civil War, 1927–1934*. Chicago: University of Chicago Press, 1983.
Ramos, Valeriano, Jr. "The Concepts of Ideology, Hegemony, and Organic Intellectuals in Gramsci's Marxism." *Theoretical Review* 30 (September–October 1982).
Ramstad, Yngve. "Reasonable Value Versus Instrumental Value." *Journal of Economic Issues*, 23, no. 3 (September 1989): 761–77.
Rapoport, Anatol. "Methodology in the Physical, Biological and Social Sciences." In *Global Systems Dynamics*, ed. Ernest O. Attinger. Basel: S. Karger, 1970.
Rauch, Leo, ed. *Hegel and the Human Spirit: A Translation of the Jena Lectures*. Detroit: Wayne State University Press, 1983.
Reist, Benjamin A. *Toward a Theology of Involvement: The Thought of Ernst Troeltsch*. n.p., 1966.
Rey, Abel. *The Physical Theory of the Modern Physicists*. Paris: F. Alcan, 1907.
Rifkin, Jeremy and Howard, Ted. *Entropy: A New World View*. New York: Bantam Books, 1980.
Riviere, Claude. "Aux sources de la sociologie dynamique" (The sources of dynamic sociology). *Ethnopsychologie* 31, no. 2 (September 1976): 100–23.
Rorty, Richard. *Philosophy and the Mirror of Nature*. Oxford: Basil Blackwell, 1980.
Rosenthal, John. "Who Practices Hegemony? Class Division and the Subject of Politics." *Cultural Critique* 9 (Spring 1988): 25–52.
Rousseau, J.-J. *Emile*. New York: Basic Books, 1979.
———. *The Social Contract*, ed. Ronald Grimsley. Oxford: Clarendon Press, 1972.
Salk, Jonas. *The Survival of the Wisest*. New York: Harper & Row, 1973.
Samnadyatyi s'exd VKP(b). *Stenografisheskii otchet* (Seventeenth Party Congress: stenographic record). Moscow, 1934.
Scanlan, James P. *Marxism in the USSR: A Critical Survey of Current Soviet Thought*. Ithaca, N.Y.: Cornell University Press, 1985.

Schlipp, P.A., ed. *Albert Einstein: Philosopher Scientist*, 7 vols. New York: Harper & Row, 1954.
Schmidt, Alfred. *The Concept of Nature in Marx*, trans. Ben Fowkes. London: New Left Books, 1971.
Schrödinger, Erwin. *Nature and the Greeks*. Cambridge: Cambridge University Press, 1954.
———. *What Is Life? and Other Scientific Essays*. Garden City, N.Y.: Doubleday, 1956.
Serbyn, Roman. "In Defense of an Independent Ukrainian Socialist Movement: Three Letters from Serhii Podolinsky to Valerian Smirnov." *Journal of Ukranian Studies* 7, no. 2 (1982).
Silverberg, Gerald. "Embodied Technical Progress in a Dynamic Economic Model: The Self-Organization Paradigm." *Lecture Notes in Economics and Mathematical Systems* 228 (1984): 192–208.
Simmel, Georg. *The Philosophy of Money*. Trans. Tom Bottomo and David Frisby. New York: Routledge, 1990.
Slosson, Edwin E. *Major Prophets of Today*. Freeport, N.Y.: Books for Libraries, 1914.
Smart, Barry. "Phenomenological Marxism and Critical Theory." *Research in Sociology of Knowledge, Science and Art* 2 (1979): 53–72.
Smith, Adam. *Wealth of Nations*, New York: Penguin Books, 1976.
Smuts, Jan. *Holism and Evolution*. Westport, CT: Greenwood Press, 1973.
Sochor, Zenovia A. *Revolution and Culture: The Bogdanov-Lenin Controversy*. Ithaca, New York: Cornell University Press, 1988.
———. "Was Bogdanov Russia's Answer to Gramsci?" *Studies in Soviet Thought* 22 (February 1981): 59–81.
Soddy, Frederick. *Cartesian Economics: The Bearing of Physical Science Upon State Stewardship*. London: Hendersons, 1922.
Sorokin, Pitirim A. *Contemporary Sociological Theories Through the First Quarter of the Twentieth Century*. New York: Harper & Row, 1928.
———. *Fads and Foibles in Modern Sociology*. Chicago: Henry Regnery, 1965.
———. *Social and Cultural Dynamics*. New York: American Books, 1943.
Spencer, Herbert. *First Principles*, 1st ed. London: Williams and Norgate, 1863.
———. *The Principles of Biology*, rev. ed. New York: D. Appleton, 1898.
———. *The Principles of Sociology*. New York: D. Appleton, 1909.
———. *The Study of Sociology*. New York: D. Appleton, 1886.
Stalin, J.V. *J.V. Stalin, Works*, 9 vols. Moscow: Foreign Languages Publishing House, 1954.
———. "The Question of Permanent Revolution." In *J.V. Stalin, Works*, vol. 8. Moscow: Foreign Languages Publishing House, 1954.
Stanley, John L. and Zimmerman, Ernst. "On the Alleged Differences Between Marx and Engels." *Political Studies* 32 (1984): 226–48.
Stokes, Kenneth M. *Critique of Economic Reason*. International University of Japan, Niigata, Monograph Series, 6, 1992.
———. *The Empire of Reason*. Unpublished manuscript, International University of Japan, Tokyo, 1994.
———. *Man and the Biosphere: Toward a Coevolutionary Political Economy*. Armonk, N.Y.: M.E. Sharpe, 1992.
———. "The Marx-Engels Conception of Darwin's Theory." Unpublished working paper, 1989. Stong College, York University, Toronto.
———. *Methodological Issues in Coevolutionary Political Economy*, unpublished manuscript, International University of Japan, Tokyo, 1994.
———. "Social Ethics and Reflections on Socio-Economic Transition." Working Paper, Center for Advanced Political Economy, International University of Japan, Niigata, 1994.

Strumilin, S. "K khozyaistvennomu planu na 1921–22 g." *Narodnoe shozyaistvo* no. 5 (1921).
Struve, Peter. *Sotsial'naya i ekonomicheskaya istoriya Rossi.* Paris, 1952.
Susiluoto, Ilmari. *The Origins and Development of Systems Thinking in the Soviet Union: Political and Philosophical Controversies from Bogdanov and Bukharin to Present-Day Reevaluations.* Helsinki: Suomalinen Tiedeakatemia, Annales Academiae Scientiarium Fennicae, 1982.
Suvorov, S. *Studies in the Philosophy of Marxism.* n.p., n.d.
Takhazhdian, A.L. "Tektologia: Istoriya i Problemy" (Tektology: history and problems). *Sistemnye Issledovaniya* (1972): 200–277.
Takhtajan, Ya. *Evgraph Fyodorov.* Moscow, 1971
Talmon, J.L. *The Origins of Totalitarian Democracy.* New York: Secker and Warburg, 1952.
Tamanoi, Yoshiro. "Living Systems as the Basis for Human Economy." *Japanese Economist* (March 20, 1984). Trans. M. Maruyama in 1987.
Tamanoi, Yoshiro; Tsuchida, Atsushi; and Murota, Takeshi. "Towards an Entropic Theory of Economy and Ecology: Beyond the Mechanistic Equilibrium Approach." *Economie Applique'e* 37, no. 2 (1984): 279–94.
Tarbuck, K.J. *Bukharin's Theory of Equilibrium.* London, 1989.
———. *Rosa Luxemburg and Nikolai Bukharin.* n.p., n.d.
Teilhard de Chardin, Pierre. *The Appearance of Man.* New York: Harper & Row, 1965.
———. *The Phenomenon of Man.* New York: Harper & Row, 1959.
Thompson, Silvanus P. *The Life of Lord Kelvin,* 2 vols. New York: Chelsea, 1976.
Tismananue, Vladimir. "Critical Marxism and Eastern Europe." *Praxis International* 3, no. 3 (October 1983): 248–61.
Toffler, Alvin. *The Third Wave.* Toronto: Bantam Books, 1981.
Trotsky, L.D. *The Challenge of the Left Oppostion (1928–29).* New York: Pathfinder Press, 1981.
Tucker, Robert C. *The Marxian Revolutionary Idea.* New York: W.W. Norton, 1969.
———, ed. *The Marx-Engels Reader,* 2nd. ed. New York: W.W. Norton, 1978.
Tugan-Baranovsky, M.I. *The Theoretical Basis of Marxism.* n.p., n.d.
Turner, Jonathan H. and Powers, Charles H. "Some Elementary Principles of Political Organization: Insights from Sociology's First Masters." *Research in Political Sociology* 2 (1986): 1–17.
Ulrich, Werner. "Systems Thinking, Systems Practice and Practical Philosophy: A Program of Research." *System Practice* 1, no. 2 (1988).
Unger, Robert M. *Knowledge and Politics.* New York: Free Press, 1975.
Utechin, I.V. "Philosophy and Society: Alexandr Bogdanov." In *Revisionism: Essays on the History of Marxist Ideas,* ed. L. Labedz. New York: Praeger, 1962.
Valentinov, Nikolay. *Encounters with Lenin.* London: Oxford University Press, 1968.
Varela, F.G.; Maturana, H.R.; and Uribe, R. "Autopoiesis: The Organization of Living Systems, Its Characterization and a Model." *Bio-Systems* 5 (1974): 187–96.
Vernadsky, Vladimir I. "Problems of Biogeochemistry: The Fundamental Matter-Energy Difference Between the Living and the Inert Natural Bodies of the Biosphere." *Transactions of the Connecticut Academy of Arts and Sciences* 35 (June 1944): 483–517.
Vico, Giambattista. *The New Science,* trans. Thomas Goddar. Ithaca, N.Y.: Cornell University Press, 1968.
Vranicki, Predrag. "Socialism and the Problem of Alienation." In *Socialist Humanism,* ed. Erich Fromm. Garden City, N.Y.: Doubleday, 1965.
Vucinich, Alexander. *Social Thought in Tsarist Russia: The Quest for a General Science of Society, 1861–1917.* Chicago: University of Chicago Press, 1976.

Vyshinsky, P. "Obrazchik vreditel'skoi filosofii (bazarovshchina)." *Pod znamenem marksizma*, nos. 1–2 (1931).
Watnick, Morris. "Relativism and Class Consciousness." In *Revisionism: Essays in the History of Marxist Ideas*, ed. L. Labedz. New York: Praeger, 1962.
Weaver, Warren. "Science and Complexity." *American Scientist* (October 1948): 536–44.
Weber, Max. *Energetische Kulturtheoriem*. n.p., n.d.
Weintraub, E. Roy. "Methodology Doesn't Matter, but the History of Thought Might." In *The State of Macroeconomics*, ed. Seppo Honkapohja, 263–79. Oxford: Basil Blackwell, 1989.
Weisskopf, Walter. *The Psychology of Economics*. London: Routledge and Kegan Paul, 1955.
White, James D. "Bogdanov in Tula." *Studies in Soviet Thought* 22 (1981): 33–58.
———. "Early Soviet Historical Interpretation of the Russian Revolution 1918–24." *Soviet Studies* 37, no. 3 (July 1985).
———. "The First Pravda and the Russian Marxist Tradition." *Soviet Studies* 26 (April 1974).
———. "Theories of Imperialism in Russian Socialist Thought from the First World War to the Stalin Era." *Coexistence* 30 (1993): 87–109.
Wiener, Norbert. *Cybernetics: Or Control and Communication in the Animal and Machine*. New York: John Wiley, 1948.
Williamson, Oliver E. *The Economic Institutions of Capitalism*. New York: Free Press, 1985.
———. *Markets and Hierarchies: Analysis and Antitrust Implications*. New York: Free Press, 1975.
Winiarsky, L. "L'energie sociale et ses mensurations." *Revue Philosophique* 49 (1900): 124–27.
———. "La Method mathematique dans la sociologie et dans l'economie." *La Revue Socialiste* 20 (1894).
Winner, Langdon. *Autonomous Technology: Technics-out-of-Control as a Theme in Political Thought*. Cambridge, Mass.: MIT Press, 1977.
Wittgenstein, Ludwig. *Remarks on Frazer's Golden Bough*, trans. A.C. Miles, ed. Rush Rees. Highland, N.J.: Humanities Press, 1979.
Woolcock, Joseph A. "Politics, Ideology and Hegemony in Gramsci's Theory." *Social and Economic Studies* 34, no. 3 (September 1985): 199–210.
Wright, Georg Henrik von. *Technology and the Legitimation Crisis of Industrialized Society*. Helsinki, 1983.
Yassour, Avraham. "Lenin and Bogdanov: Protagonists in the 'Bolshevik Center.'" *Studies in Soviet Thought* 22 (1981): 3–32.
Zeleny, Milan. "A Paradigm Lost?" In *Autopoisesis, Dissipative Structures, and Spontaneous Social Orders*, ed. M. Zeleny. Boulder, Col.: Westview, 1980.
———. "Spontaneous Social Orders." In *The Science and Praxis of Complexity*. Tokyo: United Nations University, 1985.
———. ed. *Autopoisesis, Dissipative Structures, and Spontaneous Social Orders*. Boulder, Col.: Westview, 1980.
Zenkovsky, V.V. *A History of Russian Philosophy*, trans. George L. Kline. New York: Columbia University Press, 1953.
Zimmerman, Michael E. *Heidegger's Confrontation with Modernity*, Indianapolis: Indiana University Press, 1990.

Index

Afansev, L.B., 330
Alienation, 219, 262–63, 265, 332
Althusser, Louis, 67
The Analysis of Sensations (Mach), 185
Analytical sum, 283–84
Anarchy, 36
Anti-Dühring (Engels), 94, 176, 209, 211, 289
Aristotle, 45–46, 48, 60–63, 83, 339–40
Art, 231, 236
Artificial selection, 286
Asceticism, 148–49
Assimilation, 295
Atheist radical individualism, 151–52
Atomism, 6, 7, 60, 339
Authority, 13
Automation, 321
Avenarius, Richard, 185, 188
The Axe (revolutionary society), 152
Axelos, Kostas, 219

Bacon, Francis, 46
Bailey, Kenneth, 302
Ballestrem, Karl, 179
Ban, Erwin, 100
The Basic Elements of the Historical View of Nature (Bogdanov), 166, 268
Bazarov, V.A., 308–9
Bello, Ralph, 277
Belov, N., 278
Bente, Herman, 317
Bergson, Henri, 125
Bernard Instability, 293
Bernstein, Eduard, 114, 165, 199, 242
Bertalanffy, Ludwig von, 277, 295–96, 303

Blauberg, I.V., 278
Blei, Franz, 179
Bloch, Ernst, 109
Bogdanov, Alexandr A., 3, 4, 8–11, 14–15, 110, 302, 343–44, 346–47
  arrest of, 179
  break with Lenin, 184
  and bureaucracy, 260
  and causality, 190–91
  and class, 204, 243
  condemnation of, 182
  and dialectical materialism, 204–13
  different élite theories of, 13
  dystopian warnings of, 10–11, 330–34
  energy theory of, 170
  equilibrium theory, 290–95
  and evolution of philosophy and ideology, 193
  fatal experiment, 335
  historicism of, 237
  and institutions, 319–20
  intellectual biography of, 163–68
  and materialism, 187
  monism of, 179
  organizational science of. See Tektology
  Ostwald's influence on, 169
  phenomenological Marxism of, 178–213, 373n.73
  and production forces, 217–22
  and proletariat transformation, 227–28
  and science, 166–67, 192
  social-class dynamics theory, 244–66
  social consciousness, ideology, and culture, 222–66
  and social energetics, 169–77

413

Bogdanov, Alexandr A. *(continued)*
  sociological theory of, 170
  suppression of material relating to, 163
  systems practice of, 214–17
  and techno-utopias, 320–22, 327–29
  and worker control, 266
Bolshevik (magazine), 337
Bolsheviks, 16, 112, 157, 179, 182, 224, 305, 316
Boltzmann, Ludwig, 121
Boulding, Kenneth, 120, 122
Bourgeoisie, 58, 250–51, 252
Brecht, Bertolt, 228
Bukharin, Nikolai I., 3, 4, 11–13, 14, 110, 182, 184, 210, 222, 307–8, 344–46
  on Bogdanov, 335
  and command management, 315–18
  and culture, 240
  denunciation of, 336–38
  and elites, 13
  equilibrium theory of, 12, 287–95, 296–97
  and open systems analysis, 296–302
  and Preobrazhenzky, 312–13
  and technology, 300–301
Bureaucracy, 246, 259–60, 317, 332, 386n.83

Caldwell, Bruce, 24
Canon, W.B., 302
Capital (Marx), 62, 158, 172, 220, 245, 319
Capitalism, 13, 87–88, 103, 104, 107, 108, 112, 114, 157, 158, 221, 243, 320
  basic contradictions of, 218
  for Bogdanov, 323
  class system, 248–49
  collapse of, 225–26
  crisis of, 197–98
  state, 285–86
Carey, H.C., 130
Carnot, Sadi, 118–19
Cartesian dualisms, 80
Carver, Terrel, 97
Cassirer, Ernst, 63
Causality, 47–49, 121–22, 170, 188, 190–91
Cells (biological), 98
Chaadaev, Peter, 141
Chain linkage, law of, 306–7
Change, 47

Chernishevsky, Nikolai, 147–48, 330
Chicherin, Boris Nikoláyevich, 159
Cicero, 48
City of Pigs (Plato), 50, 351n.10
Civil society, 88, 224, 253
Class, 202, 203–4
  formation, 247–48
  organizational, 13
  struggle, 12–13, 316–17
Clausius, Rudolf, 119–20
Coal, 130–32
The Coal Question (Jevons), 119, 130, 132
Cognitive dissonance, 29–30
Cohen, Stephen F., 289, 307
Collectivism, 10, 270
Collectivization, 311
Command management, 315–18
Commodity economy, 382n.194
Communal solidarity, 143
Communes. See Peasant communes
Communications, 247
The Communist Manifesto (Marx and Engels), 57, 149, 248–49
Comte, Auguste, 61
Conjunction, 283–84
Conjunctive crisis, 292
Conscience, work of, 145–46
Consumption, 103
Contra-differentiation, 296
Contribution to the Critique of Political Economy (Marx), 216, 236
Copleston, Frederick, 134, 178, 179, 292
Corporatism, 265
Correspondence principle, 42
Cosmological monism, 115, 129
Counter-revolutionary organizations, 331–32
Crime and Punishment (Dostoevsky), 149
Crises, 284
The Crisis of European Sciences (Husserl), 126
Critical Empiricism, 185
Critical Marxism, 3, 4–5, 8, 56, 107–8, 222, 341, 343
  critical kernel in, 155–62
  and cultural theory, 223
  defined, 109–14
  and holism, 7, 57–58, 63
  internal quarreling of, 4–5
  keystone in, 162–68
  Narodnok influences on, 141–46

Critical Marxism *(continued)*
  nihilist strains in, 146–55
  philosophical heritage of, 102–14
Critical theory, 102, 340
  defined, 59
  and political economy, 104–9
  primary aim of, 105
Critique of Judgment (Kant), 70
Critique of Political Economy (Marx), 89
A Critique of Pure Reason (Kant), 48, 69, 71–74
Critique of the Gotha Programme (Marx), 89
Culture, 111, 222–66
  and fetishism, 231
  and hegemony, 223–24
  progress in, 138
  proletarian, 232–43, 320
  and revolution, 226, 259
  transformation of, 252
Cybernetics, 13, 278, 309–10, 385*n.43*

Darwinism. See Evolution
Das Finanzkapital (Hilferding), 360*n.7*
Deborin, A.M., 183
Dehumanization, 201
Democracy, 375–76*n.2*
Descartes, René, 46, 72
Despotism, 258
Determinism, 50, 75, 101, 108–9, 120, 121–22, 123, 219
Developmentalism, 157
Development of Capitalism (1896–98) (Lenin), 322
The Development of Life in Nature and Society (Bogdanov), 179
Dewey, John, 21
Dialectical materialism, 96–97, 100, 251–52, 269, 272, 275
  rival conceptions of, 204–13
Dialectics, 78, 95, 96, 213, 289
  developmental, 212
  fundamental laws of, 94
  and motion, 99
Dialectics of Nature (Engels), 97, 176, 271, 289
Diderot, Denis, 76
Die Metaphysik in der National-ökonomie (Blei), 179
Different élite theories, 13
Diffused structures, 304

Disassimilation, 295
Disingression, 284
Dostoevsky, Fyodor, 146, 148, 149, 151–52, 153, 336, 367*n.12*
Dualisms. See Cartesian dualisms
Dühring, Eugen, 96
Durkheim, Emile, 301
Dzerzhinsky, Felix, 153

Economic and Philosophical Manuscripts (Marx), 201, 267
Economic rationalism, 53
Economics, 49–50
  analysis inversion, 52–55
  doctrinal basis of, 18
  durability of conventional, 17
  and ecology, 368–69*n.42*
  formalism in, 30–31, 340–41
  irreversibility of, 120
  and logical empiricism, 22
  as metabolic system, 295–96
  neoclassical, 18
  preindustrial, 51
  scientific status of, 19
  as statistical discipline, 122
  systems theoretical approach to, 22, 128–29
  See also Political economy
Economics of the Transition Period (Bukharin), 287, 310
The Economic Theory of the Leisure Class (Bukharin), 317
Economism, 53
Eddington, Arthur, 123
Efficiency, 15, 136
The Eighteenth Brumaire (Marx), 66
Einstein, Albert, 362*n.37*
Elite theories. *See* Different élite theories
Emancipatory reason, 15
Emile (Rousseau), 67, 68–69
Empiricism, 71–72, 73, 91
  See also Logical empiricism
Empirio-criticism, 186–88, 190
Empirio-monism, 177, 178–79, 187, 189, 190, 191, 221, 269–70
Empirio-monism (Bogdanov), 179–80, 190, 191
Encyclopediasts, 63, 98
Energeticism, 115, 116–17, 128–33, 220
  See also Social energetics

Energetische Grundlagen der Kulturwissenschaften (Ostwald), 129, 136
Energy, 117–20, 129, 169–70, 217, 221, 267, 270
  Bogdanov's theory of, 170
  conservation of, 117–18, 124, 131
  society as tranformations of, 133–39, 297–98
Engels, Friedrich, 57, 84, 90, 92, 174, 206, 211, 219, 271, 289, 292–93
  and civil society, 253
  developmentalism of, 157
  and dialectics, 209, 358n.35
  and energy theory, 175–76
  and entropy, 176
  and holism, 94–101, 103
  and nature, 357–58n.26
  role in Marxism, 100
Engelsism, 158–59, 186
Engineer Menni (Bogdanov), 276, 332–33
Engineers, 321
England, 130–32
Enlightenment, 6, 7, 54, 56, 62–63, 102–3, 341
  historical sense of, 64
  mechanicalism of, 49–52
Enquiry Concerning Human Understanding (Hume), 48–49
Entrepreneurs, 248
Entropy, 119–20, 121, 125, 174
  maximum, 124
  trap, 120
Environment, 12, 51, 96, 124, 267, 290
  and economic production, 292
  for Kant, 81
  and Marx, 92–93, 97
  and motion, 95
  relationship of man to, 51–52, 79, 92–93
Equilibrium, 11–12, 52–53, 287, 301, 308, 310
  Bukharin's theory of, 287–95, 345
  defined, 302
  dynamic, 275–76, 308
  internal and external, 12, 290–91
  mechanical, 308
  moving, 280
  thermodynamic, 124
Essays in Tektology (Bogdanov), 244, 264, 287

Essays in the Psychology of Society and Empirio-monism (Bogdanov), 167
Ethics, 73, 82, 136–37
Evolution, 26, 92, 96, 98, 118–20, 272
  reversibility of, 123
Experience, 25, 187–88, 189–90
  See also Sensory experience
Experts, 18–19
Extraordinary science, 32

Factory committees, 266
Factory councils, 239, 381–82n.176
Faraday, Michael, 117
Fathers and Sons (Turgenev), 148
Feedback mechanisms, 12, 298, 306–7
Festinger, Leo, 29–30
Fetishism, 230–32, 238
Feuerbach, Ludwig, 207
Feyerabend, Paul, 24, 25–26, 28, 36–37
Foucault, Michel, 19
Fourier, Jean-Joseph, 116–17
Frankfurt School, 110, 222
Free trade, 132
Frolov, Ivan, 268
Functionalism, 294, 301
The Fundamental Elements of the Historical outlook on Nature (Bogdanov), 169
Fused structures, 304
Fyodorov, E., 278–79, 333–34
Fyodorov, N.F., 335

Galbraith, John Kenneth, 17
Galileo Galilei, 48
Gastev, Alexie, 323–24, 325, 326
General Systems Theory (Bertalanffy), 277
German Idealism, 69, 141–42, 342
German Ideology (Marx), 86–87
Girolemi, Remigio de, 61
Goldman, Lucien, 71, 193–94
Goodness, 105–6
Gorelik, George, 277, 284, 303, 304
Gorky, Maxsim, 165
Graham, L.R., 330, 335
Gramsci, Antonio, 109, 240–43, 245, 252–53, 258, 259, 266
  and civil society, 253
  and Critical Marxism, 112, 222
  and factory councils, 239
  and hegemony, 223, 253–56
  and intellectuals, 228, 235

Great Purge, 338
Greek philosophy, 59–60
Grundrisse (Marx), 62, 84, 85, 111, 218, 220
Guilt, 145

Habermas, J., 26, 332
Haeckel, Ernst, 269
Hegel, Georg Wilhelm Friedrich, 65, 88, 102–3, 104, 108, 121, 142, 159, 162, 196, 207, 292
 and civil society, 253
 contribution to holism, 76–83, 84
 and dialectics, 94, 208, 271
 and history, 81
Hegemony, 223, 253–56
Heisenberg, Werner, 24, 121–22
Helmholtz, Herman von, 75
Heraclitus, 290
Hertz, Heinrich, 127
Hertzen, Alexander Ivanovich, 143–44, 227
Hilferding, Rudolf, 285, 360n.7
Hisben, John Grier, 133–34
Historical Letters (Lavróv), 159–60
Historical Materialism (Bukharin), 11, 210, 289, 292, 300, 345
Historicism, 38
History, 64–65, 64–66, 96, 100, 155
 agency theory of, 137–38
 for Hegel, 81
 for Kant, 70–71
 for Marx, 93
History and Class Conciousness (Lukács), 57, 69, 251
History of Economic Analysis (Schumpeter), 27–28
Holism, 6, 7, 44, 53, 57–58, 59–61, 63, 116, 140, 162, 339, 341–43
 Hegelian, 78–83
 and Marxism, 61–62, 83–90
 Montesquieu's contribution to, 66–67
 and natural unity of science, 91–101
 personal, 68
 philosophy of, 76–77
 and Vico, 64–66
Holism and Evolution (Smuts), 58
Homeostasis, 302
Honor, work of, 145–46
Hume, David, 48–49, 63, 72
Hungary, 252

Husserl, Edmund, 126, 199–201
Huxley, T.H., 120

Idealism, 69, 190, 342
Ideology, 191–92, 222–66, 282
Ignorant Philosopher (Voltaire), 75–76
Illich, Ivan, 265
"The Immediate Tasks of the Soviet Government" (Lenin), 325
Imperialism and the World Economy (Bukharin), 12, 345
Incommensurability thesis, 36
Indeterminancy Principle, 24, 121–22
Individualism, 50, 68, 150, 270
 atheist radical, 151–52
 socialist, 144
Industrialism, 157
Industrialization, 313, 314–15, 318
Industrial Revolution, 13
Ingression, 284
Instrumental reason, 15
Intellectuals, 57, 145, 257–58
 organic, 235
 role of, 226–29, 235
 technical, 250
Irreversibility, 118–20, 124
Istpart (organization), 163
Ivanovsky, V.I., 183

Jensen, Kenneth M., 277
Jensen, Otto, 175
Jevons, W.S., 119, 130, 131–32
Joravsky, David, 94, 211
Joule, James P., 117
Journey to Mars (Afanev), 330
Junger, Ernst, 326–27

Kamar t, Jan, 303
Kant, Immanuel, 48, 62, 67, 69–71, 77, 136, 162, 196, 353n.36
 critique of reason, 71–74, 102–3, 214–15
 levels of reality, 73
 and nature, 81
 and science, 73, 74
 and systems practice, 214
Kautsky, Karl, 112, 179, 391n.20
Keynesianism, 33
Kline, G., 210
Knowledge, 36–37, 39–40, 71–76, 161, 181
 archeology of, 59–71

Knowledge *(continued)*
  Bogdanov's theory of, 170–71, 189, 190
  as class determined, 197
  instrumentality of, 150
  and Marx, 88
  objective, 73
  sociology of, 38
Knowledge from a Historical Point of View (Bogdanov), 167, 169, 170
Kornai, Janos, 14, 315
Korsch, Karl, 109
Kuhn, Thomas S., 23, 24, 26, 28–29, 33–35, 37, 42

Labor, 173, 175
  division of, 107, 245, 301
  expenses, 309–10
  wage labor, 107
Lagrange, Joseph-Louis, 117
Lakatos, Imre, 34
La Nature de la Nature (Morin), 3
Laplace, Pierre-Simon de, 75, 117
  collapse of prototype of, 124–25
Lavróv, Pyotr Lávrovich, 159–61
Law, 67
Law of Markets, 53
Lebenswelt, 200, 215
Le Chatelier's principle, 278–79, 308
Lectures on Natural Philosophy (Ostwald), 171
Legal Marxists, 186
Leibniz, Gottfried, 48
Lenin, V.I., 11, 113, 157, 164, 194, 216, 235, 266
  and alienation, 263
  and Bernstein, 242
  and Bogdanov, 177, 179–80
  and Bukharin, 288, 310
  and bureaucracy, 260
  and culture, 239–40
  and dialectical materialism, 204–6
  and energeticism, 128–29, 171–72, 176–77, 220
  and ideology, 236
  and Machism, 179
  management principles of, 324
  Marxism of, 182–83
  and materialism, 183–84, 205–6
  monism of, 179
  and proletariat, 158, 227, 228–29
  and state capitalism, 285–86

Lenin, V.I. *(continued)*
  and synoptic planning, 307
  and Taylorism, 322–25
  and technology, 320
Light industry, 311
Linkage, 284
Locke, John, 49, 125
Logical empiricism, 22, 23–24
Logical positivism, 186
The Logic of Scientific Discovery (Popper), 23
Lossky, N.U., 206, 335
Lotka, Alfred, 136, 296–97
Ludwig Feuerbach and the End of Classical German Philosophy (Engels), 96, 98–99
Luhmann, N., 26
Lukács, Georg, 4, 57, 69, 100, 109, 194, 222, 225, 226, 245–46, 258, 263–64, 300–301

Mach, Ernst, 184–86, 268, 370n.2
A Madman's Apology (Chaadaev), 141
Malinovsky, Alexander Aleksandrovich. *See* Bogdanov, Alexandr A.
Mankind
  and nature, 79, 92–93
  unity of, 63–64
Mannheim, Karl, 37, 38
Manuscripts of 1844 (Marx), 261
Marcuse, Herbert, 234, 256–57, 271, 328
Marginalist revolution, 7
Marx, Karl, 26, 57, 92, 103–4, 149, 158, 162, 186, 207–8, 226, 270–71, 289
  and bureaucracy, 260
  and capitalist class structure, 248–49
  capitalist society for, 87–88
  and civil society, 253
  and class, 245, 248–49
  concepts of change, 108
  and dialectics, 208, 213
  and emergence of socialism, 106–7
  and energy in society, 172, 176
  and history, 93
  holism of, 62, 83–90
  and knowledge, 88
  and natural resources, 291–92
  and nature, 92–93, 95–96, 97, 99
  praxis philosophy of, 107
  and production forces, 218
  and proletariat, 226–27

Marx, Karl *(continued)*
  and revolution, 201
  sociology of, 272
  and technology, 218–20
  and utopianism, 319
  Vico's influence on, 64–66, 67
  young versus mature, 110–11
Marxism, 64, 100, 106–7, 157
  aesthetics of, 223
  degeneration of, 194–95
  early Russian, 165
  and holism, 61–62, 64
  interpretation of society, 216
  of Lenin, 182–83
  and natural sciences, 172
  of Nietzsche, 149
  response to crisis in, 193–204
  and social energetics, 169–77
  Vico's influence on, 64–66
  Western versus Russian, 3–4
  See also Critical Marxism;
    Phenomenological Marxism;
    Scientific Marxism
Mass effect, 123
Materialism, 147, 148, 183, 186, 190, 205–6, 220
Materialism and Empirio-criticism (Lenin), 163, 181–82
Mathematics, 46, 74–75, 77
  and Tektology, 281
Matter, 117, 129, 134, 179
  disappearance of, 127, 205
Maximalist Group, 164
Maxwell, James Clerk, 121, 127
McCulloch, J.R., 131
Meaning, 161–62
Mechanicalism, 41, 54–55, 91, 115, 125, 126, 127, 130, 206, 341–42
  ascendancy of paradigm of, 45–49
  of Enlightenment, 49–52
  evolution versus, 118–20
  mathematization of, 77
  philosophical countercurrents to, 56–90
  and society, 49–52
  and thermodynamics, 120–21
Mechanicalistic atomism, 6, 7
Mechanical materialism, 96
Meditations on First Philosophy (Descartes), 72
Mensheviks, 157, 164
Merleau-Ponty, Maurice, 373*n*.73

Metabolism, 99
Metaphysics, 26–27, 230–32
Meta-totality, 82–83
Methods, battle of, 140
Mikhailovsky, N., 144, 145–46, 159
Militarism, 285
Mill, J.S., 131
Mitchell, Wesley Clair, 21–22
Monism. *See* Cosmological monism;
    Empirio-monism
The Monist (journal), 129
Monod, Jacques, 123
Montesquieu, Charles-Louis de, 66–67
Morality, 50, 70, 82
Morin, Edgar, 3
Motion, 94–95, 96, 98, 116, 280, 358*n*.35
  and dialectics, 99
  matter in, 117

Narodniks, 141–46, 155–56, 160, 162, 165, 228
Naturalism, 47
"Natural Philosophy" (Ostwald), 134–35
Nature. *See* Environment
The Nature of the Physical World (Eddington), 123
Nechaev, Sergei, 152–53
Negation, 212
Negative feedback, 278
Negative selection, 295–96, 303–4
NEP. *See* New Economic Policy
New Economic Policy (NEP), 311–12, 318
The New Economics (Preobrazhensky), 312
The New Life (journal), 164
New Science (Vico), 64
Newton, Isaac, 47, 48, 75, 116, 117
Nietzsche, Friedrich, 146, 149, 161, 354*n*.54
Nihilism, 146–55, 162, 228
Nodal points, 121, 293
Normal science, 31–32, 33–34, 35
Normative forms, 244
Notes from the House of the Dead (Dostoevsky), 153, 336
Notes from the Underground (Dostoevsky), 149
"Notes of an Economist" (Bukharin), 318

Objectivity, 188–89, 190
Olivetti, Gino, 258

420 INDEX

One-Dimensional Man (Marcuse), 256, 328
"On the Jewish Question" (Marx), 88
On the Notion of Cause (Russell), 49
Ontology, 5–6
Oparin, A.I., 123
Order, 45–46
Organicism, 61
Organization, general theory of. See Tektology
Organizational class, 13
Organizational integration, 304
Organizational levels, 273–74
The Origin of the Family, Private Property, and the State (Engels), 100
Ostwald, Wilhelm, 129, 133–39, 169, 171, 178, 189

Paradigm, 30, 33
  arguments for new, 33
  articulation, 28–29, 31–32
  defined, 26
  testing, 34
Pareto, Vilfredo, 24
Parmenides, 59
Parsons, Talcott, 301–2
Party schools, 235
Passet, René, 75
Peasant communes, 144, 146, 155–56
Peasantry, 156, 318, 391*n.21*
Pecherin, V.S., 141
People's Justice. *See* The Axe
Personality, 143, 148–49
  fragmentation of, 262–63, 265
Petrashevsky, Michael Butaschevich, 152, 367*n.12*
Phenomenological Marxism, 9, 178–213, 373*n.73*
  and dialectical materialism, 204–13
  Machian influences on, 178–93
  preliminary description of, 195–96
  as response to crisis in Russian Marxism, 193–204
Phenomenology of the Spirit (Hegel), 78
Philosophes, 63–64
Philosophy, 104–5
  See also specific philosophies
Philosophy of History (Hegel), 81, 159
Philosophy of Living Experience (Bogdanov), 189, 217, 221, 271

The Philosophy of the Common Task (Fydorov), 334
Physiocrats, 51
Pisarev, Dimitri, 148
Planck, Max, 124
Planning, 13
  genetic and teleological approaches to, 309
  methodological approach to, 10
  Soviet, 305–18
Plato, 50, 60, 339, 351*n.10*, 354*n.54*
Plekhanov, G.V., 157–58, 181–83, 193, 194, 220
Pluralism, 35–36
Podolinsky, Serhii, 172–76
Poincaré, H., 121
Political economy, 3, 19–20, 140, 165, 172, 264, 341–42, 382*n.194*
  conceptual framework for, 20–41
  and critical theory, 104–9
  metaphysical aspects of, 26–27
  point of departure for, 85
  and practical reason, 216–17
  synthesis and inversion in, 44–55
Politics (Aristotle), 60, 61
Polyani, Karl, 391*n.21*
Popper, Karl, 23, 24, 25, 28, 34, 42
Population, 331
Positive selection, 295–96, 303–4
Positivism, 6, 7, 15, 22, 23–24, 63, 73, 91–92, 126, 154, 167, 183, 196, 267–68
The Possessed (Dostoevsky), 151–52, 153
Post-positivism, 24
The Poverty of Philosophy (Marx), 218–20
Power, 18–19, 35, 242
Practical reason, 15, 215–16, 342
Prat, Naftali, 291
Praxis, 99, 107, 214–15, 342
  philosophy of, 267–76
Preobrazhenzky, G., 312–13, 314
Prigogine, Ilya, 116
Principles of Social Science (Carey), 130
Prison Note Books (Gramsci), 224, 254
Private property, 103
Privilege, 13
Probability theory, 121–22
Process technologies, 13
Production, 51, 92–93, 103, 131
  forces of, 217–22
  machine, 218, 220

Production *(continued)*
  modes of, 88, 202
  and proletariat, 250
  of surplus value, 291–92
Productive forces, 88–89
Progress, 221, 249–50
  cultural, 138
Proletariat, 156, 157–58, 224, 225–26, 250–51, 252, 254, 326
  consciousness of, 372–73n.66
  culture of, 232–43
  education, 235
  role in production, 250
  transformation of, 226–29
Proletariat Culture movement, 8, 225, 228, 235–36, 239–40, 343
Proletkul't. See Proletariat Culture movement
Proportionality, law of, 306, 308, 309, 314, 391n.20

The Quest for Certainty (Dewey), 21

Rapoport, Anatol, 122–23
Rationality, 44, 46, 50, 52, 71–72, 73, 122, 126, 150, 154, 203, 215, 339
Reality, 73, 185–86, 196
Reason, 62, 76, 214–15
  empire of, 15, 36, 63
  Kant's critique of, 71–74, 102–3
  practical, 15, 215–16, 342
Recognition, 82, 354n.54
Red Star (Bogdanov), 164, 319, 330, 331
Reductionism, 91, 352n.17
Reflection, theory of, 196
Regulation, 309
Republic (Plato), 339
Resource exhaustion, 132, 331
Revolution, 65, 113–14, 152, 156, 232, 242–43, 251, 293
  cultural, 226, 259
  Marx and, 201–2
  substitution of party for class in, 229
  total, 65
  violent, 107
Revolutionary Catechism (Nechaev), 152
Rey, Abel, 128, 172
Rights (political group), 311–12, 337
"The Right Deviation in the CPSU(B)" (Stalin), 336
Romanticism, 141–42

Rousseau, Jean-Jacques, 67, 70
Russell, Bertrand, 49
Russia, 141–42
  liberal tradition in, 144
  materialism in, 147
  Slavophiles, 142–43
  Western influence on, 141–42

Saint-Simon, Claude, 61
Say, J.B., 53
Schmidt, Alfred, 94, 97
Schumpeter, Joseph A., 27–28
Science, 112, 191–92
  autonomy of, 39–40
  Bacon's concept of, 46
  Bogdanov and, 166–67, 192
  and cognitive dissonance, 29–30
  crisis of, 198
  diversification of, 277
  ethical imperative of, 39–40
  Feyerabend's criticism of, 25–26
  hard, 17–18
  hard core postulates, 34–35
  history of, 35
  Kant and, 73, 74
  natural unity of, 91–101, 115–39, 267–68
  and nihilism, 146–55
  paradigm articulation in, 28–29, 31–32
  philosophical criticism of, 49
  philosophy of, 23–24
  revolutions in, 29, 32–33
  revolution versus reform in, 41–43
  self-maintenance of disciplinary communities, 37
Scientific management. *See* Taylorism
Scientific Marxism, 3, 5, 101, 107–8, 158–59
  defined, 109–14
  politics for, 111–13
Scientific method, 24, 63
Scientific Organization of Labor and Production Processes, 305
Scientific rationality, 53
Scientism, 154
Scientists, 17–18
Second International (1889–1914), 3, 4, 100, 112
Selection, 286, 295–96, 303–4
Senior, Nassau, 131
Sensory experience, 72, 73
Shakhty trial, 332

Shils, E.A., 301–2
Shock methods, 305, 306
A Short Course in Political Economy (Bogdanov), 165
A Short Course on Economic Science (Bogdanov), 165, 169, 216, 268, 308
Singular points, 121
Slavery, 247–48
Slavophiles, 142–43
Slosson, Edwin E., 137
Smith, Adam, 49, 50–51, 116, 130
Smuts, Jan, 58
Sochor, Zenovia A., 205
Social consciousness, 222–66
Social Democracy, 163–64, 183, 346
Social Democratic Party (Germany), 101
Social energetics, 133–39, 140, 162, 217–22
  Marxist variation on, 169–77
Socialism, 10–11, 106–7, 112, 156, 224, 243, 299
  and individualism, 144
  scientific, 157
  stages for realization of, 143
Socialist Youth Congress, 235
Social praxis, 9
Social processes, 217
Social sciences, 40–41, 127
Social selection, 220–22
Social structures, 38–39
The Social Contract (Rousseau), 68
Society, 65, 270
  as energy transformations, 133–39, 297–98
  Marxian interpretation of, 216
  as natural environment, 93–94
  and nature, 12
Sociology, 61, 187, 236–37
  subjective, 159
Socrates, 354–55n.54
Sorokin, Pitirim A., 301
Soviet planning, 305–18
Specialization, 277, 327
Spencer, Herbert, 125
Speshnev, N., 152
Spinoza, Baruch, 49, 62
The Spirit of the Laws (Montesquieu), 66
Stages theory, 216–17
Stalin, Joseph, 10, 158, 159, 199, 204, 294, 315, 318, 332, 336
Stalinism, 5, 13, 109, 222

Stammler, Rudolf, 309–10
State, as political entity, 79
Statistical laws, 121
Statistical mechanics, 121, 123
Statistics, 155
Stites, R., 330, 335
Structuralism, 4, 280
The Structure of Scientific Revolutions (Kuhn), 26, 28
Strumlin, S., 306
Struve, Peter, 165, 186
Studies in the Philosophy of Marxism (Suvorov), 176
Study circles, 235
Supply-demand mechanism, 51
Suvorov, S., 176, 177
Synoptic planning, 307
Systems practice, 214–17
Systems theory, 4, 8, 14–15, 384–85n.37
  first stage in development of, 60
  See also Tektology

Takhazhdian, A.L., 278
Takhtajan, Ya., 277–78
Tarbuck, K.J., 313
Tautologies, 72
Taylorism, 322–25
Technocracy, 10–11
Technocratic theory, 247
Technology, 13, 51, 88–89, 112, 136, 217–22, 247, 251, 262, 300
  deterministic, 219
  and ideology, 191–92
  and utopianism, 319–29
Tektology, 9–10, 14–15, 189, 195, 211, 217, 238, 253, 267–304, 333, 343–44
  concepts and methods, 282–83
  dimensions in, 276–82
  and economy as metabolic system, 295–96
  formulating mechanism, 283–86
  and mathematics, 281
  and open systems, 303–4
  regulating mechanism, 286–87
  and Soviet planning, 305–18
  ultimate intent of, 269, 281
  universality of, 275
  See also Systems theory
Terrorism, 156
Textbooks, 33
Theory evaluation, 24–25

Theory of Historical Materialism (Bukharin), 287
A Theory of the Heavens (Kant), 48
Theory of the Novel (Lukács), 194
Thermodynamics, 8, 115, 123, 124–25, 131, 135, 222, 342, 362n.37
  Boltzmann's formulation of, 121
  discovery of, 116–18
  equilibrium, 124
  laws of, 361n.17
  and mechanics, 120–21
  second law of, 118–20, 137
Thesis on Feuerbach (Marx), 107
Tkachev, P.N., 155–56, 157
Totality. *See* Holism
Townsend, Robert, 49, 50, 51
Trade unions, 225
Transcendental philosophy, 73–74, 102
Truth, 194, 282, 339–40
Tugan-Baranovsky, M.I., 243, 313–14
Turgenev, Ivan, 148

Unger, Robert, 57
Unions, 225
The Universal Organizational Science: Tektology (Bogdanov), 167, 213
Utechin, I.V., 274, 335
Utilitarianism, 148–49, 150

Valentinov, N., 186
Value, 136, 173, 175, 215, 230, 291–92
Veblen, Thorstein, 17
Veblenian dichotomy, 192
Vekhi group, 165

Vernadsky, V.I., 177, 357n.26
Vico, Giambattista, 64–66, 67
Vitalism, 178
Voltaire, 64, 75–76
Voluntarism, 108–9
Vorovsky, V.V., 165
Vpered group, 223–24
Vucinich, Alexander, 179, 269, 280
Vyshinsky, P., 315

Wage labor, 107
War Communism, 266, 310–11
Watt, James, 116
Weak link, law of, 306
Wealth, 134
Weber, Max, 138, 260
What Is To Be Done (Chernishevsky), 147, 330
What Is To Be Done (Lenin), 199
White, James D., 158, 181, 261–62, 268
"Why is Economics Not an Evolutionary Science?" (Veblen), 17
Wiener, Norbert, 279
The Will to Power (Nietzsche), 149
Winiarsky, L., 138–39
Winner, Langdon, 219
Wittgenstein, Ludwig, 38
Worker's Opposition, 228
Worker's Truth, 259, 261
"World Economy and Imperialism" (Bukharin), 298
World War I, 284–85

Zeleny, Milan, 303, 304
Zenkovsky, V.V., 211, 269, 333

About the Author

Kenneth Michael Stokes studied Economics as well as Social and Political Thought at York University. He is an Associate Professor of the Graduate School of International Relations at the International University of Japan, and a Senior Research Fellow of the Center for Advanced Political Economy. His earlier books include the prize-winning *Man and the Biosphere: Toward a Coevolutionary Political Economy* and *A Critique of Economic Reason*. Forthcoming books address issues on globalization (*Past as Prologue*), methodology (*Methodological Issues in Coevolutionary Political Economy*), and socioethics (*Socioethics and Coevolutionary Political Economy*).

For Product Safety Concerns and Information please contact our EU representative GPSR@taylorandfrancis.com
Taylor & Francis Verlag GmbH, Kaufingerstraße 24, 80331 München, Germany